*Cornell Posey*
*301-753-4591*

# Stallcup's Journeyman Electrician's Study Guide

based on the 1999
national electrical code®

by James G. Stallcup

# Grayboy & Associates

4308 Broadway • Fort Worth • Texas • 76117 • 817-831-6599 • Fax 817-831-6579
http://www.grayboyassociates • e-mail - grayboy 02@aol.com

© 1999 by Grayboy Publishing
All rights reserved.
Printed in the United States of America

Published by Grayboy Publishing

 2 3 4 5 6 7 8 9

Library of Congress Catalog Card Number: 99-94098

ISBN: 1-885341-42-3

Written by: James G. Stallcup
Edited by: James W. Stallcup
Design, layout, and graphics by: Billy G. Stallcup

Grayboy & Associates
4308 Broadway
Fort Worth, Texas 76117
(817) 831-6599   FAX: (817) 831-6579

# Introduction

**Journeyman** – a workman who knows his trade.
(World Book Dictionary)

Obtaining a journeyman electrician license has been the springboard for numerous careers in the electrical industry. Most electrical contractors, electrical inspectors, apprenticeship instructors, authors, and consultants began as journeyman electricians.

Most all persons who work in the electrical industry as construction electricians consider themselves journeyman electricians. However, only those electricians who have taken and passed a recognized journeyman electrician license examination can truly be called a journeyman electrician.

Stallcup's Journeyman Electrician Study Guide is designed not only for instructors who are preparing apprentice students to take the ultimate test for obtaining a journeyman electrician license but also for those apprentices and electrical workers in the trade, who have taken the test, have failed and must now resort to self-study.

This book will tell you exactly what to study by presenting in full every type of question you will get on the actual test. After testing yourself, you may find that you are weak in a particular area. Once you know what subjects you are weak in, you should concentrate on improving your skills by using the specific exercise problems in this book that apply to you. And even if your study time is very limited, you should become familiar with the type of examination you will be given as well as practicing your skills in analyzing and answering questions involving reasoning, judgement, comparison, and evaluation. This kind of selective study yields maximum test results. Above all, remember - *understanding* what you read is an important part of your ability to learn and is a crucial part of most tests. The answers to all of the problems and questions in the book are found in the Instructor's Guide, which is sold separately.

This publication is not the first study guide for journeyman electricians that the author, James G. Stallcup, has written. However, it is his sincere wish that this new publication, including a new layout and the addition of new material, will meet the needs of the people for whom it is intended and that their study process will be genuinely enhanced.

# Table Of Contents

**Chapter  1.** Electrical Theory ...................................................................... 1-1

**Chapter  2.** Direct Current Circuits .............................................................. 2-1

**Chapter  3.** Alternating Current Circuits ...................................................... 3-1

**Chapter  4.** Applying Formulas ................................................................... 4-1

**Chapter  5.** Applying The NEC ................................................................... 5-1

**Chapter  6.** Wiring Methods ....................................................................... 6-1

**Chapter  7.** Conductor Ampacities ............................................................. 7-1

**Chapter  8.** Overcurrent Protection Devices ............................................... 8-1

**Chapter  9.** Residential Calculations .......................................................... 9-1

**Chapter 10.** Commercial Calculations ....................................................... 10-1

**Chapter 11.** Diagrams and Elements ......................................................... 11-1

**Chapter 12**. Questions and Problems ........................................................ 12-1

**Calculation Tips** ......................................................................................... A-3

**Topic Index** ................................................................................................... a

# Electrical Theory

**1**

In the last few decades, the causes of electrical phenomena  have been accurately determined and due to this, electricity is used to perform many useful functions.

Today electricity is so common that its use is taken for granted. Without it there would be no refrigerators, electric irons, electric lights, radios, televisions, or any other modern pieces of electrical equipment. Without electricity, life as modern man and woman knows it could not exist. This chapter covers the fundamentals of electricity and provides a coverage of basic electrical theory at a level which is easily understood by students who do not have a thorough knowledge of mathematics.

A thorough study of this material will provide test takers a solid foundation of questions and problems that may appear on the electrical theory part of the examination.

**Quick Reference:**

ELECTRON THEORY ................................... 1-2

MOLECULES AND ATOMS ......................... 1-2

ELECTRONS, PROTONS,

AND NEUTRONS ...................................... 1-2

FREE ELECTRONS MOVING

THROUGH CONDUCTORS ......................... 1-3

ELECTROSTATIC FIELD ............................. 1-4

DIRECTION OF CURRENT

FLOW THROUGH

CONDUCTORS ........................................... 1-5

STATIC ELECTRICITY ................................ 1-5

CHARGING CONDUCTORS ........................ 1-5

ELECTRIC CURRENT FLOW ...................... 1-6

POTENTIAL DIFFERENCE

AND EMF .................................................. 1-6

VOLTAGE IN A CIRCUIT ............................. 1-8

RESISTANCE IN A CIRCUIT ........................ 1-8

RESISTANCE AND

TEMPERATURE .......................................... 1-8

INSULATORS .............................................. 1-10

CURRENT IN A CIRCUIT ............................ 1-10

APPLYING OHMS LAW ............................... 1-11

APPLYING THE FORMULA .......................... 1-12

ELECTRIC POWER AND

WORK IN A CIRCUIT .................................. 1-13

# ELECTRON THEORY

Electricians must understand the basic principles of electrons and how they are applied and used. With a few hours of study, electrical personnel with sufficient interest can understand the basic principles pertaining to electron theory.

Such principles are Ohm's law, magnetism, electromagnetic induction and inductance, capacitance, and the nature of direct and alternating currents. These fundamentals are not difficult to understand, and almost all electrical applications and phenomena can be explained in terms of these principles.

# MOLECULES AND ATOMS

**Theory Tip 1:** Everything that occupies space is considered matter. Therefore, anything that can be seen or felt constitutes matter.

Matter is defined as anything which occupies space; therefore, everything which can be seen and felt constitutes matter.

Basically, matter is composed of molecules, which in turn, are composed of atoms. If a quantity of water is divided in half, and the half is then divided, and the resulting quarter is divided, and so on, a point must be reached where any further division changes the nature of the water and turns it into something else. The smallest particle into which any compound is divided and still retains its identity is called a molecule.

If a molecule of a substance is divided, it consists of particles called atoms. An atom is the smallest possible particle of an element. An element is a substance that cannot be separated into different substances except by nuclear disintegration. Common elements are iron, oxygen, aluminum, hydrogen, copper, lead, gold, silver, etc. The smallest division of any of these elements will still have the properties of that element.

A compound is a chemical combination of two or more different elements, and the smallest possible particle of a compound is a molecule. For example, a molecule of water ($H_2O$) consists of two atoms of hydrogen and one atom of oxygen. **(See Figure 1-1)**

**Figure 1-1.** This illustration shows a water molecule with its elements.

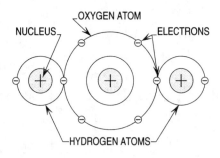

WATER MOLECULE

# ELECTRONS, PROTONS, AND NEUTRONS

A basic atom consists of infinitesimal particles known as electrons, protons, and neutrons. All matter consists of one or more of these basic components. The simplest atom is that of hydrogen, which has one electron and one proton. For simplicity sake, hydrogen is used to show such components. **(See Figure 1-2)**

There are atoms that have more than one electron and one proton. For example, the structure of an oxygen atom has eight protons, eight neutrons, and eight electrons. **(See Figure 1-3)**

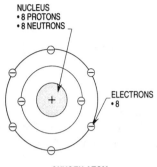

**Figure 1-3.** This illustration shows a diagram of an oxygen atom having eight protons, eight neutrons and eight electrons.

OXYGEN ATOM

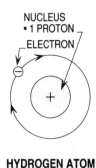

HYDROGEN ATOM

**Figure 1-2.** This illustration shows the components of hydrogen which has one electron and one proton.

The protons and neutrons from the nucleus of the atom with electrons revolving around the nucleus in orbits, vary in shape from an ellipse to a circle. For example, they can be compared to the planets as they revolve around the sun. It must be understood that a positive charge is carried by each proton, no charge is carried by the neutrons, and a negative charge is carried by each electron. The charges carried by the electron and the proton are equal, but opposite in nature. Therefore, an atom which has an equal number of protons and electrons is electrically neutral. Note that the charge carried by the electrons is balanced by the charge carried by the protons.

**Theory Tip 2:** The nucleus has a positive charge and the electron has a negative charge.

It is imperative to understand that an atom carries two opposite charges and they are as follows:

**(1)** A positive charge in the nucleus
**(2)** A negative charge in each electron

Therefore, when the charge of the nucleus is equal to the combined charges of the electrons, the atom is neutral. However, if the atom has a shortage of electrons, it is positively charged. Note that if the atom has an excess of electrons, it is negatively charged. A positively charged atom is called a positive ion, and a negatively charged atom is called a negative ion. Molecules that are charged are also called ions.

# FREE ELECTRONS MOVING THROUGH CONDUCTORS

When an atom has more than two electrons, it must have more than one shell, since the first shell will accommodate only two electrons. The number of shells in an atom depends upon the total number of electrons surrounding the nucleus. **(See Figure 1-3)**

**Theory Tip 3:** An atom with more than two electrons will have more than one shell.

The atomic structure of a substance has an important interest to the electrician because it determines the ability of the substance to conduct an electric current. Certain elements such as copper and aluminum are called conductors because an electric current can flow easily through the substance. The atoms of these elements gives up electrons or receive electrons in the outer orbits with very little difficulty. Such electrons that move from one atom to another are called free electrons. **(See Figure 1-4)**

Note that the free electrons in **Figure 1-4** pass from the outer shell of one atom to the outer shell of the next. In other words, the free electrons move from one atom to another.

For electrons to move through a conductor, a force is required, and this force is supplied in part by the electrons. When two electrons are near each other and are not acted upon by a positive charge, they repel each other with a tremendous force.

For example, if two electrons were placed a distance from each other, such electrons would repel each other with a tremendous force of power. Note that it is by this force that electrons are caused to move through conductors in an electrical circuit.

**Figure 1-4.** This diagram shows the flow of free electrons through the conductors in the branch-circuit from the panel to the industrial machinery load.

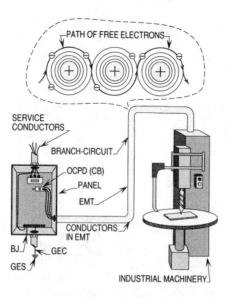

FREE ELECTRONS FLOWING
THROUGH CONDUCTORS

**Theory Tip 4:** It is the electrons that force the movement of current through a conductor.

The movement of electrons through a conductor is due to the repelling force which the electrons exert upon one another. When an extra electron enters the outer orbit of an atom, the repelling force causes another electron to move out of the orbit of that atom and into the orbit of another. If the material is a conductor such as copper or aluminum, the electrons move easily from one atom to another.

# ELECTROSTATIC FIELD

An electrostatic field is assumed to be surrounded by an invisible field of force. Such field consists of lines of force extending in all directions and terminating at a point where there is an equal and opposite charge. A field of this type is called an electrostatic field, which has two oppositely charged bodies that are in close proximity and are relatively strong. If the two bodies are joined by a conductor, the electrons from the negatively charged body flows along the conductor to the positively charged body, and the charges are neutralized. Note that when the charges are neutral, there is no electrostatic field.

**Figure 1-5.** This diagram shows the reaction between two like and unlike charges. It is by this reaction that free electrons move current through a conductor.

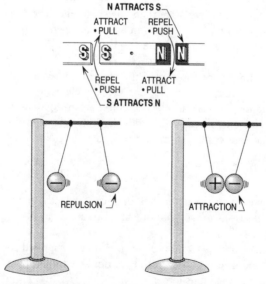

REACTION OF LIKE AND UNLIKE CHARGES

**Figure 1-5** illustrates that like charges have a repulsion reaction while unlike charges have an attraction effect.

# DIRECTION OF CURRENT FLOW THROUGH CONDUCTORS

The flow of an electric current is the movement of electrons through a conductor. Since a negatively charged body has an excess of electrons and a positively charged body a deficiency of electrons, it is clear that the electron flow will be from the negatively charged body to the positively charged body when the two are connected by a conductor. Therefore, it is fully understood, that electricity flows from negative to positive. **(See Figure 1-6)**

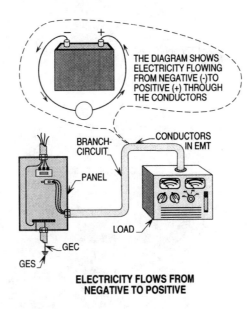

THE DIAGRAM SHOWS ELECTRICITY FLOWING FROM NEGATIVE (-) TO POSITIVE (+) THROUGH THE CONDUCTORS

CONDUCTORS IN EMT

BRANCH-CIRCUIT

PANEL

LOAD

GEC

GES

**ELECTRICITY FLOWS FROM NEGATIVE TO POSITIVE**

**Figure 1-6.** This illustration shows that electricity (current) flows from negative to positive through the conductors between the panel and load.

# STATIC ELECTRICITY

Static electricity means stationary or at rest, however, electric charges are not at rest. Static electric charges may be produced by rubbing various dissimilar substances together. The nature of the charge produced is determined by the types of substances.

For example, a glass rod rubbed with fur becomes a negative charge. However, if it is rubbed with silk, it becomes a positive charge.

For example, the insulated metal sphere in **Figure 1-7** is charged negatively, as shown, driving the positive charged electrons to the end of the rod.

The negative charged electrons in the sphere repel the electrons in the rod and drive them to the opposite end of the rod. The rod will then have a positive charge in the end nearest the charged sphere and a negative charge in the opposite end.

At the ends of the rod, there are pith balls which separate as the charged sphere is brought near one end. However, the balls near the center do not separate because the center is neutral. As the charged sphere is moved away from the rod, the balls return to their original positions. Note that the sphere was previously charged negatively.

**Theory Tip 5:** Static electricity is a charge of electricity at rest until disturbed.

# CHARGING CONDUCTORS

When a nonconductor (nonconductive) is charged by rubbing it with a dissimilar material, the charge remains at the points where the friction occurs because the electrons cannot move through the material. However, when a conductor is charged, electrons can move through the conductor. Therefore, it must be insulated from other conductors or the charge will be lost.

**Figure 1-7.** The negative charged sphere drives the positive charged electrons to the end of the rod. The rod is now charged positive at the end near the sphere and the other end is charged negative.

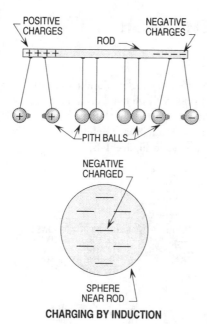

**Figure 1-8.** This illustration shows how the pressure of the voltage can charge the material of the conductors and cause electricity to flow.

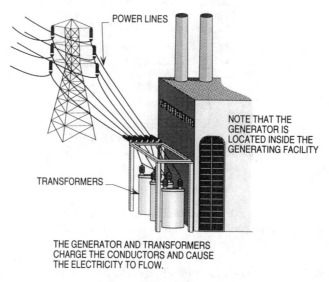

Note that an electric charge may be produced in a conductor by induction if the conductor is properly insulated to prevent short-circuits and ground-faults from occurring. **(See Figure 1-8)**

# ELECTRIC CURRENT FLOW

**Theory Tip 6:** Free electrons move through a conductor from atom to atom, due to the attraction of unlike charges and the repulsion of like charges.

An electric current is defined as a flow of electrons through a conductor. For example, the free electrons of a conducting material move from atom to atom as the result of attraction of unlike charges and the repulsion of like charges. If the terminals of a battery are connected to the ends of a conductor, the negative terminal forces electrons into the conductor and the positive terminal takes electrons from the wire and there is a continuous flow of current through the conductor. **(See Figure 1-9)**

# POTENTIAL DIFFERENCE AND EMF

Water flows in a pipe when there is a difference of pressure at the ends of the pipe, similarly an electric current flows in a conductor due to a difference in electrical pressure at the ends of the conductor.

For example, if two tanks containing water at different levels are connected by a piping system with an ON and OFF valve, water flows from the tank with the higher level to the other tank when the valve is in the open position. The difference in water pressure is due to the higher water level in the other tank.

In an electric circuit, as in the tank of water, a large number of electrons at one point will cause a current to flow to another point where there is a smaller number of electrons. To do so, two points must be connected together by a conductor. In other words, when the electron level is higher at one point than at another point, there is a difference of potential between such points. When these points are connected by a conductor, electrons will flow from the point of high potential to the point of low potential. (See Figure 1-10)

**Theory Tip 7:** The EMF or potential difference of circuits is called the volt.

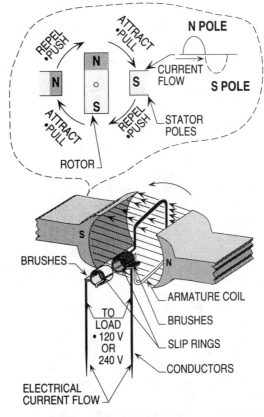

**Figure 1-9.** This illustration shows the principles of the push and pull action of the armature and field poles to cause electrons to flow through the conductors to produce electricity.

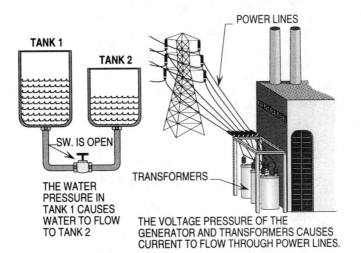

**Figure 1-10.** This illustration shows the pressure of water causing water to flow and a generator and transformer causing electricity to flow.

**Note 1:** The generator is located inside the generating facility.

Note that the force which causes electrons to flow through a conductor is called electromotive force (EMF) or electron moving force. The unit for the measurement of EMF or potential difference is called the volt.

EMF and potential difference may be considered the same for the movement of electrons through conductors (current flow). When there is a potential difference, or difference of electrical pressure, between two points, a field of force exists. Such force tends to move electrons from one point to the other. If the points are connected by a conductor, electrons will flow as long as the potential difference is available.

## VOLTAGE IN A CIRCUIT

Since potential difference and EMF are measured in volts, the word voltage is commonly related to electrical circuits. For example, it requires 1 volt of electromotive force to cause the current to flow at the rate of 1 ampere through a resistance of 1 ohm. (See Figure 1-11)

## RESISTANCE IN A CIRCUIT

**Theory Tip 8:** Resistance in circuits can be utilized to restrict the flow of current.

Resistance is that property of a conductor which tends to hold back, or restrict, the flow of electric current and every circuit has this property. Resistance may be termed as electrical friction due to its effect on the movement of electricity in a circuit. For example, if the interior of a water pipe is rough because of rust or some other material, a smaller stream of water flows through the pipe at a certain pressure than would flow if the interior of the pipe had no obstructions. Note that the resistance of conductors react to current flow in the same manner.

The unit used to measure resistance in an electric circuit is called the ohm. The resistance of a standard length and cross-sectional area of a material is called its resistivity. For example, the resistivity of a copper conductor is 10.4 ohms per circular-mil-foot (cir-mil-ft). In other words, 1 ft. of copper conductor having a cross-sectional area of 1 cir. mil. (0.001 in. diameter) will have 10.4 ohms resistance. For aluminum, the resistivity is 19.3 ohms per circular-mil-foot.

The resistance of a conductor varies inversely with the area of the cross-section. For example, if the area of the cross-section of one conductor is twice the cross-sectional area of another conductor of the same length in material, the larger conductor has one-half the resistance of the smaller conductor. When the cross-sectional area of a conductor remains constant, the resistance increases in proportion to length. For example, a conductor 2 ft. long has twice the resistance of a similar conductor 1 ft. long. **See Figure 1-11** for a testing your skills problem.

**Figure 1-11.** This illustration shows a 24 volt battery with a different potential than the load. This force of 24 volts forces the current through the wire to the light which has a lower potential.

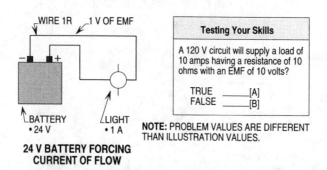

## RESISTANCE AND TEMPERATURE

In an electrical circuit, the resistance of a given conductor varies directly as its length, and inversely as the area of its cross-section. However, the temperature must remain constant. This rule may be expressed in a formula as follows:

R = KL / S

K is a constant which depends upon the resistivity of the material used. For example, copper has resistivity of 10.4 ohms at 20°C. In the formula above, L is the length of the conductor in feet, and S is the cross-sectional area in circular mils.

**For example:** To find the resistance of 400 ft. of copper conductors having a cross-sectional area of 100 circular mils, the formula is applied as follows:

**Theory Tip 9:** The constant K is usually 10.4 for copper and 19.3 for aluminum when used in certain types of circuits.

> **Step 1:** Finding R
> R = K x L / S
> R = 10.4 x 400 / 100
> R = 41.6 ohms

**Solution: The resistance of the circuit is equal to 41.6 ohms.**

Note that the cross-sectional area of a conductor is measured in circular mils with one mil equal to one-thousandth of an inch. One circular mil is the area of a circle having a diameter of 1 mil, or 0.001 in. The area of a square having sides equal to 1 mil is 1 square mil (sq. mil). See **Figure 1-12** for an illustration and exercise problem.

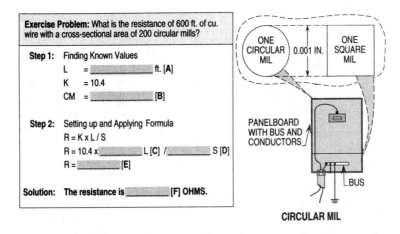

**Figure 1-12.** This diagram shows the relationship of a circular mil to a bus and conductor.

The formula for figuring the square inch area of a circle is as follows:

$\pi d^2 / 4$ or $.7854d^2$

For example, if a circle has a diameter (d) of 1 mil, the area in square mils is $0.7854 \times 1^2$, or 0.7854 sq. mil. Since a circular mil is defined as the area of a circle having a diameter of 1 mil, then 1 circular mil is equal to 0.7854 sq. mil, and

1 sq. mil = 1 / 0.7854 cir. mil or 1 sq. mil = 1.2732 cir. mil

The formula, A (area) = $.7854d^2$, gives the area of a circle in square mils when the diameter is in mils. Since:

1 sq. mil = 1 / 0.7854 cir mil.

The area of a circle in circular mils may be given as follows:

A (cir. mil) = $0.7854d^2 / 0.7854 = d^2$

The area of a circle in circular mils can be computed by merely squaring the diameter.

Resistance in electric circuits produces heat just as mechanical friction produces heat. This is called the heat of resistance. Usually the heat of resistance is dissipated as fast as it is produced, and the conductor of the circuit may become only slightly heated. However, if the current flowing in the conductor is so great that it generates heat faster than the heat can be dissipated by the surrounding air or insulation, the conductor will eventually overheat. This condition can cause burning and melting of the insulation and create a fire.

---

**Quick Calc. 1**

What is the sq. in. area of a conductor having a diameter of .121 in.?

Setting up Formula
• sq. in. A = $D^2$ x .7854
Applying Formula
• sq. in. A = $.121^2$ x .7854
• sq. in. A = .0115

**Answer : The sq in. area is .0115.**

---

**Quick Calc. 2**

What is the sq. in. fill area for a 2" EMT raceway?

Setting up Formula per columns 3 and 5 of Table 4, Ch. 9
• sq in. A = 3.356 sq in. x 40%
• sq in. A = 1.342

**Answer : The sq in. area is 1.342 for over 2 wires**

---

Consider two conductors having the same resistance and generating the same amount of heat. Note that they carry the same amount of current. If one conductor has a greater surface, it can carry more current without damage because it can dissipate the heat faster than the other. For example, if one copper conductor has a length of one ft. and a cross-sectional area of 20 circular mils, and another copper conductor has a length of two ft. and a cross-sectional area of 40 circular mils, the resistance of the two conductors is the same. However, the larger conductor can carry more current because it can dissipate heat more rapidly. **(See Figure 1-13)**

**Figure 1-13.** This illustration shows two lengths of conductors having the same current and heat. The larger conductor will carry more current than the smaller. See discussion in text.

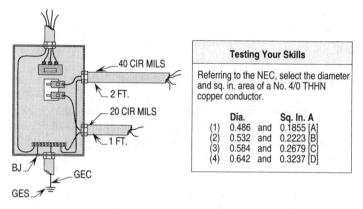

DISSIPATING HEAT

Testing Your Skills

Referring to the NEC, select the diameter and sq. in. area of a No. 4/0 THHN copper conductor.

|  | Dia. |  | Sq. In. A |
|---|---|---|---|
| (1) | 0.486 | and | 0.1855 [A] |
| (2) | 0.532 | and | 0.2223 [B] |
| (3) | 0.584 | and | 0.2679 [C] |
| (4) | 0.642 | and | 0.3237 [D] |

## INSULATORS

**Theory Tip 10:** Table 310-13 is used to determine the use of conductors and Table 310-16 is utilized for the ampacity of conductors.

Insulators are materials which have very few free electrons. However, there are no perfect insulators, but there are substances which have such high resistance that they prevent the flow of current. Substances having good insulating qualities are as follows:

**(1)** Dry air,
**(2)** Glass,
**(3)** Mica,
**(4)** Rubber, Thermoset and
**(5)** Plastics, Thermoplastic, etc.

Note that the resistance of these substances can vary but they can be utilized to effectively block the flow of current.

The atoms of an insulator do not give up electrons easily when an EMF is applied. However, if such EMF is applied strong enough that it strains the insulator beyond it elastic limit, the atoms lose electrons and the material becomes a conductor. When this occurs, the material is said to be ruptured and short-circuits or ground-faults occur.

Temperature is another factor which affects the resistance of a conductor. Normally, the resistance of a conductor increases with an increase in temperature. However, some substances decrease in resistance as the temperature is increased. Therefore, the degree of resistance change due to temperature variation is not constant, but depends upon the material.

**See Figure 1-14** for insulators of conductors which are used in modern day electrical systems, also work the testing your skills problem.

## CURRENT IN A CIRCUIT

When it is necessary to measure the flow of a liquid through a pipe, the rate of flow is often measured in gallons per minute. The gallon is a definite quantity of liquid and may be called a unit of quantity. The unit of quantity for electricity is the coulomb, and the rate of flow for an electric circuit is measured by the number of coulombs per second passing a given point in a circuit. However, the rate of flow in coulombs per second is measured by a unit called the ampere (amp).

Note that one ampere is the rate of flow of 1 coulomb per second.

Actually, the flow of electricity through a conductor is called current. When current is mentioned, it is known as a flow of electricity which is measured in amperes. **See Figure 1-15** for an illustration and work the testing your skills problem.

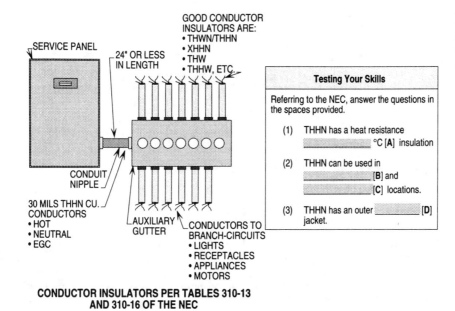

CONDUCTOR INSULATORS PER TABLES 310-13 AND 310-16 OF THE NEC

**Figure 1-14.** Good conductor insulators will hold the voltage and electron flow for the conductors and won't let it escape beyond the insulated substance.

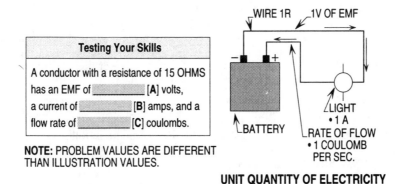

UNIT QUANTITY OF ELECTRICITY

**Figure 1-15.** This diagram shows that one ampere is the rate of flow for electricity at one coulomb per second.

# APPLYING OHMS LAW

In an electrical circuit, EMF is expressed in volts and the symbol E is used to indicate the EMF until the actual voltage is determined. R is the symbol for resistance in ohms, and I is the symbol for current or amperage.

The letter symbols E, R, and I have an exact relationship in electricity given in Ohm's law. This law may be stated as follows: The current in an electric circuit is directly proportional to the EMF (voltage) and inversely proportional to the resistance. Ohm's law can also be expressed as follows: 1 volt will cause 1 ampere to flow through a resistance of 1 ohm. The equation for Ohm's law is as follows:

$I = E / R$

Such use of the formula indicates that the current in a given circuit is equal to the voltage divided by the resistance. The volts of a circuit can be found by applying the formula using:

$E = I \times R$

By dividing the volts by the amps, the resistance of a circuit can be determined as follows:

$R = E / I$

**Note 2:** See Math Help Formulas on pg. 1-15 of this chapter.

See **Figure 1-16** for a detailed illustration of the procedure used when applying the Ohm's law formula.

**Figure 1-16.** This illustration shows the letters and how they relate to the Ohm's law formula when used to find values in an electrical circuit.

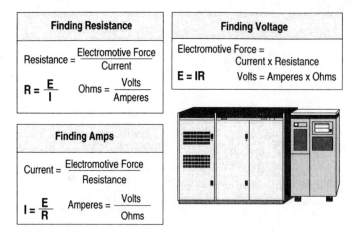

**Finding Resistance**

$\text{Resistance} = \dfrac{\text{Electromotive Force}}{\text{Current}}$

$R = \dfrac{E}{I} \qquad \text{Ohms} = \dfrac{\text{Volts}}{\text{Amperes}}$

**Finding Voltage**

$\text{Electromotive Force} = \text{Current} \times \text{Resistance}$

$E = IR \qquad \text{Volts} = \text{Amperes} \times \text{Ohms}$

**Finding Amps**

$\text{Current} = \dfrac{\text{Electromotive Force}}{\text{Resistance}}$

$I = \dfrac{E}{R} \qquad \text{Amperes} = \dfrac{\text{Volts}}{\text{Ohms}}$

**OHM'S LAW FORMULA**

By applying Ohm's law, it can be proven that the current flowing in a circuit is directly proportional to the voltage and inversely proportional to the resistance. As an example of this rule, if the voltage applied to a given circuit is doubled, the current will also double. However, if the resistance is doubled and the voltage remains the same, the current will be reduced by one-half as shown in **Figure 1-17**.

## APPLYING THE FORMULA

**Note 3:** See Math Help Formulas on page 4-8 of chapter four.

Ohm's law can be used to solve any common direct-current (DC) circuit problem when the circuit is operating with voltage, amperage, and resistance. To determine any one of the three values, if the other two are known, cover the symbol of the unknown value with the index finger and solve the problem using the known values.

**For example:** If it is desired to find the total amps of a circuit in which the voltage is 120 volts and the resistance is 10 ohms, cover the letter I in the formula. This leaves the letter E over the letter R then compute as follows:

**Step 1:** Finding amps
$I = E / R$
$I = 120 \text{ V} / 10 \text{ R}$
$I = 12 \text{ A}$

**Solution: The amps in the circuit is equal to 12 amps.**

**Figure 1-17.** If the voltage in circuit 2 is doubled, the current will be doubled. Should the resistance be doubled as in circuit 3 and the voltage remains the same, the current is reduced by one-half respectively.

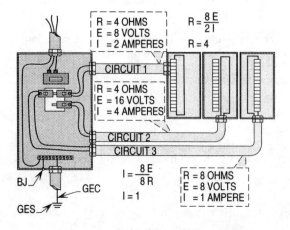

R = 4 OHMS
E = 8 VOLTS
I = 2 AMPERES

$R = \dfrac{8E}{2I}$
$R = 4$

CIRCUIT 1

R = 4 OHMS
E = 16 VOLTS
I = 4 AMPERES

CIRCUIT 2
CIRCUIT 3

BJ
GEC
GES

$I = \dfrac{8E}{8R}$
$I = 1$

R = 8 OHMS
E = 8 VOLTS
I = 1 AMPERE

**EFFECTS OF RESISTANCE AND VOLTAGE**

**For example:** If it is desired to find the voltage in a circuit when the resistance and amperage are known, cover the E in the formula. This leaves I and R adjacent to each other. Therefore, multiply the known values as follows:

**Theory Tip 11:** It is important for electricians to achieve a thorough understanding of Ohm's law. This knowledge enables him or her to compute the correct size of conductors to be used in a circuit.

**Step 1:** Finding voltage
E = I x R

**Solution: Voltage is found by multiplying amps times the resistance of the circuit.**

Likewise, resistance can be found by dividing the voltage by the amps as follows:

R = E / I

**See Figure 1-18** for a detailed illustration of applying Ohm's law, also work the testing your skills problem.

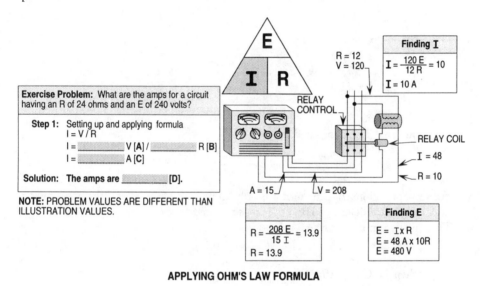

**Figure 1-18.** This illustration shows Ohm's law being used to find the resistance, voltage, and amperage of a circuit.

**Note 4:** See math help formulas on page 1-15 in this chapter and page 4-8 of Chapter four.

**APPLYING OHM'S LAW FORMULA**

**Finding R**

# ELECTRIC POWER AND WORK IN A CIRCUIT

Power means the rate of doing work. One horsepower (HP) is required to raise 550 lb. a distance of 1 ft. in 1 sec. If 1 lb. is moved through a distance of 1 ft., 1 ft. lb. of work has been done. Therefore, 1 HP is the power required to perform 550 ft. lb. of work per second.

The unit of power in electricity is the watt (W), and 1 HP is equal to 746 watts. In electrical terms, 1 watt is the power expended when 1 volt moves 1 coulomb per second through a conductor. In other words, 1 volt at 1 ampere produces 1 watt of power. The formula for electric power is as follows:

Watts = volts x amperes
W = E x I or P = E x I

An electric current flowing through a conductor always produces heat. However, in most cases, the rise in temperature is not noticeable. The heat generated in a given circuit is proportional to the square of the current, as indicated by the following formulas:

Note that wattage can be used in a calculation problem as W or VA. The NEC requires VA to be used in calculation problems.

$$W = E \times R \quad \text{or} \quad P = E \times R$$
$$W = E^2 / R \quad \text{or} \quad P = E^2 / R$$
$$W = R \times I^2 \quad \text{or} \quad P = R \times I^2$$

If energy is lost in an electric circuit in the form of heat, it is called an $I^2R$ loss because $I^2R$ represents the heat energy lost, measured in watts. Knowing the relationship between power and electrical units, it is easy to compute the approximate amperage to operate a given motor when the efficiency and operating voltage of the motor are known.

**For example:** If it is desired to install a 10 HP motor in a 240 volt system and the efficiency of the motor is 85 percent, to find the amps, compute as follows:

Step 1: Computing watts
W = I x 746
W = 10 x 746
W = 7,460 watts

Step 2: Computing amps
I = W / E
I = 7,460 W / 240 V
I = 31 A

**Theory Tip 12:** When the efficiency is less than 100 percent, the amps that the motor pulls will be higher and may require larger components

Solution: **The computed amps is 31.**

**For example:** Note that the motor is only 85 percent efficient and the amps must be divided by the efficiency to find the amps required to operate the motor at rated load. The calculation is performed as follows:

Step 1: Computing Eff.
Eff. = A / %
Eff. = 31 A / .85
Eff. = 36.5 A

Solution: **The amps after applying the operating efficiency is 36.5 amps respectively.**

See **Figure 1-19** for an exercise problem for computing the watts and efficiency of a motor.

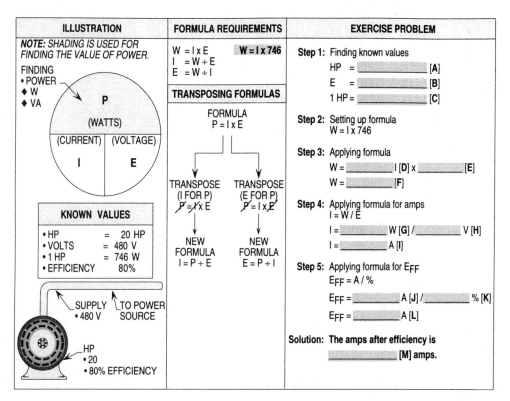

| ILLUSTRATION | FORMULA REQUIREMENTS | EXERCISE PROBLEM |
|---|---|---|

**ILLUSTRATION**

*NOTE: SHADING IS USED FOR FINDING THE VALUE OF POWER.*

FINDING
• POWER
  ◆ W
  ◆ VA

P
(WATTS)
(CURRENT)     (VOLTAGE)
I     E

**KNOWN VALUES**
• HP          = 20 HP
• VOLTS       = 480 V
• 1 HP        = 746 W
• EFFICIENCY  80%

SUPPLY     TO POWER
• 480 V     SOURCE

HP
• 20
• 80% EFFICIENCY

**FORMULA REQUIREMENTS**

$W = I \times E$          $W = I \times 746$
$I = W \div E$
$E = W \div I$

**TRANSPOSING FORMULAS**

FORMULA
$P = I \times E$

TRANSPOSE
(I FOR P)
$P = I \times E$

NEW
FORMULA
$I = P \div E$

TRANSPOSE
(E FOR P)
$P = I \times E$

NEW
FORMULA
$E = P \div I$

**EXERCISE PROBLEM**

**Step 1:** Finding known values

HP  = _____ [A]
E   = _____ [B]
1 HP = _____ [C]

**Step 2:** Setting up formula
$W = I \times 746$

**Step 3:** Applying formula
$W =$ _____ I [D] $\times$ _____ [E]
$W =$ _____ [F]

**Step 4:** Applying formula for amps
$I = W / E$
$I =$ _____ W [G] / _____ V [H]
$I =$ _____ A [I]

**Step 5:** Applying formula for $E_{FF}$
$E_{FF} = A / \%$
$E_{FF} =$ _____ A [J] / _____ % [K]
$E_{FF} =$ _____ A [L]

**Solution:** The amps after efficiency is
_____ [M] amps.

**Figure 1-19.** Exercise problem for finding the watts, when the voltage and HP are known.

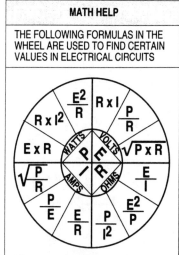

**MATH HELP**

THE FOLLOWING FORMULAS IN THE WHEEL ARE USED TO FIND CERTAIN VALUES IN ELECTRICAL CIRCUITS

# Chapter 1
# Electrical Theory

| Section | Answer | |
|---|---|---|

**Section**          **Answer**

_____     (T)  F      1. Matter is the smallest particle into which any compound is divided and still retain its identity.

_____     (T)  F      2. Hydrogen is an atom which consists of one electron and one proton.

_____     T  (F)      3. An electrostatic field has two oppositely charged bodies that are in close proximity and are relatively strong.

_____     T  (F)      4. Potential difference and EMF are measured in amps.

_____     (T)  F      5. When applying Ohms law, the symbol R is used to indicate resistance in ohms.

_____  _____    6. A basic atom consists of infinitesimal particles known as *Proton*, *electron* and *Neutron*

_____  _____    7. The flow of an electric current is the movement of *electron* through a conductor.

_____  _____    8. The unit used to measure resistance in an electric circuit is called the *Resistance*

_____  _____    9. When applying Ohms law, the symbol I is used to indicate *Current or Amp*

_____  _____    10. By applying Ohms law, it can be proven that the current flowing in a circuit is *directly* proportional to the voltage and ____ proportional to the resistance. *INversely*

_____  _____    11. What is the voltage for a circuit having a resistance (R) of 10 ohms and an amperage (I) of 24 amps?  *240*

_____  _____    12. What is the amperage for a circuit having an resistance (R) of 12 ohms and a voltage (E) of 240 volts?  *12Amp*

_____  _____    13. What is the resistance for a circuit having an amperage (I) of 16 amps and a voltage (E) of 208 volts?  *13*

_____  _____    14. What is the voltage for circuit having a resistance (R) of 12 ohms and an amperage (I) of 20 amps?  *240*

_____  _____    15. What is the amperage for a circuit having an resistance (R) of 24 ohms and a voltage (E) of 480 volts?  *20*

_____  _____    16. What is the resistance for a circuit having an amperage (I) of 26 amps and a voltage (E) of 208 volts?

_____  _____    17. What is the amperage for a 15 HP motor supplied by a 240 volt system?

_____  _____    18. What is the amperage for a 15 HP motor supplied by a 240 volt system when the efficiency of the motor is 85 percent?

_____  _____    19. What is the amperage for a 20 HP motor supplied by a 480 volt system?

_____  _____    20. What is the amperage for a 20 HP motor supplied by a 480 volt system when the efficiency of the motor is 90 percent?

# Direct Current Circuits

**2**

## Quick Reference:

TYPES OF CIRCUITS ................................. 2-2

OPEN-CIRCUITS, SHORT-CIRCUITS,

AND GROUND-FAULTS ............................... 2-2

OPEN-CIRCUITS ......................................... 2-2

SHORT-CIRCUITS ....................................... 2-2

GROUND-FAULTS ....................................... 2-3

OVERCURRENT PROTECTION

DEVICES .................................................... 2-3

FUSES ........................................................ 2-4

CIRCUIT BREAKERS .................................. 2-4

CONNECTING LOADS IN A CIRCUIT ........... 2-5

SERIES CIRCUITS ...................................... 2-5

PARALLEL CIRCUITS ................................. 2-6

SERIES / PARALLEL CIRCUITS .................. 2-6

SOLVING SERIES AND

PARALLEL CIRCUITS ................................. 2-6

COMPUTATIONS

IN A SERIES CIRCUIT ................................ 2-7

COMPUTATIONS

IN A PARALLEL CIRCUIT ........................... 2-9

COMPUTATIONS IN A SERIES /

PARALLEL CIRCUIT ................................... 2-12

This chapter covers the characteristics of DC circuits. Simple DC circuits and the different ways such circuits can be designed and used are laid out and discussed. Included in this chapter are series, parallel, and series / parallel circuits. The law, rules, and formulas for finding unknown values for resistance, current, voltage, and power are discussed in detail. The effect that open and short-circuits have in an electrical system are also presented with useful illustrations.

Electrical current is the flow of electrons in motion. When the electrons flow in one direction only, the current is called direct-current (DC). Electrons are too small to be seen, therefore, it is impossible to count them as they flow in an electrical circuit. However, circuits must be run, connected, and protected so such electrons can flow safely from the power source to the load or loads.

Due to questions and problems related to DC circuits on the journeyman examination, a thorough knowledge of these circuits is a must for someone preparing for the exam.

# TYPES OF CIRCUITS

**DC Tip 1:** For current to flow through conductors, a difference in potential must be present from the source to the load.

For a current to flow in a conductor, a difference in potential must be maintained between the ends of the conductor. In an electric circuit, this difference of potential is usually supplied by a battery or a generator. Based on this concept, both ends of the conductor must be connected to the terminals of the source (EMF) for current to flow.

With one end of the circuit connected to the positive terminal of the battery and the other end connected to the negative terminal, a circuit is formed. A switch is placed in the circuit to connect and disconnect the supply power to the load.

Note that this load can be an electric alarm, bell, relay, or any other electric device which could be operated in a such circuit. When the switch is in the closed position, current from the battery flows through the load and back to the battery. The circuit will operate only when there is a continuous path through which the current can flow from one terminal to the other. If the switch is in the open position, the path for the current is broken, and the current flow stops.

See **Figure 2-1** for a detailed illustration of the components for a simple circuit with a battery as its power supply. Note that the power source could be a generator or a transformer.

**Figure 2-1.** This illustration shows the components of a simple circuit.

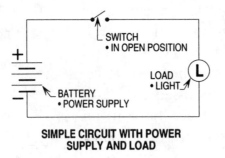

## OPEN-CIRCUITS, SHORT-CIRCUITS, AND GROUND-FAULTS

Open-circuits, short-circuits, and ground-faults create many problems for electricians. They not only have to be found, but fixed after they are discovered. To troubleshoot such circuits for these kind of defects, a journeyman electrician must be well trained on DC and AC circuits and what can cause these problems.

### OPEN-CIRCUITS

**DC Tip 2:** An open-circuit can be due to a bad switch or a broken or loose wire in the circuit or components of such circuits.

Open-circuits are the most common problems encountered when troubleshooting electrical systems. An open-circuit simply means that there is a break somewhere in the circuit and no current can flow.

As soon as the open-circuit is found and fixed, the circuit is complete and the current can flow. This type of condition is referred to as a closed-circuit. **(See Figure 2-2)**

### SHORT-CIRCUITS

A common cause of circuit failure is called a short-circuit. A short-circuit condition exists when an accidental contact between conductors permits the current to return to its power supply through a low-resistance path.

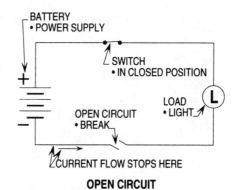

Figure 2-2. This illustration shows a circuit with an open break which interrupts the circuit and its current flow.

This type of failure can be prevented if the insulation for the conductors are in good condition and strong enough to adequately withstand the voltage of the power source.

The danger of a short-circuit condition is that an excessive amount of current can flow through limited lengths of the circuit. This additional current creates heat that causes conductors to overheat and melt the insulation.

If it were not for properly installed overcurrent protection devices, short-circuit conditions of conductors could cause a fire to occur. (See Figure 2-3)

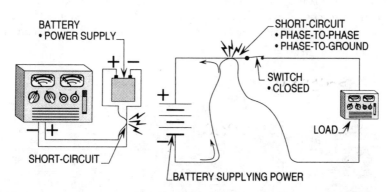

Figure 2-3. A short-circuit condition is when an ungrounded phase (hot) makes contact with another phase.

## GROUND-FAULTS

Ground-faults happen when an ungrounded phase conductor (hot) makes accidental contact with the metal of boxes, enclosures, conduits, etc. If the fault-current condition is not discovered in time, the conductors can get very hot and may melt. Equipment is damaged and fires are caused by ground-faults. However, such danger is largely overcome by the installation of protective devices such as fuses or circuit breakers which are properly sized to prevent such problems. (See Figure 2-4)

**DC Tip 3:** Ground-faults are very dangerous due to excessive current flow, which will cause conductors to get very hot and damage equipment.

## OVERCURRENT PROTECTION DEVICES

Overcurrent protection devices are used to protect circuits from dangerous short-circuits, ground-faults, and overloads. Fuses and circuit breakers are normally utilized to provide such protection.

**Figure 2-4.** A ground-fault condition is when an ungrounded phase (hot) conductor makes contact with grounded metal, etc.

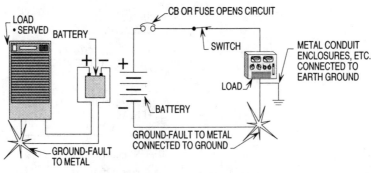

**GROUND-FAULT CONDITION**

## FUSES

A fuse is part of a circuit which is composed of a metal or alloy with a low melting point. If the current in the circuit becomes too great, the fuse will melt and open the circuit.

Fuses will normally hold 5 times their rating based upon the type used. For example, a 20 amp fuse will hold 100 amps (20 A x 5 = 100 A) for about 1/4 to 10 seconds.

Note that the time in seconds a fuse will hold 5 times its rating, is related to it being a time-delay or nontime-delay type.

A fuse will trip open and clear the circuit immediately (short-circuit conditions) when the current reaches a value above 100 amps for a 20 amp rated fuse (5 x 20 A = 100 A). When an overload condition occurs, a 20 amp fuse will clear anytime the current in amps exceeds 20 amps. **(See Figure 2-5)**

**Figure 2-5.** This illustration shows a fuse protecting circuit conductors and equipment from dangerous short-circuits, ground-faults, and overloads.

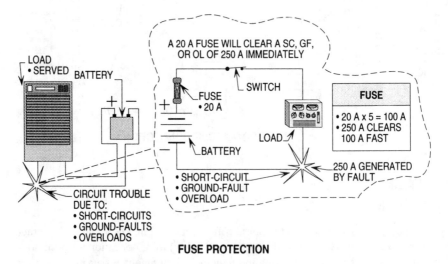

**FUSE PROTECTION**

## CIRCUIT BREAKERS

The circuit breaker is a mechanical device designed to open a circuit when the current flow exceeds a safe limit. Normally, the circuit breaker is equipped with an element which responds to heat. The heat causes the metal to expand, and the expansion trips the contact points to an open position.

A circuit breaker will hold 3 times its rating, for a period of time, based on its frame size. For example, a 20 amp, 120/240 volt circuit breaker will hold 60 amps (20 A x 3 = 60 A) for about 4 seconds without tripping open. However, such circuit breaker will trip instantly if the current in amps reaches a value above 60 amps. On the other hand, a 20 amp circuit breaker will trip open its thermal protective element for any current (amps) above its 20 amp rating. **(See Figure 2-6)**

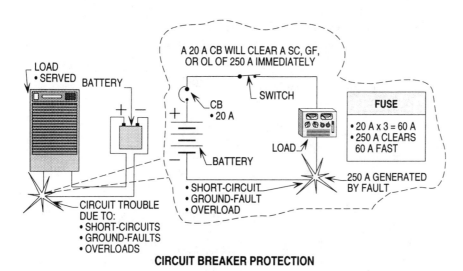

**CIRCUIT BREAKER PROTECTION**

**Figure 2-6.** This illustration shows a CB protecting circuit conductors and equipment from dangerous short-circuits, ground-faults, and overloads.

## CONNECTING LOADS IN A CIRCUIT

There are three general methods for connecting a load in an electrical system. The method used is based upon its condition of use in the circuit. The three general methods are as follows:

   **(1)** Series,
   **(2)** Parallel, and
   **(3)** Series / Parallel.

**DC Tip 4:** Current flow through circuits can be regulated by connecting such components in series, parallel, or series and parallel configurations.

## SERIES CIRCUITS

In series circuits, all the current flowing in the circuit must pass through each load in the circuit. For example, if a number of lamps are connected in series and if one of the lamps should burn out, the circuit is broken and the other lamps will stop burning.

**See Figure 2-7** for a number of lamps connected in series.

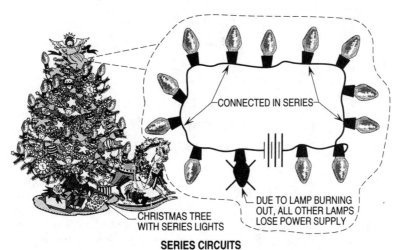

CHRISTMAS TREE WITH SERIES LIGHTS

CONNECTED IN SERIES

DUE TO LAMP BURNING OUT, ALL OTHER LAMPS LOSE POWER SUPPLY

**SERIES CIRCUITS**

**Figure 2-7.** This illustration shows a series connected circuit of lights and what happens if one should burn out.

## PARALLEL CIRCUITS

In parallel circuits, there are two or more paths for the current to travel, and if the path through one of the loads is broken accidentally, the loads will continue to operate. The loads in an electrical system are usually connected in parallel. Note that the failure of one load does not impair the operation of the other loads in the system. **(See Figure 2-8)**

**Figure 2-8.** Loads that are connected in a parallel circuit allow other loads to function if one load is lost.

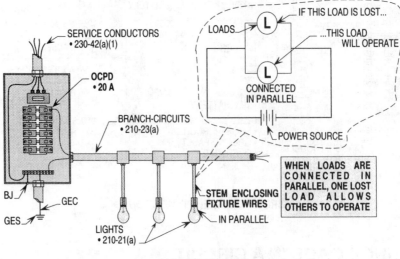

PARALLEL CIRCUITS

## SERIES / PARALLEL CIRCUITS

A circuit which has some of its loads connected in series and the other loads connected in parallel is called a series / parallel circuit or combination circuit. Certain types of equipment have such circuits, so they can be switched in and out to provide different circuitry for operation. **(See Figure 2-9)**

**Figure 2-9.** This illustration shows a series / parallel circuit which is used in certain types of equipment. **Note:** By removing load 2, the circuit becomes a series circuit. If load 3 or 4 were lost, the entire circuit is broken and no current will flow.

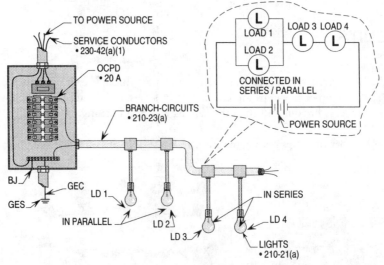

SERIES / PARALLEL CIRCUITS

## SOLVING SERIES AND PARALLEL CIRCUITS

Ohm's law can be used to determine the electrical values in any common circuit even though it may have a number of different loads. In order to solve such circuits, it is necessary to know if the loads are connected in series, parallel, or in combination. When the type of circuit is determined, the proper formula may be applied and desired values computed.

## COMPUTATIONS IN A SERIES CIRCUIT

If a current flows through a resistance, the voltage across the resistance is equal to the product of the current and the resistance. For example, the voltage in the circuit is called the IR drop and the IR drop in a complete circuit is equal to the voltage of the supply source.

**Using Figure 2-10,** consider that the resistance of a power source is .1 ohm, the resistance of three loads are 50 ohms each, the resistance of one load is 200 ohms, and the source voltage is 240 volts. When load resistances are connected in series, they are added together to determine the total resistance of the circuit.

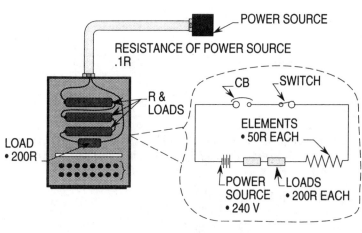

**SOLVING SERIES PROBLEM**

**Figure 2-10.** The values in the illustration are used in the text to solve problems with unknown values in a series connected circuit.

**For example:** To find the current, divide the total resistance into the voltage of the power source. The current in amps can be computed as follows:

> Step 1: Finding current
> I = 240 V / .1 + 50 + 50+ 50 + 200R
> I = 240 V / 350.1R
> I = .6855 A

**Solution: The current in amps is .6855.**

**DC Tip 5:** There will be less current flow in a circuit when the resistance of such circuit is high.

Note that the voltage drop across any load of the circuit may be easily found, due to the current being the same through each load.

**For example:** The voltage drop in the power source can be found by multiplying .6855 by .1 (resistance of service) as follows:

> Step 1: Finding VD
> VD = .6855 x .1
> VD = .06855 V

**Solution: The VD in the power source is .06855 volts.**

**Figure 2-11:** Using the known values in the series circuit, calculate the total resistance and amps in the exercise problem.

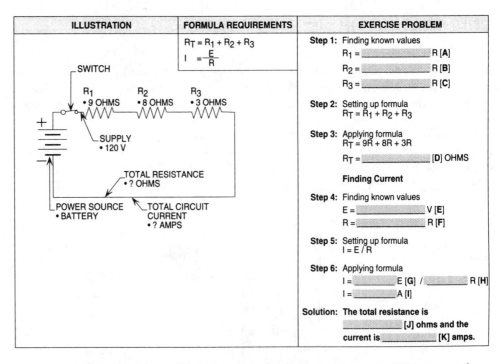

| ILLUSTRATION | FORMULA REQUIREMENTS | EXERCISE PROBLEM |
|---|---|---|

$R_T = R_1 + R_2 + R_3$

$I = \dfrac{E}{R}$

**Step 1:** Finding known values
$R_1 = $ ▓▓▓▓▓ R [A]
$R_2 = $ ▓▓▓▓▓ R [B]
$R_3 = $ ▓▓▓▓▓ R [C]

**Step 2:** Setting up formula
$R_T = R_1 + R_2 + R_3$

**Step 3:** Applying formula
$R_T = 9R + 8R + 3R$
$R_T = $ ▓▓▓▓▓ [D] OHMS

**Finding Current**

**Step 4:** Finding known values
$E = $ ▓▓▓▓▓ V [E]
$R = $ ▓▓▓▓▓ R [F]

**Step 5:** Setting up formula
$I = E / R$

**Step 6:** Applying formula
$I = $ ▓▓▓▓ E [G] / ▓▓▓▓ R [H]
$I = $ ▓▓▓▓ A [I]

**Solution:** The total resistance is ▓▓▓▓ [J] ohms and the current is ▓▓▓▓ [K] amps.

**DC Tip 6:** If the VD in the feeder is held to 3 percent overall, then the VD in the branch-circuit must be keep at 2 percent or less.

**For example:** Considering the VD in the power source, what is the VD across each individual load in the circuit? (Use values in **Figure 2-10** and text).

    **Step 1:** Finding VD
        VD = I x R
        VD = .6855 A x 50R
        VD = 34.275 V

    **Solution:** The VD in each load is 34.275 volts.

**For example:** With a VD of 34.275 volts across each 50 ohm load, what is the VD across the 200 ohm load?

    **Step 1:** Finding VD
        VD = .6855 A x 200R
        VD = 137.1 V

    **Solution:** The VD across the 200 ohm load is 137.1 volts.

**For example:** With a VD of 137.1 volts for the 200 ohm load, what is the sum of all the VD calculations for the circuit?

    **Step 1:** Finding sum of VD's
        VD    = 137.1   V
        VD    = 34.275  V
        VD    = 34.275  V
        VD    = <u>34.275</u>  V
        Total  = 239.925 V

    **Solution:** The VD rounded-up is 240 volts.

**See Figure 2-11** for a detailed illustration of computing values in series circuits

# COMPUTATIONS IN A PARALLEL CIRCUIT

In **Figure** 2-12 the load resistances are connected in parallel. For loads in parallel, a new formula is used to compute the total resistance of the circuit. Because there is more than one path through which current can flow, the total resistance must be less than it would be if there were only one resistance in the circuit. If all the resistances are equal, the resistance of one unit may be divided by the number of loads to find the total resistance.

**DC Tip 7:** The total current in a parallel circuit is equal to the sum of the currents in all the branches of the circuit.

**For example:** Assume that each resistance in the circuit in **Figure 2-12** has a value of 24 ohms. By dividing 24R / 3 = 8 the number of resistances in the parallel group is 8 ohms. The calculation is performed as follows:

**DC Tip 8:** If the branches of a parallel circuit have the same resistance, then each draws the same amount of current.

**Step 1:** Finding number of resistances
There are 3 - 8R in the circuit

**Solution: There are 3 resistances in the circuit.**

**Step 1:** Finding total R in circuit 1
8R / 3 = 2.67R

**Solution: The total resistances of the loads is 2.67 ohms.**

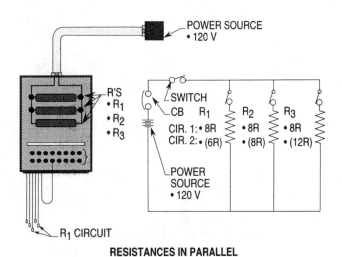

**RESISTANCES IN PARALLEL**

**Figure 2-12.** The values in the illustration are used in the text to show how to find different unknown values in a parallel connected circuit.

Note that the same results can be obtained by calculating the current flow through each resistance and then adding together each separate current which will produce the total current. By dividing applied voltage by the total current, the total resistance can be found.

For example, assume that a power source of 120 volts is connected to the circuit with 120 volts applied to each resistance, the current through each resistance is found to be 15 amp (120 V / 8R = 15 A). Then the total current is 45 amps (15 A + 15 A + 15 A = 45 A).

**DC Tip 9:** If the branches of a parallel circuit have different resistances, then each will draw a different current.

**For example:** The total current can also be found by applying the following Ohm's law formulas:

    **Step 1:** Finding amps in each R
        $I = E / R$
        $I = 120 \text{ V} / 8R$
        $I = 15 \text{ A}$

    **Step 2:** Finding total A
        $A = 15 \text{ A} \times 3$
        $A = 45 \text{ A}$

  **Solution:** **Total amps is equal to 45.**

    **Step 1:** Finding R in each circuit
        $R = E / I$
        $R = 120 \text{ V} / 15 \text{ A}$
        $R = 8$

  **Solution:** **The total resistance is 8 ohms.**

The computation proves that the previous calculation was correct.

**DC Tip 10:** The total resistance in a parallel circuit is found by applying Ohm's law to the total values of such circuits.

When parallel resistances have different values, the total resistance of the circuit may be found by using the reciprocal technique as follows: The total resistance of a parallel circuit is equal to the reciprocal of the sum of the reciprocals of the resistances.

For example, the reciprocal of a number is 1 divided by the number. Assume that the reciprocal of 8 is 1/8. Two numbers are reciprocals of each other and when multiplied, their value will be 1.

**Using Figure 2-12,** consider in circuit 2 that $R_1$ is 6 ohms, $R_2$ is 8 ohms, and $R_3$ is 12 ohms respectively and find the total resistance of the circuit.

**Note: In Figure 2-12,** such resistances are identified as 6R, 8R, and 12R.

**DC Tip 11:** The voltage across any branch in parallel is equal to the voltage across any other branch and is equal to the total voltage.

**For example:** The total resistance can be found for $R_1$ through $R_3$ by using the following formula as shown:

    **Step 1:** Finding total $R_t$ in circuit 2.
        $R_t = 1 / (1 / R_1 + 1 / R_2 + 1 / R_3)$

    **Step 2:** Applying formula
        $R_t = 1 / (1/6 + 1/8 + 1/12)$
        $R_t = 1 / (4/24 + 3/24 + 2/24)$
        $R_t = 24 / 9$
        $R_t = 2.67$

  **Solution:** **The total resistance of the circuit is 2.67 ohms.**

**Note:** $24 / 6 = 4$, $24 / 8 = 3$, and $24 / 12 = 2$ of the formula in Step 2 above.

The same result above can be derived by calculating the current through each resistance separately and then adding them together to find the value of the total current.

When the total EMF ($E_t$) is divided by 6, 8, and 12, the separate circuit currents are 20, 15, and 10 amps. See Step 1 below for calculations.

**For example:** The total current can be found by applying the following Ohm's law formula:

**Step 1:** Finding A for each resistance
I = 120 E / 6R      = 20 A
I = 120 E / 8R      = 15 A
I = 120 E / 12R     = 10 A
Total                = 45 A

**Step 2:** Finding total R
R = E / I
R = 120 E / 45 I
R = 2.67

**Solution: The total resistance is 2.67 ohms.**

Note that this value of ohms is the same as applying the formula $R_t = 1 / (1 / R_1 + 1 / R_2 + 1 / R_3)$ as previously discussed.

**For example:** Therefore, the voltage of the circuit can be determined by applying the following Ohm's law formula for computing voltage ($E_t$).

**Step 1:** Finding E
E = I x R
E = 45 I x 2.67R
E = 120.15 V

**Solution: The total supply voltage is 120 volts.**

**See Figure 2-13** for a detail illustration of computing values in parallel circuits and work the exercise problem.

**DC Tip 12:** In parallel circuits, a lot of current can flow, electricians must be careful not to overload the original circuit by adding too many loads.

| ILLUSTRATION | FORMULA REQUIREMENTS | EXERCISE PROBLEM |
|---|---|---|
| $R_1$ 30 Ω  $R_2$ 30 Ω  SWITCH $R_3$ 60 Ω  TOTAL VOLTAGE • 120 V  TOTAL CIRCUIT CURRENT • ? AMPS  + − | $R_T = 1/R_1 + 1/R_2 + 1/R_3$  $I = \frac{E}{R}$ | **Step 1:** Finding known values<br>$R_1$ = _____ R [A]<br>$R_2$ = _____ R [B]<br>$R_3$ = 60 R<br><br>**Step 2:** Setting up formula<br>$R_T = 1/R_1 + 1/R_2 + 1/R_3$<br><br>**Step 3:** Applying formula<br>$R_T$ = 1/_____ R [C] + 1/_____ R [D]<br>     + 1/_____ R [E]<br>$R_T = 2/60 + 2/60 + 1/60$<br>$R_T = 60/$_____ [F]<br>$R_T$ = _____ R [G]<br><br>**Step 4:** Finding known values<br>E = _____ V [H]<br>R = _____ R [I]<br><br>**Step 5:** Setting up formula<br>I = E / R<br><br>**Step 6:** Applying formula<br>I = _____ V [J] / _____ R [K]<br><br>**Solution:** The resistance is _____ [L] ohms<br>and the current is _____ [M] amps. |

**Figure 2-13.** Using the known values in the parallel circuit, calculate the total resistance and amps in the exercise problem.

# COMPUTATIONS IN A SERIES / PARALLEL CIRCUIT

A circuit can contain resistances in series and parallel. Such loads of the circuit must be solved separately and the results then combined.

**In Figure 2-14** there are two resistances in series and a group of three resistances in parallel. In this circuit, values of $R_1$ = 4 ohms, $R_2$ = 5 ohms, $R_3$ = 15 ohms, $R_4$ = 30 ohms, and $R_5$ = 6 ohms are assigned.

**Figure 2-14.** The values in the illustration are used in the text to solve problems with unknown values in a series / parallel circuit.

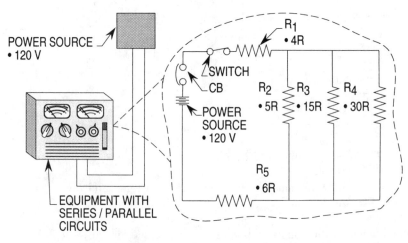

**SERIES / PARALLEL CIRCUITS**

**DC Tip 13:** The advantage of parallel circuits is if a break occurs in any branch, it will not effect the other branches.

In solving the current and voltage values for total resistance, the resistance of the parallel group must be calculated. (Use values in **Figure 2-14**).

**For example:** The total resistance of the circuit can be computed as follows:

    **Step 1:** Finding total R in circuit
        $R_t$ = 1 / 1/5 + 1/15 + 1/30
        $R_t$ = 1 / 6/30 + 2/30 + 1/30
        $R_t$ = 30/9
        $R_t$ = 3.33

    **Solution:** **The total resistance of the circuit is 3.33 ohms.**

The group of parallel resistances are equivalent to 1 resistance with a value of 3.33 ohms. To find the total, simply add together $R_1$, $R_t$, and $R_5$. The results will be as follows:

    $R_1$ 4 + $R_t$ 3.33 + $R_5$ 6 = 13.33 ohms

**DC Tip 14:** The series circuitry in series / parallel circuits can be used for reducing and controlling the current by placing resistance in series.

**For example:** Then the total current in the circuit shown in **Figure 2-14** can be determined as follows:

    **Step 1:** Finding total A in circuit
        It = E / R
        It = 120 E / 13.33R
        It = 9 A

    **Solution:** **The total amps in the circuit is 9.**

The voltage drop across each resistance can be determined by applying the Ohm's law formula (E = IR). The parallel resistances must be treated as a single resistance in series with the other two resistances.

**For example:** To find the VD of $R_1$, $R_t$, and $R_5$, the following formula can be applied:

Step 1: Finding VD of each resistance

$E_1 = 9I_t \times 4R_1 \quad = \quad 36 \quad V$

$E_t = 9I_t \times 3.33R_t \quad = \quad 29.9 \quad V$

$E_5 = 9I_t \times 6R_5 \quad = \quad \underline{54 \quad V}$

Total voltage $\quad = 119.9$ V

**Solution: The total voltage in the circuit rounded up is 120 volts.**

Note that the total voltage of the circuit above 119.9 is rounded up to 120 volts. (9I x 13.33R = 119.9E)

**For example:** By applying Ohm's law, the current in amps through $R_2$, $R_3$, and $R_4$ can be computed as follows:

Step 1: Finding A

$I_2 = E_t / R_2 = 29.9 / 5 \quad = 5.98$ A

$I_3 = E_t / R_3 = 29.9 / 15 \quad = 1.99$ A

$I_4 = E_t / R_4 = 29.9 / 30 \quad = \underline{.99}$ A

Total amps $\quad = 8.96$ A

(8.96 A is rounded up to 9 A)

**Solution: The total amperage in the circuit is 9 amps.**

**For example:** By using the above known values, each value for voltage, amps, and resistance can be found as follows:

Step 1: Finding E

E = I x R

E = 9 A x 13.33R = 120 V rounded up

Step 2: Finding I

I = E / R

I = 120 V / 13.33R

I = 9 A

Step 3: Finding R

R = E / I

R = 120 V / 9 A

R = 13.33

**Solution:** After known values are found, these values can be substituted using Ohm's law to find the unknown values as shown in Steps 1 through 3.

**DC Tip 15:** Another advantage of a series circuit used in combination circuitry, is that such series circuit can be connected with small voltages to obtain higher voltages.

**DC Tip 16:** The parallel circuitry in combination circuitry can be used to create a constant voltage and a large current supply.

Figure 2-15 illustrates a combination of series and parallel resistances. In this illustration, the symbol (R) is utilized to identify ohms.

**Figure 2-15.** The values in the illustration are used in the text to solve problems with unknown values in a combination of series and parallel resistances.

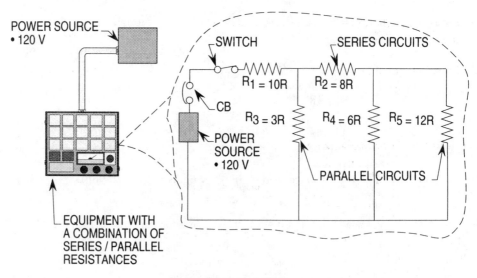

**COMBINATION OF SERIES AND PARALLEL CIRCUITS**

**DC Tip 17:** Series / parallel circuits makes it possible to obtain the different voltages of series circuits and the different currents of parallel circuits.

**For example:** By using these known values in **Figure 2-15**, unknown values can be calculated as follows:

Step 1: Combine parallel resistances $R_4$ and $R_5$, and find the resistance in ohms
$R_a = 1 / (1/6 + 1/12)$
$R_a = 1 / (2/12 + 1/12)$
$R_a = 12/3$
$R_a = 4$ ohms

Step 2: By adding $R_a$ to $R_2$, a resistance of 12 ohms ($R_b$) is obtained
$R_b = 4R + 8R$
$R_b = 12R$

Step 3: Combine $R_b$ with $R_3$ using the parallel formula and find the resistance for $R_c$
$R_c = 1 / (1/12 + 1/3)$
$R_c = 1 / (1/12 + 4/12)$
$R_c = 12/5$
$R_c = 2.4$ ohms

Step 4: The amps of $R_4$ and $R_5$ (See step 1) is found as follows
$I = 120E / 4R$
$I = 30$ A

Step 5: The voltage of $R_4$ and $R_5$ (See step 1) is found as follows
$E = 30I \times 4R$
$E = 120$ V

**DC Tip 18:** A series / parallel circuit has one or more groups of resistances in parallel which are connected in series.

As shown above in Steps 1 through 5, the solutions of solving the values of these circuits are relatively simple. However, complex circuits can be solved in a similar manner by separating the circuits into individual values and solving for each.

When solving problems for series circuits, the sum of the voltage drops are equal to the voltage applied to the circuit. However, the voltages across the loads in a parallel group are the same for each unit in the group.

In a series circuit, the current through each value of a series group is equal to the current through each of the other units in the group.

See Figure 2-16 for a detailed illustration for computing values in series / parallel circuits.

**DC Tip 19:** A parallel / series circuit has one or more groups of resistances in series which are connected in parallel.

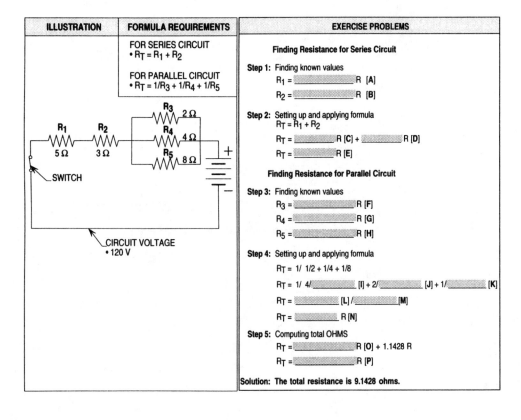

**Figure 2-16** Using the known values in the series / parallel circuit, calculate the total resistance and amps in the exercise problem.

# Chapter 2
# Direct Current Circuits

| Section | Answer | |
|---|---|---|

**Section**          **Answer**

_____  T  (F)   1. Short-circuits happen when an ungrounded phase conductor (hot) makes accidental contact with the metal of boxes, enclosures, conduits, etc.

_____  (T)  F   2. Overcurrent protection devices in circuits are use to protect such circuits from dangerous short-circuits, ground-faults, and overloads.

_____  (T)  F   3. In series circuits, all the current flowing in the circuit must pass through each load in the circuit.

_____  T  F     4. If the voltage drop (VD) in the feeder is held to 3 percent overall, than the VD in the branch-circuit must be kept at 3 percent or less.

_____  T  (F)   5. If the branches of a parallel circuit have the same resistance, then each draws the same amount of current.

_____ _____   6. A _____ condition exists when an accidental contact between conductors permits the current to return to its power supply through a low-resistance path.

_____ _____   7. Fuses will normally hold __5__ times their rating based on the type used.

_____ _____   8. A circuit breaker will hold __3__ times its rating, for a period of time, based on its frame size.

_____ _____   9. Current flow through circuits can be regulated by connecting such components in _Series_, _Parall_ or _S/P_ configurations.

_____ _____   10. A series/parallel circuit has one or more groups of resistances in parallel which are connected in _series_

_____ _____   11. How many amps will a 30 amp fuse hold for about 1/4 to 10 seconds? _150_

_____ _____   12. How many amps will a 30 amp circuit breaker hold (for about 4 seconds) without tripping its element open? _90_

_____ _____   13. What is the total resistance in a series circuit with three resistances of 6 ohms, 8 ohms, and 12 ohms supplied by a 120 volt system?

_____ _____   14. What is the total resistance in a parallel circuit with three resistance of 12 ohms supplied by a 120 volt system?

_____ _____   15. What is the total current in a parallel circuit with three resistances of 12 ohms supplied by a 120 volt system?

_____ _____   16. What is the total resistance in a parallel circuit with three resistances of 4 ohms, 6 ohms, and 8 ohms supplied by an 120 volt system?

_____  _____  17. What is the total current in a parallel circuit with three resistances of 4 ohms, 6 ohms, and 8 ohms supplied by an 120 volt system?

_____  _____  18. What is the total voltage in a parallel circuit with a total resistance of 1.846 ohms and an total current of 65 amps?

_____  _____  19. What is the total resistance in a series/parallel circuit with three parallel resistances of 3 ohms, 9 ohms, and 27 ohms and two series resistances of 6 ohms and 8 ohms supplied by an 120 volt system?

_____  _____  20. What is the total current in a series/parallel circuit with a total resistance of 16.076 ohms supplied by an 120 volt system?

# Alternating

# Current Circuits

**3**

Alternating current (AC) plays an important role in industrial and commercial operations. It is used more extensively than direct current (DC) because it has a greater range of practical applications.

Therefore, good knowledge of the principles of alternating current is essential for the understanding of various electrical devices and their operation. This is true of AC generators, transformers, and motors. This chapter covers the nature of alternating current and many of its characteristics which are used in modern day electrical systems.

Also covered are terms such as maximum, effective, and average values. These terms must be understood by journeymen electricians because they are so related to the generation and use of electricity.

Almost every Journeyman examination administered today have problems related to AC circuits in someway. Therefore, persons taking the examination must be familiar with the operation of these circuits.

**Quick Reference:**

PRINCIPLES OF AC CURRENT ................... 3-2

EFFECTIVE VALUES ..................................... 3-3

FREQUENCY ............................................... 3-3

PHASE ........................................................ 3-4

CAPACITANCE ............................................ 3-5

CAPACITIVE REACTANCE ........................... 3-7

INDUCTANCE .............................................. 3-7

INDUCTIVE REACTANCE ............................. 3-8

IMPEDANCE ................................................ 3-9

RESONANT CIRCUITS ................................. 3-9

RESISTANCE ............................................. 3-10

POWER ...................................................... 3-12

# PRINCIPLES OF AC CURRENT

Alternating current is defined as current which periodically changes direction and continuously changes in magnitude. Such current starts at zero and builds up to a maximum in one direction, then falls back to zero, builds up to a maximum in the opposite direction, and returns to zero. Note that the voltage reads a maximum in one direction, drops to zero, rises to a maximum in the opposite direction, and then returns to zero.

The values of AC and voltage can be indicated by using a sine curve. As shown in **Figure 3-1**, this curve represents a definite voltage or current value for a certain degree of rotation through the alternating cycle. One cycle begins at 0° and ends at 360°. The value of the AC is zero at 0°, maximum in one direction at 90°, zero at 180°, maximum in the opposite direction at 270°, and zero at 360°. **(See Figure 3-1)**

**Figure 3-1.** This illustration shows an AC sine curve and its relationship to an AC circuit supplying an AC machine.

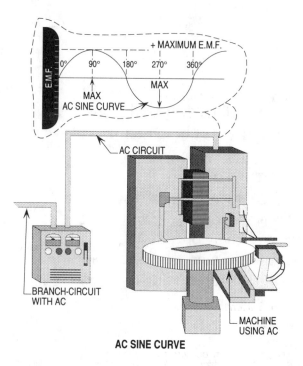

**AC SINE CURVE**

For practical purposes, the values of an alternating current may be considered to follow the sine curve. For example, a single loop of wire can be placed so that it rotates in a magnetic field. As the loop turns, the sides of the loop cut through the lines of force and an EMF is induced in the sides of the loop.

**AC Tip 1:** Note that the direction of the current in the loop C to D is now reversed from the direction in the loop A to B. **(See figure 3-2)**

**Referring to Figure 3-2,** the side AB is moving up through the field, and the side CD is moving down through the field, the voltage induced in AB causes current to flow from A to B, and the voltage induced in CD causes current to flow from C to D. Such voltages add together and cause current to flow in the direction ABCD. Note that this action takes place for as long as AB is moving up and CD is moving down. When the coil is in a vertical position, the sides are moving horizontally and parallel to the lines of force and no voltage is induced. However, as the loop moves through this position, the side AB rotates down through the field and the side CD rotates up.

When the current flow is connected to an external circuit by the action of slip rings, the current travels in one direction while the loop rotates from 0° to 180° and in the other direction while the loop rotates from 180° to 360°. While in the vertical, the loop is in either the 0° or 180° position, and no voltage is induced. When the loop rotates into the horizontal position, the maximum voltage is induced, due to the sides cutting the greatest number lines of force. The AC sine curve is utilized to represent the values of voltage or current from 0° to 360°.

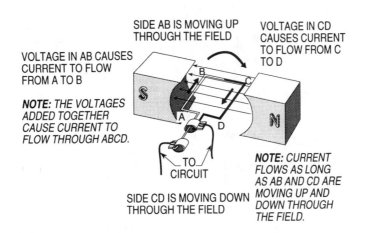

SIDE AB IS MOVING UP
THROUGH THE FIELD

VOLTAGE IN CD
CAUSES CURRENT
TO FLOW FROM C
TO D

VOLTAGE IN AB CAUSES
CURRENT TO FLOW
FROM A TO B

*NOTE: THE VOLTAGES
ADDED TOGETHER
CAUSE CURRENT TO
FLOW THROUGH ABCD.*

TO
CIRCUIT

*NOTE: CURRENT
FLOWS AS LONG
AS AB AND CD ARE
MOVING UP AND
DOWN THROUGH
THE FIELD.*

SIDE CD IS MOVING DOWN
THROUGH THE FIELD

**Figure 3-2.** This illustration shows how current flow is produced, due to induced voltage from the field poles through the loop to the external circuit.

**HOW INDUCED VOLTAGE PRODUCES CURRENT FLOW**

## EFFECTIVE VALUES

To determine the amount of power available from an AC, the effective value must be found. Obviously, effective value does not equal maximum value, because this value is reached only once in the cycle. During one-half cycle, the current is equal and opposite in direction, so that during the other half cycle, the currents do not cancel each other out. Note that work is being performed whether the current is moving in one direction or the other. Therefore, the effective value lies between the zero value and the maximum value.

The effective value of an AC is computed by comparing it with direct current. The comparison is based on the amount of heat produced by each current under the same conditions of use. The heat produced by a current is always proportional to the square of the current. Therefore, it is necessary to determine the square root of the mean square of a number of instantaneous values.

The root mean square (rms) is the resultant current value and it is calculated by the formula $(I = I_m / \sqrt{2})$. Note that I in the formula is the effective value, and $I_m$ is the maximum. If the maximum current has a value of 1, then the rms value is equal to .707 $(I = 1/1.414)$, or $I = .707I_m$. The effective value of an alternating EMF can be determined by multiplying .707 by the maximum EMF.

**AC Tip 2:** Note that in a 60 cycle current there are 120 alternations per second.

**Note:** The values of voltage or current in applications of AC are based upon their effective values rather than the maximum values.

For example, when the voltage is given as 115 volts, the maximum value of the voltage is (1 / .707 x 115 = about 162.7 V).

**See Figures 3-3(a) and (b)** for a detailed illustration pertaining to effective current values and procedures to compute such values, also work exercise problems.

## FREQUENCY

It has been explained that one cycle of AC current covers a time in which the current value increases from zero to maximum in one direction, returns to zero, increases to maximum in the opposite direction, and then returns to zero. The number of cycles per second is the frequency of the current.

**Figure 3-3(a).** This illustration shows the procedure for calculating the effective current in an AC circuit. **Note:** In the spaces provided, calculate and fill in the correct value.

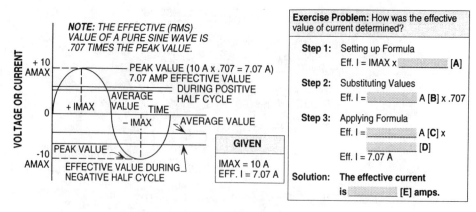

FINDING EFFECTIVE CURRENT IN AN AC CIRCUIT

**Figure 3-3(b).** This illustration shows the procedure for calculating the effective and instantaneous current values of an AC circuit. **Note:** In the spaces provided, calculate and fill in the correct value.

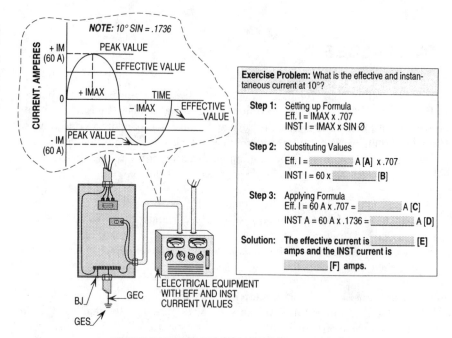

FINDING EFFECTIVE AND INSTANTANEOUS CURRENT

The frequency of an AC current effects the operation of an electrical circuit and its equipment when operating on a current with a certain frequency. Wherever such equipment is used, it must be designed for the frequency of the current in the circuit in which it is to be supplied. **In Figure 3-4,** complete each unknown value and in the spaces provided, calculate and fill in the correct value.

## PHASE

**AC Tip 3:** When voltage and current waveforms are precisely in step with each other, they are in-phase. Those that are not in-phase are considered out-of-phase with each other.

The phase of an AC current or a voltage is the angular distance it has moved from 0° in a positive direction. The phase angle is the difference in degrees of rotation between two AC currents and voltages, or between a voltage and a current. For example, when one voltage reaches a maximum value of 30° later than another, there is a phase angle of 30° between the voltages.

Note that in AC systems, the current lags or leads the voltage. This is due to the inductance or capacitance in the circuit.

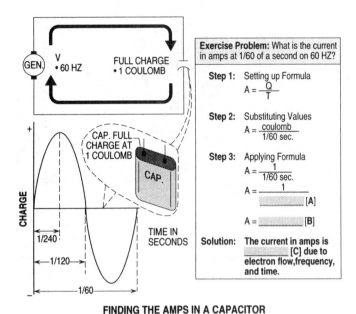

**FINDING THE AMPS IN A CAPACITOR BASED UPON FREQUENCY**

Exercise Problem: What is the current in amps at 1/60 of a second on 60 HZ?

Step 1: Setting up Formula
$$A = \frac{Q}{T}$$

Step 2: Substituting Values
$$A = \frac{coulomb}{1/60 \ sec.}$$

Step 3: Applying Formula
$$A = \frac{1}{1/60 \ sec.}$$

$$A = \frac{1}{\rule{3cm}{0.3cm}} \quad [A]$$

$$A = \rule{3cm}{0.3cm} \quad [B]$$

Solution: The current in amps is _____ [C] due to electron flow, frequency, and time.

**AC Tip 4:** Lower frequencies produce smaller currents while higher frequencies produce greater currents.

**See Figure 3-5(a)** for a detailed illustration of a sine curve representing a current lagging the voltage. Note that in circuits where the currents and voltage do not reach maximum at the same time, such currents and voltage are out-of-phase.

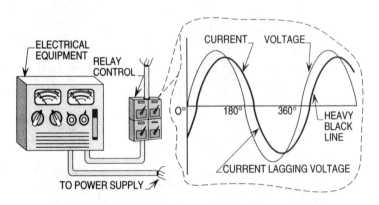

**PHASE RELATIONSHIP BETWEEN CURRENT AND VOLTAGE SUPPLYING POWER TO ELECTRICAL EQUIPMENT**

**Figure 3-5(a).** The current in the illustration is shown lagging the voltage. **Note:** If the heavy black line is the voltage, the voltage would be lagging the current and the current would be leading the voltage.

In **Figure 3-5(b),** the bolded (black) current line crosses the 0° line before the lighter line has crossed it. This indicates that the current reaches 0° before the voltage and the peak value of voltage occurs. Therefore, the current is leading the voltage in the illustration.

**AC Tip 5:** In **Figure 3-5(b)** the voltage is approximately 90° out-of-phase with the current. In other words, the voltage follows the current by approximately 90° lag.

## CAPACITANCE

When a capacitor is connected in series with an AC circuit, the AC current is allowed to flow back and forth in the circuit without actually passing through the capacitor. Note that the electrons build up on one plate of the capacitor and flow out of the other plate. An electrostatic field is established that causes the current to flow in the opposite direction. However, as the voltage from the source begins to drop, the current starts to flow out of one plate of the capacitor and into the other plate.

**Figure 3-5(b).** This illustration shows the voltage and current out-of-phase.

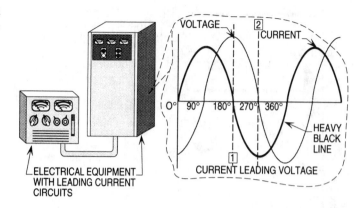

The basic effect of a capacitor in an AC circuit is to cause the current to lead the voltage. If a circuit could be designed without any resistance, the current would lead the voltage by 90°. This can be seen in **Figure 3-5(b)** by the way the electrons move through one alternation.

Note, as the voltage rises, the current begins to drop because of the dielectric stress in the capacitor. By the time the voltage has reached maximum, the capacitor is completely charged and no current flows. At point (1) the current has a value of 0°. As the voltage begins to drop, the current flows out of the capacitor in the opposite direction due to the potential of the capacitor being higher than the potential on the line. At point (2) on the curve, the voltage has dropped to 0° and the current is flowing at a maximum. **(See Figure 3-6)**

**Figure 3-6.** Where necessary in the spaces provided, calculate and fill in the correct value based upon condensers (capacitors) connected in series and parallel.

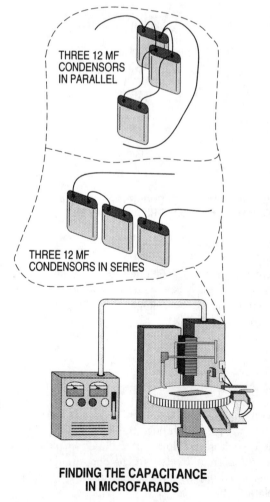

FINDING THE CAPACITANCE
IN MICROFARADS

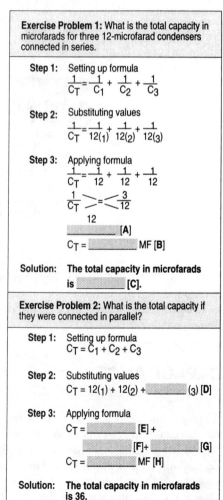

**Exercise Problem 1:** What is the total capacity in microfarads for three 12-microfarad condensers connected in series.

**Step 1:** Setting up formula

$$\frac{1}{C_T} = \frac{1}{C_1} + \frac{1}{C_2} + \frac{1}{C_3}$$

**Step 2:** Substituting values

$$\frac{1}{C_T} = \frac{1}{12_{(1)}} + \frac{1}{12_{(2)}} + \frac{1}{12_{(3)}}$$

**Step 3:** Applying formula

$$\frac{1}{C_T} = \frac{1}{12} + \frac{1}{12} + \frac{1}{12}$$

$$\frac{1}{C_T} > < \frac{3}{12}$$

12 _____ [A]

$C_T =$ _____ MF [B]

**Solution:** The total capacity in microfarads is _____ [C].

**Exercise Problem 2:** What is the total capacity if they were connected in parallel?

**Step 1:** Setting up formula

$C_T = C_1 + C_2 + C_3$

**Step 2:** Substituting values

$C_T = 12_{(1)} + 12_{(2)} +$ _____ $_{(3)}$ [D]

**Step 3:** Applying formula

$C_T =$ _____ [E] +

_____ [F] + _____ [G]

$C_T =$ _____ MF [H]

**Solution:** The total capacity in microfarads is 36.

# CAPACITIVE REACTANCE

The effect of capacitance in an AC circuit is similar to that of resistance and is called capacitive reactance. Capacitive reactance opposes the flow of current in a circuit, and is measured in ohms.

Capacitive reactance in a circuit is inversely proportional to the capacitance and the AC frequency. If the frequency increases, the capacitor charges and discharges more times per second. Therefore, more current flows in the circuit.

Note that reactance decreases as capacitance or frequency increases.

See Figure 3-7 for a detailed illustration and compute the capacitive reactance by working the exercise problem.

**AC Tip 6:** The effect of capacitance in an AC circuit is called capacitive reactance and is measured in ohms.

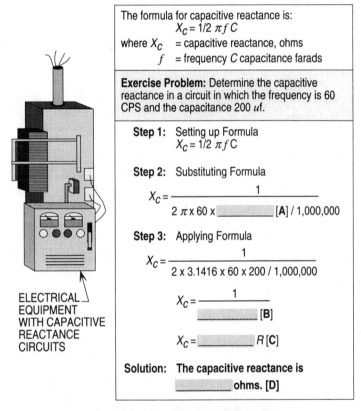

The formula for capacitive reactance is:
$$X_C = 1/2\ \pi f\, C$$
where $X_C$ = capacitive reactance, ohms
$f$ = frequency $C$ capacitance farads

**Exercise Problem:** Determine the capacitive reactance in a circuit in which the frequency is 60 CPS and the capacitance 200 $uf$.

**Step 1:** Setting up Formula
$$X_C = 1/2\ \pi f\, C$$

**Step 2:** Substituting Formula
$$X_C = \frac{1}{2\ \pi \times 60 \times \underline{\quad\quad}\ \text{[A]} / 1{,}000{,}000}$$

**Step 3:** Applying Formula
$$X_C = \frac{1}{2 \times 3.1416 \times 60 \times 200 / 1{,}000{,}000}$$

$$X_C = \frac{1}{\underline{\quad\quad}\ \text{[B]}}$$

$$X_C = \underline{\quad\quad}\ R\ \text{[C]}$$

**Solution:** The capacitive reactance is
_____ ohms. [D]

ELECTRICAL EQUIPMENT WITH CAPACITIVE REACTANCE CIRCUITS

**FINDING CAPACITIVE REACTANCE**

Figure 3-7. Where necessary in the spaces provided, calculate and fill in the correct values for the capacitive reactance in ohms.

# INDUCTANCE

The effect of inductance in an AC circuit is exactly opposite to that of capacitance. Inductance in an AC circuit causes the current to lag the voltage.

Whenever a current change in an inductance coil takes place, an EMF is induced which opposes this change in current. The EMF induced, will be maximum, when the rate of current change is the greatest. The current change is most rapid in an AC circuit when it is passing through the 0° point. This action causes the induced voltage to be maximum at this point.

**AC Tip 7:** The current lags the voltage by 90° in a purely inductive circuit. However, a purely inductive circuit is impossible due to resistance always being present. Note that the current will never lag the voltage a full 90°. (See Figure 3-8).

**Figure 3-8.** At point 0° on the same curve, the current has its most rapid change and the induced voltage at point A is maximum. When the current reaches maximum, there is momentarily no current change. Therefore, there will be no voltage induced at point B.

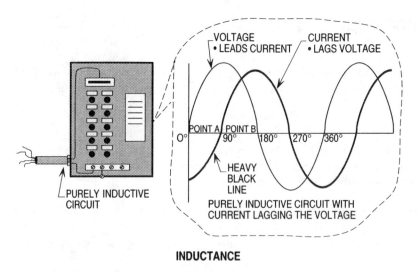

INDUCTANCE

# INDUCTIVE REACTANCE

The effect of inductance in an AC circuit is called inductive reactance and is measured in ohms because it impedes the flow of current in the circuit.

**AC Tip 8:** Since inductive reactance increases as the frequency increases and capacitive reactance decreases as the frequency increases, it is clear that capacitance and inductance has opposite characteristics.

The inductive reactance in an AC circuit is proportional to the inductance and the frequency. As inductance is increased, the induced EMF which opposes the applied EMF is increased. Therefore, the flow of current is reduced.

When the frequency of the current in the circuit is increased, the rate of current change in the inductance coil is also increased. The induced EMF, which opposes the applied EMF, is higher and the flow of current is once again reduced.

**See Figure 3-9** for a detailed illustration of how to compute inductive reactance, and where necessary in the spaces provided fill in the correct value.

**Figure 3-9.** This illustration shows the procedure for calculating inductive reactance in ohms. However, each calculation must be made and in the spaces provided each value filled in.

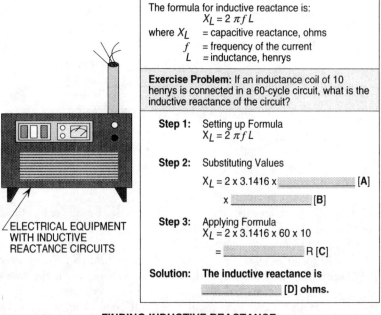

The formula for inductive reactance is:
$$X_L = 2\pi f L$$
where $X_L$ = capacitive reactance, ohms
$f$ = frequency of the current
$L$ = inductance, henrys

**Exercise Problem:** If an inductance coil of 10 henrys is connected in a 60-cycle circuit, what is the inductive reactance of the circuit?

Step 1: Setting up Formula
$X_L = 2\pi f L$

Step 2: Substituting Values
$X_L = 2 \times 3.1416 \times$ _____ [A]
$\times$ _____ [B]

Step 3: Applying Formula
$X_L = 2 \times 3.1416 \times 60 \times 10$
= _____ R [C]

Solution: **The inductive reactance is**
_____ [D] ohms.

**FINDING INDUCTIVE REACTANCE**

# IMPEDANCE

The current in a pure resistive circuit is equal to the voltage divided by the resistance. In AC circuits, capacitive reactance and inductive reactance must be considered before the total current in such a circuit can be found.

The resistance, capacitive reactance, and inductive reactance when added together is called impedance. To determine the capacitive reactance, inductive reactance, and resistance, it can't just be added together. This is mainly due to capacitive reactance and inductive reactance in AC circuits having opposite effects.

For example, to find the total reactance, the difference in the reactances must be obtained. The inductive reactance is positive, because the inductance causes the voltage to lead the current and the capacitive reactance is negative, because it causes the voltage to lag the current.

Since the resistance in a circuit does not, in effect, cause the current to lead or lag the voltage, it is 90° ahead of the inductance and 90° behind the capacitance. To find the impedance, the resistance and reactance must be added vectorially.

See **Figure 3-10** for a vector diagram representing resistance and reactance added vectorially and use such values to work the exercise problem.

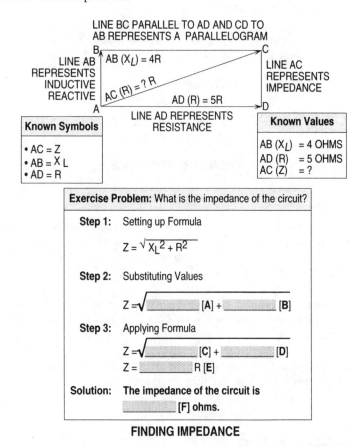

FINDING IMPEDANCE

**AC Tip 9:** Impedence is the total opposition to the flow of current in an AC circuit.

**Figure 3-10.** This illustration shows the procedure for calculating the impedance of a circuit based on resistance and inductive reactance. However, each calculation must be made and in the spaces provided, each value filled in.

See **Figure 3-11** and where necessary in the spaces provided, calculate and fill in the correct values and determine the impedence of the circuit.

# RESONANT CIRCUITS

Capacitance and inductance have opposite effects in an AC circuit and this makes it possible for one to be used to cancel the effect of the other. In AC circuits, inductive reactance

**AC Tip 10:** After the impedance is found in an AC circuit, the other values may be found by applying Ohm's law for alternating current. When applying this formula, substitute the symbol Z, meaning impedance, for the normal symbol R, meaning resistance. The formula then reads as follows:

$$I = E / R$$

**Figure 3-11.** This illustration shows the procedure for calculating the impedance based upon the resistance and capacitive reactance. However, each calculation must be made and in the spaces provided each value filled in.

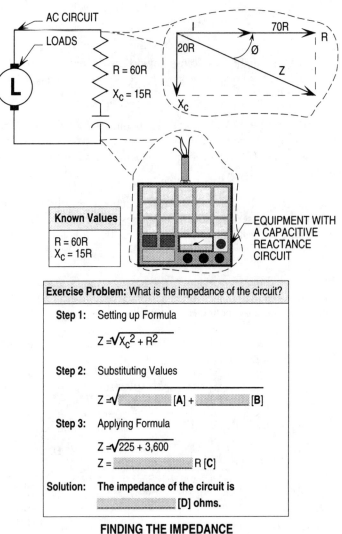

**Known Values**

R = 60R
$X_c$ = 15R

AC CIRCUIT
LOADS
L
R = 60R
$X_c$ = 15R

EQUIPMENT WITH A CAPACITIVE REACTANCE CIRCUIT

**Exercise Problem:** What is the impedance of the circuit?

Step 1: Setting up Formula

$$Z = \sqrt{X_c^2 + R^2}$$

Step 2: Substituting Values

$$Z = \sqrt{\underline{\hspace{2cm}} [A] + \underline{\hspace{2cm}} [B]}$$

Step 3: Applying Formula

$$Z = \sqrt{225 + 3{,}600}$$

$$Z = \underline{\hspace{3cm}} R [C]$$

Solution: **The impedance of the circuit is** \underline{\hspace{3cm}} **[D] ohms.**

**FINDING THE IMPEDANCE**

increases in proportion to the frequency and capacitive reactance is inversely proportional to the frequency. Due to this, frequency can be adjusted to balance any capacitance with any inductance. In other words, the capacitive reactance may be equal to the inductive reactance with the proper frequency applied.

See **Figure 3-12** and calculate the amount of frequency needed to cancel out the effects of capacitance and inductance in an AC circuit and where necessary in the spaces provided, fill in the correct values.

See **Figure 3-13** and compute the frequency in a tank circuit and where necessary in the spaces provided, fill in the correct values.

# RESISTANCE

**AC Tip 11:** Pure resistive circuits include resistors, lamps, heating elements, and other simple electrical devices which have little or no inductance or capacitance.

Resistance in an AC circuit has effects in the circuit when connected with capacitance or inductance. In a purely capacitive or inductive circuit, the current either leads or lags the voltage by 90°. If resistance is connected in series with such circuits, the resistance decreases the flow of current. Therefore, when the voltage is maximum in a positive direction, a current continues to flow in a positive direction to charge the capacitor.

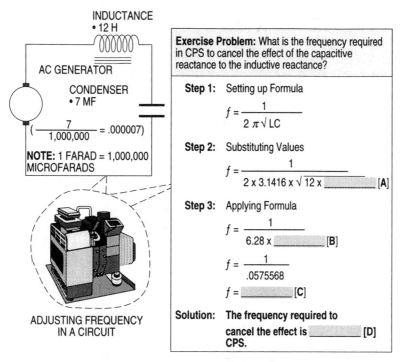

INDUCTANCE
• 12 H

AC GENERATOR

CONDENSER
• 7 MF

$(\dfrac{7}{1,000,000} = .000007)$

**NOTE:** 1 FARAD = 1,000,000 MICROFARADS

ADJUSTING FREQUENCY
IN A CIRCUIT

**Exercise Problem:** What is the frequency required in CPS to cancel the effect of the capacitive reactance to the inductive reactance?

**Step 1:** Setting up Formula

$$f = \dfrac{1}{2\,\pi\,\sqrt{LC}}$$

**Step 2:** Substituting Values

$$f = \dfrac{1}{2 \times 3.1416 \times \sqrt{12 \times \rule{1.5cm}{0.4pt}}}\quad\text{[A]}$$

**Step 3:** Applying Formula

$$f = \dfrac{1}{6.28 \times \rule{1.5cm}{0.4pt}}\quad\text{[B]}$$

$$f = \dfrac{1}{.0575568}$$

$$f = \rule{1.5cm}{0.4pt}\quad\text{[C]}$$

**Solution:** The frequency required to cancel the effect is _____ [D] CPS.

**FINDING FREQUENCY IN A SERIES CIRCUIT**

**Figure 3-12.** This illustration shows the procedure for calculating the frequency in CPS to cancel out the effect of capacitive reactance to inductive reactance. However, each calculation must be made and in the spaces provided each value filled in.

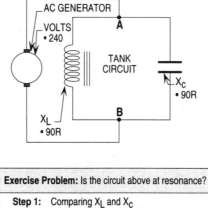

AC GENERATOR

VOLTS
• 240

TANK CIRCUIT

A

B

$X_C$
• 90R

$X_L$
• 90R

**Exercise Problem:** Is the circuit above at resonance?

**Step 1:** Comparing $X_L$ and $X_C$

$X_L = \rule{1.5cm}{0.4pt}$ [A] R

$X_C = \rule{1.5cm}{0.4pt}$ [B] R

**Solution:** Since $X_L$ and $X_C$ are equal, the circuit is at resonant frequency.

**FINDING THE RESONANCE OF A
PARALLEL RESONANT CIRCUIT**

**Figure 3-13** shows a circuit in which the capacitive reactance and inductive reactance are connected in parallel. Such a circuit is often called a "tank" circuit. The effect of a parallel resonant circuit is opposite to that of a series circuit. In other words, the impedance is provided by the parallel combination and is greatest at the resonant frequency. The current in this circuit flows between points A and B when the frequency is not the same as the resonant frequency.

In a purely capacitive circuit, the current drops to zero as soon as the voltage reaches maximum, because the capacitor is fully charged. With resistance in the circuit, the current continues to flow until the charge in the capacitor is equal to the voltage.

Note that the current is at zero. However, as the voltage continues to drop, the current starts to flow in the opposite direction, until the capacitor charge balances the applied voltage.

**See Figure 3-14** for a detailed illustration of such a circuit and how to calculate the resistance when the current leads the voltage and where necessary in the spaces provided, fill in the correct value.

**Figure 3-14.** This illustration shows the procedure for calculating the impedance of a circuit where resistance has an effect. However, each calculation must be made and in the spaces provided each value filled in.

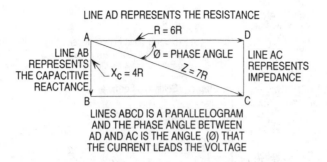

LINE AD REPRESENTS THE RESISTANCE

LINE AB REPRESENTS THE CAPACITIVE REACTANCE

$R = 6R$
$\emptyset$ = PHASE ANGLE
$X_c = 4R$
$Z = 7R$

LINE AC REPRESENTS IMPEDANCE

LINES ABCD IS A PARALLELOGRAM AND THE PHASE ANGLE BETWEEN AD AND AC IS THE ANGLE ($\emptyset$) THAT THE CURRENT LEADS THE VOLTAGE

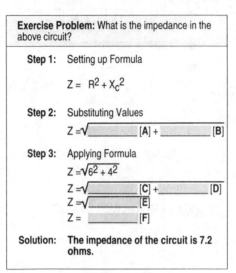

**Exercise Problem:** What is the impedance in the above circuit?

**Step 1:** Setting up Formula

$$Z = R^2 + X_c^2$$

**Step 2:** Substituting Values

$$Z = \sqrt{\rule{1cm}{0pt}}\,[A] + \rule{1.5cm}{0pt}\,[B]$$

**Step 3:** Applying Formula

$$Z = \sqrt{6^2 + 4^2}$$
$$Z = \sqrt{\rule{1cm}{0pt}}\,[C] + \rule{1.5cm}{0pt}\,[D]$$
$$Z = \sqrt{\rule{1cm}{0pt}}\,[E]$$
$$Z = \rule{1.5cm}{0pt}\,[F]$$

**Solution:** The impedance of the circuit is 7.2 ohms.

**FINDING IMPEDANCE DUE TO RESISTANCE**

# POWER

In a DC circuit, the power is equal to the product of the current and the amperage. However, this is true in an AC circuit only when the current and voltage are in-phase.

**AC Tip 12:** In most AC circuits, there is inductance and capacitive reactance present. Such reactance causes a shift in the phase relation of current and voltage, which, in turn, causes a certain inefficiency in the circuit. In such cases, it is necessary to use a power factor to calculate the true power.

Power is measured in watts. In a circuit where the voltage and current are in-phase, such power is equal to the product of the current and the voltage. If the current and voltage are out-of-phase, the product of the voltage and amperage are designated as volt-amperes and not watts. To find the power in watts, multiply the volt-amperes by the cosine of the angle.

**See Figure 3-15** for voltages and currents that are in-phase or out-of-phase with each other.

Note that the cosine of an angle is the ratio of the side or a right triangle adjacent to the angle to the hypotenuse of the triangle. **In Figure 3-16** compute the power factor and where necessary in the spaces provided, fill in the correct value.

The cosine of the phase angle ($\emptyset$) can be used to determine the power of an AC circuit when the voltage and current are out-of-phase. Such phase angle ($\emptyset$) is the power factor of the circuit. When the voltage and current are in-phase, the value of the power factor is 1 or the value of the power factor is always less than 1 or 100 percent. Power factor of an AC circuit is good if the values are in unity, which is 1 (100%).

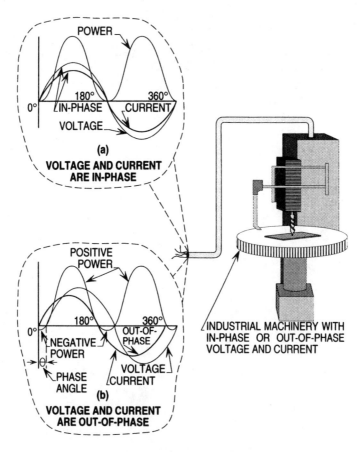

**Figures 3-15.** This illustration shows the voltage and current in-phase or out-of-phase due to the power and phase angle of the circuit.

**VOLTAGE AND CURRENT RELATIONSHIP**

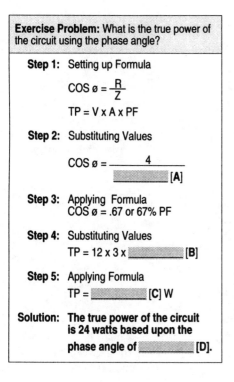

**Exercise Problem:** What is the true power of the circuit using the phase angle?

**Step 1:** Setting up Formula

$$COS\ \emptyset = \frac{R}{Z}$$

$$TP = V \times A \times PF$$

**Step 2:** Substituting Values

$$COS\ \emptyset = \frac{4}{\rule{2cm}{0.5pt}}\ [A]$$

**Step 3:** Applying Formula
COS ø = .67 or 67% PF

**Step 4:** Substituting Values
TP = 12 x 3 x _____ [B]

**Step 5:** Applying Formula
TP = _____ [C] W

**Solution:** The true power of the circuit is 24 watts based upon the phase angle of _____ [D].

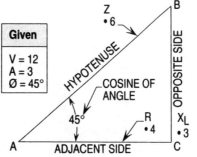

**Given**

V = 12
A = 3
Ø = 45°

**RIGHT TRIANGLE WITH PHASE ANGLE (Ø)**

**Figure 3-16.** This illustration shows a right triangle being used to demonstrate the cosine of an angle. Note that the exercise problem must be worked and in the spaces provided each calculated value filled in.

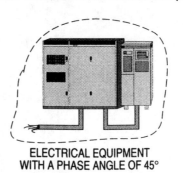

ELECTRICAL EQUIPMENT
WITH A PHASE ANGLE OF 45°

**FINDING TRUE POWER OF A CIRCUIT**

# Chapter 3
# Alternating Current Circuits

| Section | Answer | |
|---|---|---|

**Section**      **Answer**

_____      T    F      1. Alternating current is defined as current which periodically changes direction and continuously changes in magnitude.

_____      T    F      2. The values of AC and voltage begins with one cycle at 0° and ends at 180°.

_____      T    F      3. The number of cycles for AC current per second is the frequency of the current.

_____      T    F      4. The basic effect of a capacitor in an AC circuit is to cause the current to lag the voltage.

_____      T    F      5. Impedance is the total opposition to the flow of current in an AC circuit.

_____  _____      6. The values of AC current and voltage can be indicated by using a _____ curve.

_____  _____      7. In a 60 cycle current there are _____ alternations per second.

_____  _____      8. Capacitive reactance in an AC circuit is measured in _____.

_____  _____      9. Inductance in an AC circuit causes the current to _____ the voltage.

_____  _____      10. The _____ of the phase angle can be used to determine the power for an AC circuit when the voltage and current are out-of-phase.

_____  _____      11. What is the total capacity in microfarads for three 14-microfarads condensers connected in series and parallel ?

_____  _____      12. What is the capacitive reactance in a circuit in which the frequency is 60 CPS and the capacitance is 300 MF ?

_____  _____      13. What is the inductive reactance in a circuit in which an inductance coil of 20 henrys is connected in a 60 cycle circuit ?

_____  _____      14. What is the impedance in a circuit with an inductive reactance of 6 ohms and a resistance of 8 ohms ?

_____  _____      15. What is the impedance in a circuit with a capacitive reactance of 20 ohms and a resistance of 80 ohms ?

# Applying Formulas

**4**

The formulas discussed in this chapter will contain AC/DC formulas, Ohm's law formulas, PIE formulas, and voltage drop formulas. These formulas are used to solve electrical problems in this book. Other sources should be consulted for additional information pertaining to electrical formulas.

Electricians apply these formulas and others where necessary to derive values to select the components for branch-circuits, feeder-circuits and service equipment elements.

For example, electricians use the voltage drop formulas in the field to determine VD loss and they use the Ohm's law and PIE formulas to compute wattage, voltage, resistance, and amps.

Note that these formulas can appear on the electrical examination to test the competency of persons desiring to obtain a journeyman's license.

## Quick Reference:

AC/DC FORMULAS ............................................. 4-2

OHM'S LAW AND PIE FORMULAS ...................... 4-7

APPLYING OHM'S LAW ..................................... 4-7

APPLYING PIE FORMULAS ................................. 4-10

APPLYING OHM'S LAW AND PIE

FORMULAS COMBINED ...................................... 4-13

VOLTAGE DROP ............................................... 4-22

# AC/DC FORMULAS

**Formula Tip 1:** To properly calculate volts, amps, watts, HP, etc., test takers must learn how to apply the formulas in this chapter.

The following main formula and values are applied to solve electrical problems pertaining to the Journeyman's examination and to this book, which is a variation of the power formula:

$I = P / E$
$I =$ amps
$P =$ watts
$E =$ volts

Direct-current and alternating-current formulas are applied to find the following values:

(1) Amperes when horsepower is known
(2) Amperes when kilowatts is known
(3) Amperes when kilovolt amps is known
(4) Kilowatts
(5) Kilovolt amps
(6) Horsepower (output)

The following abbreviations are used when applying an AC/DC formula:

(1) $I =$ amps
(2) $E =$ volts
(3) $PF =$ power factor
(4) $kW =$ kilowatts
(5) $kVA =$ kilovolt amps
(6) $HP =$ horsepower
(7) $E_{FF} =$ efficiency

Use the following chart to apply standard electrical formulas for solving problems related to direct-current and alternating-current. **(See Figure 4-1)**

**Figure 4-1.** The chart is for applying standard electrical formulas for direct-current and alternating-current related calculations.

**Note:** Some testing authorities use 1.732 for three-phase circuits instead of 1.73 as shown in the chart for three-phase formulas.

**AC/DC FORMULAS**

| FINDING | DIRECT CURRENT | ALTERNATING CURRENT | | |
|---|---|---|---|---|
| | | 1Ø, 115 OR 120 V | 1Ø, 208, 230, or 240 V | 3Ø–ALL VOLTAGES |
| AMPERES WHEN HORSEPOWER IS KNOWN | $\dfrac{HP \times 746}{E \times E_{FF}}$ | $\dfrac{HP \times 746}{E \times E_{FF} \times PF}$ | $\dfrac{HP \times 746}{E \times E_{FF} \times PF}$ | $\dfrac{HP \times 746}{1.73 \times E \times E_{FF} \times PF}$ |
| AMPERES WHEN KILOWATTS IS KNOWN | $\dfrac{kW \times 1{,}000}{E}$ | $\dfrac{kW \times 1{,}000}{E \times PF}$ | $\dfrac{kW \times 1{,}000}{E \times PF}$ | $\dfrac{kW \times 1{,}000}{1.73 \times E \times PF}$ |
| AMPERES WHEN kVA IS KNOWN | | $\dfrac{kVA \times 1{,}000}{E}$ | $\dfrac{kVA \times 1{,}000}{E}$ | $\dfrac{kVA \times 1{,}000}{1.73 \times E}$ |
| KILOWATTS | $\dfrac{I \times E}{1{,}000}$ | $\dfrac{I \times E \times PF}{1{,}000}$ | $\dfrac{I \times E \times PF}{1{,}000}$ | $\dfrac{I \times E \times 1.73 \times PF}{1{,}000}$ |
| KILOVOLT-AMPS | | $\dfrac{I \times E}{1{,}000}$ | $\dfrac{I \times E}{1{,}000}$ | $\dfrac{I \times E \times 1.73}{1{,}000}$ |
| HORSEPOWER (OUTPUT) | $\dfrac{I \times E \times E_{FF}}{746}$ | $\dfrac{I \times E \times E_{FF} \times PF}{746}$ | $\dfrac{I \times E \times E_{FF} \times PF}{746}$ | $\dfrac{I \times E \times 1.73 \times E_{FF} \times PF}{746}$ |

What is the amperage for a 40 horsepower, 460 volt, three-phase induction motor with a power factor of 90 percent and operating efficiency of 85 percent?

**Problem 4-2:** Finding the amperes when the horsepower is known.

Step 1: Finding formula
$$I = HP \times 746 \,/\, E \times \sqrt{3} \times E_{ff} \times PF$$

Step 2: Calculating amperage
$$I = 40 \times 746 \,/\, 460\ V \times 1.732 \times 85\% \times 90\%$$
$$I = 29{,}840 \,/\, 609.5$$
$$I = 48.9$$

Solution: **The amperage is 48.9 amps when the horsepower is known.**

See **Figure 4-2** for an exercise problem when finding amperage if the horsepower is known.

| ILLUSTRATION | FORMULA REQUIREMENTS | EXERCISE PROBLEM |
|---|---|---|
| CB<br>• IN PANELBOARD<br><br>NOTE: MOTOR IS AC AND SINGLE-PHASE WHEN APPLYING FORMULA.<br><br>MOTOR<br>• 5 HP<br>• 230 V<br>• 1Ø<br>• PF = 90%<br>• E_FF = 80%<br><br>**KNOWN VALUES**<br>• HP (HORSEPOWER) = 5 HP<br>• E (VOLTAGE) = 230 V<br>• E_FF (EFFICIENCY) = 80%<br>• PF (POWER FACTOR) = 90% | I = HP x 746 ÷ E x E_FF<br>**I = HP x 746 ÷ E x E_FF x PF**<br>I = HP x 746 ÷ 1.73 x E x E_FF x PF<br><br>**ABBREVIATIONS**<br>I = AMPERAGE<br>HP = HORSEPOWER<br>E = VOLTAGE<br>E_FF = EFFICIENCY<br>PF = POWER FACTOR<br><br>**TRANSPOSING FORMULAS**<br>SEE FIGURE 4-1 IN THIS CHAPTER FOR ARRANGEMENTS OF FORMULAS | **Step 1:** Finding known values<br>HP = _____ [A]<br>E = _____ [B]<br>E_FF = _____ [C]<br>PF = _____ [D]<br><br>**Step 2:** Setting up formula<br>I = HP x 746 ÷ E x E_FF x PF<br><br>**Step 3:** Applying formula<br>I = _____ HP [E] x 746 ÷ _____ V [F]<br>_____ E_FF [G] x _____ PF [H]<br><br>I = _____ A [I]<br><br>**Solution:** The unknown value is<br>_____ [J] amps. |

**Figure 4-2.** Exercise problem for finding the amperage when the horsepower is known.

What is the amperage for a 54 kW load supplied by a 240 volt, single-phase system with a 75 percent power factor?

**Problem 4-3:** Finding the amperage when the kilowatts are known.

Step 1: Finding formula
$$I = kW \times 1{,}000 \,/\, E \times PF$$

Step 2: Calculating amperage
$$I = 54 \times 1{,}000 \,/\, 240\ V \times 75\%$$
$$I = 54{,}000 \,/\, 180$$
$$I = 300\ A$$

Solution: **The amperage is 300 amps when kilowatts is known.**

See **Figure 4-3** for an exercise problem when finding amperage if kilowatts are known.

**Figure 4-3.** Exercise problem for finding the amperage when the kilowatts are known.

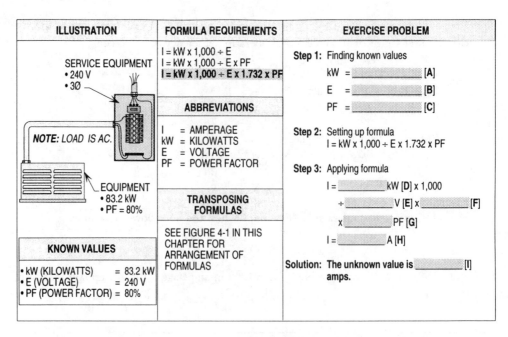

| ILLUSTRATION | FORMULA REQUIREMENTS | EXERCISE PROBLEM |
|---|---|---|
| SERVICE EQUIPMENT • 240 V • 3Ø  NOTE: LOAD IS AC.  EQUIPMENT • 83.2 kW • PF = 80% | I = kW x 1,000 ÷ E<br>I = kW x 1,000 ÷ E x PF<br>**I = kW x 1,000 ÷ E x 1.732 x PF**<br><br>**ABBREVIATIONS**<br>I = AMPERAGE<br>kW = KILOWATTS<br>E = VOLTAGE<br>PF = POWER FACTOR<br><br>**TRANSPOSING FORMULAS**<br>SEE FIGURE 4-1 IN THIS CHAPTER FOR ARRANGEMENT OF FORMULAS | **Step 1:** Finding known values<br>kW = _____ [A]<br>E = _____ [B]<br>PF = _____ [C]<br><br>**Step 2:** Setting up formula<br>I = kW x 1,000 ÷ E x 1.732 x PF<br><br>**Step 3:** Applying formula<br>I = _____ kW [D] x 1,000<br>÷ _____ V [E] x _____ [F]<br>x _____ PF [G]<br>I = _____ A [H]<br><br>**Solution:** The unknown value is _____ [I] amps. |
| **KNOWN VALUES**<br>• kW (KILOWATTS) = 83.2 kW<br>• E (VOLTAGE) = 240 V<br>• PF (POWER FACTOR) = 80% | | |

**Problem 4-4:** Finding the amperes when the kilovolt amps are known.

What is the amperage for a 72 kVA load supplied by a 240 volt, single-phase system?

**Step 1:** Finding formula
I = kVA x 1,000 / E

**Step 2:** Calculating amperage
I = 72 x 1,000 / 240 V
I = 72,000 / 240 V
I = 300 A

**Solution:** The amperage is 300 amps when kilovolt amps is known.

See **Figure 4-4** for an exercise problem when finding amperage if kilovolt amps are known.

**Figure 4-4.** Exercise problem for finding the amperage when the kilovolt amps are known.

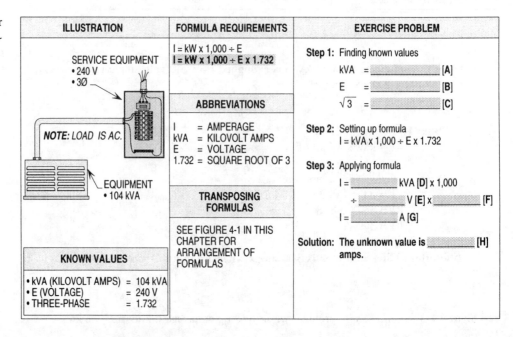

| ILLUSTRATION | FORMULA REQUIREMENTS | EXERCISE PROBLEM |
|---|---|---|
| SERVICE EQUIPMENT • 240 V • 3Ø  NOTE: LOAD IS AC.  EQUIPMENT • 104 kVA | I = kW x 1,000 ÷ E<br>**I = kW x 1,000 ÷ E x 1.732**<br><br>**ABBREVIATIONS**<br>I = AMPERAGE<br>kVA = KILOVOLT AMPS<br>E = VOLTAGE<br>1.732 = SQUARE ROOT OF 3<br><br>**TRANSPOSING FORMULAS**<br>SEE FIGURE 4-1 IN THIS CHAPTER FOR ARRANGEMENT OF FORMULAS | **Step 1:** Finding known values<br>kVA = _____ [A]<br>E = _____ [B]<br>$\sqrt{3}$ = _____ [C]<br><br>**Step 2:** Setting up formula<br>I = kVA x 1,000 ÷ E x 1.732<br><br>**Step 3:** Applying formula<br>I = _____ kVA [D] x 1,000<br>÷ _____ V [E] x _____ [F]<br>I = _____ A [G]<br><br>**Solution:** The unknown value is _____ [H] amps. |
| **KNOWN VALUES**<br>• kVA (KILOVOLT AMPS) = 104 kVA<br>• E (VOLTAGE) = 240 V<br>• THREE-PHASE = 1.732 | | |

What is the kilowatts for a 300 amp load supplied by a 240 volt, single-phase system with a 75 percent power factor?

**Problem 4-5:** Finding the kilowatts when the amperage, voltage, and power factor are known.

**Step 1:** Finding formula
kW = I x E x PF / 1,000

**Step 2:** Calculating kW
kW = 300 A x 240 V x 75% / 1,000
kW = 54,000 / 1,000
kW = 54

**Solution: The kilowatt rating is 54.**

See **Figure 4-5** for an exercise problem when finding kilowatts.

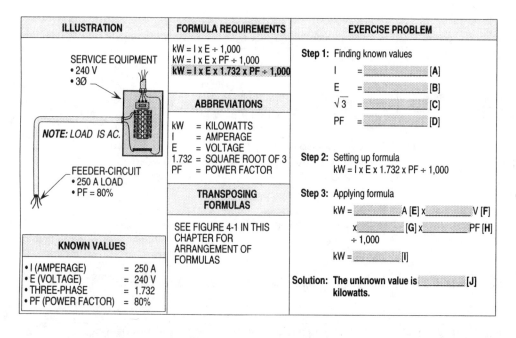

**Figure 4-5.** Exercise problem for finding the kilowatts.

What is the kilovolt amps for a 300 amp load supplied by a 240 volt, single-phase system?

**Problem 4-6:** Finding the kilovolt amps when the amperage and voltage are known.

**Step 1:** Finding formula
kVA = I x E / 1,000

**Step 2:** Calculating kVA
kVA = 300 A x 240 V / 1,000
kVA = 72,000 / 1,000
kVA = 72

**Solution: The kilovolt amp rating is 72.**

See **Figure 4-6** for an exercise problem when finding kilovolt amps.

**Figure 4-6.** Exercise problem for finding the kilovolt amps.

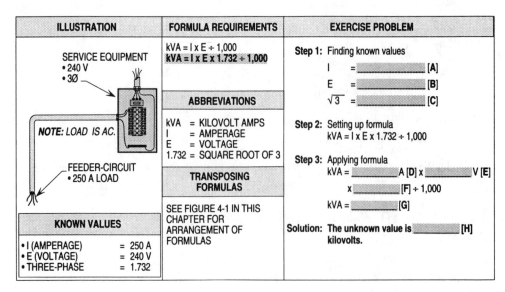

**Problem 4-7:** Finding the horsepower (output) when the amperage, voltage, power factor, and efficiency are known.

What is the horsepower for a 460 volt, three-phase induction motor with a 90 percent power factor and 85 percent efficiency that is pulling 48.9 amps?

**Step 1:** Finding formula
$$HP = I \times E \times \sqrt{3} \times E_{ff} \times PF / 746$$

**Step 2:** Calculating horsepower
$$HP = 48.9 \text{ A} \times 480 \text{ V} \times 1.732 \times 85\% \times 90\% / 746$$
$$HP = 31,086 / 746$$
$$HP = 41.7$$

**Solution:** The horsepower rating is **41.7.**

**See Figure 4-7** for an exercise problem when finding horsepower (output).

**Figure 4-7.** Exercise problem for finding the horsepower (output).

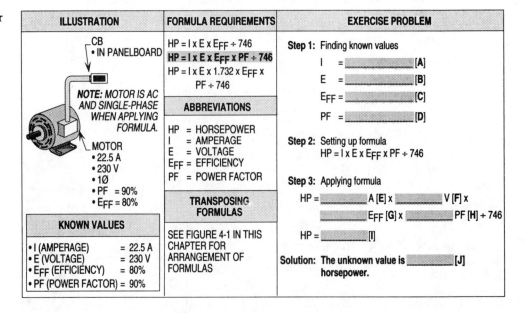

# OHM'S LAW AND PIE FORMULAS

When applying Ohm's law and PIE formulas, the following four circuit values are applied in an electrical circuit.

    **(1)** Voltage (E or V)
    **(2)** Resistance (R)
    **(3)** Current (I or A)
    **(4)** Power (P, W or VA)

**Formula Tip 2:** The voltage of a circuit provides the pressure needed to force the flow of electrons through the conductors from the source to the load.

## VOLTAGE

Voltage is abbreviated by using the letter E or V which is measured by the unit volt. Voltage is created by electron pressure which is called electromotive force. The difference of potential between any two points is also described as the term voltage.

## RESISTANCE

Resistance is abbreviated by using the letter R which is measured by the unit ohm. Resistance is created by the friction opposition to the flow of electrons. Resistance is contained in every component of an electrical circuit including the power supply.

**Formula Tip 3:** The free electrons of a circuit creates the current flow in a circuit.

## CURRENT

Current is abbreviated by using the letter I or A which is measured by the unit ampere. Current is created by free electrons moving in the same direction in a conductor. Electrical current is produced that is sometimes referred to as intensity.

## POWER

Power is abbreviated by using the letter P, W or VA which is measured by the unit watt. Power is created by the rate of work that can be produced by the movement of electrons.

**Formula Tip 4:** Power in a circuit depends on how fast a specific amount of work is performed.

## APPLYING OHM'S LAW

When applying Ohm's law, the following values are applied for finding the relationship between the voltage, current, and resistance that only supplies resistive loads in direct-current or alternating-current circuits.

**Formula Tip 5:** The electrical power in the parts of circuits are equal to the current in such parts multiplied by the voltage imposed on these parts of such circuits.

## FINDING VOLTAGE

When applying Ohm's law, the following formula is applied when finding the voltage where known values of current and resistance are given:

    • $E = I \times R$

**Problem 4-8:** Finding the voltage when the current (amperage) and resistance (ohms) are known.

What is the voltage in a circuit with a current (amperage) rating of 4 amps and a resistance (ohms) rating of 30 ohms?

Step 1: Finding formula
E = I x R

Step 2: Calculating voltage
E = 4 A x 30R
E = 120 V

Solution: **The voltage is 120 volts when applying Ohm's law.**

See **Figure 4-8** for an exercise problem when applying Ohm's law to find the voltage.

**Figure 4-8.** Exercise problem for finding the voltage when applying Ohm's law.

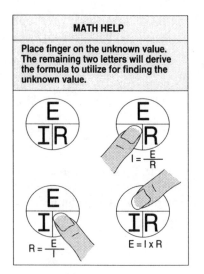

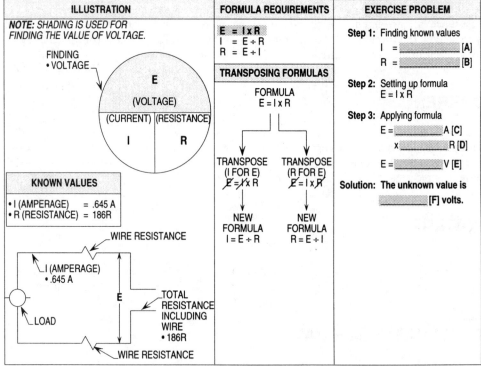

## FINDING CURRENT

To apply Ohm's law, the following formula is used for finding the amperage, if the known values of voltage and resistance are given:

• I = E / R

What is the current (amperage) in a circuit with a voltage rating of 120 volts and a resistance (ohms) rating of 30 ohms?

**Problem 4-9:** Finding the current (amperage) when the voltage and resistance (ohms) are known.

**Step 1:** Finding formula
I = E / R

**Step 2:** Calculating current (amperage)
I = 120 V / 30R
I = 4 A

**Solution:** **The amperage is 4 amps when applying Ohm's law.**

See **Figure 4-9** for an exercise problem when applying Ohm's law to find the amperage.

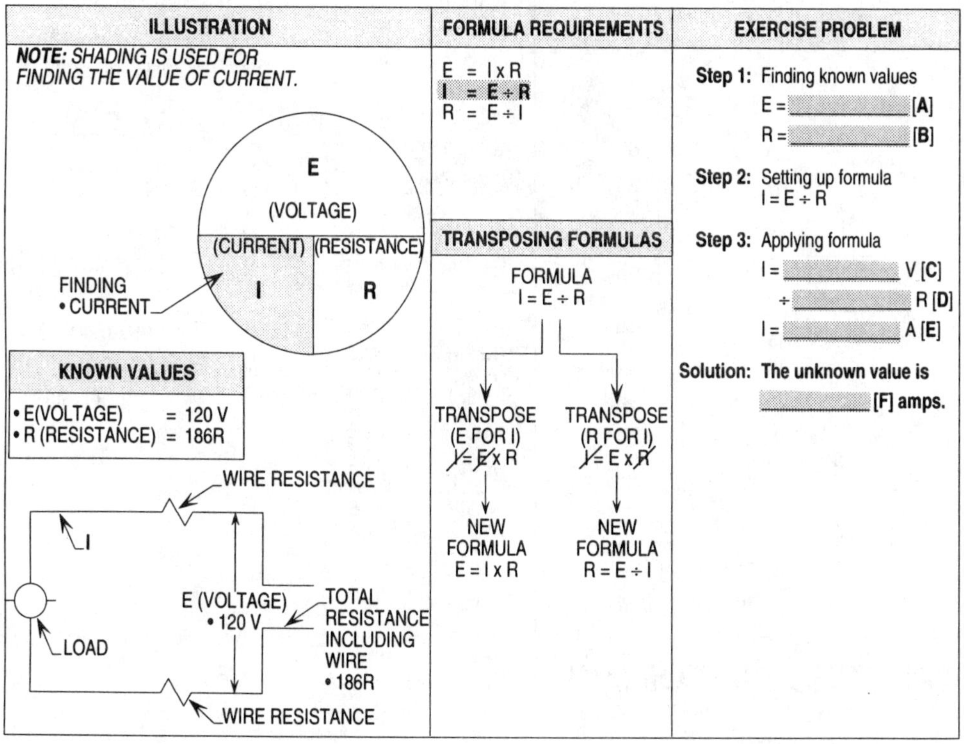

**Figure 4-9.** Exercise problem for finding the current (amperage) when applying Ohm's law.

# FINDING RESISTANCE

To apply Ohm's law, the following formula is used for finding the resistance, if the known values of voltage and current are given:

**Formula Tip 6:** The resistance of a circuit can be utilized to oppose the flow of current in such circuit.

• R = E / I

**Problem 4-10:** Finding the resistance (ohms) when the voltage and the current (amperage) are known.

What is the resistance (ohms) in a circuit with a voltage rating of 120 volts and a current (amperage) rating of 4 amps.

**Step 1:** Finding formula
R = E / I

**Step 2:** Calculating resistance (ohms)
R = 120 V / 4 A
R = 30

**Solution:** The resistance is 30 ohms when applying Ohm's law.

See **Figure 4-10** for an exercise problem when applying Ohm's law to find the resistance.

**Figure 4-10.** Exercise problem for finding the resistance (ohms) when applying Ohm's law.

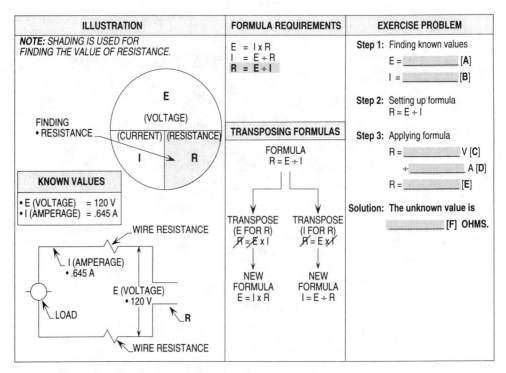

## APPLYING PIE FORMULA

To apply the PIE formulas, the following values must be used for finding the relationship between the power, current, and voltage.

## FINDING POWER

To apply the PIE formula, the following formula must be used for finding the power in watts, if the known values of current and voltage are given:

• P = E x I

What is the power (wattage) in a circuit with a voltage rating of 240 volts and a current (amperage) rating of 40 amps?

**Problem 4-11:** Finding the power (wattage) when the voltage and current (amperage) are known.

**Step 1:** Finding formula
P = E x I

**Step 2:** Calculating power (wattage)
P = 240 V x 40 A
P = 9,600 W

**Solution: The power (wattage) is 9,600 watts when applying the PIE formula.**

**See Figure 4-11** for an exercise problem when applying the PIE formula to find the power.

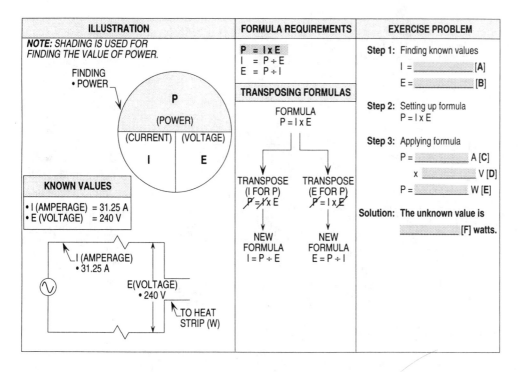

Known Values:
- I (AMPERAGE) = 31.25 A
- E (VOLTAGE) = 240 V

**Figure 4-11.** Exercise problem for finding the power (wattage) when applying the PIE formula.

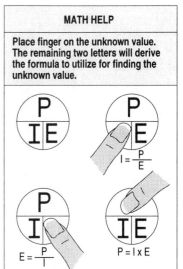

**MATH HELP**

Place finger on the unknown value. The remaining two letters will derive the formula to utilize for finding the unknown value.

# FINDING CURRENT

To apply the PIE formula, the following formula is used for finding the current, if the known values of power and voltage are given:

- I = P / E

**Problem 4-12:** Finding the current (amperage) when the power (wattage) and voltage are known.

What is the current (amperage) in a circuit with a power (wattage) rating of 9,600 watts and a voltage rating of 240 volts?

**Step 1:** Finding formula
$$I = P / E$$

**Step 2:** Calculating current (amperage)
$$I = 9,600 \text{ W} / 240 \text{ V}$$
$$I = 40 \text{ A}$$

**Solution: The current (amperage) is 40 amps when applying the PIE formula.**

See **Figure 4-12** for an exercise problem when applying the PIE formula to find the amperage.

**Figure 4-12.** Exercise problem for finding the current (amperage) when applying the PIE formula.

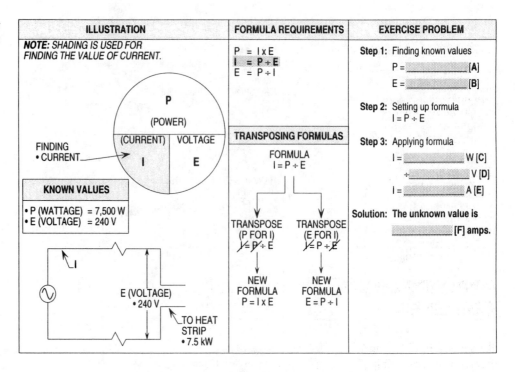

## FINDING VOLTAGE

To apply the PIE formula, the following formula is used for finding the voltage, if the known values of power and current are given:

- $E = P / I$

What is the voltage in a circuit with a power (wattage) rating of 9,600 watts and a current (amperage) rating of 40 amps?

**Problem 4-13:** Finding the voltage when the power (wattage) and current (amperage) are known.

**Step 1:** Finding formula

E = P / I

**Step 2:** Calculating voltage

E = 9,600 W / 40 A

E = 240 V

**Solution:** **The voltage is 240 volts when applying the PIE formula.**

**See Figure 4-13** for an exercise problem when finding the voltage, and applying the PIE formula.

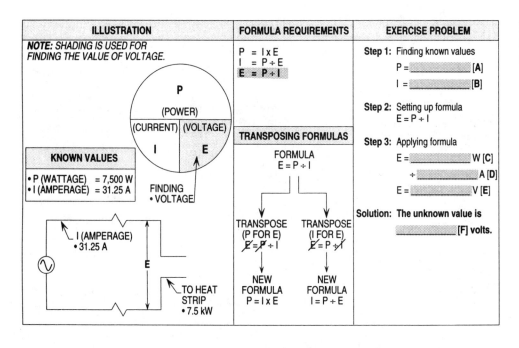

**Figure 4-13.** Exercise problem for finding the voltage when applying the PIE formula.

# APPLYING OHM'S LAW AND PIE FORMULAS COMBINED

To apply Ohm's law and the PIE formulas combined, the following values are applied for finding the relationship between power, current, voltage, and resistance.

**Note:** The following three exercise problems apply to Ohm's law and PIE formulas combined to demonstrate the relationship between the two formulas when finding power.

## FINDING POWER

To apply Ohm's law and the PIE formulas combined, the following formulas are used for finding the power, if the known values of current, voltage, and resistance are given:

- P = E x I
- P = E² / R
- P = I² x R

**Problem 4-14(a):** Finding the power (wattage) when the voltage and current (amperage) are known.

What is the power (wattage) in a circuit with a voltage rating of 240 volts and a current (amperage) rating of 30 amps?

Step 1: Finding formula
P = E x I

Step 2: Calculating power (wattage)
P = 240 V x 30 A
P = 7,200 W

Solution: The power (wattage) is 7,200 watts.

**Figure 4-14(a).** Exercise problem for finding the power (wattage) when applying Ohm's law and the PIE formulas combined.

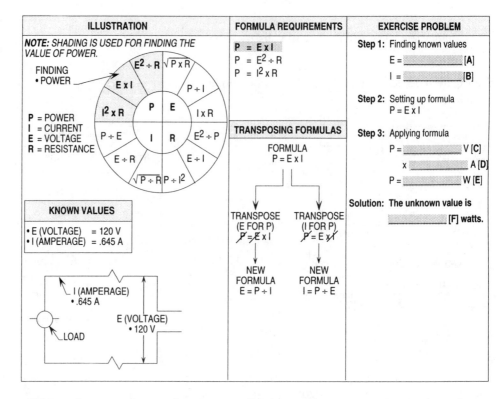

**Problem 4-14(b):** Finding the power (wattage) when the voltage and resistance (ohms) are known.

What is the power (wattage) in a circuit that has a voltage rating of 240 volts and a resistance (ohms) rating of 8 ohms?

Step 1: Finding formula
$P = E^2 / R$

Step 2: Calculating power (wattage)
P = 57,600 V / 8R
P = 7,200 W

Solution: The power (wattage) is 7,200 watts.

**Problem 4-14(c):** Finding the power (wattage) when the current (amperage) and resistance (ohms) are known.

What is the power (wattage) in a circuit that has a current (amperage) rating of 30 amps and a resistance (ohms) of 8 ohms?

Step 1: Finding formula
$P = I^2 \times R$

Step 2: Calculating power (wattage)
P = 900 A x 8R
P = 7,200 W

Solution: The power (wattage) is 7,200 watts.

See **Figures 4-14(a), (b), and (c)** for an exercise problems when applying Ohm's law and the PIE formulas combined to determine the power.

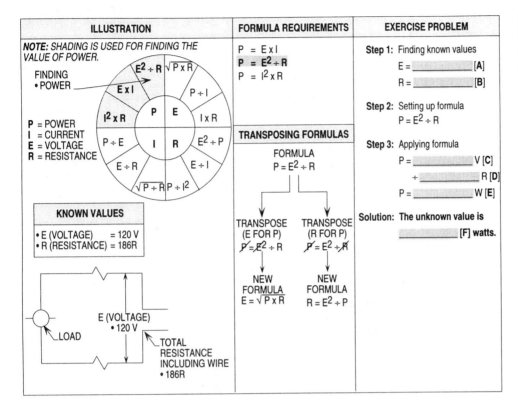

**Figure 4-14(b).** Exercise problem for finding the power (wattage) when applying Ohm's law and the PIE formulas combined.

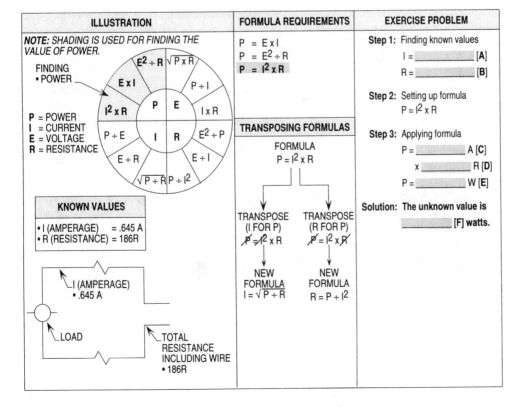

**Figure 4-14(c).** Exercise problem for finding the power (wattage) when applying Ohm's law and the PIE formulas combined.

# FINDING CURRENT

**Note:** The following three exercise problems apply to Ohm's law and PIE formulas combined to demonstrate the relationship between the two formulas when finding current.

To apply Ohm's law and the PIE formulas combined, the following formulas are used for finding the current (amperage), if the known values of power, voltage, and resistance are given:

- $I = E / R$
- $I = P / E$
- $I = \sqrt{P / R}$

**Problem 4-15(a):** Finding the current (amperage) when the voltage and resistance (ohms) are known.

What is the current (amperage) in a circuit that has a voltage rating of 240 volts and a resistance (ohms) of 8 ohms?

**Step 1:** Finding formula
$I = E / R$

**Step 2:** Calculating current (amperage)
$I = 240 \text{ V} / 8R$
$I = 30 \text{ A}$

**Solution:** The current (amperage) is 30 amps.

**Figure 4-15(a).** Exercise problem for finding the amperage when applying Ohm's law and the PIE formulas combined.

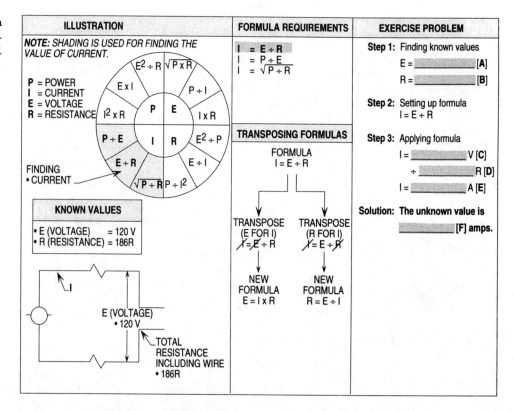

What is the current (amperage) in a circuit that has a power (wattage) rating of 7,200 watts and a voltage rating of 240 volts?

**Problem 4-15(b):** Finding the current (amperage) when the power (watts) and voltage are known.

**Step 1:** Finding formula
I = P / E

**Step 2:** Calculating current (amperage)
I = 7,200 W / 240 V
I = 30 A

**Solution: The current (amperage) is 30 amps.**

| ILLUSTRATION | FORMULA REQUIREMENTS | EXERCISE PROBLEM |
|---|---|---|
| **NOTE:** SHADING IS USED FOR FINDING THE VALUE OF CURRENT.<br><br>FINDING • CURRENT<br><br>P = POWER<br>I = CURRENT<br>E = VOLTAGE<br>R = RESISTANCE<br><br>[PIE wheel diagram: $E^2 \div R$, $\sqrt{P \times R}$, E x I, P ÷ I, $I^2$ x R, P · E, I x R, P ÷ E, I · R, $E^2 \div P$, E ÷ R, E ÷ I, $\sqrt{P \div R}$, $P \div I^2$]<br><br>**KNOWN VALUES**<br>• P (POWER) = 77.4 W<br>• E (VOLTAGE) = 120 V<br><br>[circuit diagram: I, LOAD • 77.4 W, E (VOLTAGE) • 120 V] | I = E ÷ R<br>**I = P ÷ E**<br>I = $\sqrt{P \div R}$<br><br>**TRANSPOSING FORMULAS**<br><br>FORMULA<br>I = P ÷ E<br><br>TRANSPOSE (P FOR I)<br>I = P ÷ E<br><br>TRANSPOSE (E FOR I)<br>I = P ÷ E<br><br>NEW FORMULA<br>P = E x I<br><br>NEW FORMULA<br>E = P ÷ I | **Step 1:** Finding known values<br>P = _____ [A]<br>E = _____ [B]<br><br>**Step 2:** Setting up formula<br>I = P ÷ E<br><br>**Step 3:** Applying formula<br>I = _____ W [C]<br>÷ _____ V [D]<br>I = _____ A [E]<br><br>**Solution:** The unknown value is _____ [F] amps. |

**Figure 4-15(b).** Exercise problem for finding the current (amperage) when applying Ohm's law and the PIE formulas combined.

What is the current (amperage) in a circuit that has a power (wattage) rating of 7,200 watts and a resistance (ohms) of 8 ohms?

**Problem 4-15(c):** Finding the current (amperage) when the power (watts) and resistance (ohms) are known.

**Step 1:** Finding formula
I = $\sqrt{P / R}$

**Step 2:** Calculating current (amperage)
I = $\sqrt{7,200 \text{ W}/8R}$
I = $\sqrt{900}$
I = 30 A

**Solution: The current (amperage) is 30 amps.**

**See Figures 4-15(a), (b), and (c)** for exercise problems when applying Ohm's law and the PIE formulas combined to determine the current.

**Figure 4-15(c).** Exercise problem for finding the current (amperage) when applying Ohm's law and the PIE formulas combined.

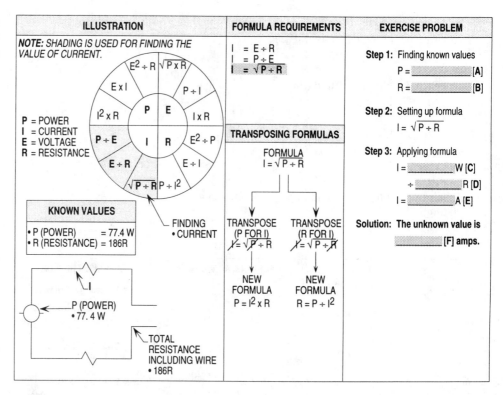

| ILLUSTRATION | FORMULA REQUIREMENTS | EXERCISE PROBLEM |
|---|---|---|

## APPLYING VOLTAGE

**Note:** The following three exercise problems apply to Ohm's law and PIE formulas combined to demonstrate the relationship between the two formulas for finding the voltage.

To apply Ohm's law and the PIE formulas combined, the following formulas are used for finding the voltage, if the known values of power, current, and resistance are given:

- $E = I \times R$
- $E = P / I$
- $E = \sqrt{P \times R}$

**Problem 4-16(a):** Finding the voltage when the current (amperage) and resistance (ohms) are known.

What is the voltage in a circuit that has a current (amperage) rating of 30 amps and a resistance (ohms) rating of 8 ohms?

**Step 1:** Finding formula
$E = I \times R$

**Step 2:** Calculating voltage
$E = 30 A \times 8R$
$E = 240 V$

**Solution:** The voltage is 240 volts.

**Problem 4-16(b):** Finding the voltage when the power (watts) and current (amperage) are known.

What is the voltage in a circuit that has a power (wattage) rating of 7,200 watts and a current (amperage) rating of 30 amps?

**Step 1:** Finding formula
$E = P / I$

**Step 2:** Calculating voltage
$E = 7,200 W / 30 A$
$E = 240 V$

**Solution:** The voltage is 240 volts.

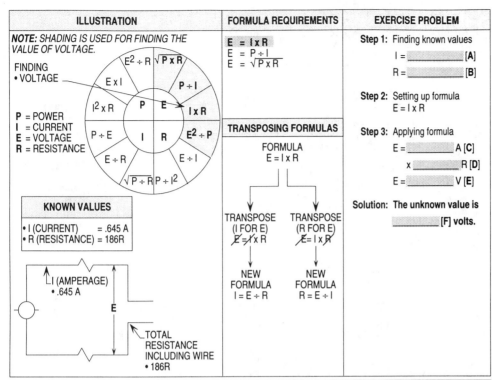

**Figure 4-16(a).** Exercise problem for finding the voltage when applying Ohm's law and the PIE formulas combined.

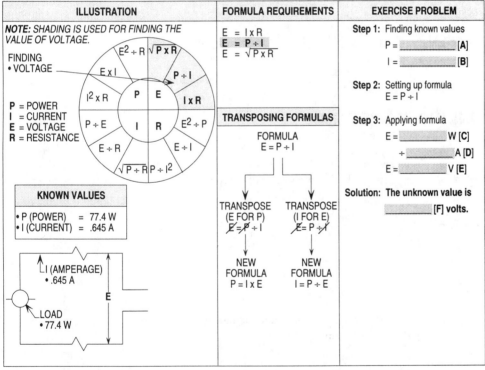

**Figure 4-16(b).** Exercise problem for finding the voltage when applying Ohm's law and PIE formulas combined.

What is the voltage in a circuit that has a power (wattage) rating of 7,200 watts and a resistance (ohms) rating of 8 ohms?

**Step 1:** Finding formula
$$E = \sqrt{P \times R}$$

**Step 2:** Calculating voltage
$$E = \sqrt{7{,}200} \times 8R$$
$$E = \sqrt{57{,}600}$$
$$E = 240 \text{ V}$$

**Solution:** The voltage is 240 volts.

**Problem 4-16(c):** Finding the voltage when the power (watts) and resistance (ohms) are known.

See Figures 4-16(a), (b), and (c) for exercise problems when applying Ohm's law and the PIE formulas combined to determine the voltage.

**Figure 4-16(c).** Exercise problem for finding the voltage when applying Ohm's law and the PIE formulas combined.

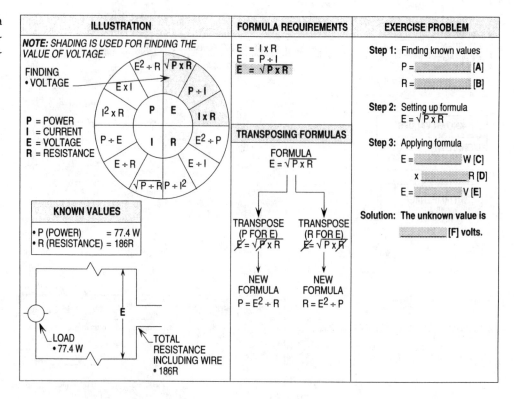

## FINDING RESISTANCE

**Note:** The following three exercise problems apply to Ohm's law and PIE formulas combined to demonstrate the relationship between the two formulas for finding the resistance.

To apply Ohm's law and the PIE formulas combined, the following formulas are used for finding the resistance, if the known values of the power, current, and voltage are given:

- $R = E / I$
- $R = E^2 / P$
- $R = P / I^2$

**Problem 4-17(a):** Finding the resistance (ohms) when the voltage and current (amperage) are known.

What is the resistance (ohms) in a circuit that has a voltage rating of 240 volts and a current (amperage) rating of 30 amps?

      **Step 1:** Finding formula
           $R = E \times I$

      **Step 2:** Calculating resistance (ohms)
           $R = 240 \text{ V} / 30 \text{ A}$
           $R = 8$

      **Solution:** The resistance (ohms) is 8 ohms.

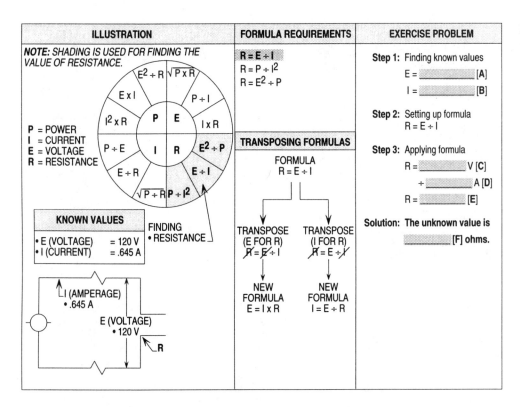

Figure 4-17(a). Exercise problem for finding the resistance (ohms) when applying Ohm's law and the PIE formulas combined.

What is the resistance (ohms) in a circuit that has a voltage rating of 240 volts and a power (wattage) rating of 7,200 watts?

Problem 4-17(b): Finding the resistance (ohms) when the voltage and power (watts) are known.

Step 1: Finding formula
$$R = E^2 / P$$

Step 2: Calculating resistance (ohms)
$$R = 57,600 \text{ V} / 7,200 \text{ W}$$
$$R = 8$$

Solution: The resistance (ohms) is 8 ohms.

What is the resistance (ohms) in a circuit that has a power (wattage) rating of 7,200 watts and a current (amperage) rating of 30 amps?

Problem 4-17(c): Finding the resistance (ohms) when the power (watts) and current (amperage) are known.

Step 1: Finding formula
$$R = P / I^2$$

Step 2: Calculating resistance (ohms)
$$R = 7,200 \text{ W} / 900 \text{ A}$$
$$R = 8$$

Solution: The resistance (ohms) is 8 ohms.

See Figures 4-17 (a), (b), and (c) for exercise problems when applying Ohm's law and the PIE formulas combined to determine the resistance.

**Figure 4-17(b).** Exercise problem for finding the resistance (ohms) when applying Ohm's law and the PIE formulas combined.

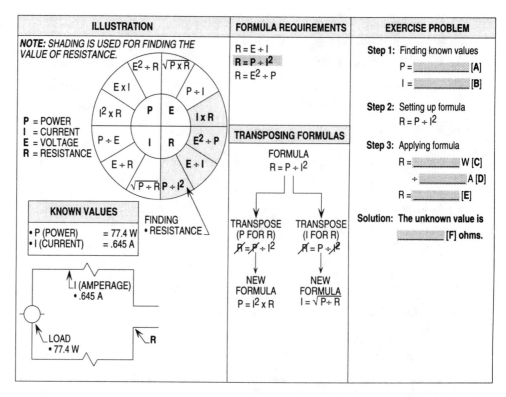

**Figure 4-17(c).** Exercise problem for finding the resistance (ohms) when applying Ohm's law and the PIE formulas combined.

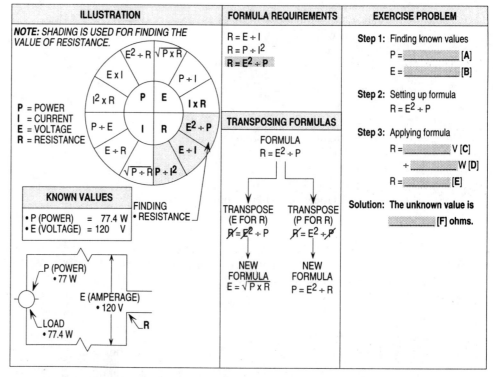

## VOLTAGE DROP
## 210-19(a), FPN 4

Due to long runs of feeder-circuit conductors, the conductors are increased in size to compensate for poor voltage drop. The voltage drop on feeder conductors should not exceed 3 percent at the farthest outlet supplying power to such loads. The voltage drop on the feeder-circuit and branch-circuit conductors should not exceed 5 percent overall.

What is the voltage drop for the branch-circuit conductors run 250 ft. with No. 2 THWN copper conductors with a 120 amp load supplied by a 240 volt, single-phase circuit that has a voltage drop of 3 percent applied? (use uncoated wire)

**Problem 4-18(a):** Finding the voltage drop when the resistivity of the wire, length of wire and amperage of load are known. Note that the circuit is single-phase.

Step 1: Selecting percentage
210-19(a), FPN 4
Branch-circuit = 3%

Step 2: Calculating VD
210-19(a), FPN 4; Table 8, Ch. 9
VD = 2 x R x L x I / 1,000
VD = 2 x 0.194 x 250 x 120 / 1,000
VD = 11,640 / 1,000
VD = 11.64 V

Step 3: Calculating allowable VD
VD = supply V x 3%
VD = 240 V x 3%
VD = 7.2 V

Step 4: Calculating percentage
210-19(a), FPN 4
% = VD / V
% = 11.64 V / 240 V
% = .0485 or 4.85%

Solution: **The voltage drop rating of 11.64 volts is greater than 7.2 volts and a larger conductor must be used to reduce the 4.85 percent to 3 percent or less.**

**Using larger conductor**
(No. 2/0 cu.)

Step 1: Selecting percentage
210-19(a), FPN 4
Branch-circuit = 3%

Step 2: Calculating VD
210-19(a), FPN 4; Table 8, Ch. 9
VD = 2 x R x L x I / 1,000
VD = 2 x 0.0967 x 250 x 120 / 1,000
VD = 5,802/ 1,000
VD = 5.802

Step 3: Checking percentage
210-19(a), FPN 4
% = 5.802 V / 240 V
% = .024175 or 2.4175

Solution: **The No. 2/0 conductor is large enough to reduce the voltage drop to 3 percent or less.**

**See Figure 4-18(a)** for an exercise problem when applying voltage drop for branch-circuit conductors using uncoated copper conductors.

**Figure 4-18(a).** Exercise problem when applying voltage drop for single-phase branch-circuit conductors.

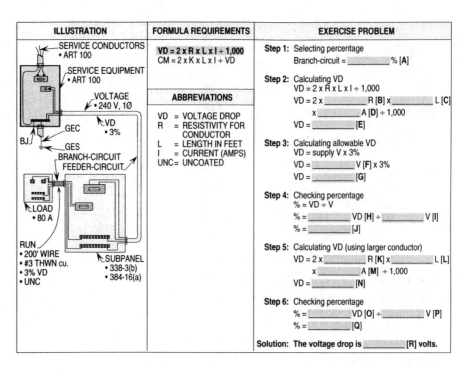

| ILLUSTRATION | FORMULA REQUIREMENTS | EXERCISE PROBLEM |
|---|---|---|

**Problem 4-18(b):** Finding the voltage drop (VD) when the resistivity of the wire, length of the wire and amperage of the load is known. Note that the circuit is three-phase.

What is the voltage drop for the branch-circuit conductors run 250 ft. with No. 1/0 THWN copper conductors with a 120 amp load supplied by a 240 volt, three-phase circuit that has a voltage drop of 3 percent applied? (use uncoated wire)

Step 1: Selecting percentage
210-19(a), FPN 4
branch-circuit = 3%

Step 2: Calculating VD
210-19(a), FPN 4; Table 8, Ch. 9
VD = 2 x R x L x I / 1,000
VD = 2 x 0.122 x 250 x 120 / 1,000
VD = 7,320 / 1,000
VD = 7.32 x .866(1.732 / 2) = 6.34

Step 3: Calculating allowable VD
VD = supply V x 3%
VD = 240 V x 3%
VD = 7.2 V

Step 4: Calculating percentage
210-19(a), FPN 4
% = VD / V
% = 6.34 V / 240 V
% = .0264 or 2.64%

Solution: The voltage drop rating of 6.34 volts is less than 7.2 volts and a larger conductor is not needed.

See Figure 4-18(b) for an exercise problem when applying voltage drop correction factors (three-phase) for the feeder circuit conductors.

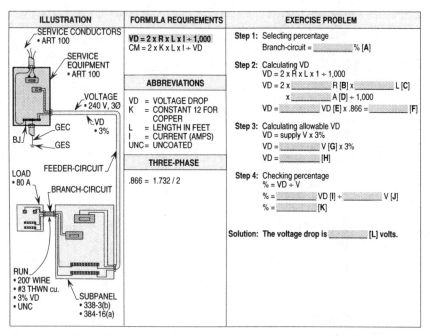

Figure 4-18(b). Exercise problem when applying voltage drop for a three-phase branch-circuit.

What is the voltage drop rating for the feeder-circuit conductors run 150 ft. with a 95 amp computed load supplied by a 240/120 volt, three-phase system that has a voltage of 3 percent applied?

    Step 1: Selecting percentages
        215-2(d), FPN 2
        Feeder-circuit = 3%
        240 x 3% = 7.2 V

    Step 2: Calculating CM
        215-2(d), FPN 2; Table 8, Ch. 9
        CM = 2 x K x L x I / VD
        CM = 2 x 12 x 150 x 95 / 7.2
        CM = 342,000 / 7.2
        CM = 47,500

    Solution: The CM rating of 47,500 requires No. 3 THWN copper conductors.

See Figure 4-18 (c) for an exercise problem when applying voltage drop correction factors for the feeder-circuit conductors.

**Problem 4-18(c):** Finding the size conductors (CM) when the constant for copper (12), the length of wire and amperage of the load are known. Note that 12 is used for the constant instead of 10.4 for figuring VD, testing authorities usually use 12 for copper (K) and not 10.4.

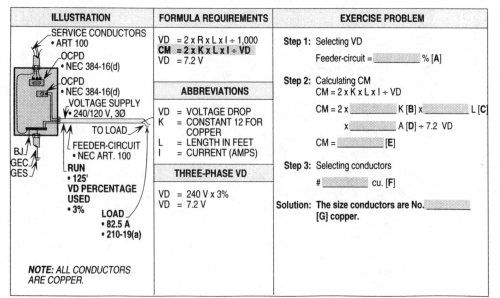

Figure 4-18 (c). Exercise problem for finding the size conductors in CM for a three-phase feeder-circuit.

# Chapter 4
## Applying Formulas

| Section | Answer | |
|---|---|---|

_____        T    F        1. When applying AC/DC formulas, the abbreviation kW is used to indicate kilovolt amps.

_____        T    F        2. When applying AC/DC formulas, the abbreviation HP is used to indicate horsepower.

_____        T    F        3. When applying Ohms law, the abbreviation E is used to indicate resistance.

_____        T    F        4. When applying Ohms law, the abbreviation I is used to indicate voltage.

_____        T    F        5. When applying PIE formulas, the abbreviation P is used to indicate power.

_____  _____        6. When applying AC/DC formulas, the abbreviation PF is used to indicate _____.

_____  _____        7. When applying AC/DC formulas, the abbreviation kVA is used to indicate _____.

_____  _____        8. When applying AC/DC formulas, the abbreviation $E_{FF}$ is used to indicate _____.

_____  _____        9. When applying Ohms law, the abbreviation R is used to indicate _____.

_____  _____        10. When applying PIE formulas, the abbreviation E is used to indicate _____.

_____  _____        11. What is the amperage for a 50 horsepower, 460 volt, three-phase induction motor with a power factor of 85 percent and operating efficiency of 80 percent?

_____  _____        12. What is the amperage for a 68 kW load supplied by a 240 volt, single-phase system with a 90 percent power factor?

_____  _____        13. What is the amperage for a 68 kVA load supplied by a 240 volt, single-phase system?

_____  _____        14. What is the kilowatts for a 200 amp load supplied by a 240 volt, single-phase system with a 90 percent power factor?

_____  _____        15. What is the kilovolt amps for a 200 amp load supplied by a 240 volt, single-phase system?

_____  _____        16. What is the horsepower for a 208 volt, three-phase induction motor with an 90 percent power factor and 80 percent efficiency which is pulling 48 amps?

_____  _____        17. What is the voltage in a circuit with a current (amperage) rating of 10 amps and a resistance (ohms) rating of 12 ohms?

_____  _____        18. What is the amperage in a circuit with a voltage rating of 120 volts and a resistance (ohms) rating of 12 ohms?

_____  _____        19. What is the resistance in a circuit with a voltage rating of 120 volts and a current (amperage) rating of 10 amps.

_____  _____        20. What is the power (wattage) in a circuit with a voltage rating of 240 volts and a current (amperage) rating of 30 amps?

_____  _____  21. What is the current (amperage) in a circuit with a power (wattage) rating of 7,200 watts and a voltage rating of 240 volts?

_____  _____  22. What is the voltage in a circuit with a power (wattage) rating of 7,200 watts and a current (amperage) rating of 30 amps?

_____  _____  23. What is the power (wattage) in a circuit with a voltage rating of 240 volts and a current (amperage) rating of 40 amps?

_____  _____  24. What is the power (wattage) in a circuit with a voltage rating of 240 volts and a resistance (ohms) rating of 6 ohms?

_____  _____  25. What is the power (wattage) in a circuit with a current (amperage) rating of 40 amps and a resistance (ohms) of 6 ohms?

_____  _____  26. What is the current (amperage) in a circuit with a voltage rating of 240 volts and a resistance (ohms) of 6 ohms?

_____  _____  27. What is the current (amperage) in a circuit with an power (wattage) rating of 9,600 watts and a voltage rating of 240 volts?

_____  _____  28. What is the current (amperage) in a circuit with an power (wattage) rating of 9, 600 watts and a resistance (ohms) of 6 ohms?

_____  _____  29. What is the voltage in a circuit with a current (amperage) rating of 40 amps and a resistance (ohms) rating of 6 ohms?

_____  _____  30. What is the voltage in a circuit with a power (wattage) rating of 9,600 watts and a current (amperage) rating of 40 amps?

_____  _____  31. What is the voltage in a circuit with a power (wattage) rating of 9,600 watts and a resistance (ohms) rating of 6 ohms?

_____  _____  32. What is the resistance (ohms) in a circuit with a voltage rating of 240 volts and a current (amperage) rating of 40 amps?

_____  _____  33. What is the resistance (ohms) in a circuit with a voltage rating of 240 volts and a power (wattage) rating of 9,600 watts?

_____  _____  34. What is the resistance (ohms) in a circuit with a power (wattage) rating of 9,600 watts and a current (amperage) rating of 40 amps?

_____  _____  35. What is the voltage drop (percentage) for the branch-circuit conductors run 200 ft. with No. 3 THWN copper conductors with a 100 amp load supplied by a 240 volt, single-phase circuit with a voltage drop of 3 percent applied? (use uncoated wire)

_____  _____  36. What is the voltage drop (percentage) for the branch-circuit conductors run 200 ft. with No. 1 THWN copper conductors with a 100 amps load supplied by a 240 volt, three-phase circuit with a voltage drop of 3 percent applied? (use uncoated wire)

_____  _____  37. What is the voltage drop (percentage) rating for the feeder-circuit conductors run 100 ft. with a 84 amp computed load supplied by a 240/120 volt, three-wire system with a voltage drop of 3 percent applied?

_____  _____  38. What is the voltage in a circuit with a current (amperage) rating of 15 amps and a resistance (ohms) rating of 8 ohms?

————————  ————————  39. What is the current (amperage) rating in a circuit with a voltage rating of 120 volts and a resistance (ohms) rating of 8 ohms?

————————  ————————  40. What is the resistance (ohms) rating in a circuit with a voltage rating of 120 volts and a current (amperage) rating of 15 amps?

# Applying
# The NEC

**5**

## Quick Reference:

LAYOUT OF THE NEC ..................................... 5-2

ARTICLES 90, 100,110 ...................................... 5-2

ARTICLE 90 ..................................................... 5-3

ARTICLE 100 ................................................... 5-3

ARTICLE 110 ................................................... 5-4

ARTICLES 200-280 ......................................... 5-4

ARTICLES 300-384 ......................................... 5-5

ARTICLES 400-490 ......................................... 5-7

ARTICLES 500-555 ......................................... 5-7

ARTICLES 600-695 ......................................... 5-7

ARTICLES 700-780 ......................................... 5-8

ARTICLES 800-830 ......................................... 5-9

TABLES .......................................................... 5-9

Electricity can be very hazardous, if proper precautions are not adhered to. The NEC is intended to give guidelines for proper installations, in order to safeguard personnel and property from the dangers of electricity.

NEC requirements are essential for safety and compliance. However, such requirements may not necessarily result in efficient, convenient, or adequate service if not used as designed.

The NEC is not intended to be used for design specifications nor as an instruction manual for untrained persons. The requirements of the NEC will, however, serve as rules which can be used to help design electrical systems properly.

The NEC is usually adopted by testing agencies and becomes effective January 1 of the year that it is published. It's rules and regulations govern wiring methods and equipment used in residential, commercial, and industrial facilities.

Questions and problems on the Journeyman electrician examination are based upon the rules and regulations of the NEC. Therefore test takers must be very familiar with certain requirements of the NEC.

## LAYOUT OF THE NEC

The rules and regulations of the NEC are laid out by Chapters, Articles, and Sections which contain the requirements for design, installation, use, and maintenance of electrical systems. The arrangement of the Chapters and what they pertain to are as follows:

- Introduction
- Chapters 1 - 4, General
- Chapter 5, Special Occupancies
- Chapter 6, Special Equipment
- Chapter 7, Special conditions
- Chapters 5 - 7, Supplement and modify the general rules presented in Chapters 1 - 4
- Chapter 8, Communications
- Chapter 8, Independent of other Chapters except as referenced
- Chapter 9, Tables

**See Figure 5-1** for a detailed illustration of how the NEC is laid out.

**Figure 5-1.** Journeyman electricians and maintenance personnel should be trained on applying the rules of the NEC as a means of providing safety for electrical or non-electrical workers that work around or near electrical circuits and components.

THE CODE IS DIVIDED INTO THE INTRODUCTION AND NINE CHAPTERS. CHAPTERS 1, 2, 3, AND 4 APPLY GENERALLY; CHAPTERS 5, 6, AND 7 APPLY TO SPECIAL OCCUPANCIES, SPECIAL EQUIPMENT, OR OTHER SPECIAL CONDITIONS. THE LATTER CHAPTERS SUPPLEMENT OR MODIFY THE GENERAL RULES. CHAPTERS 1 THROUGH 4 APPLY EXCEPT AS AMENDED BY CHAPTERS 5, 6, AND 7 FOR THE PARTICULAR CONDITIONS.

CHAPTER 8 COVERS COMMUNICATION SYSTEMS AND IS INDEPENDENT OF THE OTHER CHAPTERS EXCEPT WHERE THEY ARE SPECIFICALLY REFERENCED THEREIN.

CHAPTER 9 CONSISTS OF TABLES.

MATERIAL DEFINED BY THE SUPERSCRIPT LETTER "x" INCLUDES TEXT EXTRACTED FROM OTHER NFPA DOCUMENTS AS IDENTIFIED IN APPENDIX A OF THE NEC.

A VERTICAL LINE BESIDE A SECTION INDICATES A CHANGE IN THE RULES

• A BULLET BESIDE THE SECTION MEANS A DELETION HAS BEEN MADE IN THE SECTION

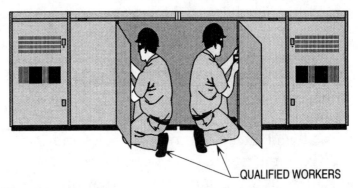

QUALIFIED WORKERS

**CHAPTER 1:** GET ACQUAINTED
**CHAPTER 2:** DESIGN
**CHAPTER 3:** INSTALLATION
**CHAPTER 4:** USER AND MAINTAINER

**CHAPTER 5:** SPECIAL OCCUPANCIES
**CHAPTER 6:** SPECIAL EQUIPMENT
**CHAPTER 7:** SPECIAL CONDITIONS
**CHAPTER 8:** COMMUNICATION CIRCUITS

**NEC 90-3**

## INTRODUCTION AND CHAPTER ONE
## ARTICLES 90, 100, 110

For many years in the electrical industry, Chapter one has been called the "get acquainted" Chapter. Everyone in the electrical industry who has the responsibility of applying the rules of the NEC must know the information and requirements of Chapter one. When using the definitions and rules of Chapter one, the "get acquainted Chapter," the user of the NEC must use either Article 90 or one of the numbers of the 100 series.

## ARTICLE 90

Article 90 contains requirements which gives the purpose of the NEC and other pertinent information that must be utilized with such purpose.

**For example:** What is "covered" and what is "not covered" by the NEC rules is found in Article 90. The word "purpose" simply means the intent, aim, or goal of the requirements of the NEC. **(See Figure 5-2)**

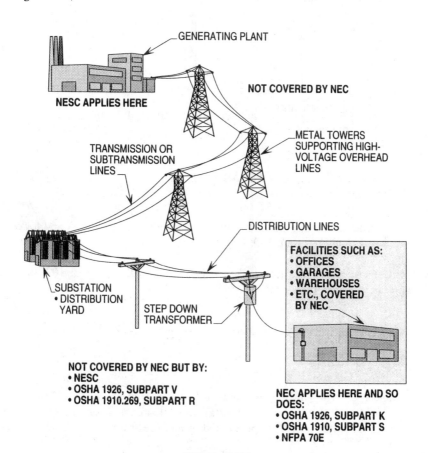

GENERATING PLANT

NOT COVERED BY NEC

**NESC APPLIES HERE**

METAL TOWERS SUPPORTING HIGH-VOLTAGE OVERHEAD LINES

TRANSMISSION OR SUBTRANSMISSION LINES

DISTRIBUTION LINES

SUBSTATION • DISTRIBUTION YARD

STEP DOWN TRANSFORMER

**FACILITIES SUCH AS:**
• OFFICES
• GARAGES
• WAREHOUSES
• ETC., COVERED BY NEC

**NOT COVERED BY NEC BUT BY:**
• NESC
• OSHA 1926, SUBPART V
• OSHA 1910.269, SUBPART R

**NEC APPLIES HERE AND SO DOES:**
• OSHA 1926, SUBPART K
• OSHA 1910, SUBPART S
• NFPA 70E

NEC 90-2(a)(5)

**Figure 5-2.** Article 90 contains requirements which gives the purpose of the NEC and other pertinent information that must be utilized with such purpose.

Note that testing agencies make-up questions for the journeyman test that are based on Articles 90, 100, and 110 of the NEC.

## CHAPTER 1
## ARTICLE 100

Article 100 breaks down the language barrier for the user of the NEC. When users of the NEC fully understand the meanings of the words, terms, or phrases that are used, they have a much better chance to comprehend the way to properly interpret the rules of the NEC.

**For example:** If the journeyman electrician wanted to run two services to a building and he or she obtain the definition of a building from Webster's Dictionary instead of Art. 100, the journeyman electrician would be very confused as to whether an individual service could be provided for such a building due to different definitions. The definition in Art. 100 is defined as the installation of wiring methods and equipment in a building.

Commonly defined terms are not included in Art. 100. Only the terms essential to the proper application or enforcement of the NEC rules are listed. **(See Figure 5-3)**

**Figure 5-3.** Article 100 contains definitions that are only essential to the proper application and enforcement of the NEC.

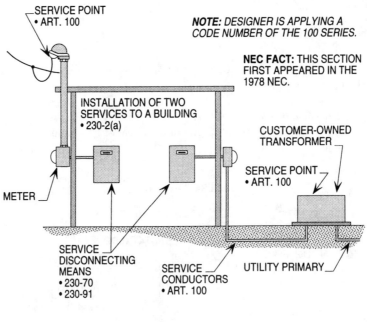

SERVICE POINT
• ART. 100

NOTE: DESIGNER IS APPLYING A
CODE NUMBER OF THE 100 SERIES.

NEC FACT: THIS SECTION
FIRST APPEARED IN THE
1978 NEC.

INSTALLATION OF TWO
SERVICES TO A BUILDING
• 230-2(a)

CUSTOMER-OWNED
TRANSFORMER

SERVICE POINT
• ART. 100

METER

SERVICE
DISCONNECTING
MEANS
• 230-70
• 230-91

SERVICE
CONDUCTORS
• ART. 100

UTILITY PRIMARY

**NEC ART. 100**

The definitions for systems of 600 volts or less are listed in Part A and for over 600 volts are listed in Part B of Article 100.

**NEC Fact:** For a definition to be eligible and included in Art. 100, such definition must appear in at least two or more Articles of the NEC.

# CHAPTER 1
# ARTICLE 110

**NEC Tip 1:** When determining clearances in front of electrical installations for 600 volts or less or over 600 volts, Art. 110 of the 100 series of Chapter one must be used.

Article 110 of the NEC covers the requirements for electrical installations. The rules of Art. 110 apply to all types of electrical installations that come after Chapter one unless there is an exception granted or it is supplemented or modified by a rule in Chapters five, six, or seven of the NEC.

**For example:** The clearance in front of a 277/480 volt panelboard is 3 ft. per Table 110-26(a), if the electrical installation falls under the provision of Condition 1. **(See Figure 5-4)**

# CHAPTER 2
# ARTICLES 200-280

Chapter two with it's accompanying Articles is used by designers to design elements and components of branch-circuits, feeder-circuits, and service equipment that make up the premises electrical system. The title of Chapter two is "Wiring Design and Protection" which pertains to designing loads for selecting wiring methods and equipment and sizing overcurrent protection devices to protect such elements as conductors, parts, and equipment.

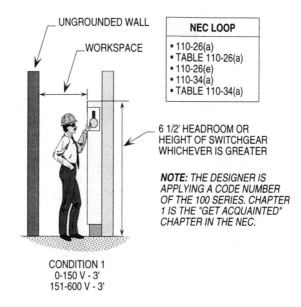

UNGROUNDED WALL

WORKSPACE

**NEC LOOP**
- 110-26(a)
- TABLE 110-26(a)
- 110-26(e)
- 110-34(a)
- TABLE 110-34(a)

6 1/2' HEADROOM OR HEIGHT OF SWITCHGEAR WHICHEVER IS GREATER

*NOTE: THE DESIGNER IS APPLYING A CODE NUMBER OF THE 100 SERIES. CHAPTER 1 IS THE "GET ACQUAINTED" CHAPTER IN THE NEC.*

CONDITION 1
0-150 V - 3'
151-600 V - 3'

**TABLE 110-26(a), CONDITION 1**

**Figure 5-4.** Article 110 contains requirements for electrical installations except those granted, supplemented, or modified by a rule in Chapters five, six, or seven of the NEC.

When journeyman electricians are in the planning stage and calculations have to be made for selecting equipment and elements based upon use, the designer must apply one of the Articles of Chapter two. In other words, one of the Articles in the 200 series must be chosen.

**For example:** If the journeyman electrician wants to know how many disconnects are allowed for each service, the Article is 230 with, Sec.'s 230-71 and 230-72 being used to determine the number.

When designing the electrical system, the designer must think Chapter two and use one of the 200 series Articles which deals with his or her particular design.

If one of the Articles in Chapter two can't be used to design a certain installation, the designer will be referred to another Chapter that covers such installation.

**For example:** Section 220-14 of the NEC refers the electrician to Art. 430 for calculating motor loads. **(See Figure 5-5)**

**NEC Tip 2:** The first six Articles of Chapter two are used for designing the electrical system and the last three for protecting people, wiring, and equipment.

# CHAPTER 3
# ARTICLES 300-384

Chapter three with its accompanying Articles is used by installers to install the electrical wiring methods and equipment after they have been designed by the designer per Chapter two of the NEC. Journeyman electricians cannot install electrical wiring methods and equipment to comply with the NEC without reading and studying the requirements of Chapter three.

The rules for routing raceways and cable systems, mounting and securing boxes, outlet boxes, junction boxes, panelboards, switchgear, etc. are covered.

**For example:** How often does a run of EMT between a process machine and panelboard have to be supported?

Section 348-13 requires supports to be provided within 3 ft. of the machine and panelboard and at intervals of 10 ft. for the run of EMT between such equipment. **(See Figure 5-6)**

**Figure 5-5.** Chapter two is used by journeyman electricians to design the elements and components of branch-circuits, feeder-circuits, and service equipment.

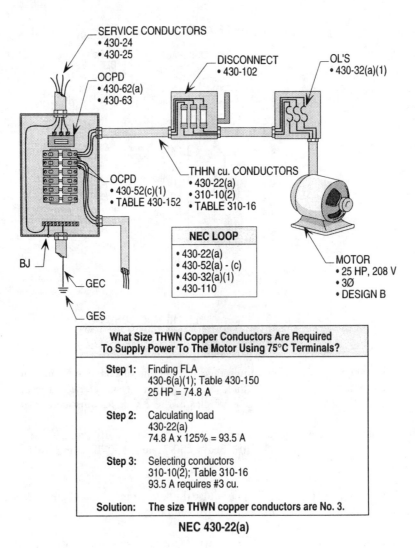

SERVICE CONDUCTORS
• 430-24
• 430-25

OCPD
• 430-62(a)
• 430-63

DISCONNECT
• 430-102

OL'S
• 430-32(a)(1)

OCPD
• 430-52(c)(1)
• TABLE 430-152

THHN cu. CONDUCTORS
• 430-22(a)
• 310-10(2)
• TABLE 310-16

BJ

GEC

GES

**NEC LOOP**
• 430-22(a)
• 430-52(a) - (c)
• 430-32(a)(1)
• 430-110

MOTOR
• 25 HP, 208 V
• 3Ø
• DESIGN B

| What Size THWN Copper Conductors Are Required To Supply Power To The Motor Using 75°C Terminals? | |
|---|---|
| **Step 1:** | Finding FLA<br>430-6(a)(1); Table 430-150<br>25 HP = 74.8 A |
| **Step 2:** | Calculating load<br>430-22(a)<br>74.8 A x 125% = 93.5 A |
| **Step 3:** | Selecting conductors<br>310-10(2); Table 310-16<br>93.5 A requires #3 cu. |
| **Solution:** | The size THWN copper conductors are No. 3. |

NEC 430-22(a)

**Figure 5-6.** Chapter three is used by installers to install the electrical wiring methods and equipment after they have been designed by Chapter two.

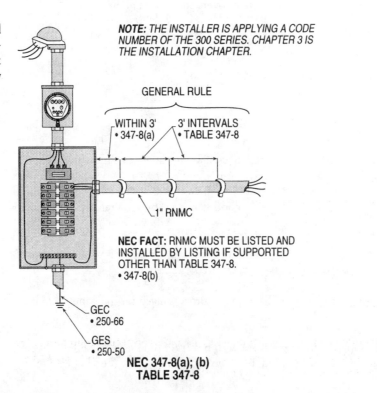

NOTE: THE INSTALLER IS APPLYING A CODE NUMBER OF THE 300 SERIES. CHAPTER 3 IS THE INSTALLATION CHAPTER.

GENERAL RULE

WITHIN 3'
• 347-8(a)

3' INTERVALS
• TABLE 347-8

1" RNMC

NEC FACT: RNMC MUST BE LISTED AND INSTALLED BY LISTING IF SUPPORTED OTHER THAN TABLE 347-8.
• 347-8(b)

GEC
• 250-66

GES
• 250-50

NEC 347-8(a); (b)
TABLE 347-8

# CHAPTER 4
# ARTICLES 400-480

Chapter four with it's accompanying Articles is used by users and maintainers. The electrical equipment in Chapter four is current consuming and requires electricity to operate. Therefore, this Chapter is usually applied after the design and installation of such systems and equipment have been done.

**For example:** What Article and Section in the 400 series is used to replace a 600 volt (output side) ballast in an electrical discharge lighting fixture?

Section 410-73(e)(1) of Article 410 in Chapter four is used to replace the ballast of 1,000 volts or less. The maintainer can use the rules of Sec. 410-73 when dealing with replacement parts in electrical-discharge lighting fixtures. **(See Figure 5-7)**

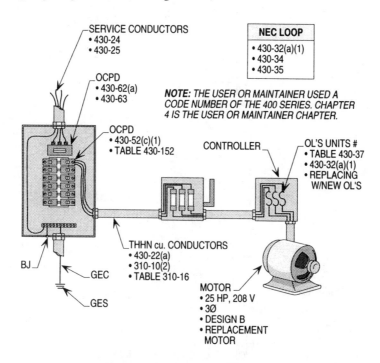

**Figure 5-7.** Chapter four with it's accompanying Articles is used by users and maintainers. Test takers must be familiar with the rules in Chapter four and how to apply them on the examination.

# CHAPTER 5
# ARTICLES 500-555

Chapter five deals with special occupancies and the first four articles deal with identifying specific classifications and general provisions. Rules and regulations pertaining to classifying these areas are discussed. The remaining Articles cover specific provisions for specific locations such as commercial garages, aircraft hangers, service stations, bulk storage plants, spray applications, etc. as well as health care facilities. **(See Figure 5-8)**

# CHAPTER 6
# ARTICLES 600-695

Chapter six is completely devoted to special equipment that requires special requirements for design and installation. In other words, the needed rules cannot be found in Chapter four which covers "equipment for general use." **(See Figure 5-9)**

If an engineer or journeyman electrician is designing the electrical system for an elevator, he or she must apply the rules and regulations of Art. 620 in Chapter six.

**For example:** To design the disconnecting means for disconnecting the power to the machine room for the elevator equipment, the journeyman electrician must consult Sec. 620-51 of the NEC for requirements which are related to sizing, selecting, and locating such disconnect.

**Figure 5-8.** Chapter five deals with special occupancies and the first four Articles deal with identifying specific classifications and general provisions.

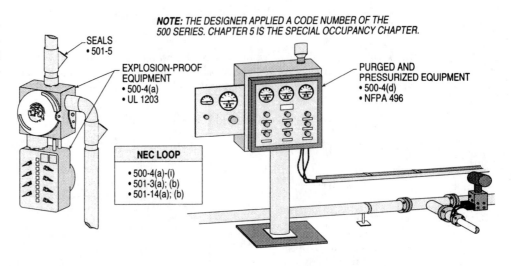

NOTE: THE DESIGNER APPLIED A CODE NUMBER OF THE 500 SERIES. CHAPTER 5 IS THE SPECIAL OCCUPANCY CHAPTER.

SEALS
• 501-5

EXPLOSION-PROOF EQUIPMENT
• 500-4(a)
• UL 1203

PURGED AND PRESSURIZED EQUIPMENT
• 500-4(d)
• NFPA 496

NEC LOOP
• 500-4(a)-(i)
• 501-3(a); (b)
• 501-14(a); (b)

NEC 500-4(a); (d)

**Figure 5-9.** Chapter six deals with special equipment that requires special requirements for design and installation.

**NEC Tip 3:** When the requirements for special equipment are not found in Chapter four, the electrician must use one of the Articles found in the 600 series of Chapter six.

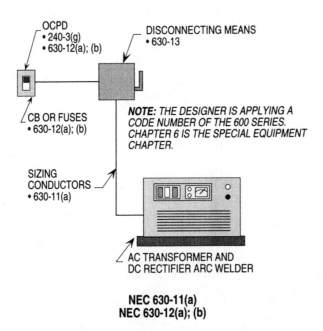

OCPD
• 240-3(g)
• 630-12(a); (b)

DISCONNECTING MEANS
• 630-13

CB OR FUSES
• 630-12(a); (b)

NOTE: THE DESIGNER IS APPLYING A CODE NUMBER OF THE 600 SERIES. CHAPTER 6 IS THE SPECIAL EQUIPMENT CHAPTER.

SIZING CONDUCTORS
• 630-11(a)

AC TRANSFORMER AND DC RECTIFIER ARC WELDER

NEC 630-11(a)
NEC 630-12(a); (b)

# CHAPTER 7
# ARTICLES 700-780

Chapter seven contains requirements for special conditions that arise from the particular type, use, and application of the power source used to supply circuits and equipment.

When special conditions pertaining to the power source, circuits, and equipment are addressed, one of the Articles of the 700 series must be used.

**For example:** The journeyman electrician wants to know if the wiring of an emergency system can be routed in the same raceway as the normal power. Special conditions are needed to verify this requirement. Article 700 of Chapter seven is used and Sec. 700-9(b) of the NEC will not allow the emergency wiring and normal wiring to be mixed in a raceway system. **(See Figure 5-10)**

**NEC Tip 4:** Journeyman electrician must take notice and carefully review how predominantly <u>the source</u>, <u>the supply</u>, and <u>the circuit(s)</u> are applied in each Article of Chapter seven to ensure the reliability of such wiring methods and equipment. Remember these "three words" are main "key words" in applying the rules and regulations of Chapter seven.

# CHAPTER 8
## ARTICLES 800-820

This Chapter covers communication circuits and equipment and is independent of the other Chapters except where they are specifically referenced.

Communication systems regulated by the Articles in Chapter eight are telephone, telegraph, radio, and alarm systems. The requirements basically cover systems which connect to a central alarm station to sound some kind of alarm.

**For example:** An alarm could communicate to a central control room that the ventilation system has failed in a hazardous location. **(See Figure 5-11)**

**NEC Tip 5:** When requirements for communication systems are needed, one of the Articles in the 800 series in Chapter eight must be utilized by the electrician.

# CHAPTER 9
## TABLES

Chapter nine is an enforceable portion of the NEC and contains Tables with dimensions of conductors. Tables 4 and 5 are utilized for conductors of different sizes with square inch rating of each conductor being multiplied by the number to derive the total square inch. The total square inch rating is used to select the raceway from Table 4 to Chapter 9.

**NEC Tip 6:** When using conduits containing different size conductors, use Table 4 and Table 5 of Chapter nine in the NEC.

**For example:** What size EMT is required for 3 - No. 4 THHN and 1 - No. 6 THHN copper conductors?

**NEC Tip 7:** When sizing conduits containing conductors of the same size, use Tables C1 through C12(A) in the Appendix C of the NEC.

Step 1: Finding sq. in. area
Table 5, Ch. 9
#4 = .0824
#6 = .0507

Step 2: Calculating sq. in. area
Table 5, Ch. 9
3 x .0824 = .2472 sq. in.
1 x .0507 = .0507 sq. in.
Total = .2979 sq. in.

Step 3: Selecting EMT
Table 4, Ch. 9
.2979 requires 1"

**Solution: A 1 in. EMT is required.**

**Figure 5-10.** Chapter seven contains requirements for special conditions that arise from the particular type, use, and application of the power source used to supply circuits and equipment.

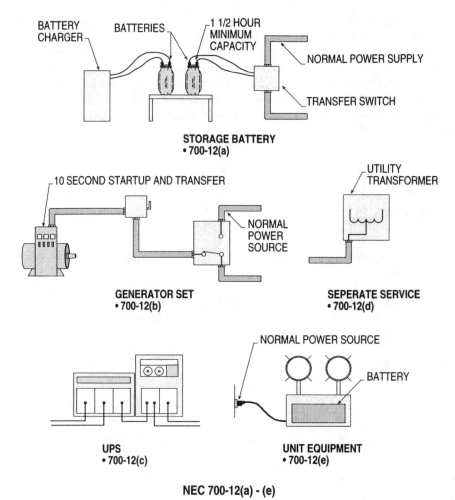

STORAGE BATTERY
• 700-12(a)

GENERATOR SET
• 700-12(b)

SEPERATE SERVICE
• 700-12(d)

UPS
• 700-12(c)

UNIT EQUIPMENT
• 700-12(e)

NEC 700-12(a) - (e)

**Figure 5-11.** Chapter eight covers communication circuits and equipment.

HIGH RISE BUILDING WITH COMMUNICATION CIRCUITS

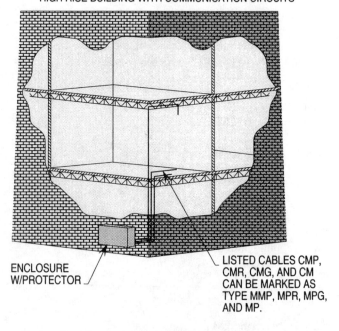

ENCLOSURE W/PROTECTOR

LISTED CABLES CMP, CMR, CMG, AND CM CAN BE MARKED AS TYPE MMP, MPR, MPG, AND MP.

*NOTE: THE DESIGNER IS APPLYING A CODE NUMBER OF THE 800 SERIES. CHAPTER 8 IS THE COMMUNICATION CHAPTER.*

NEC 800-51(g)

Appendix C is used to size the raceway where the conductors are the same size. There are approximately 82 Tables in Appendix C that can be used for the purpose of selecting raceways based upon the same size conductors. See Note (1) to Table 1 of Chapter nine.

**For example:** What size EMT is required for 4 - No. 4 THHN copper conductors?

**Step 1:** Finding number
Table C1 in Appendix C
4 #4 THHN requires 1"

**Solution: A 1 in. EMT is required.**

See **Figure 5-12** for a step-by-step procedure when sizing a raceway system.

**NEC Tip 8:** All the Tables must be reviewed very carefully by designers, installers, maintainers, and inspectors in order to be familiar with such information that may be pertinent with the duty and performance on one's job. The "new" Tables may require different size conduits based on the type of conductors and conduit used. Note that test takers must review these Tables very carefully before taking the journeyman examination.

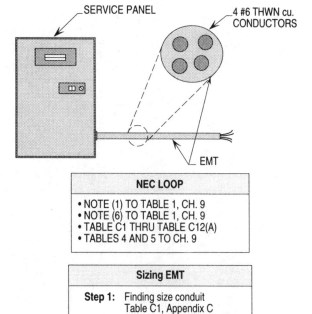

**SERVICE PANEL**

**4 #6 THWN cu. CONDUCTORS**

**EMT**

| NEC LOOP |
|---|
| • NOTE (1) TO TABLE 1, CH. 9 |
| • NOTE (6) TO TABLE 1, CH. 9 |
| • TABLE C1 THRU TABLE C12(A) |
| • TABLES 4 AND 5 TO CH. 9 |

| Sizing EMT |
|---|
| **Step 1:** Finding size conduit Table C1, Appendix C 4 #6 requires 3/4" |
| **Solution:** A 3/4 in. conduit is required. |

**NOTES (1) THROUGH (9) TO TABLE 1, CH. 9**
**TABLE C1 THROUGH 12(A), APPENDIX C**

**Figure 5-12.** Chapter nine contains Tables which are mainly used to size raceways based upon the conductor arrangement. Examples are also available to illustrate how calculations are made.

# Chapter 5
# Applying The NEC

**Section**          **Answer**

_____  _____  1. The workspace shall not be less than _____ in. wide in front of electrical equipment.

A. 30
B. 36
C. 42
D. 48

_____  _____  2. An insulated grounded conductor of No. _____ or smaller shall be identified by a continuous white or natural gray outer finish along its entire length.

A. 10
B. 8
C. 6
D. 4

_____  _____  3. A heavy-duty lampholder shall have a rating of not less than _____ watts if of the admedium type.

A. 480
B. 660
C. 750
D. 820

_____  _____  4. Overhead service drop conductors shall not be smaller than No. _____ copper.

A. 10
B. 8
C. 6
D. 4

_____  _____  5. Interior metal water piping located more than _____ ft. from the point of entrance to the building shall not be used as part of the grounding electrode system.

A. 3
B. 5
C. 8
D. 10

_____  _____  6. Nonmetallic sheathed cable installed through bored holes shall not be less than _____ in. from the nearest edge of the wood member.

A. 1/2
B. 3/4
C. 1
D. 1 1/4

_____  _____    7. Rigid nonmetallic conduit shall be installed at least _____ in. below the top surface of finished grade.

A. 6
B. 12
C. 18
D. 24

_____  _____    8. Electrical nonmetallic tubing shall be securely fastened in place within _____ ft. of each outlet box.

A. 3
B. 4 1/2
C. 5
D. 10

_____  _____    9. Nonmetallic sheathed cable shall be secured in place at intervals not exceeding _____ ft.

A. 3
B. 4 1/2
C. 5
D. 10

_____  _____    10. Rigid metal conduit shall be securely fastened within _____ ft. of each outlet box.

A. 3
B. 4 1/2
C. 5
D. 10

_____  _____    11. Surface-mounted incandescent lighting fixtures can be installed in clothes closets on the wall above the door or on the ceiling, provide there is a minimum clearance of _____ in. between the fixture and the nearest point of a storage space.

A. 3
B. 6
C. 12
D. 18

_____  _____    12. Ceiling suspended (paddle) fans that do not exceed _____ lbs. in weight shall be permitted to be supported by outlet boxes identified for such use.

A. 15
B. 20
C. 25
D. 35

_____  _____    13. For each floor in commercial garages, the entire area up to a level of _____ in. above the floor shall be considered to be a Class 1, Division 2 location.

A. 18
B. 24
C. 30
D. 36

_____  _____    14. The required branch-circuit for a sign shall be computed at a minimum of _____ volt-amperes.

A. 1,000
B. 1,200
C. 1,800
D. 2,400

_____  _____    15. All receptacles located within _____ ft. of the inside walls of a swimming pool shall be protected by ground-fault circuit-interrupter.

A. 5
B. 10
C. 15
D. 20

_____  _____    16. Underground wiring shall not be permitted under the pool or within the area extending _____ ft. horizontally from the inside wall of the pool. (General rule)

A. 5
B. 10
C. 15
D. 20

_____  _____    17. Overcurrent protection for Class 1 circuits shall not exceed _____ amperes for No. 16 conductors.

A. 5
B. 7
C. 10
D. 12

_____  _____    18. Power-limited fire alarm circuit conductors shall be separated at least _____ in. from conductors of any electric light, power, Class 1, or nonpower-limited fire alarm circuit conductors.

A. 1
B. 2
C. 6
D. 12

_____  _____    19. Communication cables shall have a vertical clearance of not less than _____ ft. from all points of roofs above which they pass.

A. 8
B. 10
C. 12
D. 18

_____  _____    20. A nipple is a conduit that is not over _____ in. in length.

A. 18
B. 24
C. 30
D. 36

# Wiring Methods

# 6

Boxes and conduits shall be sized and selected to accommodate the number of conductors required to supply power to various pieces of electrical equipment in residential, commercial, and industrial locations. Boxes, in addition to housing conductors, shall have enough fill area to provide sufficient space for receptacles, switches, dimmers, and combination devices without damaging the conductor's insulation.

When boxes and conduits are not sized properly, conductors are sometimes packed in undersized boxes and are pinched by large size devices that intrude into the box's fill area. Therefore, conductors, devices, fittings, and clamps are required to be counted and the appropriate box selected. Boxes and conduits are sized on the number of conductors being either the same size and having the same characteristics or different sizes and having different characteristics.

Journeyman electricians must learn how to size junction boxes, outlet boxes, auxiliary gutters, wireways, cable trays, nipples, and conduits by selecting and applying the appropriate Sections and Tables of the NEC.

## Quick Reference:

METHODS OF COUNTING CONDUCTORS ---------------------------- 6-2

CONDUIT BODIES -------------------------------------- 6-11

JUNCTION BOXES -------------------------------------- 6-12

SIZING CONDUITS ------------------------------------- 6-14

SIZING NIPPLES -------------------------------------- 6-16

SIZING AUXILIARY GUTTERS ---------------------- 6-17

SIZING CABLE TRAYS -------------------------------- 6-18

# METHODS OF COUNTING CONDUCTORS
## 370-16(a)(1)

**Test Tip 1:** Conductors passing through a box count as one each. Spliced conductors are counted as one each.

The size box selected is based on the number and size of conductors, devices, and fittings that are contained within the box. Electricians, installers, and inspectors must count the number of items that are in the box and select the size box from Table 370-16(a) based upon the maximum number of conductors or the minimum cubic inch capacity rating. The column for the maximum number of conductors is used when the conductors are the same size. The appropriate cubic inch capacity column is applied for combination conductors in the same box.

## CONDUCTOR FILL
## 370-16(b)(1)

Conductors passing through the box unbroken and not pulled into a loop or spliced together with scotchlocks are counted as one conductor. Conductors passing through boxes are utilized to supply power to boxes supporting lighting fixtures or receptacles, etc. Spliced conductors are counted as one each toward the fill of the box.

## CONDUCTOR FILL
## 370-16(b)(1)

**Test Tip 2:** Pigtails and bonding jumpers do not count as fill in the box.

A conductor that is not entirely within the box is not required to be counted as a conductor used toward the box fill. A pigtail from a splice within the box to a receptacle or a switch mounted to the box or a bonding jumper from the receptacle yoke bonded to the box is an example of such a conductor.

## CONDUCTOR FILL
## 370-16(b)(1), Ex.

**Test Tip 3:** Four or less fixture wires smaller than No. 14 installed in a fixture canopy do not count toward the fill in the box.

Wires from fixtures shall be counted in determining the size of the box. Fixture wire sizes from No. 18 to No. 12 or larger shall be counted to determine the size box used to support the fixture. The exception to Sec. 370-16(b)(1) allows the canopy of a fixture to be used to house the first four fixture wires smaller than No. 14. It is not necessary to count these fixture wires toward the fill of the ceiling box supporting the fixture or ceiling fan where there's a canopy. Note that No. 12 or smaller is usually used for fixture wire.

## CLAMP FILL
## 370-16(b)(2)

**Test Tip 4:** All cable clamps count as one based upon the largest conductor entering the box.

Boxes with one or more cable clamps that are installed to support cables in the box shall have one conductor added toward the fill computation to determine the size box. The conductor used to represent the one or more cable clamps is selected, based on the largest conductor in any one cable entering the box.

## SUPPORT FITTINGS FILL
## 370-16(b)(3)

**Test Tip 5:** Fixture studs and hickeys count as one each based upon the largest conductor entering the box.

Boxes that contain fixture studs or hickeys shall have one conductor added for each fitting. The conductor for each fitting is selected and based on the largest conductor entering the box. By adding a conductor for each fitting in the box, a larger box is required to be selected and such procedure will help prevent an undersized box.

## DEVICE OR EQUIPMENT FILL
## 370-16(b)(4)

A receptacle or switch that is mounted on a strap or yoke is counted as two conductors in determining the fill of the box. The count of two is based on the size conductor that is connected to the receptacle or switch. One strap could have one, two, or three receptacles mounted on it and still be counted as two conductors.

**Test Tip 6:** A yoke or a strap supporting a receptacle, switch, or pilot light counts as two based upon the sized conductors terminating to it's terminals.

## EQUIPMENT GROUNDING CONDUCTOR FILL
## 370-16(b)(5)

Equipment grounding conductors passing through or spliced together in the box count as one. It doesn't matter how many equipment grounding conductors are installed in a box. All the equipment grounding conductors added together count as one.

**Test Tip 7:** EGC's count as one except where an isolated EGC is involved, then two conductors must be counted.

The only time that equipment grounding conductors in a box count more than one is where an isolation equipment grounding conductor (IEGC) is run to an isolation receptacle and used to ground the metal enclosure of a PC, etc.

What size octagon box is required to support a lighting fixture supplied with two No. 14-2 w/ground nonmetallic sheathed cables (romex) with a fixture stud, hickey, and two No. 14 fixture wires? Neutrals are spliced with a pigtail and romex connectors are used instead of romex clamps.

**Problem 6-1:** All conductors are the same size in the octagon box.

Step 1: Same size conductors
370-16(b)(1) through (5)

| | |
|---|---|
| 2 #14 hots | = 2 |
| 2 #14 neutrals | = 2 |
| 2 #14 grounds | = 1 |
| 1 fixture stud | = 1 |
| 1 hickey | = 1 |
| 1 pigtail | = 0 |
| 2 romex connectors | = 0 |
| 2 #14 fixture wires | = 2 |
| Total | = 9 |

Step 2: Selecting box
Table 370-16(a)
9 #14 conductors requires 4" x 2 1/8" box

Solution: A 4 in. x 2 1/8 in. octagon box is required.

See Figure 6-1 for an exercise problem on sizing octagon boxes with the same size conductors.

**Figure 6-1.** Sections 370-16(b)(1) through (5) and Table 310-16(a) are utilized to size and select an octagon box based on the box containing the same size conductors. **Note:** The canopy is used for the fill of the fixture wires. **(See Test Tip 3).**

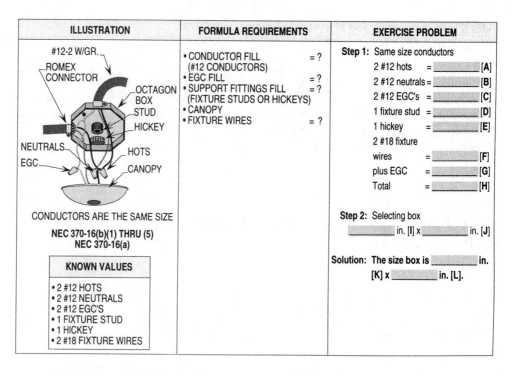

| ILLUSTRATION | FORMULA REQUIREMENTS | EXERCISE PROBLEM |
|---|---|---|

#12-2 W/GR.

ROMEX CONNECTOR

OCTAGON BOX
STUD
HICKEY

NEUTRALS
EGC
HOTS
CANOPY

CONDUCTORS ARE THE SAME SIZE

**NEC 370-16(b)(1) THRU (5)**
**NEC 370-16(a)**

**KNOWN VALUES**
- 2 #12 HOTS
- 2 #12 NEUTRALS
- 2 #12 EGC'S
- 1 FIXTURE STUD
- 1 HICKEY
- 2 #18 FIXTURE WIRES

- CONDUCTOR FILL = ?
  (#12 CONDUCTORS)
- EGC FILL = ?
- SUPPORT FITTINGS FILL = ?
  (FIXTURE STUDS OR HICKEYS)
- CANOPY
- FIXTURE WIRES = ?

Step 1:  Same size conductors
2 #12 hots = _____ [A]
2 #12 neutrals = _____ [B]
2 #12 EGC's = _____ [C]
1 fixture stud = _____ [D]
1 hickey = _____ [E]
2 #18 fixture
wires = _____ [F]
plus EGC = _____ [G]
Total = _____ [H]

Step 2:  Selecting box
_____ in. [I] x _____ in. [J]

Solution:  The size box is _____ in.
[K] x _____ in. [L].

**Problem 6-2:** All conductors in the octagon box are different sizes.

What size octagon box is required to support a lighting fixture supplied with two No. 12-2 w/ground nonmetallic sheathed cables (romex) with a fixture stud, two cable clamps, two pigtails, and two No. 18 fixture wires? (No fixture canopy)

**Test Tip 8:** A yoke is a metal strap which is used to support a switch, receptacle, or a pilot light or combination of such.

Step 1:  Combination conductors
370-16(b)(1) through (b)(5); Table 370-16(b)
**2 #12 hots**
2.25 cu. in. x 2 = 4.5 cu. in.
**2 #12 neutrals**
2.25 cu. in. x 2 = 4.5 cu. in.
**2 #12 EGC's**
2.25 cu. in. x 1 = 2.25 cu. in.
**1 fixture stud**
2.25 cu. in. x 1 = 2.25 cu. in.
**2 cable clamps**
2.25 cu. in. x 1 = 2.25 cu. in.
**2 pigtails**
= 0 cu. in.
**2 #18 fixture wires**
1.5 cu. in. x 2 = 3.0 cu. in.
Total = 18.75 cu. in.

Step 2:  Selecting box
Table 370-16(a)
18.75 cu. in. requires 4" x 2 1/8"

Solution: A 4 in. x 2 1/8 in. octagon box is required.

**See Figure 6-2** for an exercise problem on sizing octagon boxes with different size conductors.

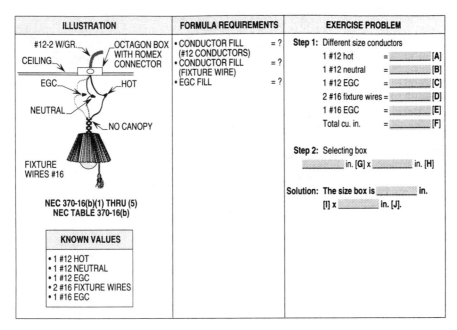

| ILLUSTRATION | FORMULA REQUIREMENTS | EXERCISE PROBLEM |
|---|---|---|
| #12-2 W/GR. OCTAGON BOX WITH ROMEX CONNECTOR  CEILING  EGC — HOT  NEUTRAL — NO CANOPY  FIXTURE WIRES #16  **NEC 370-16(b)(1) THRU (5) NEC TABLE 370-16(b)**  **KNOWN VALUES** • 1 #12 HOT • 1 #12 NEUTRAL • 1 #12 EGC • 2 #16 FIXTURE WIRES • 1 #16 EGC | • CONDUCTOR FILL (#12 CONDUCTORS) = ? • CONDUCTOR FILL (FIXTURE WIRE) = ? • EGC FILL = ? | **Step 1:** Different size conductors  1 #12 hot = _____ [A]  1 #12 neutral = _____ [B]  1 #12 EGC = _____ [C]  2 #16 fixture wires = _____ [D]  1 #16 EGC = _____ [E]  Total cu. in. = _____ [F]  **Step 2:** Selecting box  _____ in. [G] x _____ in. [H]  **Solution:** The size box is _____ in. [I] x _____ in. [J]. |

**Figure 6-2.** Sections 370-16(b)(1) through (5) and Table 370-16(b) are utilized to size and select the box based on an octagon box containing different size conductors. The cubic inch of each conductor times the number derives the size box.

What size device box with cable clamps is required for two No. 14-2 w/ground romex cables and one duplex receptacle?

**Step 1:** Same size conductors
370-16(b)(1) through (5)
2 #14 hots = 2
2 #14 neutrals = 2
2 #14 EGC's = 1
1 receptacle = 2
2 cable clamps = 1
Total = 8

**Step 2:** Selecting box
Table 370-16(a)
8 #14 conductors requires 3" x 2" x 3 1/2"

**Solution: A 3 in. x 2 in. x 3 1/2 in. device box is required.**

See Figure 6-3 for an exercise problem on sizing device boxes with the same size conductors.

**Problem 6-3:** All conductors in the device box are the same size.

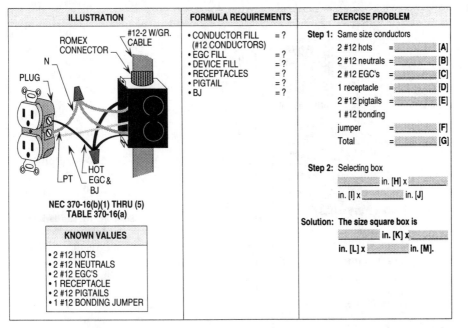

| ILLUSTRATION | FORMULA REQUIREMENTS | EXERCISE PROBLEM |
|---|---|---|
| ROMEX CONNECTOR  #12-2 W/GR. CABLE  PLUG  N  PT  HOT EGC & BJ  **NEC 370-16(b)(1) THRU (5) TABLE 370-16(a)**  **KNOWN VALUES** • 2 #12 HOTS • 2 #12 NEUTRALS • 2 #12 EGC'S • 1 RECEPTACLE • 2 #12 PIGTAILS • 1 #12 BONDING JUMPER | • CONDUCTOR FILL (#12 CONDUCTORS) = ? • EGC FILL = ? • DEVICE FILL = ? • RECEPTACLES = ? • PIGTAIL = ? • BJ = ? | **Step 1:** Same size conductors  2 #12 hots = _____ [A]  2 #12 neutrals = _____ [B]  2 #12 EGC's = _____ [C]  1 receptacle = _____ [D]  2 #12 pigtails = _____ [E]  1 #12 bonding jumper = _____ [F]  Total = _____ [G]  **Step 2:** Selecting box  _____ in. [H] x _____ in. [I] x _____ in. [J]  **Solution:** The size square box is _____ in. [K] x _____ in. [L] x _____ in. [M]. |

**Figure 6-3.** Sections 370-16(b)(1) through (5) and Table 370-16(a) are utilized to size and select a device box based on the box containing the same size conductors.

**Problem 6-4:** All conductors in the device box are different sizes.

What size device box is required to contain a No. 14-2 nonmetallic sheathed cable, two No. 12-2 nonmetallic sheathed cables passing through, and one receptacle? There is one pigtail and one bonding jumper in the box. (Romex connectors are used)

**Step 1:** Different size conductors
370-16(b)(1) through (5); Table 370-16(b)

| | | | |
|---|---|---|---|
| **1 #14 hot** | | | |
| 2 cu. in. x 1 | = | 2 | cu. in. |
| **1 #14 neutral** | | | |
| 2 cu. in. 1 | = | 2 | cu. in. |
| **2 #12 hots** | | | |
| 2.25 cu. in. x 2 | = | 4.5 | cu. in. |
| **2 #12 neutrals** | | | |
| 2.25 cu. in. x 2 | = | 4.5 | cu. in. |
| **1 receptacle** | | | |
| 2 cu. in. x 2 | = | 4 | cu. in. |
| **1 pigtail** | = | 0 | |
| **1 bonding jumper** | = | 0 | |
| Total | = 17 | | cu. in. |

**Test Tip 9:** Pigtails and bonding jumpers do not count toward the fill in the box.

**Step 2:** Selecting box
Table 370-16(a)
17 cu. in. requires 3" x 2" x 3 1/2"

**Solution: A 3 in. x 2 in. x 3 1/2 in. device box is required.**

See **Figure 6-4** for an exercise problem on sizing device boxes with different size conductors.

**Figure 6-4.** Sections 370-16(b)(1) through (5) and Table 370-16(b) are utilized to size and select a device box based on the box containing different size conductors.

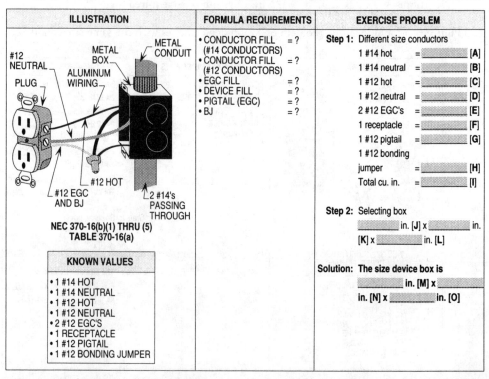

What size square box is required for two No. 12-2 w/ground romex cables connecting to a receptacle and eight No. 12-2 w/ground romex cables that pass through the box? (Use an extension ring)

**Problem 6-5:** All conductors in the square box are the same size.

**Step 1:** Same size conductors
370-16(b)(1) through (5)

| | | |
|---|---|---|
| 2 #12 hots | = | 2 |
| 2 #12 neutrals | = | 2 |
| 8 #12 hots (spliced) 4 x 2 | = | 8 |
| 8 #12 neutrals (spliced) 4 x 2 | = | 8 |
| 10 #12 EGC's | = | 1 |
| 1 Receptacle | = | 2 |
| Total | = | 23 |

**Test Tip 10:** An extention ring can be used to double the fill of a box in most cases.

**Step 2:** Selecting box
Table 370-16(a)
23 #12 requires 4" x 2 1/8"

**Solution: A 4" x 2 1/8" square box with extension ring is required.**

**Note:** Extension ring allows 26 - #12 conductors to be installed per Sec. 370-16(a). A 4 $^{11}/_{16}$ x 1 $^1/_2$ square box could also be used with an extension ring.

**See Figure 6-5** for an exercise problem on sizing square boxes with the same size conductors.

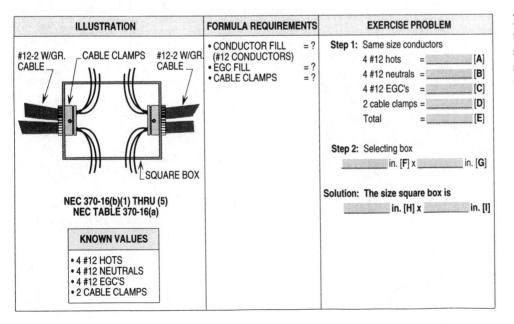

**Figure 6-5.** Sections 370-16(b)(1) through (5) and Table 370-16(a) are utilized to size and select a square box based on the box containing the same size conductors.

**Problem 6-6:** All conductors in the square box are different sizes.

What size square box is required where four No. 14-2 and four No. 12-2 romex cables w/grounds are spliced and routed to loads in the dwelling unit or building?

**Test Tip 11:** Conductors of different sizes or with different types of insulation requires the calculation to be based on cu. in. ratings.

Step 1:  Different size conductors
370-16(b)(1) through (5); Table 370-16(b)

**4 #14 hots**
2 cu. in. x 4           = 8     cu. in.
**4 #14 neutrals**
2 cu. in. x 4           = 8     cu. in.
**4 #12 hots**
2.25 cu. in. x 4       = 9     cu. in.
**4 #12 neutrals**
2.25 cu. in. x 4       = 9     cu. in.
**4 #14 EGC's**
**4 #12 EGC's**
2.25 cu. in. x 1       = 2.25 cu. in.
Total                  = 36.25 cu. in.

Step 2:  Selecting box
Table 370-16(a)
36.25 cu. in. requires 4 11/16" x 2 1/8"

**Solution:  A 4 11/16 in. x 2 1/8 in. square box is required.**

**See Figure 6-6** for an exercise problem on sizing square boxes with different size conductors.

**Figure 6-6.** Sections 370-16(b)(1) through (5) and Table 370-16(b) are utilized to size and select a square box based on the box containing different size conductors. The box is sized based upon the number of cu. in. ratings of each conductor.

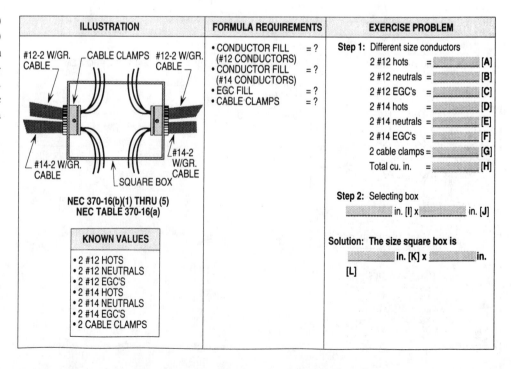

What size junction box is required to contain twelve No. 12-2 w/ground, eight No. 12-2 w/ground, and four No. 12-2 w/ground cables where all the conductors in the cables are spliced?

**Problem 6-7:** All conductors are the same size and must be installed in a box that is not found in Table 370-16(a).

**Step 1:** Same size conductors
370-16(b)(1) through (5); Table 370-16(b)

**12 #12 hots (spliced)**
2.25 cu. in. x 12 = 27 cu. in.
**12 #12 neutrals (spliced)**
2.25 cu. in. x 12 = 27 cu. in.
**12 #12 EGC's (spliced)**
2.25 cu. in. x 1 = 2.25 cu. in.
**8 #12 hots (spliced)**
2.25 cu. in. x 8 = 18 cu. in.
**8 #12 neutrals (spliced)**
2.25 cu. in. x 8 = 18 cu. in.
**8 #12 EGC's**
2.25 cu. in. x 0 = 0
**4 #12 hots (spliced)**
2.25 cu. in. x 4 = 9 cu. in.
**4 #12 neutrals (spliced)**
2.25 cu. in. x 4 = 9 cu. in.
**4 #12 EGC's (spliced)**
2.25 cu. in. x 0 = 0
Total = 110.25 cu. in.

**Test Tip 12:** If the cu. in. ratings of conductors exceed Table 370-16(a) with the use of an extension ring, a junction box must be used.

**Step 2:** Selecting box
370-16(b), Chart on page 11-45
6" x 6" x 4" box = 144 cu. in.
144 cu. in. will contain 110.25 cu. in.

**Solution: A 6 in. x 6 in. x 4 in. junction box is required.**

**See Figure 6-7** for an exercise problem on sizing other boxes with the same size conductors.

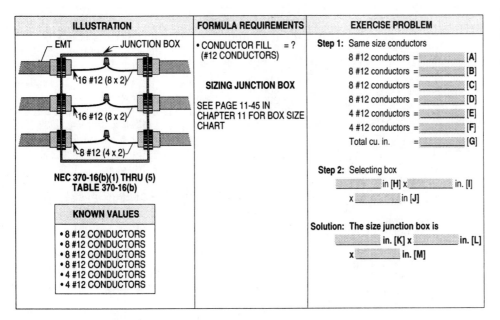

**Figure 6-7.** Sizing and selecting a junction box (see chart on page 11-45) to contain the same size conductors.

**Problem 6-8:** All conductors in the box (junction box) are different sizes (see chart on page 11-45).

What size junction box is required to contain eight No. 10-2 w/ground, twenty No. 14-2 w/ground, twelve No. 12-2 w/ground, and four No. 6-2 w/ground where all the conductors in the cables are spliced?

Step 1: Different size conductors
370-16(b)(1) through (5); Table 370-16(b)

**8 #10 hots (spliced)**
2.5 cu. in. x 8                                = 20 cu. in.
**8 #10 neutrals (spliced)**
2.5 cu. in. x 8                                = 20 cu. in.
**8 #10 EGC's (spliced)**
2.5 cu. in. x 8                                = 0
**20 #14 hots (spliced)**
2.0 cu. in. x 20                               = 40 cu. in.
**20 #14 neutrals (spliced)**
2.0 cu. in. x 20                               = 40 cu. in.
**20 #14 EGC's (spliced)**
2.0 cu. in. x 20                               = 0
**12 #12 hots (spliced)**
2.25 cu. in. x 12                              = 27 cu. in.
**12 #12 neutrals (spliced)**
2.25 cu. in. x 12                              = 27 cu. in.
**12 #12 EGC's (spliced)**
2.25 cu. in.12                                 = 0
**4 #6 hots (spliced)**
5.0 cu. in. x 4                                = 20 cu. in.
**4 #6 neutrals (spliced)**
5.0 cu. in. x 4                                = 20 cu. in.
**4 #6 EGC's (spliced)**
5.0 cu. in. x 1                                = 5 cu. in.
Total                                          = 219 cu. in.

**Test Tip 13:** Four No. 10-2 w/ ground romex cables entering and leaving a box counts as 8 conductors where spliced. However, the NEC must be applied for each conductor before final count. **Note:** Romex connectors are used to connect the cables to the box.

Step 2: Selecting box
Chart 8" x 8" x 4" = 256 cu. in.
256 cu. in. will contain 219 cu. in.

**Solution: An 8 in. x 8 in. x 4 in. junction box is required.**

See **Figure 6-8** for an exercise problem on sizing other boxes with different size conductors.

**Figure 6-8.** Sizing and selecting a junction box to contain different size conductors (see the chart on page 11-45).

| ILLUSTRATION | FORMULA REQUIREMENTS | EXERCISE PROBLEM |
|---|---|---|
| EMT — JUNCTION BOX | • CONDUCTOR FILL = ? (#10 CONDUCTORS) | Step 1: Different size conductors |
| 16 #10 (8 x 2) | • CONDUCTOR FILL = ? (#8 CONDUCTORS) | 8 #10 conductors = _____ [A] |
| 20 #8 (10 x 2) | • CONDUCTOR FILL = ? (#12 CONDUCTORS) | 8 #10 conductors = _____ [B] |
| 24 #12 (12 x 2) | • CONDUCTOR FILL = ? (#6 CONDUCTORS) | 10 # 8 conductors = _____ [C] |
| 10 #6 (5 x 2) | | 10 # 8 conductors = _____ [D] |
| | | 12 #12 conductors = _____ [E] |
| NEC 370-16(b)(1) THRU (5) TABLE 370-16(b) | | 12 #12 conductors = _____ [F] |
| | | 5 # 6 conductors = _____ [G] |
| **KNOWN VALUES** | | 5 # 6 conductors = _____ [H] |
| • 8 #10 CONDUCTORS | | Total cu. in. = _____ [I] |
| • 8 #10 CONDUCTORS | | |
| • 10 # 8 CONDUCTORS | | Step 2: Selecting box |
| • 10 # 8 CONDUCTORS | | _____ in [J] x _____ in. [K] |
| • 12 #12 CONDUCTORS | | x _____ in [L] |
| • 12 #12 CONDUCTORS | | |
| • 5 # 6 CONDUCTORS | | Solution: The size junction box is |
| • 5 # 6 CONDUCTORS | | _____ in. [M] x _____ in. [N] |
| | | x _____ in. [O] |

# CONDUIT BODIES
## 370-16(c)(1)

Conduit bodies containing No. 6 conductors and smaller are not to be less than twice the cross-sectional area of the largest conduit to which it is connected. The number of conductors that are permitted in conduit bodies are determined by the square inch area per Table 5 and Table 4 of Chapter 9.

What is the cross-sectional area of an LB (conduit body) that is connected to a 3/4 in. EMT raceway?

**Problem 6-9:** Sizing conduit bodies based upon the size raceway connecting to such body.

**Step 1:** Finding cross-sectional area
Table 4, Ch. 9
3/4" EMT raceway = .533 sq. in.

**Step 2:** Calculating size LB
370-16(c)(1)
.533 sq. in. x 2 = 1.066 sq. in.

**Solution:** **The LB (conduit body) has a cross-sectional area of 1.066 sq. in.**

See **Figure 6-9** for an exercise problem on sizing conduit bodies.

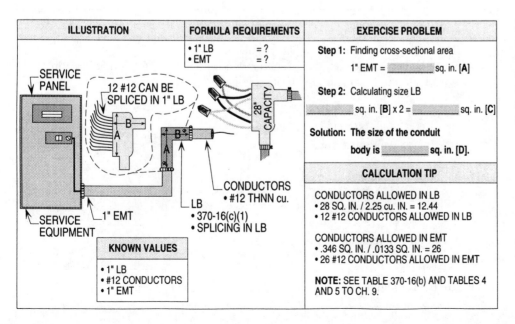

| ILLUSTRATION | FORMULA REQUIREMENTS | EXERCISE PROBLEM |
|---|---|---|

**Figure 6-9.** Conduit bodies containing No. 6 or smaller conductors shall be at least twice the cross-sectional area of the largest conduit that it is connected to. This rule is designed to provide proper room in the LB.

Note that the sq. in. areas of the 1" EMT and No. 12 conductors are found in Tables 4 and 5 to Ch. 9 of the NEC.

# JUNCTION BOXES
# 370-28

Junction boxes housing conductors No. 4 and larger that are pulled through raceways are sized based upon a straight pull or an angle pull.

**Problem 6-10:** Sizing a junction box based upon a straight pull

What is the minimum length for a straight pull consisting of one run of 2 in. raceways?

> **Step 1:** Finding the multiplier
> 370-28(a)(1)
> Multiplier = 8`

> **Step 2:** Calculating length
> 370-28(a)(1)
> 2" raceway x 8 = 16"

**Solution:  The minimum length of the junction box is 16 in.**

See **Figure 6-10** for an exercise problem on sizing straight pulls for junction boxes.

**Figure 6-10.** The size junction box for a straight pull can be found by multiplying the largest conduit by 8.

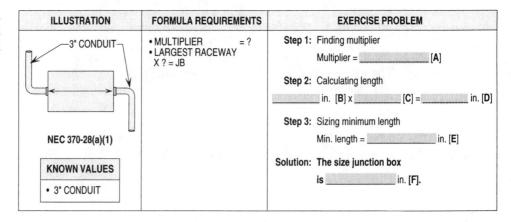

| ILLUSTRATION | FORMULA REQUIREMENTS | EXERCISE PROBLEM |
|---|---|---|
| —3" CONDUIT—<br><br>NEC 370-28(a)(1)<br><br>**KNOWN VALUES**<br>• 3" CONDUIT | • MULTIPLIER = ?<br>• LARGEST RACEWAY<br>  X ? = JB | **Step 1:** Finding multiplier<br>Multiplier = _____ [A]<br><br>**Step 2:** Calculating length<br>_____ in. [B] x _____ [C] = _____ in. [D]<br><br>**Step 3:** Sizing minimum length<br>Min. length = _____ in. [E]<br><br>**Solution:  The size junction box**<br>**is** _____ in. [F]. |

**Problem 6-11:** Sizing a junction box for a straight pull.

What is the minimum length for a junction box with a straight pull that has 4 in., 2 in., and 1 in. raceways connected to its sides?

> **Step 1:** Finding the multiplier
> 370-28(a)(1)
> Multiplier = 8

> **Step 2:** Calculating length
> 370-28(a)(1)
> 4" raceway x 8 = 32"

**Solution:  The minimum length is 32 in.**

See **Figure 6-11** for an exercise problem on sizing straight pulls for junction boxes.

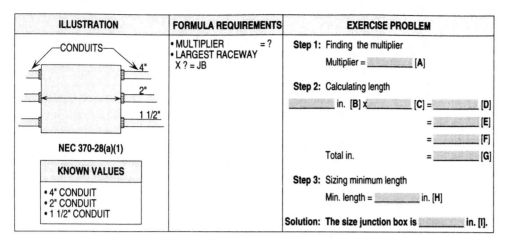

| ILLUSTRATION | FORMULA REQUIREMENTS | EXERCISE PROBLEM |
|---|---|---|
| —CONDUITS—<br>4"<br>2"<br>1 1/2"<br><br>NEC 370-28(a)(1)<br><br>**KNOWN VALUES**<br>• 4" CONDUIT<br>• 2" CONDUIT<br>• 1 1/2" CONDUIT | • MULTIPLIER = ?<br>• LARGEST RACEWAY<br>  X ? = JB | **Step 1:** Finding the multiplier<br>     Multiplier = _____ [A]<br><br>**Step 2:** Calculating length<br>_____ in. [B] x _____ [C] = _____ [D]<br>                              = _____ [E]<br>                              = _____ [F]<br>     Total in.              = _____ [G]<br><br>**Step 3:** Sizing minimum length<br>     Min. length = _____ in. [H]<br><br>**Solution:** The size junction box is _____ in. [I]. |

**Figure 6-11.** The size junction box for a straight pull can be found by multiplying the largest conduit by 8.

What is the minimum length of a junction box for an angle pull that has one run of 4 in. EMT?

**Problem 6-12:** Sizing a junction box for an angle pull.

**Step 1:** Finding the multiplier
370-28(a)(2)
Multiplier = 6

Note that the chart on page 11-45 requires the junction box in Problem 6-12 to be at least 24 in. by 24 in. by 6 in.

**Step 2:** Calculating length
370-28(a)(2)
4" raceway x 6 = 24"

**Solution: The minimum length is 24 in. x 24 in.**

See **Figure 6-12** for an exercise problem on sizing angle pulls for junction boxes.

| ILLUSTRATION | FORMULA REQUIREMENTS | EXERCISE PROBLEM |
|---|---|---|
| ANGLE PULL<br>U-PULL<br>3" CONDUIT<br>3" CONDUIT<br><br>**KNOWN VALUES**<br>• 3" CONDUIT | • MULTIPLIER = ?<br>• LARGEST RACEWAY<br>  X ? PLUS ALL REMAINING<br>  RACEWAYS = JB | **Step 1:** Finding the multiplier<br>     Multiplier = _____ [A]<br><br>**Step 2:** Calculating length<br>_____ in. [B] x _____ [C]<br>            = _____ in. [D]<br><br>**Step 3:** Sizing minimum length<br>Min. length = _____ in. [E] x _____ in. [F]<br><br>**Solution:** The size junction box is<br>_____ in. [G] x _____ in. [H] |

**Figure 6-12.** The size junction box for a angle pull can be found by multiplying the largest conduit by 6 and adding this number to the remaining conduits. Computations will determine the size junction box that is needed.

**Problem 6-13:** Sizing a junction box based upon an angle pull.

What is the minimum length of a junction box for an angle pull that has a 4 in., 3 in., 2 in., and 1 in. raceway that is connected to the right wall and bottom wall?

Step 1: Finding the multiplier
370-28(a)(2)
Multiplier = 6

Step 2: Calculating length
370-28(a)(2)
4" x 6 = 24"
        = 3"
        = 2"
        = 1"
Total = 30"

Solution: **The minimum length is 30 in. x 30 in.**

See **Figure 6-13** for an exercise problem on sizing angle pulls for junction boxes.

**Figure 6-13.** The size junction box for an angle pull can be found by multiplying the largest conduit by 6 and adding this number to the remaining conduits. Computations will determine the size junction box that is needed.

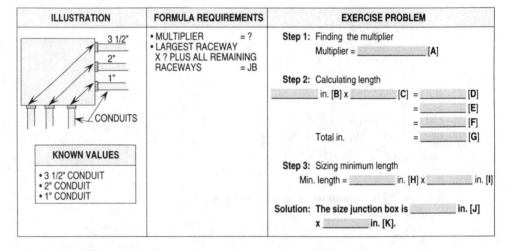

## SIZING CONDUITS
## APPENDIX C; TABLES 4 AND 5 TO CH. 9

Conduits are used to enclose conductors to supply power to various types of electrical equipment. The same size conductors with the same type of insulation may be pulled through conduits. They may also be routed through conduits with different sizes and types of insulation. Tables in Chapter 9 are used to size conduits based on the types of insulation, number, and size of conductors that are pulled through the conduit system.

**Problem 6-14:** Sizing conduits (raceways) containing the same size conductors.

What size (EMT) conduit is required for ten No. 12 XHHW copper conductors routed through the conduit to a pull box?

Step 1: Finding size conduit
Table C1, Appendix C
10 - #12 requires 3/4"

Solution: **A 3/4 in. conduit is required.**

See **Figure 6-14** for an exercise problem on sizing conduits with the same size conductors.

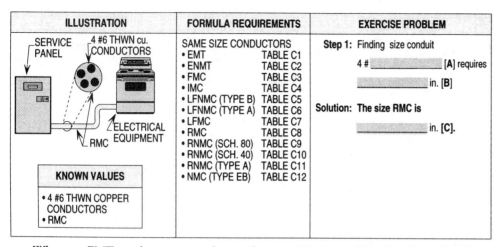

| ILLUSTRATION | FORMULA REQUIREMENTS | EXERCISE PROBLEM |
|---|---|---|
| SERVICE PANEL  4 #6 THWN cu. CONDUCTORS  ELECTRICAL EQUIPMENT  RMC | SAME SIZE CONDUCTORS<br>• EMT — TABLE C1<br>• ENMT — TABLE C2<br>• FMC — TABLE C3<br>• IMC — TABLE C4<br>• LFNMC (TYPE B) — TABLE C5<br>• LFNMC (TYPE A) — TABLE C6<br>• LFMC — TABLE C7<br>• RMC — TABLE C8<br>• RNMC (SCH. 80) — TABLE C9<br>• RNMC (SCH. 40) — TABLE C10<br>• RNMC (TYPE A) — TABLE C11<br>• NMC (TYPE EB) — TABLE C12 | **Step 1:** Finding size conduit<br><br>4 # _____ **[A]** requires<br><br>_____ in. **[B]**<br><br>**Solution:** The size RMC is<br><br>_____ in. **[C]**. |
| **KNOWN VALUES**<br>• 4 #6 THWN COPPER CONDUCTORS<br>• RMC | | |

**Figure 6-14.** Tables C1 through C12(A) in Appendix C may be used to size the conduit for conduits enclosing the same size conductors.

What size EMT conduit is required to enclose two No. 4, one No. 6, and one No. 8 THWN copper conductors?

**Problem 6-15:** Sizing conduit with different size conductors.

**Step 1:** Finding sq. in. area
Table 5, Ch. 9
#4 = .0824 sq. in.
#6 = .0507 sq. in.
#8 = .0366 sq. in.

**Step 2:** Calculating sq. in. area
Table 5, Ch. 9
.0824 sq. in. x 2      = .1648 sq. in.
.0507 sq. in. x 1      = .0507 sq. in.
.0366 sq. in. x 1      = .0366 sq. in.
Total               = .2521 sq. in.

**Step 3:** Selecting size conduit
Table 4, Ch. 9
.2521 sq. in. requires .346 sq. in.

**Solution:** A 1 in. conduit is required.

**See Figure 6-15** for an exercise problem on sizing conduits with different size conductors.

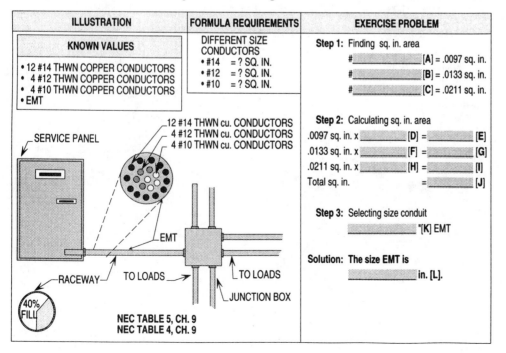

| ILLUSTRATION | FORMULA REQUIREMENTS | EXERCISE PROBLEM |
|---|---|---|
| **KNOWN VALUES**<br>• 12 #14 THWN COPPER CONDUCTORS<br>• 4 #12 THWN COPPER CONDUCTORS<br>• 4 #10 THWN COPPER CONDUCTORS<br>• EMT | DIFFERENT SIZE CONDUCTORS<br>• #14 = ? SQ. IN.<br>• #12 = ? SQ. IN.<br>• #10 = ? SQ. IN. | **Step 1:** Finding sq. in. area<br># _____ **[A]** = .0097 sq. in.<br># _____ **[B]** = .0133 sq. in.<br># _____ **[C]** = .0211 sq. in. |
| SERVICE PANEL  12 #14 THWN cu. CONDUCTORS  4 #12 THWN cu. CONDUCTORS  4 #10 THWN cu. CONDUCTORS  EMT  RACEWAY  TO LOADS  TO LOADS  JUNCTION BOX  40% FILL  NEC TABLE 5, CH. 9  NEC TABLE 4, CH. 9 | | **Step 2:** Calculating sq. in. area<br>.0097 sq. in. x ____ **[D]** = ____ **[E]**<br>.0133 sq. in. x ____ **[F]** = ____ **[G]**<br>.0211 sq. in. x ____ **[H]** = ____ **[I]**<br>Total sq. in.      = ____ **[J]**<br><br>**Step 3:** Selecting size conduit<br>_____ "**[K]** EMT<br><br>**Solution:** The size EMT is<br>_____ in. **[L]**. |

**Figure 6-15.** Table 5, Ch. 9 and Table 4, Ch. 9 can be used to size the conduit for conduits enclosing different size conductors.

## SIZING NIPPLES
## NOTE (4) TO TABLE 1, CH. 9

The difference in a nipple and a conduit is that a nipple is 24 in. or less in length. A conduit system is any run over 24 in. in length.

A conduit system with more than two conductors is allowed 40 percent fill per Table 4, Chapter 9, while a nipple is permitted to have 60 percent fill per Note (4) to Chapter 9.

**Problem 6-16:** Sizing nipples. Note that if a raceway was used instead of a nipple, the size EMT would be 1 1/4 in..

**Test Tip 14:** For a nipple to be considered a nipple, it must be 24 in. or less in length.

What size EMT nipple is required to enclose thirty-six No. 12 THWN copper conductors that are installed between a panelboard and junction box?

**Step 1:** Finding sq. in. area
Table 5, Ch. 9
#12 = .0133 sq. in.

**Step 2:** Calculating sq. in. area
Table 5, Ch. 9
.0133 sq. in. x 36 = .4788 sq. in.

**Step 3:** Finding conduit at 100% total fill
Table 4, Ch. 9
1 in. conduit that has a 100% total of .864 sq. in.
(diameter squared x .7854 = sq. in. area)
1.049 x 1.049 x .7854 = .864 sq. in.

**Step 4:** Applying 60% fill
Note (4) to Table 1, Ch. 9
sq. in. area x 60% = fill area
.864 sq. in. x 60% = .5184 sq. in.

**Step 5:** Selecting the nipple
Table 4, Ch. 9
.5184 sq. in. is greater than .4788 sq. in.

**Solution: The size nipple is 1 in.**

See Figure 6-16 for an exercise problem on sizing nipples.

**Figure 6-16.** Table 5, Ch. 9 and Table 4, Ch. 9 and Note (4) to Ch. 9, Tables may be used to calculate the size of nipples.

**Test Tip 15:** Derating for four or more current-carrying conductors is not required for nipples.

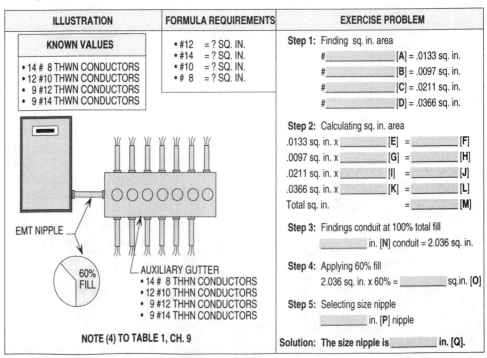

# SIZING AUXILIARY GUTTERS
## 374-5

The number of current-carrying conductors permitted in an auxiliary gutter without derating per Sec. 310-15(b)(2)(a) is 30 or less per Sec. 374-6.

The size of an auxiliary gutter is determined by dividing the total square inch area of the conductors by 20 percent fill area for installing conductors. The total square inch of the conductors is found by multiplying the square inch area per Table 5, Ch. 9 of each conductor which is based on the size and insulation of each conductor placed in the auxiliary gutter.

What size auxiliary gutter is required to house three No. 350 KCMIL THWN copper conductors (feeder-circuit) that have three No. 1/0, three No. 1, and three No. 2 THWN copper conductors spliced to them?

**Problem 6-17:** Sizing auxiliary gutters.

**Step 1:** Finding sq. in. area
Table 5, Ch. 9
#350 KCMIL = .5242 sq. in.
#1/0 THWN = .1855 sq. in.
#1 THWN = .1562 sq. in.
#2 THWN = .1158 sq. in.

**Test Tip 16:** Auxiliary gutters and wireways are allowed to have a 20 percent fill area.

**Step 2:** Calculating sq. in. area
Table 5, Ch. 9
.5242 sq. in. x 3 = 1.5726 sq. in.
.1855 sq. in. x 3 = .5565 sq. in.
.1562 sq. in. x 3 = .4686 sq. in.
.1158 sq. in. x 3 = .3474 sq. in.
Total = 2.9451 sq. in.

**Test Tip 17:** Auxiliary gutters and wireways can contain 30 or less current-carrying conductors without applying derating factors.

**Step 3:** Sizing gutter
374-5(a)(3)
sq. in. area divided by 20% = total fill
2.9451 sq. in. / 20% = 14.7255 sq. in.

**Step 4:** Selecting gutter
Chart on page 11-45
4" x 4" = 16"

Note that the different sizes of auxiliary gutters and wireways are found in the chart on page 11-45.

**Step 5:** Applying 75% fill for splices
374-8(a)
sq. in. of gutter x 75% = fill area
16" x 75% = 12 sq. in.

**Solution:** A 4 in. x 4 in. auxiliary gutter is required with only 12 in. of the gutter space used for splicing conductors.

**Test Tip 18:** Splices and taps may take up to 75 percent of the gutter or wireway fill area.

See Figure 6-17 for an exercise problem on sizing auxiliary gutters.

**Figure 6-17.** Table 5, Ch. 9 and Table 4, Ch. 9 and Sec. 374-5 is used to calculate and size auxiliary gutters.

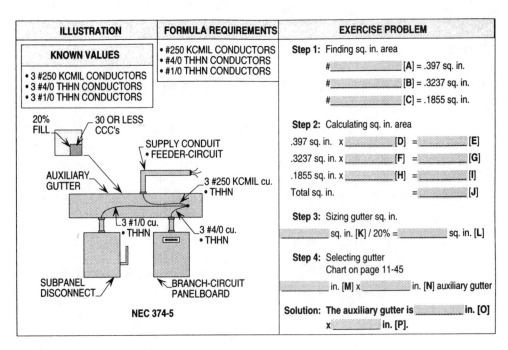

| ILLUSTRATION | FORMULA REQUIREMENTS | EXERCISE PROBLEM |
|---|---|---|

**KNOWN VALUES**
- 3 #250 KCMIL CONDUCTORS
- 3 #4/0 THHN CONDUCTORS
- 3 #1/0 THHN CONDUCTORS

FORMULA REQUIREMENTS
- #250 KCMIL CONDUCTORS
- #4/0 THHN CONDUCTORS
- #1/0 THHN CONDUCTORS

**Step 1:** Finding sq. in. area

\# _____ [A] = .397 sq. in.

\# _____ [B] = .3237 sq. in.

\# _____ [C] = .1855 sq. in.

**Step 2:** Calculating sq. in. area

.397 sq. in. x _____ [D] = _____ [E]

.3237 sq. in. x _____ [F] = _____ [G]

.1855 sq. in. x _____ [H] = _____ [I]

Total sq. in. = _____ [J]

**Step 3:** Sizing gutter sq. in.

_____ sq. in. [K] / 20% = _____ sq. in. [L]

**Step 4:** Selecting gutter
Chart on page 11-45

_____ in. [M] x _____ in. [N] auxiliary gutter

**Solution:** The auxiliary gutter is _____ in. [O]
x _____ in. [P].

Illustration labels: 20% FILL; 30 OR LESS CCC's; SUPPLY CONDUIT • FEEDER-CIRCUIT; AUXILIARY GUTTER; 3 #250 KCMIL cu. • THHN; 3 #1/0 cu. • THHN; 3 #4/0 cu. • THHN; SUBPANEL DISCONNECT; BRANCH-CIRCUIT PANELBOARD; NEC 374-5

# SIZING CABLE TRAYS
# ART. 318

Cable trays can be used for the installation of a number of cables that are installed in a single run from one location to another. Steel or aluminum cable tray sections are used with the ends bolted together to form a single run of the required length. Where installing and routing cables in cable trays, the cables are laid on racks, troughs, or hangers.

**Problem 6-18:** Sizing cable trays. **Note:** To select the proper size cable tray, match Sec. 318-10(a)(2) to column 1 of Table 318-10 and pick the correct sq. in. area and cable tray width.

What size ventilated cable tray is required for twelve No. 250 KCMIL and eight No. 1,000 KCMIL THHN copper conductors?

**Step 1:** Finding sq. in. area
Table 5, Ch. 9
#250 KCMIL THHN = .397 sq. in.
#1,000 KCMIL THHN = 1.3478 sq. in.

**Step 2:** Calculating sq. in. area
318-10(a)(2); Table 318-10, Col. 1
.397 sq. in. x 12 = 4.764 sq. in.
1.3478 sq. in. x 8 = 10.7824 sq. in.
Total = 15.5464 sq. in.

**Step 3:** Selecting size cable tray
Table 318-10, Col. 1
15.5464 sq. in. requires 18 in. width
18 in. wide tray allows 19.5 sq. in.

**Solution:** A 18 in. wide cable tray has 19.5 sq. in. per Table 318-10.

**See Figure 6-18** for an exercise problem on sizing cable trays.

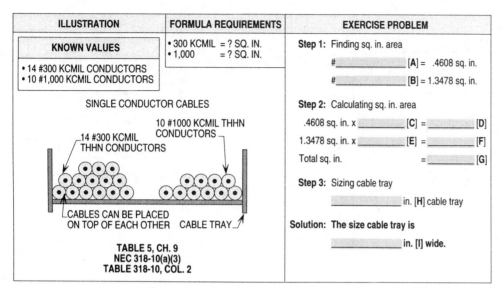

| ILLUSTRATION | FORMULA REQUIREMENTS | EXERCISE PROBLEM |
|---|---|---|

**KNOWN VALUES**
- 14 #300 KCMIL CONDUCTORS
- 10 #1,000 KCMIL CONDUCTORS

• 300 KCMIL = ? SQ. IN.
• 1,000 = ? SQ. IN.

SINGLE CONDUCTOR CABLES

10 #1000 KCMIL THHN CONDUCTORS

14 #300 KCMIL THHN CONDUCTORS

CABLES CAN BE PLACED ON TOP OF EACH OTHER    CABLE TRAY

TABLE 5, CH. 9
NEC 318-10(a)(3)
TABLE 318-10, COL. 2

**Step 1:** Finding sq. in. area

#_____ [A] = .4608 sq. in.

#_____ [B] = 1.3478 sq. in.

**Step 2:** Calculating sq. in. area

.4608 sq. in. x _____ [C] = _____ [D]

1.3478 sq. in. x _____ [E] = _____ [F]

Total sq. in.    = _____ [G]

**Step 3:** Sizing cable tray

_____ in. [H] cable tray

**Solution:** The size cable tray is

_____ in. [I] wide.

**Figure 6-18.** When installing cables in ladder or ventilated-trough trays, the total diameter of all cables No. 1,000 KCMIL or larger and less than 1,000 KCMIL, must not exceed the width of the cable tray.

Note that Sec. 318-10(a)(3) must be aligned to column 2 to Table 318-10 of the NEC.

# Chapter 6
# Wiring Methods

| Section | Answer |
|---|---|

_____   T   F    1. Spliced conductors are counted as two each toward the fill of the box.

_____   T   F    2. A pigtail from a splice within the box to a receptacle or switch mounted to the box is not required to be counted as a conductor.

_____   T   F    3. The first four fixture wires smaller than No. 14 installed in a fixture canopy do not count toward the fill in the box.

_____   T   F    4. All cable clamps count as two conductors based upon the largest conductor entering the box.

_____   T   F    5. An isolated equipment grounding conductor is to count as one conductor.

_____   T   F    6. Junction boxes housing conductors No. 6 and larger that are pulled through raceways are sized based upon a straight pull or an angle pull.

_____   T   F    7. A conduit system is any run over 18 in. in length.

_____   T   F    8. A conduit system with more than two conductors is allowed 60 percent fill.

_____   T   F    9. Auxiliary gutter and wireways can contain 30 or less current-carrying conductors without applying derating factors.

_____   T   F    10. Splices or taps may take up to 80 percent of the auxiliary gutter or wireway.

_____ _____    11. Conductors passing through the box unbroken and not spliced together with scotchlocks are counted as _____ conductor.

_____ _____    12. Boxes with one or more cable clamps that are installed to support cables in the box shall have _____ conductor added toward the fill computation.

_____ _____    13. Boxes that contain fixture studs or hickeys shall have _____ conductor added for each fitting.

_____ _____    14. A receptacle or switch that is mounted on a strap or yoke is counted as _____ conductors.

_____ _____    15. Equipment grounding conductors passing through, or spliced together in the box count as _____ conductor.

_____ _____    16. All equipment grounding conductors added together count as _____ conductor.

_____ _____    17. Conduit bodies containing No. _____ conductors and smaller are not to be less than twice the cross-sectional area of the largest conduit to which it is connected.

_____ _____    18. A nipple is _____ in. or less in length.

_____ _____    19. Derating for four or more conductors is not required for _____.

_____ _____    20. Auxiliary gutters and wireways are allowed to have a _____ percent fill area.

_____  _____

_____

21. What size octagon box is required to support a lighting fixture with the following:

- 2 #12-2 w/ground nonmetallic sheathed cables
- 2 #14 fixture wires with fixture canopy
- Two pigtails
- Fixture stud
- Hickey
- 2 Romex connectors

_____  _____

_____

22. What size octagon box is required to support a lighting fixture with the following:

- 1 #12-2 w/ground nonmetallic sheathed cables
- 2 #14 fixture wires with no fixture canopy
- Two pigtails
- Fixture stud
- Hickey
- 2 romex connectors

_____  _____

23. What size device box is required for a receptacle outlet with the following:

- 2 #12 w/ground nonmetallic sheathed cables
- 2 romex connectors
- 1 duplex receptacle outlet

_____  _____

_____

24. What size device box is required for a receptacle outlet with the following:

- 2 #12 passing through
- 1 #14 hot
- 1 #14 neutral
- 2 #12 EGC's
- 1 duplex receptacle outlet w/ No. 14
- 1 #12 pigtail
- 1 #12 bonding jumper

_____  _____

_____

25. What size square box is required to enclose the following:

- 4 #10 hots
- 4 #10 neutrals
- 4 #10 EGC's
- 2 cable clamps

_____  _____

26. What size square box is required to enclose the following:

- 2 #10 hots
- 2 #10 neutrals
- 2 #10 EGC's
- 2 #12 hots
- 2 #12 neutrals
- 2 #12 EGC's
- 2 cable clamps

_____  _____

_____

27. What size junction box is required to enclose the following:

- 18 #12 conductors (9 x 2)
- 18 #12 conductors (9 x 2)
- 6 #12 conductors (3 x 2)
- All conductors are spliced

| Section | Answer |
|---------|--------|
| _____ | _____ |
| _____ | |

28. What size junction box is required to enclose the following:

- 12 #8 conductors (6 x 2)
- 18 #10 conductors (9 x 2)
- 22 #12 conductors (11 x 2)
- 28 #14 conductors (14 x 2)
- All conductors are spliced

| _____ | _____ |

29. What is the cross-sectional area of an LB (conduit body) that is connected to a 1 1/2 in. EMT raceway?

| _____ | _____ |

30. What is the minimum length for a junction box with a straight pull consisting of one run of 3 in. raceways?

| _____ | _____ |

31. What is the minimum length for a junction box with a straight pull consisting of 3 in., 2 in., and 1 in. raceways connected to its sides?

| _____ | _____ |

32. What is the minimum length for a junction box with an angle pull consisting of one run of 3 in. raceways?

| _____ | _____ |

33. What is the minimum length for a junction box with an angle pull consisting of 4 in., 3 in., 2 in., and 1in. raceways which are connected to the right wall and bottom wall?

| _____ | _____ |

34. What size (EMT) conduit is required to enclose twelve No. 10 THWN copper conductors?

| _____ | _____ |

35. What size (RMC) conduit is required to enclose eighteen No. 10 THWN copper conductors?

| _____ | _____ |

36. What size (FMC) conduit is required to enclose eight No. 10 THWN copper conductors?

| _____ | _____ |

37. What size (RMC) conduit is required to enclose twenty No. 12 XHHW copper conductors?

| _____ | _____ |
| _____ | |

38. What size (EMT) conduit is required to enclose the following THWN copper conductors?

- 2 #6 THWN copper
- 2 #8 THWN copper
- 4 #10 THWN copper

| _____ | _____ |
| _____ | |

39. What size (RMC) conduit is required to enclose the following THWN copper conductors?

- 4 #8 THWN copper
- 8 #10 THWN copper
- 12 #12 THWN copper

| _____ | _____ |
| _____ | |

40. What size (IMC) conduit is required to enclose the following THWN copper conductors?

- 2 #2 THWN copper
- 4 #4 THWN copper
- 4 #6 THWN copper

_____  _____

_____

41. What size (RMC) conduit is required to enclose the following XHHW copper conductors?

- 4 #1/0 XHHW copper
- 4 #2 XHHW copper
- 4 #6 XHHW copper

_____  _____

_____

_____

42. What size EMT nipple is required to enclose twenty-eight No. 12 THWN copper conductors that are installed between a panelboard and junction box?

_____  _____

_____

_____

43. What size EMT nipple is required to enclose the following THWN copper conductors?

- 28 #10 THWN copper
- 16 #12 THWN copper
- 12 #14 THWN copper

_____  _____

_____

44. What size auxiliary gutter is required to enclose three No. 500 KCMIL THWN copper conductors (feeder-circuit) that have three No. 4/0, three No. 2, and three No. 4 THWN copper conductors spliced to them?

_____  _____

_____

45. What size ventilated cable tray is required for twelve No. 300 KCMIL and ten No. 1,000 KCMIL THWN copper conductors?

# Conductor Ampacities

**7**

In selecting the proper size conductors and overcurrent protection devices for supplying power in a circuit from the source to the load, it is most important that the designer apply the appropriate rules of the National Electrical Code (NEC). Rules require the overcurrent protection device (OCPD) for conductors and equipment to be sized in such a manner to open the circuit if current reaches a value that causes excessive or dangerous temperatures in conductors or insulation. Such OCPD must be selected, sized, and wired, to protect both conductors and equipment or a second stage of protection must be provided. The ampacities of conductors can vary depending upon their conditions of use, which are mainly based upon number and exposure to surrounding ambient temperatures.

Conductors routed a long distance between overcurrent devices and equipment may need to be increased in size to maintain ampacity ratings, due to voltage drop problems. Sometimes, conductors are upsized to compensate for terminal ratings. For example, a $60^0$ C terminal will usually require a larger conductor than a $75^0$ C terminal. Those taking the Journeyman's examination must learn to recognize such problems and size conductors accordingly.

## Quick Reference:

TERMINAL RATINGS ....................................... 7-2

OCPD'S RATED 100 AMPS OR LESS ........... 7-2

CALCULATING LOAD ..................................... 7-3

DERATING AMPACITY

OF CONDUCTORS ......................................... 7-4

PROTECTION OF CIRCUIT

CONDUCTORS ............................................... 7-9

TAP CONDUCTORS ...................................... 7-14

MOTOR CIRCUIT CONDUCTORS .................. 7-24

SIZING THE CONDUCTORS FOR

PHASE CONVERTERS ................................. 7-28

A/C AND REFRIGERATION

EQUIPMENT CIRCUIT CONDUCTORS .......... 7-29

TRANSFORMER SECONDARY

CONDUCTORS .............................................. 7-31

SIZING CONDUCTORS FOR A TWO-WIRE

PRIMARY TO TWO-WIRE SECONDARY ....... 7-31

SIZING CONDUCTORS FOR

THE SECONDARY

OF A TRANSFORMER .................................. 7-32

CAPACITOR CIRCUIT CONDUCTORS .......... 7-33

WELDER LOADS .......................................... 7-34

CONTROL CIRCUIT CONDUCTORS ............. 7-38

PROTECTING FIXTURE

CONDUCTORS .............................................. 7-41

## TERMINAL RATINGS
## 110-14(c); 310-10, ITEMS (1) THRU (4)

The procedure used in verifying a terminal's overcurrent protection device rating is to check the rating listed on the overcurrent protection device to see if it is 60°C, 60°C / 75°C, or 75°C. Where the rating of the overcurrent protection device is 100 amps or less, the terminal rating is 60°C if it is not marked as mentioned above. Overcurrent protection devices rated over 100 amps are rated at 75°C and can be loaded to the 75°C ampacities of conductors that are found in Tables 310-16 through 310-19 of the NEC.

## OCPD'S RATED 100 AMPS OR LESS
## 110-14(c)(1); 310-10, ITEM (3)

Note that motor's which leads and terminals are rated at 100 amps or less are rated at 75°C when selecting conductor ampacity.

Termination's for circuits that are rated 100 amps or less, and which use conductors from No. 14 through No. 1, are limited to 60°C ampacities. Conductors that have higher temperature ratings, such as THHN conductors, can be used for these circuits. However, the ampacity of such conductors must be determined by the 60°C columns of Tables 310-16 through 310-19 if not marked 60°C / 75°C or 75°C. In cases, where the termination devices for such circuits are listed for operation at higher temperatures, conductors can have their ampacity selected at the higher temperatures per Sec. 110-14(c)(1)(b) and (c).

**Problem 7-1:** OCPD's rated 100 amps or less are 60°C terminals if not marked 60°/75°C. Therefore, the ampacities of conductors must be selected from the 60°C column of Table 310-16.

What is the ampacity of a No. 4 THHN copper conductor connected to an overcurrent protection device supplying power to equipment where all terminals are rated 75°C?

Step 1: Finding ampacity
110-14(c)(1)(b) and (c)
75°C terminals per Table 310-16 permits #4
THHN cu. to have an ampacity of 85 A

Solution: **A No. 4 THHN copper conductor can be loaded to 85 amps with 75°C terminals.**

See Figure 7-1 for an exercise problem when selecting the terminal ratings to determine the conductors' ampacity based upon 100 amps or less devices.

## OCPD'S RATED OVER 100 AMPS
## 110-14(c)(2); 310-10, ITEM (3)

Termination's for circuits that are rated over 100 amps, and which use conductors larger than No. 1, are limited to 75°C. Conductors that have higher temperature ratings, such as THHN conductors, can be used for these circuits. However, the ampacity of such conductors must be determined by the 75°C columns of Tables 310-16 through 310-19. In cases, where the termination devices for the circuit are listed for operation at higher temperatures, the conductors can have their ampacity calculated at the higher temperatures per Sec. 110-14(c)(2)(b).

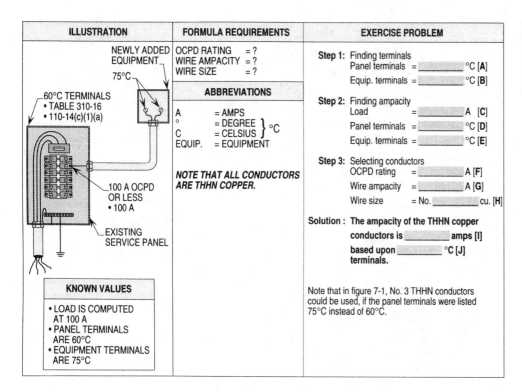

| ILLUSTRATION | FORMULA REQUIREMENTS | EXERCISE PROBLEM |
|---|---|---|

**NEWLY ADDED EQUIPMENT** 75°C

**60°C TERMINALS**
• TABLE 310-16
• 110-14(c)(1)(a)

**100 A OCPD OR LESS**
• 100 A

**EXISTING SERVICE PANEL**

OCPD RATING = ?
WIRE AMPACITY = ?
WIRE SIZE = ?

**ABBREVIATIONS**

A = AMPS
° = DEGREE
C = CELSIUS } °C
EQUIP. = EQUIPMENT

*NOTE THAT ALL CONDUCTORS ARE THHN COPPER.*

**Step 1:** Finding terminals
Panel terminals = _____ °C [A]
Equip. terminals = _____ °C [B]

**Step 2:** Finding ampacity
Load = _____ A [C]
Panel terminals = _____ °C [D]
Equip. terminals = _____ °C [E]

**Step 3:** Selecting conductors
OCPD rating = _____ A [F]
Wire ampacity = _____ A [G]
Wire size = No. _____ cu. [H]

**Solution :** The ampacity of the THHN copper conductors is _____ amps [I] based upon _____ °C [J] terminals.

Note that in figure 7-1, No. 3 THHN conductors could be used, if the panel terminals were listed 75°C instead of 60°C.

**KNOWN VALUES**

• LOAD IS COMPUTED AT 100 A
• PANEL TERMINALS ARE 60°C
• EQUIPMENT TERMINALS ARE 75°C

**Figure 7-1.** Exercise problem for selecting the ampacity of conductors, which are determined by the markings on the terminals of the OCPD's and equipment supplied.

What is the ampacity of a No. 1/0 THHN copper conductor connected to an overcurrent protection device supplying a subpanel?

**Step 1:** Finding ampacity
110-14(c)(2)(b)
75°C terminals per Table 310-16
permits #1/0 THHN cu. to have an ampacity of 150 A

**Solution:** A No. 1/0 THHN copper conductor can be loaded to 150 amps with 75°C terminals.

**Problem 7-2.** OCPD's rated over 100 amps have terminal ampacities selected from the 75°C column per Table 310-16 of the NEC.

See **Figure 7-2** for an exercise problem when selecting the terminal ratings to determine the conductors' ampacity based upon devices rated over 100 amps.

# CALCULATING LOAD
## 210-19(a); 215-2(a); 230-42(a)(1)

Loads that are continuous shall have their full-load currents increased by 125 percent and this value added to noncontinuous loads at 100 percent, if any are present.

The above concept is utilized to compute the load for branch-circuits, feeders and services. Loads are calculated in VA and amps to size and select the elements of such systems.

**Figure 7-2.** Exercise problem for selecting the ampacity of conductors, which are determined by the markings on the terminals of the OCPD's and equipment supplied.

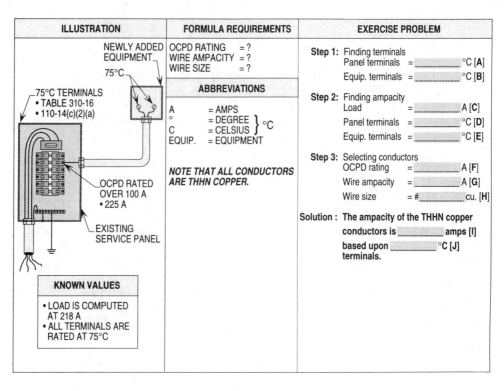

| ILLUSTRATION | FORMULA REQUIREMENTS | EXERCISE PROBLEM |
|---|---|---|

**Test Tip 1:** Continuous load is any load that can operate for three hours or more per Article 100 of the NEC.

**For example:** What is the computed load in amps to serve a continuous operated load of 14 amps and noncontinuous load of 2.5 amps.

Step 1: Finding amperage
210-19(a)
14 A x 125%    = 17.5 A
2.5 x 100%     =  2.5 A
Total load     = 20   A

Solution: The computed load is 20 amps.

# DERATING AMPACITY OF CONDUCTORS
# 310-10, ITEMS (1) THRU (4)

**Test Tip 2:** Correction factors are based upon the temperature surrounding the cable or conduit.

The ampacity of a conductor is the current rating (amps) that a conductor can carry continuously without exceeding its temperature rating which is determined by its condition of use. Such condition of use, is too many current-carrying conductors in a raceway or cable or surrounding ambient temperature which exceeds 86°F. Note that both of these conditions may exist in a circuit.

# APPLYING ADJUSTMENT FACTORS
# 310-10, ITEM (4); 310-15(b)(2)(a)

**Test Tip 3:** When there are four or more current-carrying conductors in a cable or raceway (adjustment factors), a derating factor must be applied and the ampacity of the conductors reduced.

If four or more current-carrying conductors are pulled through a raceway or bundled in a cable for a distance greater than 24 in., the allowable ampacity of such conductors shall be reduced (derated) by the factors (percentages) listed in Sec. 310-15(b)(2)(a).

For example, nine current-carrying conductors in a raceway shall have their ampacities listed in Table 310-16 and reduced by 70 percent so they will not overheat their insulation ratings if they should become fully loaded.

What is the current-carrying ampacity of nine No. 12 THHN copper conductors pulled through 3/4 in. EMT? (all current-carrying)

**Example Problem 7-3.** Applying adjustment factors based upon the number of current-carrying conductors in a cable or raceway.

Step 1: Finding amperage of conductor
Table 310-16
#12 THHN cu. = 30 A

Step 2: Finding adjustment factor
310-15(b)(2)(a)
9 conductors requires 70%

Step 3: Finding amperage
310-15(b)(2)(a)
30 A x 70% = 21 A

Solution: **The ampacity is limited to 21 amps for each conductor.**

See **Figure 7-3** for an exercise problem when derating the ampacity of conductors in a raceway or cable based upon the number that are current-carrying.

| ILLUSTRATION | FORMULA REQUIREMENTS | EXERCISE PROBLEM |
|---|---|---|
| #12 THHN cu. CONDUCTORS<br><br>CONDUCTORS<br>• COPPER<br>• THHN<br><br>FOUR CURRENT-CARRYING CONDUCTORS<br>• 310-10(4)<br><br>**KNOWN VALUES**<br>CONDUCTORS<br>• #12 THHN<br>• COPPER<br>• 4 CURRENT-CARRYING | CONDUCTORS<br>• #12 THHN<br>• COPPER<br>• 4 CURRENT-CARRYING DERATING FACTOR = ?%<br><br>**ABBREVIATIONS**<br>INSULATION = THHN<br>COPPER = cu.<br>ALUMINUM = alu.<br>CIRCULAR MIL. = CM<br>CONDUCTORS = WIRE<br>AMPS = A<br>AMPACITY = A<br>TEMPERATURE = TEMP. | Step 1: Finding amperage of conductor<br>  #12 THHN = _____ A [A]<br><br>Step 2: Finding adjustment factors<br>  4 conductors = _____ % [B]<br><br>Step 3: Finding amperage<br>  _____ A [C] x _____ % [D]<br>  = _____ A [E]<br><br>Solution: The ampacity is limited to _____ amps [F] for each conductor. |

**Figure 7-3.** Exercise problem for adjustment factors per Sec. 310-15(b)(2)(a) where there are four or more current-carrying conductors in a raceway or cable.

# APPLYING CORRECTION FACTORS
## 310-10, ITEM (1); TABLE 310-16

Conductors routed through ambient temperatures exceeding 86°F are required to be derated according to the correction factors of Table 310-16. The derating factors are listed in the ampacity correction factor chart below Table 310-16 and they are selected based on the ambient temperature that the conductors are exposed to. The ampacity correction factors are based on the material, insulation, and the size of the conductors utilized.

**Test Tip 4:** A raceway is a conduit that is over 24 in. in length.

**Problem 7-4.** Applying correction factors based upon the temperature surrounding the cable or conduit.

What is the ampacity of four No. 10 THHN copper conductors routed through an ambient temperature of 120°F?

Step 1: Finding amperage of conductors
Table 310-16
#10 THHN cu. = 40 A

Step 2: Finding correction factors
Table 310-16
120°F requires 82%

Step 3: Finding amperage
Ampacity correction factors
Table 310-16
40 A x 82% = 32.8 A

Solution: **The ampacity is limited to 32.8 amps for each conductor.**

See **Figure 7-4** for an exercise problem which deals with derating the ampacity of conductors in raceway or cable where they are exposed to ambient temperatures exceeding 86°F (30°C).

**Figure 7-4.** Exercise problem for calculating the ampacity of conductors where they are routed through ambient temperatures above 86°F.

**Test Tip 5:** After derating a conductor for condition of use, the reduced ampacity must be capable of supplying the computed load.

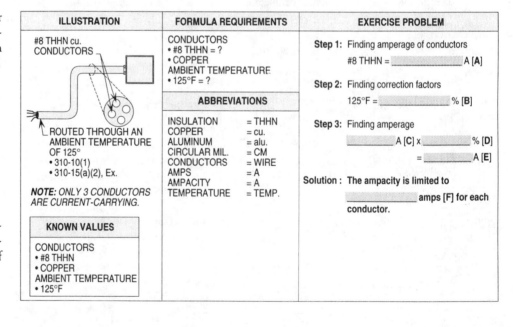

| ILLUSTRATION | FORMULA REQUIREMENTS | EXERCISE PROBLEM |
|---|---|---|
| #8 THHN cu. CONDUCTORS | CONDUCTORS<br>• #8 THHN = ?<br>• COPPER<br>• AMBIENT TEMPERATURE<br>• 125°F = ? | Step 1: Finding amperage of conductors<br>#8 THHN = _____ A [A]<br><br>Step 2: Finding correction factors<br>125°F = _____ % [B] |
| ROUTED THROUGH AN AMBIENT TEMPERATURE OF 125°<br>• 310-10(1)<br>• 310-15(a)(2), Ex.<br><br>*NOTE: ONLY 3 CONDUCTORS ARE CURRENT-CARRYING.* | **ABBREVIATIONS**<br><br>INSULATION = THHN<br>COPPER = cu.<br>ALUMINUM = alu.<br>CIRCULAR MIL. = CM<br>CONDUCTORS = WIRE<br>AMPS = A<br>AMPACITY = A<br>TEMPERATURE = TEMP. | Step 3: Finding amperage<br>_____ A [C] x _____ % [D]<br>= _____ A [E]<br><br>Solution : The ampacity is limited to<br>_____ amps [F] for each<br>conductor. |
| **KNOWN VALUES**<br><br>CONDUCTORS<br>• #8 THHN<br>• COPPER<br>AMBIENT TEMPERATURE<br>• 125°F | | |

# APPLYING BOTH ADJUSTMENT AND CORRECTION FACTORS
## 310-15(b)(2)(a); TABLE 310-16

Four or more current-carrying conductors enclosed in cables and raceways and routed through an ambient temperature above 86°F are required to have their ampacities derated twice.

Too many current-carrying conductors in a cable or raceway have problems dissipating heat into the surrounding ambient medium. The load on the conductors must heat the cable or raceway above the surrounding ambient temperature before harmful heat can be dissipated.

What is the ampacity of six current-carrying No. 14 THHN copper conductors routed through an ambient temperature of 106°F?

**Problem 7-5.** Applying both adjustment and correction factors based upon the number of current-carrying conductors and temperature surrounding the cable or raceway.

Step 1: Finding amperage of conductors
Table 310-16
#14 THHN cu. = 25 A

Step 2: Finding adjustment factor
310-15(b)(2)(a)
6 conductors requires 80%

Step 3: Finding correction factor
Table 310-16
106°F requires 87%

Step 4: Finding amperage
310-15(b)(2)(a); Table 310-16
25 A x 80% x 87% = 17.4 A

Solution: **The ampacity is limited to 17.4 amps for each conductor.**

**See Figure 7-5** for an exercise problem when applying both adjustment and correction factors.

| ILLUSTRATION | FORMULA REQUIREMENTS | EXERCISE PROBLEM |
|---|---|---|
| 8 CONDUCTORS IN RACEWAY CURRENT-CARRYING<br>• 310-15(b)(2)(a)<br>• 310-10(4)<br><br>#12 THHN cu. CONDUCTORS<br><br>ROUTED THROUGH AN AMBIENT TEMPERATURE OF 100°F<br>• 310-10(1); (4)<br>• 310-15(a)(2), Ex. | CONDUCTORS<br>• 8 CURRENT-CARRYING = ?%<br>• #12 THHN<br>• COPPER<br>AMBIENT TEMPERATURE<br>• 100°F = ?% | Step 1: Finding amperage of conductors<br>#12 THHN = _____ A [A]<br><br>Step 2: Finding adjustment factor<br>8 conductors = _____ % [B]<br><br>Step 3: Finding correction factor<br>100°F = _____ % [C]<br><br>Step 4: Finding amperage<br>A = _____ A [D] x _____ % [E]<br>x _____ % [F]<br>A = _____ A [G] |
| **KNOWN VALUES**<br>CONDUCTORS<br>• 8 CURRENT-CARRYING<br>• #12 THHN<br>• COPPER<br>AMBIENT TEMPERATURE<br>• 100°F | **ABBREVIATIONS**<br>INSULATION = THHN<br>COPPER = cu.<br>ALUMINUM = alu.<br>CIRCULAR MIL. = CM<br>CONDUCTORS = WIRE<br>AMPS = A<br>AMPACITY = A<br>TEMPERATURE = TEMP. | Solution : **The ampacity is limited to _____ amps [H] for each conductor.** |

**Figure 7-5.** Exercise problem for determining the ampacity for conductors routed through an ambient temperature above 86°F with more than three current-carrying conductors in a cable or raceway.

# APPLYING 50 PERCENT LOAD DIVERSITY FACTOR TABLE B-310-11

A 50 percent load diversity can be applied to conductor ampacity when all the conductors are not loaded at the same time, if allowed by the AHJ.

**Problem 7-6.** Applying 50 percent load factor based upon only half of the conductors being loaded at the same time.

What is the ampacity of sixteen No. 12 THHN copper conductors, with diversity, located in the same raceway?

> **Step 1:** Finding amperage
> #12 THHN cu. = 30 A

> **Step 2:** Calculating amperage
> Table B-310-11
> 16 conductors = 70%
> 30 A x 70% = 21 A

> **Solution:** The ampacity of each conductor is 21 amps, however, only eight can have this ampacity rating.

**See Figure 7-6** for an exercise problem when applying the 50 percent diversity factor based upon loading only half of the conductors in the raceway or cable.

**Figure 7-6.** Exercise problem for applying derating factors to ampacities of conductors when there is a load diversity.

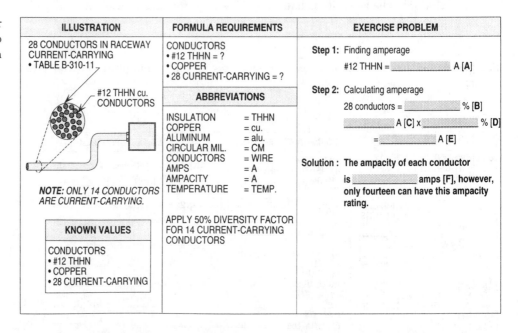

# LOADING MORE THAN HALF OF THE CONDUCTORS FORMULA TO TABLE B-310-11

Diversity can be applied to more than half of the conductors in a raceway or cable if they are limited to a certain calculated ampacity.

What is the ampacity for twelve No. 12 THHN copper conductors where there are 16 conductors pulled through a raceway?

Step 1:  Applying formula
Table B-310-11
$A_2 = \sqrt{.5 \times N / E}$
$A_2 = \sqrt{.5 \times 16 / 12}$
$A_2 = 82\%$
$A_2 = 82\% \times 70\% \times 30\ A$
$A_2 = 17.22\ A$

Solution:  **The ampacity for twelve No. 12 THHN copper conductors is 17.22 amps.**

See Figure 7-7 for an exercise problem for applying the 50 percent diversity factor value, where more than half of the conductors are current-carrying, but are not fully loaded per 310-15(b)(2)(a).

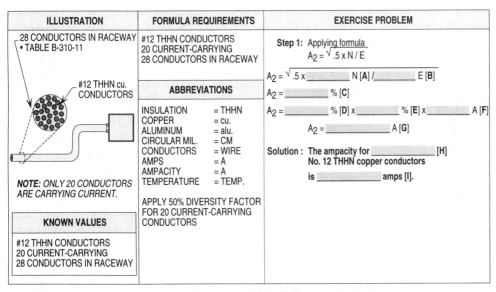

**Problem 7-7.** Loading more than half of the conductors in a raceway or cable when applying diversity factors.

**Figure 7-7.** Exercise problem for applying derating factors to ampacities of conductors when there is a load diversity.

# PROTECTION OF CIRCUIT CONDUCTORS
## 240-3

The general rule is that conductors shall be protected against overcurrent by a fuse or circuit breaker setting rated no higher than the ampacity of the conductor. Conductors have specific current-carrying ampacities for different sizes of conductors, for different insulation's, and for different ambient temperature conditions. The overcurrent protection device shall be sized to protect the insulation of the conductors from damage, caused by the current reaching an excessive value.

# SERVICE CONDUCTORS
## 230-42(a)(1)

Service-entrance conductors shall be of sufficient size to carry the loads as computed in Art. 220. Ampacity is usually determined from Table 310-16 of the NEC. In other words, the ampacity of the service conductors must not be smaller than required to serve the load, and in no case be smaller than the sum of the loads of the branch-circuits which it serves, as computed in Sec.'s 220-10 through 220-22. This rule is subject to applicable demand factors which may apply in Sec.'s 220-11 through 220-41.

**Test Tip 6:** For some types of loads, the OCPD must be sized larger than the ampacity of the conductor to allow starting and running of the equipment. Such equipment is motors, A/C units, welders, etc.

**Problem 7-8.** Service conductor ampacities are computed at continuous and noncontinuous operation. Note that both load operations can exist.

What size THWN copper conductors are required to supply a service with a continuous load of 78 amps and noncontinuous load of 72 amps?

Step 1: Computing load
230-42(a)(1)
78 A x 125%  = 97.5 A
72 A x 100%  = 72   A
Total load   = 169.5 A

Step 2: Selecting conductors
310-10(2); Table 310-16
169.5 A requires #2/0 cu.

**Solution: The size THWN conductors must be No. 2/0 copper.**

See **Figure 7-8** for an exercise problem when calculating the total load in amps to size and select the service conductors.

**Figure 7-8.** Exercise problem for determining the service load in amps and selecting conductors based upon continuous and noncontinuous operation.

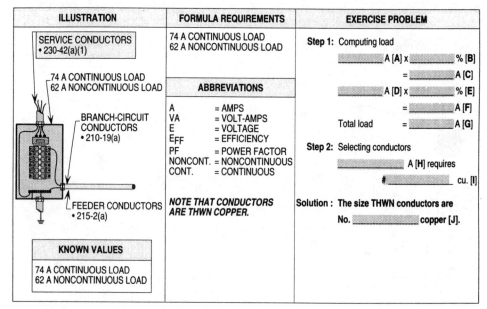

## FEEDER-CIRCUIT CONDUCTORS 215-2(a)

If all of the feeder load is a continuous load, the feeder must be sized to carry 125 percent of the load. However, in cases where part of the feeder load is continuous and part noncontinuous, only the continuous part of the load is subjected to the 125 percent rule.

**Problem 7-9.** Feeder-circuit conductor ampacities are computed at continuous and noncontinuous operation. Note that both load operations can be present.

What size THWN copper conductors are required to supply a continuous load of 130 amps and a noncontinuous load of 35 amps?

Step 1: Computing load
215-2(a)
130 A x 125%  =  162.5 A
35 A x 100%   =   35   A
Total load    =  197.5 A

Step 2: Selecting conductors
310-10(2); Table 310-16
197.5 A requires #3/0 cu.

**Solution: The size THWN conductors are No. 3/0 copper.**

See **Figure 7-9** for an exercise problem for calculating the total load in amps to size and select the feeder-circuit conductors to supply a subpanel.

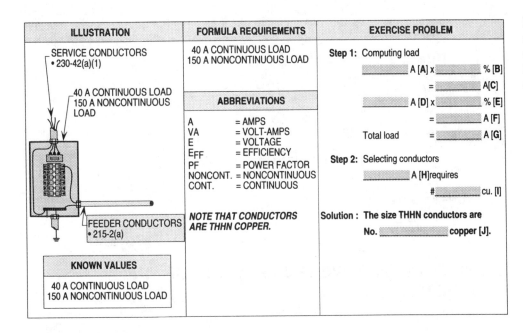

**Figure 7-9.** Exercise problem for determining the feeder load in amps and selecting conductors based upon continuous and noncontinuous operation.

## BRANCH-CIRCUIT CONDUCTORS
## 210-19(a)

Where a branch-circuit supplies continuous loads or any combination of continuous or noncontinuous loads, the ampacity of such conductors shall be the ampacity of the noncontinuous load plus 125 percent of all continuous loads. In other words, the computed continuous load shall not exceed 80 percent of the branch-circuit rating per Sec.'s 384-16(d) and 210-3.

What size THWN copper conductors are required to supply a continuous load of 18 amps and noncontinuous load of 6 amps?

**Problem 7-10.** Branch-circuit conductor ampacities are computed at continuous and noncontinuous operations. Note that both load operations can exist at the same time.

      Step 1: Computing load
            210-19(a)
            18 A x 125%     =  22.5 A
              6 A x 100%     =    6  A
            Total load       =  28.5 A

      Step 2: Selecting conductors
            Table 310-16
            28.5 A requires #10 cu.

     **Solution: The size THWN conductors are No. 10 copper.**

See **Figure 7-10** for an exercise problem when calculating the total load in amps to size and select the branch-circuit conductors.

**Figure 7-10.** Exercise problem for determining the branch-circuit load in amps and selecting conductors based upon continuous and non-continuous operation.

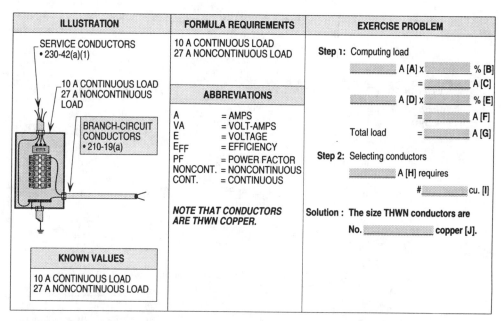

## SIZING OCPD'S ABOVE THE AMPACITY OF THE CONDUCTORS
### 240-3(b)

The general rule is that conductors shall be protected against overcurrent by a fuse or circuit breaker setting rated no higher than the ampacity of the conductor. However, in some installations, the NEC allows the fuse or circuit breaker setting to be above the ampacity of the conductor.

Such an installation, is where the ampacity of the conductor does not correspond with a standard size fuse or circuit breaker setting, which the next higher size may be used.

For example, a No. 4 THHN copper conductor connected to 75°C terminals has an ampacity of 85 amps. A 80 amp fuse or circuit breaker setting would be the largest size permitted for protection of this conductor per Sec. 240-3.

Note that Sec. 240-3(b) permits the next size OCPD which is a 90 amp fuse or circuit breaker to be connected ahead of the circuit.

**Problem 7-11.** Sizing OCPD's above the ampacity of the conductors to supply a branch-circuit load as permitted per Sec. 240-3(b).

What size THWN copper conductors and OCPD are required for a branch-circuit supplying a continuous load of 90 amps and terminated to 75°C terminals?

    **Step 1:** Computing load
           220-3(a)
           90 A x 125% = 112.5 A

    **Step 2:** Terminal ratings
           110-14(c)(1)
           112.5 A can be terminated at 75°C

    **Step 3:** Sizing conductors and OCPD
           310-10(2); Table 310-16; 240-3(b)
           112.5 A requires #2 cu. (115A)
           and 125 A OCPD

    **Solution:** **The size THWN conductors are No. 2 copper (115A) with a 125 amp OCPD.**

See **Figure 7-11** for an exercise problem pertaining to upsizing an OCPD based upon the ampacity of the conductors or the load in amps.

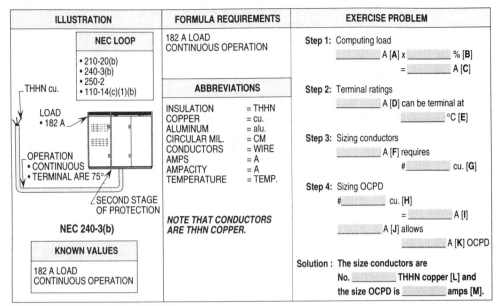

**Figure 7-11.** Exercise problem for sizing the OCPD above the ampacity of the conductors or loads in amps.

# SIZING OCPD'S BELOW THE AMPACITY OF THE CONDUCTORS
## 240-3(c)

If the overcurrent protection device is greater than 800 amps, the ampacity of the conductors shall be equal to or greater than the ampacities of the overcurrent protection device per Sec. 240-6(a).

For example, a paralleled hook-up of five No. 250 KCMIL THWN copper conductors per phase have an ampacity of 1,275 amps (255 A x 5 = 1,275 A). By applying Sec. 240-3(c) of the NEC, a 1,200 amp OCPD must be used.

What size THWN copper conductors and OPCD are required for a subpanel supplying a continuous load of 678 amps and terminated to 75°C terminals which are paralleled 4 times?

**Problem 7-12.** Sizing OCPD's below the ampacity of the conductors.

Step 1: Computing load
215-2(a)
678 A x 125% = 847.5 A

Step 2: Terminal ratings
110-14(c)(1)
847.5 A can be terminated at 75°C

Step 3: Sizing OCPD and conductor
240-3(c); 240-6(a); Table 310-16
#4/0 = 230 A x 4 = 920 A
920 A requires 900 A OCPD

Solution: **The size THWN conductors are No. 4/0 copper and the OCPD is 900 amps.**

See **Figure 7-12** for an exercise problem when sizing OCPD's below the ampacity of the conductors.

# TAP CONDUCTORS
## 240-21

**Test Tip 7:** A tapped conductor is usually from a feeder-circuit having larger conductors sufficient to supply the tapped loads.

The general rule for installing fuses or circuit breakers in a circuit is that they must be installed at the source of the circuit.

For example, where a tap is made from a feeder, the fuses or circuit breaker protecting the tap conductors, can be installed in the equipment enclosure, where such conductors are terminated.

# TAPS 10 FT. OR LESS IN LENGTH
## 240-21(b)(1)

An example of applying this rule, is a tap feeding a lighting and appliance branch-circuit panelboard. The tap conductors cannot be over 10 ft. long and must terminate at such panel. Mechanical protection by conduit, tubing, or metal gutter is required and conductors must be sized to carry the total load. If these requirements are followed, no overcurrent protection device is required at the point of such tap.

**Problem 7-13.** Sizing taps 10 ft. or less in length to supply a load at a given point in a facility.

What size THWN copper conductors are required for a 10 ft. tap when supplied by a feeder-circuit that is protected by a 400 amp OCPD?

Step 1: Calculating min. size tap
240-21(b)(1)(d)
A = 400 A OCPD / 10
A = 40

Step 2: Sizing conductors at 1000%
Table 310-16
#8 THWN cu. = 50 A
50 A x 10 = 500 A

Step 3: Verifying size per OCPD
240-21(b)(1)(d)
500 A is greater than 400 A

Solution: **The size THWN conductors are No. 8 copper. Note: The No. 8 at 50 amps is greater than the 40 amp minimum tap.**

See Figure 7-13 for an exercise problem pertaining to the application of the 10 ft. tap rule.

# TAPS OVER 10 FT. TO 25 FT. IN LENGTH
## 240-21(b)(2)

**Test Tip 8:** When applying the 25 ft. tap rule, conductors must terminate in an OCPD.

A tap from a larger conductor to a smaller conductor may extend over 10 ft. up to a distance of 25 ft., provided the current-carrying capacity of the tap is at least 1/3 that of the OCPD. Overcurrent protection is not required at the point of the tap, but the tap must have overcurrent protection at the end of the run. Such tap must be properly sized and protected from physical damage and enclosed in a raceway system.

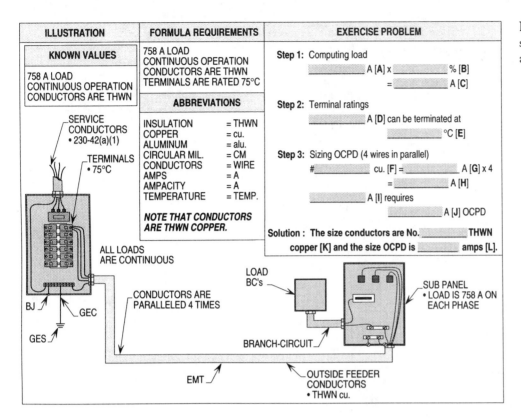

**Figure 7-12.** Exercise problem for sizing the OCPD below the ampacity of the conductors.

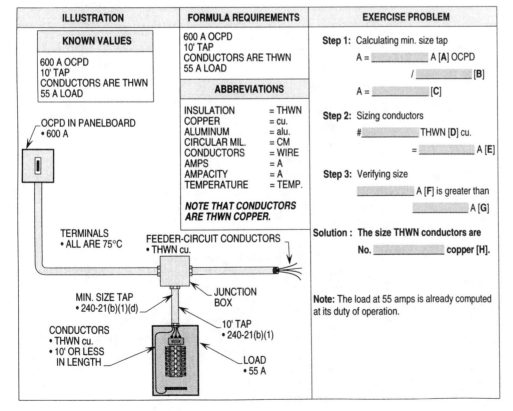

**Figure 7-13.** Exercise problem for sizing the conductors for a tap that is 10 ft. or less in length.

**Problem 7-14.** Sizing taps over 10 ft. to 25 ft. in length to supply equipment and loads at a specific location.

What size THWN copper conductors are required for a 25 ft. tap when supplied by a feeder-circuit with a 400 amp OCPD?

**Step 1:** Calculating min. size tap
240-21(b)(2)(a)
1/3 x 400 A OCPD = 133.3 A

**Step 2:** Selecting conductors
Table 310-16
133.3 A requires #1/0 cu.

**Solution:** The size THWN conductors are No. 1/0 copper.

See **Figure 7-14** for an exercise problem pertaining to the application of the over 10 ft. to 25 ft. tap rule.

## TAPS INCLUDING TRANSFORMER
## 240-21(b)(3); (c)(5)

Transformer taps with primary plus secondary conductors which are not over 25 ft. in. length can be made without overcurrent protection at the point of such taps. Conductors must be sized and based on the primary and secondary side of the transformer.

**Problem 7-15.** Sizing taps including the transformer, primary conductors, and secondary conductors respectively.

What size THWN copper conductors are required for the primary and secondary when applying the 25 ft. tap. Note that they are supplied by a 250 amp OCPD having a 480 volt primary and 208 volt secondary?

**Step 1:** Calculating primary tap
240-21(b)(3)(a)
1/3 x 250 A = 83.3 A

**Step 2:** Selecting primary conductors
Table 310-16
83.3 A requires #4 cu.

**Step 3:** Calculating secondary tap
240-21(b)(3)(b)
A = 480 V / 208 V x 1/3 x 250 A
A = 192

**Step 4:** Selecting secondary conductors
Table 310-16
192 A requires #3/0 cu.

**Solution:** The size THWN conductors for the primary side are No. 4 copper and the secondary side are No. 3/0 copper.

See **Figure 7-15** for an exercise problem pertaining to connections which include primary tap, transformer, and secondary connected conductors.

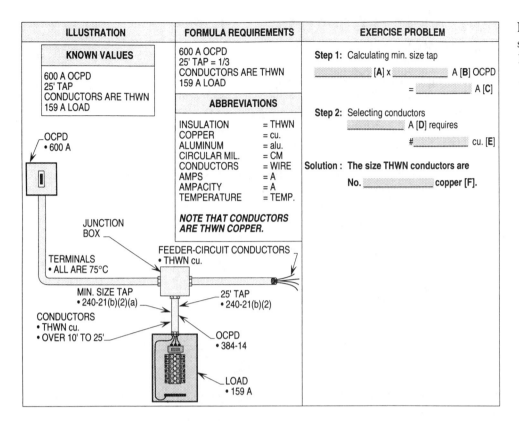

**Figure 7-14.** Exercise problem for sizing the conductors for a tap over 10 ft. up to 25 ft. in length.

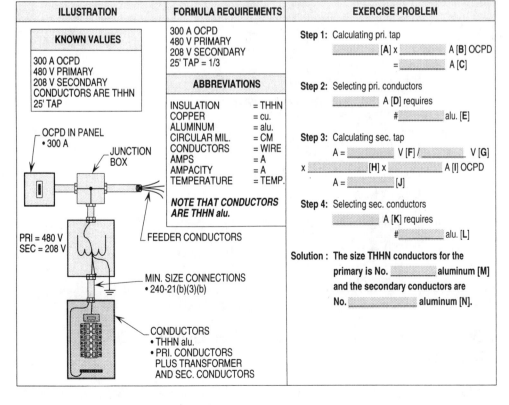

**Figure 7-15.** Exercise problem for sizing the conductors for a 25 ft. tap including the primary tap, transformer, and secondary connected conductors.

## TAPS OVER 25 FT. UP TO 100 FT. IN LENGTH
## 240-21(b)(4)

For taps in high bay manufacturing buildings, the protection for the tap may be at the end of the tapped conductors, if the tap is not over 25 ft. long horizontally, and not over 75 ft. long vertically. Note that the total run, both horizontally and vertically, is limited to 100 ft. or less in length.

**Problem 7-16.** Sizing taps over 25 ft. up to 100 ft. in length

What size THWN copper conductors are required for a 100 ft. tap when supplied by a feeder-circuit having a 350 amp OCPD?

**Step 1:** Calculating min. size tap
240-21(b)(4)(c)
1/3 x 350 A = 116.7 A

**Step 2:** Selecting conductors
Table 310-16
116.7 A requires #1 cu.

**Solution:** The size THWN conductors are No. 1 copper.

**See Figure 7-16** for an exercise problem pertaining to the application of the over 25 ft. up to 100 ft. tap rule.

**Figure 7-16.** Exercise problem for sizing the conductors for a tap over 25 ft. up to 100 ft. in length.

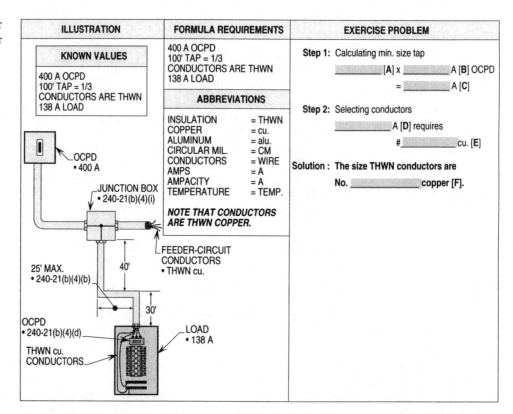

**Test Tip 9:** The tapped box (junction) must be at least 30 ft. above the finished grade.

## CONNECTIONS OF 10 FT. FROM SECONDARY OF XTMR
## 240-21(c)(2)

Conductors of 10 ft. or less may be connected from the secondary of a separately derived system.

What size OCPD is required to protect 4 No. 4/0 THWN copper conductors paralleled 4 times when supplying a 300 kVA transformer with a 480 volt primary and 208 volt secondary? **Note:** OCPD based on output of transformer.

**Step 1:** Calculating FLA (sec.)
FLA = 300 kVA x 1,000 / 208 V x 1.732
FLA = 833 A

**Step 2:** Sizing secondary OCPD
240-21(c)(2)(a); (b); 240-6(a)
800 A secondary OCPD is less than the 833 A output

**Solution:** The secondary OCPD rated at 800 amps protects the secondary output (833 A) and the 4 No. 4/0 conductors parallel per phase (920 A) is equal to and greater than the output.

**Problem 7-17.** Sizing connections rated 10 ft. or less in length from the secondary of a transformer.

| Quick Calc. |
|---|
| • #4/0      =   230 A |
| • 230 A x 4   =   920 A |
| **Solution: Parallel hook-up of 4- #4/0 per phase is 920 amps.** |

See **Figure 7-17** for an exercise problem pertaining to a 10 ft. connection that is made from the secondary side of a separately derived system.

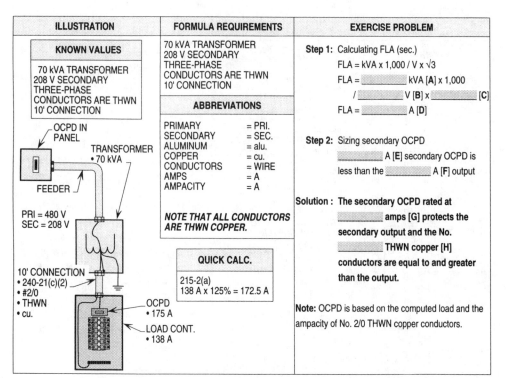

| ILLUSTRATION | FORMULA REQUIREMENTS | EXERCISE PROBLEM |
|---|---|---|
| **KNOWN VALUES**<br><br>70 kVA TRANSFORMER<br>208 V SECONDARY<br>THREE-PHASE<br>CONDUCTORS ARE THWN<br>10' CONNECTION<br><br>OCPD IN PANEL<br>TRANSFORMER • 70 kVA<br>FEEDER<br><br>PRI = 480 V<br>SEC = 208 V<br><br>10' CONNECTION<br>• 240-21(c)(2)<br>• #2/0<br>• THWN<br>• cu.<br><br>OCPD • 175 A<br>LOAD CONT. • 138 A | 70 kVA TRANSFORMER<br>208 V SECONDARY<br>THREE-PHASE<br>CONDUCTORS ARE THWN<br>10' CONNECTION<br><br>**ABBREVIATIONS**<br><br>PRIMARY   = PRI.<br>SECONDARY  = SEC.<br>ALUMINUM  = alu.<br>COPPER    = cu.<br>CONDUCTORS = WIRE<br>AMPS     = A<br>AMPACITY  = A<br><br>*NOTE THAT ALL CONDUCTORS ARE THWN COPPER.*<br><br>**QUICK CALC.**<br>215-2(a)<br>138 A x 125% = 172.5 A | Step 1: Calculating FLA (sec.)<br>FLA = kVA x 1,000 / V x √3<br>FLA = _____ kVA [A] x 1,000<br>/ _____ V [B] x _____ [C]<br>FLA = _____ A [D]<br><br>Step 2: Sizing secondary OCPD<br>_____ A [E] secondary OCPD is less than the _____ A [F] output<br><br>Solution : The secondary OCPD rated at _____ amps [G] protects the secondary output and the No. _____ THWN copper [H] conductors are equal to and greater than the output.<br><br>**Note:** OCPD is based on the computed load and the ampacity of No. 2/0 THWN copper conductors. |

**Figure 7-17.** Exercise problem for connecting conductors from the secondary of a transformer using the 10 ft. connection rule.

**Note:** For voltage values in calculation problems, use 360 volts for (208 V x 1.732) instead of 360.256 volts.

# CONNECTIONS OF 25 FT. FROM SECONDARY OF XTMR 240-21(c)(3)

Connected conductors are permitted to be connected to the transformer secondary of a separately derived system for industrial installations, without overcurrent protection at the connection, where the OCPD in the panel protects the conductors and output of the transformer.

**Problem 7-18.** Sizing connections of 25 ft. from secondary of transformer.

What size OCPD is required to protect 3 No. 300 KCMIL THWN copper conductors paralleled 3 times that supplies a 300 kVA transformer with a 480 volt primary and 208 volt secondary? **Note:** OCPD is based on output of a transformer.

**Step 1:** Calculating FLA (sec.)
FLA = 300 kVA x 1,000 / 208 V x 1.732
FLA = 833 A

**Step 2:** Sizing secondary OCPD
240-21(c)(3)(a); (b); 240-6(a)
800 A secondary OCPD is less than the 833 A output

**Solution:** The secondary OCPD rated at 800 amps protects the secondary output (833 A) and the 3 No. 300 KCMIL parallel per phase (855 A) is equal to and greater than the output.

**See Figure 7-18** for an exercise problem pertaining to making 25 ft. connections from the secondary of a separately derived system.

**Figure 7-18.** Exercise problem for connecting conductors from the secondary of a transformer using the 25 ft. connection rule.

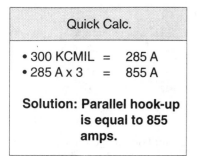

**Quick Calc.**

- 300 KCMIL = 285 A
- 285 A x 3 = 855 A

**Solution: Parallel hook-up is equal to 855 amps.**

**Test Tip 10:** The OCPD at the end of the connected conductors must protect both the output of the transformer and the conductors from overloads.

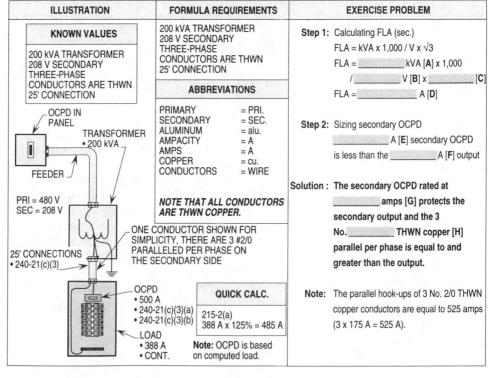

# OUTSIDE FEEDER CONNECTIONS
## 240-21(c)(4)

Outside conductors are allowed to be connected to a feeder or to be connected at the transformer secondary, without overcurrent protection at the connection. However, to apply this rule, the OCPD must protect the connected conductors and output of the transformer from overloads.

What size OCPD is required to protect a No. 250 KCMIL THWN copper conductor parallel 3 times that are tapped from a 600 kVA customer-owned transformer with a 13,800 volt primary and 480 volt secondary?

**Problem 7-19.** Sizing outside connections from the secondary side of an outdoor transformer.

Step 1:    Calculating FLA (sec.)
           FLA = 600 kVA x 1,000 / 480 V x 1.732
           FLA = 722 A

Step 2:    Sizing secondary OCPD
           240-21(c)(4)(b); (c); 240-6(a)
           700 A secondary OCPD is less than the 722 amp output

Solution:  **The 700 amp OCPD protects the secondary of a transformer (722 A) and the 3 No. 250 KCMIL THWN copper conductors per phase (765 A) are equal to and greater than the output.**

| Quick Calc. | | |
|---|---|---|
| • #250 | = | 255 A |
| • 255 A x 3 | = | 765 A |

**Solution: Parallel hook-ups of 3 #250 KCMIL per phase is equal to 765 amps.**

See **Figure 7-19** for an exercise problem pertaining to making connections from the secondary side of transformers located outside of the premises.

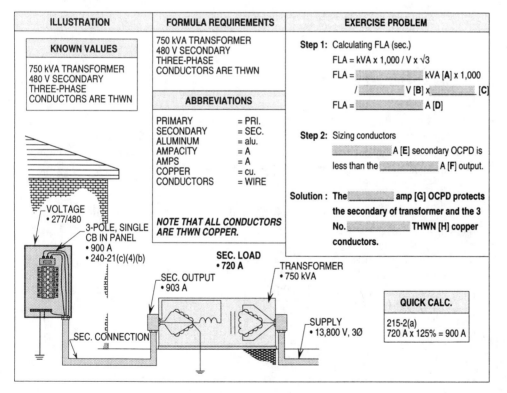

**Figure 7-19.** Exercise problem for connecting conductors from the secondary of a transformer using the outside connection rule.

Note that the ampacity of the conductors in Figure 7-21 is 930 amps (310 A x 3 = 930 A).

## BUSWAY TAPS
## 240-21(e)

Section 364-11 permits a reduction in the size of a busway. In such cases, an additional overcurrent protection device is not required for smaller busways at the point of the tap.

**Problem 7-20.** Sizing busway taps based upon the OCPD ahead of the system.

Can a 200 amp busway be tapped to a 600 amp busway?

**Step 1:** Sizing tap
240-21(e); 364-11, Ex.
600 A x 1/3 = 200 A

**Step 2:** Verifying size
200 A busway is equal to 200 A

**Solution:** The 200 amp busway tap is equal to 200 amps, therefore, the tap complies with the NEC.

See **Figure 7-20** for an exercise problem when sizing a busway tap from a larger busway.

**Figure 7-20.** Exercise problem for sizing a smaller busway that is tapped from a larger busway.

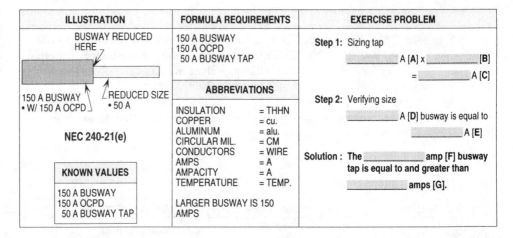

| ILLUSTRATION | FORMULA REQUIREMENTS | EXERCISE PROBLEM |
|---|---|---|
| BUSWAY REDUCED HERE / REDUCED SIZE • 50 A / 150 A BUSWAY • W/ 150 A OCPD / NEC 240-21(e) | 150 A BUSWAY / 150 A OCPD / 50 A BUSWAY TAP | **Step 1:** Sizing tap / _____ A [A] x _____ [B] / = _____ A [C] |
| **KNOWN VALUES** / 150 A BUSWAY / 150 A OCPD / 50 A BUSWAY TAP | **ABBREVIATIONS** / INSULATION = THHN / COPPER = cu. / ALUMINUM = alu. / CIRCULAR MIL. = CM / CONDUCTORS = WIRE / AMPS = A / AMPACITY = A / TEMPERATURE = TEMP. / LARGER BUSWAY IS 150 AMPS | **Step 2:** Verifying size / _____ A [D] busway is equal to / _____ A [E] / Solution : The _____ amp [F] busway tap is equal to and greater than _____ amps [G]. |

# MOTOR CIRCUIT TAPS
## 240-21(f)

Where more than one motor is on a feeder-circuit, each motor circuit is tapped from the feeder conductors. The tap is protected by the motor's branch-circuit protection. The motor's branch-circuit protection is located where the tap conductors terminate in a circuit breaker or set of fuses.

**Problem 7-21.** Sizing motor circuit taps based upon the OCPD ahead of the system.

What size THWN copper conductors are required for a 10 ft. motor circuit tap when supplied by a 600 amp OCPD?

**Step 1:** Calculating min. size tap
240-21(f); 430-28(1)
A = 600 A OCPD / 10
A = 60

**Step 2:** Sizing conductors
Table 310-16
#6 THWN cu. = 65 A

**Step 3:** Verifying size
240-21(f); 430-28(1)
65 A is greater than 60 A

**Solution:** The size THWN conductors are No. 6 copper.

See **Figure 7-21** for an exercise problem pertaining to taps used for motor circuits.

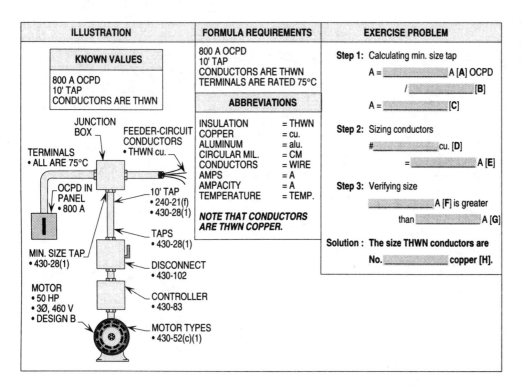

**Figure 7-21.** Exercise problem for sizing the conductors for a 10 ft. tap to supply a motor.

# CONDUCTORS FROM GENERATOR TERMINALS
## 240-21(g)

According to the general rule, generator conductors must have an ampacity equal to at least 115 percent of the nameplate current rating of the generator.

What size THWN copper conductors are required for a generator with an output of 250 kW, with a three-phase, 480 volt primary and 277 volt secondary?

**Problem 7-22.** Sizing conductors from generator terminals to supply equipment and loads.

Step 1: Finding FLA of generator
445-5
FLA = 250 kVA x 1,000 / 480 V x 1.732
FLA = 300.8 A

Step 2: Calculating FLA for conductors
445-5
300.8 A x 115% = 345.9 A

Step 3: Selecting conductors
310-10(2); Table 310-16
345.9 A requires #500 KCMIL cu.

Solution: The size THWN conductors are to be at least No. 500 KCMIL copper because there is no OCPD at the generator.

See Figure 7-22 for an exercise problem when making a secondary tap from the output of a generator to supply equipment and loads.

**Figure 7-22.** Exercise problem for tapping conductors from the secondary of a generator.

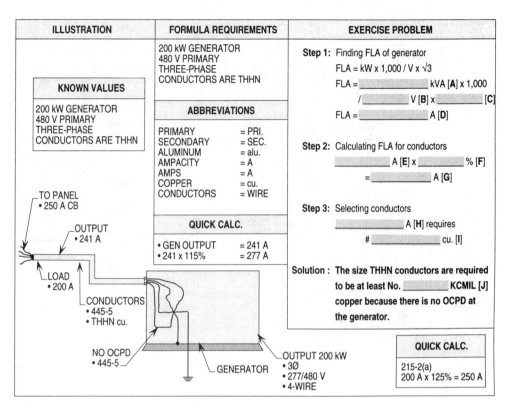

## MOTOR CIRCUIT CONDUCTORS
## 430-6(a)(1); 430-22(a)

Branch-circuit conductors supplying a single motor shall have an ampacity not less than 125 percent of the motor's full-load current rating per Tables 430-147, 430-148, 430-149, and 430-150 respectively.

Conductors supplying a feeder-circuit must have the largest motor multiplied by 125 percent and this value added to the full-load amps of each remaining motor of the group.

## SIZING CONDUCTORS FOR SINGLE-PHASE MOTORS
## 430-22(a); Table 430-148

**Test Tip 11:** Conductors must be sized at 125 percent of the motor's full load current so they are protected from overload conditions.

Section 430-6(a)(1) of the NEC requires the full-load current in amps for single-phase motors to be obtained from Table 430-148. This FLC rating in amps is then multiplied by 125 percent per Sec. 430-22(a) to derive the total amps to select the conductors from Table 310-16 to supply power to the motor windings. Conductors sized in this manner are considered protected from overloads, by the overloads in the controller. The ampacities of such conductors are selected from Table 310-16 based upon 60°C or 75°C terminals or loads.

What size THWN copper conductors are required to supply power to a 115 volt, single-phase, 3/4 HP, Design B motor that is installed in a commercial building?

**Problem 7-23.** Sizing conductors to supply single-phase motors

**Step 1:** Finding FLA
430-6(a)(1); Table 430-148
3/4 HP = 13.8 A

**Step 2:** Sizing conductors
430-22(a)
13.8 A x 125% = 17.25 A

**Step 3:** Selecting conductors
310-10(2); Table 310-16
17.25 A requires #14 cu.

**Solution: The size THWN copper conductors are No. 14.**

**See Figure 7-23** for an exercise problem when computing and selecting the size conductors for a single-phase motor that is installed in an industrial plant.

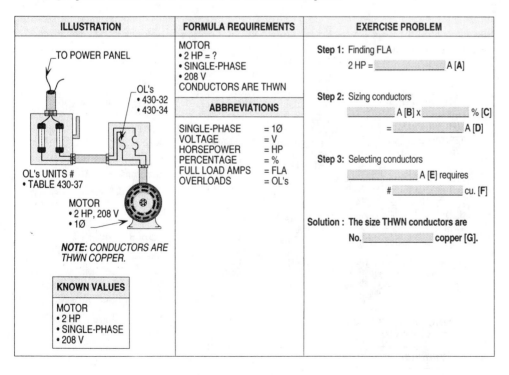

| ILLUSTRATION | FORMULA REQUIREMENTS | EXERCISE PROBLEM |
|---|---|---|
| TO POWER PANEL<br><br>OL's<br>• 430-32<br>• 430-34<br><br>OL's UNITS #<br>• TABLE 430-37<br><br>MOTOR<br>• 2 HP, 208 V<br>• 1Ø<br><br>*NOTE: CONDUCTORS ARE THWN COPPER.*<br><br>**KNOWN VALUES**<br>MOTOR<br>• 2 HP<br>• SINGLE-PHASE<br>• 208 V | MOTOR<br>• 2 HP = ?<br>• SINGLE-PHASE<br>• 208 V<br>CONDUCTORS ARE THWN<br><br>**ABBREVIATIONS**<br><br>SINGLE-PHASE = 1Ø<br>VOLTAGE = V<br>HORSEPOWER = HP<br>PERCENTAGE = %<br>FULL LOAD AMPS = FLA<br>OVERLOADS = OL's | **Step 1:** Finding FLA<br>2 HP = _____ A [A]<br><br>**Step 2:** Sizing conductors<br>_____ A [B] x _____ % [C]<br>= _____ A [D]<br><br>**Step 3:** Selecting conductors<br>_____ A [E] requires<br># _____ cu. [F]<br><br>**Solution :** The size THWN conductors are<br>No. _____ copper [G]. |

**Figure 7-23.** Exercise problem for calculating and sizing the conductors for supplying power to a single-phase motor.

## SIZING CONDUCTORS FOR THREE-PHASE MOTORS
### 430-22(a)

Section 430-6(a)(1) of the NEC requires the full-load current in amps for three-phase motors to be obtained from Table 430-150. This FLC rating in amps is multiplied by 125 percent per Sec. 430-22(a) to derive the total amps to select the conductors for the motor windings.

**Problem 7-24.** Sizing conductors for three-phase motors.

What size THHN copper conductors are required to supply power to a 208 volt, three-phase, 15 HP, Design B motor having 75°C terminals?

**Step 1:** Finding FLA
430-6(a)(1); Table 430-150
15 HP = 46.2 A

**Step 2:** Sizing conductors
430-22(a)
46.2 A x 125% = 57.75 A

**Step 3:** Selecting conductors
310-10(2); Table 310-16
57.75 A requires #6 cu.

**Solution:** **The size THHN copper conductors based on 75°C terminals are No. 6.**

See **Figure 7-24** for an exercise problem when computing and selecting the size conductors for a three-phase motor.

**Figure 7-24.** Exercise problem for calculating and sizing the conductors for supplying power to a three-phase motor. **Note:** The THWN rating is used instead of the THHN rating due to the 75°C rating of the terminals.

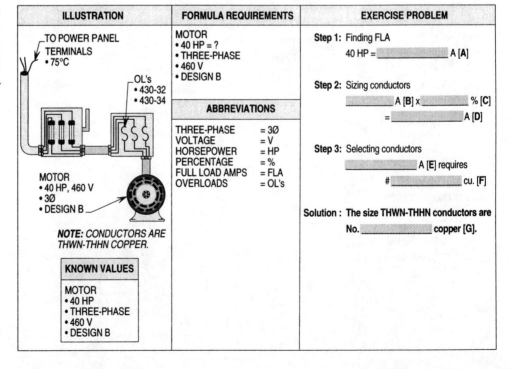

## SIZING CONDUCTORS FOR SEVERAL MOTORS 430-24

The full-load current rating of the largest motor must be multiplied by 125 percent to select the size conductors for a feeder supplying a group of two or more motors. The remaining motors of the group must have their full-load current ratings added to this value and this total amperage is then used to size the conductors.

What size THHN copper conductors are required to supply a group of three-phase, 460 volt, Design B motors which are rated at 10 HP, 20 HP, and 30 HP respectively?

**Problem 7-25.** Sizing conductors for several motors that are supplied from a feeder-circuit. Note that the terminals are 75° C.

**Step 1:** Finding FLA
430-6(a)(1); Table 430-150
10 HP = 14 A
20 HP = 27 A
30 HP = 40 A

**Step 2:** Sizing conductors
430-24
40 A x 125% = 50 A
27 A x 100% = 27 A
14 A x 100% = 14 A
Total load = 91 A

**Step 3:** Selecting conductors
310-10(2); Table 310-16
91 A requires #3 cu.

**Solution: The size THHN copper conductors are No. 3. Note: THHN copper conductor ampacities were selected based on 75°C terminal ratings and not 90°C terminals.**

See **Figure 7-25** for an exercise problem when computing and sizing the conductors for a feeder-circuit supplying a group of motors.

**ILLUSTRATION**

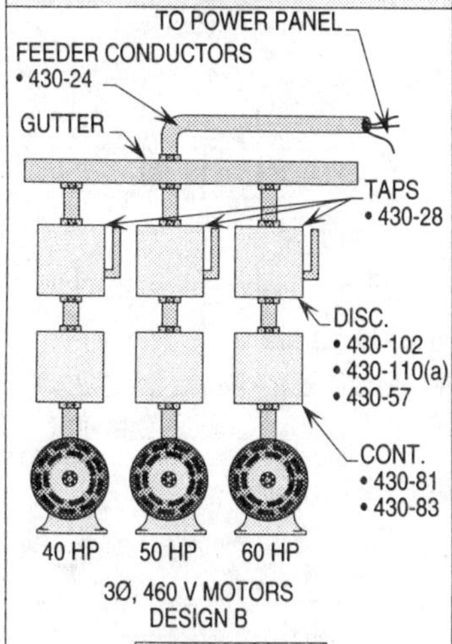


**KNOWN VALUES**

MOTORS
- 40 HP
- 50 HP
- 60 HP
- THREE-PHASE
- 460 V
- DESIGN B

**FORMULA REQUIREMENTS**

MOTORS
- 40 HP = ?
- 50 HP = ?
- 60 HP = ?
- THREE-PHASE
- 460 V
- DESIGN B

**ABBREVIATIONS**

LARGEST MOTOR = LRG. MT.
FULL LOAD AMPS = FLA
DISCONNECT = DISC.
CONTROLLER = CONT.
HORSEPOWER = HP
PERCENTAGE = %
VOLTAGE = V

**EXERCISE PROBLEM**

**Step 1:** Finding FLA
40 HP = ______ A [A]
50 HP = ______ A [B]
60 HP = ______ A [C]

**Step 2:** Sizing conductors
______ A [D] x ______ % [E]
= ______ A [F]
______ A [G] x ______ % [H]
= ______ A [I]
______ A [J] x ______ % [K]
= ______ A [L]
Total load = ______ A [M]

**Step 3:** Selecting conductors
______ A [N] requires
# ______ cu. [O]

**Solution : The size THWN conductors are No. ______ [P] copper.**

**Figure 7-25.** Exercise problem for calculating and sizing the conductors for a feeder-circuit supplying power to a group of motors.

# SIZING THE CONDUCTORS FOR PHASE CONVERTERS 455-6

Phase converters are used to convert single-phase power to three-phase power. Where the voltage is not the same, the output to input ratio shall be applied per Sec. 455-6.

Branch-circuit elements such as OCPD's and conductors supplying specific loads are calculated at 250 percent of the equipment's full-load amp rating.

**Problem 7-26.** Sizing the conductors for phase converters.

What size THWN copper conductors are required to supply a phase converter which supplies a 230 volt, three-phase, 20 HP, Design B motor?

> **Step 1:** Finding FLA
> 430-6(a)(1); Table 430-150
> 20 HP = 54 A

> **Step 2:** Sizing conductors
> 455-6(a)(2)
> 54 A x 250% = 135 A

> **Step 3:** Selecting conductors
> 310-10(2); Table 310-16
> 135 A requires #1/0 cu.

**Solution: The size THWN copper conductors are No. 1/0.**

**See Figure 7-26** for an exercise problem when sizing of conductors supplying power to a phase converter.

**Figure 7-26.** Exercise problem for calculating and sizing the conductors supplying power to a three-phase motor using a phase converter.

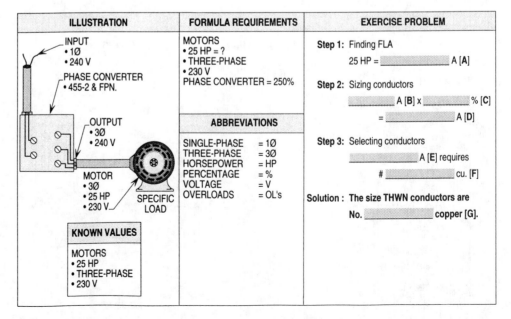

# A/C AND REFRIGERATION EQUIPMENT CIRCUIT CONDUCTORS
## 440-32 THRU 440-34

In general, to prevent conductors and motor elements of the branch-circuit from overheating, the conductors must be sized with enough capacity to allow a hermetic motor to start and run. To ensure adequate sizing, a derating factor of 80 percent must be applied to the branch-circuit conductors or such conductors must be sized at 125 percent of the motor's FLA.

## SIZING CONDUCTORS TO AN A/C UNIT
## 440-32

The conductors supplying power to an air-conditioning or refrigeration unit shall be sized to carry the load of the unit plus an overload for a period of time that won't damage the elements. The full-load current rating of the nameplate or branch-circuit selection current, whichever is greater, must be calculated at 125 percent to size and select the conductors supplying hermetically sealed motors.

What size THWN copper conductors are required to supply power to a compressor with a full-load current of 33 amps and a condenser motor having a nameplate of 2 amps with terminals rated at 75°C.

**Problem 7-27.** Sizing conductors to an individual A/C unit.

Step 1: Calculating amps
440-32
33 A x 125%  = 41.25 A
2 A x 100%   = <u>2   A</u>
Total load   = 43.25 A

Step 2: Selecting conductors
310-10(2); Table 310-16
43.25 A requires #8 cu.

Solution: **The size THWN conductors are No. 8 copper. Note: Terminal ratings are 75°C.**

See Figure 7-27 for an exercise problem when the sizing conductors for an A/C unit with a hermetic compressor motor and a condenser motor.

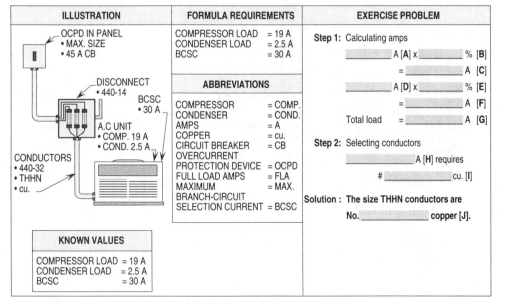

<table>
<tr><th colspan="3">ILLUSTRATION</th><th colspan="2">FORMULA REQUIREMENTS</th><th colspan="2">EXERCISE PROBLEM</th></tr>
</table>

**Figure 7-27.** Exercise problem for calculating and sizing the conductors to a compressor motor and a condenser motor in an A/C unit.

Note that the 30 amp BCSC is usually computed per Sec. 440-32 of the NEC.

## SIZING THE CONDUCTORS FOR SEVERAL A/C UNITS
## 440-33

Two or more compressors plus other motor loads can be connected to a feeder-circuit. The largest compressor is computed at 125 percent of it's FLA and the remaining compressor loads are added to this total at 100 percent of their FLA ratings. For units with a branch-circuit selection current, the circuit conductors are selected and based upon the nameplate values.

**Problem 7-28.** Sizing the conductors for several A/C units that are supplied by a feeder-circuit.

**Test Tip 12:** All terminals in Figure 7-28 are rated at 75°C.

What size THHN copper conductors are required to supply three compressors with full-load currents of 42 amps each plus the condenser motor's having nameplate current ratings of 3 amps each?

Step 1: Calculating amps
440-33
42 A x 125% +3 A     =   55.5 A
42 A x 100% +3 A     =   45   A
42 A x 100% +3 A     =   45   A
Total load           = 145.5  A

Step 2: Selecting conductors
310-10(2); Table 310-16
145.5 A requires #1/0 cu.

Solution: **The size THHN conductors are No. 1/0 copper. Note: Terminal ratings are 75°C.**

See **Figure 7-28** for an exercise problem when sizing conductors for a feeder-circuit supplying power to three A/C units.

**Figure 7-28.** Exercise problem for calculating and sizing the conductors for a feeder-circuit supplying three A/C units.

**Test Tip 13:** For simplicity, only one A/C unit (unit 3) is shown in Figure 7-28.

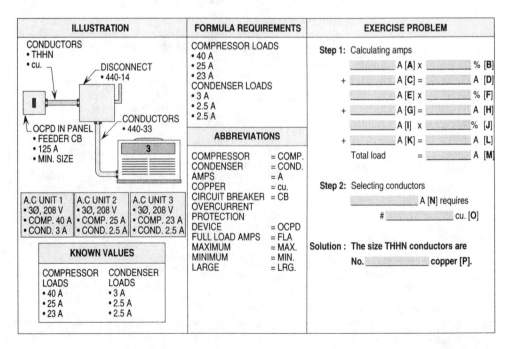

# TRANSFORMER SECONDARY CONDUCTORS
## 215-2(a)

The primary and secondary conductors of transformers must be sized to handle continuous or noncontinuous loads or a combination of such. When taking an examination to obtain a journeyman license, test takers must learn how to distinguish between these two loads.

**Test Tip 14:** Continuous loads that are computed at 125 percent will derate the loading of the OCPD to 80 percent of it's rating.

**Example Problem:** What size THWN copper conductors are required to supply the secondary side of a transformer supplying a continuous load of 40 amps and noncontinuous load of 25 amps?

Step 1: Finding amps of loads
215-2(a)
40 A x 125%  = 50 A
25 A x 100%  = 25 A
Total load      = 75 A

Step 2: Sizing conductors
310-10(2); Table 310-16
75 A requires #4 cu.

Solution: **The size of the secondary conductors are No. 4 THWN copper.**

# SIZING CONDUCTORS FOR A TWO-WIRE PRIMARY TO TWO-WIRE SECONDARY
## 240-3(f); 384-16(e), Ex.

If the primary side of a 480 volt, single-phase transformer is protected by a 125 amp OCPD, by the ratio of the primary voltage and current, three No. 250 KCMIL THWN copper conductors and a 250 amp panelboard on the 240 volt, single-phase secondary are considered protected. This protection can be verified by the following calculation:

What size OCPD is required on the primary side to protect the secondary conductors and panelboard in the example above?

Step 1: Verifying protection
240-3(f); 384-16(e), Ex.
480 V/ 240 V x 125 A OCPD = 250 A

Step 2: Comparing protection of conductors and panel
240-3(f); Table 310-16
• #250 KCMIL THWN cu. = 255 A each
• 255 A supplies 250 A panel

Solution: **The 125 amp OCPD on the primary side protects the secondary conductors and panelboard. Note: A three-wire to three-wire delta can be protected in the same manner.**

See **Figure 7-29** for an exercise problem when protecting the secondary conductors and panelboard of a transformer with the primary OCPD.

**Problem 7-29.** Sizing conductors and protection for a two-wire primary and a two-wire secondary.

| Quick Calc. |
|---|
| Pri. = 480 V / Sec. = 240 V = 2 |
| Pri. OCPD = 125 A x 2  Sec. OCPD = 250 A |
| **Solution: The primary OCPD rated at 125 amps protects the secondary panelboard of 250 amps.** |

**Figure 7-29.** Exercise problem to verify if the primary OCPD of a transformer can protect the secondary conductors supplying a panelboard.

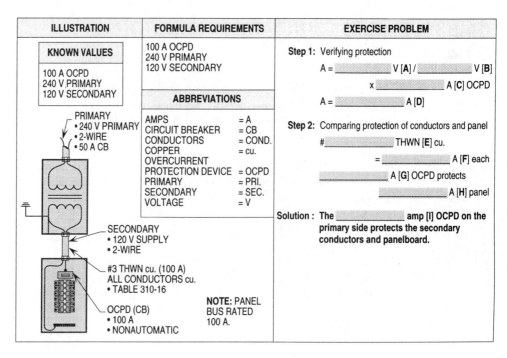

## SIZING CONDUCTORS FOR THE SECONDARY OF A TRANSFORMER
### 215-2(a); 450-3(b); TABLE 450-3(b)

A transformer 600 volt or less, nominal, having an individual overcurrent protection device on the secondary side shall be sized at no more than 125 percent of the transformer's full-load current rating or load supplied. Note, with the OCPD and conductors sized at 125 percent or less of the transformer's FLC, the supply conductors and transformer windings are considered protected from overload conditions.

**Problem 7-30.** Sizing the conductors for the secondary of a transformer that supplies equipment and loads.

What size THWN copper conductors are required to supply the secondary side of a transformer having a continuous load output of 181 amps?

> **Step 1:** Computing load
> 215-2(a); 450-3(b); Table 450-3(b)
> 181 A x 125% = 226 A

> **Step 2:** Sizing conductors
> 310-10(2); Table 310-16
> 226 A requires #4/0 cu.

**Solution: The size THWN conductors are No. 4/0 copper.**

**See Figure 7-30** for an exercise problem when sizing the secondary conductors of a transformer to supply a panelboard.

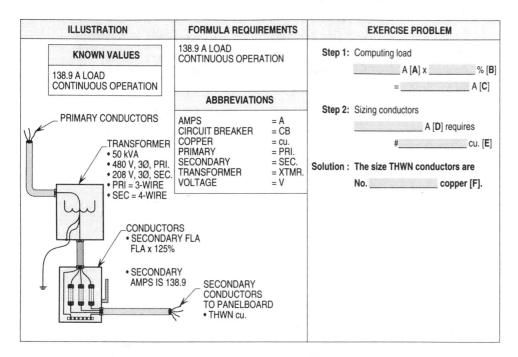

Figure 7-30. Exercise problem for calculating and sizing the conductors to supply a panelboard from the secondary side of a transformer.

Within the figure:

| ILLUSTRATION | FORMULA REQUIREMENTS | EXERCISE PROBLEM |
|---|---|---|

**KNOWN VALUES**

138.9 A LOAD
CONTINUOUS OPERATION

PRIMARY CONDUCTORS

TRANSFORMER
• 50 kVA
• 480 V, 3Ø, PRI.
• 208 V, 3Ø, SEC.
• PRI = 3-WIRE
• SEC = 4-WIRE

CONDUCTORS
• SECONDARY FLA
  FLA x 125%

• SECONDARY
  AMPS IS 138.9

SECONDARY
CONDUCTORS
TO PANELBOARD
• THWN cu.

138.9 A LOAD
CONTINUOUS OPERATION

**ABBREVIATIONS**

AMPS = A
CIRCUIT BREAKER = CB
COPPER = cu.
PRIMARY = PRI.
SECONDARY = SEC.
TRANSFORMER = XTMR.
VOLTAGE = V

**Step 1:** Computing load

_____ A [A] x _____ % [B]

= _____ A [C]

**Step 2:** Sizing conductors

_____ A [D] requires

# _____ cu. [E]

**Solution :** The size THWN conductors are

No. _____ copper [F].

# CAPACITOR CIRCUIT CONDUCTORS
## 460-8

The size conductors supplying power to capacitors must be sized and selected, based either upon the FLA of the capacitor times 135 percent or 1/3 of the conductors ampacity servicing the motor, whichever is greater.

What size THHN copper conductors are required to supply power to a 460 volt, three-phase, 10 kVA capacitor serving a 460 volt, three-phase, 50 HP motor? (Motor supplied by 480 volts and No. 4 THHN copper conductors)

**Problem 7-31.** Sizing circuit conductors for a capacitor to improve the power factor.

**Step 1:** Calculating conductors at 1/3
460-8(a); Table 310-16
#4 = 85 A x 1/3 = 28 A

**Step 2:** Selecting conductors
310-10(2); Table 310-16
28 A requires #10 cu.

**Step 3:** Calculating FLA of capacitor
460-8(a)
FLA = kVA x 1,000 / V x √3
FLA = 10 kVA x 1,000 / 480 V x 1.732
FLA = 12 A
FLA = 12 x 135%
FLA = 16 A

Note that supply voltage is used instead of motor voltage for the calculation in the problem.

**Step 4:** Selecting conductors
310-10(2); Table 310-16
16 A requires #14 cu.

**Solution:** The size THHN conductors are No. 10 copper.

**See Figure 7-31** for an exercise problem when calculating the amps to size the conductors of a capacitor serving a motor.

**Test Tip 15:** Size the conductors in Problem 7-31, using 75°C ampacities from Table 310-16.

**Figure 7-31.** Exercise problem for calculating and sizing the conductors for a capacitor serving a motor.

In Figure 7-31, an additional disconnecting means is required between the capacitor and controller, if the conductors of the capacitor are connected to the load side of the controller.

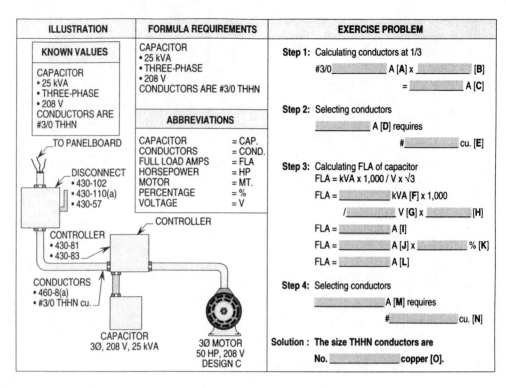

# WELDER LOADS
## ART. 630, PARTS B AND C

There are three types of welders used in modern day welding shops. The type used determines how the circuit elements must be designed and selected.

The procedure for calculating the full-load amps for welders is to obtain the duty-cycle factor and select the multiplier. The primary amps of the welder is multiplied by the multiplier to derive the full-load amps to size the elements of the branch-circuit.

## SIZING CONDUCTORS TO AC/DC ARC WELDERS
### 240-3(g); 630-11(a)

**Test Tip 16:** The multiplier for an AC/DC arc welder can be determined by taking the square root of the welder's duty-cycle.

When sizing the branch-circuit conductors for AC/DC arc welders, the current-carrying capacity shall not be less than the primary current of the welder times a duty cycle factor listed in Table 630-11(a). The OCPD can be sized larger than the ampacity of the conductors to allow the welder to operate. The ON and OFF welding cycles of the welder will protect the conductors from being overloaded.

What size THWN copper conductors are required to supply an AC transformer and DC rectifier arc welder rated at 68 amps having a 50 percent duty cycle?

**Problem 7-32.** Sizing conductors to an AC/DC arc welder based upon the duty cycle rating of the welder.

**Step 1:** Finding FLC
630-11(a)
Welder = 68 A

**Step 2:** Finding multiplier
630-11(a)
Multiplier = .71

**Step 3:** Calculating amps
630-11(a)
68 A x 71% = 48.28 A

**Step 4:** Selecting conductors
Table 310-16
48.28 A requires #8 cu.

**Solution:** **The size THWN copper conductors are No. 8.**

See **Figure 7-32** for an exercise problem when calculating the amps to size the conductors for an AC/DC arc welder.

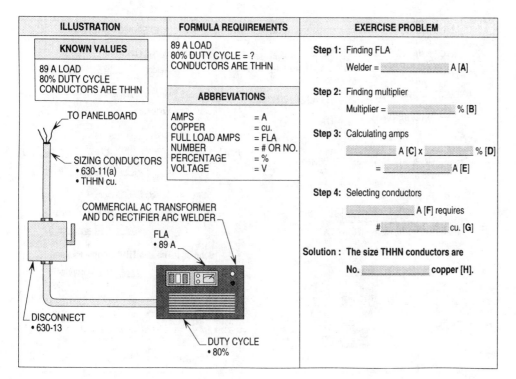

| ILLUSTRATION | FORMULA REQUIREMENTS | EXERCISE PROBLEM |
|---|---|---|
| **KNOWN VALUES** | 89 A LOAD<br>80% DUTY CYCLE = ?<br>CONDUCTORS ARE THHN | **Step 1:** Finding FLA<br>Welder = _____ A [A] |
| 89 A LOAD<br>80% DUTY CYCLE<br>CONDUCTORS ARE THHN | | **Step 2:** Finding multiplier<br>Multiplier = _____ % [B] |
| | **ABBREVIATIONS** | **Step 3:** Calculating amps |
| TO PANELBOARD | AMPS = A<br>COPPER = cu.<br>FULL LOAD AMPS = FLA<br>NUMBER = # OR NO.<br>PERCENTAGE = %<br>VOLTAGE = V | _____ A [C] x _____ % [D]<br>= _____ A [E] |
| SIZING CONDUCTORS<br>• 630-11(a)<br>• THHN cu. | | **Step 4:** Selecting conductors<br>_____ A [F] requires |
| COMMERCIAL AC TRANSFORMER<br>AND DC RECTIFIER ARC WELDER | | #_____ cu. [G] |
| FLA<br>• 89 A | | **Solution :** The size THHN conductors are<br>No. _____ copper [H]. |
| DISCONNECT<br>• 630-13 | | |
| DUTY CYCLE<br>• 80% | | |

**Figure 7-32.** Exercise problem for calculating the amps to size the conductors to an AC/DC arc welder.

**Test Tip 17:** The ampacity of conductors are based upon 75°C terminals.

# SIZING CONDUCTORS TO MOTOR-GENERATOR ARC WELDERS
## 240-3(g); 630-11(a)

When sizing the branch-circuit conductors for motor-generator arc welders, the current-carrying capacity shall not be less than the rated primary current of the welder times a duty cycle factor listed in Table 630-11(a).

**Problem 7-33.** Sizing conductors to motor-generator arc welders.

What size THWN copper conductors are required to supply a motor-generator arc welder rated at 76 amps with a 90 percent duty cycle?

Step 1: Finding FLC
630-11(a)
Welder = 76 A

Step 2: Finding multiplier
630-11(a)
Multiplier = .96

Step 3: Calculating amps
630-11(a)
76 A x 96% = 72.96 A

Step 4: Selecting conductors
Table 310-16
72.96 A requires #4 cu.

Solution: The size THWN copper conductors are No. 4.

See Figure 7-33 for an exercise problem when calculating the amps to size the conductors for a motor-generator arc welder.

**Figure 7-33.** Exercise problem for calculating the amps when sizing the conductors to a motor-generator arc welder.

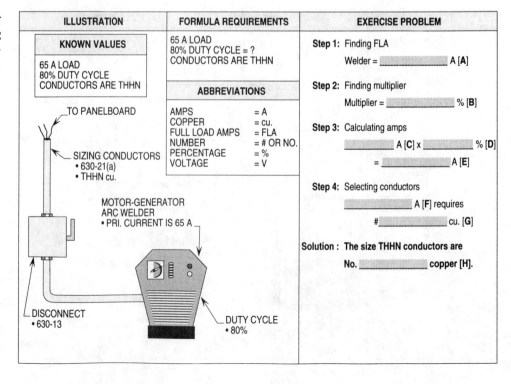

| ILLUSTRATION | FORMULA REQUIREMENTS | EXERCISE PROBLEM |
|---|---|---|
| **KNOWN VALUES** | 65 A LOAD<br>80% DUTY CYCLE = ?<br>CONDUCTORS ARE THHN | Step 1: Finding FLA<br><br>Welder = ▨▨▨ A [A] |
| 65 A LOAD<br>80% DUTY CYCLE<br>CONDUCTORS ARE THHN | **ABBREVIATIONS** | Step 2: Finding multiplier<br><br>Multiplier = ▨▨▨ % [B] |
| TO PANELBOARD | AMPS = A<br>COPPER = cu.<br>FULL LOAD AMPS = FLA<br>NUMBER = # OR NO.<br>PERCENTAGE = %<br>VOLTAGE = V | Step 3: Calculating amps<br><br>▨▨▨ A [C] x ▨▨▨ % [D]<br><br>= ▨▨▨ A [E] |
| SIZING CONDUCTORS<br>• 630-21(a)<br>• THHN cu. | | Step 4: Selecting conductors<br><br>▨▨▨ A [F] requires<br><br>#▨▨▨ cu. [G] |
| MOTOR-GENERATOR<br>ARC WELDER<br>• PRI. CURRENT IS 65 A | | Solution : The size THHN conductors are<br><br>No. ▨▨▨ copper [H]. |
| DISCONNECT<br>• 630-13 | DUTY CYCLE<br>• 80% | |

# SIZING CONDUCTORS TO RESISTANCE WELDERS
## 240-3(k); 630-31(a)

When sizing the branch-circuit conductors for resistance welders, the current-carrying capacity shall not be less than the primary current of the welder times a duty cycle factor listed in Table 630-31(a).

What size THWN copper conductors are required to supply a resistance welder rated at 91 amps with a 40 percent duty cycle?

**Problem 7-34.** Sizing conductors for resistance welders.

Step 1: Finding FLC
630-31(a)
Welder = 91 A

Step 2: Finding multiplier
630-31(a)
Multiplier = .63

Step 3: Calculating amps
630-31(a)
91 A x 63% = 57.33 A

Step 4: Selecting conductors
Table 310-16
57.33 A requires #6 cu.

**Solution:  The size THWN copper conductors are No. 6.**

See **Figure 7-34** for an exercise problem when calculating the amps to size the conductors to a resistance welder.

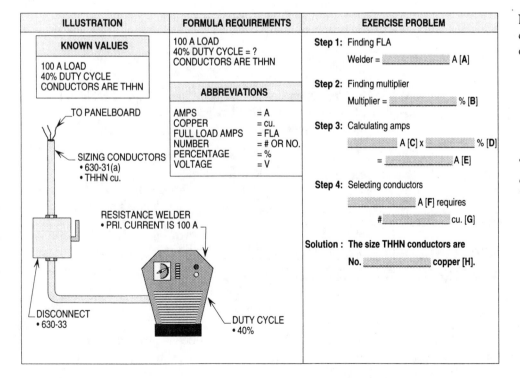

**Figure 7-34.** Exercise problem for calculating the amps to size the conductors to a resistance welder.

**Test Tip 18:** The ampacities of all conductors are selected from the 75°C column in Table 310-16.

# CONTROL CIRCUIT CONDUCTORS
## 430-72(b)(2); Table 430-72(b)

**Test Tip 19:** Ampacities of control conductors that are installed inside of enclosures are selected from Table 310-17.

A motor control circuit tapped on the load side of fuses and circuit breakers utilized for motor branch-circuits shall protect such conductors at their ampacities or supplementary protection devices must be provided.

## SIZING CONTROL CIRCUIT CONDUCTORS INSIDE ENCLOSURES
## 430-72(b)(2); Table 430-72(b), Col. B

Motor control circuit conductors that do not extend beyond the control equipment enclosure are permitted to be protected by the motor branch-circuit fuses or circuit breaker. Table 430-72(b), Col. B allows this type of installation where the devices do not exceed 400 percent of the ampacity rating of sizes No. 14 and larger conductors. Overcurrent protection for conductors smaller than No. 14 shall not exceed the values listed in Table 430-72(b), Col. B. Conductors rated No. 18 through No. 10 can be protected with the following size OCPD's:

**Problem 7-35.** Sizing control circuit conductors that are located inside enclosures.

What size THHN copper conductors are allowed in a controller where the upstream OCPD protecting the branch-circuit is rated 90 amps?

Step 1: Verifying OCPD upstream
430-72(b)(2); Table 430-72(b), Col. B
Upstream OCPD = 90 A

Step 2: Determining size conductors from Table
Table 430-72(b), Col. B
90 A allows #14 cu.

Step 3: Calculating size conductors
430-72(b)(2); Table 430-72(b), Note 2; Table 310-17
• #14 cu. = 25 A x 400% = 100 A OCPD
• 100 A OCPD allows #14 cu.
• 90 A OCPD is allowed to protect #14 cu.

Solution: **The size THHN copper control circuit conductors are No. 14 copper based on 90 amp OCPD ahead of the motor's branch-circuit conductors.**

See Figure 7-35 for an exercise problem on how to size, select, and protect control circuit conductors with an OCPD ahead of the motor's branch-circuit conductors.

## SIZING REMOTE CONTROL CIRCUIT CONDUCTORS
## 430-72(b)(2); Table 430-72(b), Col. C

**Test Tip 20:** The ampacities of conductors are selected from the 60°C column in Table 310-16.

Motor control circuit conductors that extend beyond the control equipment enclosure can be protected by the motor branch-circuit fuses or circuit breaker. Table 430-72(b), Col. C allows this type of installation where the devices do not exceed 300 percent of the ampacity rating for conductors smaller than No. 14. Conductors rated No. 18 through No. 10 can be protected with the following size OCPD's:

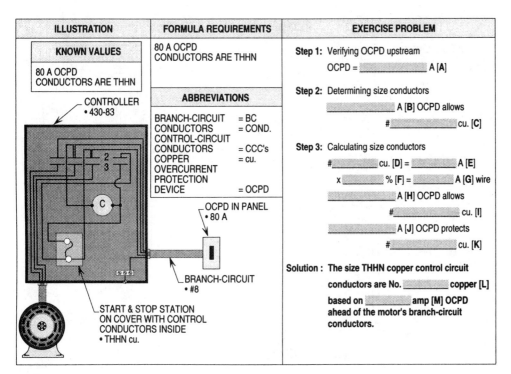

**Figure 7-35.** Exercise problem for calculating and sizing the control circuit conductors inside the enclosure of the controller cabinet.

What size THWN copper control circuit conductors are allowed to be routed remote from the magnetic starter where the upstream OCPD is rated 90 amps?

**Problem 7-36.** Sizing remote control circuit conductors which extends beyond the controller enclosure.

**Step 1:** Verifying OCPD upstream
430-72(b)(2): Table 430-72(b), Col. C
Upstream OCPD = 90 A

**Step 2:** Determining size conductors from Table
Table 430-72(b), Col. C
90 A allows #10 cu.

**Step 3:** Calculating size conductors
430-72(b)(2); Table 430-72(b), Note 3; Table 310-16*
• #10 cu. requires 30 A OCPD
• 30 A OCPD x 300% = 90 A
• 90 A OCPD is allowed to protect #10 cu.

**Solution:** The size THHN copper control circuit conductors are No. 10 based upon a 90 amp OCPD ahead of the motor's branch-circuit conductors.

**See Figure 7-36** for an exercise problem on how to size, select, and protect control circuit conductors with an OCPD ahead of the motor's branch-circuit conductors.

**Figure 7-36.** Exercise problem for calculating and sizing the control circuit conductors extending beyond the controller enclosure.

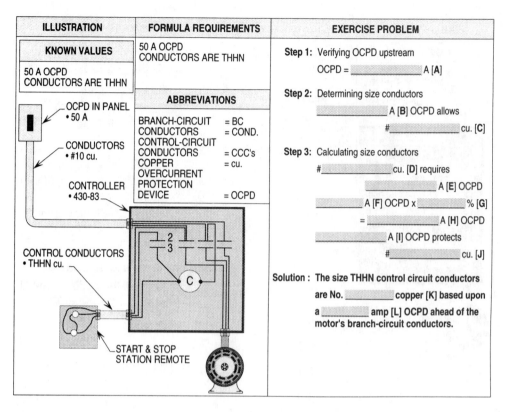

## CONTROL TRANSFORMER CIRCUIT CONDUCTORS 430-72(c)(4)

When a motor control circuit transformer is provided, the transformer and conductors shall be protected by the rules and regulations of Art. 430. A fuse or circuit breaker is permitted to be installed in the secondary circuit of the transformer per Sec. 430-72(c)(4). The primary OCPD may be used to provide the protection for the conductors tapped from the secondary side of a control transformer, if it's rating does not exceed the secondary-to-primary ratio of the transformer.

**Problem 7-37.** Sizing control transformer circuit conductors.

Could No. 14 THHN copper conductors be used on the primary side of a control transformer having a FLC of 1 amp (Transformer and control circuit conductors are inside controller enclosure)?

    **Step 1:** Calculating FLA
        430-72(c)(4)
        1 A x 500% = 5 A

    **Step 2:** Verifying A of #14 cu.
        Table 310-17
        • #14 cu. = 25 A
        • 25 A handles 5 A

    **Solution:** Yes, No. 14 THHN copper control circuit conductors can be used.

**See Figure 7-37** for an exercise problem when sizing the control circuit conductors on the primary side of a control transformer.

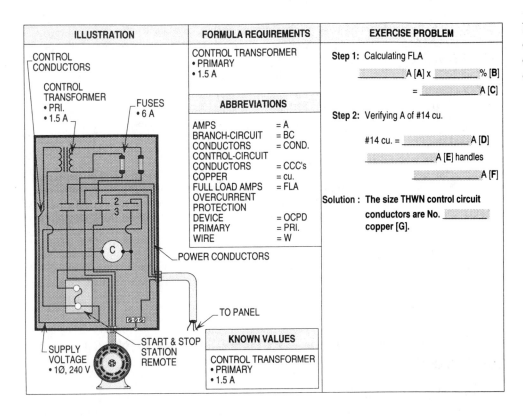

| ILLUSTRATION | FORMULA REQUIREMENTS | EXERCISE PROBLEM |
|---|---|---|

**Figure 7-37.** Exercise problem for calculating and sizing the control circuit conductors from the primary of a control transformer.

# PROTECTING FIXTURE CONDUCTORS
## 240-4(b)(2); 410-67(c); 410-15(b)

A 20 amp overcurrent protection device is considered as being adequate protection for fixture wires or flexible cords or for tinsel cord, in sizes No. 16 or No. 18 respectively. Fixture wire taps that comply with Sec. 210-19(d) are permitted to be protected if they are tapped from 30, 40, and 50 amp branch-circuits per Article 210.

# SIZING FIXTURE WIRE TO FLUORESCENT LAY-INS
## 240-4(b)(2); 410-67(c)

Fixture wires shall be considered as protected by the overcurrent protection device of the branch-circuit if sized and selected per Art. 210 and complies as follows:

20 amp circuits, No. 14 and greater
30 amp circuits, No. 14 and greater
40 amp circuits, No. 12 and greater
50 amp circuits, No. 12 and greater

Note that No. 18 fixture wire can run up to 50 ft. if protected by a 20 amp OCPD or less. No. 16 fixture wire can be run up to 100 ft. if protected by a 20 amp OCPD or less.

**Test Tip 21:** Fixture wires in fixture whips are allowed in lengths of 18 in. to 6 ft. respectively per Sec. 410-67(c).

**Problem 7-38.** Sizing fixture wire to connected fluorescent lay-ins in a suspended ceiling.

What size fixture wire (min. size) can be used with a branch-circuit having No. 14 copper conductors that are protected by a 15 amp OCPD? (Whip from junction box to fixture is 6 ft. in length)

Step 1: Determining protection
240-4(b)(2); 410-67(c)
#18 cu. can be protected by 15 A OCPD and #14 wire

Solution: **The minimum size fixture wire allowed in the whip is No. 18 copper when protected by 15 amp OCPD and supply conductors are No. 14 copper.**

See Figure 7-38 for an exercise problem pertaining to fixture wire being protected by the branch-circuit OCPD and conductors where used as a fixture whip.

## SUPPLY FIXTURE WIRES FOR OUTSIDE LIGHTING STANDARDS
## 240-4(b)(2); 410-15(b)

For 20 amp circuits, No. 18, up to a tapped length of 50 ft. and No. 16, up to a tapped length of 100 ft. can be used as fixture whips per Sec. 410-67(c) and outside lighting standards per Sec. 410-15(b). Note that the fixture wires can be routed from the fixtures to the base of the pole and terminated in the hand hole to the branch-circuit conductors.

**Problem 7-39.** Sizing fixture wires for outside lighting standards.

Can two No. 16 copper fixture wires be run for 60 ft. inside of a metal pole and terminated to two No. 10 copper conductors protected by a 20 amp OCPD?

Step 1: Determining protection
240-4(b)(2); 410-15(b)
#16 can be run 60 ft. and terminated to 20 A BC

Solution: **Yes, fixture wire rated at No. 16 copper can be routed up to 100 ft. or less if protected by a 20 amp branch-circuit.**

See Figure 7-39 for an exercise problem when fixture wire is routed inside the metal pole of an outside (listed) lighting standard, where protected by 15 or 20 amp OCPD.

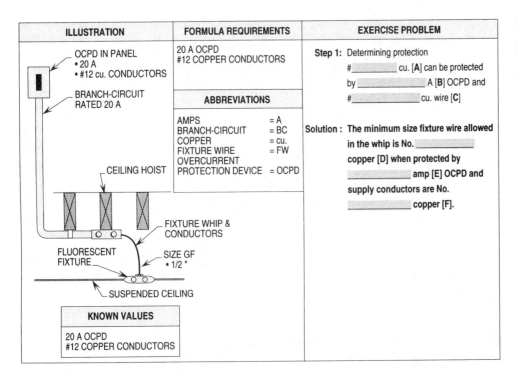

**Figure 7-38.** Exercise problem for determining the branch-circuit OCPD and conductors protect the smaller tapped fixture wires.

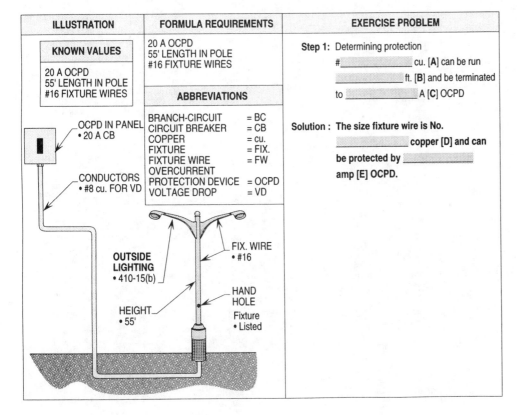

**Figure 7-39.** Exercise problem for determining if the branch-circuit OCPD and conductors protect the smaller tapped fixture wires.

Name _____          Date _____

# Chapter 7
# Conductor Ampacities

| Section | Answer | |
|---|---|---|

**Section**      **Answer**

_____     T   F     1. Continuous loads shall have their full-load currents increased by 125 percent.

_____     T   F     2. A continuous load is any load that can operate for two hours or more.

_____     T   F     3. Correction factors are based upon temperature surrounding the cable or conduit.

_____     T   F     4. When there are three or more current-carrying conductors in a cable or raceway, a derating factor must be applied and the ampacity of the conductors reduced.

_____     T   F     5. Conductors routed through ambient temperatures exceeding 82°F are required to be derated according to the correction factors of Table 310-16.

_____     T   F     6. Diversity can be applied to more than half of the conductors in a raceway or cable if they are limited to a certain calculated ampacity.

_____     T   F     7. If the overcurrent protection device is greater than 800 amps, the ampacity of the conductors shall be equal to or greater than the ampacities of the overcurrent protection device.

_____     T   F     8. Generator conductors must have an ampacity equal to at least 115 percent of the nameplate current of the generator.

_____     T   F     9. Branch-circuit conductors supplying a single motor shall have an ampacity not less than 100 percent of the motors full-load current rating.

_____     T   F     10. The size conductors supplying power to capacitors must be sized and selected, based either upon the FLA of the capacitor times 135 percent or 1/3 of the conductors ampacity servicing the motor, whichever is greater.

_____ _____     11. Terminations for circuits that are rated 100 amps or less, and which use conductors from No. 14 through No. 1 are limited to _____°C. (General rule)

_____ _____     12. Terminations for circuits that are rated over 100 amps, and use conductors larger than No. 1 are limited to _____°C.

_____ _____     13. A _____ percent load diversity can be applied to conductor ampacity when all the conductors are not loaded at the same time, if allowed by the AHJ.

_____ _____     14. A tap feeding a lighting and appliance branch-circuit panelboard cannot be over _____ ft. long. (Use the tap allowing the minimum length)

_____ _____     15. A tap from a larger conductor to a smaller conductor may extend over 10 ft. up to a distance of 25 ft., provided the current-carrying capacity of the tap is at least _____ that of the OCPD.

_____ _____     16. Transformer taps with primary plus secondary conductors, which are not over _____ ft. in length, can be made without overcurrent protection at the point of such conductors.

_____ _____     17. The full-load current rating of the largest motor must be multiplied by _____ percent and the remaining motors of the group must have their full-load current ratings added to this value and this total amperage is then used to size the conductors.

——————  ——————  18. Phase converters are used to convert single-phase power to _____ power.

——————  ——————  19. The full-load current rating of the nameplate or branch-circuit selection current, which-ever is greater, must be sized at _____ percent to size and select the conductors supplying hermetically sealed motors for air-conditioners.

——————  ——————  20. Fixture wires in fixture whips are allowed in lengths not exceeding _____ ft.

——————  ——————  21. What is the ampacity of a No. 2 THWN copper conductor connected to an overcurrent protection device supplying power to equipment where all terminals are rated 60°C?

——————  ——————  22. What is the ampacity of a No. 1 THWN copper conductor connected to an overcurrent protection device supplying power to equipment where all terminals are rated 75°C?

——————  ——————  23. What is the ampacity of a No. 4/0 THWN copper conductor connected to an overcurrent protection device (250 A CB) supplying a subpanel where all terminals are rated 75°C?

——————  ——————  24. What is the computed load in amps to serve a continuous operated load of 12 amps and a noncontinuous load of 3 amps?

——————  ——————  25. What is the current-carrying ampacity of fourteen No. 12 THHN copper conductors pulled through 3/4 in. EMT? (all current-carrying)

——————  ——————  26. What is the current-carrying ampacity of six No. 10 THHN copper conductors pulled through 3/4 in. EMT? (all current-carrying)

——————  ——————  27. What is the ampacity of four No. 8 THHN copper conductors routed through an ambient temperature of 122°F? (Only three are current-carrying)

——————  ——————  28. What is the ampacity of twelve No. 12 THHN copper conductors routed through an ambient temperature of 128°F? (All are current-carrying)

——————  ——————  29. What is the ampacity of six current-carrying No. 12 THHN copper conductors routed through an ambient temperature of 110°F?

——————  ——————  30. What is the ampacity of twelve current-carrying No. 10 THHN copper conductors routed through an ambient temperature of 125°F?

——————  ——————  31. What is the ampacity of twelve No. 10 THHN copper conductors, with diversity, located in the same raceway?

——————  ——————  32. What size THWN copper conductors are required to supply a feeder-circuit with a continuous load of 150 amps and a noncontinuous load of 40 amps?

——————  ——————  33. What size THWN copper conductors are required to supply a feeder-circuit with a continuous load of 120 amps and a noncontinuous load of 80 amps?

——————  ——————  34. What size THWN copper conductors are required to supply a branch-circuit with a continuous load of 20 amps and a noncontinuous load of 4 amps?

——————  ——————  35. What size THWN copper conductors are required to supply a branch-circuit with a continuous load of 16 amps and a noncontinuous load of 10 amp?

——————  ——————  36. What size THWN copper conductors are required to supply a branch-circuit with a continuous load of 84 amps and terminated to 75°C terminals?

——————  ——————  37. What size THWN copper conductors and OCPD are required for a subpanel supplying a continuous load of 694 amps and terminated to 75°C terminals which are paralleled 4 times?

_____  _____  38. What size THWN copper conductors are required for a 10 ft. tap when supplied by a 300 amp OCPD?

_____  _____  39. What size THWN copper conductors are required for a 25 ft. tap when supplied by a feeder-circuit with a 300 amp OCPD?

_____  _____  40. What size THWN copper conductors for the primary and secondary are required for the 25 tap when supplied by a 400 amp OCPD with a 480 volt primary and 208 volt secondary?

_____  _____  41. What size THWN copper conductors are required for the primary, when using a 100 ft. tap supplied by a 600 amp OCPD?

_____  _____  42. Can a 150 amp busway be tapped to a 450 amp busway?

_____  _____  43. What size THWN copper conductors are required for a 10 ft. motor circuit tap when supplied by a 400 amp OCPD? (Terminals are 75°C)

_____  _____  44. What size OCPD is required for a 10 ft. tap from the secondary to protect 4 - #1/0 THWN copper conductors paralleled 3 times when supplying a 150 kVA separately derived transformer with a 480 volt primary and 208 volt secondary? (Protect Sec. conductors)

_____  _____  45. What size OCPD is required for a 25 ft. tap from the secondary to protect 4 - #1/0 THWN copper conductors paralleled 3 times when supplying a 150 kVA separately derived transformer with a 480 volt primary and 208 volt secondary? (Protect Sec. output)

_____  _____  46. What size THWN copper conductors are required for a generator with an output of 200 kW, with a three-phase, 480 volt primary and 277 volt secondary?

_____  _____  47. What size THWN copper conductors are required to supply power to a 208 volt, single-phase, 3 HP, Design B motor that is installed in a commercial building?

_____  _____  48. What size THWN copper conductors are required to supply power to a 230 volt, single-phase, 5 HP, Design B motor that is installed in a commercial building?

_____  _____  49. What size THWN copper conductors are required to supply power to 115 volt, single-phase, 1/2 HP, Design B motor that is installed in a commercial building?

_____  _____  50. What size THWN copper conductors are required to supply power to 230 volt, three-phase, 10 HP, Design B motor having 75°C terminals?

_____  _____  51. What size THWN copper conductors are required to supply power to a 208 volt, three-phase, 30 HP, Design B motor having 75°C terminals?

_____  _____  52. What size THWN copper conductors are required to supply power to a 480 volt, three-phase, 50 HP, Design B motor having 75°C terminals?

_____  _____  53. What size THWN copper conductors are required to supply a group of 230 volt, three-phase, Design B motors which are rated 5 HP, 10 HP, and 20 HP?

_____  _____  54. What size THWN copper conductors are required to supply a group of 460 volt, three-phase, Design B motors which are rated 50 HP, 40 HP, and 30 HP?

_____  _____  55. What size THWN copper conductors are required to supply a phase converter which supplies a 230 volt, three-phase, 20 HP, Design B motor?

_____  _____  56. What size THWN copper conductors are required to supply power to an A/C unit with a compressor having a full-load current of 22 amps and a condenser motor having a nameplate of 2.5 amps with terminals rated at 75°C?

—————— ——————  57. What size THWN copper conductors are required to supply power to an A/C unit with a compressor having a full-load current of 18 amps and a condenser motor having a nameplate of 2 amps with terminals rated at 75°C?

—————— ——————  58. What size THWN copper conductors are required to supply power to an A/C unit with a compressor having a full-load current of 37 amps plus the condenser motor having a nameplate current rating of 3 amps?

—————— ——————  59. What size THWN copper are required to supply power to an A/C unit with the following:

A/C unit #1
• Compressor with full-load current of 32 amps
• Condenser with nameplate current of 3 amps

A/C unit #2
• Compressor with full-load current of 26 amps
• Condenser with nameplate current of 2.5 amps

A/C unit #3
• Compressor with full-load current of 24 amps
• Compressor with nameplate current of 2.5 amps

—————— ——————  60. What size THWN copper conductors are required to supply the secondary side of a transformer with a continuous load of 50 amps and noncontinuous load of 20 amps?

—————— ——————  61. What size THWN copper conductors are required to supply the secondary side of a transformer with a continuous load 68 amps and noncontinuous load of 38 amps?

—————— ——————  62. What size THWN copper conductors are required to supply the secondary side of a transformer having a continuous load output of 194 amps?

—————— ——————  63. What size THWN copper conductors are required to supply the secondary side of a transformer having a continuous load output of 212 amps?

—————— ——————  64. What size THHN copper conductors are required to supply power to a 460 volt, three-phase, 20 kVA capacitor serving a 460 volt, three-phase, 60 HP motor? (Motor supplied by No. 3 THHN copper conductors)

—————— ——————  65. What size THWN copper conductors are required to supply an AC transformer and DC rectifier arc welder rated at 58 amps having a 70 percent duty cycle?

—————— ——————  66. What size THWN copper conductors are required to supply and AC transformer and DC rectifier arc welder rated at 42 amps having a 50 percent duty cycle?

—————— ——————  67. What size THWN copper conductors are required to supply an motor-generator arc welder rated at 68 amps having a 80 percent duty cycle?

—————— ——————  68. What size THWN copper conductors are required to supply an resistance welder rated at 84 amps having a 50 percent duty cycle?

—————— ——————  69. What size THHN copper conductors are allowed in a controller where the upstream OCPD protecting the branch-circuit is rated 80 amps?

—————— ——————  70. What size THWN copper conductors are allowed to be routed remote from the magnetic starter where the upstream OCPD is rated 80 amps?

# 8

# Overcurrent Protection Devices

The purpose of overcurrent protection devices is to monitor the current in a circuit and keep it at a level that will prevent overheating of conductors, elements, and equipment. Excessive current flowing in an electrical circuit generates heat, which raises the circuits temperature. Such temperature depends entirely upon the amount of current flowing through the electrical circuit.

For example, if the temperature of the conductor is high, due to excessive current flow, insulation can melt and cause short-circuits or ground-faults. Current flowing through a conductor generates heat that is proportional to the square of the current. In other words, if the current is doubled, the amount of heat is increased to four times the original amount. Therefore, overcurrent protection devices must be sized and selected to match the current-carrying capacity (ampacity) of the conductors and elements of the equipment or stages of circuit protection must be provided.

## PROTECTION OF EQUIPMENT
## 240-2

For overcurrent protection of appliances, motors, generators, etc. it is necessary to refer to the different Articles listed in this section. In all installations, there are three main parts to be protected and they are as follows:

(1) The circuit conductors
(2) Circuit elements, and
(3) The equipment

The fuses or circuit breaker protecting an installation must be of a rating small enough to protect both, according to the rules and regulations of Sec.'s 240-2 and 240-3 of the NEC.

**Quick Reference:**

PROTECTION OF EQUIPMENT ..................... 8-1

ROUNDING UP OR DOWN OF OCPD ........... 8-2

DEVICES RATED 800 AMPS OR LESS .......... 8-3

DEVICES RATED OVER 800 AMPS ............... 8-4

OCPD FOR TAPS ............................................ 8-5

OCPD FOR TRANSFORMER
SECONDARY CIRCUITS ............................... 8-9

OCPD FOR MOTOR-OPERATED
APPLIANCE CIRCUITS .................................. 8-19

OCPD FOR MOTOR AND MOTOR
CONTROL CIRCUITS ..................................... 8-20

OCPD FOR PHASE CONVERTERS ............... 8-30

OCPD FOR A/C AND REFRIGERATION
EQUIPMENT CIRCUITS ................................. 8-31

OCPD FOR ELECTRIC WELDER
CIRCUITS ...................................................... 8-32

OCPD FOR REMOTE-CONTROL,
SIGNALING, AND POWER-LIMITED .............. 8-36

OCPD FOR FIRE ALARM CIRCUITS .............. 8-39

FEEDER-CIRCUIT PROTECTION -
OVER 600 VOLTS ......................................... 8-40

# ROUNDING UP OR DOWN OF OCPD
# 240-3

The general rule is that conductors shall be protected against overcurrent by a fuse or circuit breaker setting rated no higher than the ampacity of the conductor. Conductors have specific current-carrying ampacities for different sizes of conductors, for different insulations, and for different ambient-temperature conditions. The overcurrent protection device shall be sized to protect the insulation of the conductors from damage, caused by the current reaching an excessive value.

**Problem 8-1.** Rounding up or down of OCPD is based on the ampacity.

What size OCPD is required for a branch-circuit with a continuous load of 21.5 amps with 75°C terminals? (Rounding up calculations.)

Step 1: Computing load
210-19(a); 220-2(b)
21.5 A x 125% = 26.875 A
(26.875 A rounded up to 27 A)

**Test Tip 1:** In a calculation problem, test takers must learn when to round a number up or down.

Step 2: Terminal ratings
110-14(c)(1)(a)
27 A can be terminated at 60°C or 75°C

Step 3: Sizing OCPD
210-20(a); 240-2; 240-3(b); 240-6(a)
27 A requires 30 A OCPD

Solution: **The size OCPD is 30 amp, based on the computed load.**

**See Figure 8-1** for an exercise problem when sizing and selecting the OCPD to protect the electrical equipment served.

**Figure 8-1.** The OCPD must be sized and selected to properly protect the electrical equipment served.

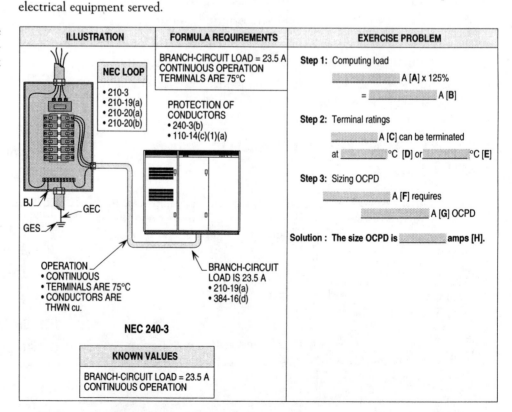

# DEVICES RATED 800 AMPS OR LESS
## 240-3(b)

If the standard current ratings of fuses or nonadjustable circuit breakers do not conform to the ampacity of the conductors being used, it is permissible to use the next larger standard rating when rated 800 amps or less.

What size OCPD is required for a branch-circuit with a continuous load of 100 amps with 75°C terminals?

      Step 1:  Computing load
                210-19(a)
                100 A x 125% = 125 A

      Step 2:  Terminal ratings
                110-14(c)(2)(b)
                125 A can be terminated at 75°C

      Step 3:  Sizing conductors
                310-10(2); Table 310-16
                125 A requires #1 cu.

      Step 4:  Sizing OCPD
                240-3(b); 240-6(a)
                #1 = 130 A
                130 A allows 150 A OCPD

    Solution:  **The size conductors are No. 1 THWN copper and the OCPD is 150 amps.**

**Problem 8-2.** Devices rated 800 amps or less can be rounded up or down, based upon ampacity of conductors.

Note that motor leads and terminals are considered 75°C for determining ampacities per Sec. 110-14(c)(1)(d).

Note that the OCPD can be sized to protect the load or the ampacity of the conductors.

See **Figure 8-2** for an exercise problem when sizing and selecting the OCPD rated 800 amps or less.

| ILLUSTRATION | FORMULA REQUIREMENTS | EXERCISE PROBLEM |
|---|---|---|
| PROTECTION OF CONDUCTORS • 240-2 • 240-3(b) <br><br> BJ <br> GEC <br> GES <br><br> SECOND STAGE OF PROTECTION <br><br> OPERATION • CONTINUOUS • TERMINALS ARE 75°C • CONDUCTORS ARE THWN cu. <br><br> BRANCH-CIRCUIT LOAD IS 90 A • 210-20(a) • 210-19(a) • 384-16(d) <br><br> **NEC 240-3(b)** | BRANCH-CIRCUIT LOAD = 90 A CONTINUOUS OPERATION TERMINALS ARE 75°C <br><br> **NEC LOOP** <br> • 210-20(b) <br> • 240-3(b) <br> • 250-2(b) <br> • 110-14(c)(2)(b) | **Step 1:** Computing load <br> _____ A [A] x 125% <br> = _____ A [B] <br><br> **Step 2:** Terminal ratings <br> _____ A [C] can be terminated <br> at _____°C [D] <br><br> **Step 3:** Sizing conductors <br> _____ A [E] requires <br> #_____ cu. [F] <br><br> **Step 4:** Sizing OCPD <br> #_____ cu. [G] <br> = _____ A [H] <br> _____ A [I] allows <br> _____ A [J] OCPD <br><br> **Solution :** The size OCPD is _____ amps [K]. |

| KNOWN VALUES |
|---|
| BRANCH-CIRCUIT LOAD = 90 A CONTINUOUS OPERATION |

**Figure 8-2.** Where the ampacity of conductor(s) do not correspond to a standard device per Sec. 240-6(a), the next higher rating can be used, if 800 amps or less in rating.

## DEVICES RATED OVER 800 AMPS
## 240-3(c)

If the overcurrent protection device is greater than 800 amps, the ampacity of the conductors shall be equal to or greater than the ampacities of the overcurrent protection device per Sec. 240-6(a).

**Problem 8-3.** Devices rated over 800 amps must be rounded down and not up.

What size OCPD is required for a feeder-circuit with a continuous load of 724 amps which is paralleled 4 times and terminated to 75°C terminals?

Step 1: Computing load
215-2(a)
724 A x 125% = 905 A

Step 2: Terminal ratings
110-14(c)(2)(a)
905 A can be terminated at 75°C

Step 3: Sizing OCPD
240-3(c); 240-6(a); Table 310-16
#4/0 = 230 A x 4 = 920 A
920 A requires 900 A OCPD

Solution: **The size OCPD is 900 amps.**

See **Figure 8-3** for an exercise problem when sizing and selecting the OCPD rated over 800 amps.

**Figure 8-3.** Where the ampacity of conductor(s) do not correspond with a standard device per Sec. 240-6(a), the next lower size must be used if rated over 800 amps.

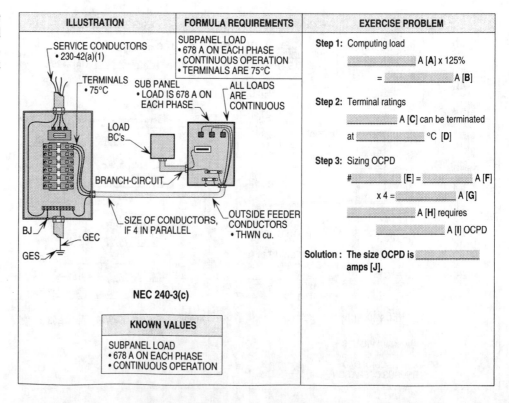

# OCPD FOR TAPS 240-3(e)

Smaller conductors can be tapped from larger conductors under certain conditions. Sec.'s 240-4, 240-21(a), and 210-19(d) of the NEC have tap rules which allow an 18 in., 10 ft., 25 ft., or 100 ft. tap respectively. Review these requirements carefully before attempting to calculate and make such taps on the journeyman examination.

**Problem 8-4.** Taps 10 ft. or less in length must be sized and protected by specific rules of the NEC.

What size OCPD is required for a 10 ft. tap from a junction box that is supplied by a feeder-circuit with a 500 amp OCPD?

**Step 1:** Calculating min. size tap
240-21(b)(1)(d)
A = 500 A OCPD / 10
A = 50

**Step 2:** Sizing conductors
Table 310-16
#8 THWN cu. = 50 A

**Step 3:** Verifying size based on wire A
240-21(b)(1)(d)
50 A is equal to 50 A
(50 A x 10 = 500 A OCPD)

**Step 4:** Calculating OCPD
240-3(e); 240-21(b)(1)(a); 240-3(b)
50 A conductors allows 50 A OCPD

**Solution: The size OCPD is 50 amps.**

See **Figure 8-4** for an exercise problem when sizing and selecting the OCPD for taps 10 ft. or less in length.

**ILLUSTRATION**

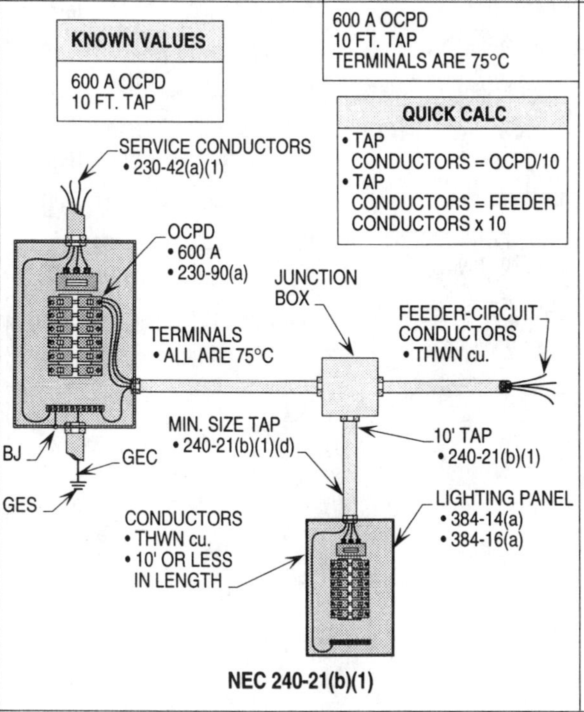


**FORMULA REQUIREMENTS**

600 A OCPD
10 FT. TAP
TERMINALS ARE 75°C

**EXERCISE PROBLEM**

**Step 1:** Calculating min. size tap
A = ________ A [A] OCPD
/ ________ [B]
A = ________ A [C]

**Step 2:** Sizing conductors
# ________ THWN [D] cu.
= ________ A [E]

**Step 3:** Verifying size
________ A [F] is greater than
________ A [G]

**Step 4:** Calculating OCPD
________ A [H] OCPD is required

**Solution: The OCPD is ________ amps [I].**

**Note:** A 70 A OCPD can be used per Sec. 240-6(b) under certain conditions of use.

**Figure 8-4.** This illustration shows an exercise problem for sizing and selecting the OCPD for taps 10 ft. or less in length.

**Problem 8-5.** Taps over 10 ft. to 25 ft. in length must be sized and protected by specific rules of the NEC.

What size OCPD is required for a tap over 10 ft. and up to 25 ft. in length from a junction box that is supplied from a feeder-circuit with a 500 amp OCPD?

> **Step 1:** Calculating min. size tap
> 240-21(b)(2)(a)
> 1/3 x 500 A OCPD = 166.7 A

> **Step 2:** Selecting conductors
> Table 310-16
> 166.7 A requires #2/0 cu.

> **Step 3:** Selecting OCPD
> 240-3(e); 240-21(b)(2)(b); 240-3(b)
> #2/0 requires 175 A OCPD

> **Solution: The size OCPD is 175 amps.**

See **Figure 8-5** for an exercise problem when sizing and selecting the OCPD for taps over 10 ft. up to 25 ft. in length.

**Figure 8-5.** This illustration shows an exercise problem for sizing and selecting the OCPD for taps over 10 ft. to 25 ft. in length.

**Test Tip 2:** When making a tap over 10 ft. and up to 25 ft. in length, the tapped conductors must be equal to 1/3 of the feeder's OCPD rating.

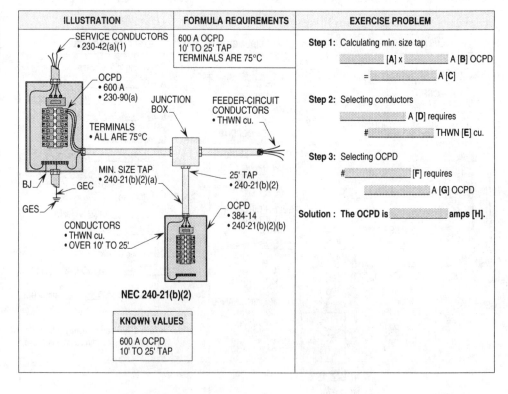

What size secondary OCPD (max.) is required for a 25 ft. tap, including transformer, which is supplied from a feeder-circuit with a 300 amp OCPD and having a 480 volt primary and 208 volt secondary?

**Problem 8-6:** Taps including the transformer must not exceed 25 ft. in total length from the point that they are tapped.

**Step 1:** Calculating secondary tap
240-21(b)(3)(b)
480 V / 208 V x 1/3 x 300 A = 230.7 A
(Rounded up to 231 A)

**Note:** A 250 amp OCPD would normally be used and not a 300 amp OCPD. However, for testing purposes, the 300 amp OCPD would be selected.

**Step 2:** Selecting conductors
Table 310-16
231 A requires #250 KCMIL

**Step 3:** Selecting OCPD in secondary tap
240-3(e); 240-21(b)(3)(e); 240-6(a); 240-3(b)
255 A (#250 KCMIL) requires 300 A OCPD

**Solution: The size OCPD is 300 amps.**

See **Figure 8-6** for an exercise problem when sizing and selecting the OCPD for a tap and connection including the primary tap, transfomer, and secondary connection.

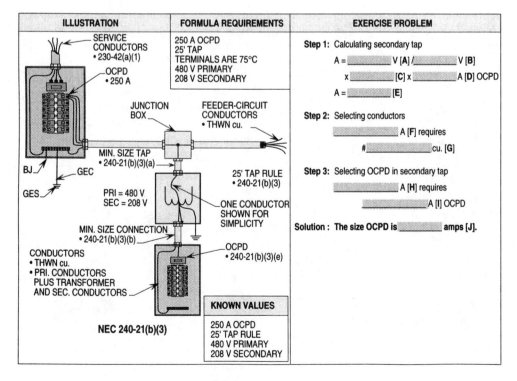

| ILLUSTRATION | FORMULA REQUIREMENTS | EXERCISE PROBLEM |
|---|---|---|
| SERVICE CONDUCTORS • 230-42(a)(1) OCPD • 250 A JUNCTION BOX FEEDER-CIRCUIT CONDUCTORS • THWN cu. MIN. SIZE TAP • 240-21(b)(3)(a) BJ GEC GES PRI = 480 V SEC = 208 V 25' TAP RULE • 240-21(b)(3) ONE CONDUCTOR SHOWN FOR SIMPLICITY MIN. SIZE CONNECTION • 240-21(b)(3)(b) OCPD • 240-21(b)(3)(e) CONDUCTORS • THWN cu. • PRI. CONDUCTORS PLUS TRANSFORMER AND SEC. CONDUCTORS NEC 240-21(b)(3) | 250 A OCPD 25' TAP TERMINALS ARE 75°C 480 V PRIMARY 208 V SECONDARY KNOWN VALUES 250 A OCPD 25' TAP RULE 480 V PRIMARY 208 V SECONDARY | **Step 1:** Calculating secondary tap A = _____ V [A] / _____ V [B] x _____ [C] x _____ A [D] OCPD A = _____ [E] **Step 2:** Selecting conductors _____ A [F] requires # _____ cu. [G] **Step 3:** Selecting OCPD in secondary tap _____ A [H] requires _____ A [I] OCPD **Solution :** The size OCPD is _____ amps [J]. |

**Figure 8-6.** This illustration shows an exercise problem for sizing and selecting the OCPD for taps and connections including transformer.

**Test Tip 3:** The secondary connected conductors and OCPD must be sized at least 1/3 the ratio of the secondary to primary voltage based upon the feeder's OCPD.

**Problem 8-7.** Taps over 25 ft. up to 100 ft. in length must be sized and protected by specific rules of the NEC.

What size OCPD is required for a 25 ft. up to 100 ft. tap that is supplied from a feeder-circuit with a 300 amp OCPD?

**Step 1:** Calculating min. size tap
240-21(b)(4)(c)
1/3 x 300 A = 100 A

**Step 2:** Selecting conductors
Table 310-16
100 A requires #3

**Test Tip 4:** Tapped conductors must be equal to 1/3 of the feeder's OCPD.

**Step 3:** Selecting OCPD
240-3(e); 240-21(b)(4)(d); 240-3
100 A (#3 THWN cu.) requires 100 A OCPD

**Solution:  The size OCPD is 100 amps.**

See **Figure 8-7** for an exercise problem when sizing and selecting the OCPD for taps over 25 ft. up to 100 ft. in length.

**Figure 8-7.** The illustration shows an exercise problem for sizing and selecting taps over 25 ft. and up to 100 ft. in length.

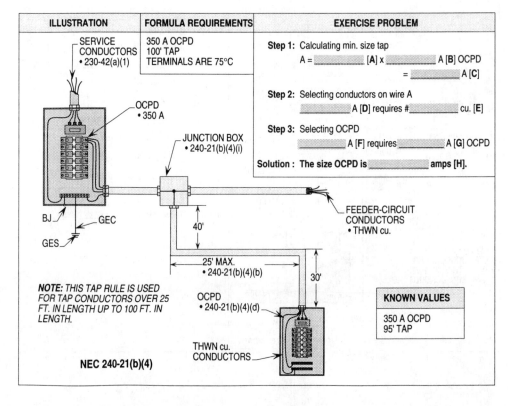

**Test Tip 5:** The junction box for tapping conductors must be at least 30 ft. from the finished floor.

What size OCPD is required for a tap of 25 ft. from the secondary of a 150 kVA transformer which is supplied by a 200 amp OCPD having a three-phase, 480 volt primary and 208 volt secondary.

Step 1: Calculating FLA (sec.)
FLA = 150 kVA x 1,000 / 208 V x 1.732
FLA = 416.7 A

Step 2: Sizing secondary OCPD
240-21(c)(3)(a); (b); 240-6(a)
400 A secondary OCPD is less than the 416.7 amp output

Solution: **The size OCPD is 400 amps.**

See **Figure 8-8** for an exercise problem when sizing and selecting the OCPD for connections of 25 ft. from the secondary of a transformer based upon the output of the transformer.

**Problem 8-8.** Taps of 25 ft. from the secondary of a transformer must be sized and protected by specific rules of the NEC.

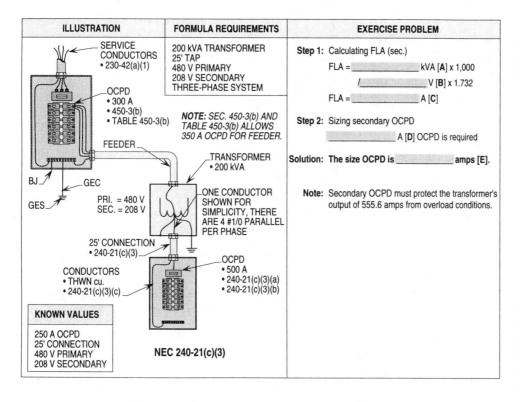

| ILLUSTRATION | FORMULA REQUIREMENTS | EXERCISE PROBLEM |
|---|---|---|
| SERVICE CONDUCTORS • 230-42(a)(1) OCPD • 300 A • 450-3(b) • TABLE 450-3(b) FEEDER BJ GEC GES PRI. = 480 V SEC. = 208 V 25' CONNECTION • 240-21(c)(3) CONDUCTORS • THWN cu. • 240-21(c)(3)(c) **KNOWN VALUES** 250 A OCPD 25' CONNECTION 480 V PRIMARY 208 V SECONDARY | 200 kVA TRANSFORMER 25' TAP 480 V PRIMARY 208 V SECONDARY THREE-PHASE SYSTEM **NOTE:** SEC. 450-3(b) AND TABLE 450-3(b) ALLOWS 350 A OCPD FOR FEEDER. TRANSFORMER • 200 kVA ONE CONDUCTOR SHOWN FOR SIMPLICITY, THERE ARE 4 #1/0 PARALLEL PER PHASE OCPD • 500 A • 240-21(c)(3)(a) • 240-21(c)(3)(b) **NEC 240-21(c)(3)** | **Step 1:** Calculating FLA (sec.) FLA = _____ kVA [A] x 1,000 / _____ V [B] x 1.732 FLA = _____ A [C] **Step 2:** Sizing secondary OCPD _____ A [D] OCPD is required **Solution: The size OCPD is _____ amps [E].** **Note:** Secondary OCPD must protect the transformer's output of 555.6 amps from overload conditions. |

**Figure 8-8.** This illustration shows an exercise problem for sizing and selecting a connection of 25 ft. from the secondary of a transformer.

**Note:** When applying the 25 ft. connection rule from the secondary of a transformer, both the transformer output and secondary conductors must be protected from overloads.

# OCPD FOR TRANSFORMER SECONDARY CIRCUITS 240-3(f)

Conductors supplied by the secondary side of a single-phase transformer having a two-wire (single voltage) secondary or a three-wire delta secondary shall be considered protected by overcurrent protection provided on the primary (supply) side of the transformer, providing this protection is in accordance with Sec. 450-3 and does not exceed the value determined by multiplying the secondary conductor ampacity by the secondary-to-primary transformer voltage ratio.

**Problem 8-9.** Two-wire to two-wire transformers can be protected by the primary OCPD. Note that No. 2 has an ampacity of 115 amps.

What size OCPD is required for a single-phase, 480 volt primary and 240 volt secondary, two-wire to two-wire system with No. 2 THWN copper conductors?

**Step 1:** Finding ratio A
OCPD = 240 V / 480 V x 115 A
OCPD = 57.5 A

**Solution:** **The size OCPD is 50 amps.**

**See Figure 8-9** for an exercise problem when sizing and selecting the OCPD for a two-wire to two-wire system.

**Figure 8-9.** This illustration shows an exercise problem for sizing and selecting the OCPD for a two-wire to two-wire system.

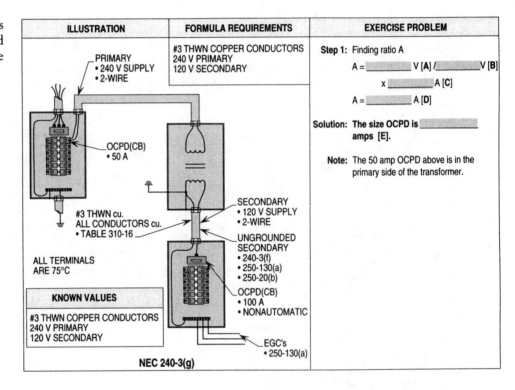

**Problem 8-10.** Three-wire to three-wire transformers can be protected by the primary OCPD.

What size OCPD is required for a three-phase, 480 volt primary and 240 volt secondary, three-wire to three-wire system with No. 500 KCMIL copper conductors?

**Step 1:** Finding ratio A
OCPD = 240 V / 480 V x 380 A
OCPD = 190 A

**Solution:** **The size OCPD is 175 amps.**

**See Figure 8-10** for an exercise problem when sizing and selecting the OCPD for a three-wire to three-wire transformer.

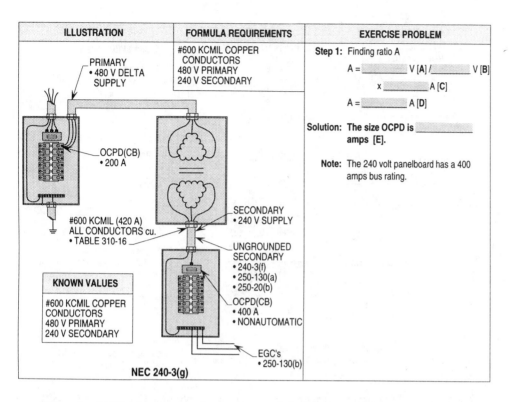

| ILLUSTRATION | FORMULA REQUIREMENTS | EXERCISE PROBLEM |
|---|---|---|
| PRIMARY • 480 V DELTA SUPPLY | #600 KCMIL COPPER CONDUCTORS 480 V PRIMARY 240 V SECONDARY | **Step 1:** Finding ratio A<br><br>A = _____ V [A] / _____ V [B]<br><br>x _____ A [C]<br><br>A = _____ A [D] |
| OCPD(CB) • 200 A | | **Solution:** **The size OCPD is** _____ **amps [E].** |
| #600 KCMIL (420 A) ALL CONDUCTORS cu. • TABLE 310-16 | SECONDARY • 240 V SUPPLY | **Note:** The 240 volt panelboard has a 400 amps bus rating. |
| | UNGROUNDED SECONDARY • 240-3(f) • 250-130(a) • 250-20(b) | |
| **KNOWN VALUES** #600 KCMIL COPPER CONDUCTORS 480 V PRIMARY 240 V SECONDARY | OCPD(CB) • 400 A • NONAUTOMATIC | |
| NEC 240-3(g) | EGC's • 250-130(b) | |

Figure 8-10. This illustration shows an exercise problem for sizing and selecting the OCPD for a three-wire to three-wire system.

What size OCPD (circuit breaker) is required for the primary side of a 2,000 kVA transformer with a three-phase supply voltage of 12,470 volts?

Problem 8-11. Primary over 600 volts can have OCPD in the primary side of the transformer.

Step 1: Finding FLA of primary
450-3(a)
FLA = kVA x 1,000 / V x √3
FLA = 2,000 kVA x 1,000 / 12,470 V x 1.732
FLA = 92.6 A

Step 2: Calculating FLA for OCPD
450-3(a); Table 450-3(a)
92.6 A x 300% = 277.8 A

Note that the OCPD is based upon individual primary protection.

Step 3: Selecting OCPD
Table 450-3(a), Note 1; 240-6(a)
277.8 A requires 300 A

Solution: **The size circuit breaker is 300 amps.**

See Figure 8-11 for an exercise problem when sizing and selecting the OCPD for the primary side of the transformer only.

**Figure 8-11.** This illustration shows an exercise problem for sizing and selecting the OCPD for the primary only.

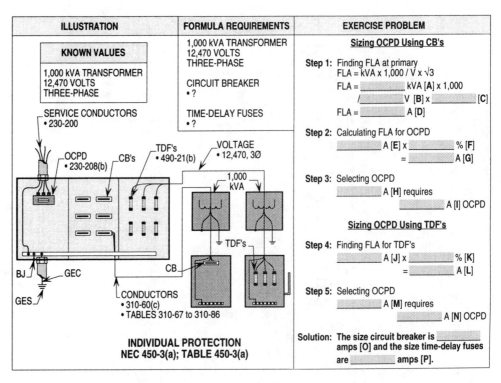

| ILLUSTRATION | FORMULA REQUIREMENTS | EXERCISE PROBLEM |
|---|---|---|

**KNOWN VALUES**

1,000 kVA TRANSFORMER
12,470 VOLTS
THREE-PHASE

SERVICE CONDUCTORS
• 230-200

OCPD
• 230-208(b)   CB's   TDF's • 490-21(b)   VOLTAGE • 12,470, 3∅

1,000 kVA

TDF's

BJ   GEC
CB
GES

CONDUCTORS
• 310-60(c)
• TABLES 310-67 to 310-86

**INDIVIDUAL PROTECTION**
**NEC 450-3(a); TABLE 450-3(a)**

*FORMULA REQUIREMENTS:*

1,000 kVA TRANSFORMER
12,470 VOLTS
THREE-PHASE

CIRCUIT BREAKER
• ?

TIME-DELAY FUSES
• ?

*EXERCISE PROBLEM:*

**Sizing OCPD Using CB's**

Step 1: Finding FLA at primary
FLA = kVA x 1,000 / V x √3
FLA = _____ kVA [A] x 1,000
/ _____ V [B] x _____ [C]
FLA = _____ A [D]

Step 2: Calculating FLA for OCPD
_____ A [E] x _____ % [F]
= _____ A [G]

Step 3: Selecting OCPD
_____ A [H] requires _____ A [I] OCPD

**Sizing OCPD Using TDF's**

Step 4: Finding FLA for TDF's
_____ A [J] x _____ % [K]
= _____ A [L]

Step 5: Selecting OCPD
_____ A [M] requires _____ A [N] OCPD

Solution: The size circuit breaker is _____ amps [O] and the size time-delay fuses are _____ amps [P].

**Problem 8-12.** Primary and secondary protection for transformers rated over 600 volts located in nonsupervised locations.

**Note:** The OCPD in the secondary side of the transformer would most likely be sized at 600 amps.

What size OCPD (circuit breaker) is required for a three-phase, 4,160 volt primary and 480 volt secondary for a 400 kVA transformer with a 5.9 percent impedance in a nonsupervised location?

Step 1: Finding FLA of transformer (primary)
FLA = kVA x 1,000 / V x √3
FLA = 400 kVA x 1,000 / 4,160 x 1.732
FLA = 55.5 A

Step 2: Calculating FLA for OCPD (primary)
450-3(a); Table 450-3(a)
FLA = 55.5 A x 600%
FLA = 333 A

Step 3: Selecting OCPD (primary)
Table 450-3(a), Note 1; 240-6(a)
333 A requires 350 A OCPD

Step 4: Finding FLA of transformer (secondary)
FLA = kVA x 1,000 / V x √3
FLA = 400 kVA x 1,000 / 480 V x 1.732
FLA = 481.4 A

Step 5: Calculating FLA for OCPD (secondary)
450-3(a); Table 450-3(a)
FLA = 481.4 A x 125%
FLA = 601.8 A

Step 6: Selecting OCPD (secondary)
Table 450-3(a), Note 1; 240-6(a)
601.8 A allows 700 A OCPD

Solution: **The size OCPD for the primary side is 350 amps and the secondary side is 700 amps.**

See **Figure 8-12** for an exercise problem when sizing and selecting the OCPD for the primary and secondary side of a transformer in a nonsupervised location.

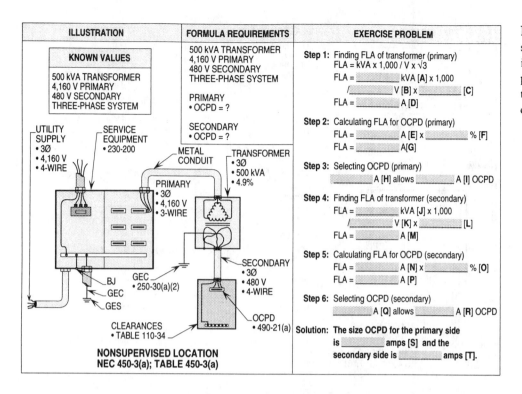

| ILLUSTRATION | FORMULA REQUIREMENTS | EXERCISE PROBLEM |
|---|---|---|

**KNOWN VALUES**

500 kVA TRANSFORMER
4,160 V PRIMARY
480 V SECONDARY
THREE-PHASE SYSTEM

500 kVA TRANSFORMER
4,160 V PRIMARY
480 V SECONDARY
THREE-PHASE SYSTEM

PRIMARY
• OCPD = ?

SECONDARY
• OCPD = ?

UTILITY SUPPLY
• 3Ø
• 4,160 V
• 4-WIRE

SERVICE EQUIPMENT
• 230-200

METAL CONDUIT

PRIMARY
• 3Ø
• 4,160 V
• 3-WIRE

TRANSFORMER
• 3Ø
• 500 kVA
• 4.9%

SECONDARY
• 3Ø
• 480 V
• 4-WIRE

BJ
GEC
GES

GEC
• 250-30(a)(2)

OCPD
• 490-21(a)

CLEARANCES
• TABLE 110-34

**NONSUPERVISED LOCATION**
**NEC 450-3(a); TABLE 450-3(a)**

**Step 1:** Finding FLA of transformer (primary)
FLA = kVA x 1,000 / V x √3
FLA = ___ kVA **[A]** x 1,000 / ___ V **[B]** x ___ **[C]**
FLA = ___ A **[D]**

**Step 2:** Calculating FLA for OCPD (primary)
FLA = ___ A **[E]** x ___ % **[F]**
FLA = ___ A**[G]**

**Step 3:** Selecting OCPD (primary)
___ A **[H]** allows ___ A **[I]** OCPD

**Step 4:** Finding FLA of transformer (secondary)
FLA = ___ kVA **[J]** x 1,000 / ___ V **[K]** x ___ **[L]**
FLA = ___ A **[M]**

**Step 5:** Calculating FLA for OCPD (secondary)
FLA = ___ A **[N]** x ___ % **[O]**
FLA = ___ A **[P]**

**Step 6:** Selecting OCPD (secondary)
___ A **[Q]** allows ___ A **[R]** OCPD

**Solution:** The size OCPD for the primary side is ___ amps **[S]** and the secondary side is ___ amps **[T]**.

**Figure 8-12.** This illustration shows an exercise problem for sizing and selecting the OCPD for the primary and secondary side of a transformer in a nonsupervised location.

What size OCPD (circuit breaker) is required for a three-phase, 4,160 volt primary and 480 volt secondary for a 400 kVA transformer with a 5.9 percent impedance in a supervised location?

**Step 1:** Finding FLA of transformer (primary)
FLA = kVA x 1,000 / V x √3
FLA = 400 kVA x 1,000 / 4,160 x 1.732
FLA = 55.5 A

**Step 2:** Calculating FLA for OCPD (primary)
450-3(a); Table 450-3(a)
FLA = 55.5 A x 600%
FLA = 333 A

**Step 3:** Selecting OCPD (primary)
450-3(a), Note 3; 240-6(a)
333 A requires 300 A OCPD

**Step 4:** Finding FLA of transformer (secondary)
FLA = kVA x 1,000 / V x √3
FLA = 400 kVA x 1,000 / 480 V x 1.732
FLA = 481.4 A

**Step 5:** Calculating FLA for OCPD (secondary)
450-3(a); Table 450-3(a)
FLA = 481.4 A x 250%
FLA = 1,203.5 A

**Step 6:** Selecting OCPD (secondary)
Table 450-3(a), Note 3; 240-6(a)
1,203.5 A allows 1,200 A OCPD

**Solution:** The size OCPD for the primary side is 300 amps and the secondary side is 1,200 amps.

**Problem 8-13.** Primary and secondary protection for transformers rated over 600 volts located in a supervised location.

See **Figure 8-13** for an exercise problem when sizing and selecting the OCPD for the primary and secondary side of the transformer in a supervised location.

**Figure 8-13.** This illustration shows an exercise problem for sizing and selecting the OCPD for the primary and secondary side of the transformer in a supervised location.

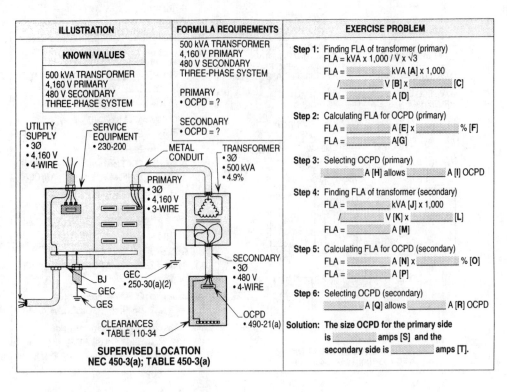

**Problem 8-14.** Primary 9 amps or more with OCPD in the primary side only.

What size OCPD (circuit breaker) is required for a single-phase, 240 volt primary and 120 volt secondary for a 25 kVA transformer?

**Step 1:** Finding FLA of primary
FLA = kVA x 1,000 / V
FLA = 25 kVA x 1,000 / 240 V
FLA = 104 A

**Step 2:** Calculating OCPD
450-3(b); Table 450-3(b)
104 A x 125% = 130 A

**Step 3:** Selecting OCPD
Table 450-3(b), Note 1; 240-6(a)
130 A allows 150 A

**Solution:** The size OCPD in the primary side is 150 amps.

**See Figure 8-14** for an exercise problem when sizing and selecting the OCPD for the primary side of the transformer.

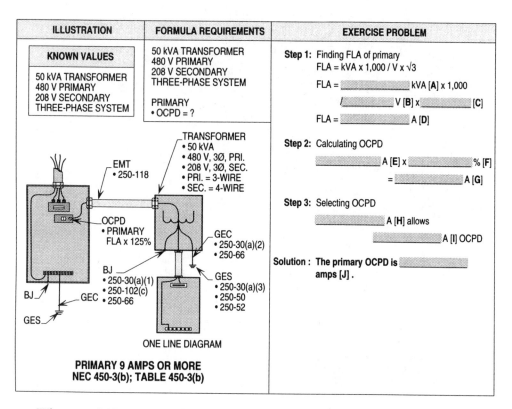

**Figure 8-14.** This illustration shows an exercise problem for sizing and selecting the OCPD for the primary side of the transformer.

What size OCPD is required for a 480 volt, single-phase, two-wire to two-wire 2 kVA transformer?

**Problem 8-15.** Primary 2 amps or more but less than 9 amps with protection in the primary side.

Step 1:  Finding FLA of primary
FLA = kVA x 1,000 / V
FLA = 2 kVA x 1,000 / 480 V
FLA = 4.17 A

Step 2:  Calculating OCPD
450-3(b); Table 450-3(b)
4.17 A x 167% = 6.96 A

Step 3:  Selecting OCPD
Table 450-3(b); 240-6(a)
6.96 A allows 6 A

Solution:  **The size OCPD is 6 amps.**

**See Figure 8-15** for an exercise problem when sizing and selecting the OCPD for the primary side of the transformer.

**Figure 8-15.** This illustration shows an exercise problem for sizing and selecting the OCPD for the primary side of the transformer.

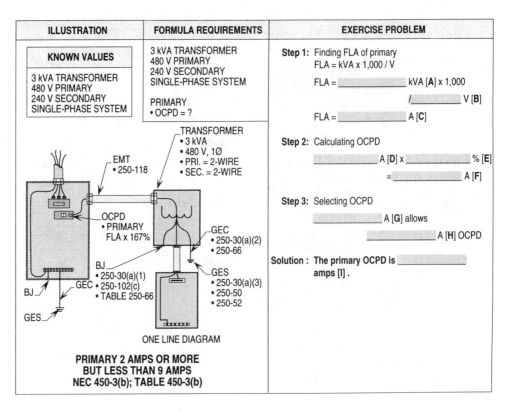

| ILLUSTRATION | FORMULA REQUIREMENTS | EXERCISE PROBLEM |
|---|---|---|

**Problem 8-16.** Primary less than 2 amps with protection in the primary side of the transformer.

What is the minimum and maximum size OCPD required for a 480 volt, single-phase, two-wire to two-wire .7 kVA transformer?

**Step 1:** Finding FLA of transformer
FLA = kVA x 1,000 / V
FLA = .7 kVA x 1,000 / 480 V
FLA = 1.46 A

**Step 2:** Calculating OCPD (minimum)
450-3(b); Table 450-3(b)
1.46 A x 300% = 4.38 A

Note that the maximum size OCPD in steps 4 and 5 are used for motor control circuits.

**Step 3:** Selecting OCPD (minimum)
450-3(b); 240-6(a)
4.38 A allows 3 A

**Step 4:** Calculating OCPD (maximum)
430-72(c)(4)
1.46 A x 500% = 7.3 A

**Step 5:** Selecting OCPD (maximum)
430-72(c)(4); 240-6(a)
7.3 A allows 6 A

**Solution:** **The minimum size OCPD in the primary is 3 amps and the maximum size OCPD is 6 amps.**

**See Figure 8-16** for an exercise problem when sizing and selecting the minimum and maximum OCPD for the primary side of the transformer.

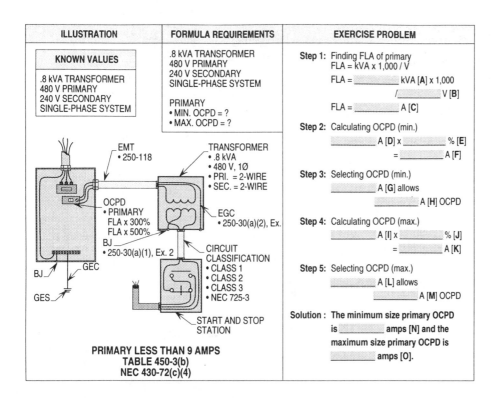

| ILLUSTRATION | FORMULA REQUIREMENTS | EXERCISE PROBLEM |
|---|---|---|

Figure 8-16. This illustration shows an exercise problem for sizing and selecting the minimum and maximum size OCPD for the primary side of the transformer.

What size OCPD is required for a 480 volt primary and 240 volt secondary, three-phase, 40 kVA transformer? (using the maximum size in the primary side).

Step 1: Finding FLA of primary
FLA = kVA x 1,000 / V x √3
FLA = 40 kVA x 1,000 / 480 V x 1.732
FLA = 48.1 A

Step 2: Calculating OCPD (primary)
450-3(b); Table 450-3(b)
48.1 A x 250% = 120.25 A

Step 3: Selecting OCPD (primary)
450-3(b); 240-6(a)
120.25 A allows 110 A

Step 4: Finding FLA of secondary
FLA = kVA x 1,000 / V x √3
FLA = 40 kVA x 1,000 / 240 V x 1.732
FLA = 96.2 A

Step 5: Calculating OCPD (secondary)
450-3(b); Table 450-3(b), Note 1
96.2 A x 125% = 120.25 A

Step 6: Selecting OCPD (secondary)
450-3(b); 240-6(a)
120.25 A allows 125 A

Solution: The size OCPD for the primary side is 110 amps and the size OCPD for the secondary side is 125 amps.

See Figure 8-17 for an exercise problem when sizing and selecting the OCPD for the primary and secondary side of the transformer.

Problem 8-17. Primary and secondary rated - 600 volts or less with protection in both sides of the transformer.

Note that the 125 percent protection in steps 5 and 6, must be placed in either the primary or secondary side of the transformer.

**Figure 8-17.** This illustration shows an exercise problem for sizing and selecting the OCPD for the primary and secondary side of the transformer.

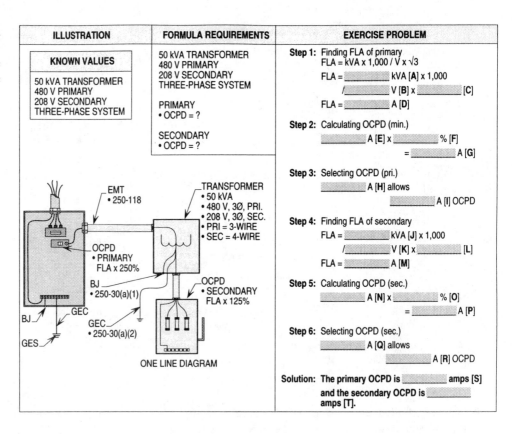

| ILLUSTRATION | FORMULA REQUIREMENTS | EXERCISE PROBLEM |
|---|---|---|
| **KNOWN VALUES**<br><br>50 kVA TRANSFORMER<br>480 V PRIMARY<br>208 V SECONDARY<br>THREE-PHASE SYSTEM | 50 kVA TRANSFORMER<br>480 V PRIMARY<br>208 V SECONDARY<br>THREE-PHASE SYSTEM<br><br>PRIMARY<br>• OCPD = ?<br><br>SECONDARY<br>• OCPD = ? | **Step 1:** Finding FLA of primary<br>FLA = kVA x 1,000 / V x √3<br>FLA = _____ kVA [A] x 1,000<br>/ _____ V [B] x _____ [C]<br>FLA = _____ A [D] |

**Step 2:** Calculating OCPD (min.)
_____ A [E] x _____ % [F]
= _____ A [G]

**Step 3:** Selecting OCPD (pri.)
_____ A [H] allows
_____ A [I] OCPD

**Step 4:** Finding FLA of secondary
FLA = _____ kVA [J] x 1,000
/ _____ V [K] x _____ [L]
FLA = _____ A [M]

**Step 5:** Calculating OCPD (sec.)
_____ A [N] x _____ % [O]
= _____ A [P]

**Step 6:** Selecting OCPD (sec.)
_____ A [Q] allows
_____ A [R] OCPD

**Solution:** The primary OCPD is _____ amps [S]
and the secondary OCPD is _____ amps [T].

Illustration labels: EMT • 250-118; TRANSFORMER • 50 kVA • 480 V, 3Ø, PRI. • 208 V, 3Ø, SEC. • PRI = 3-WIRE • SEC = 4-WIRE; OCPD • PRIMARY FLA x 250%; BJ • 250-30(a)(1); OCPD • SECONDARY FLA x 125%; BJ; GEC; GES; GEC • 250-30(a)(2); ONE LINE DIAGRAM

**Problem 8-18.** Motor circuit taps are sized and protected by the rules of the NEC.

What size OCPD is required for a motor circuit tap from a junction box that is supplied from a feeder-circuit with an 800 amp OCPD?

**Step 1:** Calculating min. size tap
240-21(f); 430-28(l)
A = 800 A OCPD / 10
A = 80 A

**Note:** The calculation load of 850 amps (85 A x 10 = 850 A) is greater than the 800 amp OCPD on the feeder-circuit.

**Step 2:** Sizing conductors
Table 310-16
#4 THWN cu. = 85 A

**Step 3:** Verifying size
240-21(f); 430-28(l)
85 A is greater than 80 A
(85 A x 10 = 850 A)

**Step 4:** Selecting OCPD
240-3(b); 240-6(a)
85 A conductors allows 90 A OCPD

**Solution: The size OCPD is 90 amps.**

See Figure 8-18 for an exercise problem when sizing and selecting the OCPD for motor circuit taps using the 10 or 25 ft. tap rule.

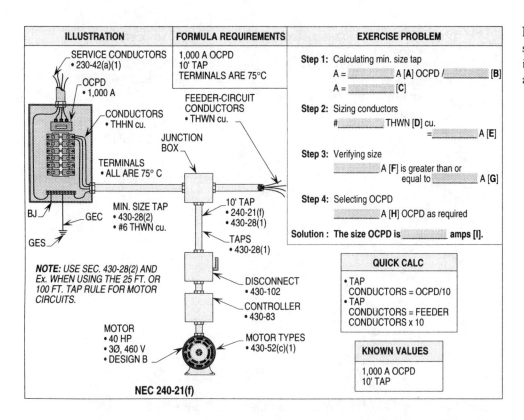

| ILLUSTRATION | FORMULA REQUIREMENTS | EXERCISE PROBLEM |
|---|---|---|

**Figure 8-18.** This illustration shows an exercise problem for sizing and selecting a circuit tap for a motor.

# OCPD FOR MOTOR-OPERATED APPLIANCE CIRCUITS 240-3(g)

Motor-operated appliance circuit conductors are normally protected against overcurrent by the provisions listed in Parts B and D of Article 422.

What size OCPD is required for a continuous branch-circuit load of 14 amps?

**Problem 8-19.** Motor-operated appliance circuits are sized and protected by specific rules of the NEC.

Step 1:  Computing load
  422-10(a); 210-19(a)
  14 A x 125% = 17.5 A

Step 2:  Sizing OCPD
  422-11(a); 240-3(b)
  17.5 A requires 20 A

Solution:  **The size OCPD is 20 amps.**

**See Figure 8-19** for an exercise problem when sizing an OCPD for a motor-operated appliance.

**Figure 8-19.** This illustration shows an exercise problem for sizing and selecting the OCPD for a motor-operated appliance.

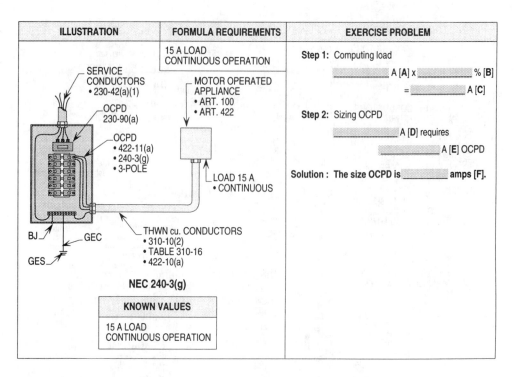

## OCPD FOR MOTOR AND MOTOR CONTROL CIRCUITS 240-3(g)

Motor circuits are another exception listed in Subpart (f), to the general rule, where the OCPD can be sized above the conductors ampacity. Motor circuits are sized according to the requirements of Article 430. A study of these requirements will reveal that for motor circuits, a fuse size or circuit breaker setting in excess of the ampacity of the conductor is permitted by the NEC. This exception is intended to provide fuse or circuit breaker protection large enough to hold the high momentary inrush current required for starting and running the driven load.

**Problem 8-20.** Minimum and next size nontime-delay fuses sized to start and run a motor.

Note that the next size OCPD is usually required on the test. Test takers must read the problem very carefully before making the decision to round up or down the size of the OCPD.

What size nontime-delay fuses are required to start and run a 40 HP, three-phase, 460 volt, Design B motor?

**Step 1:** Finding FLA
430-6(a)(1); Table 430-150
40 HP = 52 A

**Step 2:** Finding percentage
430-52(c)(1); Table 430-152
Min. size = 300%

**Step 3:** Calculating min. size
430-52(c)(1)
Min. size = 52 A x 300%
Min. size = 156 A

**Step 4:** Calculating next size
430-52(c)(1), Ex. 1
156 A requires 175 A

**Step 5:** Selecting NTDF's
Min. size = 150 A
Next size = 175 A

**Solution:** The minimum size nontime-delay fuse is 150 amps and the next size is 175 amps.

See **Figure 8-20** for an exercise problem when sizing and selecting the nontime-delay fuses to start and run a motor.

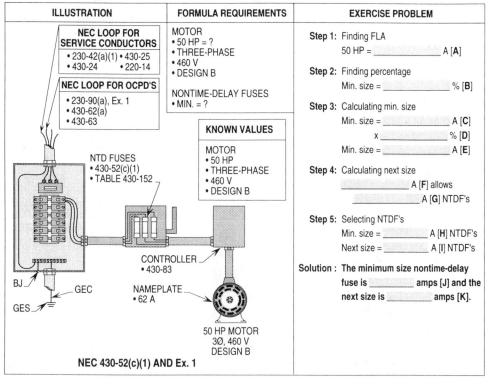

| ILLUSTRATION | FORMULA REQUIREMENTS | EXERCISE PROBLEM |
|---|---|---|

**NEC LOOP FOR SERVICE CONDUCTORS**
• 230-42(a)(1) • 430-25
• 430-24    • 220-14

**NEC LOOP FOR OCPD'S**
• 230-90(a), Ex. 1
• 430-62(a)
• 430-63

NTD FUSES
• 430-52(c)(1)
• TABLE 430-152

BJ
GEC
GES

CONTROLLER
• 430-83

NAMEPLATE
• 62 A

50 HP MOTOR
3Ø, 460 V
DESIGN B

**NEC 430-52(c)(1) AND Ex. 1**

MOTOR
• 50 HP = ?
• THREE-PHASE
• 460 V
• DESIGN B

NONTIME-DELAY FUSES
• MIN. = ?

**KNOWN VALUES**

MOTOR
• 50 HP
• THREE-PHASE
• 460 V
• DESIGN B

Step 1: Finding FLA
   50 HP = _____ A [A]

Step 2: Finding percentage
   Min. size = _____ % [B]

Step 3: Calculating min. size
   Min. size = _____ A [C]
   x _____ % [D]
   Min. size = _____ A [E]

Step 4: Calculating next size
   _____ A [F] allows
   _____ A [G] NTDF's

Step 5: Selecting NTDF's
   Min. size = _____ A [H] NTDF's
   Next size = _____ A [I] NTDF's

Solution : The minimum size nontime-delay
   fuse is _____ amps [J] and the
   next size is _____ amps [K].

**Figure 8-20.** This illustration is an exercise problem for sizing and selecting the minimum and next size nontime-delay fuses to start and run a motor.

**Note:** Unless the problem states otherwise on the test, round up the calculation of 195 amps up to a 200 amp OCPD.

**Problem 8-21.** Minimum and next size time-delay fuses required to start and run a motor.

What size time-delay fuses are required to start and run a 40 HP, three-phase, 460 volt, Design B motor?

**Step 1:** Finding FLA
   430-6(a)(1); Table 430-150
   40 HP = 52 A

**Step 2:** Finding percentage
   430-52(c)(1); Table 430-152
   Min. size = 175%

**Step 3:** Calculating min. size
   430-52(c)(1)
   Min. size = 52 A x 175%
   Min. size = 91 A

**Step 4:** Calculating next size
   430-52(c)(1), Ex. 1
   91 A requires 100 A

**Step 5:** Selecting TDF's
   Min. size =  90 A
   Next size = 100 A

**Solution:** **The minimum size time-delay fuse is 90 amps and the next size is 100 amps.**

See **Figure 8-21** for an exercise problem for sizing and selecting the minimum and next size time-delay fuses to start and run a motor.

**Figure 8-21.** This illustration is an exercise problem for sizing and selecting the minimum and next size time-delay fuses to start and run a motor.

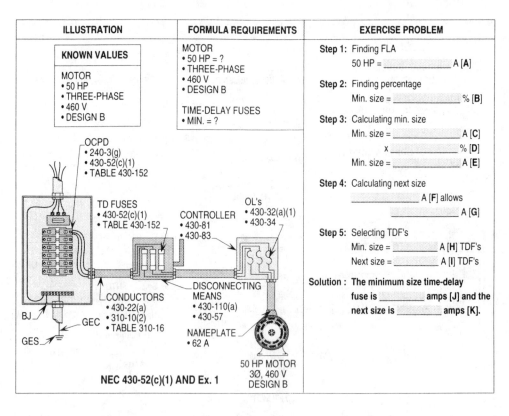

| ILLUSTRATION | FORMULA REQUIREMENTS | EXERCISE PROBLEM |
|---|---|---|
| **KNOWN VALUES** <br><br> MOTOR <br> • 50 HP <br> • THREE-PHASE <br> • 460 V <br> • DESIGN B | MOTOR <br> • 50 HP = ? <br> • THREE-PHASE <br> • 460 V <br> • DESIGN B <br><br> TIME-DELAY FUSES <br> • MIN. = ? | **Step 1:** Finding FLA <br> 50 HP = _____ A [A] <br><br> **Step 2:** Finding percentage <br> Min. size = _____ % [B] <br><br> **Step 3:** Calculating min. size <br> Min. size = _____ A [C] <br> x _____ % [D] <br> Min. size = _____ A [E] <br><br> **Step 4:** Calculating next size <br> _____ A [F] allows <br> _____ A [G] <br><br> **Step 5:** Selecting TDF's <br> Min. size = _____ A [H] TDF's <br> Next size = _____ A [I] TDF's <br><br> **Solution :** The minimum size time-delay fuse is _____ amps [J] and the next size is _____ amps [K]. |

OCPD
• 240-3(g)
• 430-52(c)(1)
• TABLE 430-152

TD FUSES
• 430-52(c)(1)
• TABLE 430-152

CONTROLLER
• 430-81
• 430-83

OL's
• 430-32(a)(1)
• 430-34

CONDUCTORS
• 430-22(a)
• 310-10(2)
• TABLE 310-16

DISCONNECTING MEANS
• 430-110(a)
• 430-57

NAMEPLATE
• 62 A

BJ
GEC
GES

50 HP MOTOR
3Ø, 460 V
DESIGN B

**NEC 430-52(c)(1) AND Ex. 1**

**Problem 8-22.** Minimum and maximum setting instantaneous trip circuit breakers required to start and run a motor.

What size instantaneous trip circuit breakers are required to start and run a 40 HP, three-phase, 460 volt, Design E motor?

**Step 1:** Finding FLA
430-6(a)(1); Table 430-150
40 HP = 52 A

**Step 2:** Finding percentage
430-52(c)(3); Table 430-152
Min. size = 1,100%

**Step 3:** Calculating min. size
430-52(c)(3)
Min. size = 52 A x 1,100%
Min. size = 572 A

**Step 4:** Calculating next size
430-52(c)(3), Ex. 1
Max. size = 52 A x 1,700%
Max. size = 884 A

**Step 5:** Selecting inst. trip circuit breaker
Min. size = 572 A
Max. size = 884 A

**Solution:** The minimum instantaneous trip circuit breaker setting is 572 amps and the maximum size is 884 amps.

**See Figure 8-22** for an exercise problem when sizing and selecting the minimum and maximum setting for an instantaneous trip circuit breaker to start and run a motor.

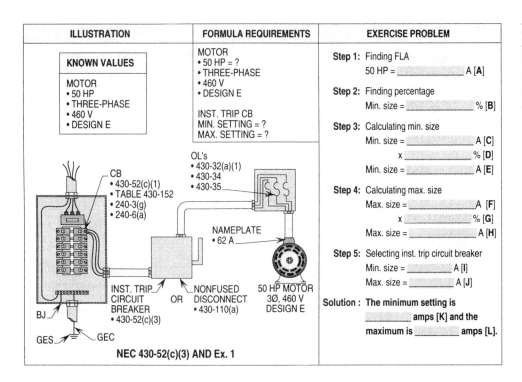

| ILLUSTRATION | FORMULA REQUIREMENTS | EXERCISE PROBLEM |
|---|---|---|
| **KNOWN VALUES**<br><br>MOTOR<br>• 50 HP<br>• THREE-PHASE<br>• 460 V<br>• DESIGN E | MOTOR<br>• 50 HP = ?<br>• THREE-PHASE<br>• 460 V<br>• DESIGN E<br><br>INST. TRIP CB<br>MIN. SETTING = ?<br>MAX. SETTING = ? | **Step 1:** Finding FLA<br>50 HP = _____ A **[A]**<br><br>**Step 2:** Finding percentage<br>Min. size = _____ % **[B]**<br><br>**Step 3:** Calculating min. size<br>Min. size = _____ A **[C]**<br>x _____ % **[D]**<br>Min. size = _____ A **[E]**<br><br>**Step 4:** Calculating max. size<br>Max. size = _____ A **[F]**<br>x _____ % **[G]**<br>Max. size = _____ A **[H]**<br><br>**Step 5:** Selecting inst. trip circuit breaker<br>Min. size = _____ A **[I]**<br>Max. size = _____ A **[J]**<br><br>**Solution :** **The minimum setting is _____ amps [K] and the maximum is _____ amps [L].** |

CB
• 430-52(c)(1)
• TABLE 430-152
• 240-3(g)
• 240-6(a)

OL's
• 430-32(a)(1)
• 430-34
• 430-35

NAMEPLATE
• 62 A

INST. TRIP CIRCUIT BREAKER
• 430-52(c)(3)

OR

NONFUSED DISCONNECT
• 430-110(a)

50 HP MOTOR
3Ø, 460 V
DESIGN E

BJ

GES — GEC

**NEC 430-52(c)(3) AND Ex. 1**

**Figure 8-22.** This illustration is an exercise problem for sizing and selecting the minimum and maximum setting for an instantaneous trip circuit breaker to start and run a motor.

What size inverse time circuit breakers are required to start and run a 40 HP, three-phase, 460 volt, Design B motor?

**Problem 8-23.** Minimum and next size inverse time circuit breakers required to start and run a motor.

**Step 1:** Finding FLA
430-6(a)(1); Table 430-150
40 HP = 52 A

**Step 2:** Finding percentage
430-52(c)(1), Table 430-152
Min. size = 250%

**Step 3:** Calculating min. size
430-52(c)(1)
Min. size = 52 A x 250%
Min. size = 130 A

**Step 4:** Calculating next size
430-52(c)(1), Ex. 1
130 A requires 150 A OCPD

**Step 5:** Selecting inverse time circuit breaker
Min. size = 125 A
Next size = 150 A

**Solution:** **The minimum size inverse time circuit breaker is 125 amps and the next size is 150 amps.**

See **Figure 8-23** for an exercise problem when sizing and selecting the minimum and next size inverse time circuit breaker to start and run a motor.

**Figure 8-23.** This illustration is an exercise problem for sizing and selecting the minimum and next size inverse time circuit breaker to start and run a motor.

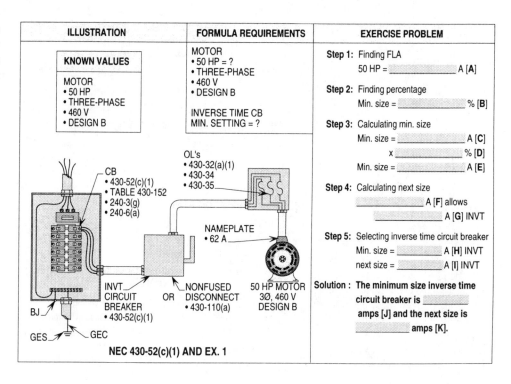

| ILLUSTRATION | FORMULA REQUIREMENTS | EXERCISE PROBLEM |
|---|---|---|
| **KNOWN VALUES**<br><br>MOTOR<br>• 50 HP<br>• THREE-PHASE<br>• 460 V<br>• DESIGN B | MOTOR<br>• 50 HP = ?<br>• THREE-PHASE<br>• 460 V<br>• DESIGN B<br><br>INVERSE TIME CB<br>MIN. SETTING = ? | **Step 1:** Finding FLA<br>50 HP = _____ A [A]<br><br>**Step 2:** Finding percentage<br>Min. size = _____ % [B]<br><br>**Step 3:** Calculating min. size<br>Min. size = _____ A [C]<br>x _____ % [D]<br>Min. size = _____ A [E]<br><br>**Step 4:** Calculating next size<br>_____ A [F] allows<br>_____ A [G] INVT<br><br>**Step 5:** Selecting inverse time circuit breaker<br>Min. size = _____ A [H] INVT<br>next size = _____ A [I] INVT<br><br>**Solution :** **The minimum size inverse time circuit breaker is _____ amps [J] and the next size is _____ amps [K].** |

OL's
• 430-32(a)(1)
• 430-34
• 430-35

CB
• 430-52(c)(1)
• TABLE 430-152
• 240-3(g)
• 240-6(a)

NAMEPLATE
• 62 A

INVT
CIRCUIT
BREAKER
• 430-52(c)(1)

OR

NONFUSED
DISCONNECT
• 430-110(a)

50 HP MOTOR
3Ø, 460 V
DESIGN B

BJ

GES — GEC

**NEC 430-52(c)(1) AND EX. 1**

**Problem 8-24.** Maximum size nontime-delay fuses required to start and run motor.

What size nontime-delay fuses are required to start and run a 40 HP, three-phase, 460 volt, Design B motor? (Determine maximum size)

**Step 1:** Finding FLA
430-6(a)(1); Table 430-150
40 HP = 52 A

**Note:** When selecting an OCPD using the maximum percentages, such percentages times the motor's FLA must not be exceeded.

**Step 2:** Finding percentage
430-52(c)(1), Ex. 2(a); Table 430-152
Max. size = 400%

**Step 3:** Calculating min. size
430-52(c)(1), Ex. 2(a)
Max. size = 52 A x 400%
Max. size = 208 A

**Step 4:** Selecting NTDF's
Max. size = 200 A

**Solution:** **The maximum size nontime-delay fuse is 200 amps.**

**See Figure 8-24** for an exercise problem when sizing and selecting the maximum size nontime-delay fuses to start and run a motor.

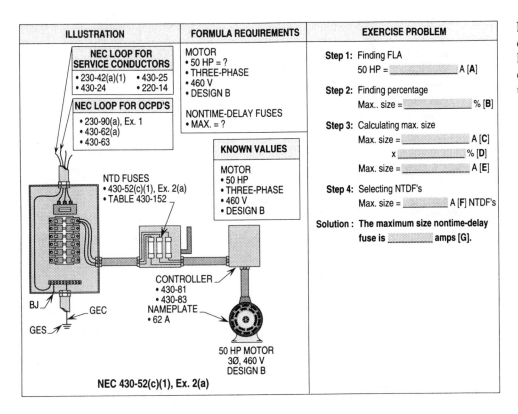

| ILLUSTRATION | FORMULA REQUIREMENTS | EXERCISE PROBLEM |
|---|---|---|

**NEC LOOP FOR SERVICE CONDUCTORS**
• 230-42(a)(1)    • 430-25
• 430-24          • 220-14

**NEC LOOP FOR OCPD'S**
• 230-90(a), Ex. 1
• 430-62(a)
• 430-63

NTD FUSES
• 430-52(c)(1), Ex. 2(a)
• TABLE 430-152

BJ
GEC
GES

CONTROLLER
• 430-81
• 430-83
NAMEPLATE
• 62 A

50 HP MOTOR
3Ø, 460 V
DESIGN B

**NEC 430-52(c)(1), Ex. 2(a)**

MOTOR
• 50 HP = ?
• THREE-PHASE
• 460 V
• DESIGN B

NONTIME-DELAY FUSES
• MAX. = ?

**KNOWN VALUES**

MOTOR
• 50 HP
• THREE-PHASE
• 460 V
• DESIGN B

**Step 1:** Finding FLA
    50 HP = _____ A [A]

**Step 2:** Finding percentage
    Max.. size = _____ % [B]

**Step 3:** Calculating max. size
    Max. size = _____ A [C]
            x _____ % [D]
    Max. size = _____ A [E]

**Step 4:** Selecting NTDF's
    Max. size = _____ A [F] NTDF's

**Solution :** The maximum size nontime-delay fuse is _____ amps [G].

**Figure 8-24.** This illustration is an exercise problem for sizing and selecting the maximum size nontime-delay fuses to start and run a motor.

What size time-delay fuses are required to start and run a 40 HP, three-phase, 460 volt, Design B motor? (Determine maximum size)

**Problem 8-25.** Maximum size time-delay fuses required to start and run a motor.

**Step 1:** Finding FLA
        430-6(a)(1); Table 430-150
        40 HP = 52 A

**Step 2:** Finding percentage
        430-52(c)(1), Ex. 2(b); Table 430-152
        Max. size = 225%

**Step 3:** Calculating max. size
        430-52(c)(1), Ex. 2(b)
        Max. size = 52 A x 225%
        Max. size = 117 A

**Step 4:** Selecting TDF's
        Max. size = 110 A

**Solution: The maximum size time-delay fuse is 110 amps.**

See **Figure 8-25** for an exercise problem when sizing and selecting the maximum size time-delay fuses to start and run a motor.

**Figure 8-25.** This illustration is an exercise problem for sizing and selecting the maximum size time-delay fuses to start and run a motor.

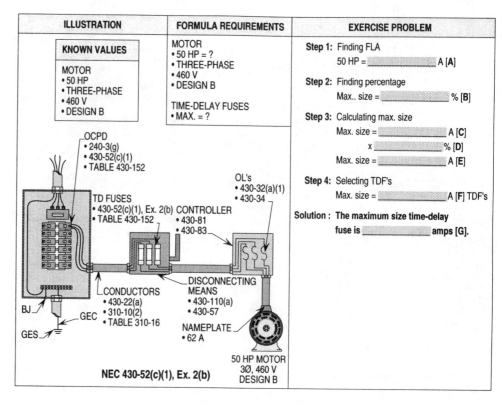

| ILLUSTRATION | FORMULA REQUIREMENTS | EXERCISE PROBLEM |
|---|---|---|

**KNOWN VALUES**

MOTOR
• 50 HP
• THREE-PHASE
• 460 V
• DESIGN B

MOTOR
• 50 HP = ?
• THREE-PHASE
• 460 V
• DESIGN B

TIME-DELAY FUSES
• MAX. = ?

OCPD
• 240-3(g)
• 430-52(c)(1)
• TABLE 430-152

TD FUSES
• 430-52(c)(1), Ex. 2(b)
• TABLE 430-152

CONTROLLER
• 430-81
• 430-83

OL's
• 430-32(a)(1)
• 430-34

CONDUCTORS
• 430-22(a)
• 310-10(2)
• TABLE 310-16

DISCONNECTING MEANS
• 430-110(a)
• 430-57

NAMEPLATE
• 62 A

BJ

GEC

GES

NEC 430-52(c)(1), Ex. 2(b)

50 HP MOTOR
3Ø, 460 V
DESIGN B

**Step 1:** Finding FLA
50 HP = _____ A [A]

**Step 2:** Finding percentage
Max.. size = _____ % [B]

**Step 3:** Calculating max. size
Max. size = _____ A [C]
x _____ % [D]
Max. size = _____ A [E]

**Step 4:** Selecting TDF's
Max. size = _____ A [F] TDF's

**Solution :** The maximum size time-delay fuse is _____ amps [G].

---

**Problem 8-26.** Maximum size inverse time circuit breaker required to start and run a motor.

What size inverse time circuit breaker is required to start and run a 40 HP, three-phase, 460 volt, Design B motor? (Determine maximum size)

**Step 1:** Finding FLA
430-6(a)(1); Table 430-150
40 HP = 52 A

**Step 2:** Finding percentage
430-52(c)(1), Ex. 2(c); Table 430-152
Max. size = 400%

**Step 3:** Calculating max. size
430-52(c)(1), Ex. 2(c)
Max. size = 52 A x 400%
Max. size = 208 A

**Step 4:** Selecting inverse time circuit breaker
Max. size = 200 A

**Solution:** The maximum size inverse time circuit breaker is 200 amps.

See Figure 8-26 for an exercise problem when sizing and selecting the maximum size inverse time circuit breaker to start and run a motor.

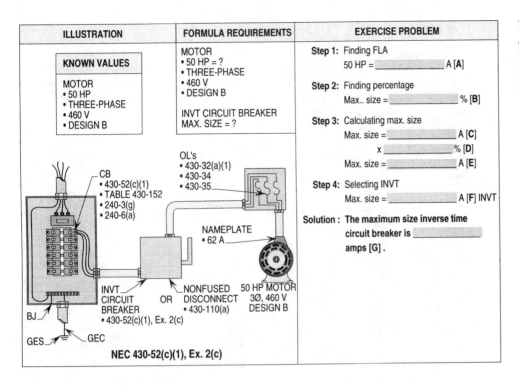

| ILLUSTRATION | FORMULA REQUIREMENTS | EXERCISE PROBLEM |
|---|---|---|
| **KNOWN VALUES** <br><br> MOTOR <br> • 50 HP <br> • THREE-PHASE <br> • 460 V <br> • DESIGN B | MOTOR <br> • 50 HP = ? <br> • THREE-PHASE <br> • 460 V <br> • DESIGN B <br><br> INVT CIRCUIT BREAKER <br> MAX. SIZE = ? | **Step 1:** Finding FLA <br> 50 HP = _____ A [A] <br><br> **Step 2:** Finding percentage <br> Max.. size = _____ % [B] <br><br> **Step 3:** Calculating max. size <br> Max. size = _____ A [C] <br> x _____ % [D] <br> Max. size = _____ A [E] <br><br> **Step 4:** Selecting INVT <br> Max. size = _____ A [F] INVT <br><br> **Solution:** **The maximum size inverse time circuit breaker is** _____ **amps [G]** . |

CB
• 430-52(c)(1)
• TABLE 430-152
• 240-3(g)
• 240-6(a)

OL's
• 430-32(a)(1)
• 430-34
• 430-35

NAMEPLATE
• 62 A

INVT CIRCUIT BREAKER
• 430-52(c)(1), Ex. 2(c)

NONFUSED DISCONNECT
• 430-110(a)

50 HP MOTOR
3Ø, 460 V
DESIGN B

BJ

GES — GEC

**NEC 430-52(c)(1), Ex. 2(c)**

**Figure 8-26.** This illustration is an exercise problem for sizing and selecting the maximum size inverse time circuit breaker to start and run a motor.

---

What size OCPD is required for a feeder-circuit supplying a 10 HP, 15 HP, 20 HP, and 25 HP, three-phase, 460 volt, Design B group of motors?

**Problem 8-27.** Sizing OCPD for two or more motors on a feeder-circuit.

**Step 1:** Finding FLA of motors
430-6(a)(1); Table 430-150
10 HP = 14 A
15 HP = 21 A
20 HP = 27 A
25 HP = 34 A

**Step 2:** Calculating feeder OCPD
430-52(a); Table 430-152; 430-62(a)
34 A x 250%  = 85 A
= 80 A (rounded down)
= 14 A
= 21 A
= 27 A
Total load  = 142 A

**Note:** There are no exceptions to Sec. 430-62(a), which allows a feeder-circuit OCPD to be rounded-up.

**Step 3:** Selecting OCPD
430-62(a); 240-3(g); 240-6(a)
142 A requires 125 A OCPD (rounded down)

**Solution: The size OCPD is 125 amps.**

See **Figure 8-27** for an exercise problem when sizing and selecting the OCPD for two or more motors supplied by a feeder-circuit.

**Figure 8-27.** This illustration is an example problem for sizing and selecting the OCPD for two or more motors.

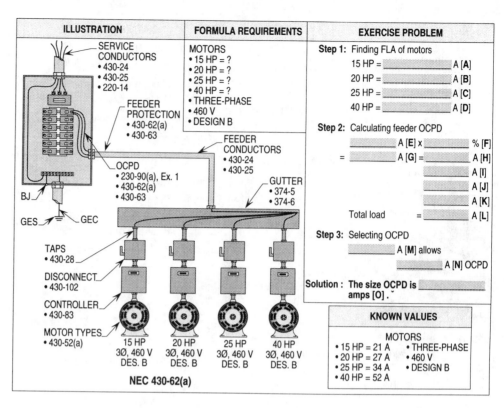

**Problem 8-28.** Minimum size overload protection for a feeder-circuit supplying two or more motors.

What is the minimum overload protection (OLR's) for a 20 HP, three-phase, 460 volt, Design B motor with a nameplate rating of 58 amps, temperature rise of 40°C, and a service factor of 1.15? (Overload relay = OLR)

Step 1: Finding FLA
430-6(a)(2)
Nameplate = 58 A

Step 2: Finding percentage
430-32(a)(1)
SF = 125%
TR = 125%

Step 3: Calculating FLA
430-32(a)(1)
58 A x 125% = 72.5 A

Step 4: Selecting OL relays
430-32(a)(1); 240-6(a)
72.5 A requires 72.5 A

Solution: **The minimum size overload protection is 72.5 amps.**

**See Figure 8-28** for an exercise problem when sizing and selecting the minimum overload protection to protect a motor from overload.

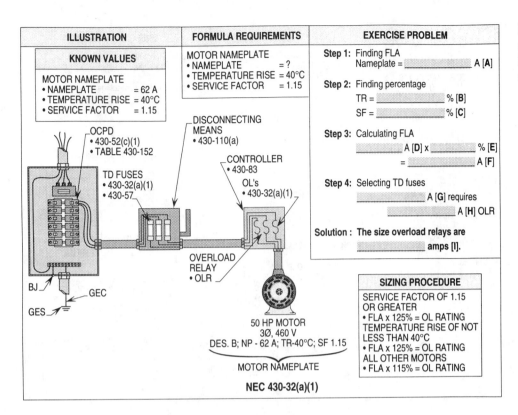

**Figure 8-28.** This illustration is an example problem for sizing and selecting the minimum overload protection.

What is the maximum overload protection (OLR's) for a 20 HP, three-phase, 460 volt, Design B motor with a nameplate rating of 58 amps, temperature rise of 40°C, and a service factor of 1.15? (Overload relay = OLR)

**Problem 8-29.** Maximum size overload protection required to protect a motor from overloads.

**Step 1:** Finding FLA
430-6(a)(2)
Nameplate = 58 A

**Step 2:** Finding percentage
430-34
SF = 140%
TR = 140%

**Note:** When using the maximum size overloads, only overload relays can be used at this greater percentage of 130 or 140 percent.

**Step 3:** Calculating FLA
430-34
58 A x 140% = 81.2 A

**Step 4:** Selecting OL relay
430-34; 240-6(a)
81.2 A requires 80 A

**Solution: The maximum size overload protection is 80 amps.**

**See Figure 8-29** for an exercise problem when sizing and selecting the maximum overload protection to allow a motor to start and run.

**Figure 8-29.** This illustration is an example problem for sizing and selecting the maximum overload protection.

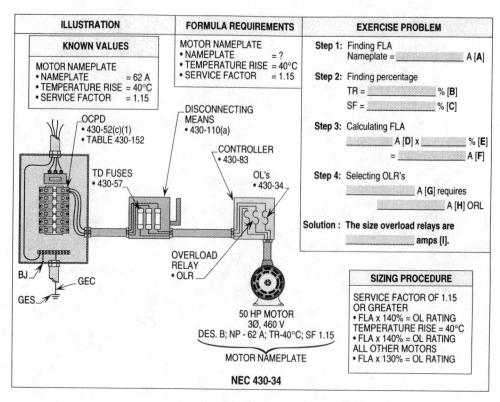

| ILLUSTRATION | FORMULA REQUIREMENTS | EXERCISE PROBLEM |

**KNOWN VALUES**

MOTOR NAMEPLATE
• NAMEPLATE = 62 A
• TEMPERATURE RISE = 40°C
• SERVICE FACTOR = 1.15

OCPD
• 430-52(c)(1)
• TABLE 430-152

TD FUSES
• 430-57

BJ
GEC
GES

DISCONNECTING MEANS
• 430-110(a)

CONTROLLER
• 430-83

OL's
• 430-34

OVERLOAD RELAY
• OLR

50 HP MOTOR
3Ø, 460 V
DES. B; NP - 62 A; TR-40°C; SF 1.15

MOTOR NAMEPLATE

**MOTOR NAMEPLATE**
• NAMEPLATE = ?
• TEMPERATURE RISE = 40°C
• SERVICE FACTOR = 1.15

**Step 1:** Finding FLA
Nameplate = _____ A **[A]**

**Step 2:** Finding percentage
TR = _____ % **[B]**
SF = _____ % **[C]**

**Step 3:** Calculating FLA
_____ A **[D]** x _____ % **[E]**
= _____ A **[F]**

**Step 4:** Selecting OLR's
_____ A **[G]** requires
_____ A **[H]** ORL

**Solution :** The size overload relays are
_____ amps **[I]**.

**SIZING PROCEDURE**

SERVICE FACTOR OF 1.15 OR GREATER
• FLA x 140% = OL RATING
TEMPERATURE RISE = 40°C
• FLA x 140% = OL RATING
ALL OTHER MOTORS
• FLA x 130% = OL RATING

NEC 430-34

# OCPD FOR PHASE CONVERTERS
## 240-3(g)

Phase converters supply conductors for motor related loads and nonmotor related loads which can be protected against overcurrent by the rules and regulations of Sec. 455-7. Before sizing the OCPD for such loads, review Art. 455, which contains different rules than the requirements of Art. 430 for sizing the elements of motor circuits.

**Problem 8-30.** OCPD for phase converters must be sized and selected by the rules and regulations of the NEC.

What size OCPD is required for the phase converter when supplying a 20 HP, three-phase, 230 volt, Design B motor?

Step 1: Finding FLA of motor
430-6(a)(1); Table 430-150
20 HP = 54 A

Step 2: Sizing OCPD
455-7(b)
54 A x 250% = 135 A

Step 3: Selecting OCPD
455-7; 240-3(g); 240-6(a)
135 A requires 150 A

Solution: The OCPD for the phase converter is 150 amps.

See Figure 8-30 for an exercise problem when sizing and selecting the OCPD for phase converters, which will allow the motor to start and run.

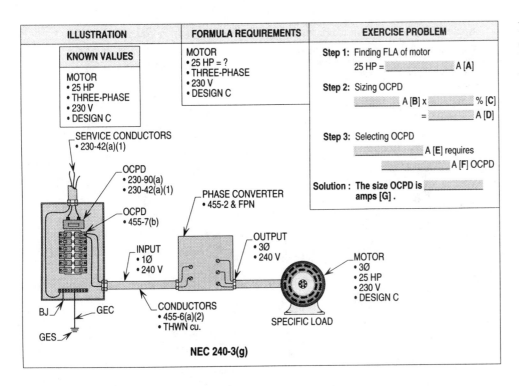

**Figure 8-30.** This illustration is an exercise problem for sizing and selecting the OCPD for phase converters.

# OCPD FOR A/C AND REFRIGERATION EQUIPMENT CIRCUITS 240-3(g)

Circuit conductors that supply air-conditioning and refrigeration equipment shall be protected against overcurrent by the provisions of Parts C and F of Article 440. Note that these rules are used only for hermetically sealed motors and not individual motors per Art. 430.

What is the minimum and maximum size OCPD required for an A/C unit with a compressor load of 21 amps and a condenser load of 1.5 amps?

**Problem 8-31.** An OCPD for A/C and refrigeration equipment circuits must be sized by the rules of the NEC.

**Step 1:** Sizing minimum OCPD
440-22(a)
21 A x 175% + 1.5 A = 38.25 A

**Step 2:** Selecting OCPD
240-3(g); 240-6(a)
38.25 A requires 35 A OCPD

**Step 3:** Sizing maximum OCPD
440-22(a)
21 A x 225% + 1.5 A = 48.75 A
48.75 A requires 45 A OCPD

**Solution:** The minimum size OCPD is 35 amps and the maximum size is 45 amps.

See **Figure 8-31** for an exercise problem when sizing and selecting the minimum and maximum size OCPD for A/C and refrigeration equipment circuits.

**Figure 8-31.** This illustration shows an exercise problem for sizing and selecting the minimum and maximum size OCPD for A/C and refrigeration equipment circuits.

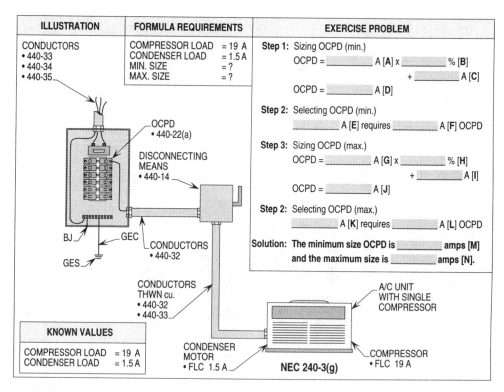

## OCPD FOR ELECTRIC WELDER CIRCUITS 240-3(g)

Circuit conductors supplying welders shall be protected against overcurrent by the provisions of Parts B and C of Article 630. AC transformer and DC rectifier arc welders and conductors are protected per Sec.'s 630-12(a) and (b). Motor-generator arc welders and conductors are protected per Sec.'s 630-12(a) and (b). Resistance welders and conductors are protected per Sec.'s 630-32(a) and (b).

**Problem 8-32.** AC transformer and DC rectifier arc welders with OCPD sized and based upon the ampacity of the conductors supplying the welder.

What size OCPD is required for an AC transformer and DC rectifier arc welder with a 54 amp load and 80 percent duty cycle?

**Step 1:** Finding FLC to size conductors
630-11(a)
Welder = 54 A

**Step 2:** Finding multiplier
Table 630-11(a)
80% = 89%

**Step 3:** Calculating A
630-11(a)
54 A x 89% = 48.06 A

**Step 4:** Selecting conductors
Table 310-16
48.06 requires #8 cu.

**Step 5:** Finding FLC to size disconnect
630-12(a); 630-12(b)
Welder = 54 A

Step 6: Finding multiplier
630-12(a); 630-12(b)
Multiplier = 200%

Step 7: Calculating A for disconnect
630-12(a); 630-12(b)
54 A x 200% = 108 A

Step 8: Selecting OCPD for disconnecting means
240-3(g); 240-6(a); 630-12(a)
108 A requires 100 A

Step 9: Protecting conductors
630-12(b)
#8 THWN cu. = 50 A
50 A x 200% = 100 A
100 A requires 100 A OCPD

Solution: **The size OCPD required for the conductors is 100 amps based upon amps of conductors times 200 percent.**

See **Figure 8-32** for an exercise problem when sizing and selecting the size OCPD required for the conductors supplying an AC transformer and DC rectifier arc welder.

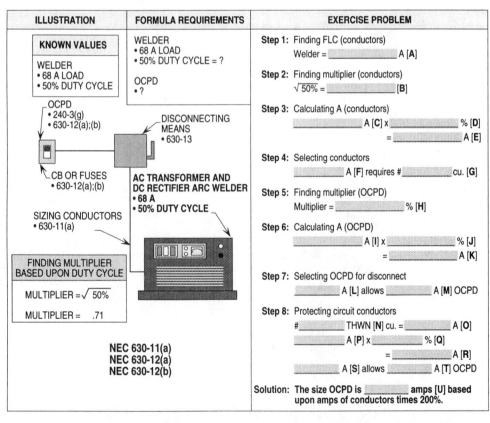

**Figure 8-32.** This illustration is an exercise problem for sizing and selecting the size OCPD required for an AC transformer and DC rectifier arc welder.

What size OCPD is required as a disconnect for a motor-generator arc welder with a 68 amp load and 70 percent duty cycle?

Step 1: Finding FLC
630-11(a); 630-11(b)
Welder = 68 A

**Problem 8-33.** A motor-generator arc welder with OCPD sized and based upon the ampacity (FLA) of the welder.

Step 2: Finding multiplier
630-12(a); 630-12(b)
Multiplier = 200%

Step 3: Calculating A
630-12(a); 630-12(b)
68 A x 200% = 136 A

Step 4: Selecting OCPD for disconnect
240-3(g); 240-6(a); 630-12(a)
136 A requires 125 A

Solution: **The size OCPD required is 125 amps.**

See **Figure 8-33** for an exercise problem when sizing and selecting the size OCPD required for a motor-generator arc welder. Note that OCPD is used as a disconnect.

**Problem 8-34.** Resistance welders with OCPD sized and based upon the ampacity of the conductors.

What size OCPD is required for a resistance welder with an 84 amp load and 50 percent duty cycle?

Step 1: Finding FLC
630-31(a)
Welder = 84 A

Step 2: Finding multiplier
Table 630-31(a)
50% = 71%

Step 3: Calculating A for conductors
630-31(a)
84 A x 71% = 59.64

Step 4: Selecting conductors
Table 310-16
59.64 A requires #6 cu.

Step 5: Finding FLC
630-32(a)
Welder = 84 A

Step 6: Finding multiplier
630-32(a)
Multiplier = 300%

Step 7: Calculating A for disconnect
630-32(a)
84 A x 300% = 252 A

Step 8: Selecting OCPD for disconnecting means
240-3(g); 240-6; 630-32(a)
252 A requires 250 A

**Test Tip 6:** The multiplier for a welder can be found by taking the square root of the demand factor that is listed on the welder's nameplate.

Step 9: Protecting conductors
630-32(b)
#6 THWN cu. = 65 A
65 A x 300% = 195 A
195 A requires 175 A

Solution: **The size OCPD required is 175 amps based upon amps of conductors times 300 percent.**

See **Figure 8-34** for an exercise problem when sizing and selecting the size OCPD required for a resistance welder.

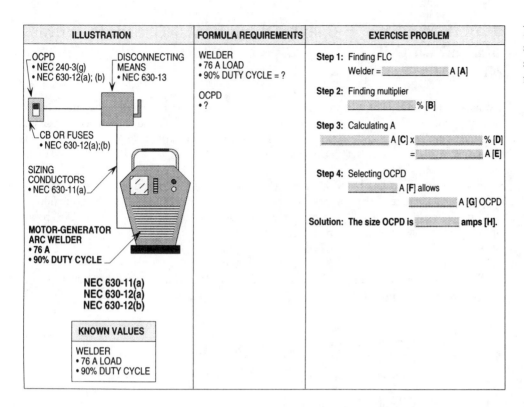

**Figure 8-33.** This illustration is an exercise problem for sizing and selecting the size OCPD required for a motor-generator arc welder.

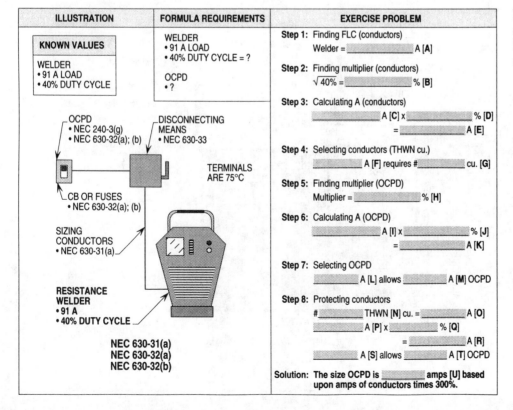

**Figure 8-34.** This illustration is an exercise problem for sizing and selecting the size OCPD required for a resistance welder.

## OCPD FOR REMOTE-CONTROL, SIGNALING, AND POWER-LIMITED CIRCUITS
## 240-3(g)

Remote-control circuits have overcurrent protection, sized up to three times the ampacity of the conductors per Sec. 725-23, Ex.. Motor-control circuits may be fused above their ampacity. A good example of a motor-control circuit is a circuit to a push-button station (start-stop) derived from a magnetic motor controller.

For motor-control circuits, the NEC allows the protection of the control circuit to be sized up to 300 or 400 percent of the ampacity of the control circuit conductors. Such protection is based upon control circuits remaining in the control enclosure or leaving the enclosure to supply a remote feed stop and start station, etc.

**Problem 8-35.** Control circuit conductors installed in the magnetic starter enclosure.

What size branch-circuit OCPD is required for No. 12 control circuit conductors located in the controller?

Step 1: Finding amperage
Table 310-17
No. 12 = 30 A

Step 2: Applying percentage
430-72(b)(2); Table 430-72(b)
30 A x 400% = 120 A

Solution: The size OCPD is 110 amps.

See **Figure 8-35** for an exercise problem when sizing and selecting the size OCPD for control circuits in the enclosure of a magnetic starter or motor control center.

**Figure 8-35.** This illustration is an exercise problem for sizing and selecting the size OCPD for circuits in the enclosure.

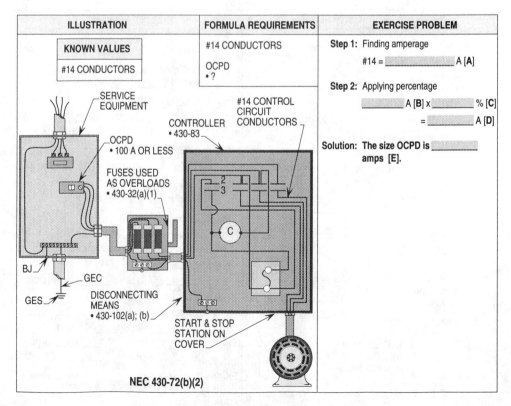

What size branch-circuit OCPD is required for No. 12 control circuit conductors that are run remote?

Step 1: Finding amperage
Table 310-16
No. 12 = 25 A

Step 2: Applying percentage based on OCPD
430-72(b)(2); Table 430-72(b)
20 A x 300% = 60 A

Solution: **The size OCPD is 60 amps.**

See Figure 8-36 for an exercise problem when sizing and selecting the size OCPD for remote control circuits.

**Problem 8-36.** Remote circuits leaving the inside area of the magnetic starter enclosure or motor control center.

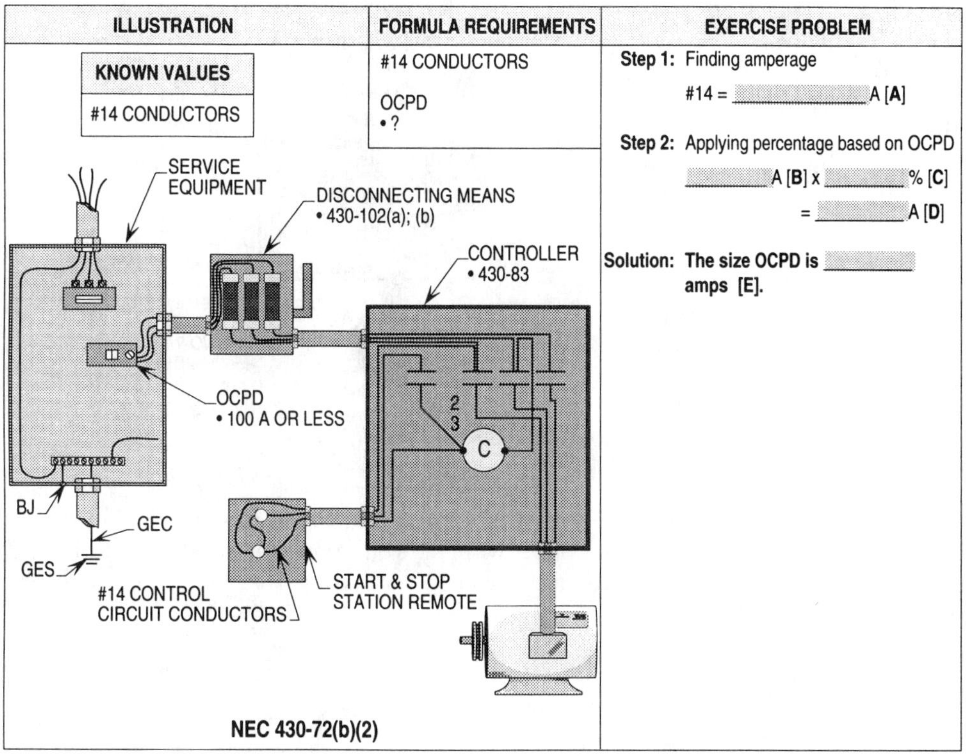

**Figure 8-36.** This illustration is an exercise problem for sizing and selecting the size OCPD for remote control circuits.

What size OCPD is required for an two-wire, 480 volt, 2,400 VA control transformer?

Step 1: Finding amperage
430-72(b), Ex. 2
$I = VA / V$
$I = 2,400 \text{ VA} / 480 \text{ V}$
$I = 5 \text{ A}$

Step 2: Applying percentage
450-3(b); Table 450-3(b)
5 A x 167% = 8.35 A

Step 3: Selecting OCPD
240-6(a)
8.35 A requires 6 A

Solution: **The size OCPD is 6 amps.**

**Problem 8-37.** Installing OCPD in the primary side of a control transformer.

See **Figure 8-37** for an exercise problem for sizing and selecting the size OCPD for the primary circuits of a control transformer.

**Figure 8-37.** This illustration is an exercise problem for sizing and selecting the size OCPD for the primary circuits of a control transformer.

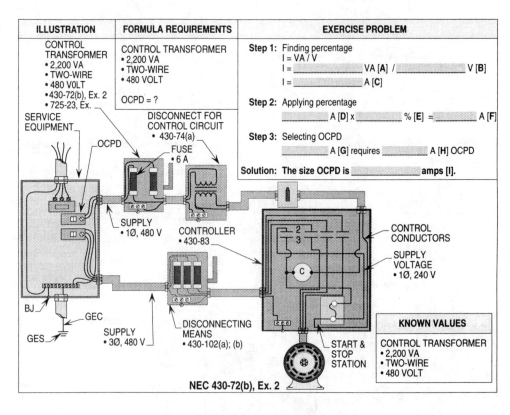

**Problem 8-38.** OCPD installed in the secondary side of a control transformer.

What size OCPD is required for No. 12 control circuit conductors tapped from the secondary side of a control transformer with 480 volt primary and 240 volt secondary? (No. 12 THWN cu. has an ampacity of 25 amps).

Step 1: Finding ratio of transformer
Pri. and Sec.
725-23, Ex.; Table 310-16
Ratio = 240 V Sec. / 480 V Pri. x 25 A
Ratio = 12.5 A

Step 2: Selecting OCPD for control circuit
725-23, Ex.; 240-6(a)
12.5 A requires 10 A

Solution: **The size OCPD is 10 amps.**

See **Figure 8-38** for an exercise problem when sizing and selecting the size OCPD for the secondary side of a control transformer.

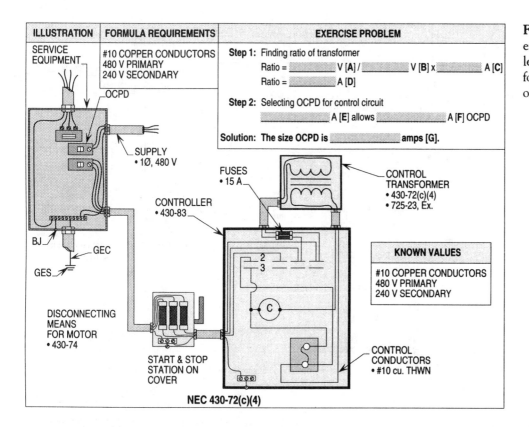

| ILLUSTRATION | FORMULA REQUIREMENTS | EXERCISE PROBLEM |
|---|---|---|
| SERVICE EQUIPMENT | #10 COPPER CONDUCTORS<br>480 V PRIMARY<br>240 V SECONDARY | **Step 1:** Finding ratio of transformer<br>Ratio = _____ V [A] / _____ V [B] x _____ A [C]<br>Ratio = _____ A [D]<br><br>**Step 2:** Selecting OCPD for control circuit<br>_____ A [E] allows _____ A [F] OCPD<br><br>**Solution:** The size OCPD is _____ amps [G]. |

FUSES
• 15 A

CONTROL TRANSFORMER
• 430-72(c)(4)
• 725-23, Ex.

CONTROLLER
• 430-83

**KNOWN VALUES**

#10 COPPER CONDUCTORS
480 V PRIMARY
240 V SECONDARY

SUPPLY
• 1Ø, 480 V

OCPD

BJ

GEC

GES

DISCONNECTING
MEANS
FOR MOTOR
• 430-74

START & STOP
STATION ON
COVER

CONTROL
CONDUCTORS
• #10 cu. THWN

**NEC 430-72(c)(4)**

**Figure 8-38.** This illustration is an exercise problem for sizing and selecting the size OCPD necessary for protecting the secondary side of a control transformer.

# OCPD FOR FIRE ALARM CIRCUITS
## 240-3(g)

Circuit conductors used in fire alarm systems shall be protected against overcurrent conditions by the provisions of Parts B and C of Art. 760. For further information when sizing and selecting OCPD's for fire alarm circuits, see Sec.'s 760-23, 760-24, and 760-41 of the NEC. These circuits are special and such rules and regulations must be studied and well understood.

What size OCPD is required for a No. 16 THWN copper fire-signaling circuit when supplying a detector?

**Problem 8-39.** OCPD for fire alarm circuits must be sized and selected by the rules of the NEC.

**Step 1:** Finding conductor A
760-23; Table 310-16; Table 430-72(b)
#16 cu. = 10 A

**Step 2:** Selecting OCPD
Table 310-16; 760-23
10 A requires 10 A OCPD

**Solution: The size OCPD is 10 amps.**

See Figure 8-39 for an exercise problem when sizing and selecting the size OCPD for fire alarm circuits.

**Figure 8-39.** This illustration is an exercise problem for sizing and selecting the size OCPD for fire alarm circuits.

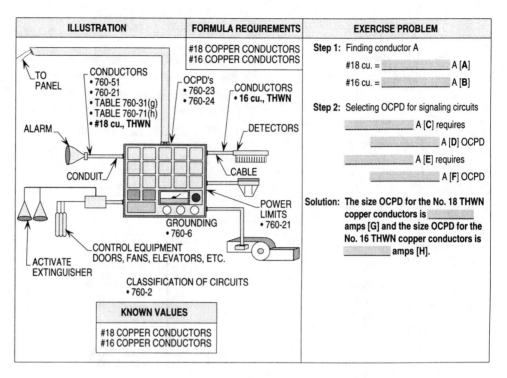

| ILLUSTRATION | FORMULA REQUIREMENTS | EXERCISE PROBLEM |
|---|---|---|

FEEDER REQUIREMENTS:
#18 COPPER CONDUCTORS
#16 COPPER CONDUCTORS

TO PANEL

CONDUCTORS
• 760-51
• 760-21
• TABLE 760-31(g)
• TABLE 760-71(h)
• #18 cu., THWN

ALARM

CONDUIT

OCPD's
• 760-23
• 760-24

CONDUCTORS
• 16 cu., THWN

DETECTORS

CABLE

POWER LIMITS
• 760-21

GROUNDING
• 760-6

CONTROL EQUIPMENT
DOORS, FANS, ELEVATORS, ETC.

ACTIVATE EXTINGUISHER

CLASSIFICATION OF CIRCUITS
• 760-2

**KNOWN VALUES**
#18 COPPER CONDUCTORS
#16 COPPER CONDUCTORS

**Step 1:** Finding conductor A

#18 cu. = _____ A [A]

#16 cu. = _____ A [B]

**Step 2:** Selecting OCPD for signaling circuits

_____ A [C] requires

_____ A [D] OCPD

_____ A [E] requires

_____ A [F] OCPD

**Solution:** The size OCPD for the No. 18 THWN copper conductors is _____ amps [G] and the size OCPD for the No. 16 THWN copper conductors is _____ amps [H].

# FEEDER-CIRCUIT PROTECTION - OVER 600 VOLTS 240-100

For short-circuit protection of high-voltage feeders, the fuse rating may be increased up to three times the conductor ampacity. Circuit breaker setting may be increased up to six times the conductor ampacity.

**Problem 8-40.** Circuit breakers sized and selected to protect high-voltage systems rated over 600 volts.

What size OCPD is required for three No. 1/0 alu. conductors (Type MV-90) with a three-phase supply voltage of 12,470 volts?

**Step 1:** Finding cable ampacity
Table 310-74 (90°C)
No. 1/0 alu. = 150 A

**Step 2:** Calculating CB rating
240-100
150 A x 600% = 900 A

**Solution:** The circuit breaker setting is 900 amps.

See **Figure 8-40** for an exercise problem when sizing and selecting the circuit breaker setting.

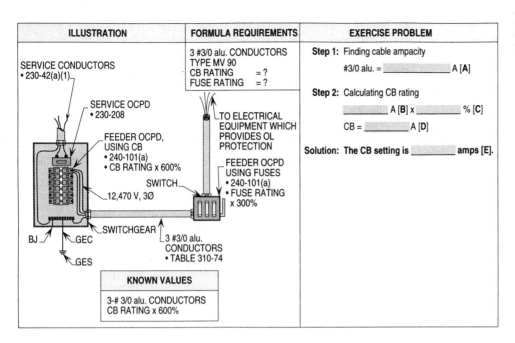

**Figure 8-40.** This illustration is an exercise problem for sizing and selecting the circuit breaker setting.

What size fuses are required for three No. 1/0 alu. conductors (Type MV-90) with a three-phase supply voltage of 12,470 volts?

**Problem 8-41.** Fuses sized and selected to protect high-voltage conductors rated over 600 volts.

     **Step 1:** Finding cable ampacity
            Table 310-74 (90°)
            No. 1/0 alu. = 150 A

     **Step 2:** Calculating fuse rating
            240-101(a)
            150 A x 300% = 450 A

     **Solution: The fuse rating is 450 amps.**

See **Figure 8-41** for an exercise problem when sizing and selecting the size fuse ratings.

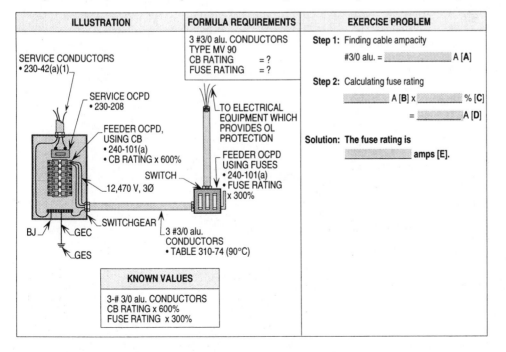

**Figure 8-41.** This illustration is an exercise problem for sizing and selecting the size fuse ratings.

# Chapter 8
## Overcurrent Protection Devices

| Section | Answer | |
|---|---|---|
| _____ | T    F | 1. If the standard current ratings of fuses or nonadjustable circuit breakers do not conform to the ampacity of the conductors being used, it is permissible, to use the next larger standard rating when below 800 amps. |
| _____ | T    F | 2. Taps over 10 ft. and up to 25 ft. in length must be equal to 1/3 of the feeder OCPD rating. |
| _____ | T    F | 3. The minimum size nontime-delay fuse shall be sized at 250 percent to start and run a motor. |
| _____ | T    F | 4. The minimum size instantaneous trip circuit shall be sized at 1,100 percent to start and run a Design E motor. |
| _____ | T    F | 5. The maximum size time-delay fuse shall be sized at 250 percent to start and run a motor. |
| _____ | T    F | 6. The maximum size inverse time circuit breaker shall be sized at 300 percent to start and run a motor, if full load current is less than 100 amps. |
| _____ | T    F | 7. The maximum size OCPD for an A/C unit shall be sized at 225 percent. |
| _____ | T    F | 8. Two-wire to two-wire transformers can be protected by the primary OCPD. |
| _____ | T    F | 9. Where the rated primary current of a transformer is less than 2 amperes, an overcurrent protection device rated or set at not more than 400 percent shall be permitted. |
| _____ | T    F | 10. The OCPD for an AC transformer and DC rectifier arc welder shall be rated or set at not more than 200 percent of the rated primary current of the welder. |
| _____ _____ | | 11. The junction box for taps up to 100 ft. in length must be at least _____ ft. from the finished floor. |
| _____ _____ | | 12. The minimum size time-delay fuse shall be sized at _____ percent to start and run a motor. |
| _____ _____ | | 13. The minimum size inverse time circuit breaker shall be sized at _____ percent to start and run a motor. |
| _____ _____ | | 14. The maximum size nontime-delay fuse shall be sized at _____ percent to start and run a motor. |
| _____ _____ | | 15. The minimum size OCPD for an A/C unit shall be sized at _____ percent. |
| _____ _____ | | 16. Where the rated primary current is more than 2 amperes but less than 9 amperes, an overcurrent protection device rated or set at not more than _____ percent of the primary current shall be permitted. |
| _____ _____ | | 17. The OCPD for an resistance welder shall be rated or set at not more than _____ percent of the rated primary current of the welder. |
| _____ _____ | | 18. Circuit breakers shall be sized at _____ percent to protect feeder-circuits in high-voltage systems rated over 600 volts. (maximum setting) |

———————  ———————  19. Fuses shall be sized at _____ percent to protect feeder-circuits in high-voltage systems rated over 600 volts.

———————  ———————  20. The branch-circuit OCPD for No. 12 control circuit conductors located in the controller shall be sized at _____ percent of the conductor's ampacity.

———————  ———————  21. What size OCPD is required for a branch-circuit with a continuous load 18.6 amps with 75°C terminals? (round up calculation)

———————  ———————  22. What size OCPD is required for a branch-circuit with a continuous load of 120 amps with 75°C terminals?

———————  ———————  23. What size OCPD is required for a feeder-circuit with a continuous load of 652 amps which is paralleled 4 times and terminated to 75°C terminals?

———————  ———————  24. What size OCPD is required for a 10 ft. tap from a junction box which is supplied by a feeder-circuit with a 400 amp OCPD?

———————  ———————  25. What size OCPD is required for a 25 ft. tap from a junction box which is supplied by a feeder-circuit with a 400 amp OCPD?

———————  ———————  26. What size secondary tap OCPD (max) is required for a tap including transformer which is supplied from a feeder-circuit with a 350 amp OCPD having a 480 volt primary and 208 volt secondary?

———————  ———————  27. What size OCPD is required for a 100 ft. tap which is supplied from a feeder-circuit with a 400 amp OCPD? (Size tap for primary side)

———————  ———————  28. What size OCPD is required for a motor circuit tap from a junction box which is supplied from a feeder-circuit with a 400 amp OCPD?

———————  ———————  29. What size OCPD is required for a connection of 25 ft. from the secondary of 100 kVA transformer which is supplied by a 150 amp OCPD with a three-phase, 480 volt primary and 208 volt secondary? (Do not exceed secondary output with OCPD)

———————  ———————  30. What size OCPD is required for a motor-operated appliance with a continuous branch-circuit load of 15 amps?

———————  ———————
———————  31. What is the minimum and next size nontime-delay fuses required to start and run a 30 HP, three-phase, 230 volt, Design B motor?

———————  ———————
———————  32. What is the minimum and next size time-delay fuses required to start and run a 30 HP, three-phase, 460 volt, Design B motor?

———————  ———————
———————  33. What is the minimum and maximum setting instantaneous trip circuit breaker required to start and run a 30 HP, three-phase, 460 volt, Design E motor?

———————  ———————
———————  34. What is the minimum and next size inverse time circuit breaker required to start and run a 30 HP, three-phase, 208 volt, Design B motor?

———————  ———————  35. What is the maximum size nontime-delay fuses required to start and run a 30 HP, three-phase, 230 volt, Design B motor?

———————  ———————  36. What is the maximum size time-delay fuses required to start and run a 30 HP, three-phase, 460 volt, Design B motor?

———————  ———————  37. What is the maximum size inverse time circuit breaker required to start and run a 30 HP, three-phase, 208 volt, Design B motor?

38. What size OCPD (CB) is required for a feeder-circuit supplying a 5 HP, 10 HP, 15, HP, and 20 HP, three-phase, 230 volt, Design B motors?

39. What size OCPD (CB) is required for a feeder-circuit supplying a 20 HP, 30 HP, and 40 HP, three-phase, 460 volt, Design B motor?

40. What is the minimum overload protection (OLR's) for a 40 HP, three-phase, 460 volt, Design B motor with a nameplate rating of 45 amps, temperature rise of 40°C, and a service factor of 1.15?

41. What is the maximum overload protection (OLR's) for a 40 HP, three-phase, 460 volt, Design B motor with a nameplate rating of 45 amps, temperature rise 40°C, and a service factor of 1.15?

42. What size OCPD is required for the phase converter when supplying an 25 HP, three-phase, 230 volt, Design B motor?

43. What is the minimum size OCPD required for an A/C unit with a compressor load of 24 amps and a condenser load of 2.5 amps?

44. What is the minimum size OCPD required for an A/C unit with a compressor load of 32 amps and a condenser load of 3 amps?

45. What is the maximum size OCPD required for an A/C unit with a compressor load of 24 amps and a condenser load of 2.5 amps?

46. What is the maximum size OCPD required for an A/C unit with a compressor load of 32 amps and a condenser load of 3 amps?

47. What size OCPD is required for a single-phase, 480 volt primary and 240 volt secondary, two-wire to two-wire system with No. 1/0 THWN copper conductors?

48. What size OCPD is required for a three-phase, 480 volt primary and 240 volt secondary, three-wire to three-wire system with No. 400 KCMIL copper conductors?

49. What size individual OCPD (circuit breaker) is required for the primary side of a 1,500 kVA transformer with a three-phase supply voltage of 12,470 volts? (Impedance is 4.9%)

50. What size OCPD (circuit breaker) is required for a three-phase, 4,160 volt primary and 480 volt secondary for a 450 kVA transformer with a 5.9 percent impedance in a nonsupervised location?

51. What size OCPD (circuit breaker) is required for a three-phase, 4,160 volt primary and 480 volt secondary for a 450 kVA transformer with a 5.9 percent impedance in a supervised location? (Dont apply FPN to 240-6)

52. What size OCPD (circuit breaker) is required for a single-phase, 240 volt primary and 120 volt secondary for a 20 kVA transformer? (Primary protection only)

53. What size OCPD is required for a 480 volt, single-phase, two-wire to two-wire 3 kVA transformer?

54. What is the minimum and maximum size OCPD required for a 480 volt, single-phase, two-wire to two-wire .6 kVA transformer?

55. What size OCPD is required for a 480 volt primary and 240 volt secondary, three-phase, 30 kVA transformer? (Using the maximum size in the primary side).

56. What size OCPD is required to protect the conductors for an AC transformer and DC rectifier arc welder with a 62 amp load and 90 percent duty cycle?

57. What size OCPD is required for an motor-generator arc welder with a 58 amp load and 80 percent duty cycle? (Size as a disconnect for welder)

58. What size OCPD is required for a resistance welder with an 78 amps load and 40 percent duty cycle? (Size to protect conductors)

59. What size branch-circuit OCPD (maximum) is required for No. 14 control circuit conductors located in controller?

60. What size branch-circuit OCPD (maximum) is required for No. 14 control circuit conductors that are run remote?

61. What size OCPD is required for an two-wire, 480 volt, 2,800 VA control transformer?

62. What size OCPD is required for No. 14 control circuit conductors tapped from the secondary side of a control transformer with 480 volt primary and 240 volt secondary?

63. What size OCPD is required for a No. 18 THWN copper fire-signaling circuit when supplying a detector?

64. What size OCPD is required for three No. 3/0 alu. conductors with a three-phase supply voltage of 12,470 volts? (Feeder-circuit)

65. What size fuses are required for three No. 3/0 alu. conductors with a three-phase supply voltage of 12,470 volts? (Feeder-circuit)

# Residential Calculations

9

**Quick Reference:**

APPLYING THE STANDARD CALCULATION .. 9-2

DEMAND FACTORS ......................................... 9-2

STANDARD CALCULATION ............................ 9-14

OPTIONAL CALCULATION .............................. 9-16

APPLYING THE STANDARD

CALCULATION FOR MULTIFAMILY ................. 9-17

MULTIFAMILY - STANDARD

CALCULATION ................................................ 9-18

APPLYING THE OPTIONAL

CALCULATION FOR MULTIFAMILY ................. 9-20

MULTIFAMILY - OPTIONAL

CALCULATION ................................................ 9-20

APPLYING THE STANDARD

CALCULATION FOR FEEDER TO MOBILE

HOMES ........................................................... 9-21

FEEDER TO MOBILE HOME -

STANDARD CALCULATION ............................ 9-22

APPLYING THE OPTIONAL

CALCULATION FOR MOBILE HOME

PARK SERVICE AND FEEDERS ..................... 9-22

MOBILE HOME PARK SERVICE AND

FEEDERS - OPTIONAL CALCULATION .......... 9-24

SIZING ELEMENTS ......................................... 9-25

Residential calculations are the most difficult to perform, due to the rules and regulations of the NEC being more restrictive than those for commercial or industrial facilities. The standard or optional calculation can be used to compute the loads to size and select the elements of the feeder or service. The optional calculation seems to be the favorite of the designers and electricians. This is true, because once loads are calculated, it produces smaller VA or amps than the longer complicated standard calculation method. Therefore, smaller components are required in the electrical system and greater savings in wiring methods are achieved. The procedure for laying out residential calculations will be different, in some ways, than those used for commercial and industrial.

When using the standard calculation, there are six loads to be found. Four of the loads, under certain conditions of use, can have demand factors applied. The optional calculation consist of two computed loads. Each load is calculated and demand factors applied as approximate. For test takers to pass the Journeyman Electrician examination, they must be capable of computing such loads properly.

## APPLYING THE STANDARD CALCULATION
## PART B TO ART. 220

**Test Tip 1:** The total VA for general lighting and receptacle loads are derived by multiplying the square footage by 3 VA and applying demand factors, where appropriate.

Residential occupancies are known in the electrical industry as dwelling units. This chapter mainly deals with computing loads for one and two family dwelling units.

When using the standard calculation method for computing loads for a residential occupancy, all loads are divided into three groups and four columns. The groups are as follows:

    Group 1: General lighting and receptacle loads
    Group 2: Small appliance loads
    Group 3: Special appliance loads

## DEMAND FACTORS
## PART B TO ART. 220

**Test Tip 2:** The small appliance circuits can be added to the VA per square foot calculation and demand factors applied.

The following four loads are separated into two columns of loads and demand factors are applied, as permitted by the NEC:

    Column 1: General lighting and receptacle loads and small appliance loads
        Table 220-11

    Column 2: Cooking equipment loads        220-19, Table 220-19
        Fixed appliance loads                220-17
        Dryer loads                          220-18, Table 220-18

    **Note:** For columns 3 and 4, see pages 9-10 and 9-11.

**Test Tip 3:** Cooking equipment loads can have demand factors applied based upon the number of units.

General lighting and receptacle loads and the small appliance circuits plus laundry circuit can have demand factors applied based upon square footage and number.

The total number of fixed appliance loads can have demand factors applied, according to the number of units. The total number of ranges and dryers in a dwelling unit may be reduced by a percentage.

## GENERAL LIGHTING AND RECEPTACLE LOADS AND
## SMALL APPLIANCE PLUS LAUNDRY LOADS
## COLUMN 1 - TABLE 220-11; 220-16(a); (b)

**Test Tip 4:** When there are four or more fixed appliances, a demand factor of 75 percent can be applied to the total VA.

The general lighting load for a dwelling unit is computed by multiplying the square footage by 3 VA per sq. ft. per Table 220-3(b). The required square footage per unit load (volt-amps) is found in Table 220-3(b). All small appliance and laundry loads are computed at 1,500 VA per Sec. 220-16(a) and (b). A demand factor is permitted per Table 220-11. The demand factors for the general lighting and receptacle loads per Table 220-11 for dwelling units are as follows:

| Volt-amps | |
|---|---|
| 0 - 3,000 | 100% |
| 3,001 - 120,000 | 35% |
| 120,001 + | 25% |

Compute the demand load for the general lighting load for a 2,800 sq. ft. dwelling unit?

**Example Problem 9-1.** Finding the general lighting and receptacle loads and the small appliance plus laundry loads.

### Column 1 and Demand load 1

**Step 1:** General lighting load
Table 220-3(a)
2,800 sq. ft. x 3 VA        = 8,400 VA

**Step 2:** Small appliance load
220-16(a)
1,500 VA x 2        = 3,000 VA

**Step 3:** Laundry load
220-16(b)
1,500 VA x 1        = 1,500 VA

**Test Tip 5:** For four or less dryers, the total VA must be calculated at 100 percent with no demand factors applied.

**Step 4:** Total load
General lighting load        = 8,400 VA
Small appliance load        = 3,000 VA
Laundry load        = 1,500 VA
Total load        = 12,900 VA

**Step 5:** Applying demand factors
Table 220-11
First 3,000 VA x 100%        = 3,000 VA
Next 9,900 VA x 35%        = 3,465 VA
Total load        = 6,465 VA

**Solution:** **Demand load 1 requires 6,465 VA for the general lighting and receptacle loads including the small appliance plus laundry loads.**

**See Figure 9-1** for an exercise problem when determining the general-purpose lighting and receptacle loads including the small appliance plus laundry loads.

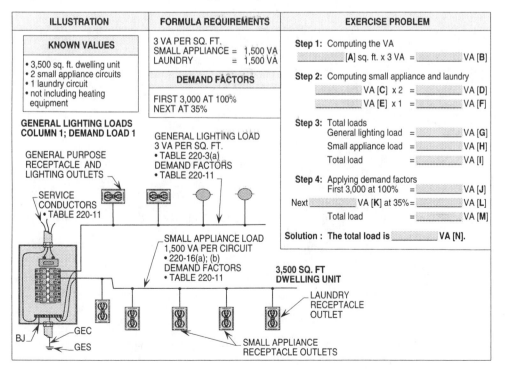

**Figure 9-1.** This figure illustrates an exercise problem for determining the general-purpose lighting and receptacle loads including the small appliance plus laundry loads.

## COOKING EQUIPMENT LOADS
## COLUMN 2 - 220-19; TABLE 220-19

The cooking equipment loads and Demand load 2 are separated from Group 3 and placed in Column 2 and demand factors applied accordingly.

The demand factors listed in Table 220-19 apply to the demand loads for cooking equipment. The Footnotes are based on the kW rating and number of units. Ranges, wall-mounted ovens, and counter-mounted cooktops are units of cooking equipment per Table 220-19.

**Example Problem 9-2.** Finding cooking equipment loads based upon number of units.

What is the demand load for a 12 kW and 10 kW cooking unit?

**Column 2 and Demand load 2**

Step 1: Computing kVA
Table 220-19, Col. A
12 kW and 10 kW = 11 kVA

**Solution: Col. A allows 11 kVA for the two cooking units.**

See Figure 9-2 for an exercise problem of demand loads that can be applied per Table 220-19, Col. A, based upon the size and number of units.

**Figure 9-2.** This figure illustrates an exercise problem for demand loads that can be applied per Table 220-19, Col. A.

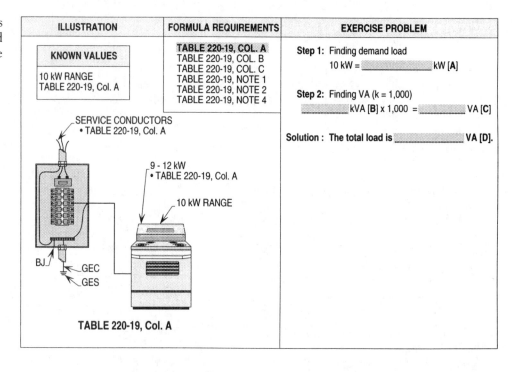

**Example Problem 9-3.** Finding cooking equipment loads based upon number of units.

What is the demand load for a piece of cooking equipment with a 2.5 kW rating?

**Column 2 and Demand load 2**

Step 1: Computing the kVA
Table 220-19, Col. B
2.5 kW x 80% = 2 kVA

**Solution: Col. B allows 2 kVA for the cooking equipment.**

See **Figure 9-3** for an exercise problem for the demand loads to be applied per Table 220-19, Col. B, based upon the size and number of units.

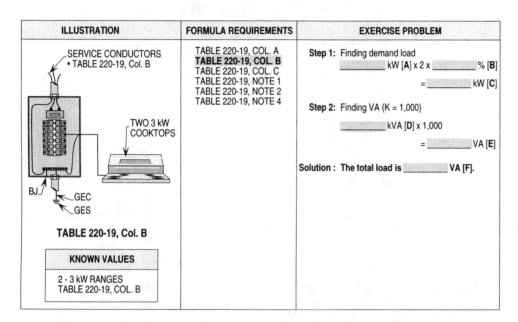

| ILLUSTRATION | FORMULA REQUIREMENTS | EXERCISE PROBLEM |
|---|---|---|
| SERVICE CONDUCTORS • TABLE 220-19, Col. B<br><br>TWO 3 kW COOKTOPS<br><br>BJ GEC GES<br><br>**TABLE 220-19, Col. B**<br><br>**KNOWN VALUES**<br>2 - 3 kW RANGES<br>TABLE 220-19, COL. B | TABLE 220-19, COL. A<br>**TABLE 220-19, COL. B**<br>TABLE 220-19, COL. C<br>TABLE 220-19, NOTE 1<br>TABLE 220-19, NOTE 2<br>TABLE 220-19, NOTE 4 | **Step 1:** Finding demand load<br>_____ kW [A] x 2 x _____ % [B]<br>= _____ kW [C]<br><br>**Step 2:** Finding VA (K = 1,000)<br>_____ kVA [D] x 1,000<br>= _____ VA [E]<br><br>**Solution :** The total load is _____ VA [F]. |

**Figure 9-3.** This figure illustrates an exercise problem for demand loads that can be applied per Table 220-19, Col. B.

What is the demand load for a piece of cooking equipment with a 8.5 kW rating?

**Column 2 and Demand load 2**

**Step 1:** Computing the kVA
Table 220-19, Col. C
8.5 kW x 80% = 6.8 kVA

**Solution: Col. C allows 6.8 kVA for the cooking equipment.**

**Example Problem 9-4.** Finding cooking equipment loads based upon the number of units.

See **Figure 9-4** for an exercise problem of the demand loads to be applied per Table 220-19, Col. C, based upon the size and number of units.

| ILLUSTRATION | FORMULA REQUIREMENTS | EXERCISE PROBLEM |
|---|---|---|
| SERVICE CONDUCTORS • TABLE 220-19, Col. C<br><br>8 3/4 kW OVEN<br><br>BJ GEC GES<br><br>**TABLE 220-19, Col. C**<br><br>**KNOWN VALUES**<br>8 3/4 kW OVEN<br>TABLE 220-19, COL. C | TABLE 220-19, COL. A<br>TABLE 220-19, COL. B<br>**TABLE 220-19, COL. C**<br>TABLE 220-19, NOTE 1<br>TABLE 220-19, NOTE 2<br>TABLE 220-19, NOTE 4 | **Step 1:** Finding demand load<br>_____ kW [A] x _____ % [B]<br>= _____ kW [C]<br><br>**Step 2:** Finding VA (K = 1,000)<br>_____ kVA [D] x 1,000<br>= _____ VA [E]<br><br>**Solution :** The total load is _____ VA [F]. |

**Figure 9-4.** This figure illustrates an exercise problem for demand loads that can be applied per Table 220-19, Col. C.

**Example Problem 9-5.** Finding cooking equipment loads based upon the size and number of units.

What is the demand load for a range with a 25 kW rating?

**Column 2 and Demand load 2**

Step 1: Computing the percentage
Table 220-19, Note 1
25 kW - 12 kW = 13 kW
13 kW x 5% = 65%

Step 2: Computing the kVA
Table 220-19, Col. A
8 kW x 165% = 13.2 kVA

**Solution: Col. C allows 13.2 kVA for the range.**

See **Figure 9-5** for an exercise problem of the demand loads to be applied per Table 220-19, Note 1, based upon the size and number of units.

**Figure 9-5.** This figure illustrates an exercise problem for demand loads that can be applied per Table 220-19, Note 1.

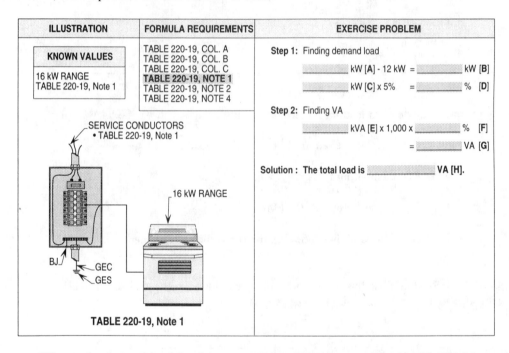

**Example Problem 9-6.** Finding cooking equipment loads based upon the size and number of units.

What is the demand load for three pieces of cooking equipment with a 12 kW, 14 kW, and 20 kW rating?

**Column 2 and Demand load 2**

Step 1: Computing the percentage
Table 220-19, Note 2
12 kW + 14 kW + 20 kW = 46 kW
Average rating
46 kW / 3 = 15.3 (round up)
16 kW - 12 kW = 4 kW
4 kW x 5% = 20%

Step 2: Computing the kVA
Table 220-19, Col. A
14 kW x 120% = 16.8 kVA

**Solution: Note 2 allows 16.8 kVA demand load for three pieces of cooking equipment.**

See **Figure 9-6** for an exercise problem of the demand loads to be applied per Table 220-19, Note 2, based upon the size and number of units.

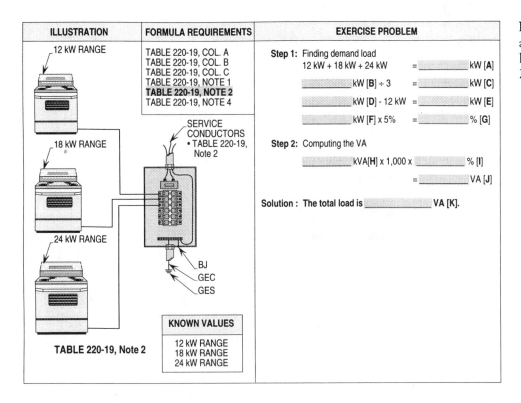

| ILLUSTRATION | FORMULA REQUIREMENTS | EXERCISE PROBLEM |
|---|---|---|

12 kW RANGE

18 kW RANGE

24 kW RANGE

**TABLE 220-19, Note 2**

TABLE 220-19, COL. A
TABLE 220-19, COL. B
TABLE 220-19, COL. C
TABLE 220-19, NOTE 1
**TABLE 220-19, NOTE 2**
TABLE 220-19, NOTE 4

SERVICE CONDUCTORS
• TABLE 220-19, Note 2

BJ
GEC
GES

**KNOWN VALUES**

12 kW RANGE
18 kW RANGE
24 kW RANGE

**Step 1:** Finding demand load

12 kW + 18 kW + 24 kW = _____ kW [A]

_____ kW [B] ÷ 3 = _____ kW [C]

_____ kW [D] - 12 kW = _____ kW [E]

_____ kW [F] x 5% = _____ % [G]

**Step 2:** Computing the VA

_____ kVA[H] x 1,000 x _____ % [I]

= _____ VA [J]

**Solution :** The total load is _____ VA [K].

**Figure 9-6.** This figure illustrates an exercise problem for demand loads that can be applied per Table 220-19, Note 2.

What is the branch-circuit demand load for a 12 kW cooktop and two 6 kW ovens installed in a dwelling unit?

**Example Problem 9-7.** Finding cooking equipment loads based upon the size and number of units.

**Column 2 and Demand load 2**

**Step 1:** Computing the percentage
Table 220-19, Note 4
12 kW + 6 kW + 6 kW = 24 kW
24 kW - 12 kW = 12 kW
12 kW x 5% = 60%

**Step 2:** Computing the kVA
Table 220-19, Col. A
8 kW x 160% = 12.8 kVA

**Solution:** Note 4 allows 12.8 kVA demand load for one cooktop and two ovens.

See **Figure 9-7** for an exercise problem of the demand loads to be applied per Table 220-19, Note 4, based upon the size and number of units.

**Figure 9-7.** This figure illustrates an exercise problem for demand loads that can be applied per Table 220-19, Note 4.

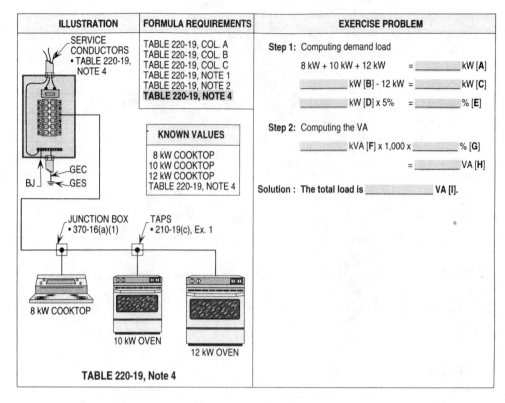

| ILLUSTRATION | FORMULA REQUIREMENTS | EXERCISE PROBLEM |
|---|---|---|

SERVICE CONDUCTORS
• TABLE 220-19, NOTE 4

TABLE 220-19, COL. A
TABLE 220-19, COL. B
TABLE 220-19, COL. C
TABLE 220-19, NOTE 1
TABLE 220-19, NOTE 2
**TABLE 220-19, NOTE 4**

**KNOWN VALUES**

8 kW COOKTOP
10 kW COOKTOP
12 kW COOKTOP
TABLE 220-19, NOTE 4

BJ ┘ ⏚ ← GEC
⏚ ← GES

JUNCTION BOX
• 370-16(a)(1)

TAPS
• 210-19(c), Ex. 1

8 kW COOKTOP

10 kW OVEN

12 kW OVEN

**TABLE 220-19, Note 4**

**Step 1:** Computing demand load

8 kW + 10 kW + 12 kW = _____ kW [A]

_____ kW [B] - 12 kW = _____ kW [C]

_____ kW [D] x 5% = _____ % [E]

**Step 2:** Computing the VA

_____ kVA [F] x 1,000 x _____ % [G]

= _____ VA [H]

**Solution :** The total load is _____ VA [I].

# DRYER LOAD
## COLUMN 2 - 220-18; TABLE 220-18

The demand load for a household dryer is computed at 5 kVA or the nameplate rating, whichever is greater. Dryer equipment of four or less is calculated at 100 percent of the nameplate rating. Dryer equipment of five or more dryers can have a percentage applied based on the number of units per Table 220-18.

**Example Problem 9-8(a).** Finding the dryer load based upon the size and number of units.

What is the demand load for a 4 kW dryer?

**Column 2 and Demand load 3**

**Step 1:** Computing the kW
220-18
4 kW = 5 kW

**Step 2:** Applying demand factors
Table 220-18
Four or fewer dryers = 100%
5 kW x 100% = 5 kVA

**Solution:** Table 220-18 allows 5 kVA demand load for the dryer.

What is the demand load for 5 dryers rated at 8,000 VA each?

**Example Problem 9-8(b).** Finding the dryer load based upon the size and number of units.

**Column 2 and Demand load 3**

Step 1: Selecting percentage
220-18; Table 220-18
5 dryers = 80%

Step 2: Applying demand factors
Table 220-18
8,000 VA x 5 x 80% = 32,000 VA

Solution: Table 220-18 allows 32,000 VA demand load for 5 dryers.

See Figure 9-8 for an exercise problem of demand factors to be applied per Sec. 220-18 and Table 220-18 based upon the size and number of units.

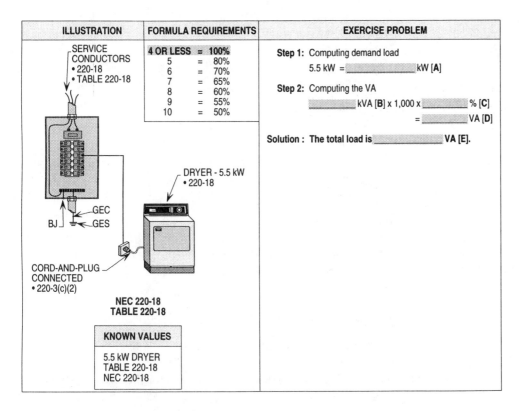

**Figure 9-8.** This figure illustrates an exercise problem for demand factors to be applied per Sec. 220-18 and Table 220-18.

# FIXED APPLIANCE LOADS
## COLUMN 2 - 220-17

Fixed appliances of four or more grouped into the special appliance load are found by adding wattage ratings from appliance nameplates and multiplying the total wattage (volt-amps) by 75 percent to obtain demand load. Three or less fixed appliance loads are calculated at 100 percent to determine the total VA.

**Test Tip 6:** Three or less fixed appliances must be calculated at 100 percent of their total VA.

**Column 2 and Demand load 4**

**Example Problem 9-9.** Finding fixed appliance loads based upon the size and number of units.

What is the demand load for the following fixed appliances.

| | |
|---|---|
| 6,000 VA A/C | 240 volt, single-phase |
| 10,000 VA heating unit | 240 volt, single-phase |
| 5,000 VA water heater | 240 volt, single-phase |
| 8,000 VA oven | 240 volt, single-phase |
| 8,500 VA cooktop | 240 volt, single-phase |
| 2,600 VA water pump | 240 volt, single-phase |
| 1,000 VA disposal | 120 volt, single-phase |
| 1,200 VA compactor | 120 volt, single-phase |
| 1,600 VA dishwasher | 120 volt, single-phase |
| 1,000 VA microwave | 120 volt, single-phase |
| 5,000 VA dryer | 240 volt, single-phase |
| 800 VA blower motor | 240 volt, single-phase |

**Test Tip 7:** A demand factor of 75 percent can be applied to four or more fixed appliances installed in a dwelling unit.

**Step 1:** Special appliance loads
Removing the following loads
220-17
Heating load
• 10,000 VA heating unit
Air-conditioning load
• 6,000 VA A/C unit
Dryer load
• 5,000 VA dryer
Cooking equipment load
• 8,000 VA oven
• 8,500 VA cooktop

**Test Tip 8:** No demand factor can be applied to three or less fixed appliances.

**Step 2:** Totaling the VA
220-17

| | | |
|---|---|---|
| Water heater load | 5,000 | VA |
| Water pump load | 2,600 | VA |
| Disposal load | 1,000 | VA |
| Compactor load | 1,200 | VA |
| Dishwasher load | 1,600 | VA |
| Microwave load | 1,000 | VA |
| Blower motor load | 800 | VA |
| Total load     = | 13,200 | VA |

**Step 3:** Applying demand factors
220-17
13,200 VA x 75% = 9,900 VA

**Solution:** Sec. 220-17 allows 9,900 VA demand load for the fixed appliance loads.

See **Figure 9-9** for an exercise problem of demand factors to be applied per Sec. 220-17.

# LARGEST LOAD BETWEEN HEAT AND A/C
# COLUMN 3 - 220-21

Section 220-21 is applied when determining the largest load between heat and A/C. The heating and A/C loads are computed at 100 percent and the smaller of the two loads is dropped.

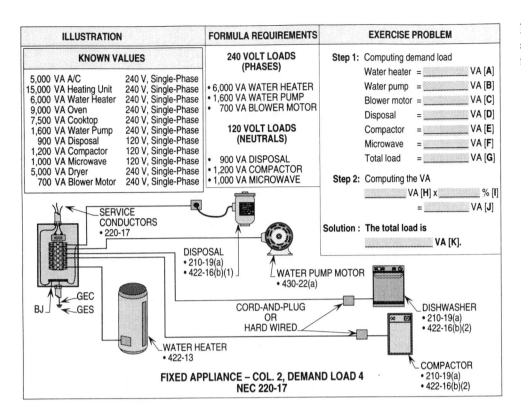

Figure 9-9. This figure illustrates an exercise problem for demand factors to be applied per Sec. 220-17.

What is the load for a 10 kW heating unit and a 5.5 kW A/C unit installed in a dwelling unit?

Example Problem 9-10. Finding largest load between the heat and A/C, based upon the size of each unit.

**Column 3**

Step 1: Computing the VA
220-21
Heating load
10 kW x 100% = 10 kVA
A/C load
5.5 kW x 100% = 5.5 kVA

Solution: Sec. 220-21 requires 10 kVA load to be used for the largest load between the heating and A/C load.

Note: Where it is unlikely that two or more noncoincident loads will be in use simultaneously, it shall be permissible to use only the largest load(s) that will be used at one time, in computing the total load of a service.

See Figure 9-10 for an exercise problem of demand factors to be applied per Sec. 220-21.

## LARGEST MOTOR LOAD
## COLUMN 4 - 220-14

The motor's total full-load current rating is computed at 25 percent per Sec. 220-14, which is required per Sec.'s 430-24 and 430-25, for computing the load of one or more motors with other loads. See Sec. 430-22(a) where one motor is involved.

Test Tip 9: The largest motor load can be selected from the A/C unit load, if not dropped, or from one of the fixed appliance motors.

**Figure 9-10.** This figure illustrates an exercise problem for demand factors to be applied per Sec. 220-21.

Note that an attic fan motor is considered a noncoincident load and is dropped per Sec. 220-21.

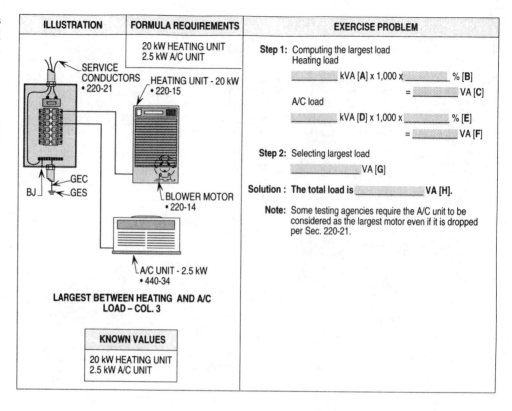

| ILLUSTRATION | FORMULA REQUIREMENTS | EXERCISE PROBLEM |
|---|---|---|

**Example Problem 9-11.** Finding the largest motor load based upon the largest motor that is eligible to be used.

What is the VA load for a 3 HP, 230 volt, single-phase motor which is to be used for the largest load?

**Column 4**

**Step 1:** Finding FLA
Table 430-148
3 HP = 17 A

**Step 2:** Calculating VA
220-14; 430-22(a); 430-24
17 A x 25% = 4.25 A

**Step 3:** Text
4.25 A x 240 V = 1,020 VA

**Test Tip 10:** The largest motor load must be computed for both the phases and the neutrals.

**Solution:** Sec. 220-14 requires 1,020 VA load to be used for the largest motor load.

**See Figures 9-11(a) and (b)** for exercise problems of the demand factors to be applied in Sec. 220-14 to determine the largest motor load.

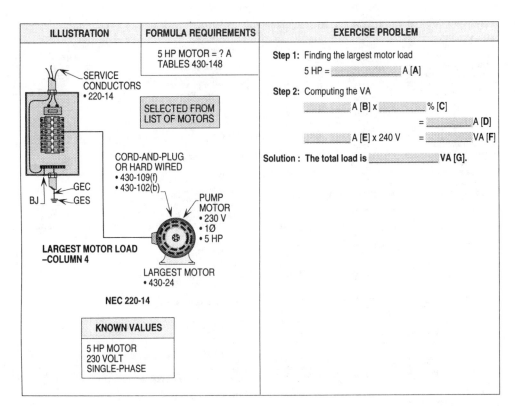

**Figure 9-11(a).** This figure illustrates an exercise problem for demand factors to be applied in Sec. 220-14 when finding the VA for a single-phase, 230 volt motor.

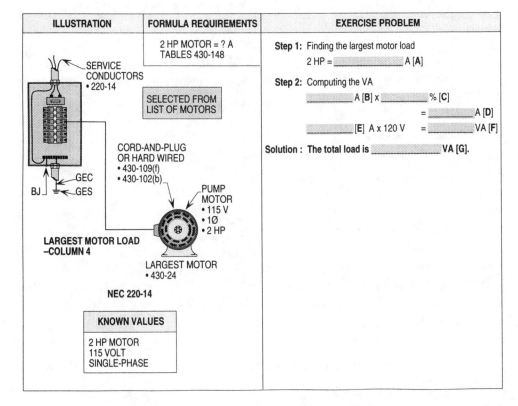

**Figure 9-11(b).** This figure illustrates an exercise problem for demand factors to be applied in Sec. 220-14 when finding the VA for a single-phase, 115 volt motor.

Example Problem 9-12. What is the load in VA and amps for a residential dwelling unit with the following loads?

| | |
|---|---|
| **Given Loads:** | **240 V, single-phase loads** |
| General lighting and receptacle load | • 6,000 VA A/C unit |
| • 2,800 sq. ft. dwelling unit | • 10,000 VA heating unit |
| • 2 small appliance circuits | • 5,000 VA water heater |
| • 1 laundry circuit | • 12,000 VA oven |
| | • 16,000 VA cooktop |
| **120 V, single-phase loads** | • 5,000 VA dryer |
| | • 800 VA blower motor |
| • 2,600 VA water pump | |
| • 1,000 VA disposal | |
| • 1,200 VA compactor | |
| • 1,600 VA dishwasher | |
| • 1,000 VA microwave | |

Sizing phases = •
Sizing neutral = √

**Form Tip 1:** Column 1 consist of the general lighting and receptacle load and small appliance plus laundry load.

**Column 1**
**Calculating general lighting and receptacle load**

Step 1: General lighting and receptacle load
Table 220-3(a)
2,800 sq. ft. x 3 VA       =       8,400   VA

Step 2: Small appliance and laundry load
220-16(a); (b)
1,500 VA x 2       =       3,000   VA
1,500 VA x 1       =       1,500   VA
Total load       =       4,500   VA

Step 3: Applying demand factors
Table 220-11
General lighting load       =       8,400   VA
Small appliance load       =       3,000   VA
Laundry load       =       1,500   VA
Total load       =       12,900   VA

First 3,000 VA x 100%       =       3,000   VA
Next 9,900 VA x 35%       =       3,465   VA
Total load       =       6,465   VA • √

**Column 2**
**Calculating cooking equipment load**

Step 1: Applying demand factors
Table 220-19, Note 2
Total kW rating
12 kW + 16 kW       =       28   kW
28 kW - 12 kW       =       16   kW
16 kW x 5%       =       80%
Table 220-19, Col. A
Total kVA rating
8 kW x 180% x 1,000       =       14,400   VA •

**Calculating fixed appliance load**

Step 1: Applying demand factors
220-17
Water heater       =       5,000   VA
Water pump       =       2,600   VA √
Disposal       =       1,000   VA √
Compactor       =       1,200   VA √
Dishwasher       =       1,600   VA √
Microwave       =       1,000   VA √
Blower motor       =       800   VA
Total load       =       13,200   VA
13,200 VA x 75%       =       9,900   VA •

**Calculating dryer load**

Step 1: Applying demand factors
220-18; Table 220-18
5,000 VA x 100%       =       5,000   VA •

**Column 3**
**Largest load between heating or A/C**

Step 1: Selecting the largest load
220-21
Heating load
10,000 VA x 100%       =       10,000   VA •

**Column 4**
**Calculating largest motor load**

Step 1: Selecting largest motor load
220-14
Water pump
2,600 VA x 25%       =       650   VA •

**Total VA loads (phases)**

General lighting load       =       6,465   VA •

Cooking equipment       =       14,400   VA •
Fixed appliance load       =       9,900   VA •
Dryer load       =       5,000   VA •
Heating load       =       10,000   VA •
Largest motor load       =       650   VA •
Six total loads       =       46,415   VA

**Finding amps**

I = VA / V
I = 46,415 VA / 240 V
I = 193 A

**Total VA loads (neutral)**

**Column 1**
**General lighting load and demand load 1**

220-22
6,465 VA √       =       6,465   VA √

**Column 2**
**Cooking equipment load and demand load 2**

(Use 70% of cooking load)
220-22
14,400 VA x 70%       =       10,080   VA √

**Column 2**
**Fixed appliance load and demand load 3**

(Use 75% of 120 volt load)
220-17
Water pump       =       2,600   VA
Disposal       =       1,000   VA
Compactor       =       1,200   VA
Dishwasher       =       1,600   VA
Microwave       =       1,000   VA
Total load       =       7,400   VA
7,400 VA x 75%       =       5,550   VA √

**Column 2**
**Dryer load and demand load 4**

(Use 70% of dryer load)
220-22
5,000 VA x 70%       =       3,500   VA √

**Column 4**
**Largest motor load**

(Use 25% of largest motor load)
2,600 VA x 25%       =       650   VA √

**Total VA loads (neutral)**

General lighting load       =       6,465   VA √
Cooking equipment load       =       10,080   VA √
Dryer load       =       3,500   VA √
Fixed appliance load       =       5,550   VA √
Largest motor load       =       650   VA √
Five total loads       =       26,245   VA

**Finding amps**

I = VA / V
I = 26,245 VA / 240 V
I = 109 A

**Finding conductor size**

Table 310-16 and 310-15(b)(6)
Phases A and B  #3/0 THWN copper
310-15(b)(6) allows  #2/0 THWN copper
Neutral #2 THWN copper

**Form Tip 2:** Column 2 consist of the cooking equipment load and fixed appliance load plus dryer load.

**Form Tip 3:** Column 3 is the largest between the heating or the A/C load.

**Form Tip 4:** Column 4 consist of the largest motor load.

See Figure 9-12 for an exercise problem for calculating the loads of a dwelling unit using the standard calculation.

**Exercise Problem 9-12. What is the load in VA and amps for a residential dwelling unit with the following loads?**

**Given loads:**

**General lighting and receptacle load**

- 2,500 sq. ft. dwelling unit
- 2 small appliance circuits
- 1 laundry circuit

**120 V, single-phase loads**

- 2,600 VA water pump
- 1,000 VA disposal
- 1,200 VA compactor
- 1,600 VA dishwasher

**240 V, single-phase loads**

- 5,000 VA dryer
- 6,000 VA A/C unit
- 20,000 VA heating unit
- 6,000 VA water heater
- 10,000 VA oven
- 9,000 VA cooktop
- 800 VA blower motor
- 1,000 VA water pump

**Column 1**
**Calculating general lighting and receptacle load**

**Step 1:** General lighting and receptacle load
Table 220-3(a)
2,500 sq. ft. x 3 VA = _____ VA [A]

**Step 2:** Small appliance and laundry load
220-16(a); (b)
1,500 VA x 2 = _____ VA [B]
1,500 VA x 1 = _____ VA [C]
Total load = _____ VA [D]

**Step 3:** Applying demand factors
Demand load 1; Table 220-11
First 3,000 VA x 100% = 3,000 VA
Next 9,000 VA x 35% = _____ VA [E]
Total load = _____ VA [F] • √

**Column 2**
**Calculating cooking equipment load**

**Step 1:** Applying demand factors for phases
Demand load 2; Table 220-19, Col. A
9 kW and 10 kW = _____ VA [G] •

**Step 2:** Applying demand factors for neutral
220-22
11,000 VA x 70% = _____ VA [H] √

**Column 2**
**Calculating dryer load**

**Step 1:** Applying demand factors for phases
Demand load 3; Table 220-18
5,000 VA x 100% = _____ VA [I] •

**Step 2:** Applying demand factors for neutral
220-22
5,000 VA x 70% = _____ VA [J] √

**Column 2**
**Calculating fixed appliance load**

**Step 1:** Applying demand factors for phases
Demand load 4; 220-17
2,600 VA x 75% = _____ VA [K]
1,000 VA x 75% = _____ VA [L]
1,200 VA x 75% = _____ VA [M]
1,600 VA x 75% = _____ VA [N]
800 VA x 75% = _____ VA [O]
1,000 VA x 75% = _____ VA [P]
6,000 VA x 75% = _____ VA [Q]
Total load = _____ VA [R] •

**Step 2:** Applying demand factors for neutral
Demand load 4; 220-22; 220-17
2,600 VA x 75% = _____ VA [S]
1,000 VA x 75% = _____ VA [T]
1,200 VA x 75% = _____ VA [U]
1,600 VA x 75% = _____ VA [V]
Total load = _____ VA [W] √

**Column 3**
**Largest load between heating and A/C load**

**Step 1:** Selecting largest load
Demand load 5; 220-21
Heating unit
20,000 VA x 100% = _____ VA [X] •

**Column 4**
**Calculating largest motor load**

**Step 1:** Selecting largest motor load for phases
220-14; 430-24
2,600 VA x 25% = _____ VA [Y] •

**Step 2:** Selecting largest motor load for neutral
220-14; 430-24
2,600 VA x 25% = _____ VA [Z] √

**Calculating phases (six loads)**

- General lighting load = _____ VA [AA] •
- Cooking equipment load = _____ VA [BB] •
- Dryer load = _____ VA [CC] •
- Appliance load = _____ VA [DD] •
- Heating load = _____ VA [EE] •
- Largest motor load = _____ VA [FF] •
Six total loads = _____ VA [GG]

**Calculating neutral (five loads)**

- General lighting load = _____ VA [HH] √
- Cooking equipment load = _____ VA [II] √
- Dryer load = _____ VA [JJ] √
- Appliance load = _____ VA [KK] √
- Largest motor load = _____ VA [LL] √
Five total loads = _____ VA [MM]

**Finding amps for phases**

I = VA / V
I = _____ VA [NN] / 240 V
I = _____ A [OO]

**Finding amps for neutral**

I = VA / V
I = _____ VA [PP] / 240 V
I = _____ A [QQ]

**Finding conductor size**

Table 310-16 and 310-15(b)(6)
Phases A and B # _____ THWN copper [RR]
310-15(b)(6) allows # _____ THWN copper [SS]
Neutral _____ THWN copper [TT]

**Figure 9-12.** The above is an exercise problem for calculating the loads of a dwelling unit when applying the standard calculation.

**Example Problem 9-13.** What is the load in VA and amps for a residential dwelling unit with the following loads? (See standard calculation in Example Problem 9-12 for sizing the neutral.)

| | |
|---|---|
| **Given Loads:** | **240 V, single-phase loads** |

**Sizing phases = •**

**General lighting and receptacle load**
- 2,800 sq. ft. dwelling unit
- 2 small appliance circuits
- 1 laundry circuit

**240 V, single-phase loads**
- 6,000 VA A/C unit
- 10,000 VA heating unit
- 5,000 VA water heater
- 12,000 VA oven
- 16,000 VA cooktop
- 5,000 VA dryer
- 800 VA blower motor

**120 V, single-phase loads**
- 2,600 VA water pump
- 1,000 VA disposal
- 1,200 VA compactor
- 1,600 VA dishwasher
- 1,000 VA microwave

**Column 1**
**Other loads**

**Step 1:** General lighting load
Table 220-3(a)
2,800 sq. ft. x 3 VA    =    8,400   VA

**Step 2:** Small appliance and laundry load
220-16(a); (b)
1,500 VA x 2    =    3,000   VA
1,500 VA x 1    =    1,500   VA

**Step 3:** Appliance load
Table 220-30(b)(3); (4)

| | | | |
|---|---|---|---|
| Water heater | = | 5,000 | VA |
| Oven | = | 12,000 | VA |
| Cooktop | = | 16,000 | VA |
| Water pump | = | 2,600 | VA |
| Disposal | = | 1,000 | VA |
| Compactor | = | 1,200 | VA |
| Dishwasher | = | 1,600 | VA |
| Microwave | = | 1,000 | VA |
| Dryer | = | 5,000 | VA |
| Blower motor | = | 800 | VA |
| Total load | = | 59,100 | VA |

**Step 4:** Applying demand load
220-30(b)

| | | | |
|---|---|---|---|
| First 10,000 VA x 100% | = | 10,000 | VA |
| Next 49,100 VA x 40% | = | 19,640 | VA |
| Total load | = | 29,640 | VA • |

**Column 2**
**Largest load between heating and A/C load**

**Step 5:** Selecting largest load
220-30(c)(1); (2); (4)

| | | | |
|---|---|---|---|
| Heating load = 10,000 VA x 1 x 65% | = | 6,500 | VA • |
| A/C load = 6,000 VA x 1 x 100% | = | 6,000 | VA |
| Total load | = | 6,500 | VA • |

**Totaling Column 1 and 2**
**220-30(b); (c)**

| | | | |
|---|---|---|---|
| Col. 1 ld. | = | 29,640 | VA • |
| Col. 2 ld. | = | 6,500 | VA • |
| Total load | = | 36,140 | VA |

**Finding amps for phases**

I = VA / VA
I = 36,140 VA / 240 V
I = 151 A

**Finding maximum conductor size**

Table 310-16
Phases A and B   #2/0 THWN copper
Neutral #2 THWN copper

**Note:** Section 310-15(b)(6) allows No. 1/0 THWN copper conductors (min. size) to be used for the phases.

See **Figure 9-13** for an exercise problem when calculating the loads of a dwelling unit using the optional calculation.

**Exercise Problem 9-13. What is the load in VA and amps for a residential dwelling unit with the following loads? (See Standard Calculation in Exercise Problem 9-12 for sizing the neutral)**

**Given loads:**

**General lighting and receptacle load**

• 2,500 sq. ft. dwelling unit
• 2 small appliance circuits
• 1 laundry circuit

**120 V, single-phase loads**

• 2,600 VA water pump
• 1,000 VA disposal
• 1,200 VA compactor
• 1,600 VA dishwasher

**240 V, single-phase loads**

• 5,000 VA dryer
• 6,000 VA A/C unit
• 20,000 VA heating unit
• 6,000 VA water heater
• 10,000 VA oven
• 9,000 VA cooktop
• 800 VA blower motor
• 1,000 VA water pump

**Sizing phases = •**

**Column 1**
**Other loads**

**Step 1:** General lighting load
Table 220-3(a)
2,500 sq. ft. x 3 VA    = _____ VA [A]

**Step 2:** Small appliance and laundry load
220-16(a); (b)
1,500 VA x 2    = _____ VA [B]
1,500 VA x 1    = _____ VA [C]

**Step 3:** Appliance load
220-30(b)(3); (4)
Cooktop load    = _____ VA [D]
Oven load    = _____ VA [E]
Dryer load    = _____ VA [F]
Water heater load    = _____ VA [G]
Disposal load    = _____ VA [H]
Compactor load    = _____ VA [I]
Dishwasher load    = _____ VA [J]
Water pump load    = _____ VA [K]
Blower motor load    = _____ VA [L]
Water pump load    = _____ VA [M]
Total load    = _____ VA [N]

**Step 4:** Applying demand load
220-30(b)
First 10,000 VA x 100%    = _____ VA [O]
Next 40,200 VA x 40%    = _____ VA [P]
Total load    = _____ VA [Q] •

**Column 2**
**Largest load between heating and A/C load**

**Step 5:** Selecting largest load
220-30(c)(1); (2); (4)
Heating load = 20,000 VA x 1 x 65%    = _____ VA [R] •
A/C load = 6,000 VA x 1 x 100%    = _____ VA [S]
Total load    = _____ VA [T] •

**Totaling Column 1 and 2**
**220-30(b); (c)**

Col. 1 ld.    = _____ VA [U]
Col. 2 ld.    = _____ VA [V] •
Total load    = _____ VA [W]

**Finding amps for phases**

$I = VA / V$

$I =$ _____ VA [X] / 240 V
$I =$ _____ A [Y]

**Finding conductor size**

Table 310-16
Phases A and B # _____ THWN [Z] copper
Neutral # _____ THWN [AA] copper

**Figure 9-13.** The above is an exercise problem for calculating the loads of a dwelling unit when applying the optional calculation.

## APPLYING THE STANDARD CALCULATION FOR MULTIFAMILY DWELLING UNITS
## PART B AND C TO ART. 220

When applying the standard calculation for multifamily dwelling units, the loads are computed the same as using the standard calculation for one family dwellings. The only difference is to compute the loads of each unit and multiply the total number of dwelling units and pieces of electrical equipment together to derive the total VA or amps to size the elements of the service or feeder-circuit.

**Example Problem 9-14.** What is the load in VA and amps for 25 multifamily dwelling units with the following loads? Note: Parallel service conductors, 6 times per phase.

| Given loads: | 240 V, single-phase loads | Sizing phases = •<br>Sizing neutral = √ |
|---|---|---|

**Given loads:**

• 25 - 1,000 sq. ft. dwelling units
• 2 small appliance circuits per unit
• 1 laundry circuit per unit

**120 V, single-phase loads**

• 25 - 1,000 VA dishwashers
• 25 - 1,200 VA disposals

**240 V, single-phase loads**

• 25 - 12,000 VA ranges
• 25 -  6,000 VA water heaters
• 25 - 20,000 VA heating units
• dryer facilities furnished by
  apartment complex

**Sizing phases = •**
**Sizing neutral = √**

---

**Column 1**
**Calculating general lighting and receptacle load**

**Step 1:** General lighting and receptacle load
Table 220-3(a)
1,000 sq. ft. x 3 VA x 25     =     75,000  VA

**Step 2:** Small appliance and laundry load
220-16(a); (b)
1,500 VA x 2 x 25     =     75,000  VA
1,500 VA x 1 x 25     =     37,500  VA
Total load     =     187,500  VA

**Step 3:** Applying demand factors
Demand load 1; Table 220-11
First 3,000 VA x 100%     =     3,000  VA
Next 117,000 VA x 35%     =     40,950  VA
Remaining 67,500 VA x 25% =     16,875  VA
Total load     =     60,825  VA • √

**Column 2**
**Calculating cooking equipment load**

**Step 1:** Applying demand factors for phases
Demand load 2; Table 220-19, Col. A
25 - 12,000 VA ranges     =     40,000  VA •

**Step 2:** Applying demand factors for neutral
220-22
40,000 VA x 70%     =     28,000  VA √

**Column 2**
**Calculating fixed appliance load**

**Step 1:** Applying demand factors for phases
Demand load 4; 220-17
1,000 VA x 25 x 75%     =     18,750  VA
1,200 VA x 25 x 75%     =     22,500  VA
6,000 VA x 25 x 75%     =     112,500  VA
Total load     =     153,750  VA •

**Step 2:** Applying demand factors for neutral
Demand load 4; 220-22
1,000 VA x 25 x 75%     =     18,750  VA
1,200 VA x 25 x 75%     =     22,500  VA
Total load     =     41,250  VA √

**Column 3**
**Largest load between heating and A/C load**

**Step 1:** Selecting largest load
Demand load 5; 220-21
Heating unit
20,000 VA x 25 x 100%     =     500,000  VA •

**Column 4**
**Calculating largest motor load**

**Step 1:** Selecting largest motor load for phases
220-14; 430-24
1,200 VA x 25%     =     300  VA •

**Step 2:** Selecting largest motor load for neutral
220-14; 430-24
1,200 VA x 25%     =     300  VA √

**Calculating phases**

General lighting load     =     60,825  VA •
Cooking equipment load     =     40,000  VA •
Appliance load     =     153,750  VA •
Heating load     =     500,000  VA •
Largest motor load     =     300  VA •
Five total loads     =     754,875  VA

**Calculating neutral**

General lighting load     =     60,825  VA √
Cooking equipment load     =     28,000  VA √
Appliance load     =     41,250  VA √
Largest motor load     =     300  VA √
Four total loads     =     130,375  VA

**Finding amps for phases**

I = VA / V
I = 754,875 VA / 240 V
I = 3,145 A

**Finding amps for neutral**

I = VA / V
I = 130,375 VA / 240 V
I = 543 A

**Finding conductors**

Phases A and B
310-4
I = 3,145 / 6 (No. run per phase)
I = 524 A

**Neutral**
220-22

543 A
First 200 A x 100%     =     200  A
Next 343 A x 70%     =     240  A
Total load     =     440  A
310-4
I = 440 A / 6 (No. run per phase)
I = 73 A (#1/0 per 310-4)

**Sizing conductors (6 per phase)**

Phases A and B  #1,000 KCMIL THWN copper
Neutral #1/0 THWN copper

---

**See Figure 9-14** for an exercise problem when calculating the loads of a multifamily dwelling unit using the standard calculation.

Exercise Problem 9-14. What is the load in VA and amps for 20 multifamily dwelling units with the following loads? Note: Parallel service conductors, 6 times per phase.

**Given loads:**

- 20 - 1,200 sq. ft. dwelling units
- 2 small appliance circuits per unit
- 1 laundry circuit per unit

**120 V, single-phase loads**

- 20 - 1,600 VA dishwashers
- 20 - 1,200 VA disposals

**240 V, single-phase loads**

- 20 - 10,000 VA ranges
- 20 -  5,000 VA water heaters
- 20 - 20,000 VA heating units
- Dryer facilities furnished by apartment complex

Sizing phases = •
Sizing neutral = √

**Column 1**
**Calculating general lighting and receptacle load**

Step 1:   General lighting and receptacle load
Table 220-3(a)
1,200 sq. ft. x 3 VA x 20        = _____ VA [A]

Step 2:   Small appliance and laundry load
220-16(a); (b)
1,500 VA x 2 x 20        = _____ VA [B]
1,500 VA x 1 x 20        = _____ VA [C]
Total load        = _____ VA [D]

Step 3:   Applying demand factors
Demand load 1; Table 220-11
First 3,000 VA x 100%        =        3,000  VA
Next 117,000 VA x 35%        = _____ VA [E]
Remaining 42,000 VA x 25%=        _____ VA [F]
Total load        = _____ VA [G] • √

**Column 2**
**Calculating cooking equipment load**

Step 1:   Applying demand factors for phases
Demand load 2; Table 220-19, Col. A
20 - 10,000 VA ranges        = _____ VA [H] •

Step 2:   Applying demand factors for neutral
220-22
35,000 VA x 70%        = _____ VA [I] √

**Column 2**
**Calculating fixed appliance load**

Step 1:   Applying demand factors for phases
Demand load 4; 220-17
1,600 VA x 20 x 75%        = _____ VA [J]
1,200 VA x 20 x 75%        = _____ VA [K]
5,000 VA x 20 x 75%        = _____ VA [L]
Total load        = _____ VA [M] •

Step 2:   Applying demand factors for neutral
Demand load 4; 220-22
1,600 VA x 20 x 75%        = _____ VA [N]
1,200 VA x 20 x 75%        = _____ VA [O]
Total load        = _____ VA [P] √

**Column 3**
**Largest load between heating and A/C load**

Step 1:   Selecting largest load
Demand load 5; 220-21
Heating unit
20,000 VA x 20 x 100%        = _____ VA [Q] •

**Column 4**
**Calculating largest motor load**

Step 1:   Selecting largest motor load for phases
220-14; 430-24
1,200 VA x 25%        = _____ VA [R] •

Step 2:   Selecting largest motor load for neutral
220-14; 430-24
1,200 VA x 25%        = _____ VA [S] √

**Calculating phases**

- General lighting load        = _____ VA [T] •
- Cooking equipment load        = _____ VA [U] •
- Appliance load        = _____ VA [V] •
- Heating load        = _____ VA [W] •
- Largest motor load        = _____ VA [X] •
- Five total loads        = _____ VA [Y]

**Calculating neutral**

- General lighting load        = _____ VA [Z] √
- Cooking equipment load        = _____ VA [AA] √
- Appliance load        = _____ VA [BB] √
- Largest motor load        = _____ VA [CC] √
- Four total loads        = _____ VA [DD]

**Finding amps for phases**

I = VA / V
I = _____ VA [EE] / 240 V
I = _____ A [FF]

**Finding amps for neutral**

I = VA / V
I = _____ VA [GG] / 240 V
I = _____ A [HH]

**Finding conductors**

Phases A and B
310-4
I = _____ A [II] / 6
I = _____ A [JJ]

**Neutral**
220-22

_____ A [KK]
First 200 A x 100%        =        200  A
Next 305 A x 70%        = _____ A [LL]
Total load        = _____ A [MM]

**310-4**

I = _____ A [NN] / 6
I = _____ A [OO]

**Table 310-16**

Phases A and B
#_____ KCMIL [PP] THWN copper conductors
Neutral
#_____ KCMIL [QQ] copper conductor

**Figure 9-14.** The above is an exercise problem for calculating the load of a multifamily dwelling unit when applying the standard calculation.

# APPLYING THE OPTIONAL CALCULATION FOR MULTIFAMILY PART B AND C TO ART. 220

When applying the optional calculation for multifamily dwelling units, the loads are computed the same as when using the optional calculation for one family dwellings. The only difference would be to compute the total number of dwelling units and pieces of electrical equipment together and apply a percentage based upon the number to derive the total VA or amps to size the elements of the service or feeder-circuit.

**Example Problem 9-15.** What is the load in VA and amps for 25 multifamily dwelling units with the following loads? (See Standard Calculation in Example Problem 9-14 for sizing the neutral) Note: Parallel service conductors, 6 times per phase.

**Given loads:**

- 25 - 1,000 sq. ft. dwelling units
- 2 small appliance circuits per unit
- 1 laundry circuit per unit

**120 V, single-phase loads**

- 25 - 1,000 VA dishwashers
- 25 - 1,200 VA disposals

**240 V, single-phase loads**

- 25 - 12,000 VA ranges
- 25 - 6,000 VA water heaters
- 25 - 20,000 VA heating units

Sizing phases = •
Sizing neutral = √

**Column 1**
**Calculating general lighting and receptacle load**

Step 1: General lighting and receptacle load
Table 220-3(a)
1,000 sq. ft. x 3 VA x 25     =     75,000 VA

Step 2: Small appliance and laundry load
220-16(a); (b)
1,500 VA x 2 x 25     =     75,000 VA
1,500 VA x 1 x 25     =     37,500 VA
Total load     =     187,500 VA •

**Column 2**
**Calculating cooking equipment load**

Step 1: Applying demand factors for phases
Demand load 2; Table 220-19, Col. A
12,000 VA x 25     =     300,000 VA •

**Calculating fixed appliance load**

Step 1: Applying demand factors for phases
Demand load 4; 220-17
1,000 VA x 25     =     25,000 VA
1,200 VA x 25     =     30,000 VA
6,000 VA x 25     =     150,000 VA
Total load     =     205,000 VA •

**Column 3**
**Largest load between heat and A/C**

Step 1: Selecting largest load
Demand load 5; 220-21
Heating unit
20,000 VA x 25     =     500,000 VA •

**Calculating phases**

General lighting load     =     187,500 VA •
Cooking load     =     300,000 VA •
Appliance load     =     205,000 VA •
Heating load     =     500,000 VA •
Total load     =     1,192,500 VA

**Applying demand factors**

Table 220-32
I = VA / V
I = 1,192,500 VA / 240 V
I = 4,969 A

**Finding amps for phases**
**Table 220-32**

I = A x %
I = 4,969 A x 35%
I = 1,739 A

**Finding conductors**

Phases A and B
310-4
I = 1,739 A / 6 (No. runs per phase)
I = 290 A

Table 310-16
Phases A and B
#350 KCMIL THWN copper

Neutral
#1/0 THWN copper

See **Figure 9-15** for an exercise problem when calculating the loads of a multifamily dwelling unit using the optional calculation.

Exercise Problem 9-15. What is the load in VA and amps for 20 multifamily dwelling units with the following loads? (See Standard Calculation in Exercise Problem 9-14 for sizing the neutral) Note: Parallel service conductors, 6 times per phase.

**Given loads:**

• 20 - 1,200 sq. ft. dwelling units
• 2 small appliance circuits per unit
• 1 laundry circuit per unit

**120 V, single-phase loads**

• 20 - 1,600 VA dishwashers
• 20 - 1,200 VA disposals

**240 V, single-phase loads**

• 20 - 10,000 VA ranges
• 20 -  5,000 VA water heaters
• 20 - 20,000 VA heating units

Sizing phases = •
Sizing neutral = √

**Column 1**
**Calculating general lighting and receptacle load**

**Step 1:** General lighting and receptacle load
Table 220-3(a)
1,200 sq. ft. x 3 VA x 20     =  _____ VA [A]

**Step 2:** Small appliance and laundry load
220-16(a); (b)
1,500 VA x 2 x 20     =  _____ VA [B]
1,500 VA x 1 x 20     =  _____ VA [C]
Total load     =  _____ VA [D] •

**Column 2**
**Calculating cooking equipment load**

**Step 1:** Applying demand factors for phases
Demand load 2; Table 220-19, Col. A
10,000 VA x 20     =  _____ VA [E] •

**Column 2**
**Calculating fixed appliance load**

**Step 1:** Applying demand factors for phases
Demand load 4; 220-17
1,600 VA x 20     =  _____ VA [F]
1,200 VA x 20     =  _____ VA [G]
5,000 VA x 20     =  _____ VA [H]
Total load     =  _____ VA [I] •

**Column 3**
**Largest load between heating and A/C load**

**Step 1:** Selecting largest load
Demand load 5; 220-21
Heating unit
20,000 VA x 20 x 100%     =  _____ VA [J] •

**Calculating phases**

• General lighting load     =  _____ VA [K] •
• Cooking equipment load     =  _____ VA [L] •
• Appliance load     =  _____ VA [M] •
• Heating load     =  _____ VA [N] •
Total load     =  _____ VA [O]

**Applying demand factors**
**Table 220-32**

I = VA / V

I =  _____ VA [P] / 240 V

I =  _____ A [Q]

**Finding amps for phases**
**Table 220-32**

I = A x %

I =  _____ A [R] x 38%

I =  _____ A [S]

**Finding conductors**

Phases A and B
310-4
I =  _____ A [T]  / 6
I =  _____ A [U]

Table 310-16
Phases A and B
# _____ THWN [V] copper conductors

Neutral
# _____ THWN [W] copper conductors

**Figure 9-15.** The above is an exercise problem for calculating the loads of a multifamily dwelling unit when applying the optional calculation.

# APPLYING THE STANDARD CALCULATION FOR FEEDER TO MOBILE HOMES
# 550-13

Service calculations for mobile homes are performed at the factory. However, it is the responsibility of the designer or electrician to size and select the proper size feeder-circuit to supply power to the mobile home using the standard calculation. Such feeder-circuit must be a four-wire circuit with all conductors insulated. The size of the conductors can be selected from Table 310-16 or Sec. 310-15(b)(6). The service equipment on a pole or pedestal must be rated at least 100 amps.

**Example Problem 9-16.** What is the load in VA and amps for a mobile home with the following loads?

| | |
|---|---|
| **Given Loads:** | **Sizing phases = •**<br>**Sizing neutral = √** |

- 800 sq. ft. dwelling unit (mobile homes)
- 2 small appliance circuits
- 1 laundry circuit
- 8,500 VA range — 240 volt, single-phase
- 6,000 VA water heater — 240 volt, single-phase
- 540 VA disposal — 120 volt, single-phase
- 800 VA dishwasher — 120 volt, single-phase
- 5,500 VA heating unit — 240 volt, single-phase

**Calculating general lighting and receptacle load**

Step 1: General lighting and receptacle load
550-13
800 sq. ft. x 3 VA = 2,400 VA

Step 2: Small appliance and laundry load
220-16(a);(b)
1,500 VA x 2 = 3,000 VA
1,500 VA x 1 = 1,500 VA
Total load = 6,900 VA

Step 3: Applying demand factors
550-13(a)
First 3,000 VA x 100% = 3,000 VA
Next 3,900 VA x 35% = 1,365 VA
Total load = 4,365 VA • √

**Calculating special appliance loads**

Step 1: Applying demand factors for phases
550-13(b)(2); (3); (4)
Water heater = 6,000 VA
Dishwasher = 800 VA √
Disposal = 540 VA √
Heating = 5,500 VA
Largest motor = 135 VA √
(540 VA x 25% = 135 VA)
Total load = 12,975 VA •

**Calculating range load**

Step 1: 550-13(b)(5)
8,500 VA x 80% = 6,800 VA •
6,800 VA x 70% = 4,760 VA √

**Calculating phases**

General lighting load = 4,365 VA •
Special appliance load = 12,975 VA •
Range load = 6,800 VA •
Three total loads = 24,140 VA

**Finding amps for phases**

$I = VA / V$
$I = 24,140\ VA / 240\ V$
$I = 101\ A$

**Calculating neutral**

General lighting load = 4,365 VA √
Dishwasher load = 800 VA √
Disposal load = 540 VA √
Largest motor = 135 VA √
Range = 4,760 VA √
Five total loads = 10,600 VA

**Finding amps for neutral**

$I = VA / V$
$I = 10,600\ VA / 240\ V$
$I = 44\ A$

**Finding conductors based on max. size**

Table 310-16
Phases
101 A requires #2 THWN copper
Neutral
44 A requires #8 THWN copper

310-15(b)(6) allows min. size
Phases
101 A requires #3 THWN copper
Neutral
44 A requires #8 THWN copper

See Figure 9-16 for an exercise problem when calculating the feeder to mobile homes using the standard calculation.

# APPLYING THE OPTIONAL CALCULATION FOR MOBILE HOME PARK SERVICE AND FEEDER
# 550-22

The elements of the service can be computed using the optional calculation. All loads are added together based upon the total number of mobile homes and multiplied by a percentage to derive the total load. Use 16,000 VA for each mobile home, if the computed load per Sec. 550-13 produces a lower VA rating.

**Exercise Problem 9-16:** What is the load in VA and amps for a mobile home with the following loads?

**Given loads:**

Sizing phases = •
Sizing neutral = √

- 800 sq. ft. dwelling unit
- 2 small appliance circuits
- 1 laundry circuit
- 8,500 VA range      240 volt, single-phase
- 5,000 VA water heater    240 volt, single-phase
- 540 VA disposal       120 volt, single-phase
- 1,000 VA dishwasher     120 volt, single-phase
- 6,000 VA heating unit     240 volt, single-phase

### Calculating general lighting and receptacle load

**Step 1:** General lighting and receptacle load
550-13
800 sq. ft. x 3 VA      = _____ VA [A]

**Step 2:** Small appliance and laundry load
220-16(a); (b)
1,500 VA x 2      = _____ VA [B]
1,500 VA x 1      = _____ VA [C]
Total load      = _____ VA [D]

**Step 3:** Applying demand factor
550-13(a)
First 3,000 VA x 100%      =      3,000   VA
Next 3,900 VA x 35%      = _____ VA [E]
Total load      = _____ VA [F] • √

### Calculating special appliance loads

**Step 1:** Applying demand factors for phases
550-13(b)(2); (3); (4)
Water heater      = _____ VA [G]
Dishwasher      = _____ VA [H] √
Disposal      = _____ VA [I] √
Heating      = _____ VA [J]
Total load      = _____ VA [K] •

### Calculating range load

**Step 1:** 550-13(b)(5)
8,500 VA x 80%      = _____ VA [L] •
6,800 VA x 70%      = _____ VA [M] √

### Calculating phases

- General lighting load      = _____ VA [N] •
- Special appliance load      = _____ VA [O] •
- Range load      = _____ VA [P] •
- Largest motor load (540 VA x 25%)    = _____ VA [Q] •
- Four total loads      = _____ VA [R]

### Finding amps for phases

$I = VA / V$

$I =$ _____ VA [S] / 240 V

$I =$ _____ A [T]

### Calculating neutral

- General lighting load      = _____ VA [U] √
- Dishwasher load      = _____ VA [V] √
- Disposal load      = _____ VA [W] √
- Largest motor      = _____ VA [X] √
- Range      = _____ VA [Y] √
- Five total loads      = _____ VA [Z]

### Finding amps for neutral

$I = VA / V$

$I =$ _____ VA [AA] / 240

$I =$ _____ A [BB]

### Finding conductors based on max. size
**Table 310-16**

Phases
# _____ THWN [CC] copper conductors
Neutral
# _____ THWN [DD] copper conductors

### 310-15(b)(6) allows min. size

Phases
# _____ THWN [EE] copper conductors
Neutral
# _____ THWN [FF] copper conductors

**Figure 9-16.** The above is an exercise problem for calculating the feeder to mobile homes when applying the standard calculation.

**Example Problem 9-17.** What is the load in VA and amps for 28 mobile homes with the following loads? Note: Parallel service conductors, 3 times per phase.

| Given loads | Sizing phases = • |
| --- | --- |
| 28 units<br>17,000 VA each based on computed load | Sizing neutral = √ |

**Finding total VA load**

Step 1: Finding VA load
550-22
Mobile home      =      17,000    VA

Step 2: Calculating VA load
Table 550-22
17,000 VA x 28 x 24%    =     114,240    VA

**Sizing conductors**

Step 1: Finding VA
550-22
Total VA      =      114,240    VA

Step 2: Calculating A
A = 114,240 VA / 240 V
A = 476

Step 3: Selecting conductors
Table 310-16; 310-4
Phases A and B (Parallel)
A = 476 A / 3 (No. runs per phase)
A = 158.7
158.7 A requires #2/0 THWN copper

**Sizing neutral based upon computed load**

Step 1: Finding VA
550-22
Total VA      =      114,240    VA

Step 2: Calculating A
A = 114,240 VA / 240 V
A = 476

Step 3: Applying demand factors
220-22
First 200 A x 100%    =      200   A
Next 276 A x 70%      =      193   A
Total load           =      393   A

Step 4: Selecting conductors
Table 310-16; 310-4
Neutral (parallel)
A = 393 A / 3 (No. runs per phase)
A = 131
131 A requires #1/0 THWN copper

See **Figure 9-17** for an exercise problem when calculating the mobile home park service or feeder when using the optional calculation.

**Exercise Problem 9-17:** What is the load in VA and amps for 26 mobile homes with the following loads? Note: Parallel service conductors, 3 times per phase.

---

**Given loads:**

• 26 units
• 19,000 VA each based upon computed load

Sizing phases = •
Sizing neutral = √

**Finding total VA load**

**Step 1:** Finding VA load
550-22
Mobile home = _____ VA [A]

**Step 2:** Calculating VA load
Table 550-22
19,000 VA x 26 x 24% = _____ VA [B]

**Sizing conductors**

**Step 1:** Finding VA
550-22
Total VA = _____ VA [C]

**Step 2:** Calculating A
A = _____ VA [D] / 240 V
A = _____ [E]

**Step 3:** Selecting conductors
Table 310-16; 310-4
Phases A and B (Parallel)
A = _____ A [F] / 3
A = _____ [G]
# _____ THWN [H] copper conductors

**Sizing neutral based upon computed load**

**Step 1:** Finding VA
550-22
Total VA = _____ VA [I]√

**Step 2:** Calculating A
A = _____ VA [J] / 240 V
A = _____ [K]

**Step 3:** Applying demand factors
220-22
First 200 A x 100% = _____ A [L]
Next 294 A x 70% = _____ A [M]
Total load = _____ A [N]

**Step 4:** Selecting conductors
Table 310-16; 310-4
Neutral (parallel)
A = _____ A [O] / 3
A = _____ [P]
# _____ THWN [Q] copper conductors

**Figure 9-17.** The above is an exercise problem for calculating the mobile home park service or feeder when applying the optional calculation.

# SIZING ELEMENTS
# EXAMPLE PROBLEM 9-12

Using the service amps of Example Problem 9-12 on page 9-14, size the elements of the following:

(1) Size THWN copper conductors per Table 310-16 and Sec. 310-15(b)(6)
(2) Size overcurrent protection device
(3) Size panelboard
(4) Size conduit
(5) Sizing grounding electrode conductor (copper)
(6) Size supplementary grounding electrode conductor (copper)

## SIZING THE CONDUCTORS FOR THE SERVICE PER TABLE 310-16 AND 310-15(b)(6)

**Test Tip 11:** The maximum size conductors are sized and selected from Table 310-16. However, the minimum size is selected from Sec. 310-15(b)(6).

**Step 1:** Calculated loads (See page 9-14)
Phases = 193 A
Neutral = 109 A

**Step 2:** Selecting conductors
Table 310-16
Phases
193 A requires #3/0 THWN copper
Neutral
109 A requires #2 THWN copper

**Step 3:** Applying Sec. 310-15(b)(6)
Phases
193 A requires #2/0 THWN copper
Neutral
109 A requires #2 THWN copper

**Solution:** The phase conductors are No. 3/0 THWN copper conductors and the Neutral is No. 2 copper.

**Note:** No. 3/0 THWN copper conductors were selected based upon Step 2 above.

## SIZING THE OCPD FOR THE SERVICE CONDUCTORS PER TABLE 310-16 AND SEC. 110-14(c)(1) AND (c)(2)

**Test Tip 12:** The OCPD must protect the service or feeder conductors from short-circuits per Sec.'s 230-42 and 240-3.

**Step 1:** Amperage of load or conductor
240-3(a) - (g); 240-6(a)
193 A requires 200 A OCPD

**Solution:** The size OCPD required is 200 amps.

## SIZING PANELBOARD FOR SERVICE PER SEC.'S 240-3(a) - (g); 384-14; 384-16(a)

**Step 1:** Amperage of load or conductor
240-3(a) - (g); 240-6(a); chart on pg 11-45
193 A requires 200 A panelboard

**Solution:** The size panelboard required is 200 amps.

## SIZING THE CONDUIT FOR THE SERVICE CONDUCTORS USING RIGID METAL CONDUIT PER TABLES 5 AND 4 TO CH. 9

**Step 1:** Different size conductors (max. size)
Table 5 and Table 4 to Ch. 9
#3/0 THWN
.2679 sq. in. x 2      = .5358
#2 THWN
.1158 sq. in. x 1      = .1158
Total sq. in. area      = .6516

**Test Tip 13:** Conduits containing four or more conductors are allowed 40 percent fill area, based upon .7854 times the diameter square.

**Step 2:** Selecting size conduit
Table 4 to Ch. 9
.6516 sq. in. requires 1 1/2" conduit

**Solution:** The size rigid metal conduit required is 1 1/2 in.

## SIZING THE GEC TO GROUND THE SERVICE TO METAL WATER PIPE PER SEC. 250-66 AND TABLE 250-66

**Step 1:** Size of phase conductors (max. size)
250-66; Table 250-66
#3/0 THWN requires #4 copper

**Solution:** The size GEC required is No. 4 copper.

## WHAT SIZE GEC IS REQUIRED TO GROUND THE SERVICE TO A DRIVEN ROD TO SUPPLEMENT THE METAL WATER PIPE PER SEC.'S 250-104(a) AND 250-50(a)(2)

**Step 1:** Size of phase conductors (max. size)
250-66(a)
#3/0 THWN requires #6 copper

**Test Tip 14:** Grounding electrode conductors are sized from Sec. 250-66(a), (b) and (c) and Table 250-66 based upon the size of the phase conductors.

**Solution:** The size of the grounding electrode conductor is No. 6 copper.

See **Figures 9-18(a) through (f)** for exercise problems when sizing the elements for exercise problem 9-12.

**Figure 9-18(a).** This figure illustrates an exercise problem for sizing the THWN copper conductors for exercise problem 9-12.

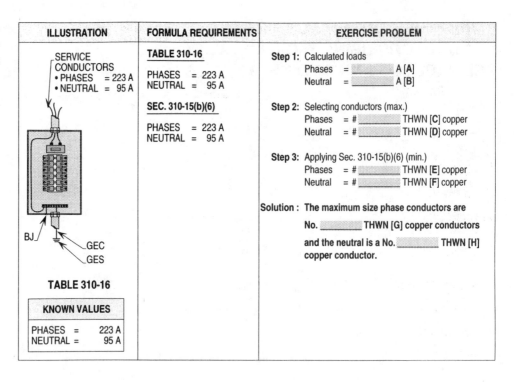

| ILLUSTRATION | FORMULA REQUIREMENTS | EXERCISE PROBLEM |
|---|---|---|
| SERVICE CONDUCTORS<br>• PHASES = 223 A<br>• NEUTRAL = 95 A<br><br>BJ<br>GEC<br>GES<br><br>**TABLE 310-16**<br><br>**KNOWN VALUES**<br>PHASES = 223 A<br>NEUTRAL = 95 A | **TABLE 310-16**<br><br>PHASES = 223 A<br>NEUTRAL = 95 A<br><br>**SEC. 310-15(b)(6)**<br><br>PHASES = 223 A<br>NEUTRAL = 95 A | **Step 1:** Calculated loads<br>Phases = _____ A **[A]**<br>Neutral = _____ A **[B]**<br><br>**Step 2:** Selecting conductors (max.)<br>Phases = # _____ THWN **[C]** copper<br>Neutral = # _____ THWN **[D]** copper<br><br>**Step 3:** Applying Sec. 310-15(b)(6) (min.)<br>Phases = # _____ THWN **[E]** copper<br>Neutral = # _____ THWN **[F]** copper<br><br>**Solution :** The maximum size phase conductors are<br>No. _____ THWN **[G]** copper conductors<br>and the neutral is a No. _____ THWN **[H]**<br>copper conductor. |

**Figure 9-18(b).** This figure illustrates an exercise problem for sizing the overcurrent protection device for exercise problem 9-12.

| ILLUSTRATION | FORMULA REQUIREMENTS | EXERCISE PROBLEM |
|---|---|---|
| SERVICE CONDUCTORS<br>• PHASES = 223 A<br>• NEUTRAL = 95 A<br><br>BJ<br>GEC<br>GES<br><br>**NEC 110-14(c)(1); (c)(2)**<br><br>**KNOWN VALUES**<br>PHASES = 223 A<br>NEUTRAL = 95 A | PHASES = 223 A<br>NEUTRAL = 95 A<br><br>**Note:** Size OCPD based on computed load in amps. | **Step 1:** Amperage of load<br>223 A requires _____ A **[A]** OCPD<br><br>**Solution :** The size OCPD required is<br>_____ amps **[B]**. |

| ILLUSTRATION | FORMULA REQUIREMENTS | EXERCISE PROBLEM |
|---|---|---|
| 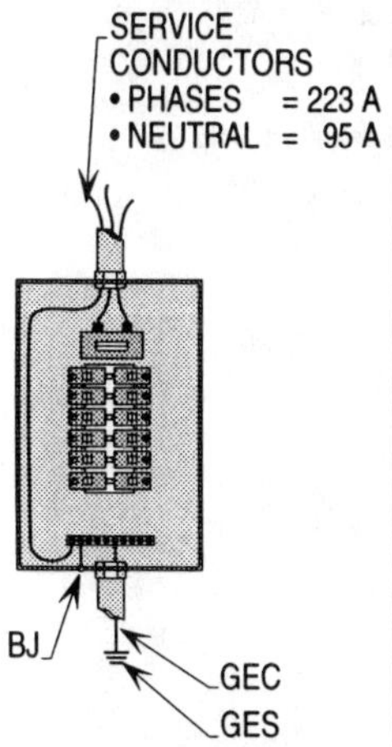 SERVICE CONDUCTORS<br>• PHASES = 223 A<br>• NEUTRAL = 95 A<br><br>BJ<br>GEC<br>GES<br><br>**NEC 240-3(a) - (g)**<br>**NEC 384-14**<br>**NEC 384-16(a)**<br><br>**KNOWN VALUES**<br>PHASES = 223 A<br>NEUTRAL = 95 A | PHASES = 223 A<br>NEUTRAL = 95 A | **Step 1:** Amperage of load<br> 223 A requires _____ A [A] panelboard<br><br>**Solution :** The size panelboard required is<br> _____ amps [B]. |

**Figure 9-18(c).** This figure illustrates an exercise problem for sizing the panelboard for exercise problem 9-12.

| ILLUSTRATION | FORMULA REQUIREMENTS | EXERCISE PROBLEM |
|---|---|---|
| 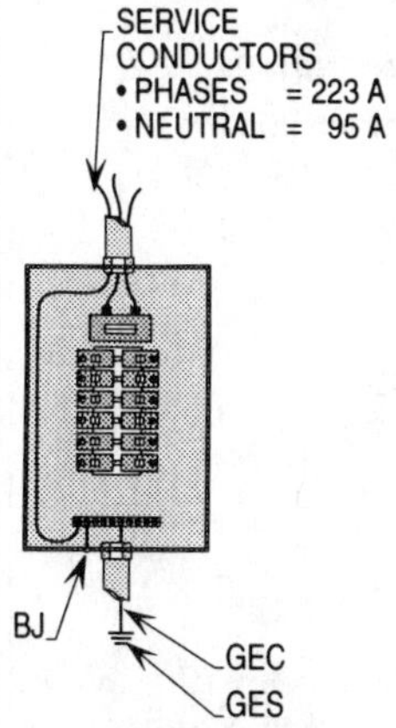 SERVICE CONDUCTORS<br>• PHASES = 223 A<br>• NEUTRAL = 95 A<br><br>BJ<br>GEC<br>GES<br><br>**TABLE 5, CH. 9**<br>**TABLE 4, CH. 9**<br><br>**KNOWN VALUES**<br>PHASES = 223 A<br>NEUTRAL = 95 A | PHASES<br>• 223 A = #4/0 cu.<br><br>NEUTRAL<br>• 95 A = #3 cu. | **Step 1:** Different size conductors (max. size)<br> #4/0 copper<br> _____ sq. in. [A] x 2 = _____ sq. in. [B]<br> #3 copper<br> _____ sq. in. [C] x 1 = _____ sq. in. [D]<br> Total sq. in. = _____ sq. in. [E]<br><br>**Step 2:** Selecting size<br> _____ sq. in.[F] requires _____ in. [G] conduit<br><br>**Solution :** The size rigid metal conduit required is<br> _____ in. [H]. |

**Figure 9-18(d).** This figure illustrates an exercise problem for sizing the rigid metal conduit for exercise problem 9-12.

**Figure 9-18(e).** This figure illustrates an exercise problem for sizing the copper grounding electrode conductor for exercise problem 9-12.

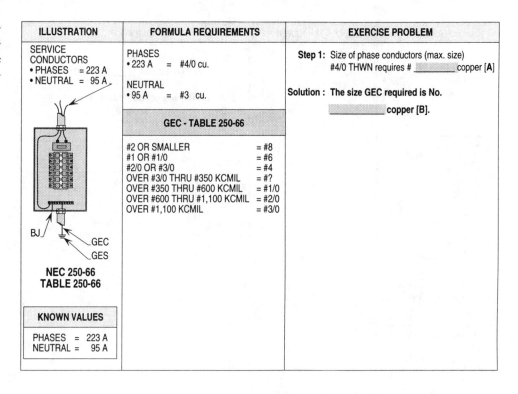

| ILLUSTRATION | FORMULA REQUIREMENTS | EXERCISE PROBLEM |
|---|---|---|
| SERVICE CONDUCTORS<br>• PHASES = 223 A<br>• NEUTRAL = 95 A | PHASES<br>• 223 A = #4/0 cu.<br><br>NEUTRAL<br>• 95 A = #3 cu. | **Step 1:** Size of phase conductors (max. size)<br>#4/0 THWN requires # _____ copper [A]<br><br>**Solution:** The size GEC required is No. _____ copper [B]. |

**GEC - TABLE 250-66**

| | |
|---|---|
| #2 OR SMALLER | = #8 |
| #1 OR #1/0 | = #6 |
| #2/0 OR #3/0 | = #4 |
| OVER #3/0 THRU #350 KCMIL | = #? |
| OVER #350 THRU #600 KCMIL | = #1/0 |
| OVER #600 THRU #1,100 KCMIL | = #2/0 |
| OVER #1,100 KCMIL | = #3/0 |

NEC 250-66
TABLE 250-66

| KNOWN VALUES |
|---|
| PHASES = 223 A<br>NEUTRAL = 95 A |

**Figure 9-18(f).** This figure illustrates an exercise problem for sizing the supplementary grounding electrode conductor for exercise problem 9-12.

| ILLUSTRATION | FORMULA REQUIREMENTS | EXERCISE PROBLEM |
|---|---|---|
| SERVICE CONDUCTORS<br>• PHASES = 223 A<br>• NEUTRAL = 95 A | PHASES<br>• 223 A = #4/0 COPPER<br><br>NEUTRAL<br>• 95 A = #3 COPPER<br><br>**Note:** Use a driven rod for supplementary ground. | **Step 1:** Size of phase conductors (max. size)<br>#4/0 THWN requires # _____ copper [A]<br><br>**Solution:** The size GEC required is No. _____ copper [B]. |

NEC 250-104(a)
NEC 250-50(a)(2)

| KNOWN VALUES |
|---|
| PHASES = 223 A<br>NEUTRAL = 95 A |

# Chapter 9
# Residential Calculations

| Section | Answer | |
|---|---|---|
| _____ | T   F | 1. The total VA for the general lighting and receptacle loads are derived by multiplying the square footage by 3 VA and applying demand factors. |
| _____ | T   F | 2. All small appliance branch-circuit loads are computed at 1,500 VA. |
| _____ | T   F | 3. For three or less dryers, the total VA must be calculated at 100 percent with no demand factors applied. |
| _____ | T   F | 4. Three or less fixed appliances are calculated at 100 percent of their total VA. |
| _____ | T   F | 5. The heating and A/C loads are computed at 125 percent and the smaller of the two loads is dropped. |
| _____ _____ | | 6. All laundry branch-circuit loads are computed at _____ VA |
| _____ _____ | | 7. Dryer equipment loads of four or fewer is calculated at _____ percent of the nameplate rating. |
| _____ _____ | | 8. The demand load for a household dryer is computed at _____ kVA or the nameplate rating, whichever is greater. |
| _____ _____ | | 9. When there are four or more fixed appliances, a demand factor of _____ percent can be applied to the total VA. |
| _____ _____ | | 10. The motor's total full-load current rating is computed at _____ percent when computing the largest motor load. |
| _____ _____ | | 11. What is the general lighting and receptacle loads and small appliance and laundry loads for a 3,200 sq. ft. dwelling unit? (Compute the load in VA) |
| _____ _____ | | 12. What is the demand load in VA for a 12 kW range? |
| _____ _____ | | 13. What is the demand load in VA for a 12 kW and 11 kW cooking unit? |
| _____ _____ | | 14. What is the demand load in VA for a piece of cooking equipment with a 3.5 kW rating? |
| _____ _____ | | 15. What is the demand load in VA for two pieces of cooking equipment with a 3.5 kW rating? |
| _____ _____ | | 16. What is the demand load in VA for a piece of cooking equipment with a 8 3/4 kW rating? |
| _____ _____ | | 17. What is the demand load in VA for two pieces of cooking equipment with a 8 3/4 kW rating? |
| _____ _____ | | 18. What is the demand load in VA for a range with a 18 kW rating? |
| _____ _____ | | 19. What is the demand load in VA for three pieces of cooking equipment with a 10 kW, 12 kW, and 18 kW rating? |
| _____ _____ | | 20. What is the branch-circuit demand load in VA for a 10 kW cooktop, 6 kW oven, and 4 kW oven installed in a dwelling unit? |

_____ _____ 21. What is the demand load in VA for a 4.5 kW dryer?

_____ _____ 22. What is the demand load in VA for a 5 kW dryer?

_____ _____ 23. What is the demand load in VA for 8 dryers rated at 7,500 VA each?

_____ _____ 24. What is the fixed appliance load in VA for the following:

- 5,000 VA water heater     240 volt, single-phase
- 1,200 VA disposal        120 volt, single-phase
- 1,000 VA compactor     120 volt, single-phase

_____ _____ 25. What is the fixed appliance load in VA for the phases and neutral for the following:

           _____

- 6,000 VA water heater     240 volt, single-phase
- 2,400 VA water pump     240 volt, single-phase
- 1,200 VA disposal        120 volt, single-phase
- 1,400 VA compactor     120 volt, single-phase
- 1,400 VA dishwasher     120 volt, single-phase
- 800 VA microwave       120 volt, single-phase

_____ _____ 26. What is the fixed appliance load in VA for the phases and neutral for the following:

           _____

- 6,000 VA water heater     240 volt, single-phase
- 1,200 VA water pump     240 volt, single-phase
- 1,000 VA disposal        120 volt, single-phase
- 1,600 VA dishwasher     120 volt, single-phase
- 800 VA blower motor     120 volt, single-phase

_____ _____ 27. What is the load in VA for 20 kW heating unit and 6 kW A/C unit installed in a dwelling unit?

_____ _____ 28. What is the load in VA for a 1 HP, 240 volt, single-phase motor which is to be used for the largest motor load?

_____ _____ 29. Compute the following loads of a 3,000 sq. ft. dwelling unit using the standard calculation and size the service-entrance conductors required for Phases A and B and the neutral? (Compute with or without the use of the residential calculation form)

           _____

- 3,000 sq. ft. dwelling unit     (120/240 volt system using
- 2 small appliance circuits      THWN copper conductors)
- 1 laundry circuit
- 6,000 VA A/C unit        240 volt, single-phase
- 10,000 VA heating unit     240 volt, single-phase
- 6,000 VA water heater     240 volt, single-phase
- 11,000 VA cooktop        240 volt, single-phase
- 12,000 VA oven           240 volt, single-phase
- 4,500 VA dryer           240 volt, single-phase
- 1,000 VA blower motor     240 volt, single-phase
- 2,400 VA water pump     240 volt, single-phase
- 1,200 VA disposal        120 volt, single-phase
- 1,400 VA compactor     120 volt, single-phase
- 1,600 VA dishwasher     120 volt, single-phase
- 1,200 VA microwave     120 volt, single-phase

_____  _____

_____

30. Compute the following loads of a 2,800 sq. ft. dwelling unit using the standard calculation and size the service-entrance conductors required for Phases A and B and the neutral? (Compute with or without the use of the residential calculation form)

| | |
|---|---|
| • 2,800 sq. ft. dwelling unit | (120/240 volt system using |
| • 2 small appliance circuits | THWN copper conductors) |
| • 1 laundry circuit | |
| • 6,000 VA A/C unit | 240 volt, single-phase |
| • 20,000 VA heating unit | 240 volt, single-phase |
| • 8,000 VA water heater | 240 volt, single-phase |
| • 8,000 VA cooktop | 240 volt, single-phase |
| • 8,500 VA oven | 240 volt, single-phase |
| • 5,000 VA dryer | 240 volt, single-phase |
| • 800 VA blower motor | 240 volt, single-phase |
| • 2,400 VA water pump | 240 volt, single-phase |
| • 1,000 VA disposal | 120 volt, single-phase |
| • 1,200 VA compactor | 120 volt, single-phase |
| • 1,600 VA dishwasher | 120 volt, single-phase |
| • 1,000 VA microwave | 120 volt, single-phase |

_____  _____

_____

31. Compute the following loads of a 3,000 sq. ft. dwelling unit using the optional calculation and size the service-entrance conductors required for Phases A and B and the neutral? (Compute with or without the use of the residential calculation form)

| | |
|---|---|
| • 3,000 sq. ft. dwelling unit | (120/240 volt system using |
| • 2 small appliance circuits | THWN copper conductors) |
| • 1 laundry circuit | |
| • 6,000 VA A/C unit | 240 volt, single-phase |
| • 10,000 VA heating unit | 240 volt, single-phase |
| • 6,000 VA water heater | 240 volt, single-phase |
| • 11,000 VA cooktop | 240 volt, single-phase |
| • 12,000 VA oven | 240 volt, single-phase |
| • 4,500 VA dryer | 240 volt, single-phase |
| • 1,000 VA blower motor | 240 volt, single-phase |
| • 2,400 VA water pump | 240 volt, single-phase |
| • 1,200 VA disposal | 120 volt, single-phase |
| • 1,400 VA compactor | 120 volt, single-phase |
| • 1,600 VA dishwasher | 120 volt, single-phase |
| • 1,200 VA microwave | 120 volt, single-phase |

**Note:** See standard calculation No. 29 for sizing the neutral.

_____  _____

_____

32. Compute the following loads of a 2,800 sq. ft. dwelling unit using the optional calculation and size the service-entrance conductors required for Phases A and B and the neutral? (Compute with or without the use of the residential calculation form)

| | |
|---|---|
| • 2,800 sq. ft. dwelling unit | (120/240 volt system using |
| • 2 small appliance circuits | THWN copper conductors) |
| • 1 laundry circuit | |
| • 6,000 VA A/C unit | 240 volt, single-phase |
| • 20,000 VA heating unit | 240 volt, single-phase |
| • 8,000 VA water heater | 240 volt, single-phase |
| • 8,000 VA cooktop | 240 volt, single-phase |
| • 8,500 VA oven | 240 volt, single-phase |
| • 5,000 VA dryer | 240 volt, single-phase |
| • 800 VA blower motor | 240 volt, single-phase |
| • 2,400 VA water pump | 240 volt, single-phase |
| • 1,000 VA disposal | 120 volt, single-phase |
| • 1,200 VA compactor | 120 volt, single-phase |
| • 1,600 VA dishwasher | 120 volt, single-phase |
| • 1,000 VA microwave | 120 volt, single-phase |

**Note:** See standard calculation No. 30 for sizing the neutral

—————— ——————

——————

33. What is the load in VA and amps for 20 multifamily dwelling units using the standard calculation and the size service-entrance conductors required for Phases A and B and the neutral with the following loads. **Note:** Parallel service conductors, 6 times per phase. (Compute with or without the use of the residential calculation form))

- 20 - 1,000 sq. ft. dwelling units    (120/240 volt system using
- 2 small appliance circuits per unit    THWN copper conductors)
- 1 laundry circuit per unit
- 20 - 10,000 VA ranges    240 volts, single-phase
- 20 - 5,000 VA water heaters    240 volts, single-phase
- 20 - 10,000 VA heating units    240 volts, single-phase
- 20 - 1,000 VA disposals    120 volts, single-phase
- 20 - 1,600 VA dishwashers    120 volts, single-phase

—————— ——————

——————

34. What is the load in VA and amps for 20 multifamily dwelling units using the optional calculation and the size service-entrance conductors required for Phases A and B and the neutral with the following loads. **Note:** Parallel service conductors, 6 times per phase. (Compute with or without the use of the residential calculation form)

- 20 - 1,000 sq. ft. dwelling units    (120/240 volt system using
- 2 small appliance circuits per unit    THWN copper conductors)
- 1 laundry circuit per unit
- 20 - 10,000 VA ranges    240 volts, single-phase
- 20 - 5,000 VA water heaters    240 volts, single-phase
- 20 - 10,000 VA heating units    240 volts, single-phase
- 20 - 1,000 VA disposals    120 volts, single-phase
- 20 - 1,600 VA dishwashers    120 volts, single-phase

**Note:** See standard calculation No. 33 for sizing the neutral

—————— ——————

——————

35. Compute the following loads of a 900 sq. ft. mobile home using the standard calculation and size the service-entrance conductors required for Phases A and B and the Neutral? (Compute with or without the use of the residential calculation form)

- 900 sq. ft. mobile home    (120/240 volt system using
- 2 small appliance circuits    THWN copper conductors)
- 1 laundry circuit
- 8,750 VA range    240 volts, single-phase
- 5,500 VA water heater    240 volts, single-phase
- 680 VA disposal    120 volts, single-phase
- 1,000 VA compactor    120 volts, single-phase
- 6,000 VA heating unit    240 volts, single-phase

—————— ——————

——————

36. Compute the following of 24 mobile homes using the optional calculation and size the service-entrance conductors required for Phases A and B and the Neutral? (120/240 volt system). **Note:** Parallel service conductors, 3 times per phase.

- 24 mobile home units
- 18,000 VA each based on computed load

The following Problems will be determined by using Problem No. 29

—————— ——————

——————

37. In problem 36 above, what size service-entrance conductors are required if Note 3 to Table 310-16 is applied

—————— ——————

38. What size OCPD is required for the service conductors?

—————— ——————

39. What size panelboard for the service is required?

—————— ——————

40. What size conduit is required for the service-entrance conductors using rigid metal conduit.

# Commercial Calculations

**10**

Commercial facilities such as offices, banks, stores, and restaurants have diverse loads. These loads are classified as continuous or noncontinuous. Such loads may also cycle on and off, allowing demand factors to be applied.

The procedure and manner in which the lighting, receptacle, and equipment loads are used in the electrical system determines how they are classified.

Loads must be computed based upon the type of occupancy and the requirements of the equipment supplied. Either the standard or optional calculation is utilized to compute the loads in VA or amps to size the service equipment and associated elements.

## Quick Reference:

APPLYING THE STANDARD
CALCULATION ............................................. 10-2

LIGHTING LOADS ......................................... 10-3

RECEPTACLE LOADS ................................. 10-8

SPECIAL APPLIANCE LOADS ..................... 10-10

COMPRESSOR LOADS ............................... 10-12

MOTOR LOADS ............................................ 10-14

HEAT OR A/C LOADS .................................. 10-15

LARGEST MOTOR LOAD ........................... 10-15

STANDARD CALCULATIONS ....................... 10-16

APPLYING THE OPTIONAL
CALCULATION ............................................ 10-34

KITCHEN EQUIPMENT ................................. 10-34

APPLYING THE OPTIONAL
CALCULATION ............................................ 10-34

# APPLYING THE STANDARD CALCULATION
# PARTS A AND B TO ART. 220

The standard calculation can be used to compute the VA or amp rating to size and select the elements of the service equipment and associated components. The selection of loads, to apply the standard calculation, is arranged in a different manner for commercial loads than for the loads used in residential occupancies. There are seven loads utilized to determine the service load. Based upon conditions of use, demand factors can be applied to certain loads.

The loads are grouped into seven individual loads, and the proper NEC rules are applied to each of these loads based upon use. The loads are grouped and classified as follows:

(1) Lighting loads
   • General lighting load per Sec. 220-3(a)
   • Show window load per Sec. 220-12(a)
   • Lighting track load per Sec. 220-12(b)
   • Low-voltage lighting load per Art. 411
   • Outside lighting load per Sec. 230-42(a)(1)
   • Outside sign lighting load per Sec.'s 220-3(b)(6); 600-5(b)(3)

(2) Receptacle loads
   • General-purpose receptacle load
   (Noncontinuous per Sec.'s 220-3(b)(9), 230-42(a)(1), and Table 220-13)
   • General-purpose receptacle load
   (Continuous per Sec.'s 220-3(b)(9), 230-42(a)(1))
   • Multioutlet assembly load
   (Used simultaneously per Sec. 220-3(b)(8)(b))
   (Not used simultaneously per Sec. 220-3(b)(8)(a))

(3) Special appliance loads
   • Noncontinuous load per Sec. 230-42(a)(1)
   • Continuous load per Sec. 230-42(a)(1)
   • Demand factors per various sections of the NEC

(4) Compressor loads
   • Refrigeration per Sec.'s 440-34 and 230-42(a)(1)
   • Cooling per Sec.'s 440-34 and 230-42(a)(1)

(5) Motor loads
   • Single-phase per Sec. 430-24 and Table 430-148
   • Three-phase per Sec. 430-24 and Table 430-150

(6) Heating or A/C loads
   • Heating per Sec. 220-15
   • A/C per Sec. 440-34
   • Heat pump per Sec. 440-34

(7) Largest motor loads
   • Taken from loads (4), (5) or (6) per Sec. 220-14

The seven loads are computed at continuous operation or noncontinuous operation. Demand factors are applied to the noncontinuous operated loads by specific sections of the NEC.

Generally, no demand factors can be applied to the loads for commercial occupancies, as the loads are usually used at continuous operation. However, Table 220-11 permits the general lighting loads in hospitals, hotels, motels, and warehouses to have demand factors applied because of load diversity.

# LIGHTING LOADS
# ART. 220; ART. 410; ART. 411

Lighting loads are the first of the loads to be computed. Six lighting loads are computed to derive the total lighting load in commercial facilities. These six loads are as follows:

**(1)** General lighting loads
**(2)** Show window loads
**(3)** Lighting track loads
**(4)** Low-voltage lighting loads
**(5)** Outside lighting loads
**(6)** Sign lighting loads

Each lighting load is computed by the method in which it is used. Loads are calculated at continuous or noncontinuous operation and other lighting loads can have demand factors applied, where permitted.

What is the general lighting load for a noncontinuous lighting load of 60 amps and a continuous load of 100 amps?

**Example Problem 10-1:** Finding general lighting loads.

Step 1: Computing load
220-42(a)(1)
60 A x 100%    =  60  A
100 A x 125%   = 125  A
Total load     = 185  A

Solution: **The computed load for the lighting is 185 amps.**

See **Figure** 10-1 for an exercise problem when computing the general lighting load.

| ILLUSTRATION | FORMULA REQUIREMENTS | EXERCISE PROBLEM |
|---|---|---|
| GENERAL LIGHTING LOAD<br>• 220-3(a)<br>• TABLE 220-3(a)<br>• 230-42(a)(1)<br><br>ELECTRIC DISCHARGE LIGHTING<br>• 90 A<br>• CONTINUOUS<br><br>INCANDESCENT LIGHTING<br>• 70 A<br>• NONCONTINUOUS DISCHARGE<br><br>GENERAL LIGHTING LOAD IS SELECTED FROM THE LIGHTING LOADS<br><br>KNOWN VALUES<br>70 A NONCONTINUOUS<br>90 A CONTINUOUS | NONCONTINUOUS<br>• 70 A LOAD<br><br>CONTINUOUS<br>• 90 A LOAD | Step 1: Computing load<br>_____ A [A] x 100% = _____ A [B]<br>_____ A [C] x 125% = _____ A [D]<br>Total load = _____ A [E]<br><br>Solution: The lighting load is _____ A [F]. |

Figure 10-1. This figure illustrates an exercise problem for computing the general lighting load.

**Example Problem 10-2:** Finding the lighting load for listed occupancies.

What is the load in VA for the general-purpose lighting load in an 8,000 sq. ft. office facility located in a ten story building?

Step 1: Computing load
Table 220-3(a)
8,000 sq. ft. x 3.5 = 28,000 VA

Solution: The general-purpose lighting load is 28,000 VA

See Figure 10-2 for an exercise problem when computing the lighting load of a listed occupancy.

**Figure 10-2.** This figure illustrates an exercise problem for computing the lighting load for a listed occupancy.

**Note:** The total VA in a test problem is only increased by 125 percent when the problem specifically states continuous use.

| ILLUSTRATION | FORMULA REQUIREMENTS | EXERCISE PROBLEM |
|---|---|---|
| GENERAL LIGHTING LOAD<br>• 220-3(a)<br>• TABLE 220-3(a)<br><br>LISTED OCCUPANCY<br><br>ELECTRIC DISCHARGE LIGHTING<br>• 220-4(b)<br>• 230-42(a)(1)<br><br>INCANDESCENT LIGHTING<br>• 220-3(b)(4)<br>• 230-42(a)(1)<br><br>SQUARE FOOTAGE<br>• 6,000 SQ. FT.<br>• STORE BUILDING<br><br>GENERAL PURPOSE LIGHTING IS SELECTED FROM THE LIGHTING LOADS<br><br>KNOWN VALUES<br>6,000 SQ. FT. STORE<br>? VA PER SQ. FT. | 6,000 SQ. FT. STORE<br>? VA PER SQ. FT. | Step 1: Finding lighting load<br>_____ sq. ft. [A] x _____ VA [B]<br>= _____ VA [C]<br><br>Solution: The general lighting load is _____ VA [D].<br><br>Note: For continuous use, 18,000 VA must be multiplied by 125 percent to derive total VA (18,000 VA x 125% = 22,500 VA). |

**Example Problem 10-3:** Finding the lighting load for unlisted occupancies.

What is the load in VA for 60, 120 volt, lighting ballast's rated at 1.5 amps each and used for 12 hours a day?

Step 1: Computing load in A
220-4(b)
60 x 1.5 A = 90 A

Step 2: Computing continuous load
230-42(a)(1)
90 A x 125% = 112.5 A

Step 3: Computed VA
220-2(a)
112.5 A x 120 V = 13,500 VA

Solution: The lighting loads for the unlisted occupancy is 13,500 VA.

See Figure 10-3 for an exercise problem when computing the lighting load of an unlisted occupancy.

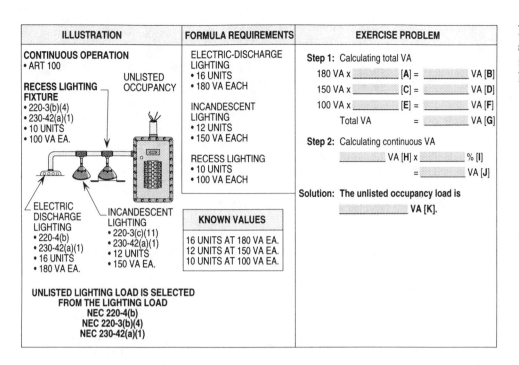

Figure 10-3. This figure illustrates an exercise problem for computing the lighting load for an unlisted occupancy.

What is the lighting load in VA for 80 ft. of show window lighting, used at noncontinuous or continuous operation?

Example Problem 10-4: Finding the show window lighting load.

Step 1: Computing noncontinuous load
220-12(a); 230-42(a)(1)
80' x 200 VA x 100% = 16,000 VA

Step 2: Computing continuous load
220-12(a); 230-42(a)(1)
80' x 200 VA x 125% = 20,000 VA

Solution: **The noncontinuous load is 16,000 VA and the continuous load is 20,000 VA.**

See Figure 10-4 for an exercise problem when computing the show window lighting load.

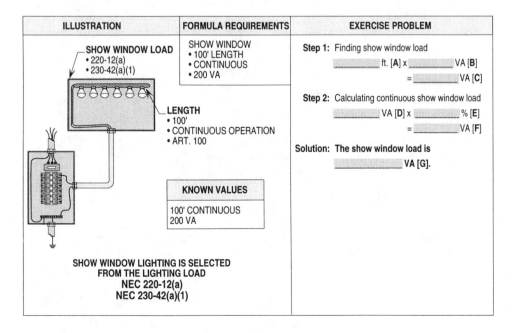

Figure 10-4. This figure illustrates an exercise problem for computing the show window lighting load.

**Example Problem 10-5.** Finding the track lighting load.

What is the load in VA for 80 ft. of lighting track used at noncontinuous or continuous operation?

Step 1: Computing noncontinuous load
220-12(b); 230-42(a)(1)
80' / 2 x 150 VA x 100% = 6,000 VA

Step 2: Computing continuous load
220-12(b); 230-42(a)(1)
80' / 2 x 150 VA x 125% = 7,500 VA

Solution: **The noncontinuous load is 6,000 VA and the continuous load is 7,500 VA.**

See **Figure 10-5** for an exercise problem when computing the track lighting load.

**Figure 10-5.** This figure illustrates an exercise problem for computing the track lighting load.

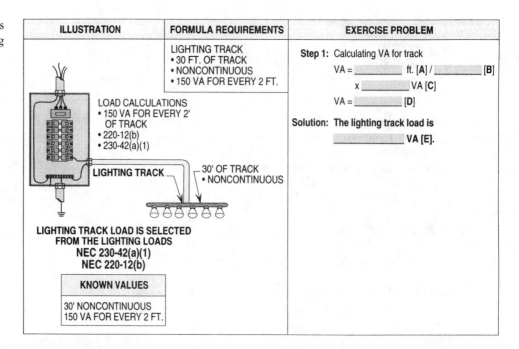

**Example Problem 10-6.** Finding the low-voltage lighting load.

What is the load in VA for a low-voltage lighting system supplied by an isolation transformer with a FLC of 50 amps used at noncontinuous or continuous operation?

Step 1: Computing noncontinuous load
Art. 411; 230-42(a)(1)
50 A x 100% = 50 A

Step 2: Computing continuous load
Art. 411; 230-42(a)(1)
50 A x 125% = 62.5 A

Solution: **The noncontinuous load is 50 amps and the continuous load is 62.5 amps.**

See **Figure 10-6** for an exercise problem when computing the low-voltage lighting load.

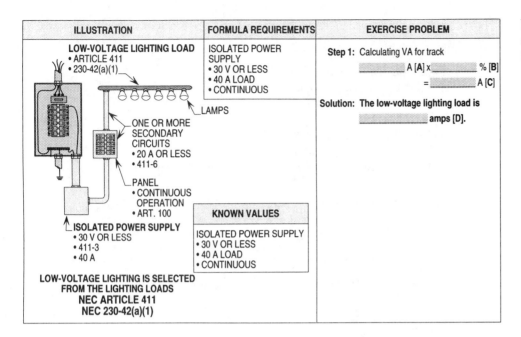

**Figure 10-6.** This figure illustrates an exercise problem for computing the low-voltage lighting load.

What is the lighting load in VA for 30 continuous operated lighting fixtures with a 75 VA ballast in each unit and 10 noncontinuous operated lighting fixtures with each ballast having a rating of 75 VA rating?

**Example Problem 10-7.** Finding the outside lighting load.

Step 1: Computing load
220-4(b); 230-42(a)(1)
75 x 30 x 125%    = 2,812.5 VA
75 x 10 x 100%    =   750   VA
Total load        = 3,562.5 VA

Solution: **The total outside lighting load is 3,562.5 VA.**

See Figure 10-7 for an exercise problem when computing the outside lighting load.

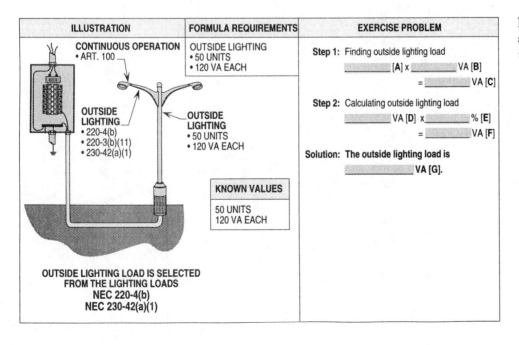

**Figure 10-7.** This figure illustrates an exercise problem for computing the outside lighting load.

**Example Problem 10-8.** Finding the outside sign lighting load.

What is the lighting load in VA for a sign rated at 1,800 VA operating at three hours or more?

Step 1: Computing load
220-3(b)(6); 600-5(b)(3); 230-42(a)(1)
1,800 VA x 125% = 2,250 VA

**Solution: The sign load is 2,250 VA.**

**See Figure 10-8** for an exercise problem when computing the sign lighting load.

**Figure 10-8.** This figure illustrates an exercise problem for computing the sign lighting load.

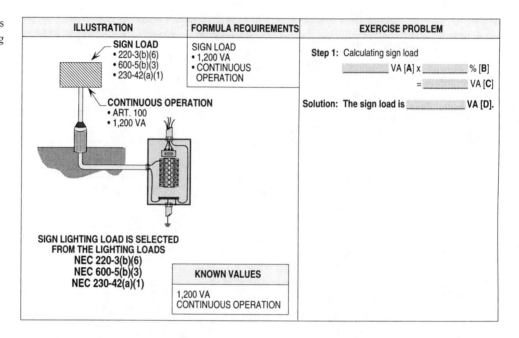

| ILLUSTRATION | FORMULA REQUIREMENTS | EXERCISE PROBLEM |
|---|---|---|
| SIGN LOAD<br>• 220-3(b)(6)<br>• 600-5(b)(3)<br>• 230-42(a)(1) | SIGN LOAD<br>• 1,200 VA<br>• CONTINUOUS OPERATION | Step 1: Calculating sign load<br>_____ VA [A] x _____ % [B]<br>= _____ VA [C]<br>Solution: The sign load is _____ VA [D]. |

CONTINUOUS OPERATION
• ART. 100
• 1,200 VA

SIGN LIGHTING LOAD IS SELECTED
FROM THE LIGHTING LOADS
NEC 220-3(b)(6)
NEC 600-5(b)(3)
NEC 230-42(a)(1)

**KNOWN VALUES**

1,200 VA
CONTINUOUS OPERATION

## RECEPTACLE LOADS
## 220-3(b)(9); TABLE 220-13

Receptacle loads are the second group of loads to be computed. Such loads are divided into two subgroups as follows:

(1) General-purpose receptacle outlets
(2) Multioutlet assemblies

**Example Problem 10-9.** Finding the general-purpose receptacle outlet load.

What is the load in VA for 48 general-purpose receptacles used to serve noncontinuous and continuous related loads?

Step 1: Computing noncontinuous loads
220-3(b)(9); 230-42(a)(1)
180 VA x 48 x 100% = 8,640 VA

Step 2: Computing continuous loads
220-3(b)(9); 230-42(a)(1)
180 VA x 48 x 125% = 10,800 VA

**Solution: The noncontinuous load is 8,640 VA and the continuous load is 10,800 VA.**

**See Figure 10-9** for an exercise problem when computing the general-purpose outlet load.

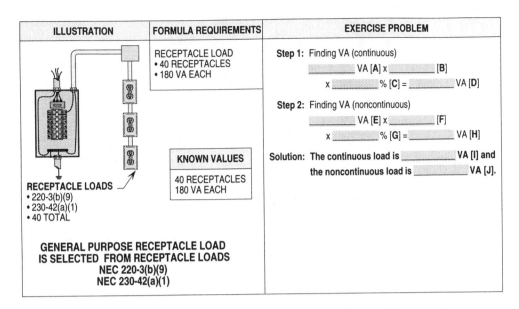

Figure 10-9. This figure illustrates an exercise problem for computing the general-purpose outlet load.

What is the VA rating for 125 general-purpose receptacle outlets to cord-and-plug connect loads used at noncontinuous operation?

**Example Problem 10-10.** Finding the general-purpose receptacle outlet load (noncontinuous operation) when applying demand factors.

**Step 1:**  Computing load
220-3(b)(9)
125 x 180 VA  = 22,500 VA

**Step 2:**  Applying demand factors
Table 220-13
First 10,000 VA x 100%     = 10,000  VA
Next 12,500 VA x 50%     = <u>  6,250  VA</u>
Total load     = 16,250  VA

**Solution:**  **The demand load is 16,250 VA.**

See Figure 10-10 for an exercise problem when computing the general-purpose receptacle outlet load and applying demand factors.

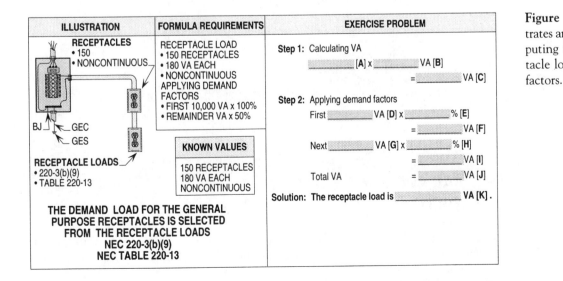

Figure 10-10. This figure illustrates an exercise problem for computing the general-purpose receptacle load when applying demand factors.

**Example Problem 10-11.** Finding the multioutlet assemblies load.

**Note:** The fixed multioutlet assemblies load shall be permitted to be added to the noncontinuous receptacle load for nondwelling units and demand factors applied per Table 220-13.

What is the load in VA for 100 ft. of multioutlet assembly used to cord-and-plug connect loads that are not used simultaneously and used simultaneously?

Step 1: Connecting load for nonsimultaneous use
220-3(b)(8)(a)
VA = length / 5' x 180 VA
VA = 100' / 5' x 180 VA
VA = 3,600

Step 2: Computing load for simultaneous use
220-3(b)(8)(b)
VA = length x 180 VA
VA = 100' x 180 VA
VA = 18,000 VA

Solution: The load in VA for nonsimultaneous load is 3,600 VA and for simultaneous load is 18,000 VA.

See Figure 10-11 for an exercise problem when computing the multioutlet assembly load.

**Figure 10-11.** This figure illustrates an exercise problem for computing the multioutlet assembly load.

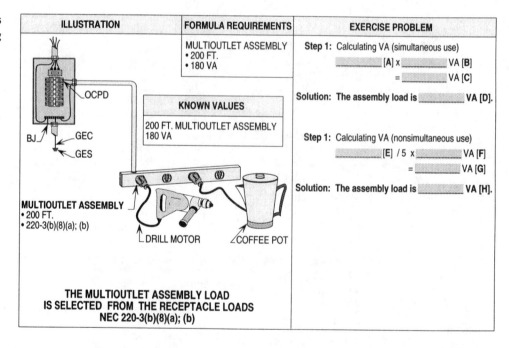

| ILLUSTRATION | FORMULA REQUIREMENTS | EXERCISE PROBLEM |
|---|---|---|
| OCPD BJ GEC GES MULTIOUTLET ASSEMBLY • 200 FT. • 220-3(b)(8)(a); (b) DRILL MOTOR COFFEE POT THE MULTIOUTLET ASSEMBLY LOAD IS SELECTED FROM THE RECEPTACLE LOADS NEC 220-3(b)(8)(a); (b) | MULTIOUTLET ASSEMBLY • 200 FT. • 180 VA KNOWN VALUES 200 FT. MULTIOUTLET ASSEMBLY 180 VA | Step 1: Calculating VA (simultaneous use) _____ [A] x _____ VA [B] = _____ VA [C] Solution: The assembly load is _____ VA [D]. Step 1: Calculating VA (nonsimultaneous use) _____ [E] / 5 x _____ VA [F] = _____ VA [G] Solution: The assembly load is _____ VA [H]. |

# SPECIAL APPLIANCE LOADS
## 230-42(a)(1)

Special appliance loads are the third group to be computed. These loads, which include computers, processing machines, etc. are usually served by individual circuits.

What is the VA rating for a 208 volt, three-phase, 65 amp special appliance load operating for ten hours and supplied by an individual branch-circuit?

Step 1: Computing VA
220-2(a)
VA = V x 1.732 x I
VA = 208 V x 1.732 (360 V) x 65
VA = 23,400

Step 2: Computing continuous load
230-42(a)(1)
23,400 VA x 125% = 29,250 VA

Solution: **The load at continuous operation is 29,250 VA.**

See **Figure 10-12** for an exercise problem when computing the special appliance load at continuous operation.

**Example Problem 10-12.** Finding the special appliance load at continuous operation.

Note that 360 volts are used for the calculation and not 360.256 volts. Check with the testing agencies and verify if 360 volts is used or if the full square root of 3 is used. (208 V x 1.732 = 360.256 V)

| ILLUSTRATION | FORMULA REQUIREMENTS | EXERCISE PROBLEM |
|---|---|---|
| OCPD<br>• 230-42(a)(1)<br>• 230-90(a)<br><br>GEC<br>BJ<br>GES<br>APPLIANCE<br>• LOAD IS 13,728 VA<br>• CONTINUOUS USE<br><br>THE SPECIAL APPLIANCE LOAD CONSISTS OF ALL THE SPECIAL APPLIANCE LOADS NEC 230-42(a)(1)<br><br>**KNOWN VALUES**<br>13,728 VA LOAD<br>CONTINUOUS OPERATION | APPLIANCE LOAD<br>• 13,728 VA LOAD<br>• CONTINUOUS OPERATION | **Step 1:** Calculating VA<br>_____ VA [A] x _____ % [B]<br>= _____ VA [C]<br><br>**Solution:** The appliance load is<br>_____ VA [D]. |

**Figure 10-12.** This figure illustrates an exercise problem for computing the special appliance load at continuous operation.

Consider and compute the VA rating for a special appliance load of 52 amps operating at 480 volts, three-phase, for a period of 2 1/2 hours every four hours?

Step 1: Computing VA
220-2(a)
VA = V x 1.732 x I
VA = 480 V x 1.732 (831 V) x 52 A
VA = 43,212

Step 2: Computing noncontinuous load
230-42(a)(1)
43,212 VA x 100% = 43,212 VA

Solution: **The load in VA for the noncontinuous load is 43,212 VA.**

See **Figure 10-13** for an exercise problem when computing the special appliance load at noncontinuous operation.

**Example Problem 10-13.** Finding the special appliance load at noncontinuous operation.

**Figure 10-13.** This figure illustrates an exercise problem for computing the special appliance load at non-continuous operation.

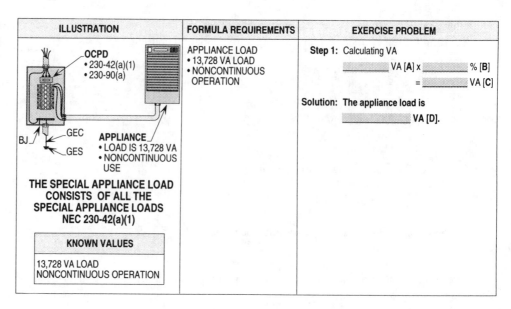

| ILLUSTRATION | FORMULA REQUIREMENTS | EXERCISE PROBLEM |
|---|---|---|
| **OCPD**<br>• 230-42(a)(1)<br>• 230-90(a)<br><br>BJ — GEC<br>— GES<br>**APPLIANCE**<br>• LOAD IS 13,728 VA<br>• NONCONTINUOUS USE<br><br>**THE SPECIAL APPLIANCE LOAD CONSISTS OF ALL THE SPECIAL APPLIANCE LOADS NEC 230-42(a)(1)**<br><br>**KNOWN VALUES**<br>13,728 VA LOAD<br>NONCONTINUOUS OPERATION | APPLIANCE LOAD<br>• 13,728 VA LOAD<br>• NONCONTINUOUS OPERATION | **Step 1:** Calculating VA<br><br>_____ VA [A] x _____ % [B]<br>= _____ VA [C]<br><br>**Solution:** The appliance load is<br>_____ VA [D]. |

**Example Problem 10-14.** Finding the special appliance load when applying demand factors.

What is the demand load in VA and amps for ten, 208 volt, three-phase cooking units rated 8 kW each?

Step 1: Computing VA
220-20
8 kW x 10 = 80 kW

Step 2: Computing amps
220-2
I = kW x 1,000 / V x 1.732
I = 80 kW x 1,000 / 208 V x 1.732 (360 V)
I = 222 A

Step 3: Applying demand factors
Table 220-20
222 A x 65%          = 144.3   A
144.3 A x 360 V     = 51,948  VA

Solution: **The demand load is 51,948 VA.**

See **Figure 10-14** for an exercise problem when computing the special appliance load and applying demand factors based upon the number of units.

# COMPRESSOR LOADS
## 440-34

Compressor loads are the fourth group of loads to be computed. Special considerations must be applied when computing loads for hermetically sealed compressors.

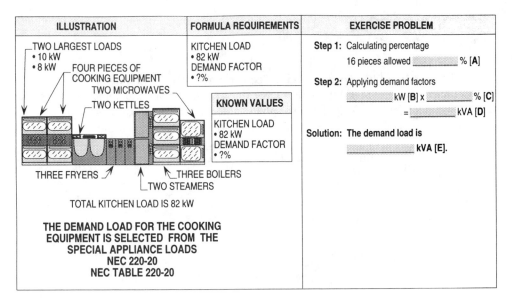

**Figure 10-14.** This figure illustrates an exercise problem for computing the special appliance load when demand factors are applied.

What is the total load in VA for six compressors rated at 26.5 amps each and supplied by a 480 volt, three-phase supply?

**Example Problem 10-15.** Finding the compressor load in VA.

Step 1: Computing VA
220-2
26.5 A x 6 x 480 V x 1.732 (831 V) = 132,129 VA

Note all motors are calculated at 100 percent and the largest motor related load in the fourth, fifth, or sixth loads is calculated at 25 percent in the seventh load.

Step 2: Computing total VA
230-42(a)(1)
132,129 VA x 100% = 132,129 VA

Solution: **The continuous load rating is 132,129 VA.**

See **Figure 10-15** for an exercise problem when computing the compressor load.

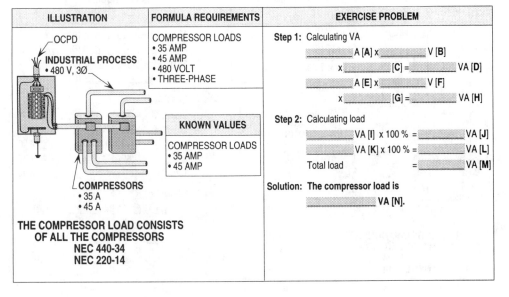

**Figure 10-15.** This figure illustrates an exercise problem for computing the compressor load in VA.

## MOTOR LOADS
## 220-14; 430-24

Motor loads are the fifth group of loads to be computed. The VA rating of a motor is converted from amperage to VA by multiplying the amperage from Table 430-148 for single-phase motors or Table 430-150 for three-phase motors by the supply voltage.

**Example Problem 10-16.** Finding the motor loads in VA.

What is the VA rating for a group of 480 volt, three-phase motors rated at 30 HP, 20 HP, and 15 HP respectively?

Step 1: Finding FLA
Table 430-150
30 HP = 40 A
20 HP = 27 A
15 HP = 21 A

Step 2: Computing total VA
220-2(a)
VA = V x 1.732 x I
30 HP motor
480 V x 1.732 x 40 A      = 33,240 VA
20 HP motor
480 V x 1.732 x 27 A      = 22,437 VA
15 HP motor
480 V x 1.732 x 21 A      = 17,451 VA
Total load      = 73,128 VA

Solution: The total load for the motors is 73,128 VA.

See Figure 10-16 for an exercise problem when computing the motor loads.

**Figure 10-16.** This figure illustrates an exercise problem for computing the motor loads in VA.

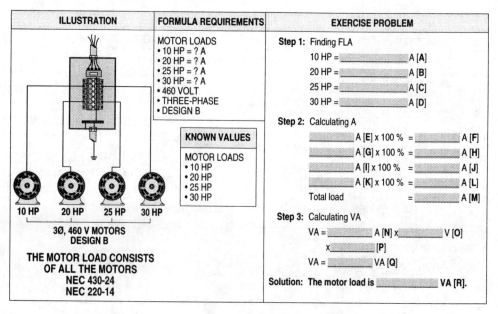

# HEAT OR A/C LOADS
## 220-21

Heating or A/C loads is the sixth group of loads to be computed. The largest VA rating between the heating or A/C load is selected and the smaller of the two loads is dropped. To determine the largest of the two loads, the VA rating for each is computed at 100 percent and the largest load of the two is selected. The load dropped is not used again in the calculation.

**Note:** Where it is unlikely that two or more noncoincident loads will be in use simultaneously, it shall be permissible to use only the largest load(s) that will be used at one time in computing the total of a service.

What is the largest load between a 30 kW heating unit and a 32.5 amp A/C unit? The voltage is supplied by 208 volts, three-phase system.

**Example Problem 10-17.** Finding largest load between the heat or A/C.

Step 1: Selecting largest load
220-21
Heating load
30 kW x 1,000 x 100% = 30,000 VA
A/C load
32.5 A x 208 V x 1.732 = 11,700 VA

Solution: **The 30,000 VA heating unit is the largest load.**

See **Figure 10-17** for an exercise problem when computing largest load between the heat or A/C.

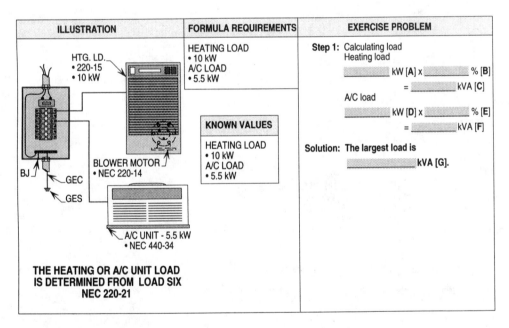

**Figure 10-17.** This figure illustrates an exercise problem for computing the largest load between the heat or A/C.

Note that an attic fan motor is considered a noncoincident load and can be dropped per Sec. 220-17.

# LARGEST MOTOR LOAD
## 220-14; 430-24

The largest motor load in VA is the seventh group of loads to be computed. The largest motor load is selected from one of the motor related loads listed in the fourth, fifth, or sixth loads. The VA rating of the largest motor is computed by multiplying the amperage of the unit by the voltage times 25 percent.

**Example Problem 10-18.** Finding the largest motor load in amps.

What is the largest motor load from the following loads?

Fourth load = compressor of 35 A
Fifth load = motor of 40 A
Sixth load = A/C unit = 30 A

Step 1: Selecting largest load
220-14; 440-34; 430-24
The motor load of 40 A is the largest motor

Solution: **The largest motor load is 40 amps.**

See Figure 10-18 for an exercise problem when computing the largest motor load.

**Figure 10-18.** This figure illustrates an exercise problem for computing the largest motor load in VA.

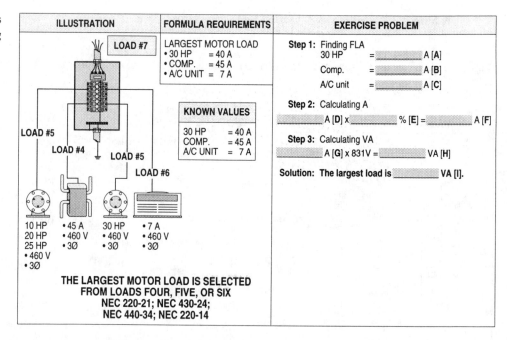

# STANDARD CALCULATIONS
# PARTS A, B AND C TO ART. 220

The elements of electrical systems can be computed by using the standard calculation. The size of these elements are determined by which method the designer chooses to compute these loads. The following computations are typical examples of how these loads are calculated, sized, and selected. The step-by-step procedures are easy to follow and have condensed the more complicated rules pertaining to calculating loads into a compact listing, that provides easier understanding of how to perform calculations according to the provisions of the NEC. A broad assortment of basic code calculations have been selected to represent the main principles of designing electrical systems that may appear on the test.

# ADDING ADDITIONAL LOADS TO EXISTING INSTALLATIONS 220-35

When additional loads are added to existing facilties having feeders and service as originally computed, the maximum kVA computations in determining the load on the existing feeders and service can be used, if the maximum data of the demand in kVA is available for a minimum of one year. If the demand ratings for that period of one year is at 125 percent and the addition of the new load does not exceed the rating of the service, such a load can be added to the existing service.

Note that a new load can be added to an existing feeder under certain conditions of use per Sec. 220-35, Ex.

**Example Problem 10-19.** Determining if a new load can be added to an existing service.

**For Example:** Can a load of 15.1 kVA be added to an existing service with No. 400 KCMIL THW copper conductors having a maximum demand of 78.4 kVA?

**Step 1:** Finding demand
220-35
Maximum demand = 78.4 kVA

**Step 2:** Calculating existing demand
220-35
78.4 kVA x 125% = 98 kVA

**Step 3:** Calculating total kVA
230-42(a)(1)
98 kV + 15.1 kVA = 113.1 kVA

Note that the 15.1 kVA load has already been computed at continuous and noncontinuous operation.

**Step 4:** Calculating amperage
Table 310-16
No. 400 KCMIL THW copper = 335A
113.1 x 1,000 = 113,100 VA
113,100 VA / 208 x 1.732 = 314 A
314 A is less than 335 A

**Solution:** **The 15.1 kVA load can be applied to the existing service without upgrading the elements.**

See **Figure 10-19** for an exercise problem when determining if a new load can be added to an existing service without having to upgrade the components.

**Figure 10-19.** This figure illustrates the calculations to determine if a new load can be added to an existing service.

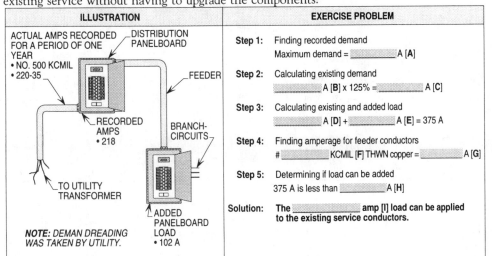

| ILLUSTRATION | EXERCISE PROBLEM |
|---|---|
| ACTUAL AMPS RECORDED FOR A PERIOD OF ONE YEAR • NO. 500 KCMIL • 220-35 DISTRIBUTION PANELBOARD — FEEDER — RECORDED AMPS • 218 — BRANCH-CIRCUITS — TO UTILITY TRANSFORMER — ADDED PANELBOARD LOAD • 102 A **NOTE:** DEMAN DREADING WAS TAKEN BY UTILITY. | **Step 1:** Finding recorded demand<br>Maximum demand = _____ A [A]<br><br>**Step 2:** Calculating existing demand<br>_____ A [B] x 125% = _____ A [C]<br><br>**Step 3:** Calculating existing and added load<br>_____ A [D] + _____ A [E] = 375 A<br><br>**Step 4:** Finding amperage for feeder conductors<br># _____ KCMIL [F] THWN copper = _____ A [G]<br><br>**Step 5:** Determining if load can be added<br>375 A is less than _____ A [H]<br><br>**Solution:** The _____ amp [I] load can be applied to the existing service conductors. |

**Example Problem 10-20.** What is the load in VA and amps to compute and size the elements for a 120 / 240 volt, single-phase service supplying a 50,000 sq. ft. store including a 30,000 sq. ft. warehouse space with the following loads?

| 120 V, single-phase loads | 240 V, single-phase loads | |
|---|---|---|
| • 100 linear feet of show window (noncontinuous operation) <br> • 120 ft. of lighting track (noncontinuous operation) <br> • 40 - 180 VA ballast's outside lighting (continuous operation) <br> • 4,200 VA sign lighting (continuous operation) <br> • 74 receptacles (noncontinuous operation) <br> • 24 receptacles (continuous operation) <br> • 50 ft. multioutlet assembly (heavy-duty) | • 12,000 VA water heater <br> • 60,000 VA heating unit <br> • 24,800 VA A/C unit <br> • 7,240 VA freezer <br> • 6,480 VA ice cream box <br> • 9,560 VA walk-in cooler <br> • 1 - 1/2 HP exhaust fan <br> • 1 - 2 HP water pump | Sizing phases = • <br> Sizing neutral = √ <br> Sizing total load = * |

**Calculating lighting load**

Step 1: General lighting load
Table 220-3(a); 230-42(a)(1)

| | | | |
|---|---|---|---|
| 50,000 sq. ft. x 3 VA | = | 150,000 | VA √ |
| 150,000 VA x 125% | = | 187,500 | VA * |
| 30,000 sq. ft. x 1/4 VA | = | 7,500 | VA √ |
| 7,500 VA x 125% | = | 9,375 | VA * |

Step 2: Show window load
220-12(a)

| | | | |
|---|---|---|---|
| 100' x 200 VA | = | 20,000 | VA * √ |

Step 3: Track lighting load
220-12(b)

| | | | |
|---|---|---|---|
| 120' / 2 x 150 VA | = | 9,000 | VA * √ |

Step 4: Outside lighting load
230-42(a)(1)

| | | | |
|---|---|---|---|
| 40 x 180 VA | = | 7,200 | VA √ |
| 7,200 VA x 125% | = | 9,000 | VA * |

Step 5: Sign lighting load
600-5(b)(3); 230-42(a)(1)

| | | | |
|---|---|---|---|
| 4,200 VA x 100% | = | 4,200 | VA √ |
| 4,200 VA x 125% | = | 5,250 | VA * |
| Total load | = | 240,125 | VA • |

**Calculating receptacle loads**

Step 1: Noncontinuous operation
220-3(b)(9); 220-3(b)(8)(b)

| | | | |
|---|---|---|---|
| 74 x 180 VA | = | 13,320 | VA |
| 100' x 180 VA | = | 18,000 | VA |
| Total Load | = | 31,320 | VA |
| Table 220-13 | | | |
| First 10,000 VA x 100% | = | 10,000 | VA |
| Next 21,320 VA x 50% | = | 10,660 | VA |
| Total load | = | 20,660 | VA * √ |

Step 2: Continuous operation
220-3(b)(9); 230-42(a)(1)

| | | | |
|---|---|---|---|
| 24 x 180 VA | = | 4,320 | VA √ |
| 4,320 VA x 125% | = | 5,400 | VA * |
| Totalo Load | = | 26,060 | VA • |

**Calculating special loads**

Step 1: 12,000 VA x 100% = 12,000 VA * •

**Calculating compressor loads**

Step 1: Freezer load
230-42(a)(1)

| | | | |
|---|---|---|---|
| 7,240 VA x 100% | = | 7,240 | VA * |

Step 2: Ice cream boxes
230-42(a)(1)

| | | | |
|---|---|---|---|
| 6,480 VA x 100% | = | 6,480 | VA * |

Step 3: Walk-in cooler
230-42(a)(1)

| | | | |
|---|---|---|---|
| 9,560 VA x 100% | = | 9,560 | VA * |
| Total load | = | 23,280 | VA • |

**Calculating motor loads**

Step 1: Water pump load
430-24; Table 430-148

| | | | |
|---|---|---|---|
| 12 A x 240 V x 100% | = | 2,880 | VA * |

Step 2: Exhaust fan load
430-24; Table 430-148

| | | | |
|---|---|---|---|
| 4.9 A x 240 V x 100% | = | 1,176 | VA * |
| Total load | = | 4,056 | VA • |

**Calculating heating or A/C load**

Step 1: Heating load selected
220-21

| | | | |
|---|---|---|---|
| 60,000 VA x 100% | = | 60,000 | VA * • |
| 24,800 VA x 100% | = | 24,800 | VA |

**Calculating largest motor load**

Step 1: Walk-in cooler
220-14; 430-24

| | | | |
|---|---|---|---|
| 9,560 VA x 25% | = | 2,390 | VA * • |

**Calculating phases (Total loads)**

| | | | |
|---|---|---|---|
| Lighting loads | = | 240,125 | VA • |
| Receptacle loads | = | 26,060 | VA • |
| Special loads | = | 12,000 | VA • |
| Compressor loads | = | 23,280 | VA • |
| Motor loads | = | 4,056 | VA • |
| Heating loads | = | 60,000 | VA • |
| Largest motor load | = | 2,390 | VA • |
| Total load | = | 367,911 | VA |

**Calculating Neutral**

| | | | |
|---|---|---|---|
| Lighting load | = | 197,900 | VA √ |
| Receptacle load | = | 24,980 | VA √ |
| Total load | = | 222,880 | VA |

**Finding amps for Phases A and B**

I = VA / V
I = 367,911 VA / 240 V
I = 1,533 A

**Finding amps for Neutral**

I = VA / V
I = 222,880 VA / 240 V
I = 929 A

**See Figure 10-20** for an exercise problem when computing a 120/240 volt, single-phase service supplying a store and warehouse space.

Exercise Problem 10-20. What is the load in VA and amps to compute and size the elements for a 120 / 240 volt, single-phase service supplying a 40,000 sq. ft. store with 20,000 sq. ft. of warehouse space with the following loads?

| 120 V, single-phase loads | 240 V, single-phase loads | |
|---|---|---|
| • 80 linear feet of show window (noncontinuous operation)<br>• 120' of lighting track (noncontinuous operation)<br>• 30 - 180 VA ballast's outside lighting (continuous operation)<br>• 3,600 VA sign lighting (continuous operation)<br>• 65 receptacles (noncontinuous operation)<br>• 28 receptacles (continuous operation)<br>• 40' multioutlet assembly (heavy-duty) | • 10,000 VA water heater<br>• 50,000 VA heating unit<br>• 23,320 VA A/C unit<br>• 7,380 VA freezer<br>• 5,580 VA ice cream boxes<br>• 1 - 1/2 HP exhaust fan<br>• 1 - 2 HP water pump<br>• 9,540 VA walk-in cooler | Sizing phases = •<br>Sizing neutral = √<br>Sizing total load = * |

**Calculating lighting load**

Step 1: General lighting load
Table 220-3(a); 230-42(a)(1)
40,000 sq. ft. x 3 VA = _____ VA [A] √
120,000 VA x 125% = _____ VA [B] *
20,000 sq. ft. x 1/4 VA = _____ VA [C] √
5,000 VA x 125% = _____ VA [D] *

Step 2: Show window load
220-12(a)
80' x 200 = _____ VA [E] * √

Step 3: Track lighting load
220-12(b)
120' / 2 x 150 VA = _____ VA [F] * √

Step 4: Outside lighting load
230-42(a)(1)
30 x 180 VA = _____ VA [G] √
5,400 VA x 125% = _____ VA [H] *

Step 5: Sign lighting load
600-5(b)(3); 230-42(a)(1)
3,600 VA x 100% = _____ VA [I] √
3,600 VA x 125% = _____ VA [J] *
Total load = _____ VA [K] •

**Calculating receptacle loads**

Step 1: Noncontinuous operation
220-3(b)(9); 220-3(b)(8)(b)
65 x 180 VA = _____ VA [L]
80' x 180 VA = _____ VA [M]
Total Load = _____ VA [N]
Table 220-13
First 10,000 VA x 100% = _____ VA [O]
Next 16,100 VA x 50% = _____ VA [P]
Total load = _____ VA [Q] *√

Step 2: Continuous operation
220-3(b)(9); 230-42(a)(1)
28 x 180 VA = _____ VA [R]
5,040 VA x 125% = _____ VA [S] *
Total Load = _____ VA [T]

**Calculating special loads**

Step 1: Water heater load
10,000 VA x 100% = _____ VA [U] * •

**Calculating compressor loads**

Step 1: Freezer load
230-42(a)(1)
7,380 VA x 100% = _____ VA [V] *

Step 2: Ice cream boxes
5,580 VA x 100% = _____ VA [W] *

Step 3: Walk-in cooler
9,540 VA x 100% = _____ VA [X] *
Total load = _____ VA [Y] •

**Calculating motor loads**

Step 1: Water pump load
430-24; Table 430-148
12 A x 240 V x 100% = _____ VA [Z] *

Step 2: Exhaust fan load
4.9 A x 240 V x 100% = _____ VA [AA] *
Total load = _____ VA [BB] •

**Calculating heating or A/C load**

Step 1: Heating load selected
220-21
50,000 VA x 100% = _____ VA [CC] * •
23,320 VA x 100% = _____ VA [DD]

**Calculating largest motor load**

Step 1: Walk-in cooler
220-14; 430-24
9,540 VA x 25% = _____ VA [EE] * •

**Calculating phases (Total loads)**

Lighting loads = _____ VA [FF] •
Receptacle loads = _____ VA [GG] •
Special loads = _____ VA [HH] •
Compressor loads = _____ VA [II] •
Motor loads = _____ VA [JJ] •
Heating load = _____ VA [KK] •
Largest motor load = _____ VA [LL] •
Total load for facility = _____ VA [MM]

**Finding amps for phases A and B**

I = VA / V
I = _____ VA [NN] / _____ V [OO]
I = _____ A [PP]

**Calculating neutral**

Lighting load = _____ VA [QQ] √
Receptacle load = _____ VA [RR] √
Total load = _____ VA [SS]

**Finding amps for neutral**

I = VA / V
I = _____ VA [TT] / _____ V [UU]
I = _____ A [VV]

**Figure 10-20.** The above is an exercise problem for computing the amps of a store and warehouse space that is supplied by a 120/240 volt, single-phase service.

**Example Problem 10-21.** What is the load in VA and amps to compute and size the elements for a 120 / 208 volt, three-phase service supplying a 50,000 sq. ft. store including a 30,000 sq. ft. warehouse space with the following loads?

| 120 V, single-phase loads | 208 V, three-phase loads | Sizing phases = • |
|---|---|---|
| | | Sizing neutral = √ |
| | | Sizing total load = * |

**120 V, single-phase loads**
- 100 linear feet of show window (noncontinuous operation)
- 120 ft. of lighting track (noncontinuous operation)
- 40 - 180 VA ballast's outside lighting (continuous operation)
- 4,200 VA sign lighting (continuous operation)
- 74 receptacles (noncontinuous operation)
- 24 receptacles (continuous operation)
- 50 ft. multioutlet assembly (heavy-duty)

**208 V, three-phase loads**
- 12,000 VA water heater
- 60,000 VA heating unit
- 24,800 VA A/C unit
- 7,240 VA freezer
- 6,480 VA ice cream box
- 9,560 VA walk-in cooler
- 1 - 1/2 HP exhaust fan
- 1 - 2 HP water pump

**Calculating lighting load**

Step 1: General lighting load
Table 220-3(a); 230-42(a)(1)

| | | |
|---|---|---|
| 50,000 sq. ft. x 3 VA | = | 150,000 VA √ |
| 150,000 VA x 125% | = | 187,500 VA * |
| 30,000 sq. ft. x 1/4 VA | = | 7,500 VA √ |
| 7,500 VA x 125% | = | 9,375 VA * |

Step 2: Show window load
220-12(a)

| | | |
|---|---|---|
| 100' x 200 VA | = | 20,000 VA * √ |

Step 3: Track lighting load
220-12(b)

| | | |
|---|---|---|
| 120' / 2 x 150 VA | = | 9,000 VA * √ |

Step 4: Outside lighting load
230-42(a)(1)

| | | |
|---|---|---|
| 40 x 180 VA | = | 7,200 VA √ |
| 7,200 VA x 125% | = | 9,000 VA * |

Step 5: Sign lighting load
600-5(b)(3); 230-42(a)(1)

| | | |
|---|---|---|
| 4,200 VA x 100% | = | 4,200 VA √ |
| 4,200 VA x 125% | = | 5,250 VA * |
| Total load | = | 240,125 VA • |

**Calculating receptacle loads**

Step 1: Noncontinuous operation
220-3(b)(9); 220-3(b)(8)(b)

| | | |
|---|---|---|
| 74 x 180 VA | = | 13,320 VA |
| 100' x 180 VA | = | 18,000 VA |
| Total Load | = | 31,320 VA |

Table 220-13

| | | |
|---|---|---|
| First 10,000 VA x 100% | = | 10,000 VA |
| Next 21,320 VA x 50% | = | 10,660 VA |
| Total load | = | 20,660 VA * √ |

Step 2: Continuous operation
220-3(b)(9); 230-42(a)(1)

| | | |
|---|---|---|
| 24 x 180 VA | = | 4,320 VA √ |
| 4,320 VA x 125% | = | 5,400 VA * |
| Total load | = | 26,060 VA • |

**Calculating special load**

Step 1: 12,000 VA x 100%    =    12,000 VA * •

**Calculating compressor loads**

Step 1: Freezer load
230-42(a)(1)

| | | |
|---|---|---|
| 7,240 VA x 100% | = | 7,240 VA * |

Step 2: Ice cream boxes
230-42(a)(1)

| | | |
|---|---|---|
| 6,480 VA x 100% | = | 6,480 VA * |

Step 3: Walk-in cooler
230-42(a)(1)

| | | |
|---|---|---|
| 9,560 VA x 100% | = | 9,560 VA * |
| Total load | = | 23,280 VA • |

**Calculating motor loads**

Step 1: Water pump load
430-24; Table 430-150

| | | |
|---|---|---|
| 7.5 A x 360 V x 100% | = | 2,700 VA * |

Step 2: Exhaust fan load
430-24; Table 430-150

| | | |
|---|---|---|
| 2.4 A x 360 V x 100% | = | 864 VA * |
| Total load | = | 3,564 VA • |

**Calculating heating or A/C load**

Step 1: Heating load selected
220-21

| | | |
|---|---|---|
| 60,000 VA x 100% | = | 60,000 VA * • |
| 24,800 VA x 100% | = | 24,800 VA |

**Calculating largest motor load**

Step 1: Walk-in cooler
220-14; 430-24

| | | |
|---|---|---|
| 9,560 VA x 25% | = | 2,390 VA * • |

**Calculating phases (Total loads)**

| | | |
|---|---|---|
| Lighting loads | = | 240,125 VA • |
| Receptacle loads | = | 26,060 VA • |
| Special loads | = | 12,000 VA • |
| Compressor loads | = | 23,280 VA • |
| Motor loads | = | 3,564 VA • |
| Heating load | = | 60,000 VA • |
| Largest motor load | = | 2,390 VA • |
| Total load | = | 367,419 VA |

**Calculating neutral**

| | | |
|---|---|---|
| Lighting load | = | 197,900 VA √ |
| Receptacle load | = | 24,980 VA √ |
| Total load | = | 222,880 VA |

**Finding amps for Phases A and B**

I = VA / V
I = 367,419 VA / 360 V
I = 1,021 A

**Finding amps for neutral**

I = VA / V
I = 222,880 VA / 360 V
I = 619 A

Note that the 360 volt is used (208 V x 1.732) instead of 360.256 volt.

See **Figure 10-21** for an exercise problem when computing a 120/208 volt, single-phase service supplying a store and warehouse space.

Exercise Problem 10-21.What is the load in VA and amps to compute and size the elements for a 120 / 208 volt, three-phase, four-wire service supplying a 40,000 sq. ft. store with 20,000 sq. ft. of warehouse space with the following loads?

| 120 V, single-phase loads | 208 V, three-phase loads | |
|---|---|---|
| • 80 linear feet of show window (noncontinuous operation)<br>• 120' of lighting track (noncontinuous operation)<br>• 30 - 180 VA ballast's outside lighting (continuous operation)<br>• 3,600 VA sign lighting (continuous operation)<br>• 65 receptacles (noncontinuous operation)<br>• 28 receptacles (continuous operation)<br>• 40' multioutlet assembly (heavy-duty) | • 7,380 VA freezer<br>• 5,580 VA ice cream boxes<br>• 1 - 1/2 HP exhaust fan<br>• 10,000 VA water heater<br>• 9,540 VA walk-in cooler<br>• 50,000 VA heating unit<br>• 23,320 VA A/C unit<br>• 1 - 2 HP water pump | Sizing phases = •<br>Sizing neutral = √<br>Sizing total load = * |

**Calculating lighting load**

Step 1: General lighting load
Table 220-3(a); 230-42(a)(1)
40,000 sq. ft. x 3 VA = _____ VA [A] √
120,000 VA x 125% = _____ VA [B] *
20,000 sq. ft. x 1/4 VA = _____ VA [C] √
5,000 VA x 125% = _____ VA [D] *

Step 2: Show window load
220-12(a)
80' x 200 = _____ VA [E] * √

Step 3: Track lighting load
220-12(b)
120' / 2 x 150 VA = _____ VA [F] * √

Step 4: Outside lighting load
230-42(a)(1)
30 x 180 VA = _____ VA [G] √
5,400 VA x 125% = _____ VA [H] *

Step 5: Sign lighting load
600-5(b)(3); 230-42(a)(1)
3,600 VA x 100% = _____ VA [I] √
3,600 VA x 125% = _____ VA [J] *
Total load = _____ VA [K] •

**Calculating receptacle load**

Step 1: Noncontinuous operation
220-3(b)(9); 220-3(b)(8)(b)
65 x 180 VA = _____ VA [L]
80' x 180 VA = _____ VA [M]
Total Load = _____ VA [N]

Table 220-13
First 10,000 VA x 100% = _____ VA [O]
Next 16,100 VA x 50% = _____ VA [P]
Total load = _____ VA [Q] * √

Step 2: Continuous operation
220-3(b)(9); 230-42(a)(1)
28 x 180 VA = _____ VA [R] √
5,040 VA x 125% = _____ VA [S] *
Total load = _____ VA [T] •

**Calculating special loads**

Step 1: Water heater load
10,000 VA x 100% = _____ VA [U] * •

**Calculating compressor loads**

Step 1: Freezer load
230-42(a)(1)
7,380 VA x 100% = _____ VA [V] *

Step 2: Ice cream boxes
5,580 VA x 100% = _____ VA [W] *

Step 3: Walk-in cooler
9,540 VA x 100% = _____ VA [X] *
Total load = _____ VA [Y] •

**Calculating motor loads**

Step 1: Water pump load
430-24; Table 430-150
7.5 A x 360 V x 100% = _____ VA [Z] *

Step 2: Exhaust fan load
2.4 A x 360 V x 100% = _____ VA [AA] *
Total load = _____ VA [BB] •

**Calculating heating or A/C load**

Step 1: Heating load selected
220-21
50,000 VA x 100% = _____ VA [CC] * •
23,320 VA x 100% = _____ VA [DD]

**Calculating largest motor load**

Step 1: Walk-in cooler
220-14; 430-24
9,540 VA x 25% = _____ VA [EE] * •

**Calculating phases (Total loads)**

Lighting loads = _____ VA [FF] •
Receptacle loads = _____ VA [GG] •
Special loads = _____ VA [HH] •
Compressor loads = _____ VA [II] •
Motor loads = _____ VA [JJ] •
Heating load = _____ VA [KK] •
Largest motor load = _____ VA [LL] •
Total load for facility = _____ VA [MM]

**Finding amps for phases A and B**

I = VA / V
I = _____ VA [NN] / _____ V [OO]
I = _____ A [PP]

**Calculating neutral**

Lighting load = _____ VA [QQ] √
Receptacle load = _____ VA [RR] √
Total load = _____ VA [SS]

**Finding amps for neutral**

I = VA / V
I = _____ VA [TT] / _____ V [UU]
I = _____ A [VV]

**Figure 10-21.** The above is an exercise problem for computing a store and warehouse space that is supplied by a 120/208 volt, single-phase service.

**Example Problem 10-22.** What is the load in VA and amps to compute and size the elements for a 277 / 480 volt, three-phase service supplying a 50,000 sq. ft. store including a 30,000 sq. ft. warehouse space with the following loads?

| 120 V, single-phase loads | 480 V, three-phase loads | Sizing phases = •<br>Sizing neutral = √<br>Sizing total load = * |
|---|---|---|

**120 V, single-phase loads**
- 100 linear feet of show window (noncontinuous operation)
- 120 ft. of lighting track (noncontinuous operation)
- 40 - 180 VA ballast's outside lighting (continuous operation)
- 4,200 VA sign lighting (continuous operation)
- 74 receptacles (noncontinuous operation)
- 24 receptacles (continuous operation)
- 50 ft. multioutlet assembly (heavy-duty)
- office area is 277 V lighting
- warehouse is 277 V lighting

**480 V, three-phase loads**
- 12,000 VA water heater
- 60,000 VA heating unit
- 24,800 VA A/C unit
- 7,240 VA freezer
- 6,480 VA ice cream box
- 9,560 VA walk-in cooler
- 1 - 1/2 HP exhaust fan
- 1 - 2 HP water pump

### Calculating lighting load

**Step 1:** General lighting load
Table 220-3(a); 230-42(a)(1)
50,000 sq. ft. x 3 VA = 150,000 VA √
150,000 VA x 125% = 187,500 VA *
30,000 sq. ft. x 1/4 VA = 7,500 VA √
7,500 VA x 125% = 9,375 VA *

**Step 2:** Show window load
220-12(a)
100' x 200 VA = 20,000 VA *

**Step 3:** Track lighting load
220-12(b)
120' / 2 x 150 VA = 9,000 VA *

**Step 4:** Outside lighting load
230-42(a)(1)
40 x 180 VA = 7,200 VA
7,200 VA x 125% = 9,000 VA *

**Step 5:** Sign lighting load
600-5(b)(3); 230-42(a)(1)
4,200 VA x 100% = 4,200 VA
4,200 VA x 125% = 5,250 VA *
Total load = 240,125 VA •

### Calculating receptacle loads

**Step 1:** Noncontinuous operation
220-3(b)(9); 220-3(b)(8)(b)
74 x 180 VA = 13,320 VA
100' x 180 VA = 18,000 VA

Total Load = 31,320 VA
Table 220-13
First 10,000 VA x 100% = 10,000 VA
Next 21,320 VA x 50% = 10,660 VA
Total load = 20,660 VA *

**Step 2:** Continuous operation
220-3(b)(9); 230-42(a)(1)
24 x 180 VA = 4,320 VA
4,320 VA x 125% = 5,400 VA *
Total load = 26,060 VA •

### Calculating special loads

**Step 1:** 12,000 VA x 100% = 12,000 VA * •

### Calculating compressor loads

**Step 1:** Freezer load
230-42(a)(1)
7,240 VA x 100% = 7,240 VA *

**Step 2:** Ice cream boxes
230-42(a)(1)
6,480 VA x 100% = 6,480 VA *

**Step 3:** Walk-in cooler
230-42(a)(1)
9,560 VA x 100% = 9,560 VA *
Total load = 23,280 VA •

### Calculating motor loads

**Step 1:** Water pump load
430-24; Table 430-150
3.4 A x 831 V x 100% = 2,825 VA *

**Step 2:** Exhaust fan load
430-24; Table 430-150
1.1 A x 831 V x 100% = 914 VA *
Total load = 3,739 VA •

### Calculating heating or A/C load

**Step 1:** Heating load selected
220-21
60,000 VA x 100% = 60,000 VA * •
24,800 VA x 100% = 24,800 VA

### Calculating largest motor load

**Step 1:** Walk-in cooler
220-14; 430-24
9,560 VA x 25% = 2,390 VA * •

### Calculating phases (Total loads)

| | | |
|---|---|---|
| Lighting loads | = | 240,125 VA • |
| Receptacle loads | = | 26,060 VA • |
| Special loads | = | 12,000 VA • |
| Compressor loads | = | 23,280 VA • |
| Motor loads | = | 3,739 VA • |
| Heating load | = | 60,000 VA • |
| Largest motor load | = | 2,390 VA • |
| Total load | = | 367,594 VA |

### Calculating neutral

| | | |
|---|---|---|
| Lighting load | = | 157,500 VA √ |
| Total load | = | 157,500 VA |

### Finding amps for Phases A and B

I = VA / V
I = 367,594 VA / 831 V
I = 442 A

### Finding amps for neutral

I = VA / V
I = 157,500 VA / 831 V
I = 190 A

**See Figure 10-22** for an exercise problem when computing a 277/480 volt, single-phase service supplying a store and warehouse space.

**Exercise Problem 10-22.** What is the load in VA and amps to compute and size the elements for a 277 / 480 volt, three-phase, four-wire service supplying a 40,000 sq. ft. store with 20,000 sq. ft. of warehouse space having 277 volt lighting with the following loads?

| 120 V, single-phase loads | 480 V, three-phase loads | Sizing phases = • |
|---|---|---|
| | | Sizing neutral = √ |
| | | Sizing total load = * |

**120 V, single-phase loads**
- 80 linear feet of show window (noncontinuous operation)
- 120' of lighting track (noncontinuous operation)
- 30 - 180 VA ballast's outside lighting (continuous operation)
- 3,600 VA sign lighting (continuous operation)
- 65 receptacles (noncontinuous operation)
- 28 receptacles (continuous operation)
- 40' multioutlet assembly (heavy-duty)
- store lighting is 277 V
- warehouse lighting is 277 V

**480 V, three-phase loads**
- 7,380 VA freezer
- 5,580 VA ice cream boxes
- 1 - 1/2 HP exhaust fan
- 10,000 VA water heater
- 9,540 VA walk-in cooler
- 50,000 VA heating unit
- 23,320 VA A/C unit
- 1 - 2 HP water pump

**Calculating lighting load**

Step 1: General lighting load
Table 220-3(a); 230-42(a)(1)
40,000 sq. ft. x 3 VA = _____ VA [A] √
120,000 VA x 125% = _____ VA [B] *
20,000 sq. ft. x 1/4 VA = _____ VA [C] √
5,000 VA x 125% = _____ VA [D] *

Step 2: Show window load
220-12(a)
80' x 200 = _____ VA [E] *

Step 3: Track lighting load
220-12(b)
120' / 2 x 150 VA = _____ VA [F] *

Step 4: Outside lighting load
230-42(a)(1)
30 x 180 VA = _____ VA [G] *
5,400 VA x 125% = _____ VA [H] *

Step 5: Sign lighting load
600-5(b)(3); 230-42(a)(1)
3,600 VA x 100% = _____ VA [I]
3,600 VA x 125% = _____ VA [J] *
Total load = _____ VA [K] •

**Calculating receptacle loads**

Step 1: Noncontinuous operation
220-3(b)(9); 220-3(b)(8)(b)
65 x 180 VA = _____ VA [L]
80' x 180 VA = _____ VA [M]
Total Load = _____ VA [N]
Table 220-13
First 10,000 VA x 100% = _____ VA [O]
Next 16,100 VA x 50% = _____ VA [P]
Total load = _____ VA [Q] *

Step 2: Continuous operation
220-3(b)(9); 230-42(a)(1)
28 x 180 VA = _____ VA [R]
5,040 VA x 125% = _____ VA [S] *
Total load = _____ VA [T] •

**Calculating special loads**

Step 1: Water heater load
10,000 VA x 100% = _____ VA [U] * •

**Calculating compressor loads**

Step 1: Freezer load
230-42(a)(1)
7,380 VA x 100% = _____ VA [V] *

Step 2: Ice cream boxes
5,580 VA x 100% = _____ VA [W] *

Step 3: Walk-in cooler
9,540 VA x 100% = _____ VA [X] *
Total load = _____ VA [Y] •

**Calculating motor loads**

Step 1: Water pump load
430-24; Table 430-150
3.4 A x 831 V x 100% = _____ VA [Z] *

Step 2: Exhaust fan load
1.1 A x 831 V x 100% = _____ VA [AA] *
Total load = _____ VA [BB] •

**Calculating heating or A/C load**

Step 1: Heating load selected
220-21
50,000 VA x 100% = _____ VA [CC] * •
23,320 VA x 100% = _____ VA [DD]

**Calculating largest motor load**

Step 1: Walk-in cooler
220-14; 430-24
9,540 VA x 25% = _____ VA [EE] * •

**Calculating phases (Total loads)**

Lighting loads = _____ VA [FF] •
Receptacle loads = _____ VA [GG] •
Special loads = _____ VA [HH] •
Compressor loads = _____ VA [II] •
Motor loads = _____ VA [JJ] •
Heating load = _____ VA [KK] •
Largest motor load = _____ VA [LL] •
Total load for facility = _____ VA [MM]

**Finding amps for phases A and B**

I = VA / V
I = _____ VA [NN] / _____ V [OO]
I = _____ A [PP]

**Calculating neutral**

Lighting load = _____ VA [QQ] √
Total load = _____ VA [RR]

**Finding amps for neutral**

I = VA / V
I = _____ VA [SS] / _____ V [TT]
I = _____ A [UU]

**Figure 10-22.** The above is an exercise problem for computing a store and warehouse space that is supplied by a 277/480 volt, single-phase service.

**Example Problem 10-23.** What is the load in VA and amps to compute and size the elements for a 120 / 240 volt, three-phase, four-wire service supplying a 50,000 sq. ft. store including a 30,000 sq. ft. warehouse space with the following loads?

| 120 V, single-phase loads | 240 V, three-phase loads | Sizing phases = • |
|---|---|---|
| | | Sizing neutral = √ |
| | | Sizing total load = * |

**120 V, single-phase loads**
- 100 linear feet of show window (noncontinuous operation)
- 120 ft. of lighting track (noncontinuous operation)
- 40 - 180 VA ballast's outside lighting (continuous operation)
- 4,200 VA sign lighting (continuous operation)
- 74 receptacles (noncontinuous operation)
- 24 receptacles (continuous operation)
- 50 ft. multioutlet assembly (heavy-duty)

**240 V, three-phase loads**
- 12,000 VA water heater
- 60,000 VA heating unit
- 24,800 VA A/C unit
- 7,240 VA freezer
- 6,480 VA ice cream box
- 9,560 VA walk-in cooler
- 1 - 1/2 HP exhaust fan
- 1 - 2 HP water pump

**Calculating lighting loads**

| Step 1: | General lighting load | | | |
|---|---|---|---|---|
| | Table 220-3(a); 230-42(a)(1) | | | |
| | 50,000 sq. ft. x 3 VA | = | 150,000 | VA √ |
| | 150,000 VA x 125% | = | 187,500 | VA * |
| | 30,000 sq. ft. x 1/4 VA | = | 7,500 | VA √ |
| | 7,500 VA x 125% | = | 9,375 | VA * |

| Step 2: | Show window load | | | |
|---|---|---|---|---|
| | 220-12(a) | | | |
| | 100' x 200 VA | = | 20,000 | VA * √ |

| Step 3: | Track lighting load | | | |
|---|---|---|---|---|
| | 220-12(b) | | | |
| | 120' / 2 x 150 VA | = | 9,000 | VA * √ |

| Step 4: | Outside lighting load | | | |
|---|---|---|---|---|
| | 230-42(a)(1) | | | |
| | 40 x 180 VA | = | 7,200 | VA √ |
| | 7,200 VA x 125% | = | 9,000 | VA * |

| Step 5: | Sign lighting load | | | |
|---|---|---|---|---|
| | 600-5(b)(3); 230-42(a)(1) | | | |
| | 4,200 VA x 100% | = | 4,200 | VA √ |
| | 4,200 VA x 125% | = | 5,250 | VA * |
| | Total load | = | 240,125 | VA • |

**Calculating receptacle loads**

| Step 1: | Noncontinuous operation | | | |
|---|---|---|---|---|
| | 220-3(b)(9); 220-3(b)(8)(b) | | | |
| | 74 x 180 VA | = | 13,320 | VA |
| | 100' x 180 VA | = | 18,000 | VA |
| | Total Load | = | 31,320 | VA |
| | Table 220-13 | | | |
| | First 10,000 VA x 100% | = | 10,000 | VA |
| | Next 21,320 VA x 50% | = | 10,660 | VA |
| | Total load | = | 20,660 | VA * √ |

| Step 2: | Continuous operation | | | |
|---|---|---|---|---|
| | 220-3(b)(9); 230-42(a)(1) | | | |
| | 24 x 180 VA | = | 4,320 | VA √ |
| | 4,320 VA x 125% | = | 5,400 | VA * |
| | Total load | = | 26,060 | VA • |

**Calculating special loads**

| Step 1: | 12,000 VA x 100% | = | 12,000 | VA * • |
|---|---|---|---|---|

**Calculating compressor loads**

| Step 1: | Freezer load | | | |
|---|---|---|---|---|
| | 230-42(a)(1) | | | |
| | 7,240 VA x 100 % | = | 7,240 | VA * |

| Step 2: | Ice cream boxes | | | |
|---|---|---|---|---|
| | 230-42(a)(1) | | | |
| | 6,480 VA x 100% | = | 6,480 | VA * |

| Step 3: | Walk-in cooler | | | |
|---|---|---|---|---|
| | 230-42(a)(1) | | | |
| | 9,560 VA x 100% | = | 9,560 | VA * |
| | Total load | = | 23,280 | VA • |

**Calculating motor loads**

| Step 1: | Water pump load | | | |
|---|---|---|---|---|
| | 430-24; Table 430-150 | | | |
| | 6.8 A x 416 V x 100% | = | 2,829 | VA * |

| Step 2: | Exhaust fan load | | | |
|---|---|---|---|---|
| | 430-24; Table 430-150 | | | |
| | 2.2 A x 416 V x 100% | = | 915 | VA * |
| | Total load | = | 3,744 | VA • |

**Calculating heating or A/C load**

| Step 1: | Heating load selected | | | |
|---|---|---|---|---|
| | 220-21 | | | |
| | 60,000 VA x 100% | = | 60,000 | VA * • |
| | 24,800 VA x 100% | = | 24,800 | VA |

**Calculating largest motor load**

| Step 1: | Walk-in cooler | | | |
|---|---|---|---|---|
| | 220-14; 430-24 | | | |
| | 9,560 VA x 25% | = | 2,390 | VA * • |

**Single-phase loads**

| Lighting loads | = | 240,125 | VA • |
|---|---|---|---|
| Receptacle loads | = | 26,060 | VA • |
| Total load | = | 266,185 | VA |

**Three-phase loads**

| Special loads | = | 12,000 | VA • |
|---|---|---|---|
| Compressor loads | = | 23,280 | VA • |
| Motor loads | = | 3,744 | VA • |
| Heating load | = | 60,000 | VA • |
| Largest motor load | = | 2,390 | VA • |
| Total load | = | 101,414 | VA |

**Calculating neutral**

| Lighting loads | = | 197,900 | VA √ |
|---|---|---|---|
| Receptacle loads | = | 24,980 | VA √ |
| Total load | = | 222,880 | VA |

**Finding single-phase load**

I = VA / V
I = 266,185 VA / 240 V
I = 1,109 A

**Finding three-phase load**

I = VA / V
I = 101,414 VA / 416 V
I = 244 A

**Finding amps for neutral**

I = VA / V
I = 222,880 VA / 240 V
I = 929 A

**Finding Phases A and C**

| Single-phase load | = | 1,109 | A |
|---|---|---|---|
| Three-phase load | = | 244 | A |
| Total load | = | 1,353 | A |

**Calculating Phase B**

| Three-phase load | = | 244 | A |
|---|---|---|---|

**See Figure 10-23.** for an exercise problem when computing a 120/240 volt, three-phase service supplying a store and warehouse space.

Exercise Problem 10-23. What is the load in VA and amps to compute and size the elements for a 120 / 240 volt, three-phase, four-wire service supplying a 40,000 sq. ft. store with 20,000 sq. ft. of warehouse space with the following loads?

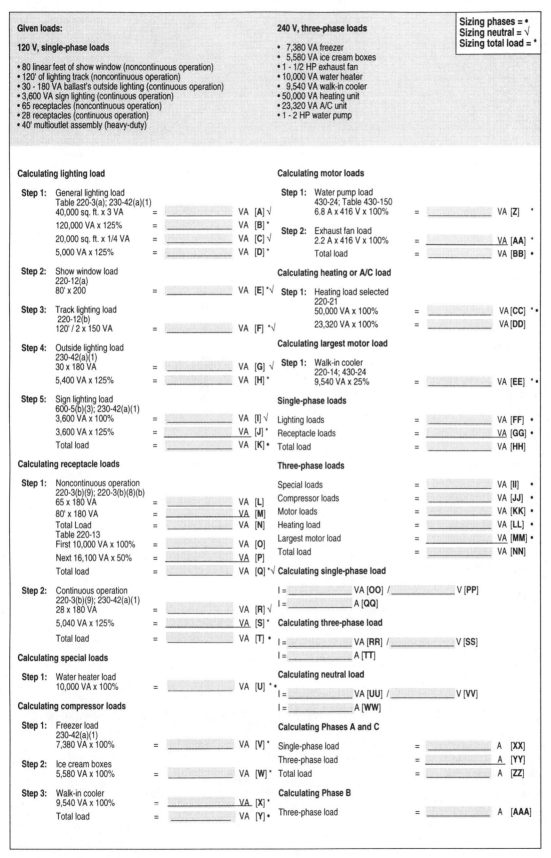

**Given loads:**

**120 V, single-phase loads**

- 80 linear feet of show window (noncontinuous operation)
- 120' of lighting track (noncontinuous operation)
- 30 - 180 VA ballast's outside lighting (continuous operation)
- 3,600 VA sign lighting (continuous operation)
- 65 receptacles (noncontinuous operation)
- 28 receptacles (continuous operation)
- 40' multioutlet assembly (heavy-duty)

**240 V, three-phase loads**

- 7,380 VA freezer
- 5,580 VA ice cream boxes
- 1 - 1/2 HP exhaust fan
- 10,000 VA water heater
- 9,540 VA walk-in cooler
- 50,000 VA heating unit
- 23,320 VA A/C unit
- 1 - 2 HP water pump

Sizing phases = •
Sizing neutral = √
Sizing total load = *

**Calculating lighting load**

**Step 1:** General lighting load
Table 220-3(a); 230-42(a)(1)
40,000 sq. ft. x 3 VA = _____ VA [A] √
120,000 VA x 125% = _____ VA [B] *
20,000 sq. ft. x 1/4 VA = _____ VA [C] √
5,000 VA x 125% = _____ VA [D] *

**Step 2:** Show window load
220-12(a)
80' x 200 = _____ VA [E] *√

**Step 3:** Track lighting load
220-12(b)
120' / 2 x 150 VA = _____ VA [F] *√

**Step 4:** Outside lighting load
230-42(a)(1)
30 x 180 VA = _____ VA [G] √
5,400 VA x 125% = _____ VA [H] *

**Step 5:** Sign lighting load
600-5(b)(3); 230-42(a)(1)
3,600 VA x 100% = _____ VA [I] √
3,600 VA x 125% = _____ VA [J] *
Total load = _____ VA [K] •

**Calculating receptacle loads**

**Step 1:** Noncontinuous operation
220-3(b)(9); 220-3(b)(8)(b)
65 x 180 VA = _____ VA [L]
80' x 180 VA = _____ VA [M]
Total Load = _____ VA [N]
Table 220-13
First 10,000 VA x 100% = _____ VA [O]
Next 16,100 VA x 50% = _____ VA [P]
Total load = _____ VA [Q] *√

**Step 2:** Continuous operation
220-3(b)(9); 230-42(a)(1)
28 x 180 VA = _____ VA [R] √
5,040 VA x 125% = _____ VA [S] *
Total load = _____ VA [T] •

**Calculating special loads**

**Step 1:** Water heater load
10,000 VA x 100% = _____ VA [U] * •

**Calculating compressor loads**

**Step 1:** Freezer load
230-42(a)(1)
7,380 VA x 100% = _____ VA [V] *

**Step 2:** Ice cream boxes
5,580 VA x 100% = _____ VA [W] *

**Step 3:** Walk-in cooler
9,540 VA x 100% = _____ VA [X] *
Total load = _____ VA [Y] •

**Calculating motor loads**

**Step 1:** Water pump load
430-24; Table 430-150
6.8 A x 416 V x 100% = _____ VA [Z] *

**Step 2:** Exhaust fan load
2.2 A x 416 V x 100% = _____ VA [AA] *
Total load = _____ VA [BB] •

**Calculating heating or A/C load**

**Step 1:** Heating load selected
220-21
50,000 VA x 100% = _____ VA [CC] * •
23,320 VA x 100% = _____ VA [DD]

**Calculating largest motor load**

**Step 1:** Walk-in cooler
220-14; 430-24
9,540 VA x 25% = _____ VA [EE] * •

**Single-phase loads**

Lighting loads = _____ VA [FF] •
Receptacle loads = _____ VA [GG] •
Total load = _____ VA [HH]

**Three-phase loads**

Special loads = _____ VA [II] •
Compressor loads = _____ VA [JJ] •
Motor loads = _____ VA [KK] •
Heating load = _____ VA [LL] •
Largest motor load = _____ VA [MM] •
Total load = _____ VA [NN]

**Calculating single-phase load**

I = _____ VA [OO] / _____ V [PP]
I = _____ A [QQ]

**Calculating three-phase load**

I = _____ VA [RR] / _____ V [SS]
I = _____ A [TT]

**Calculating neutral load**

I = _____ VA [UU] / _____ V [VV]
I = _____ A [WW]

**Calculating Phases A and C**

Single-phase load = _____ A [XX]
Three-phase load = _____ A [YY]
Total load = _____ A [ZZ]

**Calculating Phase B**

Three-phase load = _____ A [AAA]

**Figure 10-23.** The above is an exercise problem when computing a store and warehouse space with a 120/240 volt, three-phase, four-wire service.

**Example Problem 10-24.** What is the load in VA and amps to size the elements for a 277 / 480 volt, three-phase, four-wire service supplying a 140,000 sq. ft. office with a 2,500 sq. ft. meeting hall with the following loads? (All lighting is 277 volt)

**120 V, single-phase loads**

- 50 ft. of lighting track (noncontinuous operation)
- 20 - 180 VA ballast's outside lighting (continuous operation)
- 4,200 VA sign lighting (continuous operation)
- 174 receptacles (noncontinuous operation)
- 114 receptacles (continuous operation)
- 6,000 VA isolation transformer for LVLS (continuous operation)
- 80 ft. multioutlet assembly (heavy-duty)

**Note:** All lighting is 277 volt.

**208 V, three-phase loads**

- 4 - 1,275 VA copying machines
- 1 - 8,000 VA water heater
- 22 - 225 VA data processors
- 8 - 175 VA work processors
- 2 - 1,000 VA printers

**480 V, three-phase loads**

- 40 HP elevator (15 minute intermittent duty)
- 40 kW heating unit

Sizing phases = •
Sizing neutral = √
Sizing total load = *

**Calculating lighting loads**

Step 1:   General lighting load
          Table 220-3(a); 230-42(a)(1)
          140,000 sq. ft. x 3.5 VA     =     490,000  VA √
          490,000 VA x 125%            =     612,500  VA *
          2,500 sq. ft. x 1/2 VA       =       1,250  VA √
          1,250 VA x 125%              =       1,563  VA *

Step 2:   Track lighting load
          220-12(b)
          50' / 2 x 150 VA             =       3,750  VA * √

Step 3:   Low-voltage lighting load
          Art. 411; 230-42(a)(1)
          6,000 VA x 100%              =       6,000  VA √
          6,000 VA x 125%              =       7,500  VA *

Step 4:   Outside lighting load
          230-42(a)(1)
          20 x 180 VA                  =       3,600  VA √
          3,600 VA x 125%              =       4,500  VA *

Step 5:   Sign lighting load
          600-5(b)(3); 230-42(a)(1)
          4,200 VA x 100%              =       4,200  VA √
          4,200 VA x 125%              =       5,250  VA *
          Total load                   =     635,063  VA •

**Calculating receptacle loads**

Step 1:   Noncontinuous operation
          220-3(b)(9); 220-3(b)(8)(b)
          174 x 180 VA                 =      31,320  VA
          160' x 180 VA                =      28,800  VA
          Total Load                   =      60,120  VA
          Table 220-13
          First 10,000 VA x 100%       =      10,000  VA
          Next 50,120 VA x 50%         =      25,060  VA
          Total load                   =      35,060  VA *

Step 2:   Continuous operation
          220-3(b)(9); 230-42(a)(1)
          114 x 180 VA                 =      20,520  VA
          20,520 VA x 125%             =      25,650  VA *
          Total load                   =      60,710  VA •

**Calculating special loads**

Step 1:   Copying machine load
          230-42(a)(1)
          1,275 VA x 4                 =       5,100  VA
          5,100 VA x 125%              =       6,375  VA *

Step 2:   Water heater load
          422-13; 230-42(a)(1)
          8,000 VA x 100%              =       8,000  VA *

Step 3:   Data processor load
          230-42(a)(1)
          225 VA x 22                  =       4,950  VA
          4,950 VA x 125%              =       6,188  VA *

Step 4:   Word processor load
          230-42(a)(1)
          175 VA x 8                   =       1,400  VA
          1,400 VA x 125%              =       1,750  VA *

Step 5:   Printer load
          230-42(a)(1)
          1,000 VA x 2                 =       2,000  VA
          2,000 VA x 125%              =       2,500  VA *
          Total load                   =      24,813  VA •

**Calculating motor loads**

Step 1:   40 HP elevators
          430-24; 430-22(b); Table 430-22(b)
          52 A x 831 V x 85%           =      36,730  VA * •

**Calculating heating or A/C load**

Step 1:   Heating load selected
          220-21; 220-15
          40,000 VA x 100%             =      40,000  VA * •

**Calculating largest motor load**

Step 1:   40 HP elevator
          220-14; 430-24
          36,730 VA x 25%              =       9,183  VA * •
          Total load of facility       =     806,499  VA •

**Finding amps for Phases A, B, and C**

I = VA / V x √3
I = 806,499 VA / 831 V
I = 971 A

**Calculating Neutral**

General lighting load
(office building)              =     490,000  VA √
(halls)                       =       1,250  VA √
Track lighting load           =       3,750  VA √
Low-voltage lighting load     =       6,000  VA √
Outside lighting load         =       3,600  VA √
Sign lighting load            =       4,200  VA √
Total load                    =     508,800  VA

**Finding amps for Neutral**

I = VA / V x √3
I = 508,800 VA / 831 V
I = 612 A

See **Figure 10-24** for an exercise problem when computing a 277/480 volt, three-phase service supplying an office and meeting hall.

**Exercise Problem 10-24.** What is the load in VA and amps to compute and size the elements for a 277 / 480 volt, three-phase, four-wire service supplying a 150,000 sq. ft. office facility with 3,000 sq. ft. hall area equipped with 277 volt lighting units with the following loads?

| | |
|---|---|
| **120 V, single-phase loads** | **480 V, three-phase loads** |

Sizing phases = •
Sizing neutral = √
Sizing total load = *

**120 V, single-phase loads**

- 60' of lighting track (noncontinuous operation)
- 20 - 180 VA ballast's outside lighting (continuous operation)
- 4,800 VA sign lighting (continuous operation)
- 182 receptacles (noncontinuous operation)
- 121 receptacles (continuous operation)
- 6,000 VA isolation transformer for LVLS (continuous operation)
- 100' multioutlet assembly (heavy duty)

**480 V, three-phase loads**

- 40 kW heating units
- 40 HP elevator (15 minute intermittent duty)

**208 V, three-phase loads**

- 5 - 1,450 VA copying machine
- 1 - 8,500 VA water heater
- 25 - 225 VA data processors
- 10 - 175 VA word processor
- 4 - 1,200 VA printers

## Calculating lighting load

**Step 1:** General lighting load
Table 220-3(a); 230-42(a)(1)
150,000 sq. ft. x 3.5 VA = _____ VA **[A]** √

525,000 VA x 125% = _____ VA **[B]** *

3,000 sq. ft. x 1/2 VA = _____ VA **[C]** √

1,500 VA x 125% = _____ VA **[D]** *

**Step 2:** Track lighting load
220-12(b)
60' / 2 x 150 VA = _____ VA **[E]** *

**Step 3:** Low-voltage lighting load
Art. 411; 230-42(a)(1)
6,000 VA x 100% = _____ VA **[F]**

6,000VA x 125% = _____ VA **[G]** *

**Step 4:** Outside lighting load
230-42(a)(1)
20 x 180 VA = _____ VA **[H]**

3,600 VA x 125% = _____ VA **[I]** *

**Step 5:** Sign lighting load
600-5(b)(3); 230-42(a)(1)
4,800 VA x 100% = _____ VA **[J]**

4,800 VA x 125% = _____ VA **[K]** *

Total load = _____ VA **[L]** •

## Calculating receptacle loads

**Step 1:** Noncontinuous operation
220-3(b)(9); 220-3(b)(8)(b)
182 x 180 VA = _____ VA **[M]**

200' x 180 VA = _____ VA **[N]**

Total Load = _____ VA **[O]**
Table 220-13
First 10,000 VA x 100% = _____ VA **[P]**

Next 58,760 VA x 50% = _____ VA **[Q]**

Total load = _____ VA **[R]** *

**Step 2:** Continuous operation
220-3(b)(9); 230-42(a)(1)
121 x 180 VA = _____ VA **[S]**

21,780 VA x 125% = _____ VA **[T]** *

Total load = _____ VA **[U]** •

## Calculating special loads

**Step 1:** Copying machine load
230-42(a)(1)
1,450 VA x 5 = _____ VA **[V]**

7,250 VA x 125% = _____ VA **[W]** *

**Step 2:** Water heater load
422-13; 230-42(a)(1)
8,500 VA x 100% = _____ VA **[X]** *

**Step 3:** Data processor load
225 VA x 25 = _____ VA **[Y]**

5,625 VA x 125% = _____ VA **[Z]** *

**Step 4:** Word processor load
230-42(a)(1)
175 VA x 10 = _____ VA **[AA]**

1,750 VA x 125% = _____ VA **[BB]** *

**Step 5:** Printer load
230-42(a)(1)
1,200 VA x 4 = _____ VA **[CC]**

4,800 VA x 125% = _____ VA **[DD]** *

Total load = _____ VA **[EE]** •

## Calculating motor loads

**Step 1:** 40 HP elevator
430-24; 430-22(b); Table 430-22(b)
52 A x 831 V x 85% = _____ VA **[FF]** * •

## Calculating heating or A/C load

**Step 1:** Heating load selected
220-21; 220-15
40,000 VA x 100% = _____ VA **[GG]** * •

## Calculating largest motor

**Step 1:** 40 HP elevator
220-14; 430-24
36,730 VA x 25% = _____ VA **[HH]** * •

Total load of facility = _____ VA **[II]** •

## Finding amps for phases A, B, and C

I = VA / V x √3

I = _____ VA **[JJ]** / _____ V **[KK]**

I = _____ A **[LL]**

## Calculating neutral

General lighting load
(office building) = _____ VA **[MM]** √

(halls) = _____ VA **[NN]** √

Total load = _____ VA **[OO]**

## Finding amps for neutral

I = VA / V x √3

I = _____ VA **[PP]** / _____ V **[QQ]**

I = _____ A **[RR]**

**Figure 10-24.** The above is an exercise problem for computing an office and meeting hall that is supplied by a 277/480 volt, three-phase service.

**Example Problem 10-25.** What is the load in VA and amps to size the elements for a 277 / 480 volt, three-phase, four-wire service supplying a 20,000 sq. ft. classroom, 4,000 sq. ft. auditorium area, and 1,000 sq. ft. assembly hall area with the following loads? (school building lighting is supplied by 277 volt fixtures)

**120 V, single-phase loads**

- 170 receptacles (noncontinuous duty)
- 40 receptacles (continuous duty)
- 80 ft. multioutlet assembly (heavy-duty)

**208 V, single-phase cooking equipment**

- 2 - 1 kW toasters
- 4 - 1.5 kW refrigerators
- 2 - 1.5 kW freezers

**208 V, single-phase cooking equipment**

- 4 - 9 kW ranges
- 3 - 10 kW ovens
- 4 - 3 kW fryers

**208 V, single-phase motor loads**

- 3 - 1 HP vent-hood fans
- 3 - 3/4 HP grill-vent fans

**480 V, three-phase motor loads**

- 18 - 3/4 HP exhaust fans

| Sizing phases = • |
|---|
| Sizing neutral = √ |
| Sizing total load = * |

**Calculating lighting loads**

**Step 1:** General lighting load
Table 220-3(a)

| | | | |
|---|---|---|---|
| 20,000 sq. ft. x 3 VA | = | 60,000 | VA √ |
| 60,000 VA x 125% | = | 75,000 | VA * |
| 4,000 sq. ft. x 1 | = | 4,000 | VA √ |
| 4,000 VA x 125% | = | 5,000 | VA * |
| 1,000 sq. ft. x 1 | = | 1,000 | VA √ |
| 1,000 VA x 125% | = | 1,250 | VA * |
| Total load | = | 81,250 | VA • |

**Calculating receptacle loads**

**Step 1:** Noncontinuous operation
220-3(b)(9); 220-3(b)(8)(b)

| | | | |
|---|---|---|---|
| 170 x 180 VA | = | 30,600 | VA |
| 160' x 180 VA | = | 28,800 | VA |
| Total Load | = | 59,400 | VA |
| Table 220-13 | | | |
| First 10,000 VA x 100% | = | 10,000 | VA |
| Next 49,400 VA x 50% | = | 24,700 | VA |
| Total load | = | 34,700 | VA * |

**Step 2:** Continuous operation
220-3(b)(9); 230-42(a)(1)

| | | | |
|---|---|---|---|
| 40 x 180 VA | = | 7,200 | VA |
| 7,200 VA x 125% | = | 9,000 | VA * |
| Total load | = | 43,700 | VA • |

**Calculating special loads**

**Step 1:** Kitchen equipment
220-20
Toasters

| | | | |
|---|---|---|---|
| 2 x 1 kW x 1,000 | = | 2,000 | VA |
| Refrigerators | | | |
| 4 x 1.5 kW x 1,000 | = | 6,000 | VA |
| Freezers | | | |
| 2 x 1.5 kW x 1,000 | = | 3,000 | VA |
| Ranges | | | |
| 4 x 9 kW x 1,000 | = | 36,000 | VA |
| Ovens | | | |
| 3 x 10 kW x 1,000 | = | 30,000 | VA |
| Fryers | | | |
| 4 x 3 kW x 1,000 | = | 12,000 | VA |
| Total load | = | 89,000 | VA |

**Step 2:** Applying demand factors
Table 220-20

| | | | |
|---|---|---|---|
| 89,000 VA x 65% | = | 57,850 | VA * • |

**Calculating motor loads**
Tables 430-148 and 430-150

**Step 1:** Exhaust fans

| | | | |
|---|---|---|---|
| 28.8 x 100% x 480 V | = | 13,824 | VA |
| 13,824 VA x 1.732 | = | 23,943 | VA * |
| (1.6 A x 18 = 28.8 A) | | | |

**Step 2:** Hood fans

| | | | |
|---|---|---|---|
| 26.4 x 100% x 208 V | = | 5,491 | VA * |
| (8.8 A x 3 = 26.4 A) | | | |

**Step 3:** Grill vent fans

| | | | |
|---|---|---|---|
| 22.8 x 100% x 208 V | = | 4,742 | VA * |
| (7.6 A x 3 = 22.8 A) | | | |
| Total load | = | 34,176 | VA • |

**Calculating largest motor load**

**Step 1:** Hood fan

| | | | |
|---|---|---|---|
| 8.8 A x 100% x 208 V | = | 1,830 | VA |
| 1,830 VA x 25% | = | 458 | VA * • |
| Total load of facility | = | 217,434 | VA • |

**Finding amps for phases**

$I = VA / V \times \sqrt{3}$
$I = 217,434 \ VA / 831 \ V$
$I = 262 \ A$

**Calculating neutral**

| | | | |
|---|---|---|---|
| General lighting load | = | 65,000 | VA √ |
| Total load | = | 65,000 | VA |

**Finding amps for neutral**

$I = VA / V \times \sqrt{3}$
$I = 65,000 \ VA / 831 \ V$
$I = 78 \ A$

**See Figure 10-25** for an exercise problem when computing a 277/480 volt, three-phase service supplying a classroom, auditorium area, and assembly hall area.

Exercise Problem 10-25. What is the load in VA and amps to compute and size the elements for a 277 / 480 volt, three-phase, four-wire service supplying a 30,000 sq. ft. classroom area, 5,000 sq. ft. auditorium area, and 1,000 sq. ft. assembly hall area with the following loads? (School building lighting is supplied by 277 volt fixtures)

**120 V, single-phase loads**

- 200 receptacles (noncontinuous duty)
- 50 receptacles (continuous duty)
- 100' multioutlet assembly (heavy-duty)

**208 V, single-phase motor loads**

- 4 - 1 HP hood fans
- 3 - 3/4 HP grill vent fans

**480 V, three-phase motor loads**

- 20 - 3/4 HP exhaust fans

**208 V, single-phase cooking equipment**

- 2 - 1 kW toaster
- 4 - 1.5 kW refrigerators
- 3 - 1.5 kW freezers

**208 V, single-phase cooking equipment**

- 4 - 12 kW ranges
- 3 - 9 kW ovens
- 4 - 4 kW fryers

Sizing phases = •
Sizing neutral = √
Sizing total load = *

**Calculating lighting load**

Step 1: General lighting load
Table 220-3(a)

| | | | |
|---|---|---|---|
| 30,000 sq. ft. x 3 VA | = _____ | VA | [A] √ |
| 90,000 VA x 125% | = _____ | VA | [B] * |
| 5,000 sq. ft. x 1 | = _____ | VA | [C] √ |
| 5,000 VA x 125% | = _____ | VA | [D] * |
| 1,000 sq. ft. x 1 | = _____ | VA | [E] √ |
| 1,000 VA x 125% | = _____ | VA | [F] * |
| Total load | = _____ | VA | [G] • |

**Calculating receptacle loads**

Step 1: Noncontinuous operation
220-3(b)(9); 220-3(b)(8)(b)

| | | | |
|---|---|---|---|
| 200 x 180 VA | = _____ | VA | [H] |
| 200' x 180 VA | = _____ | VA | [I] |
| Total Load | = _____ | VA | [J] |
| Table 220-13 | | | |
| First 10,000 VA x 100% | = _____ | VA | [K] |
| Next 62,000 VA x 50% | = _____ | VA | [L] |
| Total load | = _____ | VA | [M] * |

Step 2: Continuous operation
220-3(b)(9); 230-42(a)(1)

| | | | |
|---|---|---|---|
| 50 x 180 VA | = _____ | VA | [N] |
| 9,000 VA x 125% | = _____ | VA | [O] * |
| Total load | = _____ | VA | [P] • |

**Calculating special loads**

Step 1: Kitchen equipment
220-20
Toasters

| | | | |
|---|---|---|---|
| 2 x 1 kW x 1,000 | = _____ | VA | [Q] |
| Refrigerators | | | |
| 4 x 1.5 kW x 1,000 | = _____ | VA | [R] |
| Freezers | | | |
| 3 x 1.5 kW x 1,000 | = _____ | VA | [S] |
| Ranges | | | |
| 4 x 12 kW x 1,000 | = _____ | VA | [T] |
| Ovens | | | |
| 3 x 9 kW x 1,000 | = _____ | VA | [U] |
| Fryers | | | |
| 4 x 4 kW x 1,000 | = _____ | VA | [V] |
| Total load | = _____ | VA | [W] |

Step 2: Applying demand factors

| | | | |
|---|---|---|---|
| 103,500 VA x 65% | = _____ | VA | [X] * • |

**Calculating motor loads**
Tables 430-148 and 430-150

Step 1: Exhaust fans

| | | | |
|---|---|---|---|
| 32 A x 100% x 480 V | = _____ | VA | [Y] |
| 15,360 VA x 1.732 | = _____ | VA | [Z] * |
| (1.6 A x 20 = 32 A) | | | |

Step 2: Hood fans

| | | | |
|---|---|---|---|
| 35.2 A x 100% x 208 V | = _____ | VA | [AA] * |
| (8.8 A x 4 = 35.2 A) | | | |

Step 3: Grill vent fans

| | | | |
|---|---|---|---|
| 22.8 A x 100% x 208 V | = _____ | VA | [BB] * |
| (7.6 A x 3 = 22.8) | | | |
| Total load | = _____ | VA | [CC] • |

**Calculating largest motor load**

Step 1: Hood fan

| | | | |
|---|---|---|---|
| 8.8 A x 100% x 208 V | = _____ | VA | [DD] |
| 1,830 VA x 25% | = _____ | VA | [EE] * • |
| Total load of facility | = _____ | VA | [FF] • |

**Finding amps for phases**

I = VA / V x √3

I = _____ VA [GG] / _____ V [HH]

I = _____ A [II]

**Calculating neutral**

| | | | |
|---|---|---|---|
| General lighting load | = _____ | VA | [JJ] |
| Total load | = _____ | VA | [KK] |

**Finding amps for neutral**

I = VA / V x √3

I = _____ VA [LL] / _____ V [MM]

I = _____ A [NN]

**Figure 10-25.** The above is an exercise problem for computing a classroom, auditorium area, and assembly hall area that is supplied by a 277/480 volt, three-phase service.

**Example Problem 10-26.** What is the load in VA and amps to size the elements for a 120 / 208 volt, three-phase, four-wire service supplying a restaurant with an area of 6,000 sq. ft. with the following loads?

**120 V, single-phase loads**

**Lighting Load**

- 35 ft. of lighting track (continuous operation)
- 10 - 180 VA outside lighting (continuous operation)
- 1,200 VA sign lighting (continuous operation)

**Receptacle Load**

- 35 receptacles (noncontinuous operation)
- 30 receptacles (continuous operation)
- 20 ft. multioutlet assembly (heavy duty)

Sizing phases = •
Sizing neutral = √
Sizing total load = *

**208 V, single-phase loads**

**Motor Loads**

- 6,950 VA vent hood fans
- 4,758 VA grill vent fans

**208 V, three-phase loads**

**Special Loads**

- 2 - 25 kW heating units
- 2 - 7,850 VA A/C units

**208 V, three-phase loads**

**Kitchen Equipment**

- 1 - 3,600 VA boiler
- 2 - 2,600 VA deep fat fryer
- 1 - 20 A walk-in cooler
- 1 - 6,500 VA water heater

**208 V, single-phase loads**

- 1 - 13 A freezer
- 1 - 8,000 VA cooktop
- 2 -10,000 VA ovens
- 1 -11,000 VA range
- 1 - 14 A refrigerator
- 1 - 3,750 VA ice cream box

**Calculating lighting load**

**Step 1:** General lighting load
Table 220-3(a); 230-42(a)(1)
| | | |
|---|---|---|
| 6,000 sq. ft. x 2 VA | = | 12,000 VA √ |
| 12,000 VA x 125% | = | 15,000 VA * |

**Step 2:** Track lighting load
220-12(b)
| | | |
|---|---|---|
| 35 / 2 x 150 VA | = | 2,625 VA √ |
| 2,625 VA x 125% | = | 3,281 VA * |

**Step 3:** Outside lighting load
230-42(a)(1)
| | | |
|---|---|---|
| 10 x 180 VA | = | 1,800 VA √ |
| 1,800 VA x 125% | = | 2,250 VA * |

**Step 4:** Sign lighting load
600-5(b)(3); 230-42(a)(1)
| | | |
|---|---|---|
| 1,200 VA x 100% | = | 1,200 VA √ |
| 1,200 VA x 125% | = | 1,500 VA * |
| Total load | = | 22,031 VA • |

**Calculating receptacle load**

**Step 1:** Receptacle load (noncontinuous)
220-3(b)(9); 230-42(a)(1)
| | | |
|---|---|---|
| 35 x 180 VA | = | 6,300 VA * √ |

**Step 2:** Receptacle load (continuous)
220-3(b)(9); 230-42(a)(1)
| | | |
|---|---|---|
| 30 x 180 VA | = | 5,400 VA √ |
| 5,400 VA x 125% | = | 6,750 VA * |

**Step 3:** Multioutlet assembly
220-3(b)(8)(b)
| | | |
|---|---|---|
| 20' x 180 VA | = | 3,600 VA * √ |
| Total load | = | 16,650 VA • |

**Calculating special loads**

**Step 1:** Kitchen equipment
220-20
| | | |
|---|---|---|
| Freezer | = | 2,704 VA |
| Cooktop | = | 8,000 VA |
| Ovens | = | 20,000 VA |
| Range | = | 11,000 VA |
| Refrigerator | = | 2,912 VA |
| Ice cream box | = | 3,750 VA |
| Boiler | = | 3,600 VA |
| Deep fat fryer | = | 5,200 VA |

| | | |
|---|---|---|
| Walk-in cooler | = | 7,200 VA |
| Water heater | = | 6,500 VA |
| Total load | = | 70,866 VA |

**Step 2:** Applying demand factors
Table 220-20
| | | |
|---|---|---|
| 70,866 VA x 65% | = | 46,063 VA * • |

**Calculating motor loads**

**Step 1:** Hood fans
430-22(a); 430-24; 430-25
| | | |
|---|---|---|
| 6,950 VA x 100% | = | 6,950 VA * |

**Step 2:** Grill vent fans
| | | |
|---|---|---|
| 4,758 VA x 100% | = | 4,758 VA * |
| Total load | = | 11,708 VA • |

**Calculating heating or A/C load**

**Step 1:** Heating load
| | | |
|---|---|---|
| 25 kW x 2 x 1,000 | = | 50,000 VA * • |

**Calculating largest motor load**

**Step 1:** Walk-in cooler
220-14
| | | |
|---|---|---|
| 20 A x 100% x 360 V | = | 7,200 VA |
| 7,200 VA x 25% | = | 1,800 VA * • |
| Total load of facility | = | 148,252 VA • |

**Finding amps for phases**

$I = VA / V \times \sqrt{3}$
$I = 148,252\ VA / 360\ V$
$I = 412\ A$

**Calculating neutral**
220-22; 230-42(a)(1)
| | | |
|---|---|---|
| Lighting load | = | 17,625 VA √ |
| Receptacle load | = | 15,300 VA √ |
| Total load | = | 32,925 VA |

**Finding amps for neutral**

$I = VA / V \times \sqrt{3}$
$I = 32,925\ VA / 360\ V$
$I = 91\ A$

**See Figure 10-26** for an exercise problem when computing a 120/208 volt, three-phase service supplying a restaurant.

**Exercise Problem 10-26:** What is the load in VA and amps to compute and size the elements for a 120 / 208 volt, three-phase, four-wire service supplying a restaurant with an area of 5,600 sq. ft. with the following loads?

---

**120 V, single-phase loads**

**Lighting load**

- 30' lighting track (continuous)
- 10 - 180 VA outside lighting (continuous)
- 1,200 VA sign lighting (continuous)

**Receptacle load**

- 30 receptacles (noncontinuous)
- 25 receptacles (continuous)
- 25' multioutlet assembly (heavy-duty)

Sizing phases = •
Sizing neutral = √
Sizing total load = *

**208 V, three-phase loads**

**Special loads**

- 2 - 20 kW heating units
- 2 - 8,650 VA A/C units

**208 V, single-phase loads**

**Motor loads**

- 7,322 VA hood fans
- 4,742 VA grill vent fans

**208 V, three-phase loads**

**Kitchen Equipment**

- 1 - 3,600 VA boiler
- 2 - 2,700 VA deep fat fryer
- 1 - 20 A walk-in cooler
- 1 - 6,000 VA water heater

**208 V, single-phase loads**

- 1 - 13 A freezer
- 1 - 11,000 VA cooktop
- 2 - 9,000 VA ovens
- 1 - 12,000 VA range
- 1 - 14 A refrigerator
- 1 - 3,650 VA ice cream box

---

**Calculating lighting loads**

**Step 1:** General lighting load
Table 220-3(a); 230-42(a)(1)
5,600 sq. ft. x 2 VA = _____ VA [A] √
11,200 VA x 125% = _____ VA [B] *

**Step 2:** Track lighting load
220-12(b)
30' / 2 x 150 VA = _____ VA [C] √
2,250 VA x 125% = _____ VA [D] *

**Step 3:** Outside lighting load
230-42(a)(1)
180 VA x 10 = _____ VA [E] √
1,800 VA x 125% = _____ VA [F] *

**Step 4:** Sign lighting load
600-5(b)(3); 230-42(a)(1)
1,200 VA x 100% = _____ VA [G] √
1,200 VA x 125% = _____ VA [H] *
Total load = _____ VA [I] •

**Calculating receptacle loads**

**Step 1:** Receptacle load (noncontinuous)
220-3(b)(9); 230-42(a)(1)
30 x 180 VA = _____ VA [J] * √

**Step 2:** Receptacle load (continuous)
220-3(b)(9); 230-42(a)(1)
25 x 180 VA = _____ VA [K] √
4,500 VA x 125% = _____ VA [L] *

**Step 3:** Multioutlet assembly
220-3(b)(8)(b)
25' x 180 VA = _____ VA [M] * √
Total load = _____ VA [N] •

**Calculating special load**

**Step 1:** Kitchen equipment
220-20
Boiler = _____ VA [O]
Deep fat fryer = _____ VA [P]
Walk-in cooler = _____ VA [Q]
Water heater = _____ VA [R]
Ice cream box = _____ VA [S]
Freezer = _____ VA [T]
Cooktop = _____ VA [U]

Ovens = _____ VA [V]
Range = _____ VA [W]
Refrigerator = _____ VA [X]
Total load = _____ VA [Y]

**Step 2:** Applying demand factor
Table 220-20
72,466 VA x 65% = _____ VA [Z] * •

**Calculating motor load**

**Step 1:** Hood fans
430-22(a); 430-24; 430-25
7,322 VA x 100% = _____ VA [AA] *

**Step 2:** Grill vent fans
4,742 VA x 100% = _____ VA [BB] *
Total load = _____ VA [CC] •

**Calculating heating or A/C load**

**Step 1:** Heating load
220-21
20 kW x 2 x 1,000 = _____ VA [DD] * •

**Calculating largest motor load**

**Step 1:** Walk-in cooler
220-14
20 A x 100% x 360 V = _____ VA [EE]
7,200 VA x 25% = _____ VA [FF] * •
Total load of facility = _____ VA [GG] •

**Calculating VA load (neutral)**
220-22; 230-42(a)(1)

Lighting load = _____ VA [HH] √
Receptacle load = _____ VA [II] √
Total load = _____ VA [JJ]

**Finding amps for phases**

I = VA / V x √3
I = _____ VA [KK] / _____ V [LL]
I = _____ A [MM]

**Finding amps for neutral**

I = VA / V x √3
I = _____ VA [NN] / _____ V [OO]
I = _____ A [PP]

**Figure 10-26.** The above is an exercise problem for computing a restaurant that is supplied by a 120/208 volt, three-phase service.

Example Problem 10-27. What is the load in VA and amps to size the elements for a 120 / 208 volt, three-phase service supplying a welding shop with the following loads?

| 120 V, single-phase loads | 208 V, three-phase loads | Sizing phases = • <br> Sizing neutral = √ <br> Sizing total load = * |
|---|---|---|
| • 8,500 VA inside lighting loads (continuous operation) <br> • 6 - 180 VA outside lighting loads (continuous operation) <br> • 1,200 VA sign lighting load (noncontinuous operation) <br> • 50 receptacles (continuous duty) | • 2 - 12 kW heating units <br> • 6,000 VA A/C unit <br> • 7.5 HP air-compressor <br> • 1 1/2 HP grinder <br> • 2 welders - resistance (30% duty cycle) <br> • 11 kW <br> • 9 kW <br> • 2 welders - motor generator arc (80% duty cycle) <br> • 12 kW <br> • 10 kW <br> • 2 welders - AC transformer and DC rectifier (90% duty cycle) <br> • 12 kW <br> • 9 kW | |
| Note: A welding shop is not a listed occupancy per Table 220-3(b) | | |

**Calculating lighting loads**

Step 1: Inside lighting load
230-42(a)(1)
8,500 VA x 100%  =  8,500 VA √
8,500 VA x 125%  =  10,625 VA *

Step 2: Outside lighting load
230-42(a)(1)
6 x 180 VA  =  1,080 VA √
1,080 VA x 125%  =  1,350 VA *

Step 3: Sign lighting load
600-5(b)(3); 230-42(a)(1)
1,200 VA x 100%  =  1,200 VA * √
Total load  =  13,175 VA •

**Calculating receptacle load**

Step 1: Continuous duty
220-3(b)(9); 230-42(a)(1)
50 x 180 VA  =  9,000 VA √
9,000 VA x 125%  =  11,250 VA * •

**Calculating special loads**

Step 1: Welders - resistance
630-31(a); (b)
11,000 VA x 55%  =  6,050 VA *
9,000 VA x 55% x 60%  =  2,970 VA *

Step 2: Welders - motor-generator arc
630-11(a); (b)
12,000 VA x 91%  =  10,920 VA *
10,000 VA x 91%  =  9,100 VA *

Step 3: Welders - AC transformer and DC rectifier
630-11(a); (b)
12,000 VA x 95%  =  11,400 VA *
9,000 VA x 95%  =  8,550 VA *
Total load  =  48,990 VA •

**Calculating compressor and motor loads**

Step 1: Air compressor
430-24; 430-22(b); Table 430-22(b)
24.2 A x 100% x 360 V  =  8,712 VA *

Step 2: Grinders
6.6 A x 100% x 360 V  =  2,376 VA *
Total load  =  11,088 VA •

**Calculating heating or A/C load**

Step 1: Heating load
220-21; 220-15
24,000 VA x 100%  =  24,000 VA * •

**Calculating largest motor load**

Step 1: Air compressor
24.2 A x 360 V x 25%  =  2,178 VA * •

**Calculating total load**

Lighting loads  =  13,175 VA •
Receptacle loads  =  11,250 VA •
Special loads  =  48,990 VA •
Motor loads  =  11,088 VA •
Heating load  =  24,000 VA •
Largest motor load  =  2,178 VA •
Total load  =  110,681 VA

**Calculating neutral**

Lighting loads  =  10,780 VA √
Receptacle loads  =  9,000 VA √
Total loads  =  19,780 VA

**Finding amps for phases**

I = VA / V x √3
I = 110,681 VA / 360 V
I = 308 A

**Finding amps for neutral**

I = VA / V x √3
I = 19,780 VA / 360 V
I = 55 A

See Figure 10-27 for an exercise problem when computing a 120/208 volt, three-phase service supplying a welding shop.

**Exercise Problem 10-27:** What is the load in VA and amps to compute and size the elements for a 120 / 208 volt, three-phase service supplying a welding shop with the following loads?

| 120 V, single-phase loads | 208 V, three-phase loads | |
|---|---|---|
| | | Sizing phases = •<br>Sizing neutral = √<br>Sizing total load = * |

**120 V, single-phase loads**

- 9,000 VA inside lighting loads (continuous operation)
- 6 - 180 VA outside lighting loads (continuous operation)
- 1,200 VA sign lighting loads (noncontinuous operation)
- 60 receptacles (continuous operation)

**208 V, three-phase loads**

- 2 - 10 kW heating units
- 5,400 VA A/C unit
- 7.5 HP air-compressor
- 1 1/2 HP grinder
- Welders - resistance (50% duty cycle)
- 12 kW
- 8 kW
- Welders - motor-generator arc (90% duty cycle)
- 14 kW
- 12 kW
- Welders - AC transformer and DC rectifier (80% duty cycle)
- 13 kW
- 9 kW

**Note:** A welding shop is not a listed occupancy per Table 220-3(b).

**Calculating lighting loads**

**Step 1:** Inside lighting load
230-42(a)(1)
9,000 VA x 100% = _____ VA [A] √
9,000 VA x 125% = _____ VA [B] *

**Step 2:** Outside lighting load
230-42(a)(1)
6 x 180 VA = _____ VA [C] √
1,080 VA x 125% = _____ VA [D] *

**Step 3:** Sign lighting load
600-5(b)(3); 230-42(a)(1)
1,200 VA x 100% = _____ VA [E] * √
Total load = _____ VA [F] •

**Calculating receptacle load**

**Step 1:** Continuous duty
220-3(b)(9); 230-42(a)(1)
60 x 180 VA = _____ VA [G] √
10,800 VA x 125% = _____ VA [H] * •

**Calculating special loads**

**Step 1:** Welders - resistance
630-31(a); (b)
12,000 VA x 71% = _____ VA [I] *
8,000 VA x 71% x 60% = _____ VA [J] *

**Step 2:** Welders - motor-generator arc
630-11(a); (b)
14,000 VA x 96% = _____ VA [K] *
12,000 VA x 96% = _____ VA [L] *

**Step 3:** Welders - AC transformer and DC rectifier
630-11(a); (b)
13,000 VA x 89% = _____ VA [M] *
9,000 VA x 89% = _____ VA [N] *
Total load = _____ VA [O] •

**Calculating compressor and motor loads**

**Step 1:** Air-compressor
430-24; 430-22(b); Table 430-22(b)
24.2 A x 100% x 360 V = _____ VA [P] *

**Step 2:** Grinders
6.6 A x 100% x 360 V = _____ VA [Q] *
Total load = _____ VA [R] •

**Calculating heating or A/C load**

**Step 1:** Heating load
220-21; 220-15
20,000 VA x 100% = _____ VA [S] * •

**Calculating largest motor load**

**Step 1:** Air-compressor
24.2 A x 360 V x 25% = _____ VA [T] * •

**Calculating total load**

Lighting loads = _____ VA [U] •
Receptacle loads = _____ VA [V] •
Special loads = _____ VA [W] •
Heating loads = _____ VA [X] •
Motor loads = _____ VA [Y] •
Largest motor load = _____ VA [Z] •
Total load = _____ VA [AA]

**Finding amps for phases**

I = VA / V x √3
I = _____ VA [BB] / _____ V [CC]
I = _____ A [DD]

**Calculating neutral**

220-22
Lighting loads = _____ VA [EE] √
Receptacle loads = _____ VA [FF] √
Total load = _____ VA [GG]

**Finding amps for neutral**

I = VA / V x √3
I = _____ VA [HH] / _____ V [II]
I = _____ A [JJ]

**Figure 10-27.** The above is an exercise problem for computing a welding shop that is supplied by a 120/208 volt, three-phase service.

## APPLYING THE OPTIONAL CALCULATION
## PART C TO ART. 220

The load in VA or amps can be calculated by applying the optional calculation instead of the standard calculation. The optional calculation is based upon specific use of the electrical system or the type of occupancy.

## KITCHEN EQUIPMENT
## 220-20; TABLE 220-20

Table 220-20 in the NEC is permitted to be used for load computations for commercial cooking equipment, such as dishwashers, booster heaters, water heaters, and other kitchen equipment. The demand factors shown in the Table are applicable to all equipment that is thermostatically controlled or is only intermittently used as part of the kitchen equipment. In no way do the demand factors apply to the electric heating, ventilating, or air-conditioning equipment. In computing the demand, the demand load must never be less than the sum of the two largest kitchen equipment loads.

## APPLYING THE OPTIONAL CALCULATION
## PART C TO ART. 220

The load in VA and amps can be calculated by applying the optional calculation instead of the standard calculation. The optional calculation is based upon specific use of the electrical system or the type of occupancy.

**Example Problem 10-28.** What is the load in VA to size the elements for supplying a school with the following loads?

Total square footage of school

| | |
|---|---|
| Classroom area | = 30,000 sq. ft. |
| Auditorium area | = 5,000 sq. ft. |
| Cafeteria area | = 3,000 sq. ft. |
| Hall area | = 1,000 sq. ft. |

Total VA of school

801,693 VA

**Step 1:** Calculating sq. ft.
Classroom area = 30,000 sq. ft.
Auditorium area = 5,000 sq. ft.
Cafeteria area = 3,000 sq. ft.
Hall area = 1,000 sq. ft.
Total area = 39,000 sq. ft.

**Step 2:** Calculating VA per sq. ft.
Table 220-34
VA per sq. ft. = Total VA / Total sq. ft.
VA per sq. ft. = 801,693 VA / 39,000 sq. ft.
VA per sq. ft. = 20.55623

**Step 3:** Applying demand factors
Table 220-34
First 3 VA x sq. ft. x 100%
Next 17.55623 x 75%
3 VA x 39,000 sq. ft. x 100% = 117,000 VA
17.55623 VA x 39,000 sq. ft. x 75% = 513,519.72 VA
Total VA = 630,519.72 VA

**Solution:** The demand load in VA for the school is **630,519.72 VA.**

See **Figure 10-28** for an exercise problem when computing a school using the optional calculation method.

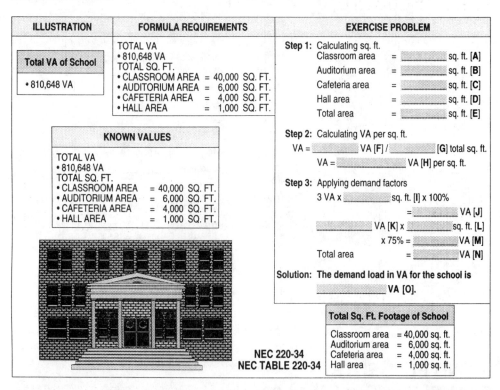

**Figure 10-28.** This figure illustrates an exercise problem for computing a school using the optional calculation method.

---

**Example Problem 10-29.** What is the load in VA to size the elements for supplying a restaurant with the following loads?

Given loads:

| | | |
|---|---|---|
| Lighting loads | = 16,450 | VA |
| Receptacle loads | = 15,300 | VA |
| Special loads | = 95,015 | VA |
| Heating or A/C loads | = 40,000 | VA |
| Motor loads | = 6,808.9 | VA |

Step 1: Computing total VA
220-36

| | | |
|---|---|---|
| Lighting loads | = 16,450 | VA |
| Receptacle loads | = 15,300 | VA |
| Special loads | = 95,015 | VA |
| Heating or A/C loads | = 40,000 | VA |
| Motor loads | = 6,808.9 | VA |
| Total loads | = 173,573.9 | VA |

Step 2: Applying demand factors
Table 220-36
Demand load = VA x demand factor
Demand load = 173,573.9 VA x 80%
Demand load = 138,859 VA

**Solution: The demand load in VA for the restaurant is 138,859 VA.**

See **Figure 10-29** for an exercise problem when computing a restaurant using the optional calculation method.

**Figure 10-29.** This figure illustrates an exercise problem for computing a restaurant using the optional calculation method.

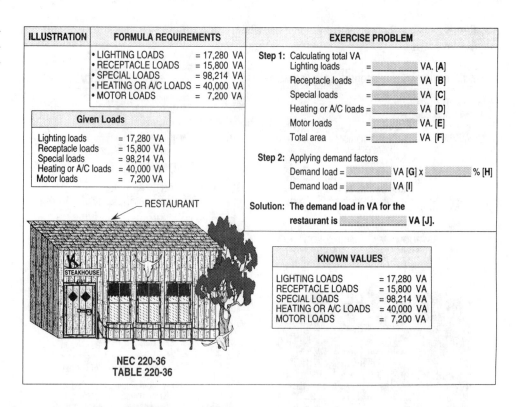

## SIZING ELEMENTS
## EXAMPLE PROBLEM 10-20

(1) What size THWN copper conductors are required for the service where they are paralleled five times per phase? (See page 10-18)

Step 1: Paralleling conductors
310-4
Amps of conductors = service amps / # in parallel
A = 1,533 A / 5
A = 307

Step 2: Selecting conductors size
Table 310-16
307 A requires #350 KCMIL
#350 KCMIL = 310 A

Solution: It takes five No. 350 KCMIL THWN copper conductors to supply a load of 1,533 amps (310 A x 5 = 1,550 A).

See **Figure 10-30** for an exercise problem when computing the size THWN copper conductors required for the service in exercise problem 10-20 on page 10-19.

(2) What size OCPD is required for the service based upon the computed load?

Step 1: Sizing OCPD
230-90(a); 240-6(a); 240-3(c)
1,550 A requires 1,500 A (See solution above)

Solution: The size OCPD based upon computed load is 1,500 amps.

See **Figure 10-31** for an exercise problem when computing the size OCPD required for the service in exercise problem 10-20 on page 10-19.

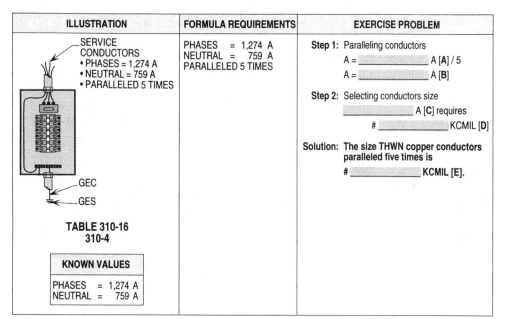

| ILLUSTRATION | FORMULA REQUIREMENTS | EXERCISE PROBLEM |
|---|---|---|
| SERVICE CONDUCTORS<br>• PHASES = 1,274 A<br>• NEUTRAL = 759 A<br>• PARALLELED 5 TIMES<br><br>GEC<br>GES<br><br>**TABLE 310-16**<br>**310-4**<br><br>**KNOWN VALUES**<br>PHASES = 1,274 A<br>NEUTRAL = 759 A | PHASES = 1,274 A<br>NEUTRAL = 759 A<br>PARALLELED 5 TIMES | **Step 1:** Paralleling conductors<br>A = _____ A [A] / 5<br>A = _____ A [B]<br><br>**Step 2:** Selecting conductors size<br>_____ A [C] requires<br># _____ KCMIL [D]<br><br>**Solution:** The size THWN copper conductors paralleled five times is<br># _____ KCMIL [E]. |

**Figure 10-30.** This figure illustrates an exercise problem for computing the size THWN copper conductors required for the service.

**Note:** See exercise problem 10-20 on page 10-19.

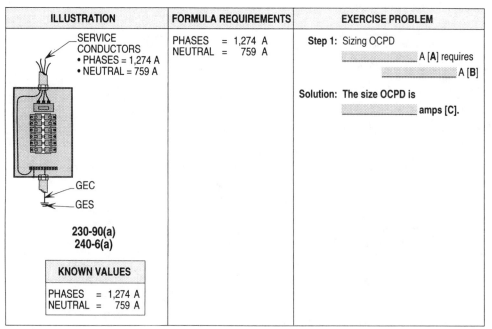

| ILLUSTRATION | FORMULA REQUIREMENTS | EXERCISE PROBLEM |
|---|---|---|
| SERVICE CONDUCTORS<br>• PHASES = 1,274 A<br>• NEUTRAL = 759 A<br><br>GEC<br>GES<br><br>**230-90(a)**<br>**240-6(a)**<br><br>**KNOWN VALUES**<br>PHASES = 1,274 A<br>NEUTRAL = 759 A | PHASES = 1,274 A<br>NEUTRAL = 759 A | **Step 1:** Sizing OCPD<br>_____ A [A] requires<br>_____ A [B]<br><br>**Solution:** The size OCPD is<br>_____ amps [C]. |

**Figure 10-31.** This figure illustrates an exercise problem for computing the size OCPD required for the service in Figure 10-30 above.

| Quick Calc. |
|---|
| • #250 KCMIL = 255 A<br>• 255 A x 5 = 1,275 A |

(3) What size neutral conductor is required for the service if they are paralleled five times per phase? (See page 10-18)

**Step 1:** Selecting conductor size
310-4
Amps of conductors = service amps / # in parallel
A = 929 A / 5
A = 186

**Step 2:** Selecting conductor size
Table 310-16
186 A requires #3/0
#3/0 = 200 A

**Solution:** It takes five No. 3/0 THWN copper conductors to supply a load of 929 amps (200 A x 5 = 1,000 A).

See **Figure 10-32** for an exercise problem when computing the size neutral conductor required for the service.

**Figure 10-32.** This figure illustrates an exercise problem for computing the size neutral conductor required for the service.

**Note:** See exercise problem 10-20 on page 10-19.

| ILLUSTRATION | FORMULA REQUIREMENTS | EXERCISE PROBLEM |
|---|---|---|
| 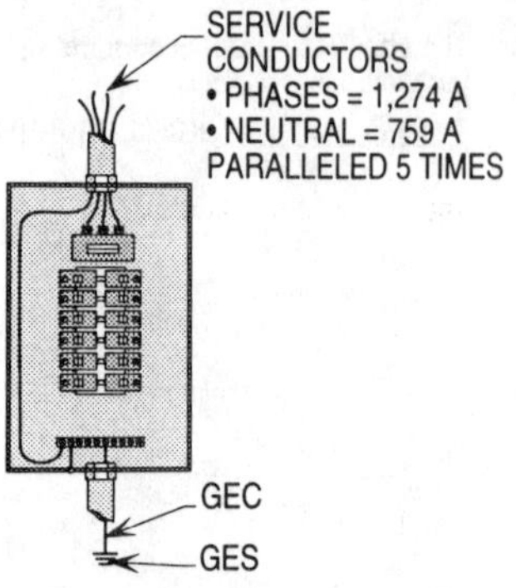 SERVICE CONDUCTORS<br>• PHASES = 1,274 A<br>• NEUTRAL = 759 A<br>PARALLELED 5 TIMES<br><br>GEC<br>GES<br><br>**TABLE 310-16**<br>**310-4**<br><br>**KNOWN VALUES**<br>PHASES = 1,274 A<br>NEUTRAL = 759 A | PHASES = 1,274 A<br>NEUTRAL = 759 A<br>PARALLELED 5 TIMES | **Step 1:** Selecting conductor size<br><br>A = _____ A [A] / 5<br><br>A = _____ A [B]<br><br>**Step 2:** Selecting conductor size<br>_____ A [C] requires<br># _____ THWN [D]<br><br>**Solution:** The size THWN copper conductors paralleled five times is<br># _____ THWN [E]. |

**(4)** What size rigid metal conduit is required for each run in question No. 1 on page 10-36?

**Step 1:** Sizing sq. in. area
Table 5, Ch. 9
#350 KCMIL = .5242
#3/0 THWN = .2679

**Step 2:** Calculating total sq. in. area
Table 5, Ch. 9
.5242 sq. in. x 3  = 1.5726  sq. in.
.2679 sq. in. x 1  = .2679  sq. in.
Total sq. in.      = 1.8405  sq. in.

**Step 3:** Selecting RMC
Table 4, Ch. 9
1.8405 sq. in. = 2 1/2"

**Solution:** The size rigid metal conduit for each is 2 1/2 in.

See **Figure 10-33** for an exercise problem when computing the size rigid metal conduit required for each run that is routed between the utilities, transformers, and service.

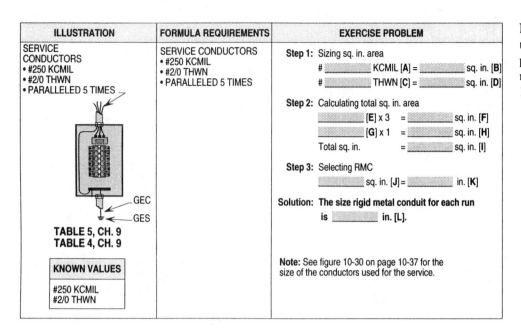

| ILLUSTRATION | FORMULA REQUIREMENTS | EXERCISE PROBLEM |
|---|---|---|
| SERVICE CONDUCTORS<br>• #250 KCMIL<br>• #2/0 THWN<br>• PARALLELED 5 TIMES | SERVICE CONDUCTORS<br>• #250 KCMIL<br>• #2/0 THWN<br>• PARALLELED 5 TIMES | **Step 1:** Sizing sq. in. area<br>   # ▨▨▨▨ KCMIL **[A]** = ▨▨▨▨ sq. in. **[B]**<br>   # ▨▨▨▨ THWN **[C]** = ▨▨▨▨ sq. in. **[D]**<br><br>**Step 2:** Calculating total sq. in. area<br>   ▨▨▨▨ **[E]** x 3  = ▨▨▨▨ sq. in. **[F]**<br>   ▨▨▨▨ **[G]** x 1  = ▨▨▨▨ sq. in. **[H]**<br>   Total sq. in.    = ▨▨▨▨ sq. in. **[I]**<br><br>**Step 3:** Selecting RMC<br>   ▨▨▨▨ sq. in. **[J]** = ▨▨▨▨ in. **[K]**<br><br>**Solution:** The size rigid metal conduit for each run<br>   is ▨▨▨▨ in. **[L]**.<br><br><br>**Note:** See figure 10-30 on page 10-37 for the size of the conductors used for the service. |

GEC
GES

**TABLE 5, CH. 9**
**TABLE 4, CH. 9**

**KNOWN VALUES**

#250 KCMIL
#2/0 THWN

**Figure 10-33.** This figure illustrates an exercise problem for computing the size rigid metal conduit required for each run. **(See figure 10-30)**

(5) What size copper grounding electrode conductor is required for the service in question No. 1 on page 10-36, if connected to the building's steel?

    **Step 1:** Finding total KCMIL
           250-66
           #350 KCMIL x 5 = 1,750 KCMIL

    **Step 2:** Finding Size GEC
           Table 250-66
           1,750 KCMIL requires #3/0 cu.

    **Solution:** The GEC is No. 3/0 copper.

(6) What size copper bonding jumper is required to ground the service raceways to the grounded neutral bar in the service panel in question No. 5 above?

    **Step 1:** Finding total KCMIL
           250-102(d)
           1,750 KCMIL x 12 1/2% = 218.75 KCMIL

    **Step 2:** Finding size BJ
           Table 250-66; Table 8, Ch. 9
           218.75 KCMIL requires #250 KCMIL

    **Solution:** The size copper BJ is No. 250 KCMIL

# Chapter 10
# Commercial Calculations

**Note:** All calculation problems can be solved with or without using the handy commercial calculation forms.

| Section | Answer | |
|---|---|---|

**Section**        **Answer**

_____    T    F    1. The general-purpose lighting load for an office building is calculated at 3.5 VA per sq. ft.

_____    T    F    2. The general-purpose lighting load for an auditorium in a school building is calculated at 1/2 VA per sq. ft.

_____    T    F    3. The lighting load for s sign shall be computed at a minimum of 1,400 volt-amperes.

_____    T    F    4. The largest VA rating between the heating and A/C load is selected and the smaller of the two loads is dropped.

_____    T    F    5. The VA rating of the largest motor is calculated by multiplying the amperage of the unit by the voltage times 125 percent.

_____  _____    6. For show window lighting, a load of not less than _____ volt-amperes shall be included for each linear foot of show window.

_____  _____    7. General-purpose receptacle outlets shall be calculated by the number of receptacles times _____ volt-amperes.

_____  _____    8. Special appliance loads that operate for more than three hours shall be calculated by the amperage of the appliance times _____ percent.

_____  _____    9. The demand load for 22 pieces of cooking equipment shall be calculated by the equipment load times _____ percent.

_____  _____    10. The volt-ampere rating for each heating and A/C load is calculated at _____ percent and the largest load of the two is selected.

_____  _____    11. What is the general lighting load, in amps, for a continuous load of 90 amps and a noncontinuous lighting load of 50 amps?

_____  _____    12. What is the load in VA for the general-purpose lighting load in an 7,000 sq. ft. office facility used continuously?

_____  _____    13. What is the load in VA for the general-purpose lighting load in an 40,000 sq. ft. store including 20,000 sq. ft. of warehouse space? (Used at continuous duty)

_____  _____    14. What is the load in VA for the general-purpose lighting load in an school building with the following area: (Compute at continuous operation)

- 20,000 sq. ft. classroom area
- 4,000 sq. ft. auditorium area
- 1,000 sq. ft. assembly hall area

_____  _____    15. What is the load in VA for 50, 120 volt, lighting ballast rated at 1.5 amps each and used for 8 hours a day?

_____ _____ 16. What is the load in VA for the following lighting fixtures:

- 12 - 100 VA each recess lighting fixtures
- 14 - 150 VA each incandescent lighting fixtures
- 20 - 180 VA each electric discharge lighting fixtures
- Compute at continuous operation

_____ _____ 17. What is the lighting load in VA for a 120 ft. of show window used at noncontinuous operation?

_____ _____ 18. What is the lighting load in VA for a 120 ft. of show window used at continuous operation?

_____ _____ 19. What is the lighting load in VA for 120 ft. of lighting track used at noncontinuous operation?

_____ _____ 20. What is the lighting load in VA for 120 ft. of lighting track used at continuous operation?

_____ _____ 21. What is the lighting load in amps for a low-voltage lighting system supplied by an isolation transformer with an FLA of 30 amps used as noncontinuous operation?

_____ _____ 22. What is the lighting load in amps for a low-voltage lighting system supplied by an isolation transformer with an FLA of 30 amps used at continuous operation?

_____ _____ 23. What is the lighting load in VA for 20 continuous operated lighting fixtures with a 75 VA ballast in each unit and 10 noncontinuous operated lighting fixtures with 75 VA ballast in each unit?

_____ _____ 24. What is the lighting load in VA for 40 continuous operated lighting fixtures with a 120 VA ballast in each unit?

_____ _____ 25. What is the lighting load in VA for a sign rated 1,200 VA operating for six hours?

_____ _____ 26. What is the lighting load in VA for a sign rated 2,400 VA operating for three hours?

_____ _____ 27. What is the load in VA for 54 general-purpose receptacles used to serve noncontinuous operated loads?

_____ _____ 28. What is the load in VA for 54 general-purpose receptacles used to serve continuous operated loads?

_____ _____ 29. What is the load in VA for 120 general-purpose receptacle outlets to cord-and-plug connect loads used at noncontinuous operation?

_____ _____ 30. What is the load in VA for 120 ft. of multioutlet assembly used to cord-and-plug connect loads that are not used simultaneously?

_____  _____  31. What is the load in VA for 120 ft. of multioutlet assembly used to cord-and-plug connect loads that are used simultaneously?

_____  _____  32. What is the load in VA for a 208 volt, three-phase, 58 amp special appliance load operating for four hours and supplied by an individual branch-circuit?

_____  _____  33. What is the load in VA for a 208 volt, three-phase, 58 amp special appliance load operating for two hours and supplied by an individual branch-circuit?

_____  _____
           _____  34. What is the demand load in VA and amps for twenty, 208 volt, three-phase cooking units rated 8 kW each?

_____  _____  35. What is the load in VA for a group of 240 volt, three-phase motors rated at 40 HP, 30 HP, and 20 HP?

_____  _____  36. What is the load in VA for four compressors rated at 24.5 amps each and supplied by a 480 volt, three-phase supply?

_____  _____  37. What is the largest load in VA between a 20 kW heating unit and a 6.5 kW A/C unit supplied by 208 volt, three-phase system?

_____  _____  38. What is the load in VA and amps for a store building including warehouse space using the standard calculation method with the following loads: (120/240 volt, single-phase service)
           _____
           _____      • 60,000 sq. ft. office space
                          • 30,000 sq. ft. warehouse space
           _____
           120 volt, single-phase loads

                          • 120 linear feet of show window (noncontinuous operation)
                          • 120 ft. lighting track (noncontinuous operation)
                          • 50 - 180 VA ballast's outside lighting (continuous operation)
                          • 2,400 VA sign lighting (continuous operation)
                          • 82 receptacles (noncontinuous operation)
                          • 30 receptacles (continuous operation)
                          • 160 ft. multioutlet assembly (heavy-duty)

           240 volt, single-phase loads

                          • 18,000   VA water heater
                          • 50,000   VA heating unit
                          • 29,400   VA A/C unit
                          • 8,640    VA freezer
                          • 5,820    VA ice cream box
                          • 9,680    VA walk-in cooler
                          • 1 - 3/4  HP exhaust fan
                          • 1 - 2    HP water pump

_____  _____  39. What size THWN copper conductors are required for the service in problem 38, where they are paralleled six times per phase?

_____  _____  40. What size OCPD is required for the service based on the computed load?

_____  _____  41. What size neutral conductor is required for the service where they are paralleled six times per phase?

_____  _____   42. What size rigid metal conduit is required for each run?

_____  _____   43. What is the load in VA and amps for a store building including warehouse space using the
                            standard calculation method with the following loads: (120/208 volt, three-phase service)

          _____
                            • 60,000 sq. ft. office space
          _____         • 30,000 sq. ft. warehouse space

          _____     120 volt, single-phase loads

                            • 120 linear feet of show window (noncontinuous operation)
                            • 120 ft. lighting track (noncontinuous operation)
                            • 50 - 180 VA ballast's outside lighting (continuous operation)
                            • 2,400 VA sign lighting (continuous operation)
                            • 82 receptacles (noncontinuous operation)
                            • 30 receptacles (continuous operation)
                            • 160 ft. multioutlet assembly (heavy-duty)

                        208 volt, three-phase loads

                            • 18,000    VA water heater
                            • 50,000    VA heating unit
                            • 29,400    VA A/C unit
                            • 8,640     VA freezer
                            • 5,820     VA ice cream box
                            • 9,680     VA walk-in cooler
                            • 1 - 3/4   HP exhaust fan
                            • 1 - 2     HP water pump

_____  _____   44. What size THWN copper conductors are required for the service where they are paral-
                            leled six times per phase?

_____  _____   45. What size OCPD is required for the service based upon the computed load?

_____  _____   46. What size neutral conductor is required for the service where they are paralleled six times
                            per phase?

_____  _____   47. What size rigid metal conduit is required for each run?

_____  _____   48. What is the load in VA and amps for a store building including warehouse space using the
                            standard calculation method with the following loads: (277/480 volt, three-phase service)
                            All VA per sq. ft. lighting is 277 volt.

          _____
                            • 60,000 sq. ft. office space
          _____         • 30,000 sq. ft. warehouse space

          _____     120 volt, single-phase loads

                            • 120 linear feet of show window (noncontinuous operation)
                            • 120 ft. lighting track (noncontinuous operation)
                            • 50 - 180 VA ballast's outside lighting (continuous operation)
                            • 2,400 VA sign lighting (continuous operation)
                            • 82 receptacles (noncontinuous operation)
                            • 30 receptacles (continuous operation)
                            • 160 ft. multioutlet assembly (heavy-duty)

                        480 volt, three-phase loads

                            • 18,000    VA water heater
                            • 50,000    VA heating unit
                            • 29,400    VA A/C unit
                            • 8,640     VA freezer
                            • 5,820     VA ice cream box
                            • 9,680     VA walk-in cooler
                            • 1 - 3/4   HP exhaust fan
                            • 1 - 2     HP water pump

_____  _____  49. What size THWN copper conductors are required for the service where they are paralleled two times per phase?

_____  _____  50. What size OCPD is required for the service based on computed load?

_____  _____  51. What size neutral conductor is required for the service where they are paralleled two times per phase?

_____  _____  52. What size rigid metal conduit is required for each run?

_____  _____  53. What is the load in VA and amps for a store building including warehouse space using the standard calculation method with the following loads: (120/240 volt, three-phase service)

_____

_____

_____

- 60,000 sq. ft. office space
- 30,000 sq. ft. warehouse space

120 volt, single-phase loads

- 120 linear feet of show window (noncontinuous operation)
- 120 ft. lighting track (noncontinuous operation)
- 50 - 180 VA ballast's outside lighting (continuous operation)
- 2,400 VA sign lighting (continuous operation)
- 82 receptacles (noncontinuous operation)
- 30 receptacles (continuous operation)
- 160 ft. multioutlet assembly (heavy-duty)

240 volt, three-phase loads

- 18,000    VA water heater
- 50,000    VA heating unit
- 29,400    VA A/C unit
- 8,640    VA freezer
- 5,820    VA ice cream box
- 9,680    VA walk-in cooler
- 1 - 3/4    HP exhaust fan
- 1 - 2    HP water pump

_____  _____  54. What is the load in VA and amps for a office building including meeting hall using the standard calculation method with the following loads: (277/480 volt, three-phase service) All lighting is 277 volt.

_____

_____

- 130,000 sq. ft. office building
- 5,000 sq. ft. meeting hall

120 volt, single-phase loads

- 100 ft. lighting track (noncontinuous operation)

- 30 - 180 VA ballast's outside lighting ( continuous operation)
- 3,800 VA sign lighting (continuous operation)
- 152 receptacles (noncontinuous operation)
- 138 receptacles (continuous operation)
- 8,000 VA isolation transformer for LVLS (continuous operation)
- 200 ft. multioutlet assembly (heavy-duty)

208 volt, three-phase loads

- 2 - 1,480 VA copying machines
- 10,000    VA water heater
- 34 - 225  VA data processors
- 10 - 175  VA work processors
- 4 - 1,200 VA printers

480 volt, three-phase loads

- 50 HP elevator (15 minute intermittent duty)
- 30 kW heating unit

55. What is the load in VA and amps for a school building using the standard calculation method with the following loads: (277/480 volt, three-phase service)

- 40,000 sq. ft. classroom area
- 8,000 sq. ft. auditorium area          } All lighting is 277 volts
- 1,500 sq. ft. assembly hall area

120 volt, single-phase loads

- 190 receptacles (noncontinuous duty)
- 60 receptacles (continuous duty)
- 200 ft. multioutlet assembly (heavy-duty)

120 volt, single-phase cooking equipment loads

- 2 - 1.2 kW toasters
- 6 - 1.4 kW refrigerators
- 4 - 1.6 kW freezers

208 volt, single-phase cooking equipment loads

- 6 - 12 kW ranges
- 4 - 9 kW ovens
- 4 - 4 kW fryers

208 volt, single-phase motor loads

- 4 - 2     HP vent hood fans
- 4 - 1/2   HP grill-vent fans

480 volt, three-phase motor loads

- 20 - 3/4 HP exhaust fans

56. What is the load in VA and amps for a restaurant using the standard calculation method with the following loads: (120/208 volt, three-phase service)

- 8,000 sq. ft. restaurant

120 volt, single-phase loads

- 40' lighting track (continuous duty)
- 14 - 180 VA outside lighting (continuous duty)
- 2,400 VA sign lighting (continuous duty)
- 30 receptacles (noncontinuous duty)
- 20 receptacles (continuous duty)
- 20' multioutlet assembly (heavy-duty)

208 volt, single-phase loads

- 6,450 VA hood fan
- 5,245 VA grill vent fan
- 15 A freezer
- 12,000 VA cooktop
- 2 - 10,000 VA ovens
- 12,000 VA range
- 18 A refrigerator
- 4,250 VA ice cream box

208 volt, three-phase loads (Use 208V x 1.732 = 360V)

- 2 - 30 kW heating units
- 2 - 6.5 kW A/C units
- 4,400 VA broiler
- 2 - 3,200 VA deep fat fryers
- 20 A walk-in cooler
- 6,000 VA water heater

_____    _____

           _____

           _____

           _____

57. What is the load in VA and amps for a welding shop using the standard calculation method with the following loads: (120/208 volt, three-phase service)

      120 volt, single-phase loads

- 8,400 VA inside lighting loads (continuous duty)
- 4 - 180 VA outside lighting loads (continuous duty)
- 1,200 VA sign lighting loads (continuous duty)
- 50 receptacles (continuous operation)

      208 volt, three-phase loads

- 2 - 10 kW heating units
- 6,500 VA A/C unit
- 5 HP air-compressor
- 2 - 2 HP grinders

Welders - resistance (40% duty cycle)
- 11 kW
- 9 kW

Welders - motor-generator arc (80% duty cycle)
- 16 kW
- 13 kW

Welders - AC transformer and DC rectifier (70% duty cycle)
- 14 kW
- 8 kW

_____    _____

58. What is the load in VA for a school building using the optional calculation method with the following loads:

| | | |
|---|---|---|
| • Classroom area | = | 40,000 sq. ft. |
| • Auditorium area | = | 5,000 sq. ft. |
| • Cafeteria area | = | 5,000 sq. ft. |
| • Hall area | = | 1,200 sq. ft. |

Total VA of school      = 845,794 VA

_____    _____

59. What is the load in VA for a restaurant using the optional calculation method with the following loads:

| | | |
|---|---|---|
| • Lighting loads | = | 18,240 VA |
| • Receptacle loads | = | 16,400 VA |
| • Special loads | = | 98,215 VA |
| • Heating or A/C loads | = | 40,000 VA |
| • Motor loads | = | 7,200 VA |

# 11

# Diagrams and Elements

There are many questions and problems on the journeyman test that requires the test taker to identify certain elements on diagrams. These elements are those found on plans in which electricians utilize to wire-in electrical equipment to the supply system.

Journeyman electricians are not only required to know such elements but they must be able to recognize them and identify them quickly.

For example, licensed electricians must know when to use a regular device box or square box with a plaster ring for the purpose of mounting a switch or receptacle. What is the difference between a circuit-breaker or fuse, and what is the benefit of selecting one over the other? These questions are answered and many other wiring methods and elements are identified with helpful exercise problems which will enhance one's ability to size and select such items.

This chapter will also aid test takers so they can recognize and identify such electrical elements without guess work. Test takers using the guess work concept, lose points if they choose and identify the wrong element by name.

It is recommended to use the NEC and a manufacturer's material catalog when studying and completing the blanks in the exercise problems.

## Quick Reference:

SERVICE ELEMENTS ................................... 11-2

BOXES, COVERS, DEVICES,

AND FITTINGS ............................................ 11-4

FIXTURE FITTINGS ...................................... 11-13

PANELBOARDS ............................................ 11-24

CONTROLLERS ............................................ 11-25

TYPES OF CABLES ...................................... 11-27

TYPES OF CONDUITS ................................... 11-30

OVERCURRENT

PROTECTION DEVICES ................................ 11-32

SWITCHES ................................................... 11-36

FLEXIBLE CORDS AND FITTINGS ................ 11-37

TERMINALS, LUGS,

AND CONNECTORS ..................................... 11-41

HELPFUL TABLES AND CHARTS ................. 11-45

## SERVICE ELEMENTS
## ART. 230 OF THE NEC

This chapter gives a complete coverage of service conductors and equipment for the control and protection of all elements of the service. In Art. 100 of the NEC, covering definitions, are the conductors and equipment from the source of power through the service-entrance equipment. Such a source might be distribution lines, transformers, or generators, etc.

A thorough knowledge of this chapter is very important since a good service is the heart of the entire installation. Branch-circuits and feeders extend the power of the service to the user end of the electrical system.

## OVERHEAD SERVICES
## ART. 100 OF THE NEC

**Test Tip 1:** The term "service-entrance" includes the service-entrance conductors, conduit and fittings, meter, service equipment with fuses or CB's, and any other equipment used between the tap to the service drop or lateral and the service disconnect.

To correctly interpret the rules relating to services, it is necessary to know precisely what is meant by their different terms as used in the NEC. Note that the following terms apply for overhead services:

(1) The service drop is the overhead conductors between the last pole and the service-entrance. The service drop ends at the point where the service-entrance conductors are connected to the service drop conductors.

(2) The service-entrance conductors are the conductors between the service drop and the service disconnect, which can be located outside or inside the building.

(3) The service conductors are the conductors between the last pole and the service disconnect. The term "service conductors" includes both the service drop conductors and the service-entrance conductors.

The service includes the service-drop conductors, service-entrance conductors, and any other equipment used between the last pole and the service disconnect.

**See Figures 11-1(a) and (b)** for a detailed illustration of an overhead service and in the spaces provided identify each item.

**Figure 11-1(a).** Identify in the spaces provided what each item represents in the diagram.

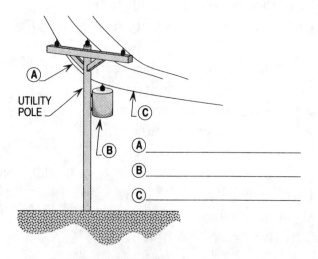

UTILITY POLE

(A) _____

(B) _____

(C) _____

**DISTRIBUTION EQUIPMENT**

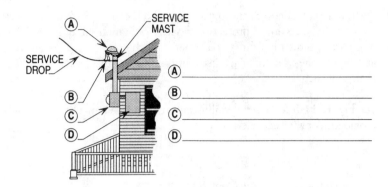

Figure 11-1(b). Identify in the spaces provided what each item represents in the diagram.

SERVICE ELEMENTS

# UNDERGROUND SERVICES
## ART. 100 OF THE NEC

For underground services, the underground lateral takes the place of the service drop as discussed above and shown in the diagrams in Figures 11-1(a) and (b).

When the service is underground, the conductors between the street main and the service-entrance are a lateral. The lateral connects to the utility company's underground protective devices or it could run underground to a pole, then routed up the pole and connected to the utilities overhead lines.

See **Figure 11-2** for a detailed illustration of an underground service and in the spaces provided identify each item.

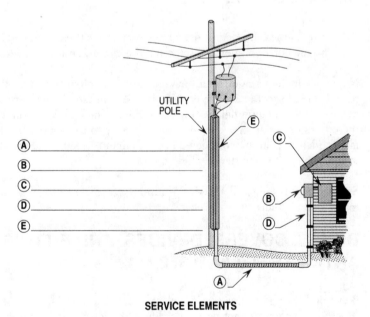

**Figure 11-2.** Identify in the spaces provided what each item represents in the diagram.

SERVICE ELEMENTS

# FEEDER ELEMENTS
## ART. 215 OF THE NEC

Article 100 of the NEC defines a feeder as all conductors between the service equipment (or generator switchboard of an isolated plant), and the final branch-circuit overcurrent protection device. An example of a feeder would be a circuit from the service equipment to a distribution panel supplying the branch-circuits.

**Test Tip 2:** For the protection of underground lateral conductors, the burial depth of conduit and cables must comply with Table 300-5 of the NEC.

For example, feeders are the conductors which carry electrical power from the service equipment to the overcurrent protection devices for branch-circuits supplying the loads. Subfeeders originate at a distribution center other than the service equipment or generator switchboard and supply one or more other distribution panelboards, branch-circuit panelboards, or combination of such.

See Figure 11-3 for a detailed illustration of the elements of a feeder-circuit and in the spaces provided identify such elements.

**Figure 11-3.** Identify in the spaces provided what each item represents in the diagram.

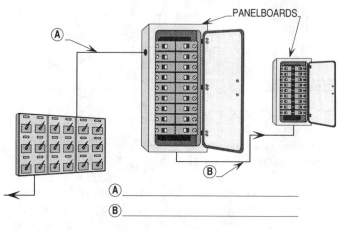

PANELBOARDS

Ⓐ

Ⓑ

Ⓐ _____

Ⓑ _____

**FEEDER-CIRCUIT ELEMENTS**

**Test Tip 3:** Conductors of feeder-circuits must be at least No. 10 copper and rated at 30 amps.

## BRANCH-CIRCUIT ELEMENTS
## ART. 210 OF THE NEC

**Test Tip 4:** Conductors of branch-circuits must be at least No. 14 copper or larger. Aluminum conductors must be at least No. 12 or larger.

According to the NEC definition, a branch-circuit is the circuit conductors between the final overcurrent protection device protecting the circuit, and the outlet(s) served.

Note that in some cases there may be no feeder-circuits and that the branch-circuits are routed directly to the service equipment. Several circuit breakers or sets of fuses are then connected to the terminal end of such service. These circuits connected to the load side of these fuses or circuit breakers are routed directly to the appliances, lighting, or other equipment. Such circuits are considered branch-circuits because they are located behind the final overcurrent protection device along the line.

See Figure 11-4 for a detailed illustration of the elements of a branch-circuit and in the spaces provided identify each element.

## BOXES, COVERS, DEVICES, AND FITTINGS
## ARTICLES 300 AND 370

**Note:** Before selecting a Box, know the following:

- Box material (metal or PVC)
- Box shape and size needed
- Type and size of knockouts needed
- Fixture studs and hickeys if needed
- Type of bracket if needed
- Type of cover if needed
- Type of clamp or connector needed
- Box extension if needed

Boxes and fittings do not conduct electric current. They are device and conductor housing structures. Before attempting to identify such items, test takers must know the difference between these items and be familiar with their use in electrical systems. The following clarifies such differences:

(1) A device connects the wiring and conducts the electricity from point to point in a circuit.

(2) A fitting or box connects the metallic or nonmetallic wiring sections together and holds such parts in place. **(See Figure 11-5)**

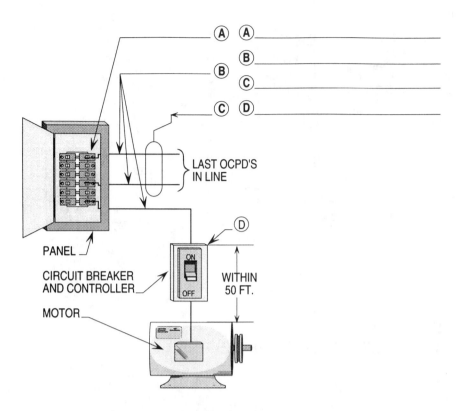

**Figure 11-4.** Identify in the spaces provided what each item represents in the diagram.

(A) (A)
(B)
(B)
(C)
(C) (D)

LAST OCPD'S
IN LINE

PANEL

CIRCUIT BREAKER
AND CONTROLLER

MOTOR

(D)
ON
OFF
WITHIN
50 FT.

**BRANCH-CIRCUITS**

**Test Tip 5:** Circuit breakers must be sized large enough to allow the motor to start and run without tripping and opening the circuit.

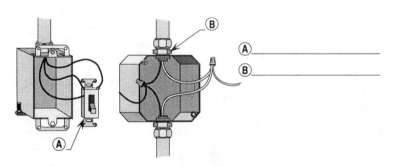

(B)
(A)
(B)
(A)

**DEVICES AND FITTINGS**

**Figure 11-5.** Identify in the spaces provided whether each item is a device or fitting by naming each.

Note that a length of at least 3 in. or 6 in. of wire must be left at each switch box per Sec. 300-14.

# BOXES
## TABLE 370-16(a) OF THE NEC

Boxes are available in four general types and shapes. They are octagonal, rectangular, square, and circular with variations of each basic configuration. All of the configurations come in many sizes with a choice of mounting brackets that can be utilized depending upon the particular type of installation.

Boxes not only must secure the ends of the conduit and house all the conductor joints but must also make a good electrical connection to the conduit system. Then the grounding of the conduit system is continuous. However, equipment grounding conductors must be used if the conduit system is nonmetallic (PVC). **(See Figure 11-6)**

**Test Tip 6:** Boxes are used not only to support the wiring but they are also used to support the devices or fixtures. Boxes may also be used where only splices or junctions in the wiring system occur.

**Figure 11-6.** Identify in the spaces provided the correct box configuration that each item represents.

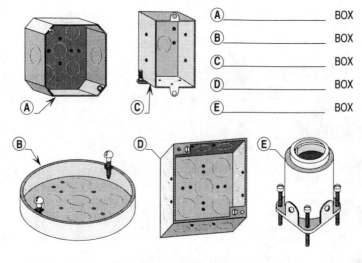

| | |
|---|---|
| Ⓐ_____ | BOX |
| Ⓑ_____ | BOX |
| Ⓒ_____ | BOX |
| Ⓓ_____ | BOX |
| Ⓔ_____ | BOX |

**BOX CONFIGURATIONS**

# DEVICE BOXES
## TABLE 370-16(a) OF THE NEC

**Test Tip 7:** Plaster rings, domed covers, and extension rings must have their fill area listed or selected from the box fill area from which they are mounted to.

There are several types of device boxes and all are available in either metallic or nonmetallic materials. The type used is based upon the type of installation.

A switch or device box can be either equipped with square or beveled corners. They are also called sectional or gangable boxes, because by loosening one screw on the side and one screw on one or more other boxes, the sides can be removed and such boxes ganged together. **(See Figure 11-7)**

**Figure 11-7.** Identify in the spaces provided what each item represents.

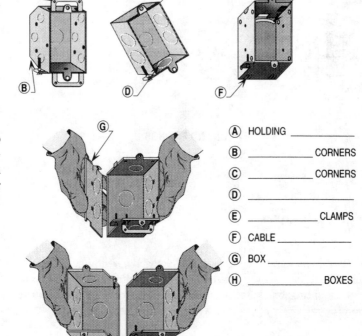

**Test Tip 8:** Boxes are ganged so that more than one switch, receptacle, pilot light, or combination of such can be mounted together in the same box area side by side.

| | |
|---|---|
| Ⓐ HOLDING _____ | |
| Ⓑ _____ CORNERS | |
| Ⓒ _____ CORNERS | |
| Ⓓ _____ | |
| Ⓔ _____ CLAMPS | |
| Ⓕ CABLE _____ | |
| Ⓖ BOX _____ | |
| Ⓗ _____ BOXES | |

**DEVICE BOXES**

**Note:** The mounting ears on boxes are adjustable for mounting on a wall and removable if needed. A sectional device box without clamps for use with conduit is also available. Such a box can be used for NM cable by adding NM cable connectors or for armored cable (AC) by adding AC connectors.

**Test Tip 9:** The ears of device boxes can be used to secure such boxes to wooden materials or hold fast bars can be utilized to hold boxes in sheetrocked walls.

# HANDY BOXES
# ART. 370 OF THE NEC

Handy boxes are usually mounted on the surface and they are not usually equipped with self contained clamps for cables. If they are used for cables, cable connectors must be used. Boxes with brackets can be nailed to a wall stud and used in place of one of the device boxes mentioned above. A box extension can be used to add more depth to the original box so that more conductors can be contained.

**Note:** Handy boxes are similar to the device boxes but they do not have ears. They are nongangable and require separate cable clamps or appropriate connectors. Their standard dimensions are 4 in. by 2 1/8 in. (See **Figure 11-8**)

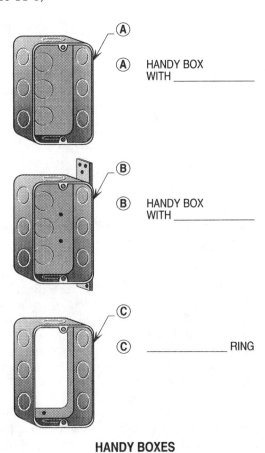

(A)  HANDY BOX
WITH _____

(B)  HANDY BOX
WITH _____

(C)  _____ RING

**HANDY BOXES**

**Figure 11-8.** Identify in the spaces provided what each item represents.

**Test Tip 10:** When direct metal to metal contact between a device yoke and surface mounted handy box is made, the device U ground is considered grounded by the No. 6-32 screws of the device yoke which bonds such straps to the metal box.

# OCTAGON BOXES
# TABLE 370-16(a) OF THE NEC

Most boxes used in ceilings for fixtures are octagon boxes. Several variations of 4 in. octagon boxes are available with knockouts for conduits or boxes with clamps for cables. Box extensions are also available to add more volume to existing or newly installed boxes when mounting. Boxes with brackets are used to nail the boxes to studs or joists and can be used with adjustable bar hangers. Note that there are other methods of mounting such boxes.

**Note:** Octagon boxes are usually used for installing ceiling or wall fixtures. They are available with or without clamps and with or without brackets. **(See Figure 11-9)**

**Figure 11-9.** Identify in the spaces provided what each item represents.

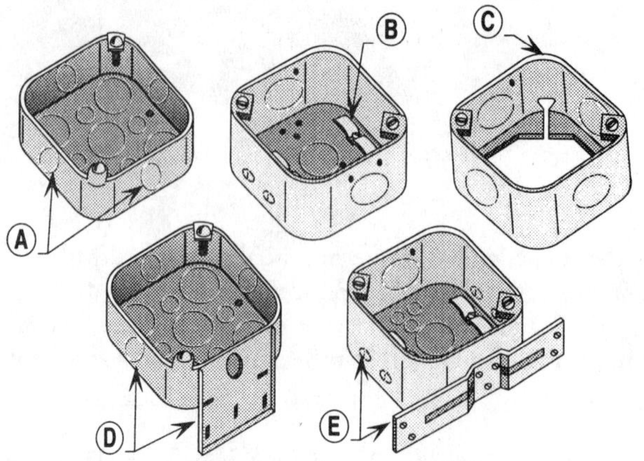

Ⓐ OCTAGON BOX WITH _____

Ⓑ OCTAGON BOX WITH _____

Ⓒ EXTENSION _____

Ⓓ OCTAGON BOX WITH _____

   AND _____ BRACKET

Ⓔ OCTAGON BOX WITH _____

   ENTERS AND _____ BRACKETS

**OCTAGON BOXES**

## ROUND BOXES
## TABLE 370-16(a) OF THE NEC

**Test Tip 12:** Lighting fixtures mounted to ceiling boxes are limited to 50 lbs or less. A listed box is allowed to support a lighting fixture weighing more than 50 lbs..

Round boxes can be used in ceiling or wall work. However, round boxes have a major restriction for conduit which can't enter through their sides. The sides are rounded and have no flat spots which makes it difficult to get a good electrical connection with a locknut or connector. When trying to tighten a locknut on the outside, the center of the nut will tend to sit flush but the edges have a space between the locknut and box. Likewise, when trying to tighten a nut on the inside, the edges of the nut seats, but the center fails to do so. Conduits and cables can be connected to the back of round boxes because this part of the box is flat. **(See Figure 11-10)**

**Test Tip 11:** The NEC prohibits the connection of conduits and cables to the round portion of boxes when using compression or set screw connectors.

**Note:** Either octagon or round boxes can be used for the installation of ceiling fixtures. Round boxes are often called ceiling boxes and must not be used with conduit connections to their sides because locknuts will not seat properly and provide good continuity.

## SQUARE BOXES
## TABLE 370-16(a) OF THE NEC

**Test Tip 13:** Ceiling (paddle) fans mounted to listed ceiling boxes must weigh 35 lbs or less.

Square boxes are available for installations where a larger volume is required for the wiring. They can be used in place of switchboxes or octagon boxes due to a variety of cover plates.

Square boxes are generally 4 in. or 4 11/16 in. in sizes and are available with different depths. An extension ring can be used to add more volume to contain additional conductors. **(See Figures 11-11(a), (b), and (c).**

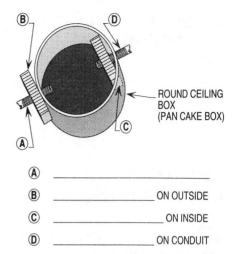

**Figure 11-10.** Identify in the spaces provided what each item represents.

ROUND CEILING BOX (PAN CAKE BOX)

Ⓐ _____

Ⓑ _____ ON OUTSIDE

Ⓒ _____ ON INSIDE

Ⓓ _____ ON CONDUIT

**IMPROPER USE OF ROUND BOX**

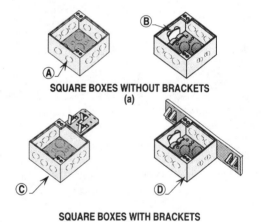

SQUARE BOXES WITHOUT BRACKETS
(a)

SQUARE BOXES WITH BRACKETS
(b)

**Figures 11-11(a), (b), and (c).** Identify in the spaces provided what each item represents.

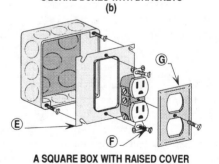

A SQUARE BOX WITH RAISED COVER
(c)

Ⓐ SQUARE BOXES WITH _____

Ⓑ SQUARE BOXES WITH CABLE _____

Ⓒ FLUSH MOUNTING _____ BRACKET

Ⓓ FLAT MOUNTING _____ BRACKET

Ⓔ SQUARE BOX _____ COVER

Ⓕ DEVICE MOUNTING _____ - 32 SCREW

Ⓖ DEVICE COVERING _____ PLATE

**Test Tip 14:** Device yokes designed for the purpose, can be used to ground the metal strap of a device to the flush mounted metal box surface.

**Note:** When junction boxes are needed, square boxes are ideal for such use. They are allowed to be concealed but are required to be accessible to the user by ladders or another acceptable means such as crawl spaces or suspended ceilings.

## BOXES WITH KNOCKOUTS
## 370-18 OF THE NEC

**Test Tip 15:** Unused openings in boxes must be closed with the proper fittings.

Boxes are equipped with two types of knockouts and they are as follows:

**(1)** Round knockouts (KO's) for conduits
**(2)** D-shaped knockouts for cables.

## ROUND KNOCKOUTS
## 370-2 OF THE NEC

The round knockout (KO) is used whenever an electrician is going to install a conduit or cable connector. Round knockouts are made for standard sizes of conduits such as 1/2, 3/4, and 1 in, etc. More than one size is often found of the same box so different size conduits can be connected without using a knockout cutter. **(See Figure 11-12)**

**Figure 11-12.** Identify in the spaces provided what each item represents.

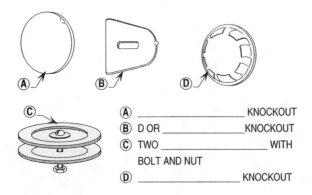

Ⓐ _____ KNOCKOUT
Ⓑ D OR _____ KNOCKOUT
Ⓒ TWO _____ WITH BOLT AND NUT
Ⓓ _____ KNOCKOUT

**TYPES OF KNOCKOUTS**

**Test Tip 16:** To prevent damage to the insulation of conductors, 1/4 in. of the cable's outer jacket should be pulled into the box and installed under the cable clamp.

The pressure-type knockout plug is more convenient, for it can be easily inserted when a mistake has been made. Multiple ring knockouts also are used, but normally they are utilized on large panelboards or junction boxes. **(See Figure 11-12)**

## D-SHAPED KNOCKOUTS
## 370-17 OF THE NEC

The D-shaped knockout is found on outlet boxes that are equipped with self-contained cable clamps. It usually has a slot in it so it can be pried out easily which is also called a pryout. Electricians normally use their screwdrivers to remove such knockouts from boxes. **(See Figure 11-12)**

## MASONRY BOXES
## 370-1 OF THE NEC

Masonry boxes are boxes constructed in standard lengths that correspond to the widths of standard size bricks and cinder blocks. Masonry boxes normally are equipped with knockouts designed only for conduit fittings.

Masonry boxes are available in different sizes and configurations. They are basically two types and they are as follows:

(1) Stud-mounted
(2) Through the wall

**See Figure 11-13** for a detailed illustration of the types of boxes and in the spaces provided identify each type.

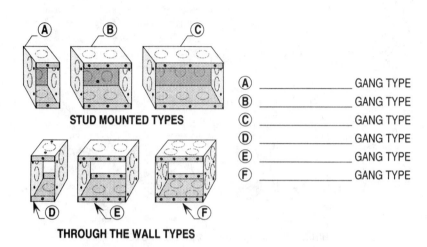

**STUD MOUNTED TYPES**

Ⓐ _____ GANG TYPE
Ⓑ _____ GANG TYPE
Ⓒ _____ GANG TYPE
Ⓓ _____ GANG TYPE
Ⓔ _____ GANG TYPE
Ⓕ _____ GANG TYPE

**THROUGH THE WALL TYPES**

**VARIOUS TYPES OF MASONARY BOXES**

**Figure 11-13.** Identify in the spaces provided what each item represents.

**Note:** The stud-mounted box is available in sizes that can be used with wet-wall or dry-wall type construction. The through the wall type boxes can serve as outlet boxes for the rooms on both sides of a wall, etc. Masonry boxes usually have concentric or eccentric knockouts so different conduit sizes can be used without having to use a knockout cutter.

**Test Tip 17:** Boxes such as FS and FD are larger cast or sheet metal boxes and are not considered conduit bodies.

# BRACKETS
# 370-23 OF THE NEC

Brackets are designed to be used for old work and new work, but most of them are used in new construction. Journeyman electricians must know the different types that are available so they can select the right bracket for each particular wiring method and installation.

**See Figure 11-14** for a detailed illustration of the different types of box brackets and in the spaces provided identify each type.

**Note:** Box brackets are available for both metallic and nonmetallic boxes.

**Test Tip 18:** Boxes without brackets can be mounted to framing members with nails if these nails are located within 1/4 in. at the back of such boxes.

# BAR HANGERS
# 370-23 OF THE NEC

Boxes can be mounted with bar hangers that can be adjusted between framing members of walls, ceilings, and floors. They are available in two types as follows:

(1) Stud type
(2) Clip type

**Figure 11-14.** Identify in the spaces provided what each item represents.

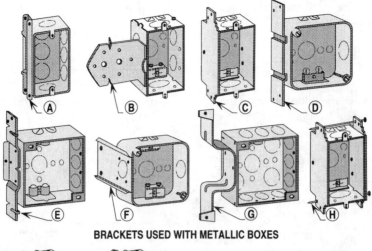

**BRACKETS USED WITH METALLIC BOXES**

**Test Tip 19:** Wooden braces used to support boxes must have a cross section not less than 1 in. by 2 in. respectively.

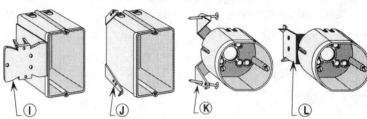

**BRACKETS USED WITH NONMETALLIC BOXES**

Ⓐ _____ BRACKETS  Ⓖ _____ BRACKETS
Ⓑ _____ BRACKETS  Ⓗ _____ BRACKETS
Ⓒ _____ BRACKETS  Ⓘ _____ BRACKETS
Ⓓ _____ BRACKETS  Ⓙ _____ BRACKETS
Ⓔ _____ BRACKETS  Ⓚ _____ BRACKETS
Ⓕ _____ BRACKETS  Ⓛ _____ BRACKETS

**DIFFERENT TYPES OF BOX BRACKETS**

**Figure 11-15.** Identify in the spaces provided what each item represents.

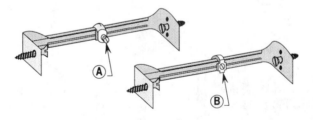

**ADJUSTABLE BAR HANGERS**

**Test Tip 20:** Boxes supported to bar hangers must be fastened to these hangers by a mechanical means such as bolts, screws, rivets, or clips.

Ⓐ _____ TYPE BAR HANGER
Ⓑ _____ TYPE BAR HANGER

**See Figure 11-15** for the different types of adjustable bar hangers and in the spaces provided identify each type.

## BOX FITTINGS
## 300-15 OF THE NEC

Box fittings are one of two types and they are as follows:

(1) Clamps
(2) Fixture fittings

## CLAMPS
## TABLE 370-16(a) OF THE NEC

Cable clamps are used in boxes to support the in-coming cable. Such cable can be NM, AC, or MC cables which are used mainly to wire feeders and branch-circuits between panelboards, lighting outlets, receptacle outlets, and equipment, etc.

**Note:** If boxes are not equipped with self-contained clamps, then proper cable connectors have to be used. The different types of connectors will be discussed later.

See **Figure 11-16** for the various types of cable clamps and in the spaces provided identify each type.

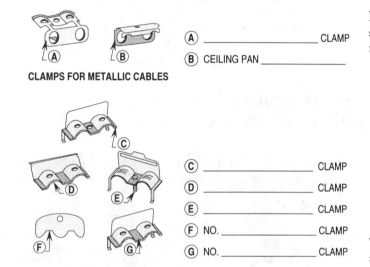

CLAMPS FOR METALLIC CABLES

(A) _____ CLAMP

(B) CEILING PAN _____

(C) _____ CLAMP

(D) _____ CLAMP

(E) _____ CLAMP

(F) NO. _____ CLAMP

(G) NO. _____ CLAMP

CLAMPS FOR NONMETALLIC CABLES

DIFFERENT TYPES OF CABLE CLAMPS

**Figure 11-16.** Identify in the spaces provided what each item represents.

**Test Tip 21:** Cable clamps count as one when determining the fill area of boxes. Such clamps, count as one, based upon the largest conductor entering the box.

## FIXTURE FITTINGS
## TABLE 370-16(a) OF THE NEC

Fixture fittings may be purchased as part of the box assembly or purchased separately and assembled as needed in actual field installations. For hanging fixtures, there are two basic methods and they are as follows:

(1) Stud, hickey, and nipple
(2) Strap, nipple, etc.

See **Figure 11-17** for a detailed illustration of the types of fixture fittings and in the spaces provided identify each type.

**Test Tip 22:** Studs and hickeys count as one each based upon the largest conductor entering the box.

## BOX PLATES AND COVERS
## 370-25 OF THE NEC

After the proper box has been selected, along with its associated fittings, a plate or cover for the box must be selected to enclose wiring and device parts.

**Figure 11-17.** Identify in the spaces provided what each item represents.

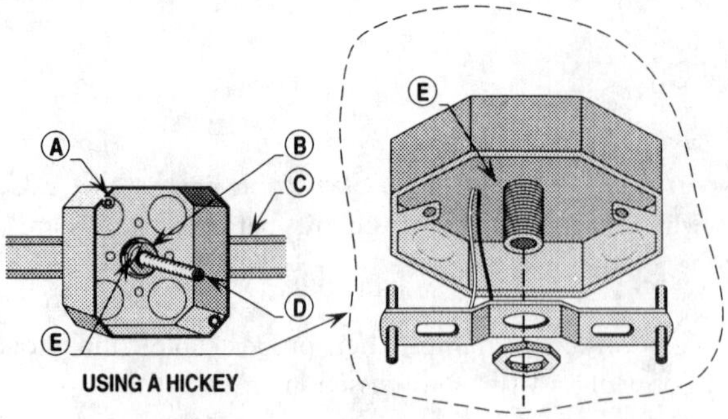

**Test Tip 23:** Boxes used to enclose flush devices must completely enclose such device on back and sides.

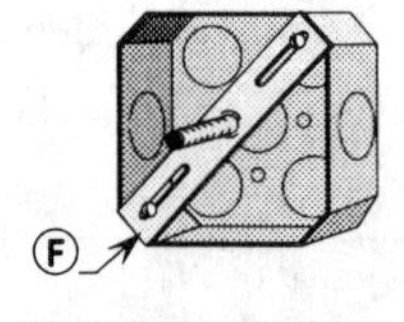

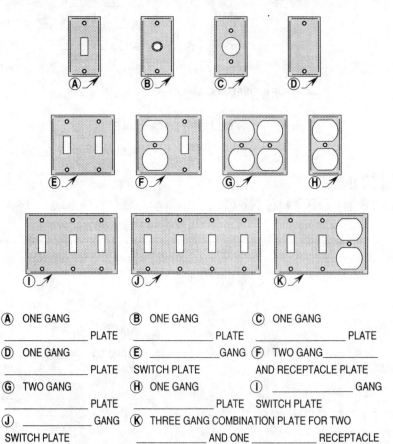

USING A HICKEY

USING A FIXTURE STRAP

Ⓐ _____ BOX

Ⓑ _____

Ⓒ _____ HANGER

Ⓓ _____

Ⓔ _____

Ⓕ FIXTURE _____

**VARIOUS TYPES OF FIXTURE FITTINGS**

## PLATE COVERS
## 370-25 OF THE NEC

The plate has to match the device that is mounted in the box. Whichever the type of box used, there are plates and covers designed for every application. **(See Figure 11-18)**

**Figure 11-18.** Identify in the spaces provided what each item represents.

**Test Tip 24:** To make an installation complete, each box must have a cover, faceplate, or fixture canopy.

Ⓐ ONE GANG
_____ PLATE

Ⓑ ONE GANG
_____ PLATE

Ⓒ ONE GANG
_____ PLATE

Ⓓ ONE GANG
_____ PLATE

Ⓔ _____ GANG
SWITCH PLATE

Ⓕ TWO GANG _____
AND RECEPTACLE PLATE

Ⓖ TWO GANG
_____ PLATE

Ⓗ ONE GANG
_____ PLATE

Ⓘ _____ GANG
SWITCH PLATE

Ⓙ _____ GANG
SWITCH PLATE

Ⓚ THREE GANG COMBINATION PLATE FOR TWO
_____ AND ONE _____ RECEPTACLE

**VARIOUS TYPES OF PLATE COVERS**

## BOX COVERS
## 370-28(c) OF THE NEC

Box covers are available in many designs to fit the large variety of round, square, oblong, and octagon shaped boxes. They come in forms of closed, slotted, or with knockouts. They also have the same shapes as the boxes on which they are used.

**See Figures 11-19(a) and (b)** for a detailed illustration of box cover configurations used to enclose a box or device mounted in the box. Note that each type must be identified in the space provided.

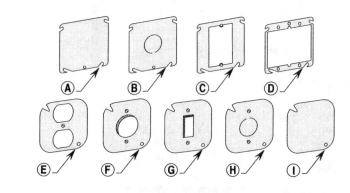

**FLAT BOX COVERS**

**Figure 11-19(a).** Identify in the spaces provided what each item represents.

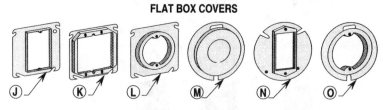

**RAISED BOX COVERS**

**Test Tip 25:** Boxes installed in walls having noncombustible material must not be set back more than 1/4 in. from the finished surface.

Ⓐ _____ COVER    Ⓑ _____ COVER W/KO    Ⓒ ONE _____ COVER

Ⓓ _____ DEVICE COVER    Ⓔ ONE _____ RECEPTACLE COVER    Ⓕ ONE _____ COVER FOR RECEPTACLE

Ⓖ ONE _____ SWITCH COVER    Ⓗ ONE _____ COVER W/KO    Ⓘ ONE _____ COVER FOR OCTAGON BOX

Ⓙ ONE _____ DEVICE COVER    Ⓚ TWO SQUARE _____ COVERS    Ⓛ ONE _____ ROUND COVER

Ⓜ ONE ROUND _____ COVER W/KO    Ⓝ ONE ROUND _____ COVER    Ⓞ ONE ROUND _____ COVER W/OPENING

**VARIOUS TYPES OF PLATE COVERS**

**Note:** When a box is used as a junction box and a service box, a raised cover will normally increase the fill area for installing extra wires.

## FS AND FD BOXES
## TABLE 370-16(a) AND ART. 100 OF THE NEC

FS and FD boxes are cast boxes for devices, and they are equipped with threaded hubs for connecting conduit or connectors instead of using locknuts and connectors. Note that these boxes do not have any mounting brackets. They are normally installed with conduit and they use the conduit for support. If supported properly, they do not need additional supports. These boxes are available in standard sizes and threaded fittings not over 100 cu. in. in size.

**Test Tip 26:** FS and FD boxes must be supported by conduits if they are not specially designed with supporting ears.

**Figure 11-19(b).** Identify in the spaces provided what each item represents.

**Test Tip 27:** Covers must completely cover the boxes and wiring within.

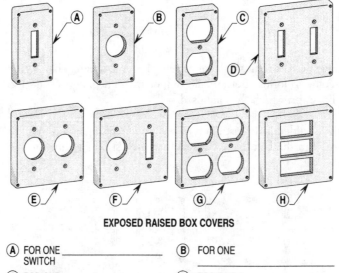

**EXPOSED RAISED BOX COVERS**

(A) FOR ONE _____ SWITCH

(B) FOR ONE _____

(C) FOR ONE _____ RECEPTACLE

(D) FOR TWO _____ SWITCHES

(E) FOR TWO_____ RECEPTACLES

(F) FOR SINGLE SWITCH AND _____

(G) FOR TWO _____ RECEPTACLES

(H) FOR THREE-GANG _____

**VARIOUS TYPES OF EXPOSED BOX COVERS**

**Figure 11-20.** Identify in the spaces provided what each item represents.

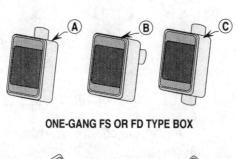

**ONE-GANG FS OR FD TYPE BOX**

**Test Tip 28:** When conduits are supported within 3 ft. of such boxes, these boxes are considered supported if not supporting fixtures or devices. If fixtures or devices are supported from such boxes, the conduits must be supported within 18 in. of such boxes.

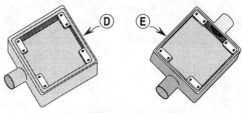

**TWO-GANG FS TYPE BOX**

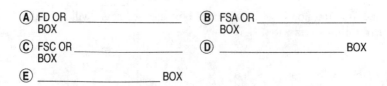

(A) FD OR _____ BOX

(B) FSA OR _____ BOX

(C) FSC OR _____ BOX

(D) _____ BOX

(E) _____ BOX

**VARIOUS TYPES OF FS AND FD BOXES**

See **Figure 11-20** for a detailed illustration of such boxes and in the spaces provided identify each type.

# CONDUIT BODIES
# 370-16(c) OF THE NEC

Conduit bodies are special fittings for a conduit system that provide access to its interior at a junction point of the system or at a terminal point. Due to such bodies having removable covers, they can be utilized for the same use as boxes. Note that many of the rules that apply to pull boxes also apply to conduit bodies. One of the most important rules is splices must not be made in conduit bodies, without such bodies having two or more conduit entries. However, some bodies are approved (listed) to contain the splicing of conductors.

When working with No. 6 and smaller conductors, a conduit body must have a cross-sectional area which is twice that of the largest size conduit connected to it. When selected as such, the conductor fill of the conduit body is considered the same as the conductor fill allowed in the connected conduit. For example, a 1/2 in. conduit that has a cross-sectional area of .3 square inches is being connected to a conduit body, such body must be at least 2 by 0.3 or 0.6 square inch area. The conduit body will now have the conductor fill permitted by the NEC for 1/2 in. conduit. However, when conduit bodies are connected to 3/4 in. or larger conduits containing No. 4 or larger conductors, the length of a conduit body must be at least eight times the trade size diameter of the attached conduit.

**Test Tip 29:** The first letter of the type designation of a conduit body describes the shape of the fitting. The second letter identifies which sides the covers are located on.

**See Figures 11-21(a) and (b)** for a detailed illustration of different types of conduit bodies and in the space provided identify each type.

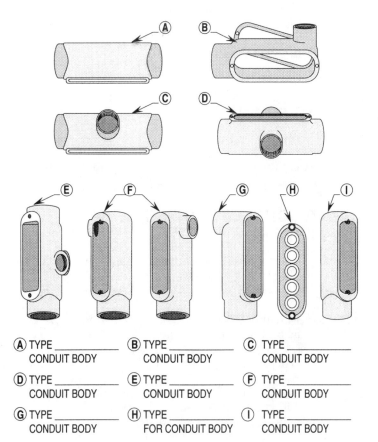

**Figure 11-21(a).** Identify in the spaces provided what each item represents.

**Test Tip 30:** Eight 90° bends can be made in a conduit run if a conduit body is installed in the run so that four bends are on one side of the body and the other four bends are on the other side.

(A) TYPE _____ CONDUIT BODY

(B) TYPE _____ CONDUIT BODY

(C) TYPE _____ CONDUIT BODY

(D) TYPE _____ CONDUIT BODY

(E) TYPE _____ CONDUIT BODY

(F) TYPE _____ CONDUIT BODY

(G) TYPE _____ CONDUIT BODY

(H) TYPE _____ FOR CONDUIT BODY

(I) TYPE _____ CONDUIT BODY

**VARIOUS TYPES OF CONDUIT BODIES**

**Figure 11-21(b).** Identify in the spaces provided what each item represents.

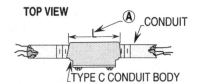

TOP VIEW

Ⓐ CONDUIT

TYPE C CONDUIT BODY

**STRAIGHT TYPE BODY**

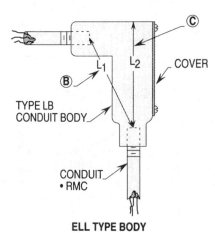

Ⓒ

$L_1$  $L_2$  COVER

Ⓑ

TYPE LB CONDUIT BODY

CONDUIT
• RMC

**ELL TYPE BODY**

**Test Tip 31:** Note that conduit bodies must be supported by the connected conduit. Holes must not be drilled into the conduit body and screws through such holes shall not be used to support the box.

Ⓐ _____ TIMES THE TRADE DIAMETER OF THE LARGEST CONDUIT

Ⓑ _____ TIMES THE INSIDE DIAMETER OF THE CONDUIT

Ⓒ _____ TIMES THE INSIDE DIAMETER OF THE CONDUIT

**RULES FOR SIZING CONDUIT BODIES**

## ACCESS FITTINGS
## 370-5

Conduit access fittings such as pulling elbows can be used to aid a conduit system where there are several bends in the run. **(See Figure 11-22)**

## CABLE CONNECTORS AND CLAMPS
## 300-10 OF THE NEC

**Test Tip 32:** Connectors and fittings can only be used with the specific wiring method for which they have been listed.

Conductors must be firmly fastened to the outlet box to prevent movement that might cause damage to its insulation. For this purpose, clamps are sometimes provided in outlet boxes.

When outlet boxes do not include clamps, self bushed cable connectors or connectors and bushings must be used. Such connectors must match the size and types of conductors used. For example, a connector for Type AC cable must not be used with Type NM cable or a flexible cord connector used with MC cable unless listed for such use.

**Note:** In general, a connector for nonmetallic cable will be fastened to the cable with a clamp, whereas a connector for armored cable may be fastened with either a setscrew or a clamp. There are connectors which are designed for specific types of cables and the correct one must be selected based upon the cable used.

**See Figure 11-23(a)** for a detailed illustration of the types of cable connectors and clamps and in the space provided identify each type.

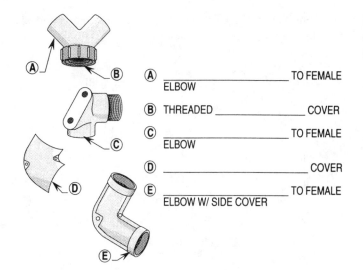

**Figure 11-22.** Identify in the spaces provided what each item represents.

Ⓐ _____ TO FEMALE
ELBOW

Ⓑ THREADED _____ COVER

Ⓒ _____ TO FEMALE
ELBOW

Ⓓ _____ COVER

Ⓔ _____ TO FEMALE
ELBOW W/ SIDE COVER

**VARIOUS TYPES OF CONDUIT ACCESS FITTINGS**

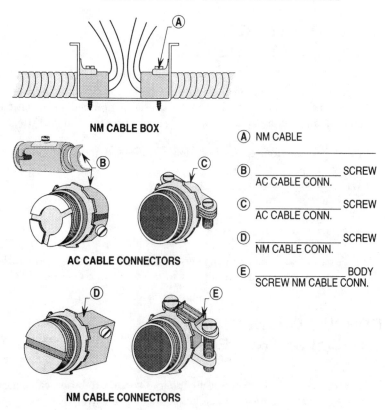

**NM CABLE BOX**

**AC CABLE CONNECTORS**

**NM CABLE CONNECTORS**

Ⓐ NM CABLE
_____

Ⓑ _____ SCREW
AC CABLE CONN.

Ⓒ _____ SCREW
AC CABLE CONN.

Ⓓ _____ SCREW
NM CABLE CONN.

Ⓔ _____ BODY
SCREW NM CABLE CONN.

**Figure 11-23(a).** Identify in the spaces provided what each item represents.

**Test Tip 33:** The reason a romex connector must not be used on an AC cable run, is because such connector does not have an inside shield to prevent the cable from entering the box.

**VARIOUS TYPES OF CABLE CONNECTORS**

**Note:** Cable connectors are available in materials such as steel, zinc, plastic, or combinations of such material. For example, combination connectors can be equipped with plastic bodies and steel clamps. Such connectors are sometimes necessary.

# CABLE SUPPORTS
# 300-4 OF THE NEC

Cables must be supported to the framing members in an approved method. Staples and straps are used for this purpose. **Note:** In some cases plastic ties can be used per the AHJ.

See **Figure 11-23(b)** for the various types of supports and identify each type in the spaces provided.

**Figure 11-23(b).** Identify in the spaces provided what each item represents.

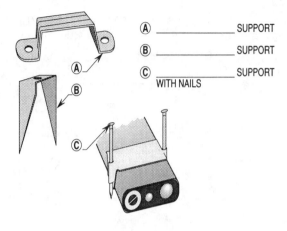

Ⓐ _____ SUPPORT

Ⓑ _____ SUPPORT

Ⓒ _____ SUPPORT
WITH NAILS

**CABLE SUPPORTS**

## CONDUIT FITTINGS
## 300-15(a) OF THE NEC

**Test Tip 34:** Conduit fittings must be installed mechanically tight to ensure the continuity of the conduit system.

To select the proper conduit fittings, the type of conduit must be known. For example, the trade size and whether it is rigid metal conduit, intermediate metal conduit, or electrical metallic tubing, etc. must be known before selecting the correct fitting.

There are basically four types of conduit fittings used and they are as follows:

(1) Threaded fittings
(2) Compression fittings
(3) Clamp or squeeze fittings
(4) Setscrew fittings

**Note:** A particular conduit fitting gets its name by the method in which it is installed on a conduit system to connect the conduit to the frame of enclosures, boxes, etc.

## CONDUIT CONNECTORS
## 300-15(a) OF THE NEC

**Test Tip 35:** When PVC is used with rigid metal conduit, an approved adapter must be used to join these conduit systems together.

In general, a conduit connector is used to join conduit to boxes, cabinets, conduit bodies, etc. Several types and variations of conduit connectors are available with insulated throats which will keep the insulation from wearing through and permitting the conductors from shorting out.

See **Figure 11-24** for a detailed illustration of the types of conduit fittings and in the spaces provided identify each type.

## CONDUIT COUPLINGS
## 300-15(a) OF THE NEC

Couplings are very similar to connectors except that they are used to join lengths of conduit together. Lengths of conduit may be of the same type or of different types. When lengths of conduit are of different types, the coupling is called a combination or adapter coupling.

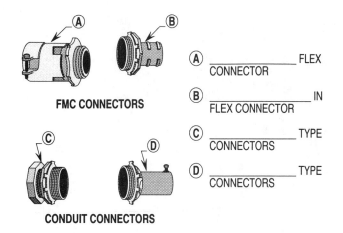

Ⓐ _____ FLEX
CONNECTOR

Ⓑ _____ IN
FLEX CONNECTOR

Ⓒ _____ TYPE
CONNECTORS

Ⓓ _____ TYPE
CONNECTORS

**VARIOUS TYPES OF CONDUIT CONNECTORS**

**Figure 11-24.** Identify in the spaces provided what each item represents.

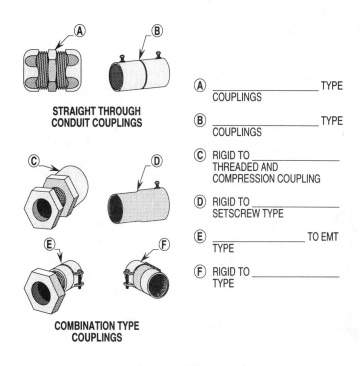

Ⓐ _____ TYPE
COUPLINGS

Ⓑ _____ TYPE
COUPLINGS

Ⓒ RIGID TO _____
THREADED AND
COMPRESSION COUPLING

Ⓓ RIGID TO _____
SETSCREW TYPE

Ⓔ _____ TO EMT
TYPE

Ⓕ RIGID TO _____
TYPE

**VARIOUS TYPES OF COUPLINGS**

**Figure 11-25.** Identify in the spaces provided what each item represents.

See **Figure 11-25** for a detailed illustration of the types of conduit couplings and in the spaces provided identify each type.

# FMC CONNECTORS
## 350-20 OF THE NEC

In general, flexible metal conduit (FMC) connectors are used to joint such conduit to boxes, cabinets, conduit bodies, etc. These connectors are available in straight through, 90° elbows, 45° elbows, and offset types.

See **Figure 11-26** for a detailed illustration of the types of flexible metal conduit connectors and in the spaces provided identify each type.

**Test Tip 36:** When a six foot length of flexible metal conduit is used for grounding a fixture to a junction box, listed FMC connectors for grounding must be used.

**Figure 11-26.** Identify in the spaces provided what each item represents.

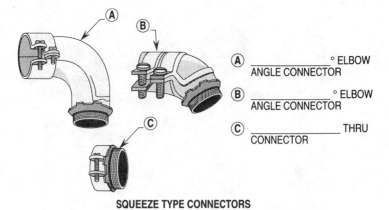

A _____° ELBOW
ANGLE CONNECTOR

B _____° ELBOW
ANGLE CONNECTOR

C _____ THRU
CONNECTOR

**SQUEEZE TYPE CONNECTORS**

**VARIOUS TYPES OF FMC CONNECTORS**

**Test Tip 37:** Angle connectors must not be concealed when used in a flexible metal conduit run between power and load.

## OFFSET CONNECTORS
## 350-20 OF THE NEC

Offset connectors are used to connect conduits to an outlet box or panel. In a conduit run, the conduit must be bent to fit or factory made offsets must be used.

**See Figure 11-27** for a detailed illustration of the types of offsets and in the spaces provided identify each type.

**Figure 11-27.** Identify in the spaces provided what each item represents.

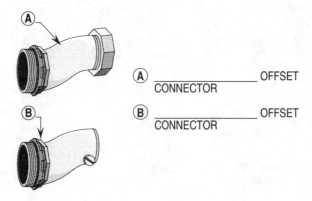

A _____ OFFSET
CONNECTOR

B _____ OFFSET
CONNECTOR

**VARIOUS TYPES OF OFFSET CONNECTORS**

## ACCESSORY FITTINGS
## 300-15(a) OF THE NEC

**Test Tip 38:** Bonding jumpers are not required to be used, if fittings connecting conduit to enclosures are listed for self grounding.

Accessory fittings are usually not purchased completely with the original fittings. For example, a grounding locknut may be needed instead of a standard locknut to prevent the use of a bonding jumper having to be installed to bond a conduit to a box, etc. However, in some applications a different type of bushing than the one that comes with the original fitting may be needed. **(See Figure 11-28)**

**Note:** There are many types of fittings and hardware which have other names, such are Ericksons, conduit pennies, nipples, bushings, locknuts, plugs, etc. The electrician must be able to recognize, identify, and use these fittings in the electrical system properly.

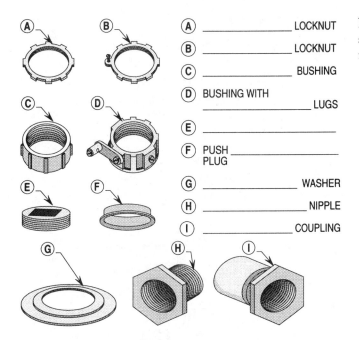

| | | |
|---|---|---|
| Ⓐ | _____ | LOCKNUT |
| Ⓑ | _____ | LOCKNUT |
| Ⓒ | _____ | BUSHING |
| Ⓓ | BUSHING WITH _____ | LUGS |
| Ⓔ | _____ | |
| Ⓕ | PUSH _____ PLUG | |
| Ⓖ | _____ | WASHER |
| Ⓗ | _____ | NIPPLE |
| Ⓘ | _____ | COUPLING |

**Figure 11-28.** Identify in the spaces provided what each item represents.

**VARIOUS TYPES OF ACCESSORY FITTINGS**

# FITTINGS FOR SUPPORTING CONDUITS
## 300-15(a) OF THE NEC

All conduit runs must be supported with fittings that will prevent them from falling. There are many types of support fittings that are available and journeyman electricians must be familiar with all the different types.

See Figure 11-29 for a detailed illustration of the different types of support fittings and in the spaces provided identify each type.

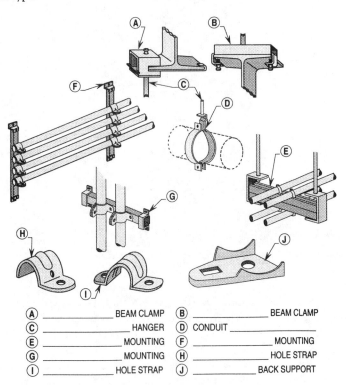

**Figure 11-29.** Identify in the spaces provided what each item represents.

| | | | |
|---|---|---|---|
| Ⓐ | _____ BEAM CLAMP | Ⓑ | _____ BEAM CLAMP |
| Ⓒ | _____ HANGER | Ⓓ | CONDUIT _____ |
| Ⓔ | _____ MOUNTING | Ⓕ | _____ MOUNTING |
| Ⓖ | _____ MOUNTING | Ⓗ | _____ HOLE STRAP |
| Ⓘ | _____ HOLE STRAP | Ⓙ | _____ BACK SUPPORT |

**VARIOUS TYPES OF SUPPORTS**

## PANELBOARDS
## ART. 384 OF THE NEC

**Test Tip 39:** OCPD's supplying continuous loads must not be loaded to more than 80 percent of their amp rating.

Panelboards are equipped with busbars and overcurrent protection devices such as circuit breakers and fuses. In general, panelboards refers only to the cabinet which contains these elements.

In a panelboard, spaces are required between the sidewalls of the panel and the terminals within the panels to which the conductors are terminated. The spaces, or gutters, are necessary for conductors terminating within the panel and also for bending space for conductors entering the panel. **(See Figure 11-30)**

**Figure 11-30.** Identify in the spaces provided what each item represents.

**Test Tip 40:** Conductors entering panelboards must be formed into an L, S, or Z-bend and then terminated to lugs and terminals.

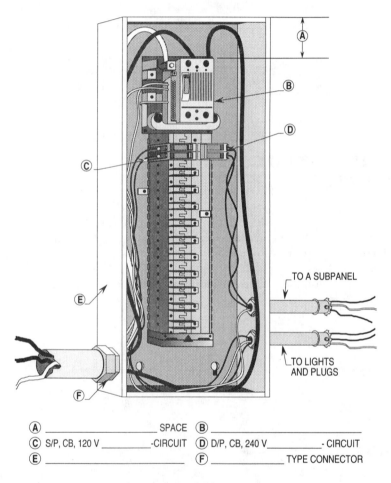

Ⓐ _____ SPACE  Ⓑ _____
Ⓒ S/P, CB, 120 V _____ -CIRCUIT  Ⓓ D/P, CB, 240 V _____ - CIRCUIT
Ⓔ _____  Ⓕ _____ TYPE CONNECTOR

**PANELBOARD WITH ELEMENTS**

## BENDS AND GUTTER SPACE
## 384-3(g) OF THE NEC

**Test Tip 41:** Conductors passing through a panelboard's gutter space must not take more than 40 percent of such fill area.

The gutter widths are measured in a straight line from the end of the lugs to the wall of the panel. Panelboards usually have a single conductor terminating to its busbars. However, some panelboards may require multiple conductors connected to a terminal or lug. When multiple connected conductors are utilized, the gutter space of the panelboard requires more room so such conductors can be terminated properly. To provide such space, the conductors entering the panelboard must be bent into a L, S, or Z-bend. **(See Figure 11-31)**

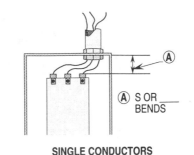

SINGLE CONDUCTORS

Ⓐ S OR ____
BENDS

**Figure 11-31.** Identify in the spaces provided what each item represents.

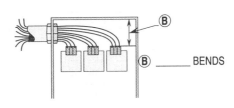

CONDUCTORS IN MULTIPLES

Ⓑ ____ BENDS

**TERMINATING CONDUCTORS**

**Test Tip 42:** Conductors supplying continuous loads must be sized by calculating the load in amps by 125 percent.

## ELEMENTS OF A PANELBOARD
## 384-16 OF THE NEC

In panelboards, there are usually two to three main busbars that run vertically. Fuses or circuit breakers plug into or they are bolted against such busbars. These overcurrent protection devices are used to protect the conductors and equipment of feeders and branch-circuits. In addition, there is a neutral bar with terminal screws. The neutral bar is grounded at zero volts potential. In some applications, there is also a grounding bar present.

**See Figure 11-32** for a detailed illustration of the elements in a panelboard and in the spaces provided identify each element.

**Test Tip 43:** If conductors are supplying noncontinuous loads and demand loads, the load in amps of these loads are taken at 100 percent.

## CONTROLLERS
## TABLE 430-72(b) OF THE NEC

Magnetic starters are the most commonly used controllers in the electrical industry and they are equipped with normally open (NO) contacts which are energized by applying voltage to the coil. Coils can range in values from 24 volts to 480 volts, and control voltage is used to energize the contacts and provide power to the motor. The devices used to control the voltage to the coil may be manually or automatically controlled. Different wiring procedures are required for each method. The windings are protected from overload conditions by an overload relay unit that is provided in the magnetic starter circuitry. **(See Figure 11-33)**

Note that control circuits operating at 1,000 VA or less and 30 V or less are called power-limited Class 1 circuits. Those operating above 30 V to 600 V are nonpower-limited circuits.

## TWO-WIRE CONTROL
## TABLE 430-72(b) OF THE NEC

Two-wire control circuits are designed and installed to eliminate a voltage release situation during a power failure. This type of installation (no voltage release) means that the coil circuit is maintained through the contacts of the pilot device until it is disconnected. The contacts of the pilot device controlling the circuit to the coil usually remains closed and

**Figure 11-32.** Identify in the spaces provided what each item represents.

**Test Tip 44:** Panelboards used for lighting and receptacles are limited to 42 OCPD plus the main.

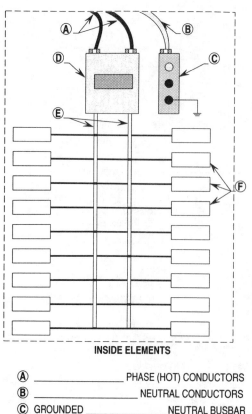

**INSIDE ELEMENTS**

Ⓐ _____ PHASE (HOT) CONDUCTORS
Ⓑ _____ NEUTRAL CONDUCTORS
Ⓒ GROUNDED _____ NEUTRAL BUSBAR
Ⓓ _____ CIRCUIT BREAKER
Ⓔ UNGROUNDED PHASE _____
Ⓕ SPACES FOR CIRCUIT- _____

**ELEMENTS OF A PANELBOARD**

**Figure 11-33.** Identify in the spaces provided what each item represents.

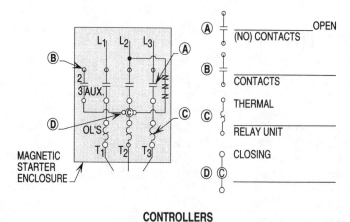

**CONTROLLERS**

**Test Tip 45:** Control circuits must be classified by use as Class 1, Class 2, or Class 3 circuits per NEC.

connects power immediately to the coil when power to the circuit is restored. Two-wire devices are designed and installed to be used for two-wire control circuits. These type of devices are single-pole switches, pressure switches, float switches, thermostats, and limit switches, etc. **(See Figure 11-34)**

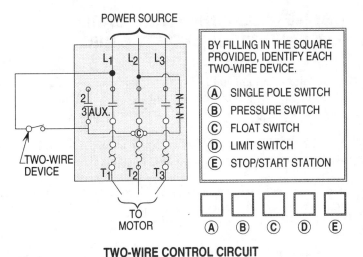

TWO-WIRE CONTROL CIRCUIT

**Figure 11-34.** Identify in the spaces provided which square represents a two-wire control device.

**Test Tip 46:** Two-wire circuits are used to prevent a voltage release condition during surges and outages.

# THREE-WIRE CONTROL
## TABLE 430-72(b) OF THE NEC

Three-wire control circuits are designed and installed to provide a voltage release during a power failure. Power is energized to the coil by pushing the starting button which is normally open (NO), causing the contacts to close and energize power to the motor.

A three-wire control circuit consists of a start button with normally open (NO) contacts and a stop button with normally closed (NC) contacts. The contacts are connected in parallel for the start button and in series for the stop button. No voltage protection means that the coil circuit is maintained through the normally closed contacts of the stop button. (See Figure 11-35)

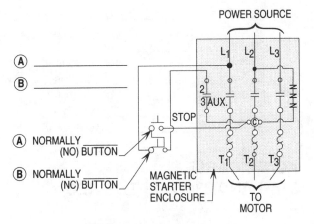

THREE-WIRE CONTROL CIRCUIT

**Figure 11-35.** Identify in the spaces provided what each item represents.

**Test Tip 47:** Control circuits designed to energize and deenergize a starter are connected in series for stopping and in parallel for starting.

# TYPES OF CABLES
## 300-4 OF THE NEC

Cable systems have a major benefit over conduit systems because conduit benders and hickeys are not required for bending and shaping the cable. Cables can be removed from the box or rolled and pulled through the framing members. In some installations, such cables can be routed on the tops of the framing members and secured with proper supports.

## NONMETALLIC SHEATHED CABLE
## 336-4 AND 336-30(b) OF THE NEC

**Test Tip 48:** NMSC must be supported within 12 in. of a box and every 4 1/2 ft. thereafter.

By definition, a nonmetallic sheathed cable is an assembly of two or more conductors having an outer sheath of moisture-resistant, flame-resistant, nonmetallic material. Such cable is commonly known in the electrical industry as **romex** or **rope**.

Nonmetallic sheathed cable must be of an approved (listed) type. This type of cable is available in sizes from No. 14 to and including No. 2.

In addition to the current-carrying conductors, NM cable may have an uninsulated conductor or a green insulated conductor for equipment grounding purposes. Table 250-122 in the NEC lists the size of this grounding conductor.

There must be a distinctive marking on the exterior of the cable for its entire length that specifies cable type and the name of the manufacturing company. The box or roll in which the cable is packaged will have the UL listing. **(See Figure 11-36)**

**Figure 11-36.** Identify in the spaces provided what each item represents.

TWO-CONDUCTOR WITH GROUND TYPE NMC CABLE

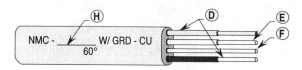

THREE-CONDUCTOR WITH GROUND TYPE NMC CABLE

**Test Tip 49:** NMSC run through framing members must be installed at least 1 1/4 in. from the face of such members.

Ⓐ ONE _____ CONDUCTOR
Ⓑ ONE _____ CONDUCTOR
Ⓒ ONE _____ CONDUCTOR
Ⓓ TWO _____ CONDUCTORS
Ⓔ ONE _____ CONDUCTOR
Ⓕ ONE _____ CONDUCTOR
Ⓖ 14/ _____ W/GROUND
Ⓗ 12/ _____ W/GROUND

## AC/MC CABLE
## 333-1 AND 334-1 OF THE NEC

**Test Tip 50:** MC cable can be installed in a place of assembly, which houses 100 people or more.

Type AC cable (BX) is a flexible metallic enclosure with circuit conductors installed at the time of manufacturing. AC cable is used in commercial buildings such as hotels, motels, offices, etc. Older electricians refer to AC cable as **BX** which is a trade name for such cable.

MC cable is factory produced and is composed of one or more conductors, each of which is individually insulated. These insulators are enclosed within a metal enclosure or interlocking tape or a smooth or corrugated tube. MC cable is mainly used in places of assembly such as theaters, clubs, conference rooms, church chapels, etc.

**See Figure 11-37** for an illustration of AC cable and identify in the spaces provided what each item represents.

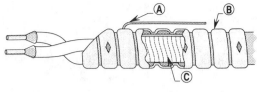

**Figure 11-37.** Identify in the spaces provided what each item represents.

**AC OR MC TYPE CABLE**

Ⓐ _____ STRIP
Ⓑ OUTER _____
Ⓒ INSIDE _____

**Test Tip 51:** AC cable is provided with an aluminum wire inside the metal-clad to prevent resistance and allow more fault-current to flow during a short-circuit condition.

# SERVICE-ENTRANCE CABLES
# 338-1 OF THE NEC

Service-entrance cables (SEC) may be a single conductor or a multiconductor assembly. It is normally equipped with an outer covering, however, it may come without the covering. Its primary use is for services and feeders.

When SE cable is used for service-entrance conductors, the requirements of Art. 230 of the NEC must be complied with.

SE cables are also permitted to be used for branch-circuits and feeders on interior wiring systems located inside of buildings where all of the circuit conductors of the cable are of rubber-covered or thermoplastic type. Where an equipment grounding conductor is required, it may be a bare or insulated conductor in the cable. **(See Figure 11-38)**

Note that under certain conditions of use, the white conductor in SEC can be used as an ungrounded phase conductor.

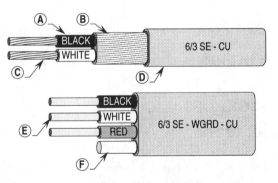

**Figure 11-38.** Identify in the spaces provided what each item represents.

**NONMETALLIC SHEATH CABLE**

Ⓐ _____ CONDUCTOR
Ⓑ BARE _____ CONDUCTOR
Ⓒ _____ CONDUCTOR
Ⓓ OUTER _____ OR SHEATH
Ⓔ _____ CONDUCTOR
Ⓕ _____ OR GREEN EGC

**Test Tip 52:** SEC cable must be terminated at a subfed panel by the provisions of Sec. 384-20 of the NEC.

Type MI cable is a high grade metal-covered cable with conductors that are embedded in a mineral type insulation (magnesium oxide) which will last for years without deterioration. MI cable also has the ability to withstand very high temperatures. The covering or sheath is sheet copper, which does not corrode and it is waterproof and gastight. The cable can be bent the same as any other type of cable and can be installed in almost any location. **(See Figure 11-39)**

**Figure 11-39.** Identify in the spaces provided what each item represents.

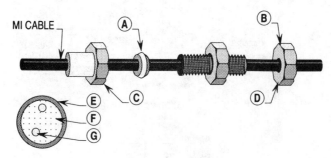

**MI CABLE AND FITTINGS**

Ⓐ COMPRESSION _____
Ⓑ SEAL W/ SEALING _____
Ⓒ COMPRESSION _____
Ⓓ NEOPRENE FITTING WITH _____
Ⓔ COPPER _____
Ⓕ MAGNESIUM _____
Ⓖ BARE _____ CONDUCTORS

**Test Tip 53:** MI cable must be supported within 6 ft. of every box and every 6 ft. thereafter.

Note that special fittings are required when using this type of cable. Extreme care must be exercised when installing these fittings for they can be very difficult to connect to such cables.

# TYPES OF CONDUITS
# 300-4 OF THE NEC

Conduit systems have the advantage over cable systems for circuits can be removed or more circuits can be added without running new conduits. Conduits of metal and PVC provide more protection for conductors and contain short-circuits and ground-faults.

## RIGID METAL CONDUIT
## 346-1 OF THE NEC

**Test Tip 54:** Applying the general rule, RMC and IMC must be supported within 3 ft. of an enclosure and every 10 ft. thereafter.

Rigid metal conduit is a very durable wiring method and it may be used in all atmospheric conditions and occupancies. Only ferrous conduit and fittings that have enamel protection from corrosion can be used indoors and even then cannot be subject to severe corrosive conditions. When practical, ferrous conduit must be used with ferrous fittings, and nonferrous conduit with fittings of similar material. This is to avoid galvanic action between the dissimilar metals where installed in the ground, etc. **(See Figure 11-40)**

## INTERMEDIATE METAL CONDUIT
## 345-1 OF THE NEC

IMC is a lightweight rigid metal conduit with integral or associated couplings, connectors, and fittings. The average weight of IMC is much lighter than that of standard rigid conduit. It is also less expensive than standard rigid metal conduit. However, it will withstand severe mechanical abuse. IMC is very similar to rigid metal conduit and has all the characteristics of use as RMC. **(See Figure 11-41)**

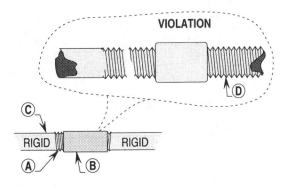

Figure 11-40. Identify in the spaces provided what each item represents.

RIGID METAL CONDUIT

Ⓐ _____ OF RMC
Ⓑ _____ FOR RMC
Ⓒ _____ COATING
Ⓓ _____ THREADS

**Test Tip 55:** Running threads on RMC or IMC is prohibited when running and connecting such conduit with regular couplings.

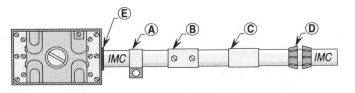

**Figure 11-41.** Identify in the spaces provided what each item represents.

INTERMEDIATE METAL CONDUIT AND FITTINGS

Ⓐ _____ HOLE STRAP
Ⓑ TYPE _____ COUPLING
Ⓒ _____ COUPLING
Ⓓ _____ COUPLING
Ⓔ _____ HUB

# ELECTRICAL METALLIC TUBING
## 348-1 OF THE NEC

EMT may be used for exposed work and concealed work. If during or after installation, EMT is subject to severe physical damage, it shall not be used. Care must be exercised and special precaution taken to keep it from contacting dissimilar metals, to eliminate the possibility of electrolysis. Note that there is a great difference among soils in their reaction to EMT and metal conduits. EMT cannot be used to support lighting fixtures or other equipment due to its light weight. **(See Figure 11-42)**

**Test Tip 56:** Where structural members do not allow EMT to be supported within 3 ft., a 5 ft. supporting means is permitted.

# RIGID NONMETALLIC CONDUIT
## 347-1 OF THE NEC

Rigid nonmetallic conduit (PVC) is a system of nonmetallic conduit having fittings that are resistant to moisture and chemicals. For above ground use, it must be sunlight resistant, crush resistant, heat resistant, and flame retardant. Certain types of rigid nonmetallic conduit are listed to be installed underground in continuous lengths from a reel.

**Test Tip 57:** Applying the general rule, RNMC must be supported within 3 ft. of enclosures and every 3 ft. thereafter.

**Figure 11-42.** Identify in the spaces provided what each item represents.

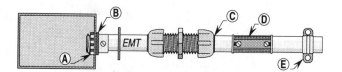

**ELECTRICAL METALLIC TUBING AND FITTINGS**

Ⓐ _____ FOR CONNECTOR
Ⓑ TYPE _____ CONNECTOR
Ⓒ _____ COUPLING
Ⓓ _____ COUPLING
Ⓔ _____ HOLE STRAP

Nonmetallic conduit is made from nonmetallic materials, such as fiber, soapstone, polyvinyl chloride, or polyethylene. The conduit is waterproof, rotproof, and rustproof, but does not have the strength of rigid metal conduit. Rigid nonmetallic conduit is also known and merchandised as PVC (plastic conduit.) **(See Figure 11-43)**

**Figure 11-43.** Identify in the spaces provided what each item represents.

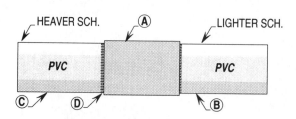

**NONMETALLIC CONDUIT AND FITTINGS**

Ⓐ PVC _____
Ⓑ SCH _____
Ⓒ SCH _____
Ⓓ JOINTED BY _____

# OVERCURRENT PROTECTION DEVICES
# ART. 240 OF THE NEC

**Test Tip 58:** OCPD's must protect conductors and equipment or a second stage of protection must be provided.

All electrical systems require protection devices and the two most common types are fuses and circuit breakers. The function of these devices is to protect electrical conductors and equipment by interrupting the current flow when the current becomes excessively high because of a short-circuit, ground-fault, or an overload.

## FUSES
## 240-60 OF THE NEC

Fuses are protective devices which are designed to be the weakest part, or link, in an electric circuit. The fuse element is a short length of metal wire or ribbon made from an alloy with a low melting point. The element is sized so that it will carry the rated current for indefinite lengths of time. However, its link will melt when excessive current flows through it. Excessive current in a circuit is caused by short-circuits (phase-to-phase), ground-faults (phase-to-ground), or overloads (slow heat build up).

Note that some fuses have renewable elements but most fuses cannot be reused.

## PLUG AND S FUSES
## 240-51 AND 240-53 OF THE NEC

One common type of **plug fuse** known in the electrical industry is an Edison base fuse type. The element is enclosed in a housing to prevent the molten metal alloy from escaping when the fuse blows. A window is provided to determine whether the fuse has blown. The fuse can be replaced by unscrewing the blown fuse and screwing in a new one. Plug fuses are available in sizes 15, 20, 25, and 30 amp respectively. **(See Figure 11-44)**

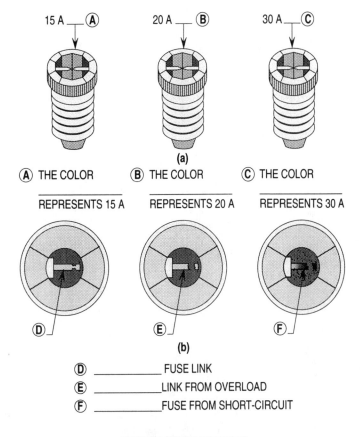

**Figure 11-44.** Identify in the spaces provided what each item represents.

Ⓐ THE COLOR _____ REPRESENTS 15 A

Ⓑ THE COLOR _____ REPRESENTS 20 A

Ⓒ THE COLOR _____ REPRESENTS 30 A

**Test Tip 59:** Fuses, if not marked, have an IC rating of 10,000 amps.

Ⓓ _____ FUSE LINK
Ⓔ _____ LINK FROM OVERLOAD
Ⓕ _____ FUSE FROM SHORT-CIRCUIT

**EDISON-BASE PLUG FUSES**

**Test Tip 60:** Edison based fuses must be used in an electrical system as replacements only.

**Type S fuses** are dual-element fuses which must be used with adapters approved for such use. Each size of fuse has an adapter which cannot be removed from the fuseholder after it is installed. It is therefore not possible to replace a fuse with one of a higher rating. However, all sizes of the standard plug fuses are interchangeable if changed by the rules of the NEC pertaining to the protection of wiring and equipment. **(See Figures 11-45)**

## CARTRIDGE FUSES
## 240-60 OF THE NEC

When fuses are used in wiring systems, both plug types and cartridge fuses are permitted to be used. Plug fuses are commonly used to protect branch-circuits, and cartridge fuses are often limited to the main fuses for feeders or service overcurrent devices. Cartridge fuses are normally used when the current flow in amps exceeds 30. **(See Figure 11-46)**

**Figure 11-45.** Identify in the spaces provided what each item represents.

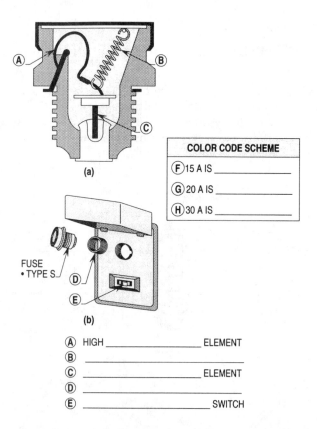

**Test Tip 61:** Type S fuses are dual-element fuses and they must be used with adapters.

Note that T-rated fuses have the same color code scheme for ratings of 15, 20, or 30 amps.

| COLOR CODE SCHEME | |
|---|---|
| Ⓕ 15 A IS | _____ |
| Ⓖ 20 A IS | _____ |
| Ⓗ 30 A IS | _____ |

Ⓐ HIGH _____ ELEMENT
Ⓑ _____
Ⓒ _____ ELEMENT
Ⓓ _____
Ⓔ _____ SWITCH

**DUAL ELEMENT FUSE TYPE S**

**Figure 11-46.** Identify in the spaces provided what each item represents.

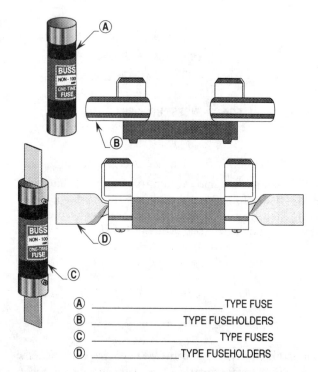

**Test Tip 62:** Cartridge fuses are usually used in electrical circuits having a current flow greater than 30 amps.

Ⓐ _____ TYPE FUSE
Ⓑ _____ TYPE FUSEHOLDERS
Ⓒ _____ TYPE FUSES
Ⓓ _____ TYPE FUSEHOLDERS

**CARTRIDGE TYPE FUSES**

**Note:** Cartridge fuses are available in ferrule or blade types to accomodate circuits.

## SUPPLEMENTARY FUSES
## 240-10 OF THE NEC

There are basically three types of supplementary fuses and they are as follows:

**(1)** Micro fuses
**(2)** Miniature fuses
**(3)** Miscellaneous fuses

**Test Tip 63:** Supplementary fuses do not have to be readily accessible.

Such fuses are used in individual pieces of electrical and electronic equipment and for protection of individual circuits or components.

**Note:** The miscellaneous type of supplementary fuses has a minimum diameter of 13/32 in. and a minimum length of 1 1/2 in. Such fuses are available in voltage ratings up to 600 volts and are designed so that they must be installed in specific type fuseholders. **(See Figure 11-47)**

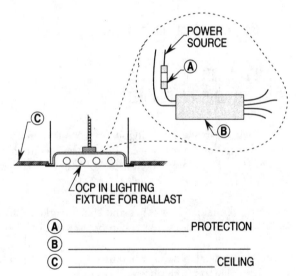

**Figure 11-47.** Identify in the spaces provided what each item represents.

POWER SOURCE

Ⓐ

Ⓑ

Ⓒ

⌐OCP IN LIGHTING FIXTURE FOR BALLAST

Ⓐ _____ PROTECTION
Ⓑ _____
Ⓒ _____ CEILING

**SUPPLEMENTARY PROTECTION**

**Test Tip 64:** Supplementary fuses have to be accessible by a ladder or other portable means, etc.

## CIRCUIT BREAKERS
## 240-83 OF THE NEC

Circuit breakers can be used for protecting conductors from excessive current flow. Circuit breakers are available in single-pole, double-pole, and three-pole configurations. Single-pole circuit breakers supply circuits with one hot conductor and neutral while double-pole and three-pole circuit breakers serve loads with or without neutral connections.

**Test Tip 65:** Circuit breakers that are not marked with an IC rating are 5000 amps respectively.

A circuit breaker is equipped with four positions, **two** of which are labeled ON and OFF. The **third** is when an overload or short-circuit occurs and the circuit breaker handle moves to the tripped position.

The circuit breaker is closed by pushing the handle past the OFF position to the RESET position, and then to the ON position. This is the **fourth** position if the overload or short-circuit has been removed, the circuit breaker will energize the power to the circuit conductors and remain closed. **(See Figure 11-48)**

**Figure 11-48.** Identify in the spaces provided what each item represents.

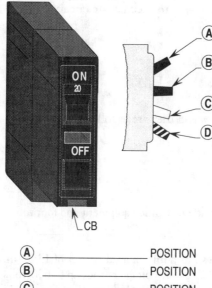

**Test Tip 66:** CB's used on an ungrounded system must be marked with a straight voltage marking.

**Test Tip 67:** CB's used on a grounded system are usually slash marked with a voltage to ground and a phase to phase voltage rating.

Ⓐ _____ POSITION
Ⓑ _____ POSITION
Ⓒ _____ POSITION
Ⓓ _____ POSITION

**PRINCIPLES OF OPERATION**

# SWITCHES
# 380-14 OF THE NEC

Some switches make a clicking sound when turned ON and OFF while others are silent. Note that all switches are rated according to the specific amperage and voltage to which they are designed for. Switches marked CO-ALR can be used with either copper or aluminum conductors.

**Warning:** Unmarked switches and those marked CU may be used with copper conductors only. Those marked CU-ALU can be used with CU or ALU.

Switches are available that when used in combination hook-ups can switch receptacle outlets or lighting outlets from different locations.

# SINGLE-POLE SWITCHES
# 200-7 OF THE NEC

**Test Tip 68:** Single-pole (T-rated) switches supplying motors must not be loaded to more than 125 percent of the FLC rating.

Single-pole switches are identified by two terminals with the words ON and OFF printed on the toggle. A single-pole switch can be used to control a light or receptacle from one location only. **(See Figure 11-49)**

# THREE-WAY SWITCHES
# 200-7 OF THE NEC

Three-way switches are identified by three terminals with a plain toggle and three-way switches operate in pairs, to control a light or receptacle from two different locations. **(See Figure 11-50)**

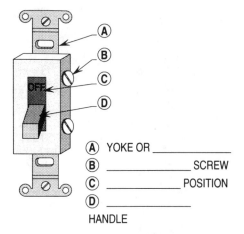

**Figure 11-49.** Identify in the spaces provided what each item represents.

Ⓐ YOKE OR _____
Ⓑ _____ SCREW
Ⓒ _____ POSITION
Ⓓ _____
HANDLE

**SINGLE-POLE SWITCHES**

Note that when A/C or NMSC cables are used, the white conductor in such cable can be used as a hot conductor from the fixture to the switch.

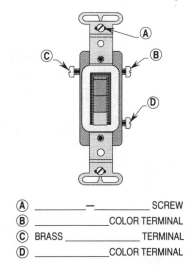

**Figure 11-50.** Identify in the spaces provided what each item represents.

Ⓐ _____ — _____ SCREW
Ⓑ _____ COLOR TERMINAL
Ⓒ BRASS _____ TERMINAL
Ⓓ _____ COLOR TERMINAL

**THREE-WAY SWITCHES**

Note that Ⓑ and Ⓓ terminals are travelers.

# FOUR-WAY SWITCHES
## 200-7 OF THE NEC

Four-way switches are identified by four terminals and no ON or OFF indicators on the toggle handle. A four-way switch is used only in combination with a pair of three-way switches to control a lighting outlet or receptacle outlet from more than two locations. Note that by adding additional four-way switches a lighting outlet, or a number of outlets, can be turned ON and OFF at a number of different locations. (See Figure 11-51)

**Test Tip 69:** Three four-way switches with two three-way switches can switch a light from five different locations.

# FLEXIBLE CORDS AND FITTINGS
## ART. 400 OF THE NEC

Flexible cords are available in different sizes and ratings. They are available with multiple conductors to accommodate the various load requirements of equipment, etc.

**See Figure 11-52** for a detailed illustration of flexible cords and fittings.

**Figure 11-51.** Identify in the spaces provided what each item represents.

**Test Tip 70:** Brass terminals are used to terminate the hot ungrounded conductors while the silver are used to connect the neutral.

**Figure 11-52.** Identify in the spaces provided what each item represents.

**Test Tip 71:** Under certain conditions of use, No. 14 and larger conductors can be spliced when a flexible cord is damaged.

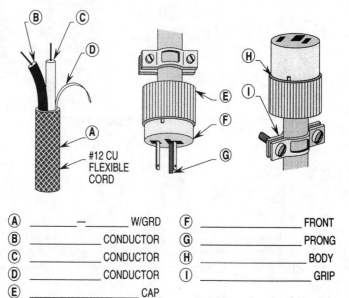

SWITCHING PROCEDURE

POSITION 1 SHOWS TOGGLE HANDLE DOWN (OFF)

POSITION 2 SHOWS TOGGLE HANDLE UP (ON)

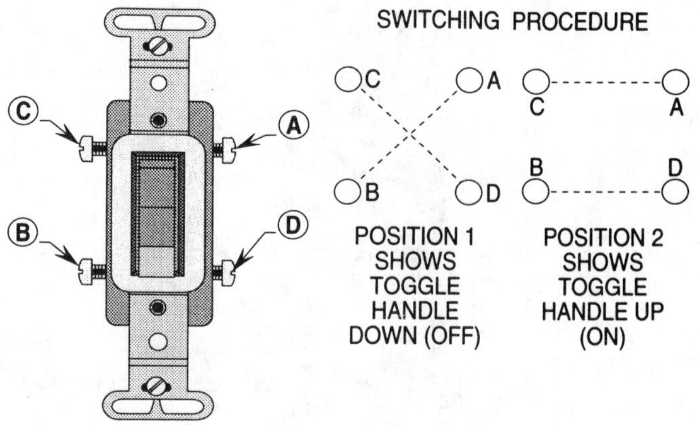

(A) FIRST _____ OF SWITCHING SET IN POSITION ONE

(B) _____ TERMINAL OF SWITCHING SET IN POSITION ONE

(C) MAKING TERMINAL OF SWITCHING SET ((C) TO (D)) IN POSITION _____

(D) MAKING ((D) TO (C)) TERMINAL OF SWITCHING SET IN POSITION _____

**FOUR-WAY SWITCHES**

#12 CU FLEXIBLE CORD

(A) _____ – _____ W/GRD
(B) _____ CONDUCTOR
(C) _____ CONDUCTOR
(D) _____ CONDUCTOR
(E) _____ CAP

(F) _____ FRONT
(G) _____ PRONG
(H) _____ BODY
(I) _____ GRIP

**FLEXIBLE CORDS AND FITTINGS**

# RECEPTACLE AND CAPS
# ARTICLES 210 AND 400 OF THE NEC

Cap fittings are used with flexible cords to cord-and-plug connect various types of electrical apparatus. When connected, attachment caps and bodies must mate.

## SINGLE RECEPTACLES AND CAPS
## TABLE 210-24 OF THE NEC

Single outlets and caps are used only for lamps and other small related appliances. In most receptacles, one slot is longer than the other. When the receptacle is correctly wired, the shorter slot is hot and the longer slot is the neutral. To comply with the NEC, connect the black phase wire to the terminal with the short slot (brass) and the white or gray wire to the long slot (silver). **(See Figure 11-53)**

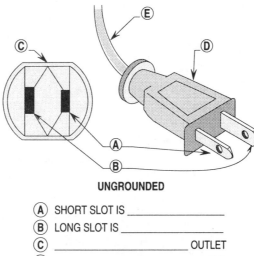

**UNGROUNDED**

Ⓐ SHORT SLOT IS _____

Ⓑ LONG SLOT IS _____

Ⓒ _____ OUTLET

Ⓓ _____ CAP

Ⓔ 14-_____ W/GRD
FLEXIBLE CORD

**UNGROUNDED SINGLE RECEPTACLE
OUTLET AND ACCESSORIES**

**Figure 11-53.** Identify in the spaces provided what each item represents.

**Test Tip 72:** When a 30 amp single-piece of equipment is cord-and-plug connected, a 30 amp individual receptacle and circuit must be installed.

**Test Tip 73:** A general purpose circuit can have 15 or 20 amp duplex receptacles connected to it if it is rated 20 amps.

## DUPLEX RECEPTACLES AND CAPS
## TABLE 210-24 OF THE NEC

Grounded duplex receptacles have an inverted U-shaped grounding slot with a matching grounding prong on the receptacle which is used to connect equipment grounding conductors for grounding and bonding electrical equipment for safety. Duplex receptacles must be used only when there are two or more outlets on such branch-circuits. **(See Figure 11-54)**

## THIRTY AMP RECEPTACLES
## TABLE 210-24 OF THE NEC

Thirty amp receptacles (L grounded) are designed especially for clothes dryers, this receptacle supplies 240 volts for the heating coils of the dryer and 120 volts for such standard accessories as the timer and the pilot light, etc. The grounding is accomplished by using the grounded conductor of the circuit wiring for neutral and grounding currents. **(See Figure 11-55)**

**Note:** Four-wire 30 amp receptacles are also available. These receptacles are equipped with two hot slots, one neutral slot, and one equipment grounding slot. Such receptacles are designed to prevent the grounded neutral conductor form being used as a neutral plus and equipment grounding conductor.

**Figure 11-54.** Identify in the spaces provided what each item represents.

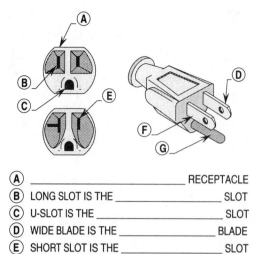

Ⓐ _____ RECEPTACLE
Ⓑ LONG SLOT IS THE _____ SLOT
Ⓒ U-SLOT IS THE _____ SLOT
Ⓓ WIDE BLADE IS THE _____ BLADE
Ⓔ SHORT SLOT IS THE _____ SLOT
Ⓕ LESS WIDE BLADE IS THE _____ BLADE
Ⓖ THE U BLADE IS THE _____ BLADE

**GROUNDING TYPE RECEPTACLE**

**Figure 11-55.** Identify in the spaces provided what each item represents.

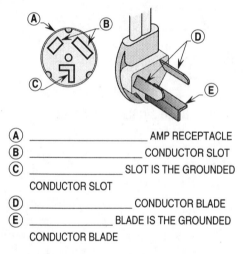

**Test Tip 74:** When running a new branch-circuit to a dryer, range, cooktop, or oven, a four wire circuit must be routed with an individual neutral conductor and EGC.

Ⓐ _____ AMP RECEPTACLE
Ⓑ _____ CONDUCTOR SLOT
Ⓒ _____ SLOT IS THE GROUNDED
CONDUCTOR SLOT
Ⓓ _____ CONDUCTOR BLADE
Ⓔ _____ BLADE IS THE GROUNDED
CONDUCTOR BLADE

**THIRTY AMP L GROUNDED RECEPTACLE**

## THIRTY AMP RECEPTACLES
## TABLE 210-24 OF THE NEC

Thirty amp receptacles of the U grounded type are designed to supply only 240 volt equipment. Such electrical equipment as hot water heaters and air-conditioners. The ground is usually furnished by using the circuits grounded conductor or an additional grounding conductor is provided if a neutral is needed.

See **Figure 11-56** and Note to thirty amp (L grounded) receptacles on page 11-39.

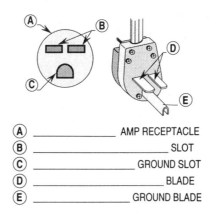

**Figure 11-56.** Identify in the spaces provided what each item represents.

(A) _____ AMP RECEPTACLE
(B) _____ SLOT
(C) _____ GROUND SLOT
(D) _____ BLADE
(E) _____ GROUND BLADE

**THIRTY AMP U GROUNDED RECEPTACLE**

**Test Tip 75:** The grounded conductor can only be used as a neutral plus an EGC in old installations, but never used as such in the wiring of a new branch-circuit.

## FIFTY AMP RECEPTACLES
## TABLE 210-24 OF THE NEC

Fifty amp receptacles are designed to provide an electric range with the required high amperage and voltage combinations necessary to operate cooktop burners, the oven coils, and other accessories. In an old installation, a grounded conductor is also used with the receptacle and plug cap for grounding and carrying any neutral related loads. **(See Figure 11-57)**

**Note:** Four-wire 50 amp receptacles are also available for the cord-and-plug connection of electrical equipment. See Note for 30 amp (L grounded) receptacles on page 11-39.

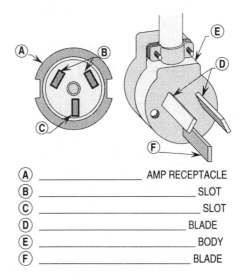

**Figure 11-57.** Identify in the spaces provided what each item represents.

(A) _____ AMP RECEPTACLE
(B) _____ SLOT
(C) _____ SLOT
(D) _____ BLADE
(E) _____ BODY
(F) _____ BLADE

**FIFTY AMP GROUNDED RECEPTACLE**

**Test Tip 76:** Blades of an attachment (connector) cap must never be bent by force in any way to match and mate to a receptacle outlet.

## TERMINALS, LUGS, AND CONNECTORS
## ART. 110 OF THE NEC

All component parts of electrical systems are connected together by conductors or wires. Insulated wires provide the connecting means between loads and such devices as lighting fixtures, lampholders, receptacles, appliances, circuit breakers and fuseholders, switches, motors, transformers, and all other electrical equipment. However, larger pieces of equipment, such as switches, receptacles, and starters is usually equipped with lugs for connecting the conductors.

## TERMINALS
## 110-14(a) AND (c) OF THE NEC

The terminals and leads on receptacles, lampholders, lighting fixtures, and other devices and loads are color coded to serve as an aid to wire them correctly. To maintain polarity, the common colors for EGC terminals are green and for grounded neutral conductors they are white or silver. For the hot ungrounded phase conductors they are a natural brass color.

See Figure 11-58 for the various types of terminals and identify each type.

**Figure 11-58.** Identify in the spaces provided, each type of terminal device.

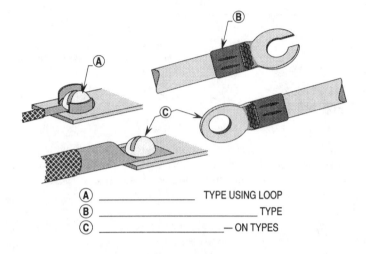

A _____ TYPE USING LOOP
B _____ TYPE
C _____— ON TYPES

**VARIOUS TYPES OF TERMINATING DEVICES**

## TERMINATING CONDUCTORS
## 110-14(a) AND (c) OF THE NEC

**Test Tip 77:** Unless the terminals are marked for such use, only one conductor per terminal or lug is permitted.

To insert the end of the conductor under the screwhead, strip the conductor and form a loop. The next step is to place the loop under the screwhead and close the loop completely by using longnose pliers. It is important that the loop be in the same direction as the screw when it is tightened. This will tighten the loop as the screw as tightened. The loop will tend to unroll and loosen if tightening the screw results in a force opposing the loop formation. Note that excessive conductor length must be cut off and never to be lapped over the lopped conductor.

See Figure 11-59 for a detailed illustration of how to terminate a conductor using a loop and identify in the spaces provide the correct and incorrect methods.

## LUGS
## 110-14(a) AND (c) OF THE NEC

**Test Tip 78:** The terminal is marked for CU-ALU, only copper can be connected to such terminals.

Lugs are used for connecting solid conductors, or wires, and stranded wires larger than No. 10. Note that lugs in the electrical industry are usually called solderless terminals, connectors, etc.

The NEC prohibits the use of soldered connections on conductors used in service-entrance equipment including grounding conductors. Heavy-duty solderless lugs or pressure connectors must be used in such installations.

See Figure 11-60 for a illustration of a solderless lug or pressure connector and identify each type in the spaces provided.

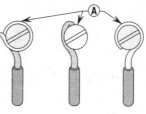

**OVERLAP METHOD**

**Figure 11-59.** Identify in the spaces provided which are correct and incorrect methods by inserting the word right or wrong.

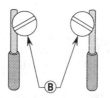

**STRAIGHT IN METHOD**

**Test Tip 79:** Terminals 100 amps or less are 60°C rated unless marked 60/75°C.

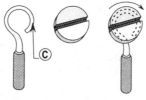

**LOOP METHOD**

Note that the straight-in method of terminating conductors is not permitted unless listed for such use.

Ⓐ OVERLAP _____ METHOD
Ⓑ STRAIGHT IN _____ METHOD
Ⓒ THREE QUARTERS _____ METHOD

**METHODS OF TERMINATING DEVICES**

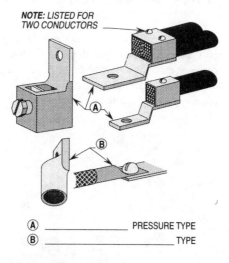

*NOTE: LISTED FOR TWO CONDUCTORS*

**Figure 11-60.** Identify in the spaces provided what each type of lug represents.

Ⓐ _____ PRESSURE TYPE
Ⓑ _____ TYPE

**SOLDER AND SOLDERLESS TYPE LUGS**

**Test Tip 80:** Lugs over 100 amps are rated 75°C and the ampacities of 90°C THHN copper conductors must be selected at the 75°C rating per Table 310-16 of the NEC.

## SOLDERLESS MECHANICAL CONNECTORS
## 110-14 OF THE NEC

Conductors and wires are joined together (spliced) with solderless mechanical connectors. Such connectors are of two basic types and they are as follows:

(1) Wirenuts
(2) Compression rings

Generally, these types come in four sizes to accommodate various wire combinations. Manufacturers have their own color code to distinguish each particular size. Once the number of conductors to be spliced is known, the proper connector must be selected.

**See Figure 11-61** for the correct procedure when splicing conductors together using a wire connector and identify in the space provided the type of connector utilized.

**Figure 11-61.** Identify in the spaces provided what type of connector is used to splice the conductors.

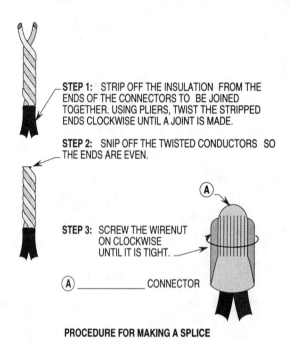

STEP 1: STRIP OFF THE INSULATION FROM THE ENDS OF THE CONNECTORS TO BE JOINED TOGETHER. USING PLIERS, TWIST THE STRIPPED ENDS CLOCKWISE UNTIL A JOINT IS MADE.

STEP 2: SNIP OFF THE TWISTED CONDUCTORS SO THE ENDS ARE EVEN.

STEP 3: SCREW THE WIRENUT ON CLOCKWISE UNTIL IT IS TIGHT.

(A) _____ CONNECTOR

**PROCEDURE FOR MAKING A SPLICE**

**Test Tip 81:** Most splicing connectors allow the conductors to be stripped a certain length and then laid side by side and the connector screwed on.

# INLINE SPLICING
# 110-14 OF THE NEC

For various reasons, sometimes splices, or joints, in the conductors are necessary. Such splices must be mechanically and electrically as good as a continuous length of wire. To make a splice, the insulation must be removed where the splice is to be made. Then an electrical and mechanical connection must be made by using either solder or a solderless connector. The splice is complete when the removed insulation has been properly replaced. **(See Figure 11-62)**

**Figure 11-62.** Identify the connector types in the spaces provided.

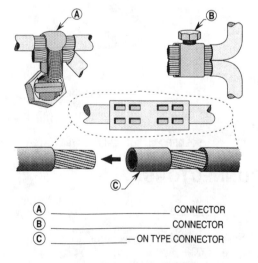

**Test Tip 82:** When using a kerney, only two spliced conductors are allowed, unless the connector is listed for more than two.

(A) _____ CONNECTOR
(B) _____ CONNECTOR
(C) _____ — ON TYPE CONNECTOR

**VARIOUS TYPES OF CONNECTORS**

# HELPFUL TABLES AND CHARTS

**See Figure 11-63** for tables and charts which list the sizes of panelboards, switchboards, disconnects, OCPD's, wireways, gutters, junction boxes, and busducts. These tables and charts can be used when selecting the various items to be installed in working problems in this book.

Note that other manufacturer's Tables and charts may have different sizes of panelboards, transformers, disconnects, etc. available.

**For example:** What size disconnect is needed to house three 70 amp fuses and three 150 amp fuses respectively. These fuses are designed for branch-circuits to motor loads.

**Step 1:** Finding disconnect for 70 amp fuses
430-57; Figure 11-63
70 A fuses require 100 A disconnect

**Step 2:** Finding disconnect for 150 amp fuses
430-57; Figure 11-63
150 A fuses requires 200 A disconnect

**Solution:** The size disconnect for the 70 amp fuses is 100 amp and for the 150 amp fuses is 200 amp.

| PANELBOARDS | | | | |
|---|---|---|---|---|
| **SINGLE/PHASE - 3-WIRE SYSTEMS** | | | | |
| 40 A | 100 A | 150 A | 225 A | 400 A |
| 70 A | 125 A | 200 A | 300 A | 600 A |
| **THREE/PHASE - 4-WIRE SYSTEMS** | | | | |
| 60 A | 150 A | 225 A | 400 A | |
| 120 A | 200 A | 300 A | 600 A | |

| GUTTERS AND WIREWAYS | | |
|---|---|---|
| 2 1/2" x 2 1/2" | 6" x 6" | 10" x 10" |
| 4" x 4" | 8" x 8" | |

*These sizes are available in 12", 24", 36", 48", and 60" lengths*

| DISCONNECTS | | | |
|---|---|---|---|
| 30 A | 200 A | 800 A | 1,600 A |
| 60 A | 400 A | 1,200 A | 1,800 A |
| 100 A | 600 A | 1,400 A | |

| BUSWAY OR BUSDUCT | |
|---|---|
| **1Ø** | **3Ø** |
| 225 A | 225 A |
| 400 A | 400 A |
| 600 A | 600 A |
| 800 A | 800 A |
| 1,000 A | 1,000 A |
| 1,200 A | 1,200 A |
| 1,350 A | 1,350 A |
| 1,600 A | 1,600 A |
| 2,000 A | 2,000 A |
| 2,500 A | 2,500 A |
| 3,000 A | 3,000 A |
| 4,000 A | 4,000 A |
| 5,000 A | 5,000 A |

| PULLBOXES AND JUNCTION BOXES | | |
|---|---|---|
| 4" x 4" x 4" | 10" x 8" x 4" | 12" x 12" x 6" |
| 6" x 4" x 4" | 10" x 8" x 6" | 12" x 12" x 8" |
| 6" x 6" x 4" | 10" x 10" x 4" | 15" x 12" x 4" |
| 6" x 6" x 6" | 10" x 10" x 6" | 15" x 12" x 6" |
| 8" x 6" x 4" | 10" x 10" x 8" | 18" x 12" x 4" |
| 8" x 6" x 6" | 12" x 8" x 4" | 18" x 12" x 6" |
| 8" x 6" x 8" | 12" x 8" x 6" | 18" x 18" x 4" |
| 8" x 8" x 4" | 12" x 10" x 4" | 18" x 18" x 6" |
| 8" x 8" x 6" | 12" x 10" x 6" | 24" x 18" x 6" |
| 8" x 8" x 8" | 12" x 12" x 4" | 24" x 24" x 6" |
| | | 24" x 24" x 8" |

| CB'S AND FUSES | | | |
|---|---|---|---|
| 15 | 70 | 225 | 800 |
| 20 | 80 | 250 | 1,000 |
| 25 | 90 | 300 | 1,200 |
| 30 | 100 | 350 | 1,600 |
| 35 | 110 | 400 | 2,000 |
| 40 | 125 | 450 | 2,500 |
| 45 | 150 | 500 | 3,000 |
| 50 | 175 | 600 | 4,000 |
| 60 | 200 | 700 | 5,000 |
| | | | 6,000 |

*For fuses only, additional standard sizes are 1,3,6, and 10.*

| SWITCHBOARDS OR SWITCHGEARS | |
|---|---|
| **1Ø** | **3Ø** |
| 200 A | 400 A |
| 400 A | 600 A |
| 600 A | 800 A |
| 800 A | 1,200 A |
| 1,200 A | 1,600 A |
| 1,600 A | 2,000 A |
| 2,000 A | 2,500 A |
| 2,500 A | 3,000 A |
| 3,000 A | 4,000 A |
| 4,000 A | |

**Figure 11-63.** Various Tables and charts that can be utilized to select items needed when designing and installing wiring methods, boxes, panelboards, OCPD's, etc.

Note that pull boxes and junction boxes that are larger than 24" x 24" x 8" must be selected from a manufacturer's catalog or be specially built.

# Chapter 11
## Diagrams and Elements

| Section | Answer | |
|---|---|---|
| _____ | T  F | 1. The service-entrance conductors are the conductors between the last pole and the service disconnect. |
| _____ | T  F | 2. Feeders are all conductors between the service equipment and the final branch-circuit overcurrent protection device. |
| _____ | T  F | 3. Branch-circuits are the circuit conductors between the final overcurrent protection device protecting the circuit, and the outlet(s) served. |
| _____ | T  F | 4. Lighting fixtures mounted to ceiling boxes are limited to 60 lbs. or less. |
| _____ | T  F | 5. Unused openings in boxes must be closed with the proper fittings. |
| _____ | T  F | 6. Boxes without brackets can be mounted to framing members with nails, if these nails are located within 1/2 in. at the back of such boxes. |
| _____ | T  F | 7. Wooden braces used to support boxes must have a cross-section not less than 1 in. x 2 in. respectively. |
| _____ | T  F | 8. Cable clamps count as two when determining the fill area of boxes. |
| _____ | T  F | 9. When a 6 ft. length of flexible metal conduit is used for grounding a fixture to a junction box, listed FMC connectors for grounding must be used. |
| _____ | T  F | 10. Overcurrent protection devices supplying continuous loads must not be loaded to more than 100 percent of their amp rating. |

11. The service _____ is the overhead conductors between the last pole and the service-entrance.

12. Feeder-circuit conductors must be at least No. 10 copper and rated at _____ amps.

13. Branch-circuit conductors must be at least No. _____ copper.

14. When direct metal-to-metal contact between a device yoke and surface mounted handy box is made, the devices U ground is considered grounded by the # _____ screws of the devices yoke (strap).

15. Ceiling fans mounted to listed ceiling boxes must weigh _____ lbs. or less.

16. Studs and hickeys count as _____ each based upon the largest conductor entering the box.

17. Boxes installed in walls having noncombustible material must not be set back more than _____ in. from the finished surface.

18. Conductors passing through a panelboard or gutter space must not take more than _____ percent of such fill area.

_____ _____

_____

_____ _____

19. Three-wire control circuits designed to energize and deenergize a starter are connected in _____ for stopping and in _____ for starting.

20. MC cable can be installed in a place of assembly, which houses _____ people or more.

21. Nonmetallic sheathed cable run through framing members must be installed at least _____ in. from the face of such members.

A. 1 1/8          C. 1 1/2
B. 1 1/4          D. 1 3/4

22. MI cable must be supported within _____ ft. of every box.

A. 3          C. 6
B. 5          D. 10

23. Rigid metal conduit must be supported every _____ ft. (General rule)

A. 5          C. 15
B. 10         D. 20

24. Intermediate metal conduit must be supported within _____ ft. of an enclosure.

A. 3          C. 6
B. 5.         D. 10

25. Fuses, if not marked, have an IC rating of _____ amps.

A. 5,000          C. 15,000
B. 10,000         D. 20,000

26. Circuit breakers, if not marked, have an IC rating of _____ amps.

A. 5,000          C. 15,000
B. 10,000         D. 20,000

27. Single-pole switches supplying motors must not be loaded more than _____ percent of the motor's FLC rating.

A. 80          C. 115
B. 100         D. 125

28. Unless the terminals are marked for such use, only _____ conductor(s) per terminal or lug is permitted.

A. 1          C. 3
B. 2          D. 4

29. Terminals _____ amps or less are rated 60°C. (General rule)

A. 50          C. 150
B. 100         D. 175

30. Terminals over _____ amps are rated 75°C.

A. 50          C. 100
B. 80          D. 150

# Questions and Problems

12

This chapter is designed as a guide in preparation for the Journeyman's license examination. These examinations are given periodically by a local licensing authority, such as state, county, municipal, or other agencies having legal jurisdiction over licensing electricians.

Numerous examples, in the form of questions and problems, are presented throughout this chapter. Thereby, enabling the test taker to gain a complete knowledge of the types of questions and problems asked on a Journeyman's examination. The importance of careful study is essential in order to master the fundamental principles of each question and problem for those preparing to take such a test. Only through such a process can an applicant prepare himself or herself to solve questions and problems appearing on the examination.

The questions and problems in this chapter must be answered by using the material in this book and the National Electrical Code.

## Quick Reference:

Article 90 ................................................................ 12-3

Articles 100-110 ..................................................... 12-3

Articles 200-250 ..................................................... 12-6

Articles 300-338 ..................................................... 12-30

Articles 345-384 ..................................................... 12-41

Articles 400-450 ..................................................... 12-51

Articles 500-550 ..................................................... 12-64

Articles 600-680 ..................................................... 12-71

Articles 700-760 ..................................................... 12-77

Article 800 ............................................................. 12-79

# Chapter 12
## Questions and Problems

### Article 90
### Introduction

_____  _____  1. The NEC covers all of the following electrical installations, except:

      A. Recreational vehicles         B. Floating buildings
      C. Carnivals                   D. Public utilities

_____  _____  2. Which of the following statements about the authority having jurisdiction of enforcement of the NEC is not true.

      A. Uses the authority given for making interpretations of the NEC rules, etc.
      B. Uses the authority given for deciding the approval of equipment and materials
      C. Uses the authority given to grant special permission
      D. Does not have the authority to waive specific requirements in the NEC

_____  _____  3. Chapters 1 through 4 of the NEC applies to _____.

      A. Generally                B. Special occupancies
      C. Special conditions        D. Communication systems

_____  _____  4. Chapter 8 of the NEC applies to _____.

      A. Generally                B. Special occupancies
      C. Special conditions        D. Communication systems

_____  _____  5. The _____ wiring of equipment is not required to be reinspected at the time of installation if the equipment is listed by a qualified testing laboratory.

      A. Associated             B. Internal
      C. External              D. None of the above

### Article 100
### Definitions

_____  _____  6. Accessible is defined as admitting close approach, not guarded by locked doors, elevation, or other effective means.

      A. True                  B. False

_____  _____  7. A bathroom can be defined as an area, including a basin with a toilet, a tub, or a shower.

      A. True                  B. False

_____  _____  8. A bonding jumper is defined per Article 100 as the permanent joining of metallic parts to form an electrically conductive path that will ensure electrical continuity and the capacity to conduct safely any current likely to be imposed.

      A. True                  B. False

9. A branch-circuit is defined as a branch-circuit that supplies a number of outlets for lighting and appliances.

   A. True                    B. False

10. A building is defined as a structure that stands alone or that is cut off from adjoining structures by fire walls with all openings therein protected by approved fire doors.

    A. True                    B. False

11. A continuous load is defined as a load where the maximum current is expected to continue for three hours or less.

    A. True                    B. False

12. A feeder is defined as the circuit conductors between the final overcurrent device protecting the circuit and the outlet(s).

    A. True                    B. False

13. Grounded is defined as a system or circuit conductor that is intentionally grounded.

    A. True                    B. False

14. The grounding conductor is defined as a conductor used to connect equipment or the grounded circuit of a wiring system to a grounding electrode or electrodes.

    A. True                    B. False

15. Where the NEC specifies that one equipment shall be "in sight from," "within sight from," or "within sight," or etc., of another equipment, the specified equipment is to be visible and not more than _____ ft. distant from the other.

16. A location not normally subject to dampness or wetness is called a _____ location.

17. The conductors from the service point to the service disconnecting means is called the _____ conductors.

18. The _____ drop conductors are the overhead conductors between the last utility pole and the service-entrance conductors.

19. The service _____ is where the premises wiring or equipment connects to the utility wiring.

## Article 110
## Requirements for electrical installations

20. The conductors and equipment required or permitted by the NEC shall be acceptable only if _____.

21. Electric equipment shall be installed in a neat and _____ manner.

22. Termination provisions of equipment for circuits rated 100 amperes or less, or marked Nos. _____ through _____, shall be used only for conductors rated 60°C. (General rule)

23. Termination provisions of equipment for circuits rated over 100 amperes, or marked for conductors larger than No. _____, shall be used only with conductors rated 75°C.

24. For the mounting of electrical equipment, the code specifically prohibits which of the following methods?

A. Machine screws
B. Sheet metal screws
C. Bolts of malleable iron
D. Wooden plugs driven into holes in masonry

25. Connections, by means of wire binding screws or studs and nuts having upturned lugs, shall be permitted for conductors of a maximum size No. _____.

A. 12
B. 10
C. 8
D. 6

26. Where used on circuits of 100 amperes or less, the load on conductors shall be limited to ampacities rated _____ degrees C, unless the terminals are rated higher.

A. 60
B. 75
C. 85
D. 90

27. The load on conductors used on circuits of over 100 amperes shall be limited to ampacities rated _____ degrees C, unless the terminals are rated higher.

A. 60
B. 75
C. 85
D. 90

28. The work space in front of electric equipment shall be at least _____ inches wide.

A. 24
B. 30
C. 36
D. 40

29. For electrical equipment operating with a nominal voltage of 150 volts-to-ground, the maximum working space clearance required in front of the equipment shall be _____ inches deep.

A. 30
B. 36
C. 42
D. 48

30. Where electrical switchboards face each other and exposed live parts of electrical equipment operating at 277/480 volts are accessible on each side of the work space, the clear working space between shall be at least _____ inches.

A. 36
B. 42
C. 48
D. 60

31. Where access is required to the back of a motor control center for working on deenergized parts, a minimum working space of _____ inches horizontally is required.

A. 24
B. 30
C. 36
D. 42

_____  _____   32. For equipment rated over 1,200 amperes or more and over 6 1/2 ft. wide, containing overcurrent devices, switching devices, or control devices, there shall be one entrance not less than _____ in. wide and _____ ft. high at each end.

A. 24 ; 6              B. 24 ; 6 1/2
C. 30 ; 6              D. 30 ; 6 1/2

_____  _____   33. Enclosures for electrical installations over 600 volts, a fence not less than _____ ft. with _____ ft. of fence fabric utilizing three or more strands of barbed wire or equivalent is permitted.

A. 6 ; 1               B. 6 ; 2
C. 7 ; 1               D. 7 ; 2

_____  _____   34. The minimum headroom about a 100 ampere panelboard in a store shall be at least _____ feet in height.

A. 6 1/4               B. 6 1/2
C. 7                   D. 8

## Article 200
## Use and identification of grounded conductors

_____  _____   35. Where one grounded and two ungrounded circuit conductors are run in a raceway, the grounded conductor shall have an outer finish of white or natural gray its entire length if it is a maximum size of No. _____ or smaller.

A. 10                  B. 8
C. 6                   D. 4

_____  _____   36. The maximum size grounded conductor that is required to be white or natural gray along its entire length is No. _____.

A. 10                  B. 8
C. 6                   D. 4

_____  _____   37. The grounded conductor of a mineral- _____ metal-sheathed cable shall be identified at the time of installation by distinctive marking at its terminations.

A. Insulated           B. Copper
C. Aluminum            D. Armored

_____  _____   38. Where a conductor with black insulation is used as a grounded conductor in a raceway, it shall be permitted to be identified with white markings at its terminations if it is at least size No. _____.

A. 8                   B. 6
C. 4                   D. 2

_____  _____   39. An insulated conductor intended for use as a grounded conductor, where contained in a flexible cord, shall be identified by a _____ outer finish.

A. White               B. Natural Gray
C. None of the above   D. All of the above

_____  _____  40. A continuous white or natural gray color identifies the _____ conductor of a branch-circuit.

    A. Bonding               B. Isolated
    C. Grounded              D. Grounding

_____  _____  41. The white conductor of a nonmetallic sheathed cable is permitted to be used in a switch loop, as an ungrounded conductor:

    A. For a single-phase switch loop only
    B. As the supply to the switched outlet
    C. As the return from the switched outlet
    D. Where reidentified as an ungrounded conductor

_____  _____  42. The identification of terminals to which a grounded conductor is to be connected shall be substantially _____ in color.

    A. Brass                 B. White
    C. Green                 D. Silver

_____  _____  43. For screw shell devices with attached leads, the conductor attached to the center terminal or contact point at the bottom of the screw shall, be _____.

    A. Bare                  B. Green
    C. White                 D. None of the above

## Article 210
## Branch-circuits

_____  _____  44. Multiwire branch-circuits shall only supply phase-to-phase loads.

    A. True                  B. False

_____  _____  45. Where more than one nominal voltage system exists in a building, each ungrounded conductor of a multiwire branch-circuit, where accessible, shall be identified by phase and system.

    A. True                  B. False

_____  _____  46. The equipment grounding conductor of a branch-circuit shall be identified by a continuous green color or a continuous green color with one or more yellow stripes unless its bare.

    A. True                  B. False

_____  _____  47. A three-phase, four-wire, _____ connected system used to supply power to nonlinear loads such as, personal computers, electric discharge lighting, data processing, etc. shall be designed to allow for the possibility of high harmonic neutral currents.

_____  _____  48. The grounding contacts of receptacles and cord connectors shall be grounded by connection to the _____ grounding conductor.

_____  _____  49. A _____ type receptacle shall be permitted to be replaced with another nongrounding type receptacle on existing systems only.

_____  _____   50. A branch-circuit that supplies only one range could be defined by the code as all of the following, except a(n) _____ branch-circuit.

A. Appliance                     B. Multiwire
C. Individual                    D. General purpose

_____  _____   51. General purpose branch-circuits are rated in accordance with the:

A. Voltage of the system
B. Sizing of the conductor used
C. Ampere rating of the overcurrent device
D. Temperature rating of the terminals on the equipment supplied

_____  _____   52. All of the following are ratings (per NEC) for general purpose branch-circuits, except _____ amps.

A. 15                            B. 20
C. 25                            D. 30

_____  _____   53. Which of the following is a rating (per NEC) only of an individual branch-circuit of _____ amps.

A. 15                            B. 20
C. 25                            D. 30

_____  _____   54. In dwelling units, the code specifically requires a means to disconnect simultaneously all ungrounded conductors at the panelboard where the circuit originated, for all _____ branch-circuits.

A. Multiwire                     B. Individual
C. Multioutlet                   D. General purpose

_____  _____   55. A metal junction box contains the following eight conductors for two multiwire branch-circuits:

2 black
2 blue
2 red
1 white
1 white with a green stripe

The white conductor with a green stripe is:

A. A grounded conductor
B. A grounding conductor
C. An insulated equipment grounding conductor
D. Not permitted by the code for either a grounded or grounding conductor

_____  _____   56. A continuous white or natural gray color identifies the _____ conductor of a branch-circuit.

_____

A. Bonding                       B. Isolated
C. Grounded                      D. Grounding

57. Where installed in a raceway, a white No. 8 insulated conductor, used as an equipment grounding conductor, is:

 A. A code violation, even it is marked with green tape
 B. Permitted if it is colored green for the entire exposed length
 C. Permitted if the white insulation is stripped from the entire exposed length
 D. Permitted if the conditions of maintenance ensure that only qualified persons will service the installation.

58. In dwelling units, the code requires that the voltage be limited to 120 volts between conductors for all branch-circuits which supply the terminals of:

 A. Receptacles
 B. Lighting fixtures
 C. Equipment of 1 HP or less
 D. Cord-and-plug connected equipment of 2,400 VA or less

59. Branch-circuits exceeding 120 volts between conductors but not more than 277 volts-to-ground, shall be permitted to supply lighting fixtures equipped with _____ base screw shell lampholders.

 A. Mogul      B. Medium
 C. Admedium    D. Intermediate

60. A nongrounding type receptacle shall be permitted to be replaced with a grounding type receptacle where supplied through a ground-fault circuit-interrupter. (General rule)

 A. True      B. False

61. Cord-and-plug connected equipment shall always be of the grounded type where grounding type receptacles are installed.

 A. True      B. False

62. In dwelling units, wet bar sinks are required to have ground-fault circuit-interrupter protection for all 120 V receptacles, where located within 6 ft. of the outside edge of the wet bar sink.

 A. True      B. False

63. Tap conductors supplying electric ranges, wall-mounted electric ovens, and counter-mounted electric cooking units from a _____ ampere branch-circuit shall have an ampacity of not less than 20 amperes.

64. Branch-circuit conductors supplying loads other than cooking appliances shall have an ampacity sufficient for the loads served and shall not be smaller than No. _____.

65. A heavy-duty lampholder shall have a rating of not less than _____ watts if of the admedium type.

66. The rating of any one cord-and-plug connected utilization equipment shall not exceed _____ percent of the branch-circuit ampere rating.

67. On a circuit that supplies electric discharge lighting fixtures at the top of poles 22 feet in height, the maximum permitted voltage is _____ volts-to-ground.

 A. 120      B. 277
 C. 300      D. 600

68. In an existing dwelling, built and wired before GFCI receptacles where required in kitchens, a receptacle serving the kitchen countertop surfaces is replaced. This replacement receptacle:

    A. Is not covered by the current edition of the code
    B. Is required to be ground-fault circuit-interrupter protected
    C. Is not required to be ground-fault circuit-interrupter protected
    D. Is required to be ground-fault circuit-interrupter protected, only if within 6 ft. of the kitchen sink

69. The grounding contacts of branch-circuit receptacles shall be grounded by connection to the _____ grounding conductor.

    A. Bonding                 B. Neutral
    C. Grounded            D. Equipment

70. Ground-fault circuit-interrupter protection is required for receptacles in all of the following locations, except receptacles:

    A. In a school kitchen
    B. In an office building restroom with a toilet and sink
    C. On the roof of a bank building for servicing an air conditioning unit
    D. In the kitchen of a dwelling to serve countertops

71. GFCI-protection is required for all receptacles, without exception or qualification, in dwelling:

    A. Garages              B. Wet bar sinks
    C. Bathrooms          D. Outdoors

72. In a dwelling unit garage, one cord-and-plug connected freezer will occupy a dedicated space, but the receptacle for the freezer will be "readily accessible" after the freezer is installed. This receptacle is:

    A. Required to be a single receptacle
    B. Not required to be a single receptacle, but if a single receptacle is used, it must be GFCI-protected
    C. Permitted to be a duplex receptacle, and if a duplex receptacle is used to connect another appliance, it must be GFCI-protected
    D. Required to be installed on the same GFCI-protected circuit as the other readily accessible garage receptacles

73. Outdoor receptacles for a dwelling are not required to be GFCI-protected if they are supplied from a dedicated branch-circuit and installed:

    A. In a weatherproof box
    B. At a second floor balcony
    C. At least six feet, six inches above grade
    D. For electric snow-melting or deicing equipment that is GFCE protected

74. Which of the following outdoor receptacles at a dwelling unit is not required to be GFCI-protected? A receptacle installed:

    A. In an open carport
    B. On a second floor balcony
    C. On the wall at a height of 7 feet above the ground level
    D. On a dedicated branch circuit to supply snow-melting equipment at the roof

75. In a store, ground-fault circuit-interrupter protection for personnel is required for 20 ampere receptacles installed at which of the following locations?

    A. Rooftops      B. Bathrooms
    C. All of the above      D. None of the above

76. A 40 or 50 ampere branch-circuit shall supply only nonlighting outlet loads.

    A. True      B. False

77. Each wall space 6 ft. or more wide shall be treated individually and separately from other wall spaces within the room.
    A. True      B. False

78. The total rating of utilization equipment fastened-in-place shall not exceed _____ percent of the branch-circuit ampere rating.

79. Appliance receptacle outlets installed in a dwelling unit for specific appliances, shall be installed within _____ ft. of the intended location of the appliance.

80. Receptacle outlets in a dwelling unit are required to be installed so that there is no point on the wall greater than _____ ft.

81. Receptacle outlets in a dwelling unit shall not serve as one of the required outlets if located over _____ ft. _____ in. from the floor.

82. Receptacles installed in the kitchen of dwelling units to serve countertop surfaces shall be supplied by not less than _____ small appliance branch-circuits.

83. An autotransformer that supplies a 480 volt circuit from a 600 volt system is not required to have a grounded conductor that is electrically connected between the supplying system and the circuit supplied where the autotransformer:

    A. Has no exposed noncurrent-carrying metal parts
    B. Is connected in a three-phase open delta arrangement
    C. Is located at least 8 feet above the floor or working surface
    D. Is in an industrial occupancy and only qualified persons will service the installation

84. Where the ampacity of multioutlet branch-circuit conductors do not correspond to the rating of a standard size overcurrent device, the next smaller size device must be used if the multioutlet branch-circuit supplies:

    A. A motor load
    B. A load of less than 800 amps
    C. Receptacles for cord-and-plug connected loads
    D. Fixed loads such as lighting units and appliances

85. The code requires that branch-circuit conductors shall have an ampacity of at least the rating of the branch-circuit, if it pertains to conductors of:

    A. All branch-circuits
    B. Only individual branch-circuits
    C. Multioutlet branch-circuits supplying fixed lighting and appliance loads
    D. Multioutlet branch-circuits supplying receptacles for cord-and-plug connected portable loads

86. Where a 30 ampere branch-circuit serves fixed lighting units, tap conductors to individual light fixtures are permitted to extend a maximum of _____ inches beyond any portion of the fixture.

    A. 6                              B. 12
    C. 18                             D. 24

87. A mogul base lampholder installed on a 30 ampere branch-circuit must have a rating of at least _____ watts.

    A. 250                            B. 300
    C. 660                            D. 750

88. All of the following are code violations, except:

    A. A single 15 ampere rated receptacle on a 20 ampere general purpose branch-circuit
    B. A single 15 ampere rated receptacle on a 20 ampere individual branch-circuit
    C. A duplex 20 ampere rated receptacle on a 15 ampere multiwire branch-circuit
    D. A single 30 ampere rated receptacle on a 40 ampere individual branch-circuit

89. Receptacles that are an integral part of a lighting fixture, appliance, or cabinet shall not be counted as one of the required receptacle outlets in a dwelling unit.

    A. True                           B. False

90. A minimum of two 20 amp, 1,500 VA small appliance circuits are required to supply receptacle outlets that are located in the kitchen, pantry, breakfast room, and dining room in a dwelling unit.

    A. True                           B. False

91. Receptacle outlets are permitted to be installed so that there is no point on the wall greater than 6 ft. from a receptacle outlet in a dwelling unit.

    A. True                           B. False

92. Sliding glass doors are considered wall space when spacing receptacles in a dwelling unit.

    A. True                           B. False

93. An outside outlet can be installed on the small appliance circuit in a dwelling unit.

    A. True                           B. False

94. A receptacle outlet shall be installed at each wall counter space _____ in. or wider in a dwelling unit.

95. Receptacle outlets shall be installed for each peninsular countertop in a dwelling unit with a long dimension of _____ in. or greater and a short dimension of _____ or greater.

96. In dwelling units, bathroom receptacle outlets shall be supplied by at least one _____ ampere branch-circuit.

97. Grade level access is considered _____ ft. _____ in. or less from finished grade in a dwelling unit.

98. Where a branch-circuit supplies continuous or any combination of continuous and non-continuous loads, the rating of the overcurrent device shall not be less than the noncontinuous load plus _____ percent of the continuous load.

99. A 20 ampere branch-circuit is permitted to supply lighting units together with utilization equipment in all of the following situations except:

    A. If the utilization equipment is fastened-in-place
    B. If the utilization equipment is cord-and-plug connected
    C. Where the 20 ampere circuit is a small appliance branch-circuit
    D. Where the circuit supplies motor-operated utilization equipment with a motor larger than 1/8 horsepower

100. Receptacle outlets are permitted to be mounted not more than 18 in. below the countertop in a dwelling unit for the physically impaired.

    A. True                B. False

101. At least one wall receptacle outlet shall be installed in the bathroom within 30 in. of the outside edge of the basin in a dwelling unit.

    A. True                B. False

102. At least one receptacle outlet shall be installed for the laundry in a dwelling unit.

    A. True                B. False

103. Hallways of 20 ft. or more in length shall have at least one receptacle outlet in a dwelling unit.

    A. True                B. False

104. At least one receptacle outlet shall be installed directly above a show window for each 12 liner ft.

    A. True                B. False

105. Receptacle outlets shall be located not more than _____ in. above the countertop in a dwelling unit.

106. Receptacle outlets shall not be installed in the _____ position in the work surfaces or countertops in a dwelling unit.

107. A 15 or 20 ampere receptacle outlet shall be installed at an _____ location for the servicing of air-conditioning equipment on rooftops.

108. A vehicle door in a _____ shall not be considered as an outdoor entrance or exit for a dwelling unit.

109. A branch-circuit in a multifamily dwelling which supplies outdoor lighting in a common area, shall:

    A. Not be supplied from a panelboard in an individual dwelling unit
    B. Be permitted to be supplied from a panelboard in the dwelling unit for the manager of the multifamily dwelling
    C. Be permitted to be supplied from a panelboard in an individual dwelling unit if the lighting is controlled by a photocell
    D. Be permitted to be supplied from a panelboard in an individual dwelling unit where the circuit is not over 20 amperes

110. A cord connector that is supported by a permanently installed cord pendant shall be considered a(n) _____ outlet.

    A. Power                    B. Lighting
    C. Individual               D. Receptacle

111. Receptacle outlets shall be spaced a maximum of 12 feet apart in all of the following rooms or areas of dwellings, except the _____.

    A. Kitchen                  B. Hallway
    C. Dining room              D. Living room

112. In the living room of a dwelling, a wall space at least _____ inches or more in width shall have a receptacle outlet installed.

    A. 12                       B. 18
    C. 24                       D. 30

113. In the family room of a dwelling, which of the following is not included in the measurement of wall space for required spacing of receptacle outlets?

    A. An open railing next to a stairway
    B. A sliding panel in an exterior door
    C. A fixed window panel next to an exterior door
    D. A free standing bar-type counter serving as a room divider

114. In dwellings, a floor outlet shall be permitted to be counted as part of the required number of receptacle outlets where located a maximum of _____ inches from the wall.

    A. 6                        B. 12
    C. 18                       D. 24

115. In a dwelling unit, a receptacle outlet which is factory-installed in a listed baseboard electric heater is permitted to serve as the required outlet for the wall space utilized by the baseboard heater, if:

    A. The heater circuit is a maximum of 120 volts.
    B. The outlet it is connected to the heater circuit.
    C. The outlet is not connected to the heater circuit.
    D. The baseboard heater is six feet or more in length.

116. For a commercial occupancy, the code requires receptacle outlets to be installed:

    A. Within 6 feet of any point along the floor line
    B. Within 6 feet of the intended location of equipment
    C. Within 12 feet of the intended location of equipment
    D. Wherever flexible cords with attachment plugs are used

117. For dwelling units, a branch-circuit supplying _____ receptacle outlet(s) may also supply receptacles in an attached garage.

    A. Outdoors          B. Bathroom
    C. Laundry room      D. Kitchen small appliance

118. In a dwelling, a separate circuit with no other outlets or loads on the same circuit, is required for all of the following locations or loads except:

    A. Bathroom receptacles
    B. Laundry room receptacles
    C. A refrigerator supplied by a 20-ampere circuit
    D. Central heating equipment other than fixed electric space-heating equipment

119. In a dwelling unit kitchen, the small appliance branch-circuits that supply countertop receptacles are not permitted to supply receptacle outlets:

    A. Outdoors
    B. In a pantry
    C. In a dining room
    D. For refrigeration equipment

120. In a dwelling unit kitchens, the two or more small appliance branch-circuits installed to serve countertop surfaces are permitted to serve which of the following cord-and-plug connected appliances?

    A. Trash compactor
    B. Built-in dishwasher
    C. Electrically operated kitchen waste disposer
    D. Gas-fired range with supplemental electrical equipment

121. In a dwelling, the receptacle outlet for the refrigerator shall be:

    A. Permitted to be supplied from an individual 15 ampere branch-circuit
    B. Permitted to be supplied from a general purpose 15 ampere branch-circuit
    C. Required to be supplied from an individual 20 ampere branch-circuit
    D. Required to be supplied from (only) one of the two or more 20 small appliance branch-circuits

122. In a dwelling, receptacle outlets installed for a specific appliance, shall be installed within at least _____ feet of the intended location of the appliance.

    A. 3            B. 6
    C. 10          D. 12

123. In the kitchen of a dwelling unit, a receptacle outlet shall be installed at each wall counter space which is at least _____ inches or wider.

    A. 10                          B. 12
    C. 18                          D. 24

124. In the kitchen of a dwelling unit, an island countertop space is 90 inches long with a width of 28 inches, and has a 30 inch wide range installed in the center, evenly dividing the space on each side of the range. How many receptacle outlets is/are required for the island?

    A. 1                           B. 2
    C. 3                           D. 4

125. In a dwelling unit kitchen, a peninsular countertop is 2 1/2 feet wide and 7 feet long measured from the connecting edge. At least _____ receptacle outlet(s) is/are required to be installed at this peninsular counter space.

    A. 0                           B. 1
    C. 2                           D. 3

126. In the kitchen of a dwelling, receptacles installed below the countertop of a peninsular counter space shall not be located where the countertop extends at least _____ inches or more beyond its support base.

    A. 6                           B. 8
    C. 10                          D. 12

127. In the kitchen of a dwelling, receptacle outlets for counter spaces shall be located a maximum of _____ inches above the countertop.

    A. 10                          B. 12
    C. 18                          D. 24

128. In a dwelling unit bathroom, the receptacle outlet or outlets shall be supplied by at least one:

    A. 15 ampere branch-circuit which supplies no other outlets
    B. 15 ampere branch-circuit which is permitted to also supply outdoor outlets
    C. 20 ampere branch-circuit which supplies no other outlets
    D. 20 ampere branch-circuit which is permitted to also supply outdoor outlets

129. The outdoor outlets for a dwelling that are required to be accessible at grade level shall be installed a maximum of _____ feet above grade.

    A. 5 1/2                       B. 6
    C. 6 1/2                       D. 8

130. In a dwelling, the receptacle outlet provided for the clothes washer shall be:

    A. Permitted to be supplied from an individual 15 ampere branch-circuit
    B. Permitted to be supplied from a general purpose 15 ampere branch-circuit
    C. Required to be supplied from a general purpose 20 ampere branch-circuit
    D. Required to be supplied from a 20 ampere branch-circuit which supplies only the outlet or outlets for the laundry

131. In dwelling units, hallways of _____ ft. or more in length shall have at least one receptacle outlet.

   A. 3                          B. 6
   C. 10                         D. 20

132. For a store, at least one receptacle shall be installed above a show window for each _____ linear feet or major fraction thereof of show window.

   A. 10                         B. 12
   C. 18                         D. 25

133. Where an air conditioning unit is located on the rooftop of an office building, a receptacle outlet shall be located on the roof on the same level and within _____ feet of the air conditioning unit.

   A. 6                          B. 12
   C. 25                         D. 50

134. In a dwelling, a light fixture over a stairway shall be controlled by a wall switch at each floor level where the difference between floor levels is _____ steps or more.

   A. 3                          B. 4
   C. 5                          D. 6

135. In which of the following rooms of a dwelling would the required lighting outlet be permitted to be a wall-switched controlled receptacle?

   A. Dining room               B. Kitchen
   C. Bathroom                  D. None of the above

136. In a dwelling unit, a lighting outlet being controlled by an occupancy sensor is:

   A. Prohibited by the code
   B. Permitted for all locations except at outdoor entrances
   C. Permitted for all rooms except rooms containing electrical equipment requiring servicing
   D. Permitted if a wall switch or manual override is also installed at the customary wall switch location

137. What size OCPD is required for a branch-circuit with a continuous load of 80 amps with 75°C terminals?

   A. 90 amp                    B. 100 amp
   C. 125 amp                   D. 150 amp

## Article 215
## Feeders

138. The feeder conductor ampacity shall not be less than that of the service-entrance conductors where the feeder conductors carry the total load supplied by the service-entrance conductors with an ampacity of _____ amperes or less.

139. On a four-wire delta-connected secondary, the phase conductor having the higher voltage-to-ground shall be identified by an outer finish that is _____ in color.

140. Ground-fault protection of equipment shall be provided for a feeder disconnect rated _____ amperes or more in a solidly grounded wye system with greater than 150 volts-to-ground, but not exceeding 600 volts phase-to-phase.

141. What size THWN feeder- circuit copper conductors are required to supply a continuous load of 140 amps and a noncontinuous load of 50 amps?

A. No. 2/0　　　　　　　　B. No. 3/0
C. No. 4/0　　　　　　　　D. No. 250

## Article 220
## Branch-circuit, Feeder, and Service Calculations

142. Except where computations result in a fraction of an ampere _____ or larger, such fractions shall be permitted to be dropped.

A. 0.3　　　　　　　　B. 0.4
C. 0.5　　　　　　　　D. 0.6

143. When calculating the general lighting load for an office building, a unit load of _____ volt-amperes shall be included for general purpose receptacle outlets when the number of outlets to be installed is unknown.

A. 1/2　　　　　　　　B. 1
C. 1 1/2　　　　　　　D. 3 1/2

144. When calculating the general lighting and receptacle load for an dwelling unit, a unit load of _____ volt-amperes shall be used.

A. 1　　　　　　　　B. 2
C. 3　　　　　　　　D. 3 1/2

145. When calculating the general lighting load for a restaurant, a unit load of _____ volt-amperes shall be used.

A. 1/4　　　　　　　　B. 1/2
C. 1　　　　　　　　D. 2

146. For the feeder calculation for a store, the load for each receptacle outlet shall be _____ volt-amperes.

A. 150　　　　　　　　B. 180
C. 200　　　　　　　　D. 300

147. For computing the load on a branch-circuit, an outlet for a heavy-duty lampholder not used for general illumination, shall be _____ volt-amperes.

A. 250　　　　　　　　B. 600
C. 660　　　　　　　　D. 750

148. For computing the load on a branch-circuit, sign and outline lighting shall be calculated at _____ volt-amperes.

A. 1,000　　　　　　　　B. 1,200
C. 1,500　　　　　　　　D. 1,800

149. When applying demand factors for nondwelling receptacle loads, the first 10 kVA is calculated at 100 percent and the remainder is calculated at _____ percent.

    A. 25            B. 50
    C. 75            D. 85

150. The largest motor load must be added to the other loads at _____ percent of the motors full load current rating.

    A. 25            B. 50
    C. 60            D. 75

151. In a dwelling, at least _____ branch-circuits shall be provided for the small appliance circuits.

    A. One 15-ampere        B. Two 15-ampere
    C. One 20 ampere        D. Two 20-ampere

152. For calculating the load on a feeder using the standard calculation method, a fixed electric space heating load shall be computed at _____ percent of the total connected load.

    A. 80            B. 100
    C. 125           D. 150

153. For fixed electric space-heating equipment, the ampacity of the branch-circuit conductors shall be at least _____ percent of the total load supplied.

    A. 80            B. 100
    C. 125           D. 150

154. In a dwelling, each small appliance branch-circuit shall be computed at _____ volt-amperes.

    A. 1,000          B. 1,500
    C. 3,000          D. 5,000

155. For calculating the service conductor size for a dwelling, at least _____ volt-amperes shall be included for each two-wire laundry branch-circuit.

    A. 500           B. 1,000
    C. 1,500         D. 3,000

156. For calculating a feeder load for a two-family dwelling, the demand factor permitted to be applied to the nameplate rating load of four or more appliances, would apply to all of the following except:

    A. Blower motors        B. Dishwashers
    C. Clothes dryers       D. Kitchen waste disposals

157. Four or more fixed appliances fastened-in-place shall have a demand factor of _____ percent applied.

    A. 50            B. 60
    C. 70           D. 75

158. Electric clothes dryers shall be _____ watts or the nameplate rating, whichever is larger, for each dryer served.

    A. 4,000                      B. 5,000
    C. 7,500                      D. 8,000

159. Demand factors for five electric clothes dryers shall be calculated at _____ percent.

    A. 65                         B. 70
    C. 80                         D. 100

160. What is the demand load for a 12 kW range?

    A. 8                          B. 10
    C. 12                         D. 16

161. A school with twelve pieces of kitchen equipment has a feeder demand factor of _____ percent applied.

    A. 65                         B. 70
    C. 80                         D. 90

162. What is the general lighting and receptacle loads and the small appliance and laundry loads for the following:

    • 3,000 sq. ft. dwelling
    • 2 small appliance circuits
    • 1 laundry circuit

    A. 6,675 VA                   B. 6,845 VA
    C. 6,925 VA                   D. 7,125 VA

163. What is the VA rating for 150 general purpose receptacle outlets to cord-and-plug connect loads used at noncontinuous operation?

    A. 16,250 VA                  B. 18,500 VA
    C. 19,400 VA                  D. 20,250 VA

164. What is the load in VA for the following fixed appliances:

    • 1,000 VA compactor
    • 1,200 VA disposal
    • 1,600 VA dishwasher
    • 1,200 VA microwave
    • 2,600 VA water pump

    A. 5,700 VA                   B. 5,925 VA
    C. 6,225 VA                   D. 6750 VA

## Article 225
## Outside Branch-circuits and Feeders

165. Open individual conductors shall not be smaller than No. 10 copper for 600 volts, nominal, or less, for spans up to _____ ft. in length.

    A. 25                         B. 40
    C. 50                         D. 75

166. Overhead conductors for festoon lighting shall not be smaller than No. _____.

    A. 14                     B. 12
    C. 10                     D. 8

167. The conductors for festoon supports shall be supported by a messenger wire in spans exceeding _____ ft.

    A. 25                     B. 40
    C. 50                     D. 75

168. Conductors on poles shall have a separation of not less than _____ ft. where not placed on racks or brackets.

    A. 1                      B. 2
    C. 3                      D. 6

169. Outside conductors shall have a clearance from television antennas not less than _____ ft.

    A. 1                      B. 2
    C. 3                      D. 6

170. What size THWN copper conductors are required for a branch-circuit having a 16 amp continuous load and a 8 amp noncontinuous load?

    A. No. 14              B. No 12
    C. No. 10              D. No. 8

171. What size THWN copper conductors are required for a feeder-circuit having a 150 amp continuous load and a 20 amp noncontinuous load?

    A. No. 1/0            B. No. 2/0
    C. No. 3/0            D. No. 4/0

172. What size THWN copper conductors are required for a feeder-circuit having a 120 amp continuous load and an 80 amp noncontinuous load?

    A. No. 3/0            B. No. 4/0
    C. No. 250 KCMIL      D. No. 300 KCMIL

## Article 230
## Services

173. A permanent plaque or directory shall be installed at each service disconnecting location where a building or structure is supplied by more than one service.

    A. True                   B. False

174. Service conductors supplying a building or other structure are permitted to run through the interior of another building or other structure.

    A. True                   B. False

175. Overhead service drop conductors shall not be smaller than No. 8 copper.

    A. True                   B. False

176. Service conductors installed as open conductors shall have a clearance of not less than _____ ft. from windows that are designed to be opened.

177. Overhead conductors that are installed to supply only limited loads of a single branch-circuit, such as controlled water heaters, shall not be smaller than No. _____ hard-drawn copper.

178. Conductors shall have a vertical clearance of not less than _____ ft. above the roof surface.

179. Service drop conductors of 240 volts-to-ground crossing residential property or drive ways must have a clearance of _____ ft. from finished grade.

180. Service drop conductors crossing over public streets which are subject to truck traffic must have a clearance of _____ ft. from finished grade.

181. Service conductors may be permitted to pass through the interior of another building, such as through the crawlspace of a multifamily dwelling, where they are:

    A. Installed in rigid conduit
    B. Installed in a cable
    C. Installed in conduit properly supported to the lower edges of the floor joists
    D. Installed in a raceway that is encased in concrete or brick at least two inches thick

182. Overhead service conductors run above the top level of a window, shall:

    A. Be enclosed in a cable or raceway
    B. Have a maximum voltage of 150 volts-to-ground
    C. Have a clearance of at least 3 feet from the window
    D. Be permitted to be less than 3 feet from the window

183. Where service conductors pass over a flat roof, the vertical clearance required above the roof level shall be maintained for a distance of at least _____ feet in all directions from the edge of the roof.

    A. 3                    B. 4
    C. 6                    D. 8

184. Where a building with a flat roof is supplied by a 240 volt service drop passing 6 feet horizontally above the roof overhang and terminated through the roof raceway, the service drop conductors shall have a clearance from the roof of at least _____ feet.

    A. 1 1/2                B. 3
    C. 4                    D. 8

185. Service drop conductors with a voltage of 240 volts-to-ground, shall have a clearance of _____ feet over a commercial driveway used by delivery trucks.

    A. 12                   B. 15
    C. 16                   D. 18

186. The point of attachment of service drop conductors to a building shall be at least _____ feet above finished grade.

    A. 10                   B. 12
    C. 16                   D. 18

_____  _____    187. Service-entrance conductors for a one-family dwelling shall have an ampacity of at least
                         _____ amperes.

                         A. 30                              B.  50
                         C. 100                             D. 125

_____  _____    188. For installations consisting of not more than two two-wire branch-circuits, the service
                         disconnecting means shall have a rating of not less than _____ amperes.

                         A. 20                              B.  30
                         C. 60                              D. 100

_____  _____    189. Service lateral conductors shall not be smaller than No. 6 copper.

                         A. True                            B. False

_____  _____    190. Service lateral conductors exposed to physical damage can be protected by Schedule 40
_____                  rigid nonmetallic conduit.

                         A. True                            B. False

_____  _____    191. Each service disconnecting means shall be permanently marked to identify it as a service
                         disconnecting means.

                         A. True                            B. False

_____  _____    192. Service-entrance cables shall be supported by straps within _____ in. of every service
_____  _____         head and at intervals not exceeding _____ in.

_____  _____    193. In a multiple occupancy building, each occupant shall have _____ to the occupant's
                         service disconnecting means.

_____  _____    194. The service disconnecting means shall be plainly marked to identify whether it is in the
_____                  _____ or _____ position.

_____  _____    195. If the service disconnecting means is located inside the building, it shall be located
                         _____ of entrance of the service conductors.

                         A. Nearest the point               B. A maximum of 10 ft. from
                         C. A maximum of 15 ft. from        D. A maximum of 25 ft. from

_____  _____    196. The code requires the service disconnecting means to be installed at a(n):

                         A. Accessible location outside the building
                         B. Accessible location either outside the building or inside the nearest point of
                            entrance of the service conductors
                         C. Readily accessible location outside the building
                         D. Readily accessible location either outside the building or inside the building
                            nearest the point of entrance of the service conductors

197. The service disconnecting means shall consist of not more than _____ switches or circuit breakers.

    A. 2                               B. 4
    C. 5                               D. 6

198. In a multiple occupancy building where electrical maintenance is not provided by the building management, the service disconnect for each occupancy shall be:

    A. Accessible to each occupant
    B. Located outside the building
    C. Located inside each occupancy
    D. Accessible only to building management personnel

199. For installations consisting of not more than two two-wire branch-circuits, the rating of the service disconnecting means shall have a rating of at least _____ amperes.

    A. 20                              B. 30
    C. 60                              D. 100

200. Ground-fault protection of equipment shall be provided for solidly grounded wye electrical services of more than 150 volts-to-ground, but not exceeding _____ volts phase-to-phase.

    A. 240                             B. 300
    C. 480                             D. 600

201. For a 1,600 ampere, solidly grounded wye electrical service, the maximum setting of the ground-fault protection shall be _____ amperes.

    A. 800                             B. 1,000
    C. 1,200                           D. 1,600

## Article 240
## Overcurrent Protection

202. Overcurrent protection for conductors and equipment is provided to open the circuit if the current reaches a value that will cause an excessive or dangerous temperature in conductors or conductor insulation.

    A. True                            B. False

203. Where a flexible cord is used as an extension cord, No. 16 and larger conductors shall be protected by 30 ampere circuits.

    A. True                            B. False

204. In grounded systems for single-phase circuits, individual single pole circuit breakers with approved handle ties shall be not be approved as the protection for each ungrounded conductor for line-to-line connected loads.

    A. True                            B. False

205. Overcurrent protection devices shall be readily accessible. (General rule)

    A. True                            B. False

_____ _____ 206. A No. 18 fixture wire run 20 ft. which is connected to a 120 volt branch-circuit shall be protected by an _____ ampere circuit. (General rule)

_____ _____ 207. Overcurrent devices shall be located where they will not be exposed to _____ damage.

_____ _____ 208. Plug fuses shall not be used in circuits exceeding _____ volts between conductors.

_____ _____ 209. Where circuit breaker handles are operated vertically, the up position of the handle shall be the _____ position.

_____ _____ 210. A No. 16 flexible cord supplying a specific listed appliance shall be protected by an _____ ampere circuit.

A. 15                   B. 20
C. 30                   D. 40

_____ _____ 211. The requirements that feeder tap conductors be at least No. 6 copper, contain no splices, and not penetrate walls, floors or ceilings, are some of the conditions for feeder taps:

A. Not over 10 ft. long          B. Not over 25 ft. long
C. Over 25 ft. long              D. Supplying a transformer

_____ _____ 212. Tap conductors supplying a wall-mounted oven from a 50 ampere branch-circuit shall have an ampacity of at least _____ amperes.

_____ 

A. 20                   B. 30
C. 40                   D. 50

_____ _____ 213. In a multifamily dwelling where electrical service and maintenance is not provided by the building manager, the branch-circuit overcurrent devices, where installed with proper clearance, would be permitted to be located in which of the following locations?

A. A laundry room
B. A clothes closet
C. The bathroom of each dwelling
D. In an electrical room kept locked where only the manager has the key

_____ _____ 214. Disconnecting means shall be provided on the supply side of cartridge fuses in circuits of _____ where accessible to other than qualified persons.

A. Over 50 volts-to-ground       B. Over 150 volts-to-ground
C. Over 300 volts-to-ground      D. Any voltage

_____ _____ 215. Where the interrupting capacity rating of _____ is other than 10,000 amperes, it must be marked on the device.

A. Plug fuses                    B. Cartridge fuses
C. Circuit breakers              D. Ground-fault sensors for equipment

_____ _____ 216. Cartridge fuses rated at _____ volts, nominal or less, shall be permitted to be used for voltages at or below their ratings.

A. 300                   B. 600
C. 800                   D. 1,000

217. What size OCPD is required for a 10 ft. tap when supplied by a 600 amp OCPD?

   A. 50                              B. 60
   C. 80                              D. 100

## Article 250
## Grounding

218. AC systems of less than 50 volts shall be grounded where supplied by transformers that exceed 150 volts-to-ground.

   A. True                           B. False

219. A neutral conductor shall be bonded to the generator frame where the generator is a component of a separately derived system.

   A. True                           B. False

220. A grounding electrode is required for the grounded system in each building or structure when two or more buildings or structures are supplied from a common AC service.

   A. True                           B. False

221. Where a submersible pump is used in a metal well casing, the well casing shall be _____ to the pump circuit equipment grounding conductor.

222. Metal raceways and enclosures shall be kept at least _____ ft. away from lightning rod conductors or be bonded together.

223. The path to ground from circuits, equipment, and metal enclosures for conductors shall be _____ and electrically continuous.

224. The grounding electrode conductor shall be connected to the grounded service conductor:

   A Within five feet of the service equipment on the load side
   B. At any point on the load side of the service disconnecting means
   C. At a subpanel outside the building
   D. At any accessible point between the load end of the service drop or lateral to and including at the service disconnecting means

225. Where a separately derived AC system provided by a transformer is required to be grounded, the connection of the grounding electrode conductor of the derived system, shall be made:

   A. At the service panel
   B. At the overcurrent device on the load side
   C. At any point on the load side of the first disconnecting means
   D. At any point on the separately derived system from the transformer to the first disconnecting means or overcurrent device

226. Where a separately derived AC system is located on the third floor of a shopping mall, the preferred or first choice for a grounding electrode is:

   A. A metal gas pipe
   B. A concrete-encased electrode
   C. A driven ground rod at the first floor of the building
   D. The nearest available effectively grounded structural member of the building

227. Exposed metal parts of fastened-in-place equipment shall be grounded where located _____ from grounded metal objects and subject to contact by persons.

    A. 7 1/2 ft. vertically and 5 ft. horizontally
    B. 7 1/2 ft. vertically and 3 ft. horizontally
    C. 8 ft. vertically and 3 ft. horizontally
    D. 8 ft. vertically and 5 ft. horizontally

228. The code permits frames of ranges and dryers to be grounded to the grounded conductor under certain conditions for _____ installations only.

    A. New                          B. Existing
    C. Commercial                   D. Residential

229. An equipment bonding jumper installed outside of a raceway is permitted to be a maximum _____ feet in length.

    A. 3                            B. 4
    C. 6                            D. 8

230. The metal water piping system in the area served by a separately derived system is not effectively grounded, therefore, a ground rod is used as the grounding electrode for this system. The metal water piping in the area shall be:

    A. Bonded to a separate ground rod
    B. Bonded to the grounded conductor of the separately derived system
    C. Used as a supplemental grounding electrode for the separately derived system
    D. Isolated from any contact with the electrical system, since it is not effectively grounded

231. The connection of the grounding electrode conductor to a metal underground water pipe used as a grounding electrode shall be at any point:

    A. Outside the building
    B. On the water piping system within the building
    C. Within 5 ft. from where the water pipe enters the building
    D. Between the water pipe entrance to the building and the first insulating joint or device such as a water meter

232. Which one of the grounding electrodes listed below is required to be supplemented by an additional electrode.

    A. Ground rod                   B. Ground ring
    C. Concrete-encased electrode    D. Metal underground water pipe

233. Any nonconductive paint, enamel, or similar coating shall be removed at threads, contact points, and contact surfaces.

    A. True                         B. False

234. Aluminum wire can be installed when used as an equipment bonding jumper.

    A. True                         B. False

235. The interior metal water piping system shall be bonded to service equipment enclosure.

    A. True                         B. False

236. A metal underground gas piping system can be used as a grounding electrode.

    A. True                 B. False

237. The grounding electrode conductor to a ground rod shall not be required to be larger than No. _____ copper wire.

238. A ground rod used as a grounding electrode that does not have a resistance of _____ ohms or less shall be augmented by one additional electrode.

239. Where multiple ground rods are installed, they shall not be less than _____ ft. apart.

240. Equipment grounding conductors run in the hollow spaces of a wall are not required to be enclosed in a raceway if installed in sizes smaller than No. _____.

241. All of the following statements are true for a concrete-encased electrode, except:

    A. It may be used as the sole grounding electrode
    B. It may serve as the supplemental electrode to a metal underground water pipe electrode
    C. If it is available on the premises, it is required to be made part of the grounding electrode system
    D. Where the concrete-encased electrode is a copper conductor, it shall be sized in accordance with Table 250-94.

242. A metal underground water pipe may serve as a grounding electrode if it is in direct contact with the earth for at least _____ ft. or more.

    A. 6                 B. 8
    C. 10              D. 12

243. In an industrial building, where the conditions of maintenance and supervision ensure that only qualified persons will service the installation:

    A. The resistance of a single-made electrode may exceed 25 ohms
    B. A metal underground water pipe is permitted to serve as the sole grounding electrode
    C. A metal underground gas piping system is permitted to serve as a grounding electrode
    D. The supplemental electrode shall be permitted to be bonded to a totally exposed interior metal water piping system at any convenient point.

244. For a bare copper conductor installed in a concrete footing as a concrete-encased grounding electrode, which of the following is not a correct code requirement? The bare copper conductor shall be:

    A. At least size No. 2
    B. At least 20 ft. in length
    C. Located near the bottom of the footing
    D. Encased by at least 2 in. of concrete

245. Where two made electrodes are installed, each of a different system, they shall be spaced at least _____ ft. apart.

    A. 3                 B. 6
    C. 8              D. 10

_____  _____

246. Where a ground rod cannot be driven to the required depth, it shall be driven at an angle or buried in a trench at least \_\_\_\_\_ ft. deep.

A. 2                          B. 2 1/2
C. 3                          D. 3 1/2

_____  _____

247. A ground shall be installed so that at least \_\_\_\_\_ ft. of the length of the rod is in contact with the soil.

A. 6                          B. 7 1/2
C. 8                          D. 10

_____  _____

248. A single ground rod which has a resistance to ground of 50 ohms has:

A. Acceptable resistance as is
B. Too low a resistance and must be replaced by a longer rod
C. Too high a resistance and must be replaced by a rod with a larger diameter
D. Too high a resistance and must be augmented by one additional grounding electrode

_____  _____

249. The minimum size grounding electrode conductor that is permitted to be run along the surface of the building construction without protection, is No. \_\_\_\_\_.

A. 8                          B. 6
C. 4                          D. 2

_____  _____

250. The size of the grounding electrode conductor for a DC system shall not be smaller than No. 6 copper.

A. True                       B. False

_____  _____

251. The size of the grounding electrode conductor connected to a concrete-encased electrode for a DC system shall not be smaller than No. 4 copper.

A. True                       B. False

_____  _____

252. The connection of a grounding electrode conductor to a grounding electrode is not required to be accessible.

A. True                       B. False

_____  _____

253. Ground clamps shall be protected from physical damage.

A. True                       B. False

_____  _____

254. The size of a direct-current grounding electrode conductor that is the sole connection to the grounding electrode (ground ring) shall not be required to be larger than No. \_\_\_\_ copper wire.

_____  _____

255. Secondary circuits of current and potential instrument transformers shall be grounded where the primary windings are connected to circuits of \_\_\_\_ volts or more to ground.

_____  _____

256. The grounding conductor for secondary circuits of instrument transformers and for instrument cases shall not be smaller than No. \_\_\_\_\_ copper.

_____ _____    257. Which of the following wiring methods is not permitted by the code to be used as an equipment grounding conductor:

       A. Rigid metal conduit
       B. Electrical metallic tubing
       C. Armor of Type AC cable
       D. Flexible metal conduit over 6 ft. in length

_____ _____    258. Bare aluminum grounding conductors that are used outside, shall not be installed within _____ in. of the earth.

       A. 6               B. 12
       C. 18             D. 24

_____ _____    259. The size of the grounding electrode conductor connected to a concrete-encased electrode for a grounded AC system shall not be smaller than No. _____ copper.

       A. 6               B. 4
       C. 2               D. 1

_____ _____    260. The minimum size copper grounding electrode conductor required for a 200 ampere service consisting of No. 3/0 THW copper service-entrance conductors is No. _____.
_____

       A. 8               B. 6
       C. 4               D. 2

_____ _____    261. A grounding electrode conductor that is the sole connection to a made electrode shall not be required to be larger than No. _____.

       A. 8               B. 6
       C. 4               D. 2

_____ _____    262. Which of the following are not allowed for the connection of grounding conductors and bonding jumpers:

       A. Exothermic welding        B. Listed pressure connectors
       C. Listed clamps              D. Sheet-metal screws

_____ _____    263. What size copper equipment grounding conductor is required for an overcurrent protection device rated at 400 amps?

       A. 8               B. 6
       C. 4               D. 3

_____ _____    264. What size copper grounding electrode conductor (to metal building steel) is required for service-entrance conductors that are sized No. 3/0?
_____

       A. 6               B. 4
       C. 2               D. 1/0

## Article 300
## Wiring methods

_____ _____    265. Conductors of circuits rated over 600 volts, can occupy the same raceway with conductors of circuits rated 600 volts or less.

       A. True                      B. False

_____  _____   266. Where a raceway is exposed to physical damage, Schedule 80 rigid nonmetallic conduit can be used.

        A. True                     B. False

_____  _____   267. Cable systems that are not run through the center of the framing members can be placed in a cut notch in the framing member and protected by a steel plate of _____ in.

_____  _____   268. Raceways are required to be provided with _____ joints where necessary to compensate for thermal expansion and contraction.

_____  _____   269. No wiring systems of any type shall be installed in _____ used to transport dust, loose stock, or flammable vapors.

_____  _____   270. For conductors rated 600 volt or less, conductors of different voltage ratings are permitted to occupy the same raceway where all conductors in the raceway:

        A. Are power conductors, with no control wires included
        B. Have an insulation rating of at least 600 volts
        C. Have an insulation rating equal to that of the lowest rated conductor in the raceway
        D. Have an insulation rating equal to at least the maximum circuit voltage applied to any conductor in the raceway

_____  _____   271. In exposed locations where a cable is run through bored holes in studs, the edge of the hole shall be at least _____ in. from the nearest edge of the stud.

        A. 1                     B. 1 1/8
        C. 1 1/4               D. 1 1/5

_____  _____   272. For raceways installed in shallow groves, where nails or screws are likely to penetrate, physical protection such as steel plates are required for all of the following raceways, except:

        A. Flexible metal conduit         B. Electrical metallic tubing
        C. Electrical nonmetallic tubing      D. Liquidtight flexible metal conduit

_____  _____   273. A fitting such as an insulating bushing or insulating material shall be provided to protect conductors where raceways containing ungrounded conductors of at least No. _____ enter a cabinet.

        A. 8                     B. 6
        C. 4                     D. 2

_____  _____   274. A 120/240 volt, 40 ampere branch-circuit from a house to an outbuilding is direct buried underground with Type UF cable. The cable shall be at least _____ in.

        A. 6                     B. 12
        C. 18                 D. 24

_____  _____   275. A direct burial cable which is run underground and emerges on the outside wall of a building and then enters the building, shall be protected by an enclosure or raceway to:

        A. At least 3 ft. above grade
        B. At least 6 ft. above grade
        C. At least 8 ft. above grade
        D. The point where it enters the building

276. A direct burial UF cable for a 24 volt circuit is installed outside an office building for landscape lighting. This cable shall be buried at least _____ in. deep.

    A. 6                              B. 12
    C. 18                             D. 24

277. A rigid nonmetallic conduit is buried under a single family dwelling and contains a 120 volt, 30 ampere circuit for an irrigation pump for the yard of the dwelling. This conduit shall be buried at least _____ in. deep.

    A. 6                              B. 12
    C. 18                             D. 24

278. Service lateral cables which are direct buried under a driveway shall be buried at least _____ in. deep.

    A. 12                             B. 18
    C. 24                             D. 36

279. A direct buried service lateral run down a utility pole and then underground to emerge at a building, shall be protected at the pole by an enclosure or raceway to a point at least _____ ft. above finished grade.

    A. 8                              B. 10
    C. 12                             D. 15

280. Where direct buried conductors emerge from the ground and are subject to physical damage, which of the following conduits provide the protection required by the code.

    A. Flexible metallic conduit
    B. Rigid metal conduit
    C. Electrical nonmetallic tubing
    D. Schedule 40 rigid nonmetallic conduit

281. Rigid metallic conduit shall be buried in the ground a minimum of _____ in.

    A. 4                              B. 6
    C. 12                             D. 18

282. In indoor wet locations, which of the following types of raceways are not required to be mounted so that there is at least 1/4 in. space between them and the mounting surface.

    A. Armored cables                 B. Rigid metal conduits
    C. Flexible metal conduits        D. Rigid nonmetallic conduits

283. A cabinet installed in a wet location shall be mounted so there is an airspace of at least _____ in. between the cabinet and the supporting surface.

    A. 1/8                            B. 1/4
    C. 1/2                            D. 3/4

284. At each lighting outlet, at least _____ in. of free conductor shall be left for the connection of light fixtures.

    A. 4                              B. 6
    C. 8                              D. 10

285. Where installed in vertical raceways, copper conductors of size No. 250 KCMIL shall be supported every _____ ft.

A. 60                          B. 80
C. 135                         D. 180

286. Which of the following wiring methods is permitted to be installed in a plenum used for environmental air. (General rule)

A. Type AC cable
B. Type MI cable
C. Rigid nonmetallic conduit
D. Type MC cable with a nonmetallic cover

287. Where installed in an environmental air duct, liquidtight flexible metal conduit shall be limited to a maximum length of _____ ft.

A. 3                           B. 4
C. 6                           D. 8

288. Conductors over 600 volts shall not be bent to a radius less than _____ times the overall diameter for nonshielded conductors.

A. 4                           B. 6
C. 8                           D. 10

## Article 305
## Temporary wiring

289. Temporary electrical power, that may be of a class less than would be required for a permanent installation, shall be permitted for a maximum of _____ days for Christmas lighting.

A. 30                          B. 60
C. 90                          D. 120

290. Temporary electrical power and lighting installations shall be permitted during emergencies for which of the following:

A. Tests                       B. Experiments
C. Developmental work          D. All of the above

291. For temporary wiring on a construction site where the voltage does not exceed 150 volts-to-ground, which of the following is not a code violation.

A. Feeders installed using nonmetallic sheathed cable
B. Receptacles installed on branch-circuits that supply temporary lighting
C. Branch-circuits run as open conductors to provide lighting throughout the period of construction
D. Receptacles connected to the same ungrounded conductor of a multiwire circuit that supplies temporary lighting

292. Where a multiconductor cord or cable is used, a box shall not be required for splices for temporary wiring:

A. On construction sites
B. Indoors or in dry locations only
C. For Christmas decorative lighting or displays
D. Only in industrial establishments where conditions of maintenance ensure that qualified personnel are involved

_____  _____  293. Where a store is being remodeled, temporary power for hand tools used by personnel during construction is supplied from an existing receptacle outlet not affected by the remodeling, This receptacle:

    A. Shall be removed and the circuit deenergized during construction
    B. Is required to be GFCI-protected during the construction period
    C. Is permitted to be used for temporary power without GFCI-protection during construction if located indoors
    D. Is permitted to be used for temporary power as is, without GFCI protection since it is part of the permanent wiring

## Article 310
## Conductors for general wiring

_____  _____  294. The largest size solid conductor permitted to be installed in raceways is No. _____.

    A. 12                B. 10
    C. 8                 D. 6

_____  _____  295. The minimum size feeder conductors permitted to be installed in parallel is No. _____.

    A. 2                 B. 1
    C. 1/0             D. 2/0

_____  _____  296. Where conductors are run in parallel, several conditions are required. Which one of the following conditions is not one of those requirements? Paralleled conductors shall:

    A. Be run in metal raceways
    B. Have the same insulation type
    C. Have the same conductor material
    D. Be the same size in circular mill area

_____  _____  297. Conductors in sizes smaller than No. _____ shall be permitted to be run in parallel to supply control power.

    A. 8                 B. 6
    C. 4                 D. 1/0

_____  _____  298. In an existing installation, where nonlinear loads are causing an increased load on neutral conductors, under an engineer's supervision, it shall be permitted to run the neutral conductors in parallel for sizes as small as No. _____.

    A. 8                 B. 6
    C. 4                 D. 2

_____  _____  299. Which of the following conductors is permitted to be used in wet locations.

    A. RH               B. XHH
    C. THHN           D. THWN

_____  _____  300. Multiconductor flat cable No. _____ or larger shall be permitted to employ an external ridge on the grounded conductor.

    A. 8                 B. 6
    C. 4                 D. 1/0

_____  _____  301. A black conductor is permitted to be used as an equipment grounding conductor where permanently and properly identified, if it is at least size No. \_\_\_\_\_.

A. 8                     B. 6
C. 4                     D. 2

_____  _____  302. The ampacity of a conductor is the current in amperes the conductor can carry continuously under the conditions of use without exceeding its \_\_\_\_\_ rating.

A. Voltage               B. Impedance
C. Temperature           D. Circuit interrupting

_____  _____  303. An derating factor of \_\_\_\_\_ percent shall be applied for THHN copper conductors running through an ambient temperature 120°F.

A. 71                    B. 76
C. 82                    D. 87

_____  _____  304. Where multiconductor cables not installed in raceways, are bundled longer than \_\_\_\_\_ in. without maintaining spacing, the allowable ampacity of each conductor shall be derated.

A. 18                    B. 24
C. 36                    D. 48

_____  _____  305. A derating factor of \_\_\_\_\_ percent shall be applied for four current-carrying conductors pulled through a raceway.

A. 45 percent            B. 50 percent
C. 70 percent            D. 80 percent

_____  _____  306. A derating factor of \_\_\_\_\_ percent shall be applied for twenty current-carrying conductors pulled through a raceway.

A. 45                    B. 50
C. 70                    D. 80

_____  _____  307. A derating factor shall not apply to conductors in nipples having a length not exceeding \_\_\_\_\_ in.

A. 6                     B. 12
C. 18                    D. 24

_____  _____  308. Where burial depths are deeper than shown in a specific underground ampacity Table, an ampacity derating factor of \_\_\_\_\_ percent per increased ft. of depth, beyond 25 percent for all values of RHO can be utilized.

A. 2                     B. 4
C. 6                     D. 8

_____  _____  309. Where a four conductor UF cable leaves an outdoor trench and is extended up a pole in rigid metal conduit, ampacity derating shall not be required if the conduit has a maximum length of \_\_\_\_\_ ft.

A. 6                     B. 8
C. 10                    D. 12

310. What is the current-carrying capacity of twelve No. 12 THHN copper conductors pulled through 3/4 in. EMT?

    A. 12 amps            B. 15 amps
    C. 16 amps            D. 18 amps

311. What is the ampacity for eight No. 10 THHN copper conductors routed through an ambient temperature of 120°F?

    A. 22.96 amps         B. 23.44 amps
    C. 23.86 amps         D. 26.24 amps

## Article 318
## Cable trays

312. Cable tray systems shall be permitted to have mechanically _____ segments between cable tray runs.

313. Supports shall be provided to prevent _____ on cables where they enter raceways.

314. Steel cable tray systems are permitted to be used as _____ grounding conductors provided certain requirements are complied with.

315. In industrial establishments where only qualified persons will service the installation, single conductors shall be permitted to be installed in cable trays but shall be at least size No. _____.

    A. 2            B. 1
    C. 1/0         D. 2/0

316. Cable trays, as covered in the code are:

    A. Raceways
    B. Raceway and cable support systems
    C. Limited to the support of cables only
    D. Limited to industrial establishments only

317. In industrial establishments, where only qualified persons will service the installation, conduits terminating at a cable tray with a listed clamp or adapter shall:

    A. Be supported within at least 1 ft. from the cable tray
    B. Be supported within at least 3 ft. from the cable tray
    C. Be supported within at least 5 ft. from the cable tray
    D. Not require any nearby support, such as within 3 ft.

318. The ampacities for No. 1/0 and larger single conductor cables in uncovered cable trays shall not exceed _____ percent of the allowable ampacities in Tables 310-69 and 310-70.

    A. 65           B. 70
    C. 75          D. 90

319. Where cable trays are covered for more than 6 ft. with solid unventilated covers, the ampacities for No. 1/0 and larger single conductor cables shall not exceed _____ percent of the allowable ampacities in Tables 310-69 and 310-70.

A. 65          B. 70
C. 75          D. 90

## Article 320
## Open wiring on insulators

320. Open wiring on insulators shall be installed within _____ in. from a tap or splice.

A. 3          B. 6
C. 12          D. 18

321. Open wiring on insulators shall be installed within _____ in. of a dead-end connection to a lampholder or receptacle.

A. 6          B. 12
C. 18          D. 24

322. Open wiring on insulators shall be installed at intervals not exceeding _____ ft.

A. 3          B. 3 1/2
C. 4 1/2          D. 6

323. Open conductors shall be separated at least _____ in. from metal raceways, piping, or other conducting material.

A. 1          B. 2
C. 3          D. 6

324. Open conductors within _____ ft. from the floor shall be considered exposed to physical damage.

A. 3          B. 6
C. 7          D. 10

## Article 324
## Concealed knob-and-tube wiring

325. Concealed knob-and-tube wiring shall have a clearance of not less than _____ in. between conductors.

A. 1          B. 2
C. 3          D. 6

326. Concealed knob-and-tube wiring shall have a clearance of not less than _____ in. between the conductor and the surface over which it passes.

A. 1          B. 2
C. 3          D. 6

327. Concealed knob-and-tube wiring passing through wood cross members shall be protected by noncombustible, nonabsorbent, insulating tubes extending not less than _____ in. beyond the wood member.

   A. 1 in.                        B. 3 in.
   C. 6 in.                        D. 12 in.

328. Concealed knob-and-tube wiring run through bored holes in joists shall be above the floor at a height of not less than _____ ft.

   A. 6                            B. 7
   C. 8                            D. 10

## Article 330
## Mineral-insulated, metal-sheathed cable

329. Type MI cable shall be installed and supported so that the nearest outside surface of the cable or raceway is not less than _____ in. from the nearest edge of the framing member.

   A. 1 1/8                        B. 1 1/4
   C. 1 1/2                        D. 1 3/4

330. Where Type MI cable is installed in notches of wood, the cable shall be protected by a steel plate at least _____ in. thickness.

   A. 1/16                         B. 1/8
   C. 1/4                          D. 1/2

331. Type MI cable shall be securely supported at intervals not exceeding _____ ft.

   A. 3                            B. 4
   C. 6                            D. 10

332. The radius of the inner edge of any bend for Type MI cable shall not be less than _____ times the diameter of the metallic sheath for cable not more than 3/4 in. in external diameter.

   A. 3                            B. 5
   C. 8                            D. 10

## Article 331
## Electrical Nonmetallic Tubing

333. Which of the following raceways is defined by the code as a pliable raceway or one that can be bent by hand with a reasonable force, but without other assistance.

   A. Flexible metal conduit       B. Rigid nonmetallic conduit
   C. Electrical metallic conduit  D. Electrical nonmetallic conduit

334. Electrical nonmetallic tubing shall be permitted in a four story building concealed in walls that have a thermal barrier of material that has at least a _____ minute finish rating.

   A. 15                           B. 30
   C. 45                           D. 60

335. The maximum size electrical nonmetallic tubing allowed to be used is _____ in.

    A. 1                   B. 2
    C. 3                   D. 4

336. Electrical nonmetallic tubing shall not be more than _____ degrees of bends between pull points, conduit bodies, and boxes.

    A. 120              B. 250
    C. 360              D. 420

337. Electrical nonmetallic tubing shall be securely fastened-in-place within _____ ft. of every outlet box.

    A. 1                   B. 2
    C. 3                   D. 5

## Article 333
## Armored cable

338. Which of the following wiring methods requires an insulating bushing to be installed that is visible for inspection where connected to a box or cabinet.

    A. AC cable            B. MC cable
    C. Flexible metal conduit       D. Electrical metallic tubing

339. Type AC cable shall be secured at intervals not exceeding _____ ft.

    A. 3                   B. 4 1/2
    C. 6                   D. 10

340. Exposed runs of AC cable shall closely follow the building surface except for a maximum length of _____ ft. to serve lighting fixtures in accessible ceilings.

    A. 3                   B. 4
    C. 6                   D. 8

341 Where AC cable is run across the face of rafters in an accessible attic that is not accessible by a permanent ladder or stairs, the cable shall be protected within _____ ft. of the nearest edge of the attic entrance.

    A. 1 1/2           B. 3
    C. 4 1/4           D. 6

342. Type AC cable installed in thermal insulation shall have conductors rated at _____ °C.

    A. 60                B. 75
    C. 80               D. 90

## Article 334
## Metal-clad cable

343. Type MC cable shall be supported and secured at maximum intervals of _____ ft.

    A. 3                   B. 4 1/2
    C. 5                   D. 6

344. MC cable shall be supported within 12 in. of boxes where it contains a maximum of _____ conductors sized a maximum of No. _____.

A. 3, 12                          B. 3, 10
C. 4, 12                          D. 4, 10

345. Type MC cable shall be installed and supported so that the nearest outside surface of the cable or raceway is not less than _____ in. from the nearest edge of the framing member.

A. 1 1/8                          B. 1 1/4
C. 1 1/2                          D. 1 3/4

346. Where Type MC cable is installed in notches of wood, the cable shall be protected by a steel plate at least _____ in. thickness.

A. 1/16                          B. 1/8
C. 1/4                           D. 1/2

347. Where MC cable is run across the face of rafters in an accessible attic that is not accessible by a permanent ladder or stairs, the cable shall be protected within _____ ft. of the nearest edge of the attic entrance.

A. 1 1/2                          B. 3
C. 4 1/4                          D. 6

## Article 336
## Nonmetallic sheathed cable

348. Where NM cable is installed exposed and passes through a floor, the cable shall be protected by a conduit extending at least _____ in. above the floor.

A. 6                             B. 12
C. 18                            D. 24

349. Where NM cable is run at angles with floor joists in an unfinished basement, the minimum size three conductor cable permitted to be secured to the lower edge of the joists is No. _____.

A. 10                            B. 8
C. 6                             D. 4

350. Where NM cable is run across the face of the rafters in an attic accessible by a permanent pull-down ladder, the cable shall be protected by guard strips within _____ ft. of the attic entrance.

A. 3                             B. 6
C. 7                             D. 8

351. Type NM cable shall be installed and supported so that the nearest outside surface of the cable or raceway is not less than _____ in. from the nearest edge of the framing member.

A. 1 1/8                          B. 1 1/4
C. 1 1/2                          D. 1 3/4

352. Where Type NM cable is installed in notches of wood, the cable shall be protected by a steel plate at least _____ in. thickness.

A. 1/16                    B. 1/8
C. 1/4                     D. 1/2

353. Type NM cable shall be secured in place at intervals not exceeding _____ ft.

A. 3                       B. 4 1/2
C. 6                       D. 10

354. Where type NM cable is run into a panelboard, it shall be secured in place within at least _____ in. of the panelboard.

A. 6                       B. 12
C. 36                      D. 54

355. The insulation of the conductors for Type NM cable shall be rated at _____ degrees C, and the allowable ampacity of NM cable shall be that of _____ degrees C conductors.

A. 60, 90                  B. 75, 75
C. 90, 75                  D. 90, 60

## Article 338 and 339
## Service-entrance and underground feeder cable

356. Which of the following is not a correct code provision for a Type SE service-entrance cable which consists of only three conductors. (General rule)

A. All three conductors shall be insulated where the cable is used inside a building
B. One conductor is permitted to be bare only if the cable is used to supply new installations of ranges or clothes dryers and originates in the service equipment
C. One conductor is permitted to be bare where the cable is used as a feeder to supply only other buildings on the same premises
D. If the cable is used inside a building, one of the three conductors is permitted to be bare only if it is used as an equipment grounding conductor.

357. Multiconductor Type UF cable shall be permitted for all of the following uses, except:

A. In corrosive locations          B. Installed in cable trays
C. In interior wet locations       D. As service-entrance cables

358. The ampacity of UF cable shall be that of _____ °C conductors.

A. 60                      B. 75
C. 85                      D. 90

## Article 345
## Intermediate metal conduit

359. The maximum size intermediate metal conduit shall not be larger than _____ in.

A. 2                       B. 3
C. 4                       D. 6

360. Where intermediate metal conduit is threaded in the field, a cutting die with a _____ in. taper per foot shall be used.

    A. 3/8               B. 1/2
    C. 3/4               D. 1

361. Intermediate metal conduit shall be supported at least every _____ ft. (General rule)

    A. 3                B. 5
    C. 10              D. 20

362. Intermediate metal conduit shall be securely fastened within _____ ft. of each outlet box.

    A. 1                B. 3
    C. 5               D. 6

363. Where intermediate metal conduit is installed as a vertical riser from industrial machinery and made up with threaded couplings, supports shall be permitted to be a maximum of every _____ ft. if supported at the top and bottom of the riser.

    A. 5                B. 10
    C. 15              D. 20

## Article 346
## Rigid metal conduit

364. The minimum size rigid metal conduit shall not be smaller than _____ in.

365. Where rigid metal conduit is threaded in the field, a standard conduit cutting die with a _____ in. taper per ft. shall be used.

366. Rigid metal conduit (1 1/2 in.) shall be supported at least every _____ ft. provided the conduit is made up with threaded couplings.

367. The maximum size rigid metal conduit shall not be larger than _____ in.

    A. 2                B. 3
    C. 4               D. 6

368. Rigid metal conduit (3/4 in.) shall be supported at least every _____ ft.

    A. 3                B. 5
    C. 6               D. 10

369. Rigid metal conduit shall be securely fastened within _____ ft. of each outlet box.

    A. 1                B. 3
    C. 6               D. 10

370. Where approved, rigid metal conduit installed as a through-the-roof mast, shall not be required to be securely fastened within _____ ft. of the service head.

    A. 1 1/2            B. 3
    C. 4 1/2           D. 5

## Article 347
## Rigid nonmetallic conduit

371. Rigid nonmetallic conduit shall not be permitted:

A. In cinder fill
B. For the support of fixtures
C. To be concealed in floors or ceilings
D. In locations subject to severe corrosive influences

372. Rigid nonmetallic conduit shall be securely fastened within _____ ft. of each box.

A. 3                      B. 5
C. 6                      D. 7

373. Where 1 1/4 in. rigid nonmetallic conduit is run horizontally along a wall, it shall be supported at least every _____ ft.

A. 3                      B. 5
C. 6                      D. 7

374. Expansion fittings shall be installed on runs of rigid nonmetallic conduit where the length change due to thermal expansion and contraction is expected to be at least _____ in.

A. 1/4                    B. 1/2
C. 3/4                    D. 1

## Article 348
## Electrical metallic tubing

375. The maximum size electrical metallic tubing shall not be larger than _____ in.

A. 3                      B. 4
C. 5                      D. 6

376. Electrical metallic tubing shall not have more than _____ degrees bends between pull points, conduit bodies, and boxes.

A. 120                   B. 250
C. 360                   D. 420

377. Electrical metallic tubing shall be securely fastened in place at least every _____ ft.

A. 3                      B. 5
C. 6                      D. 10

378. Electrical metallic tubing shall be securely fastened in place within _____ ft. each outlet box.

A. 3                      B. 5
C. 6                      D. 10

379. Electrical metallic tubing installed where structural members are spaced greater than 3 ft. apart, shall be permitted to be supported a maximum of _____ ft. to and from boxes and cabinets, if unbroken lengths are used.

A. 4                                    B. 4 1/2
C. 5                                    D. 6

## Article 350
## Flexible metal conduit

380. The maximum size flexible metal conduit shall not be larger than _____ in.

A. 1                                    B. 2
C. 3                                    D. 4

381. Listed flexible metal conduit is permitted to be installed a grounding means if the total length in any ground return path is _____ ft. or less.

A. 3                                    B. 5
C. 6                                    D. 10

382. Flexible metal conduit shall be securely fastened in place by an approved means within _____ in. of each box.

A. 6                                    B. 12
C. 18                                   D. 24

383. Flexible metal conduit shall be supported and secured at intervals not exceeding _____ ft.

A. 4                                    B. 4 1/2
C. 5                                    D. 6

384. Flexible metal conduit is not required to be supported for lengths not exceeding _____ ft. at terminals where flexibility is required.

A. 3                                    B. 4
C. 5                                    D. 6

## Article 351
## Liquidtight flexible metal conduit and liquidtight
## flexible nonmetallic conduit

385. The minimum size liquidtight flexible metal conduit shall not be smaller than _____ in. (General rule)

A. 1/2                                  B. 3/4
C. 1                                    D. 1 1/4

386. Liquidtight flexible metal conduit shall be securely fastened in place by an approved means within _____ in. of each box.

A. 6                                    B. 12
C. 18                                   D. 24

_____ _____ 387. A 6 foot run of 1 1/4 in. liquidtight flexible metal conduit is permitted to be used as a grounding means where the fittings are listed for grounding, if the branch-circuit is rated a maximum of _____ amperes.

      A. 20                     B. 40
      C. 50                     D. 60

_____ _____ 388. Liquidtight flexible nonmetallic conduit shall be securely fastened at intervals not greater than _____ ft.

      A. 3                     B. 4 1/2
      C. 5                     D. 6

_____ _____ 389. Liquidtight flexible nonmetallic conduit shall not be required to be "securely fastened" where installed horizontally through openings in framing members having a maximum spacing of _____ inches.

      A. 12                     B. 24
      C. 36                     D. 48

## Article 352
## Surface metal raceways and surface nonmetallic raceways

_____ _____ 390. For conductors installed in surface metal raceways, ampacity derating factors do not apply where certain conditions are met. Which one of the following is not one of those conditions?

      A. The maximum number of conductors does not exceed 30
      B. The maximum cross-sectional area of the raceway is 4 square inches
      C. The surface metal raceway shall not pass transversely through walls, partitions or floors
      D. The sum of the conductors cross-sectional areas does not exceed 20 percent of the cross-sectional area of the raceway

_____ _____ 391. Splices and taps shall not fill a surface metal raceway to more than _____ percent of its area at that point.

      A. 50                     B. 65
      C. 75                     D. 80

_____ _____ 392. An _____ grounding conductor shall be connected to surface metal raceway enclosures providing a transition from other wiring methods.

      A. Equipment              B. Grounded
      C. Electrode              D. Bonding

_____ _____ 393. Surface mount strut-type channel raceway shall be secured to the mounting surface at intervals not exceeding _____ ft.

      A. 3                     B. 5
      C. 6                     D. 10

_____ _____ 394. Strut-type channel raceways shall be permitted to be suspension mounted in air at intervals not to exceed _____ ft.

      A. 5                     B. 10
      C. 15                     D. 20

## Article 364
## Busways

395. Lighting busway shall not be installed less than _____ ft. above the floor.

    A. 7                    B. 8
    C. 10                  D. 12

396. Busways shall be supported at maximum intervals not exceeding _____ ft.

    A. 3                    B. 5
    C. 6                  D. 10

397. Busways are permitted to pass vertically through floors if they are totally enclosed where passing through the floor and for a distance of at least _____ ft. above the floor.

    A. 3                    B. 5
    C. 6                  D. 8

398. A cable assembly is permitted to be used as a branch from a busway where the length of the cable from the busway plug-in device to the tension take-up support device is a maximum of _____ ft.

    A. 1 1/2              B. 3
    C. 5                  D. 6

399. In industrial establishments, overcurrent protection shall not be required at the point where a busway is reduced in ampacity, if certain conditions are met. Which of the following is not one of those conditions?

    A. The smaller busway shall be a maximum of 50 ft. in length
    B. The smaller busway shall not be in contact with any combustible material
    C. The rating of the overcurrent device next back on the line shall not exceed 800 amperes
    D. The ampacity of the smaller busway shall be at least 1/3 the rating of the overcurrent device next back on the line

## Article 370
## Outlet, device, pull and junction boxes, conduit bodies and fittings

400. Metal plugs used with nonmetallic boxes shall be recessed at least 1/8 in. from the outer surface.

    A. True                    B. False

401. In straight pulls for junction boxes, the length of the box shall not be less than six times the trade diameter of the largest raceway.

    A. True                    B. False

402. Where permanent barriers are installed in a junction box, each section shall be considered as a separate box.

    A. True                    B. False

_____  _____  403. Conductors passing through the box unbroken and not pulled into a loop or spliced together with scotchlocks are counted as _____ conductor each.

_____  _____  404. Equipment grounding conductors passing through or spliced together in the box counts as _____ conductor each.

_____  _____  405. A receptacle or switch that is mounted on a strap or yoke is counted as _____ conductors.

_____  _____  406. Boxes that contain fixture studs or hickeys shall have _____ conductor added for each fitting.

_____  _____  407. Conduit bodies enclosing No. _____ or smaller conductors shall have a cross-sectional area not less than twice the cross-sectional area of the largest conduit to which it is attached.

_____  _____  408. Spliced conductors within a box count as _____ each.

A. One                    B. Two
C. Three                  D. Four

_____  _____  409. An isolated equipment grounding conductor run with an equipment grounding conductor shall count as _____ conductor.

A. Zero                   B. One
C. Two                    D. Three

_____  _____  410. Boxes with one or more cable clamps that are installed to support cables shall have _____ conductor added toward the fill.

A. One                    B. Two
C. Three                  D. Four

_____  _____  411. Where nonmetallic sheathed cable is installed in a 2 1/4 in. x 4 in. wall mounted nonmetallic box, securing the cable to the box is not required if the sheath extends inside the box at least 1/4 in. and is stapled a maximum of _____ in. from the box.

A. 6                      B. 8
C. 10                     D. 12

_____  _____  412. Boxes mounted in walls of noncombustible material, shall be installed so that the front edge of the box will be set back a maximum of ____ in.

A. 1/4                    B. 3/8
C. 1/2                    D. 3/4

_____  _____  413. The front edge of a metal switch box that is mounted in a wall covered with wood paneling, shall be _____ from the surface of the wall.

A. Flush with or project out
B. Permitted to be set back a maximum of 1/4 in.
C. Permitted to be set back a maximum of 3/8 in.
D. Permitted to be set back a maximum of 1/2 in.

414. Plasterboard that is broken around the edges of a switch box shall be repaired so there will be no gaps or open spaces greater than _____ in. at the edge of the box.

     A. 1/16                B. 1/8
     C. 1/4                D. 3/8

415. A 100 cu. in. box that does not contain devices or support fixtures, shall be permitted to be supported only by conduit threaded wrenchtight into hubs on the box, if the conduit is supported within _____ (in. or ft.) of the box and enters the box on at least two side(s) of the box.

     A. 6 in.               B. 1 ft.
     C. 2 ft.               D. 3 ft.

416. Boxes intended to enclose flush devices shall have an internal depth of not less than _____ in.

     A. 3/4                B. 1/8
     C. 15/16             D. 3/8

417. What size device box is required for the following:

     • 2 - # 12 hots
     • 2 - # 12 neutrals
     • 1 duplex receptacle
     • 1 pigtail
     • 1 bonding jumper

     A. 3" x 2" x 2 "             B. 3" x 2" x 2 1/4"
     C. 3" x 2" x 2 1/2"        D. 3" x 2" x 2 3/4"

418. What is the minimum length of a junction box for an angle pull that has one run of 3 in. raceways?

     A. 12 in. x 12 in.         B. 18 in. x 18 in.
     C. 24 in. x 24 in.         D. 30 in. x 30 in.

## Article 373
## Cabinets, cutout boxes, and meter socket enclosures

419. Cabinets installed in noncombustible material such as walls of concrete, cabinets shall be so installed that the front edge of the cabinet will not set back of the finished surface more than _____ in.

     A. 1/8                B. 1/4
     C. 1/2                D. 3/4

420. In a cabinet containing overcurrent devices, the conductors shall fill a minimum of _____ percent of the wiring space.

     A. 20                 B. 40
     C. 60                 D. 75

421. Other than at points of support, there shall be an airspace of at least _____ in. between the base of the device and the wall of any metal cabinet in which the device is mounted.

     A. 1/16               B. 1/8
     C. 1/4                D. 1/2

422. Where the voltage is 277 volts-to-ground, the airspace clearance between any metal part of a cabinet and the nearest exposed current-carrying part of an electrical device in the cabinet shall be _____ inch.

A. 1              B. 3
C. 4              D. 6

## Article 374
## Auxiliary gutters

423. Where auxiliary gutters are used at service equipment, they shall be permitted to extend a maximum of _____ feet from the equipment they supplement.

A. 10             B. 20
C. 30             D. 40

424. Nonmetallic auxiliary gutters shall be supported at intervals of _____ feet.

A. 3              B. 5
C. 8              D. 10

425. Sheet metal auxiliary gutters shall not contain more than _____ current-carrying conductors at any cross-section.

A. 10             B. 20
C. 30             D. 50

426. The sum of cross-sectional areas of all contained conductors at any cross-section of the nonmetallic auxiliary gutter shall not exceed _____ percent of the interior cross-section area of the nonmetallic auxiliary gutter.

A. 10             B. 20
C. 30             D. 40

## Article 380
## Switches

427. Switches shall be installed so that the center of the grip of the operating handle, when in its highest position, will not be more than _____ above the floor.

A. 6 feet, 3 inches       B. 6 feet, 4 inches
C. 6 feet, 6 inches       D. 6 feet, 7 inches

428. Multiple switches installed in one enclosure without barriers between switches, shall be arranged so that the voltage between adjacent switches does not exceed _____ volts.

A. 120            B. 150
C. 240            D. 300

429. A knife switch rated 800 amperes and 480 volts, shall:

A. Be used to interrupt inductive loads only
B. Be used to interrupt noninductive loads only
C. Have contacts of a renewable or quick-break type
D. Be used as an isolating switch only and not opened under load

430. AC general use snap switches can supply motor loads not exceeding _____ percent of the ampere rating of the switch at its rated voltage.

A. 50                    B. 75
C. 80                    D. 90

431. AC-DC general use snap switches can supply inductive loads not exceeding _____ percent of the ampere rating of the switch at the applied voltage.

A. 50                    B. 75
C. 80                    D. 90

## Article 384
## Switchboard and panelboards

432. No piping, ducts, or equipment foreign to the electrical installation shall be located in the dedicated space. (General rule)

A. True                  B. False

433. Suitable protection shall be provided for switchboards where installed over a combustible floor.

A. True                  B. False

434. The _____ phase shall be that phase having the higher voltage-to-ground on three-phase, four-wire, delta-connected systems.

435. Not more than _____ overcurrent devices of a lighting and appliance branch-circuit panelboard shall be installed in any one cabinet.

436. Each lighting and appliance branch-circuit panelboard shall be individually protected on the supply side by not more than _____ main circuit breakers.

437. The space equal to the width and depth of a panelboard and extending from the floor to a height of _____ ft. above the panelboard or to the structural ceiling, whichever is lower, shall be dedicated to the electrical installation.

A. 6                     B. 10
C. 25                    D. 50

438. For other than a totally enclosed switchboard, a space not less than _____ ft. shall be provided between the top of the switchboard and any combustible ceiling.

A. 1                     B. 2
C. 3                     D. 6

439. Where conduits enter a floor standing panelboard at the bottom, the conduits including their fittings, shall rise a maximum of _____ inches above the bottom of the enclosure.

A. 2                     B. 3
C. 4                     D. 6

440. Where conductors are run under the floor and enter a switchboard at the bottom, the wiring space between the bottom of the switchboard and the busbars shall be at least _____ inches if the busbars are bare.

A. 6                              B. 8
C. 10                             D. 12

441. In an industrial plant, a panelboard designed for 24 overcurrent devices contains seven three-pole circuit breakers which feed three-phase motors and three single-pole, 20 ampere circuit breakers which feed receptacles. This panelboard is:

A. Being used as a power panel
B. Being used as a split-bus panelboard
C. Being used as a lighting and appliance branch-circuit panelboard
D. In violation of the code because receptacle circuits are not permitted in a three-phase panelboard supplying motors

442. A power panelboard is one having a maximum of _____ percent of its overcurrent devices rated 30 amperes or less, for which neutral connections are provided.

A. 10                             B. 20
C. 30                             D. 50

443. A lighting and appliance branch-circuit panelboard in a store contains 10 two-pole breakers and 10 single-pole breakers. What is the maximum number of additional single-pole circuit breakers permitted to be installed in this panelboard?

A. 4                              B. 10
C. 12                             D. 22

444. The total load on any overcurrent device located in a panelboard shall not exceed_____ percent of it's rating where the load is continuous operation.

A. 50                             B. 70
C. 75                             D. 80

## Article 400
## Flexible cords and cables

445. An SO cord containing an equipment grounding conductor and two current-carrying conductors of size No. 12, has an allowable ampacity of _____ amperes.

A. 15                             B. 18
C. 20                             D. 25

446. Flexible cords shall be permitted indoors where:

A. Concealed behind a wall
B. Run through a wall to serve nonstationary equipment
C. Used for a feeder or branch-circuit for temporary wiring
D. Run along the surface of a wall and secured at the required intervals

447. A three conductor flexible cord used in a light fixture has one conductor marked with ridges or groves to identify it as the _____ conductor.

A. Grounded                       B. Grounding
C. Ungrounded                     D. Switched

448. Multiconductor portable cables used to connect mobile equipment over 600 volts shall be No. _____ copper or larger and shall employ flexible stranding.

A. 8                          B. 6
C. 4                          D. 2

## Article 402
## Fixture wires

449. The allowable ampacity of No. 14 fixture wires is _____ amperes.

A. 14                         B. 17
C. 20                         D. 23

450. The allowable ampacity of No. 12 fixture wires is _____ amperes.

A. 17                         B. 20
C. 23                         D. 28

451. The minimum size fixture wires shall not be smaller than No. _____.

A. 18                         B. 16
C. 14                         D. 12

## Article 410
## Lighting fixtures, lampholders, lamps, and receptacles

452. A recessed fluorescent light fixture is permitted to be installed in a clothes closet on the wall above the door where the clearance between the fixture and the nearest point of storage space is at least 12 in.

A. True                       B. False

453. A fixture that weighs more than 6 lbs. or exceeds 16 in. in any dimension shall not be supported by the screw shell of a lampholder.

A. True                       B. False

454. Fixtures are allowed to be used as a raceway for circuit conductors. (General rule)

A. True                       B. False

455. Recessed portions of lighting fixture enclosures shall be spaced at least 1/2 in. from combustible materials.

A. True                       B. False

456. Lighting track installed over a bathtub shall have a clearance of 3 ft. horizontally and _____ ft. vertically.

457. A recessed incandescent light fixture is permitted to be installed in a clothes closet on the wall above the door where the clearance between the fixture and the nearest point of storage space is at least _____ in.

458. Lighting fixtures supported by metal poles are required to have an accessible handhole not less than _____ in. x _____ in.

_____  _____    459. Locations, where light fixtures are installed outdoors under a canopy, they are considered _____ locations.

A. Dry                          B. Wet
C. Damp                         D. Outdoor

_____  _____    460. Where a bathroom ceiling is 9 1/2 feet high from the floor and 8 feet above the rim of the bathtub, which of the following fixtures is not permitted on the ceiling, 30 inches horizontally from the rim of the bathtub?

A. A recessed fluorescent fixture
B. A lighting track mounted fixture
C. A surface mounted fluorescent fixture
D. A surface mounted incandescent fixture

_____  _____    461. Metal poles which support light fixtures where supply conductors are installed within the pole, shall not require a handhole for access to conductors if the pole has a hinged base and is a maximum of _____ ft. in height.

A. 10                           B. 15
C. 20                           D. 25

_____  _____    462. A surface mounted incandescent light fixture is permitted to be installed in a clothes closet on the wall above the door where the clearance between the fixture and the nearest point of storage space is at least _____ in.

A. 6                            B. 10
C. 12                           D. 18

_____  _____    463. Where a light fixture weighs a maximum of _____ pounds, an outlet box is permitted to be the only support for the fixture if the outlet box meets code provisions for boxes.

A. 20                           B. 30
C. 40                           D. 50

_____  _____    464. Receptacles intended for the reduction of electrical noise shall be identified by:

A. The receptacle being an orange and blue color
B. An orange triangle on the face of the receptacle
C. A green triangle on the face of the receptacle
D. A wording on the faceplate indicating isolated ground receptacle

_____  _____    465. Thermal insulation shall not be installed within _____ in. of the recessed fixture enclosure, wiring compartment, or ballast.

A. 1                            B. 2
C. 3                            D. 6

_____  _____    466. An electric-discharge lighting system with equipment having exposed live parts and an open-circuit voltage exceeding _____ volts shall not be installed in a dwelling occupancy.

A. 120                          B. 240
C. 300                          D. 600

467. Where a surface-mounted light fixture with a ballast is installed on combustible low-density cellulose fiberboard, it shall be spaced at least _____ in. from the fiberboard.

A. 1/2                          B. 1
C. 1 1/2                        D. 3

## Article 411
## Lighting systems operating at 30 volts or less

468. Lighting systems operating at 30 volts or less shall not be installed within _____ ft. of pools.

A. 5                            B. 10
C. 15                           D. 20

469. Bare conductors for lighting systems operating at 30 volts or less shall not be installed less than _____ ft. above the finished floor.

A. 6                            B. 6 1/2
C. 7                            D. 8

470. Lighting systems operating at 30 volts or less shall be supplied from a maximum _____ ampere circuit.

A. 15                           B. 20
C. 25                           D. 30

## Article 422
## Appliances

471. A kitchen waste disposer is permitted to be connected with a flexible cord under certain conditions. Which of the following is not one of those conditions.

A. The receptacle shall be accessible
B. It is permitted only in dwelling units
C. The cord shall be at least 18 in. long
D. The rating of the disposer shall not exceed 80 percent of the branch-circuit rating

472. Built-in dishwashers shall be permitted to be cord-and-plug connected by a flexible cord with a length of _____ ft. to _____ ft.

A. 2 ; 3                        B. 3 ; 4
C. 4 ; 5                        D. 5 ; 6

473. Screw shell lampholders shall not be used with infrared lamps over _____ watts rating.

A. 150                          B. 175
C. 225                          D. 300

474. A plug and receptacle combination in the supply line to a counter-mounted cooking unit shall:

A. Not be installed as the disconnecting means
B. Be permitted as the disconnecting means if it is accessible
C. Be permitted as the disconnecting means if it is readily accessible
D. Be permitted as the disconnecting means if the cooking unit has a unit switch with marked "off" position

475. Ceiling fans are permitted to be supported by outlet boxes if the maximum weight of the ceiling fan is _____ pounds.

A. 35                                          B. 40
C. 45                                          D. 50

476. The branch-circuit overcurrent device shall be permitted to serve as the disconnecting means for a permanently connected appliance not rated over _____ volt-amperes.

A. 180                                         B. 200
C. 300                                         D. 480

477. A circuit breaker serving as the disconnecting means for a permanently connected motor driven appliance of more than _____ horsepower, shall be located within sight from the motor controller.

A. 1/8                                         B. 1/4
C. 1/2                                         D. 3/4

478. An electric heating appliance which has resistance-type heating elements rated at more than 48 amperes shall have heating elements subdivided with each subdivided load protected at a maximum of _____ amperes.

A. 50                                          B. 60
C. 75                                          D. 90

## Article 424
## Fixed electric space heating equipment

479. Wiring located above heated ceilings shall be spaced not less than _____ in. above the heated ceiling.

A. 1                                           B. 2
C. 3                                           D. 4

480. Heating elements shall be separated at least _____ in. from the edge of outlet boxes and junction boxes that are to be used for mounting surface lighting fixtures.

A. 4                                           B. 6
C. 8                                           D. 10

## Article 426
## Fixed outdoor electric deicing and
## snow-melting equipment

481. The ampacity of branch-circuit conductors supplying fixed outdoor electric deicing and snow-melting equipment shall not be less than _____ percent of the total load of the heaters.

A. 100                                         B. 115
C. 125                                         D. 150

482. Embedded snow-melting cables shall be installed at least _____ in. from the top surface.

A. 1                                           B. 1 1/2
C. 2                                           D. 3 1/2

483. For fixed outdoor deicing equipment, the disconnecting means shall be permitted to be all of the following, except:

    A. A remote temperature controller
    B. The branch-circuit breaker where readily accessible
    C. A factory-installed attachment plug rated 20 amperes and 150 volts-to-ground
    D. A temperature controlled switching device with an "off" position with a lockout provided

**Article 430**
**Motors, motor circuits, and controllers**

484. The full-load current in amps for three-phase motors shall be selected from Table 430-148.

    A. True                    B. False

485. Conductors for a motor used for periodic duty are required to be sized with a current-carrying capacity of 125 percent of the motors full-load current.

    A. True                    B. False

486. Wound-rotor motors are three-phase motors that are installed with two sets of leads.

    A. True                    B. False

487. The motor branch-circuit overcurrent device is not required to be capable of carrying the starting current of the motor.

    A. True                    B. False

488. Branch-circuit conductors supplying a single motor shall have an ampacity not less than _____ percent of the motor's full-load current rating.

489. The selection of conductors for wye start and delta run motors between the controller and motor must be based on _____ percent of the motors full-load current times 125 percent for continuous use.

490. The disconnecting means for power conversion equipment shall not be less than _____ percent of the input current rating of the conversion unit.

491. The full-load current rating of the largest motor must be multiplied by _____ percent to select the size of conductors for a feeder supplying a group of two or more motors.

492. The motor branch-circuit overcurrent device shall be capable of carrying the _____ current of the motor.

493. For general motor applications, (other than for torque motors and AC adjustable voltage motors) where the current rating of a motor is used to determine the ampacity of conductors, which of the following values shall be used. (General rule)

    A. The current rating marked on the nameplate of the motor
    B. The current values given in the Tables at the end of Article 430
    C. 125 percent of the rating of the overcurrent device
    D. 125 percent of the value of the overload protection required

494. Generally, separate motor overload protection for motors shall be based on the:

    A. Motor nameplate current rating
    B. Size of the conductors supplying the motor
    C. Rating of the branch-circuit overcurrent device
    D. Values given in the Tables at the end of Article 430

495. For torque motors, the locked-rotor current shall be used to determine all of the following, except the ampere rating of the:

    A. Overload protection
    B. Disconnecting means
    C. Ground-fault protection
    D. Branch-circuit conductors

496. The code does not specify the wire bending space within an enclosure for motor controllers where the maximum size wire used is No. _____.

    A. 12                 B. 10
    C. 8                  D. 6

497. Where an automatically started motor has a long accelerating time to arrive at normal running speed, motor overload protection is permitted to be shunted during the starting period if several conditions are met. Which of the following is not one of those conditions?

    A. Shunting will automatically be prevented in the event the motor fails to start
    B. If normal motor running condition is not reached, means shall be provided for shut down and manual restarting
    C. The time period of overload protection shunting shall be less than the locked rotor time rating of the protected motor
    D. Inverse time fuses or circuit breakers rated at a maximum of 400 percent of the motor full-load current shall be operative during the starting period of the motor

498. A motor that is used for short-time duty is considered as being protected against overcurrent by the:

    A. Overload relay
    B. Branch-circuit overcurrent device
    C. Thermal protector integral with the motor
    D. Fuses that are used for overload protection

499. A continuous duty motor is permitted to be protected solely by the branch-circuit protective device if the motor meets certain conditions. Which of the following is not one of those conditions? The motor shall be:

    A. Automatically started.
    B. Rated a maximum of 1 horsepower
    C. Within sight of the controller location
    D. Portable and not permanently installed

500. A motor _____ is where the motor operates in excess of its normal full-load current rating for a sufficient length of time so as to cause dangerous overheating.

    A. Overload             B. Short-circuit
    C. Ground-fault         D. Shunt-circuit

501. Code letters shall be marked on the nameplate and such letters are used for designing locked-rotor current.

    A. True                B. False

502. Time-delay fuses which are sized at 125 percent or less of the motor's FLC rating can provide overload protection for the motor.

    A. True                B. False

503. The maximum percentage that can be applied for a time-delay fuse is 400 percent.

    A. True                B. False

504. The full-load current ratings of the remaining motors are added to the rating of the largest overcurrent protection device when sizing for two or more motors.

    A. True                B. False

505. When a motor won't start and run, a nontime-delay fuse not exceeding 600 amperes in rating shall be permitted to be increased up to _____ percent of the full-load current.

506. When a motor won't start and run, an inverse-time circuit breaker protecting a motor greater than 100 amps shall be permitted to be increased up to _____ percent of the full-load current.

507. Code letters are installed on motors by manufacturers for calculating the _____ in amps based upon the kVA per horsepower which is selected from the motor's code letter.

508. The size of branch-circuit conductors for a three-phase motor shall be based on the:

    A. Motor nameplate current rating
    B. Rating of the overload protective devices
    C. Current rating of the motor given in Table 430-150
    D. Maximum permitted ampere rating or setting of the branch-circuit protective device

509. The maximum size or rating of a branch-circuit protective device for a motor circuit is determined by the:

    A. Starting current of the motor
    B. Rating of the overload protection devices
    C. Full-load current of the motor in amperes
    D. Size of the motor branch-circuit conductors

510. Which of the following statements is true regarding motor circuits?

    A. Motor controllers are intended to open short circuits and ground faults
    B. The motor overload protective device is intended to open short-circuits and ground-faults.
    C. Branch-circuit conductors shall be sized according to the rating of the branch-circuit protective device
    D. The branch-circuit protective device shall protect the conductors, motor and motor control apparatus from overcurrent due to short-circuits or ground-faults

511. An attachment plug and receptacle shall be permitted as the controller for a portable motor rated a maximum of _____ horsepower.

    A. 1/8                B. 1/4
    C. 1/3                D. 1/2

512. A motor control enclosure which provides a degree of protection against windblown dust where used outdoors, is Type _____.

A. 1                              B. 3
C. 3R                             D. 5

513. For a motor, the disconnecting means shall be located in sight from and not more than _____ ft. from the motor.

A. 6                              B. 10
C. 25                             D. 50

514. The branch-circuit overcurrent device shall be permitted to serve as the disconnecting means for stationary motors of a maximum _____ horsepower.

A. 1/8                            B. 1/2
C. 3/4                            D. 1

515. Which of the following switches is rated in horsepower?

A. Transfer switch                B. Isolating switch
C. Motor-circuit switch           D. Bypass isolation switch

516. The disconnecting means for motor circuits rated 600 volts or less shall have an ampere rating of at least _____ percent of the full-load current rating of the motor.

A. 100                            B. 115
C. 125                            D. 150

517. The controller shall be permitted to be an attachment plug and receptacle which is acceptable for use with a portable motor rated 1/8 horsepower or less.

A. True                           B. False

518. The controller for Design E motors rated more than 1 horsepower shall always be marked for use with Design E motors.

A. True                           B. False

519. The controller shall be permitted to be a general-use switch rated for at least twice the motor's full-load current for stationary motors rated 2 horsepower or less.

A. True                           B. False

520. An overcurrent protection device rated at _____ amps or less can protect a 120 volt or less branch-circuit supplying motors rated less than 1 horsepower.

521. The service factor or _____ rise of the motor shall be used when sizing and installing the running overload protection for motors.

522. The horsepower rating of Design E controllers shall not be less than _____ times the motor's horsepower for motors rated 3 through 100 horsepower.

523. The motor controller for a torque motor shall have a continuous duty, full-load current rating not less than the _____ current rating of the motor.

524. Power conversion equipment requires the conductors to be sized at _____ percent of the rated input of such equipment.

A. 100                          B. 115
C. 125                          D. 150

525. For Design E motors, the setting of an instantaneous circuit breaker can be adjusted up to _____ percent to allow the motor to start and run. (Maximum)

A. 1,000                        B. 1,200
C. 1,300                        D. 1,700

526. A nontime-delay fuse will hold _____ times its rating for approximately 1/4 to 2 seconds based upon the type used.

A. 2                            B. 3
C. 5                            D. 10

527. Motor's with a marked service factor not less than 1.15 shall have the minimum running overload protection sized at _____ percent.

A. 115                          B. 125
C. 130                          D. 140

528. Motor's marked with a temperature rise not over 40°C shall have the minimum running overload protection sized at _____ percent.

A. 115                          B. 125
C. 130                          D. 140

529. Motors marked with a service factor not less than 1.15 shall have the maximum running overload protection sized at _____ percent.

A. 115                          B. 125
C. 130                          D. 140

530. Motors marked with a temperature rise not over 40°C shall have the maximum running overload protection sized at _____ percent.

A. 115                          B. 125
C. 130                          D. 140

531. An AC general-use snap switch may be installed as the controller for a stationary motor where the full-load current of the switch does not exceed _____ percent of the branch-circuit rating.

A. 50                           B. 75
C. 80                           D. 90

532. Live parts of motors or controllers shall be guarded against accidental contact where operating at over _____ volts-to-ground.

A. 50                           B. 150
C. 250                          D. 600

533. What size inverse time circuit breaker is required to start and run a 30 HP, three-phase, 460 volt, Design B motor? (Determining maximum size)

A. 125 amp            B. 150 amp
C. 175 amp            D. 200 amp

534. What size OCPD is required for a feeder-circuit supplying 20 HP, 30 HP, and 40 HP, three-phase, 460 volt motor? (Use a CB)

A. 175 amp            B. 200 amp
C. 250 amp            D. 300 amp

535. What size THWN copper conductors are required to supply a group of three-phase, 460 volt, Design B motors which are rated at 40 HP, 30 HP, and 20 HP?

A. No. 3            B. No. 2
C. No. 1            D. No. 1/0

536. What is the minimum overload protection (TDF's) for a 60 HP, three-phase, 460 volt, Design B motor with a nameplate rating of 67 amps, temperature rise of 40°C, and a service factor of 1.15?

A. 70 amps            B. 75 amps
C. 80 amps            D. 90 amps

## Article 440
## Air-conditioning and refrigerating equipment

537. The overcurrent protection device is sized and selected by the information provided on the nameplate listing for air-conditioning and refrigeration equipment.

A. True            B. False

538. A horsepower rated switch may be used as a disconnecting means for air-conditioners.

A. True            B. False

539. Cord-and-plug connected room air-conditioners are not permitted to serve as the disconnecting means for hermetic motors.

A. True            B. False

540. When sizing the conductors for a feeder supplying A/C units and motors, the full-load current in amps of the largest motor is multiplied by _____ percent.

541. The full-load current rating of the nameplate or the nameplate branch-circuit selection current of the compressor, whichever is greater, must be sized at _____ percent of the disconnecting means.

542. The disconnecting means for air-conditioning equipment shall be located within sight and within _____ ft. and shall be readily accessible to the user.

543. The full-load current rating of the nameplate or the branch-circuit selection current rating of the largest motor, whichever is greater, must be sized at _____ percent (for CB) if there are two or more hermetic sealed motors installed on the same feeder-circuit.

544. Two or more motor compressors can be connected for a feeder-circuit with the largest motor compressor computed at _____ percent of it's FLA and the remaining compressor loads added to this total at _____ percent of their FLA rating.

545. The overload relay for the motor compressor must trip at not more than _____ percent of the full-load current rating.

A. 100                                      B. 125
C. 130                                      D. 140

546. When attachment plugs and receptacles are used for circuit connection they must be rated no higher than _____ amps, for 208 or 240 volt, single-phase branch-circuits.

A. 15                                       B. 20
C. 25                                       D. 30

547. The full-load current rating of the room air-conditioner must be marked on the name-plate and must not operate at more than _____ amps on 250 volts.

A. 20                                       B. 30
C. 40                                       D. 50

548. A cord-and-plug may serve as the disconnecting means even if the room air-conditioner manual controller is above _____ ft.

A. 4                                        B. 5
C. 6                                        D. 7

549. Room air-conditioners installed with flexible cords are required to be a length that is limited to _____ ft. for 120 volt circuits.

A. 6                                        B. 8
C. 10                                       D. 12

550. The OCPD for hermetic sealed compressors are selected at _____ percent (for minimum) of the compressor's FLA rating or the branch-circuit selection current, whichever is greater.

A. 125                                      B. 150
C. 175                                      D. 225

551. The rating of the overcurrent protection device must be determined by using the rating of the nameplate of the cord-and-plug connected equipment having single-phase, _____ volt or less hermetic sealed motors.

A. 120                                      B. 250
C. 480                                      D. 600

552. Room air-conditioners are required to be grounded where operating over _____ volts-to-ground.

A. 120                                      B. 150
C. 250                                      D. 300

553. A cord-and-plug may serve as the disconnecting means for the room air-conditioner if it operates at _____ volts or less.

A. 120          B. 150
C. 250          D. 300

554. What size THWN copper conductors are required to supply power to a compressor with a full-load current of 24 amps and a condenser motor having a nameplate of 1.5 amps having terminals rated at 75°C?

A. No. 12       B. No. 10
C. No. 8        D. No. 6

## Article 450
## Transformers and transformer vaults

555. Transformers are permitted to be connected in parallel and switched as a unit provided each transformer has overcurrent protection.

A. True          B. False

556. Transformers enclosed by fences or guards are not required to be grounded.

A. True          B. False

557. Doors to transformer vaults must be kept locked at all times to prevent access of un-qualified persons to the vault.

A. True          B. False

558. Foreign piping or duct systems are permitted to be installed in a transformer vault.

A. True          B. False

559. Storage is allowed in a transformer vault.

A. True          B. False

560. Dry-type transformers not over 600 volts, which are located on open walls or steel columns, do not have to be _____ accessible.

561. If installing fuses, the overcurrent protection device for the primary side of a transformer rated over 600 volts shall be rated not greater than _____ percent of the rated primary current of the transformer. (Individual OCP in primary)

562. A transformer in a nonsupervised location with a secondary voltage of 600 volts or less, the OCPD and conductors on the secondary side must be sized at _____ percent of the FLC rating. (Primary and secondary protection)

563. A transformer of 600 volts or less, nominal, where the rated secondary current of a transformer is less than 9 amps but 2 amps or more, an overcurrent protection device rated or set at no more than _____ percent of secondary current may be used.

564. Transformers shall be elevated at least _____ ft. above the floor to prevent unauthorized personnel from contact.

A. 6            B. 6 1/2
C. 8            D. 10

565. All indoor dry-type transformers of over _____ volts are required to be installed in a vault.

A. 10,000          B. 15,000
C. 25,000          D. 35,000

566. The walls and roof for a transformer vault must have a _____ in. thickness.

A. 3          B. 4
C. 5          D. 6

567. The door sills for a transformer vault must be at least _____ in. high.

A. 1          B. 2
C. 3          D. 4

568. Tap conductors not over _____ ft. long supplying the secondary shall have an ampacity equal to the transformer's secondary output or load served. (Maximum length)

A. 10          B. 25
C. 50          D. 100

569. A transformer in a supervised location with a secondary voltage rated 600 volts or less, the OCPD on the secondary side must be sized at not more than _____ percent of the FLC rating.

A. 100          B. 125
C. 225          D. 250

570. Dry-type transformers rated 112 1/2 kVA or less, must be separated at least _____ in. from the combustible material where the voltage is 600 volts or less.

A. 6          B. 12
C. 18          D. 24

571. Askarel-insulated transformers of over _____ kVA must be furnished with a relief vent such as a chimney.

A. 25          B. 35
C. 50          D. 75

572. The floor for a transformer vault must be at least _____ in. thick.

A. 2          B. 4
C. 6          D. 12

## Article 500
## Hazardous (classified) locations

573. Explosionproof equipment is permitted to be installed in Class I, Division 1 locations for which it is approved.

A. True          B. False

_____    _____    574. Purged and pressurized equipment is permitted to be installed in any hazardous (classified) location for which it is approved.

   A. True                      B. False

_____    _____    575. Nonincendive circuits shall be permitted for equipment in Class I, Division 1 locations for which is approved.

   A. True                      B. False

_____    _____    576. Class I, Division 1 locations are those locations in which volatile flammable liquids or flammable gases are handled, processed, or used. (Gases not normally present)

   A. True                      B. False

_____    _____    577. Class II, Division 1 locations are those locations in which combustible dust is in the air under normal operation conditions in quantities sufficient to produce explosive or ignitable mixtures.

   A. True                      B. False

_____    _____    578. An atmosphere containing acetylene is classified as Group _____.

   A. Group A                   B. Group B
   C. Group C                   D. Group D

_____    _____    579. An atmosphere containing ethyl ether, ethylene, or gases or vapors of equivalent hazard is classified as Group _____.

   A. Group A                   B. Group B
   C. Group C                   D. Group D

_____    _____    580. An atmosphere containing combustible metal dusts is classified as Group _____.

   A. Group D                   B. Group E
   C. Group F                   D. Group G

_____    _____    581. Equipment marked "Division _____" is suitable for both Division 1 and 2.

   A. 1                         B. 2
   C. 1 and 2                   D. None of the above

_____    _____    582. Class III locations are those that are hazardous because of the presence of easily ignitable _____ or _____.

   A. Vapors ; gases            B. Liquids ; combustible dusts
   C. Fibers ; flyings          D. Liquids ; vapors

## Article 501
## Class I locations

_____    _____    583. Flexible cord approved for extra-hard usage and provided with approved bushed fittings can never be used in Class I, Division 2 locations.

_____

   A. True                      B. False

584. Seals are to be provided in a conduit and cable system to minimize the passage of gases or vapors from one portion of the system to another portion.

   A. True                    B. False

585. Live parts are allowed to be exposed in Class I, Division 2 locations.

   A. True                    B. False

586. Threaded joints of rigid metal conduit shall be made up with at least _____ threads fully engaged.

   A. Four                    B. Five
   C. Six                     D. Seven

587. Rigid nonmetallic conduit may be installed in Class I, Division 1 locations if encased in a concrete envelope of at least _____ in. and provided with not less than _____ in. of cover measured from the top of the conduit to grade.

   A. 1; 12                   B. 1; 24
   C. 2; 24                   D. 2; 30

588. In Class I, Division 2 locations, pendant fixtures must be suspended by a flexible hangers unless rigid stems not over _____ in. long are used.

   A. 6                       B. 12
   C. 18                      D. 24

589. Explosionproof equipment or equipment with arcing or sparking devices must have a seal placed within _____ in. of such equipment in Class I, Division 1 locations.

   A. 6                       B. 12
   C. 18                      D. 24

590. The cross-sectional area of the conductors permitted in a seal shall not exceed _____ percent of the cross-sectional area of a conduit of the same trade size.

   A. 20                      B. 25
   C. 40                      D. 50

## Article 511
## Commercial garages, repair and storage

591. Pits or depressions below floor level, which extend up to the floor level, are not always required to be considered as Class I, Division 1 locations.

   A. True                    B. False

592. In commercial garages, EMT is permitted to be installed above the 18 in. level.

   A. True                    B. False

593. In classifying a floor of a garage where vehicles are repaired and volatile flammable fluids are present, the floor area up to _____ in. is Class I, Division 2.

A. 6
C. 18

B. 12
D. 24

594. Any equipment in commercial garages that might produce an arc or spark, and which is less than _____ ft. above the floor level, must have a tight enclosure that will prevent the escape of any arc or spark.

A. 6
C. 18

B. 12
D. 24

## Article 513
## Aircraft hangers

595. A seal is required at every point in an aircraft hanger where a conduit is routed from a hazardous area to a nonhazardous area.

A. True

B. False

596. Flexible cord shall have a separate equipment grounding conductor when used for portable equipment in aircraft hangers.

A. True

B. False

597. The entire area of an aircraft hanger shall be classified as a Class I, Division 2 location up to a level _____ in. above the floor.

A. 6
C. 18

B. 12
D. 24

598. Any equipment installed in aircraft hangers that is over _____ ft. above engines may be the general-purpose type.

A. 3
C. 10

B. 5
D. 20

599. Aircraft energizers shall be so designed and mounted that all electric equipment and fixed wiring will be at least _____ in. above the floor level.

A. 12
C. 24

B. 18
D. 30

## Article 514
## Gasoline dispensing and service stations

600. A Class I location for a service station does extend beyond an unpierced wall, roof, or other solid partition.

A. True

B. False

601. Metallic portions of dispensing pumps and all noncurrent-carrying metal parts of electric equipment must be grounded.

    A. True                           B. False

602. The surrounding space out to a distance of _____ ft., measured from a point vertically below the edge of the dispenser enclosure, is Class I, Division 2 up to a height of _____ in. above grade.

    A. 10 ; 12                    B. 20 ; 12
    C. 20 ; 18                    D. 20 ; 24

603. Where rigid nonmetallic conduit is used for underground wiring in a service station, threaded rigid metal conduit shall be used for the last _____ ft. of the underground run to emergence.

    A. 1                            B. 2
    C. 3                            D. 6

604. Emergency controls for unattended self-service stations must be more than _____ ft. but less than _____ ft. from the dispensers.

    A. 10 ; 50                    B. 20 ; 50
    C. 10 ; 100                 D. 20 ; 100

## Article 515
## Bulk storage plants

605. An indoor pit for a bulk storage tank that is located in the _____ to _____ ft. sphere around pumps, bleeders, meters, etc. is considered as a Class I, Division 2 location.

    A. 3 ; 10                    B. 5 ; 10
    C. 3 ; 25                    D. 5 ; 20

606. Storage and repair garages for tank vehicles are considered as Class I, Division 2 up to a height of _____ in. above the floor.

    A. 6                            B. 12
    C. 18                        D. 24

607. Underground wiring routed to and around aboveground storage tanks may be installed with rigid metal conduit where buried not less than _____ ft. in the earth.

    A. 1                            B. 2
    C. 3                            D. 6

## Article 517
## Health care facilities

608. The outer metal armor of listed Type AC cable is not an acceptable grounding return path when installed in patient care areas.

    A. True                           B. False

_____   _____   609. Each patient bed location in general care areas shall be supplied by at least two branch-circuits. (General rule)

A. True                           B. False

_____   _____   610. Each patient bed location in critical care areas shall be supplied by at least four branch-circuits.

A. True                           B. False

_____   _____   611. Ground-fault interrupter protection is required for receptacles installed in those critical care areas where the toilet and basin are installed within the patient room.

A. True                           B. False

_____   _____   612. The life safety branch and critical branch of the emergency system shall be kept entirely independent of all other wiring and equipment.

A. True                           B. False

_____   _____   613. Light fixtures more than _____ ft. above the floor in patient care areas shall not be required to be grounded by an insulated grounding conductor.

A. 6                              B. 6 1/2
C. 7                              D. 7 1/2

_____   _____   614. The equipment grounding terminal busses of the normal and essential branch-circuit panelboards serving the same individual patient vicinity shall be bonded together with an insulated continuous copper conductor not smaller than No. _____.

A. 12                             B. 10
C. 8                              D. 6

_____   _____   615. Each patient bed location in general care areas shall be provided with a minimum of _____ receptacles.

A. Two                            B. Four
C. Six                            D. Eight

_____   _____   616. Each patient bed location in critical care areas shall be provided with a minimum of _____ receptacles.

A. Two                            B. Four
C. Six                            D. Eight

_____   _____   617. The branches of the emergency system for hospitals shall be installed and connected to the alternate power sources so that all functions for the emergency system shall be automatically restored to operation within _____ sec. after interruption of the normal source.

A. 5                              B. 10
C. 20                             D. 30

## Article 525
### Carnivals, circuses, fairs, and similar events

618. Service equipment for carnivals shall be installed in a location that is accessible to unqualified persons.

   A. True                    B. False

619. Flexible cords or cables installed at circuses shall be continuous without splice or tap between boxes or fittings.

   A. True                    B. False

620. Approved nonconductive mats shall be used to cover flexible cords or cables run on the ground, where accessible to the public at carnivals.

   A. True                    B. False

621. All equipment requiring grounding at circuses shall be grounded by a grounding electrode conductor.

   A. True                    B. False

622. Amusement attractions (not supplying equipment) shall be maintained not less than _____ ft. in any direction from overhead conductors operating at 600 volts or less.

   A. 10                      B. 15
   C. 20                      D. 25

623. Amusement rides shall not be located under or within _____ ft. horizontally of conductors operating in excess of 600 volts.

   A. 10                      B. 15
   C. 20                      D. 25

624. Single conductor cables installed at fairs shall be permitted only in sizes No. _____ or larger.

   A. 8                       B. 6
   C. 4                       D. 2

625. Termination boxes installed outdoors shall be mounted so that the bottom of the enclosure is not less than _____ in. above the ground.

   A. 3                       B. 6
   C. 12                      D. 18

626. Each ride shall be provided with a fused disconnect switch or circuit breaker located within sight and within _____ ft. of the operator's station.

   A. 6                       B. 20
   C. 40                      D. 50

## Article 550
## Mobile homes, manufactured homes, and mobile home parks

627. The power supply to a mobile home shall be a feeder assembly consisting of not more than one listed _____ ampere mobile home power supply cord. (General rule)

A. 30                                    B. 40
C. 50                                    D. 100

621. Ground-fault circuit interrupters in mobile homes shall be provided for receptacle outlets located within _____ ft. of any sink.

A. 5                                     B. 6
C. 10                                    D. 12

629. Receptacle outlets in mobile homes shall be installed so that no point along the floor line is more than _____ ft. measured horizontally from an outlet in that space.

A. 2                                     B. 5
C. 6                                     D. 12

630. The small appliance load is calculated at _____ VA for each 20 ampere small appliance receptacle circuit.

A. 1,200                                 B. 1,500
C. 1,800                                 D. 2,000

631. The service equipment shall be located in sight from and not more than _____ ft. from the exterior wall of the mobile home it serves.

A. 10                                    B. 20
C. 25                                    D. 30

## Article 600
## Electric signs and outline lighting

632. Metal poles used to support signs are not permitted to enclose supply conductors.

A. True                                  B. False

633. Each sign shall be controlled by an circuit breaker that will open all ungrounded conductors.

A. True                                  B. False

634. The disconnecting means for a sign shall be within sight of the sign that is controls.

A. True                                  B. False

635. Portable signs are required to be provided with factory-installed ground-fault circuit-interrupter protection for personnel.

A. True                                  B. False

636. Circuits that only supply neon tubing installations shall not be rated in excess of _____ amperes.

    A. 15                  B. 20
    C. 30                  D. 40

637. The branch-circuit load for a sign shall be calculated at a minimum of _____ volt-amperes.

    A. 1,000             B. 1,200
    C. 1,800             D. 2,400

638. Where flexible nonmetallic conduit is used to install the secondary wiring of a transformer and a bonding jumper is required to bond the metal electrode receptacles, the bonding conductor shall not be smaller No. _____ copper.

    A. 14                  B. 12
    C. 10                  D. 8

639. A sign shall be at least _____ ft. above areas accessible to vehicles.

    A. 10                  B. 12
    C. 14                  D. 18

640. Each ballast shall be provided with a working space at least _____ ft. wide.

    A. 2                  B. 3
    C. 4                  D. 5

641. What is the load in VA for a sign rated at 2,400 VA operating at three hours or more?

    A. 2,250             B. 2,500
    C. 2,750             D. 3,000

## Article 610
## Cranes and hoists

642. Main contact conductors carried along runways shall be supported on insulating supports placed at intervals not exceeding _____ ft.

    A. 10                  B. 18
    C. 20                  D. 22

643. The continuous ampere rating of the circuit breaker shall not be less than _____ percent of the combined short-circuit ampere rating of the motors used for cranes.

    A. 20                  B. 40
    C. 50                  D. 75

644. When servicing cranes that are energized, a working space in the direction of access to live parts shall be a minimum of _____ ft.

    A. 2                  B. 2 1/2
    C. 3                  D. 3 1/2

## Article 620
## Elevators, dumbwaiters, escalators, moving walks, wheelchair lifts, and stairway chair lifts

_____ _____

645. Traveling cables for lighting circuits shall be permitted in parallel for conductors in sizes No. _____ or larger, provided the ampacity is equivalent to at least that of No. 14 copper.

A. 22      B. 20
C. 18      D. 16

_____ _____

646. Flexible metal conduit of 3/8 in. nominal trade size shall be permitted between control panels and machine motors in elevators when not exceeding ____ ft. in length.

A. 6      B. 10
C. 12      D. 18

_____ _____

647. Vertical runs of wireways in elevators shall be securely supported at intervals not exceeding _____ ft.

A. 10      B. 12
C. 15      D. 20

_____ _____

648. Traveling cables shall be permitted to be run without the use of a raceway for a distance not exceeding _____ ft. in length as measured from the first point of support on the elevator car.

A. 3      B. 5
C. 6      D. 10

_____ _____

649. Which of the following receptacles are required to be installed with ground-fault circuit-interrupter protection:

A. Where installed in pits
B. Where installed in machinery spaces
C. Where installed in escalators
D. All of the above

## Article 625
## Electric vehicle charging system equipment

_____ _____

650. Where cord-and-plug connected electric vehicle supply equipment is used, the ground-fault circuit-interrupter protection for personnel shall be an integral part of the attachment plug or shall be located in the power supply cable not more than _____ in. from the attachment plug.

A. 3      B. 6
C. 12      D. 18

_____ _____

651. For vehicle supply equipment rated more than _____ amperes, the disconnecting means shall be provided and installed in a readily accessible location.

A. 30      B. 40
C. 50      D. 60

652. Unless specifically listed for the purpose and location, the coupling means of the electric vehicle supply equipment shall be stored or located at a height of not less than _____ in. and not more than _____ ft. above the floor level.

A. 12 ; 2                    B. 12 ; 4
C. 18 ; 2                    D. 18 ; 4

653. Unless specifically listed for the purpose and location, the coupling means of the electric vehicle supply equipment shall be stored or located at a height of not less than _____ in. and not more than _____ ft. above the parking surface.

A. 12 ; 4                    B. 18 ; 4
C. 24 ; 4                    D. 30 ; 4

## Article 630
## Electric welders

654. AC transformer and DC rectifier arc welders that have a duty cycle of 80 percent shall have an multiplier of _____ percent.

A. 78                        B. 84
C. 89                        D. 95

655. Motor-generator arc welders shall have an overcurrent protection device rated or set at not more than _____ percent of the rated primary current of the welder.

A. 150                       B. 200
C. 300                       D. 400

656. Resistance welders that have a duty cycle of 30 percent shall have an multiplier of _____ percent.

A. 50                        B. 55
C. 63                        D. 71

657. Resistance welders shall have an overcurrent device rated or set at not more than _____ percent of the rated primary current of the welder.

A. 150                       B. 200
C. 300                       D. 400

658. Welding cables supported by cable trays shall provide supports at not greater than _____ in. intervals.

A. 3                         B. 4
C. 5                         D. 6

659. What size OCPD is required for a motor-generator arc welder with a 54 amp load and 80 percent duty cycle? (Use welder primary current in amps)

A. 100                       B. 125
C. 150                       D. 175

## Article 680
## Swimming pools, fountains, and similar installations

660. Receptacles shall be installed at least _____ ft. from the inside walls of a swimming pool.

    A. 5                          B. 10
    C. 15                       D. 20

661. Receptacles shall be installed at least a minimum of _____ ft. from and not more than _____ ft. from the inside wall of a permanently installed swimming pool for a dwelling unit.

    A. 5 ; 10                 B. 5 ; 20
    C. 10 ; 15               D. 10 ; 20

662. Receptacles shall be located not more than _____ ft. above the grade level that serves the pool for a dwelling unit.

    A. 6                          B. 6 1/2
    C. 7                          D. 7 1/2

663. Receptacles located within _____ ft. of the inside walls of a swimming pool shall be protected by a ground-fault circuit-interrupter.

    A. 5                          B. 10
    C. 15                       D. 20

664. Ceiling fans shall not be installed over the pool or over the area extending _____ ft. horizontally from the inside walls of a pool.

    A. 3                          B. 5
    C. 6                          D. 7 1/2

665. Lighting fixtures can be installed over the pool if no part of the lighting fixture is less than _____ ft. above the maximum water level.

    A. 6                          B. 7 1/2
    C. 10                       D. 12

666. Lighting fixtures can be installed over an indoor pool area if the distance from the bottom of the fixture to the maximum water level is not less than _____ ft.

    A. 6                          B. 7 1/2
    C. 10                       D. 12

667. Switching devices shall be installed at least _____ ft. horizontally from the inside walls of a pool.

    A. 3                          B. 4
    C. 5                          D. 6

668. Underground wiring shall not be installed within _____ ft. horizontally from the inside wall of the pool. (General rule)

    A. 5                          B. 10
    C. 12                       D. 18

669. The disconnecting means for a swimming pool shall be installed at least _____ ft. from the inside walls of the pool.

A. 3                              B. 5
C. 10                             D. 50

670. Lighting fixtures mounted in the walls of swimming pools shall be installed with the top of the fixture lens at least _____ in. below the normal level of the pool.

A. 4                              B. 6
C. 12                             D. 18

671. A No. _____ insulated copper conductor shall be routed in PVC conduit to ground to the metal forming shell of a wet-niche fixture.

A. 12                             B. 10
C. 8                              D. 6

672. The deck box shall have a height of _____ in. measured from the deck or _____ in. measured from the water, whichever is greater.

A. 2 ; 6                          B. 4 ; 6
C. 4 ; 8                          D. 6 ; 10

673. The deck box located behind a solid permanent barrier may be located less than _____ ft. from the inside walls of the pool.

A. 3                              B. 4
C. 5                              D. 6

674. All metallic parts of a swimming pool are required to be bonded with a No. _____ solid copper bonding conductor.

A. 12                             B. 10
C. 8                              D. 6

675. Wet-niche lighting fixtures for a swimming pool shall be connected to at least a No. _____ copper insulated equipment grounding conductor.

A. 12                             B. 10
C. 8                              D. 6

676. At least one receptacle shall be installed a minimum of _____ ft. from and not more than _____ ft. from the inside wall of a hot tub.

A. 5 ; 10                         B. 5 ; 20
C. 10 ; 15                        D. 10 ; 20

677. Receptacles located within _____ ft. of the inside walls of a hot tub shall be protected by a ground-fault circuit-interrupter.

A. 5                              B. 6
C. 10                             D. 20

678. Switches shall be installed at least _____ ft. from the inside walls of the hot tub.

    A. 5                       B. 6
    C. 10                  D. 20

679. All receptacles within _____ ft. of the inside walls of a hydromassage tub shall be protected by a ground-fault circuit-interrupter.

    A. 3                       B. 4
    C. 5                   D. 10

## Article 700
## Emergency systems

680. A sign shall be placed at the service-entrance equipment indicating type and location of on-site emergency power sources.

    A. True                   B. False

681. Feeder-circuit wiring for emergency systems shall be installed either in spaces fully protected by approved automatic fire suppression systems or shall be a listed electrical circuit protective system with a _____ hour fire rating.

    A. 1                       B. 2
    C. 3                   D. 4

682. Storage batteries used as source of power for emergency systems shall be of suitable rating and capacity to supply and maintain the total load for a period of _____ hours minimum.

    A. 1                       B. 1 1/2
    C. 2                   D. 2 1/2

## Existing Article 710 - See Articles 300 and 490
## Over 600 volts, nominal, general

683. A 600 volt feeder-circuit installed in rigid metal conduit shall have a minimum cover of at least _____ in.

    A. 6                       B. 12
    C. 18                  D. 24

684. A 600 volt feeder-circuit installed in a commercial parking garage shall have a minimum cover of _____ in.

    A. 6                       B. 12
    C. 18                  D. 24

685. Oil-filled cutouts shall be so located that they will be readily and safely accessible for refusing, with the top of the cutout not over _____ ft. above the floor or platform.

    A. 3                       B. 5
    C. 6                   D. 10

686. Control and instrument transfer switch handles shall be in a readily accessible location at an elevation not over _____ in.

    A. 48                               B. 60
    C. 72                               D. 78

## Article 725
## Class 1, Class 2, and Class 3 remote-control, signaling, and power-limited circuits

687. Remote-control circuits for safety-control equipment shall be classified as Class _____ if the failure of the equipment to operate introduces a direct fire or life hazard.

    A. 1                                B. 2
    C. 3                                D. 4

688. A Class 1 nonpower limited remote-control circuit shall not exceed _____ volts.

    A. 50                               B. 120
    C. 240                              D. 600

689. Class 1 circuit overcurrent protection shall not exceed _____ amps for No. 16 conductors.

    A. 5                                B. 7
    C. 10                               D. 12

690. Class 1 circuits and power supply circuits shall be permitted to occupy the same raceway only where _____.

    A. Equipment powered is functionally associated
    B. There is not a mixture of alternating or direct current circuits
    C. Class 1 circuits and power supply circuits are of the same voltage
    D. None of the above

691. Conductors of Class 2 and Class 3 circuits shall be separated by at least _____ in. from conductors of any Class 1 circuits.

    A. 1                                B. 2
    C. 3                                D. 4

## Article 760
## Fire alarm systems

692. Nonpower-limited fire alarm circuits shall have overcurrent protection not to exceed _____ amperes for No. 18 conductors.

    A. 5                                B. 7
    C. 10                               D. 12

693. Multiconductor nonpower-limited fire alarm circuit cables shall be located within 7 ft. of the floor, cables shall be securely fastened at intervals of not more than _____ in.

    A. 3                                B. 6
    C. 12                               D. 18

694. Power-limited fire alarm circuit conductors can be installed in the same raceway with which of the following wiring methods:

A. Power conductors
B. Class 1 conductors
C. Nonpower-limited circuit conductors
D. None of the above

695. Power-limited fire alarm circuit conductors shall be separated at least _____ in. from conductors of any electric light.

A. 1                          B. 2
C. 3                          D. 4

## Article 800
## Communications circuits

696. Communication wires and cables shall have a vertical clearance of not less than _____ ft. from all points of roofs above which they pass.

A. 8                          B. 10
C. 12                         D. 18

697. Communication wires and cables shall be separated at least _____ in. from electric power and light conductors not in a raceway or cable.

A. 2                          B. 4
C. 6                          D. 10

698. Where practicable, a separation of at least ____ ft. shall be maintained between open conductors of communication systems on buildings and lightning conductors.

A. 6                          B. 8
C. 10                         D. 12

699. A bonding jumper not smaller than No. _____ copper shall be connected between the communications grounding electrode and power grounding electrode system at the building.

A. 10                         B. 8
C. 6                          D. 4

700. A grounding electrode shall be bonded to the metal frame or available grounding terminal of the mobile home with a copper grounding conductor not smaller than No. _____.

A. 12                         B. 10
C. 8                          D. 6

# Appendix

Included in this chapter are useful calculation tips and calculation forms that may be utilized for completing service, feeder, and branch-circuit loads. These calculation tips and forms will greatly aid designers, installers, and inspectors so as to limit or eliminate errors and save time when computing such loads.

These calculation tips were designed to alert personnel using the NEC to be aware of the different interpretations of certain sections of the code. It is these different interpretations, by the authority having jurisdiction, that hinders correct computations from being calculated by the NEC.

The calculation forms in the Appendix may be reproduced for instructional use only. They shall not be reproduced and sold.

## Quick Reference:

Calculation Tips -------------------------------------- A-3

Standard Calc. ------------------------------------------- A-4

Optional Calc. ------------------------------------------- A-5

Standard Calc. Multifamily --------------------------- A-6

Optional Calc. Multifamily --------------------------- A-7

Standard Calc.

Mobile Home --------------------------------------------- A-8

Standard Calc.-Store and

Whse, Single-Phase -------------------------------------- A-9

Standard Calc.-Store and

Whse, Three-Phase ----------------------------------- A-10

Standard Calc.-Store and

Whse,Three-Phase 277/480 ---------------------------- A-11

Standard Calc.-Store and

Whse, Three-Phase 120/240 --------------------------- A-12

Standard Calc.-Office Building

277-480 volt ------------------------------------------- A-13

Standard Calc.-Schools-277/480 ------------------ A-14

Standard Calc.-Restaraunt -------------------------- A-15

Standard Calc.-Welding Shop --------------------- A-16

# CALCULATION TIPS

These calculation tips were designed to alert personnel using the NEC to be aware of the different interpretations of certain sections of the code. It is these different interpretations, by the authority having jurisdiction (AHJ), that hinders correct computations from being calculated by the NEC.

The following tips should be studied carefully and the authority having jurisdiction should be consulted as to the interpretation of each particular rule and procedure to be used in calculating volt-amps or ampacities by the NEC.

1. The AHJ may require the general lighting load calculated at 3 VA per sq. ft. to be compared to the total VA rating of the lighting fixtures and the larger load selected. This procedure is applied where the listed occupancy and the number of fixtures with VA ratings are available.

2. The AHJ may permit all cooking equipment rated over 1 3/4 kW and up to 8 3/4 kW to be grouped and the percentages in Column B or C used to determine the demand load.

3. The AHJ may interpret the NEC to allow Note 3 to Table 220-19 to be applied to cooking units grouped in Columns B and C. After demands factors are applied, the smaller load is used in the calculation.

4. The AHJ may permit the demand load for service-entrance conductors and equipment to be selected from Note 4 to Table 220-19. Most authorities only permit the demand load for the branch-circuit to be computed when Note 4 to Table 220-19 is utilized.

5. Four or less dryers must be calculated at 100 percent of 5,000 VA or the nameplate value, whichever is greater.

6. The AHJ may rule that the A/C load is eligible as the largest motor load, even when the A/C load is dropped, due to the heating unit being the largest load per NEC 220-21.

7. The AHJ may require the A/C load to be calculated at 125 percent compared to 100 percent of the heating load, and the smaller load dropped per NEC 220-21. Note, 100 percent for both is used by most of the AHJ's.

8. The AHJ may require the blower motor to be calculated as part of the heating load and added to the service load at 100 percent per NEC 220-15. However, other AHJ's may require the blower motor to be considered eligible for the largest motor per NEC 220-14..

9. The AHJ may require a sign less than 1,200 VA to be increased to a minimum of 1,200 VA.

10. Derating the current-carrying ability of the OCPD's by 80 percent is the same as multiplying the load times 125 percent. The 80 percent is derived by dividing 1 by 125 percent (1/1.25 = 80%). **Note:** If the OCPD is derated by 80 percent and the load is added to this value at 125 percent, the total rating for OCPD is calculated at 150 percent and not 125 percent.

The following is an example on how to use Calculation Tips.

**For Example:** If a 25 kW heating unit and a 6 kVA air conditioning unit are compared per NEC 220-21, the A/C unit is dropped. If the AHJ requires the A/C unit to be considered as the largest motor, 6 kVA must be compared with other motor related loads and should it be selected as the largest motor, 25 percent of the 6 kVA must be added to the total calculated load.

## STANDARD CALCULATION — SINGLE FAMILY DWELLING

**Column 1**
**Calculating general lighting and receptacle load**

Step 1: General lighting and receptacle load
Table 220-3(a)
_____ sq. ft. x 3 VA = _____ VA

Step 2: Small appliance and laundry load
220-16(a); (b)
1,500 VA x 2 = _____ VA
1,500 VA x 1 = _____ VA
Total load = _____ VA

Step 3: Applying demand factors
Demand load 1; Table 220-11
First 3,000 VA x 100% = 3,000 VA
Next _____ VA x 35% = _____ VA
Total load = _____ VA • √

**Column 2**
**Calculating cooking equipment load**

Step 1: Applying demand factors for phases
Demand load 2; Table 220-19, Col. A
_____ = _____ VA •

Step 2: Applying demand factors for neutral
220-22
_____ VA x 70% = _____ VA√

**Column 2**
**Calculating dryer load**

Step 1: Applying demand factors for phases
Demand load 3; Table 220-18
_____ VA x 100% = _____ VA •

Step 2: Applying demand factors for neutral
220-22
_____ VA x 70% = _____ VA √

**Column 2**
**Calculating fixed appliance load**

Step 1: Applying demand factors for phases
Demand load 4; 220-17
_____ VA x 75% = _____ VA
_____ VA x 75% = _____ VA
_____ VA x 75% = _____ VA
_____ VA x 75% = _____ VA
_____ VA x 75% = _____ VA
_____ VA x 75% = _____ VA
_____ VA x 75% = _____ VA
Total load = _____ VA •

Step 2: Applying demand factors for neutral
Demand load 4; 220-22
_____ VA x 75% = _____ VA
_____ VA x 75% = _____ VA
_____ VA x 75% = _____ VA
_____ VA x 75% = _____ VA
Total load = _____ VA √

**Column 3**
**Largest load between heating and A/C load**

Step 1: Selecting largest load
Demand load 5; 220-21
Heating unit
_____ VA x 100% = _____ VA •

**Column 4**
**Calculating largest motor load**

Step 1: Selecting largest motor load for phases
220-14; 430-24
_____ VA x 25% = _____ VA •

Step 2: Selecting largest motor load for neutral
220-14; 430-24
_____ VA x 25% = _____ VA √

**Calculating phases (six loads)**

• General lighting load = _____ VA •
• Cooking equipment load = _____ VA •
• Dryer load = _____ VA •
• Appliance load = _____ VA •
• Heating load = _____ VA •
• Largest motor load = _____ VA •
Six total loads = _____ VA

**Calculating neutral (five loads)**

• General lighting load = _____ VA √
• Cooking equipment load = _____ VA √
• Dryer load = _____ VA √
• Appliance load = _____ VA √
• Largest motor load = _____ VA √
Five total loads = _____ VA

**Finding amps for phases**

$I = VA / V$
$I =$ _____ VA / _____ V
$I =$ _____ A

**Finding amps for neutral**

$I = VA / V$
$I =$ _____ VA / _____ V
$I =$ _____ A

**Finding conductor size**

Table 310-16 and 310-15(b)(2)(a)

Phases A and B # _____ THWN copper

310-15(b)(2)(a) allows # _____ THWN copper

Neutral _____ THWN copper

## OPTIONAL CALCULATION — SINGLE FAMILY DWELLING

**Column 1**
**Other loads**

**Step 1:** General lighting load
Table 220-3(a)
_____ sq. ft. x 3 VA = _____ VA

**Step 2:** Small appliance and laundry load
220-16(a); (b)
1,500 VA x 2 = _____ VA
1,500 VA x 1 = _____ VA

**Step 3:** Appliance load
Table 220-30(b)(3); (4)
Cooktop load = _____ VA
Oven load = _____ VA
Dryer load = _____ VA
Water heater load = _____ VA
Disposal load = _____ VA
Compactor load = _____ VA
Dishwasher load = _____ VA
Attic fan load = _____ VA
Blower motor load = _____ VA
Water pump load = _____ VA
Total load = _____ VA

**Step 4:** Applying demand load
220-30(b)
First 10,000 VA x 100% = _____ VA
Next _____ VA x 40% = _____ VA
Total load = _____ VA •

**Column 2**
**Largest load between heating and A/C load**

**Step 5:** Selecting lagest load
220-30(c)(1); (2); (4)
Heating load = _____ VA x 1 x 65% = _____ VA •
A/C load = _____ VA x 1 x 100% = _____ VA
Total load = _____ VA •

**Totaling Column 1 and 2**
**220-30(b); (c)**
Col. 1 ld. = _____ VA •
Col. 2 ld. = _____ VA •
Total load = _____ VA

**Finding amps for phases**

I = VA / V
I = _____ VA / _____ V
I = _____ A

**Finding conductor size**

Table 310-16
Phases A and B # _____ THWN copper
Neutral # _____ THWN copper

## STANDARD CALCULATION - MULTIFAMILY

**Column 1**
**Calculating general lighting and receptacle load**

Step 1: General lighting and receptacle load
Table 220-3(a)

⬚ sq. ft. x 3 VA x ⬚ = ⬚ VA

Step 2: Small appliance and laundry load
220-16(a); (b)
1,500 VA x 2 x ⬚ = ⬚ VA
1,500 VA x 1 x ⬚ = ⬚ VA
Total load = ⬚ VA

Step 3: Applying demand factors
Demand load 1; Table 220-11
First 3,000 VA x 100% = 3,000 VA
Next ⬚ VA x 35% = ⬚ VA
Remaining ⬚ VA x 25% = ⬚ VA
Total load = ⬚ VA •√

**Column 2**
**Calculating cooking equipment load**

Step 1: Applying demand factors for phases
Demand load 2; Table 220-19
⬚ VA ranges = ⬚ VA •

Step 2: Applying demand factors for neutral
220-22
⬚ VA x 70% = ⬚ VA √

**Column 2**
**Calculating fixed appliance load**

Step 1: Applying demand factors for phases
Demand load 4; 220-17
⬚ VA x ⬚ x 75% = ⬚ VA
⬚ VA x ⬚ x 75% = ⬚ VA
⬚ VA x ⬚ x 75% = ⬚ VA
Total load = ⬚ VA •

Step 2: Applying demand factors for neutral
Demand load 4; 220-22
⬚ VA x ⬚ x 75% = ⬚ VA
⬚ VA x ⬚ x 75% = ⬚ VA
Total load = ⬚ VA √

**Column 3**
**Largest load between heating and A/C load**

Step 1: Selecting largest load
Demand load 5; 220-21
Heating unit
⬚ VA x ⬚ x 100% = ⬚ VA •

**Column 4**
**Calculating largest motor load**

Step 1: Selecting largest motor load for phases
220-14; 430-24
⬚ VA x 25% = ⬚ VA •

Step 2: Selecting largest motor load for neutral
220-14; 430-24
⬚ VA x 25% = ⬚ VA √

**Calculating phases**

• General lighting load = ⬚ VA •
• Cooking equipment load = ⬚ VA •
• Appliance load = ⬚ VA •
• Heating load = ⬚ VA •
• Largest motor load = ⬚ VA •
Five total loads = ⬚ VA

**Calculating neutral**

• General lighting load = ⬚ VA √
• Cooking equipment load = ⬚ VA √
• Appliance load = ⬚ VA √
• Largest motor load = ⬚ VA √
Four total loads = ⬚ VA

**Finding amps for phases**

I = VA / V
I = ⬚ VA / ⬚ V
I = ⬚ A

**Finding amps for neutral**

I = VA / V
I = ⬚ VA / ⬚ V
I = ⬚ A

**Finding conductors**

Phases A and B
310-4
I = ⬚ A / ⬚
I = ⬚ A

**Neutral**
**220-22**

⬚ A
First 200 A x 100% = 200 A
Next ⬚ A x 70% = ⬚ A
Total load = ⬚ A

**310-4**

I = ⬚ A / ⬚
I = ⬚ A

**Table 310-16**

Phases A and B

#⬚ KCMIL THWN copper conductors
Neutral

#⬚ KCMIL copper conductor

## OPTIONAL CALCULATION - MULTIFAMILY

**Column 1**
**Calculating general lighting and receptacle load**

Step 1: General lighting and receptacle load
Table 220-3(a)

_____ sq. ft. x 3 VA x _____ = _____ VA

Step 2: Small appliance and laundry load
220-16(a); (b)
1,500 VA x 2 x _____ = _____ VA
1,500 VA x 1 x _____ = _____ VA
Total load = _____ VA •

**Column 2**
**Calculating cooking equipment load**

Step 1: Applying demand factors for phases
Demand load 2; Table 220-19
_____ VA x _____ = _____ VA •

**Column 2**
**Calculating fixed appliance load**

Step 1: Applying demand factors for phases
Demand load 4; 220-17
_____ VA x _____ = _____ VA
_____ VA x _____ = _____ VA
_____ VA x _____ = _____ VA
Total load = _____ VA •

**Column 3**
**Largest load between heating and A/C load**

Step 1: Selecting largest load
Demand load 5; 220-21
Heating unit
_____ VA x _____ x 100% = _____ VA •

**Calculating phases**

- General lighting load = _____ VA •
- Cooking equipment load = _____ VA •
- Appliance load = _____ VA •
- Heating load = _____ VA •
Total load = _____ VA

**Applying demand factors**
**Table 220-32**

I = VA / V
I = _____ VA / _____ V
I = _____ A

**Finding amps for phases**
**Table 220-32**

I = A x %
I = _____ A x _____ %
I = _____ A

**Finding conductors**

Phases A and B
310-4
I = _____ A / _____
I = _____ A

Table 310-16
Phases A and B
# _____ THWN copper conductors

Neutral
# _____ THWN copper conductors

STANDARD CALCULATION - MOBILE HOME

## Calculating general lighting and receptacle load

**Step 1:** General lighting and receptacle load
550-13
_____ sq. ft. x 3 VA = _____ VA

**Step 2:** Small appliance and laundry load
220-16(a); (b)
1,500 VA x 2 = _____ VA
1,500 VA x 1 = _____ VA
Total load = _____ VA

**Step 3:** Applying demand factor
550-13(a)
First 3,000 VA x 100% = 3,000 VA
Next _____ VA x 35% = _____ VA
Total load = _____ VA • √

## Calculating special appliance loads

**Step 1:** Applying demand factors for phases
550-13(b)(2); (3); (4)
Water heater = _____ VA
Dishwasher = _____ VA √
Disposal = _____ VA √
Heating = _____ VA
Total load = _____ VA •

## Calculating range load

**Step 1:** 550-13(b)(5)
_____ VA x _____ % = _____ VA •
_____ VA x _____ % = _____ VA √

## Calculating phases

• General lighting load = _____ VA •
• Special appliance load = _____ VA •
• Range load = _____ VA •
• Largest motor load ( _____ VA x 25%) = _____ VA •
Four total loads = _____ VA

## Finding amps for phases

I = VA / V
I = _____ VA / _____ V
I = _____ A

## Calculating neutral

• General lighting load = _____ VA √
• Dishwasher load = _____ VA √
• Disposal load = _____ VA √
• Largest motor = _____ VA √
• Range = _____ VA √
Five total loads = _____ VA

## Finding amps for neutral

I = VA / V
I = _____ VA / _____ V
I = _____ A

## Finding conductors based on max. size
Table 310-16

Phases
# _____ THWN copper conductors
Neutral
# _____ THWN copper conductors

## Sec. 310-15(b)(2)(a) allows min. size

Phases
# _____ THWN copper conductors
Neutral
# _____ THWN copper conductors

## STANDARD CALCULATION - STORE AND WAREHOUSE SPACE - SINGLE-PHASE - 120/240

### Calculating lighting load

**Step 1:** General lighting load
Table 220-3(a); 230-42(a)(1)

_____ sq. ft. x \_\_\_\_\_ VA = _____ VA √

_____ VA x 125% = _____ VA *

_____ sq. ft. x \_\_\_\_\_ VA = _____ VA √

_____ VA x 125% = _____ VA *

**Step 2:** Show window load
220-12(a)

_____ x 200 = _____ VA *√

**Step 3:** Track lighting load
220-12(b)

_____ / 2 x 150 VA = _____ VA * √

**Step 4:** Outside lighting load
230-42(a)(1)

_____ x 180 VA = _____ VA √

_____ VA x 125% = _____ VA *

**Step 5:** Sign lighting load
600-5(b)(3); 230-42(a)(1)

_____ VA x 100% = _____ VA √

_____ VA x 125% = _____ VA *

Total load = _____ VA •

### Calculating receptacle load

**Step 1:** Noncontinuous operation
220-3(b)(9)

_____ x 180 VA = _____ VA

Table 220-13
First 10,000 VA x 100% = _____ VA

Next _____ VA x 50% = _____ VA

Total load = _____ VA * √

**Step 2:** Continuous operation
220-3(b)(9); 230-42(a)(1)

_____ x 180 VA = _____ VA √

_____ VA x 125% = _____ VA *

**Step 3:** Multioutlet assembly
220-3(b)(8)(b)

_____ x 180 VA = _____ VA * √

Total load = _____ VA •

### Calculating special loads

**Step 1:** Water heater load

_____ VA x 100% = _____ VA * •

### Calculating compressor loads

**Step 1:** Compressor load
230-42(a)(1)

_____ VA x 100% = _____ VA *

**Step 2:** Compressor load

_____ VA x 100% = _____ VA *

**Step 3:** Compressor load

_____ VA x 100% = _____ VA *

Total load = _____ VA •

### Calculating motor loads

**Step 1:** Motor load
430-24; Table 430-148

_____ A x _____ V x 100% = _____ VA *

**Step 2:** Motor load

_____ A x _____ V x 100% = _____ VA *

Total load = _____ VA •

### Calculating heating or A/C load

**Step 1:** Heating load selected
220-21

_____ VA x 100% = _____ VA * •

_____ VA x 100% = _____ VA

### Calculating largest motor load

**Step 1:** Largest motor load
220-14; 430-24

_____ VA x 25% = _____ VA * •

### Calculating phases

Lighting loads = _____ VA •

Receptacle loads = _____ VA •

Special loads = _____ VA •

Compressor loads = _____ VA •

Motor loads = _____ VA •

Heating load = _____ VA •

Largest motor load = _____ VA •

Total load for facility = _____ VA

### Finding amps for phases A and B

$I = VA / V$

I = _____ VA / _____ V

I = _____ A

### Calculating neutral

Lighting load = _____ VA √

Receptacle load = _____ VA √

Total load = _____ VA

### Finding amps for neutral

$I = VA / V$

I = _____ VA / _____ V

I = _____ A

## STANDARD CALCULATION - STORE AND WAREHOUSE SPACE - THREE-PHASE - 120/208

**Calculating lighting load**

**Step 1:** General lighting load
Table 220-3(a); 230-42(a)(1)

_____ sq. ft. x _____ VA = _____ VA √
_____ VA x 125% = _____ VA *
_____ sq. ft. x _____ VA = _____ VA √
_____ VA x 125% = _____ VA *

**Step 2:** Show window load
220-12(a)

_____ x 200 = _____ VA * √

**Step 3:** Track lighting load
220-12(b)

_____ / 2 x 150 VA = _____ VA * √

**Step 4:** Outside lighting load
230-42(a)(1)

_____ x 180 VA = _____ VA √
_____ VA x 125% = _____ VA *

**Step 5:** Sign lighting load
600-5(b)(3); 230-42(a)(1)

_____ VA x 100% = _____ VA √
_____ VA x 125% = _____ VA *
Total load = _____ VA •

**Calculating receptacle load**

**Step 1:** Noncontinuous operation
220-3(b)(9)

_____ x 180 VA = _____ VA
Table 220-13
First 10,000 VA x 100% = _____ VA
Next _____ VA x 50% = _____ VA
Total load = _____ VA * √

**Step 2:** Continuous operation
220-3(b)(9); 230-42(a)(1)

_____ x 180 VA = _____ VA √
_____ VA x 125% = _____ VA *

**Step 3:** Multioutlet assembly
220-3(b)(8)(b)

_____ x 180 VA = _____ VA * √
Total load = _____ VA •

**Calculating special loads**

**Step 1:** Water heater load

_____ VA x 100% = _____ VA * •

**Calculating compressor loads**

**Step 1:** Compressor load
230-42(a)(1)

_____ VA x 100% = _____ VA *

**Step 2:** Compressor load

_____ VA x 100% = _____ VA *

**Step 3:** Compressor load

_____ VA x 100% = _____ VA *
Total load = _____ VA •

**Calculating motor loads**

**Step 1:** Motor load
430-24; Table 430-150

_____ A x _____ V x 100% = _____ VA *

**Step 2:** Motor load

_____ A x _____ V x 100% = _____ VA *
Total load = _____ VA •

**Calculating heating or A/C load**

**Step 1:** Heating load selected
220-21

_____ VA x 100% = _____ VA * •
_____ VA x 100% = _____ VA

**Calculating largest motor load**

**Step 1:** Largest motor load
220-14; 430-24

_____ VA x 25% = _____ VA * •

**Calculating phases**

Lighting loads = _____ VA •
Receptacle loads = _____ VA •
Special loads = _____ VA •
Compressor loads = _____ VA •
Motor loads = _____ VA •
Heating load = _____ VA •
Largest motor load = _____ VA •
Total load for facility = _____ VA

**Finding amps for phases A and B**

$I = VA / V \times \sqrt{3}$
I = _____ VA / _____ V
I = _____ A

**Calculating neutral**

Lighting load = _____ VA√
Receptacle load = _____ VA √
Total load = _____ VA

**Finding amps for neutral**

$I = VA / V \times \sqrt{3}$
I = _____ VA / _____ V
I = _____ A

## STANDARD CALCULATION - STORE AND WAREHOUSE SPACE - THREE-PHASE, 277/480 VOLT

**Calculating lighting load**

**Step 1:** General lighting load
Table 220-3(a); 230-42(a)(1)

_____ sq. ft. x 3 VA = _____ VA √
_____ VA x 125% = _____ VA *
_____ sq. ft. x 1/4 VA = _____ VA √
_____ VA x 125% = _____ VA *

**Step 2:** Show window load
220-12(a)

_____ x 200 = _____ VA *

**Step 3:** Track lighting load
220-12(b)

_____ / 2 x 150 VA = _____ VA *

**Step 4:** Outside lighting load
230-42(a)(1)

_____ x 180 VA = _____ VA
_____ VA x 125% = _____ VA *

**Step 5:** Sign lighting load
600-5(b)(3); 230-42(a)(1)

_____ VA x 100% = _____ VA
_____ VA x 125% = _____ VA *
Total load = _____ VA •

**Calculating receptacle loads**

**Step 1:** Noncontinuous operation
220-3(b)(9)

_____ x 180 VA = _____ VA

Table 220-13
First 10,000 VA x 100% = _____ VA
Next _____ VA x 50% = _____ VA
Total load = _____ VA *

**Step 2:** Continuous operation
220-3(b)(9); 230-42(a)(1)

_____ x 180 VA = _____ VA
_____ VA x 125% = _____ VA *

**Step 3:** Multioutlet assembly
220-3(b)(8)(b)

_____ x 180 VA = _____ VA *
Total load = _____ VA •

**Calculating special loads**

**Step 1:** Water heater load

_____ VA x 100% = _____ VA * •

**Calculating compressor loads**

**Step 1:** Compressor load
230-42(a)(1)

_____ VA x 100% = _____ VA *

**Step 2:** Compressor load

_____ VA x 100% = _____ VA *

**Step 3:** Compressor load

_____ VA x 100% = _____ VA *
Total load = _____ VA •

**Calculating motor loads**

**Step 1:** Motor load
430-24; Table 430-150

_____ A x _____ V x 100% = _____ VA *

**Step 2:** Motor load

_____ A x _____ V x 100% = _____ VA *
Total load = _____ VA •

**Calculating heating or A/C load**

**Step 1:** Heating load selected
220-21

_____ VA x 100% = _____ VA * •
_____ VA x 100% = _____ VA

**Calculating largest motor load**

**Step 1:** Largest motor load
220-14; 430-24

_____ VA x 25% = _____ VA * •

**Calculating phases**

Lighting loads = _____ VA •
Receptacle loads = _____ VA •
Special loads = _____ VA •
Compressor loads = _____ VA •
Motor loads = _____ VA •
Heating load = _____ VA •
Largest motor load = _____ VA •
Total load for facility = _____ VA

**Finding amps for phases A and B**

I = VA / V
I = _____ VA / _____ V
I = _____ A

**Calculating neutral**

Lighting load = _____ VA √
Total load = _____ VA

**Finding amps for neutral**

I = VA / V
I = _____ VA / _____ V
I = _____ A

## STANDARD CALCULATION - STORE AND WAREHOUSE SPACE - THREE-PHASE, 120/240 VOLT

### Calculating lighting load

**Step 1:** General lighting load
Table 220-3(a); 230-42(a)(1)

_____ sq. ft. x 3 VA = _____ VA √
_____ VA x 125% = _____ VA *
_____ sq. ft. x 1/4 VA = _____ VA √
_____ VA x 125% = _____ VA *

**Step 2:** Show window load
220-12(a)

_____ x 200 = _____ VA * √

**Step 3:** Track lighting load
220-12(b)

_____ / 2 x 150 VA = _____ VA * √

**Step 4:** Outside lighting load
230-42(a)(1)

_____ x 180 VA = _____ VA √
_____ VA x 125% = _____ VA *

**Step 5:** Sign lighting load
600-5(b)(3); 230-42(a)(1)

_____ VA x 100% = _____ VA √
_____ VA x 125% = _____ VA *
Total load = _____ VA •

### Calculating receptacle loads

**Step 1:** Noncontinuous operation
220-3(b)(9)

_____ x 180 VA = _____ VA

Table 220-13
First 10,000 VA x 100% = _____ VA
Next _____ VA x 50% = _____ VA
Total load = _____ VA * √

**Step 2:** Continuous operation
220-3(b)(9); 230-42(a)(1)

_____ x 180 VA = _____ VA √
_____ VA x 125% = _____ VA *

**Step 3:** Multioutlet assembly
220-3(b)(8)(b)

_____ x 180 VA = _____ VA * √
Total load = _____ VA •

### Calculating special loads

**Step 1:** Water heater load

_____ VA x 100% = _____ VA * •

### Calculating compressor loads

**Step 1:** Compressor load
230-42(a)(1)

_____ VA x 100% = _____ VA *

**Step 2:** Compressor load

_____ VA x 100% = _____ VA *

**Step 3:** Compressor load

_____ VA x 100% = _____ VA *
Total load = _____ VA •

### Calculating motor loads

**Step 1:** Motor load
430-24; Table 430-150

_____ A x _____ V x 100% = _____ VA *

**Step 2:** Motor load

_____ A x _____ V x 100% = _____ VA *
Total load = _____ VA •

### Calculating heating or A/C load

**Step 1:** Heating load selected
220-21

_____ VA x 100% = _____ VA * •
_____ VA x 100% = _____ VA

### Calculating largest motor load

**Step 1:** Largest motor load
220-14; 430-24

_____ VA x 25% = _____ VA * •

### Single-phase loads

Lighting loads = _____ VA •
Receptacle loads = _____ VA •
Total load = _____ VA

### Three-phase loads

Special loads = _____ VA •
Compressor loads = _____ VA •
Motor loads = _____ VA •
Heating load = _____ VA •
Largest motor load = _____ VA •
Total load = _____ VA

### Calculating single-phase load

$I = $ _____ VA / _____ V
$I = $ _____ A

### Calculating three-phase load

$I = $ _____ VA / _____ V
$I = $ _____ A

### Calculating neutral load

$I = $ _____ VA / _____ V
$I = $ _____ A

### Calculating Phases A and C

Single-phase load = _____ A
Three-phase load = _____ A
Total load = _____ A

### Calculating Phase B

Three-phase load = _____ A

## STANDARD CALCULATION - OFFICE BUILDING - 277/480 VOLT

**Calculating lighting load**

**Step 1:** General lighting load
Table 220-3(a); 230-42(a)(1)

_____ sq. ft. x _____ VA = _____ VA √

_____ VA x 125% = _____ VA *

_____ sq. ft. x _____ VA = _____ VA √

_____ VA x 125% = _____ VA *

**Step 2:** Track lighting load
220-12(b)

_____ / 2 x 150 VA = _____ VA *

**Step 3:** Low-voltage lighting load
Art. 411; 230-42(a)(1)

_____ VA x 100% = _____ VA

_____ VA x 125% = _____ VA *

**Step 4:** Outside lighting load
230-42(a)(1)

_____ x 180 VA = _____ VA

_____ VA x 125% = _____ VA *

**Step 5:** Sign lighting load
600-5(b)(3); 230-42(a)(1)

_____ VA x 100% = _____ VA

_____ VA x 125% = _____ VA *

Total load = _____ VA •

**Calculating receptacle load**

**Step 1:** Noncontinuous operation
220-3(b)(9)

_____ x 180 VA = _____ VA

Table 220-13
First 10,000 VA x 100% = _____ VA

Next _____ VA x 50% = _____ VA

Total load = _____ VA *

**Step 2:** Continuous operation
220-3(b)(9); 230-42(a)(1)

_____ x 180 VA = _____ VA

_____ VA x 125% = _____ VA *

**Step 3:** Multioutlet assembly(heavy-duty)
220-3(b)(8)(b)

_____ x 180 VA = _____ VA *

Total load = _____ VA •

**Calculating special loads**

**Step 1:** Special load
230-42(a)(1)

_____ VA x _____ = _____ VA

_____ VA x 125% = _____ VA *

**Step 2:** Special load
442-13; 230-42(a)(1)

_____ VA x 100% = _____ VA *

**Step 3:** Special load

_____ VA x _____ = _____ VA

_____ VA x 125% = _____ VA *

**Step 4:** Special load
230-42(a)(1)

_____ VA x _____ = _____ VA

_____ VA x 125% = _____ VA *

**Step 5:** Special load
230-42(a)(1)

_____ VA x _____ = _____ VA

_____ VA x 125% = _____ VA *

Total load = _____ VA •

**Calculating motor loads**

**Step 1:** Motor load
430-24;430-22(b); Table 430-22(b)

_____ A x _____ V x _____ % = _____ VA * •

**Calculating heating or A/C load**

**Step 1:** Heating load selected
220-21; 220-15

_____ VA x 100% = _____ VA * •

**Calculating largest motor**

**Step 1:** Largest motor load
220-14; 430-24

_____ VA x 25% = _____ VA * •

Total load of facility = _____ VA •

**Finding amps for phases A, B, and C**

I = VA / V x √3

I = _____ VA / _____ V

I = _____ A

**Calculating neutral**

General lighting load
(office building) = _____ VA √

(halls) = _____ VA √

Total load = _____ VA

**Finding amps for neutral**

I = VA / V x √3

I = _____ VA / _____ V

I = _____ A

## STANDARD CALCULATION - SCHOOLS - 277/480 VOLT

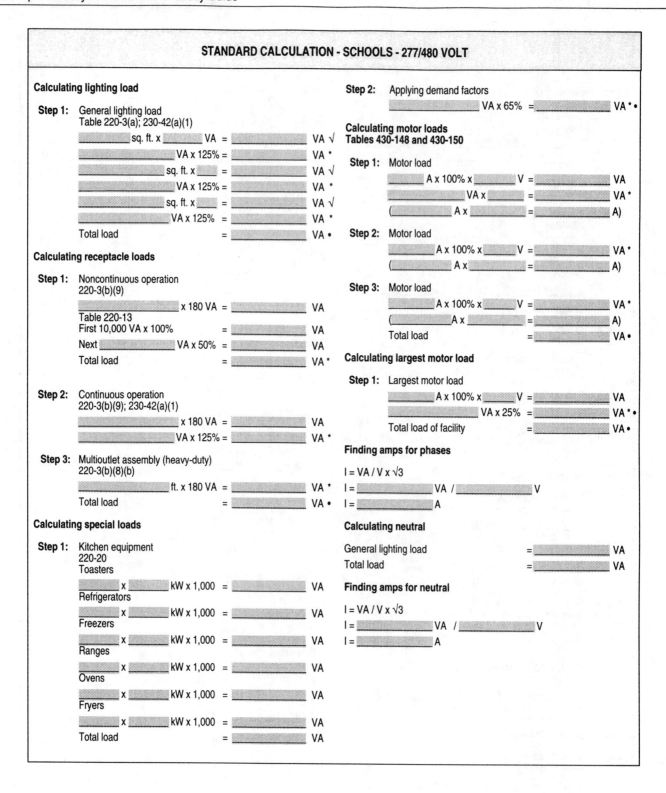

**Calculating lighting load**

Step 1: General lighting load
Table 220-3(a); 230-42(a)(1)

| | | |
|---|---|---|
| _____ sq. ft. x _____ VA = | _____ | VA √ |
| _____ VA x 125% = | _____ | VA * |
| _____ sq. ft. x _____ = | _____ | VA √ |
| _____ VA x 125% = | _____ | VA * |
| _____ sq. ft. x _____ = | _____ | VA √ |
| _____ VA x 125% = | _____ | VA * |
| Total load = | _____ | VA • |

**Calculating receptacle loads**

Step 1: Noncontinuous operation
220-3(b)(9)

_____ x 180 VA = _____ VA

Table 220-13
First 10,000 VA x 100% = _____ VA
Next _____ VA x 50% = _____ VA
Total load = _____ VA *

Step 2: Continuous operation
220-3(b)(9); 230-42(a)(1)

_____ x 180 VA = _____ VA
_____ VA x 125% = _____ VA *

Step 3: Multioutlet assembly (heavy-duty)
220-3(b)(8)(b)

_____ ft. x 180 VA = _____ VA *
Total load = _____ VA •

**Calculating special loads**

Step 1: Kitchen equipment
220-20
Toasters

_____ x _____ kW x 1,000 = _____ VA
Refrigerators

_____ x _____ kW x 1,000 = _____ VA
Freezers

_____ x _____ kW x 1,000 = _____ VA
Ranges

_____ x _____ kW x 1,000 = _____ VA
Ovens

_____ x _____ kW x 1,000 = _____ VA
Fryers

_____ x _____ kW x 1,000 = _____ VA
Total load = _____ VA

Step 2: Applying demand factors
_____ VA x 65% = _____ VA * •

**Calculating motor loads**
Tables 430-148 and 430-150

Step 1: Motor load

_____ A x 100% x _____ V = _____ VA
_____ VA x _____ = _____ VA *
( _____ A x _____ = _____ A)

Step 2: Motor load

_____ A x 100% x _____ V = _____ VA *
( _____ A x _____ = _____ A)

Step 3: Motor load

_____ A x 100% x _____ V = _____ VA *
( _____ A x _____ = _____ A)
Total load = _____ VA •

**Calculating largest motor load**

Step 1: Largest motor load

_____ A x 100% x _____ V = _____ VA
_____ VA x 25% = _____ VA * •
Total load of facility = _____ VA •

**Finding amps for phases**

$I = VA / V \times \sqrt{3}$
$I =$ _____ VA / _____ V
$I =$ _____ A

**Calculating neutral**

General lighting load = _____ VA
Total load = _____ VA

**Finding amps for neutral**

$I = VA / V \times \sqrt{3}$
$I =$ _____ VA / _____ V
$I =$ _____ A

# STANDARD CALCULATION - RESTAURANT

## Calculating lighting loads

**Step 1:** General lighting load
Table 220-3(a); 230-42(a)(1)

_____ sq. ft. x ____ VA = _____ VA √

_____ VA x 125% = _____ VA *

**Step 2:** Track lighting load
220-12(b)

_____ / 2 x 150 VA = _____ VA √

_____ VA x 125% = _____ VA *

**Step 3:** Outside lighting load
230-42(a)(1)

180 VA x _____ units = _____ VA √

_____ VA x 125% = _____ VA *

**Step 4:** Sign lighting load
600-5(b)(3); 230-42(a)(1)

_____ VA x 100% = _____ VA √

_____ VA x 125% = _____ VA *

Total load = _____ VA •

## Calculating receptacle loads

**Step 1:** Receptacle load (noncontinuous)
220-3(b)(9); 230-42(a)(1)

_____ x 180 VA = _____ VA * √

**Step 2:** Receptacle load (continuous)
220-3(b)(9); 230-42(a)(1)

_____ x 180 VA = _____ VA √

_____ VA x 125% = _____ VA *

**Step 3:** Multioutlet assembly
220-3(b)(8)(b)

_____ x 180 VA = _____ VA * √

Total load = _____ VA •

## Calculating special load

**Step 1:** Kitchen equipment
220-20
Boiler = _____ VA
Deep fat fryer = _____ VA
Walk-in cooler = _____ VA
Water heater = _____ VA
Ice cream box = _____ VA
Freezer = _____ VA
Cooktop = _____ VA

Ovens = _____ VA
Range = _____ VA
Refrigerator = _____ VA
Total load = _____ VA

**Step 2:** Applying demand factor
Table 220-20

_____ VA x 65% = _____ VA * •

## Calculating motor load

**Step 1:** Motor load
430-22(a); 430-24; 430-25

_____ VA x 100% = _____ VA *

**Step 2:** Motor load

_____ VA x 100% = _____ VA *

Total load = _____ VA •

## Calculating heating or A/C load

**Step 1:** Heating load
220-21

_____ kW x ____ x 1,000 = _____ VA * •

## Calculating largest motor load

**Step 1:** Largest motor load
220-14

_____ A x 100% x ____ V = _____ VA

_____ VA x 25% = _____ VA * •

Total load of facility = _____ VA •

## Calculating VA load (neutral)
220-22; 230-42(a)(1)

Lighting load = _____ VA √
Receptacle load = _____ VA √
Total load = _____ VA

### Finding amps for phases

$I = VA / V \times \sqrt{3}$

$I =$ _____ VA / _____ V

$I =$ _____ A

### Finding amps for neutral

$I = VA / V \times \sqrt{3}$

$I =$ _____ VA / _____ V

$I =$ _____ A

## STANDARD CALCULATION - WELDING SHOP

### Calculating lighting loads

**Step 1:** Inside lighting load
230-42(a)(1)

_____ VA x 100% = _____ VA √
_____ VA x 125% = _____ VA *

**Step 2:** Outside lighting load
230-42(a)(1)

_____ x 180 VA = _____ VA √
_____ VA x 125% = _____ VA *

**Step 3:** Sign lighting load
600-5(b)(3); 230-42(a)(1)

_____ VA x 100% = _____ VA * √
Total load = _____ VA •

### Calculating receptacle load

**Step 1:** Continuous duty
220-3(b)(9); 230-42(a)(1)

_____ x 180 VA = _____ VA √
_____ VA x 125% = _____ VA * •

### Calculating special loads

**Step 1:** Welders - resistance
630-31(a); (b)

_____ VA x _____ % = _____ VA *
_____ VA x _____% x _____%= _____ VA *

**Step 2:** Welders - motor-generator arc
630-11(a); (b)

_____ VA x _____ % = _____ VA *
_____ VA x _____ % = _____ VA *

**Step 3:** Welders - AC transformer and DC rectifier
630-11(a); (b)

_____ VA x _____ % = _____ VA *
_____ VA x _____ % = _____ VA *
Total load = _____ VA •

### Calculating compressor and motor loads

**Step 1:** Compressor load
430-24; 430-22(b); Table 430-22(b)

_____ A x 100% x _____ V = _____ VA *

**Step 2:** Motor load

_____ A x 100% x _____ V = _____ VA *
Total load = _____ VA •

### Calculating heating or A/C load

**Step 1:** Heating load
220-21; 220-15

_____ VA x 100% = _____ VA * •

### Calculating largest motor load

**Step 1:** Largest motor load

_____ A x _____ V x 25% = _____ VA * •

### Calculating total load

Lighting loads = _____ VA •
Receptacle loads = _____ VA •
Special loads = _____ VA •
Heating loads = _____ VA •
Motor loads = _____ VA •
Largest motor load = _____ VA •
Total load = _____ VA

### Finding amps for phases

$I = VA / V \times \sqrt{3}$

$I =$ _____ VA / _____ V
$I =$ _____ A

### Calculating neutral

220-22
Lighting loads = _____ VA √
Receptacle loads = _____ VA √
Total load = _____ VA

### Finding amps for neutral

$I = VA / V \times \sqrt{3}$

$I =$ _____ VA / _____ V
$I =$ _____ A

# Topic Index

AC/DC FORMULAS ...................... 4-2
A/C AND REFRIGERATION EQUIPMENT CIRCUIT CONDUCTORS .................... 7-29
ARTICLES 90, 100, 110 .................. 5-2
ARTICLES 200-280 ....................... 5-4
ARTICLES 300-384 ....................... 5-5
ARTICLES 400-480 ....................... 5-7
ARTICLES 500-555 ....................... 5-7
ARTICLES 600-695 ....................... 5-7
ARTICLES 700-780 ....................... 5-8
ARTICLES 800-820 ....................... 5-9
APPENDIX C ................................. 6-14
APPLYING OHMS LAW ................. 1-11
APPLYING THE FORMULA ........... 1-12
APPLYING OHM'S LAW ................ 4-7
APPLYING PIE FORMULA ........... 4-10
APPLYING OHM'S LAW AND PIE FORMULAS COMBINED .............. 4-13
APPLYING THE STANDARD CALCULATION ........................... 9-14
APPLYING THE OPTIONAL CALCULATION ........................... 9-16
APPLYING THE STANDARD CALCULATION FOR MULTIFAMILY ............................. 9-18
APPLYING THE OPTIONAL CALCULATION FOR MULTIFAMILY ............................. 9-20
APPLYING THE STANDARD CALCULATION FOR FEEDER TO MOBILE HOMES .................... 9-22
APPLYING THE OPTIONAL CALCULATION FOR MOBILE HOME PARK SERVICE AND FEEDER ...................................... 9-24
APPLYING THE STANDARD CALCULATION ........................... 10-2
APPLYING THE OPTIONAL CALCULATION ........................... 10-34

BOXES, COVERS, DEVICES, AND FITTINGS ........................... 11-4

CAPACITANCE ............................ 3-5
CAPACITIVE REACTANCE ............ 3-7
CALCULATING LOAD ................... 7-3
CAPACITOR CIRCUIT CONDUCTORS ........................... 7-33
CIRCUIT BREAKERS ..................... 2-4
CHARGING CONDUCTORS .......... 1-5
CURRENT IN A CIRCUIT .............. 1-10
CONDUIT BODIES ....................... 6-11
CONNECTING LOADS IN A CIRCUIT ............................. 2-5
COMPRESSOR LOADS .............. 10-12
COMPUTATIONS IN A SERIES CIRCUIT .................... 2-7
COMPUTATIONS IN A PARALLEL CIRCUIT .............. 2-9
COMPUTATIONS IN A SERIES / PARALLEL CIRCUIT ..................... 2-12
CONTROL CIRCUIT CONDUCTORS ........................... 7-38
CONTROLLERS ......................... 11-25

DIRECTION OF CURRENT FLOW THROUGH CONDUCTORS ............................ 1-5
DEMAND FACTORS ...................... 9-2
DERATING AMPACITY OF CONDUCTORS ...................... 7-4
DEVICES RATED 800 AMPS OR LESS ......................... 8-3
DEVICES RATED OVER 800 AMPS .................................. 8-4

EFFECTIVE VALUES .................... 3-3
ELECTRIC CURRENT FLOW ........ 1-6
ELECTRIC POWER AND WORK IN A CIRCUIT .................... 1-13
ELECTRON THEORY .................... 1-2
ELECTRONS, PROTONS, AND NEUTRONS ......................... 1-2

ELECTROSTATIC FIELD ............... 1-4
FEEDER-CIRCUIT PROTECTION - OVER 600 VOLTS ...................... 8-40
FEEDER TO MOBILE HOME - STANDARD CALCULATION ......... 9-24
FIXTURE FITTINGS .................... 11-13
FLEXIBLE CORDS AND FITTINGS ................................ 11-37
FOR A TWO-WIRE PRIMARY TO TWO-WIRE SECONDARY ................................ 7-31
FREE ELECTRONS MOVING THROUGH CONDUCTORS .......... 1-3
FREQUENCY ............................... 3-3
FUSES ........................................ 2-4

GROUND-FAULTS ....................... 2-3

HEAT OR A/C LOADS ................. 10-15
HELPFUL TABLES AND CHARTS ............................ 11-45

IMPEDANCE ................................ 3-9
INDUCTANCE ............................... 3-7
INDUCTIVE REACTANCE ............. 3-8
INSULATORS ............................... 1-10

JUNCTION BOXES ...................... 6-12

KITCHEN EQUIPMENT .............. 10-34

LARGEST MOTOR LOAD .......... 10-15
LAYOUT OF THE NEC ................. 5-2
LIGHTING LOADS ........................ 10-3

METHODS OF COUNTING CONDUCTORS ............................ 6-2
MOBILE HOME PARK SERVICE AND FEEDERS - OPTIONAL CALCULATION .......... 9-24
MOLECULES AND ATOMS ............ 1-2
MOTOR LOADS .......................... 10-14

a

MOTOR CIRCUIT
CONDUCTORS ........................... 7-24
MULTIFAMILY - STANDARD
CALCULATION ......................... 9-18
MULTIFAMILY - OPTIONAL
CALCULATION ......................... 9-20
NOTE (4) TO TABLE 1, CH. 9 ........ 6-16

OCPD FOR TAPS ......................... 8-5
OCPD FOR MOTOR AND
MOTOR CONTROL CIRCUITS ..... 8-11
OCPD FOR PHASE
CONVERTERS ............................ 8-21
OCPD FOR A/C AND
REFRIGERATION
EQUIPMENT CIRCUITS ............... 8-22
OCPD FOR TRANSFORMER
SECONDARY CIRCUITS ............. 8-23
OCPD FOR REMOTE-CONTROL,
SIGNALING, AND
POWER-LIMITED ........................ 8-36
OCPD FOR FIRE ALARM
CIRCUITS ................................. 8-39
OCPD'S RATED OVER
100 AMPS ........................... 7-2
OCPD'S RATED 100 AMPS
OR LESS ............................... 7-2
OHM'S LAW AND PIE
FORMULAS .................................. 4-7
OPEN-CIRCUITS,
SHORT-CIRCUITS,
AND GROUND-FAULTS ................. 2-2
OPEN-CIRCUITS ........................... 2-2
OPTIONAL CALCULATION .......... 9-17
OVERCURRENT PROTECTION
DEVICES ................................. 2-3
OVERCURRENT PROTECTION
DEVICES ................................. 11-32

PANELBOARDS .......................... 11-24
PARALLEL CIRCUITS ................... 2-6
PHASE ......................................... 3-4
POTENTIAL DIFFERENCE
AND EMF ..................................... 1-6
POWER ........................................ 3-12
PRINCIPLES OF AC CURRENT ..... 3-2
PROTECTION OF CIRCUIT
CONDUCTORS ............................ 7-9
PROTECTION OF EQUIPMENT ... 8-1
PROTECTING FIXTURE
CONDUCTORS ............................ 7-41

RECEPTACLE LOADS ................. 10-8

RESISTANCE ................................ 3-10
RESISTANCE IN A CIRCUIT ........ 1-8
RESISTANCE AND
TEMPERATURE ........................... 1-8
RESONANT CIRCUITS .................. 3-9
ROUNDING UP OR DOWN
OF OCPD ..................................... 8-2

SECONDARY OF
A TRANSFORMER ....................... 7-32
SERIES CIRCUITS ........................ 2-5
SERIES / PARALLEL CIRCUITS ..... 2-6
SERVICE ELEMENTS .................. 11-2
SHORT-CIRCUITS .......................... 2-2
SIZING THE CONDUCTORS
FOR PHASE CONVERTERS ........ 7-28
SIZING AUXILIARY GUTTERS ..... 6-17
SIZING CABLE TRAYS .................. 6-18
SIZING CONDUITS ....................... 6-14
SIZING ELEMENTS ....................... 9-25
SIZING NIPPLES ........................... 6-16
SOLVING SERIES AND
PARALLEL CIRCUITS ................... 2-6
SPECIAL APPLIANCE LOADS .... 10-10
STANDARD CALCULATIONS ..... 10-16
STANDARD CALCULATION .......... 9-14
STATIC ELECTRICITY .................. 1-5
SWITCHES ................................. 11-36

TABLES ........................................ 5-9
TAP CONDUCTORS ..................... 7-14
TERMINAL RATINGS ................... 7-2
TERMINALS, LUGS,
AND CONNECTORS ................... 11-41
TRANSFORMER SECONDARY
CONDUCTORS ............................ 7-31
TYPES OF CABLES .................... 11-27
TYPES OF CONDUITS............... 11-30

VOLTAGE DROP ......................... 4-22
VOLTAGE IN A CIRCUIT .............. 1-8

WELDER CIRCUITS ..................... 8-32
WELDER LOADS .......................... 7-34

1. Grounding 250-118
   Cond

2. MAIN Bonding Green
   Jumper
          250-28

3. Grounded Cond. 250-24B

4. Bonding Jumper 250-102

5. Grounding Electrode Cond 250-50
                              52

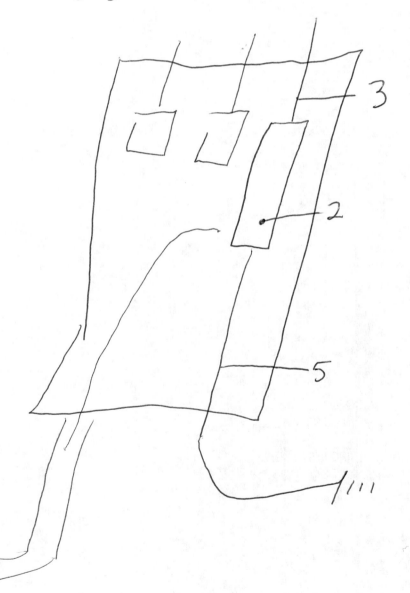